CAPE PUNCH.

CAPT BADEN-POWELI
IN
THE BALLET

No......   No......

MAFEKING SIEGE
March. NOTE 1900
ONE POUND
£1   £1

ISSUED BY AUTHORITY OF COLONEL R.S.S. BADEN POWELL.

(Commanding Rhodesian Forces)

This note is good for One Pound during the siege and will be exchanged for
coin at the Standard Bank, Mafeking, on the resumption of Civil Law.

ENTERED......   ......
                                            CHIEF PAYMASTER

THE BOY-MAN

THE BOY-MAN

THE LIFE OF LORD BADEN-POWELL

TIM JEAL

William Morrow and Company, Inc.
New York

Copyright © 1990 by Tim Jeal

Originally published in Great Britain in 1989 by Century Hutchinson Ltd.

Recognizing the importance of preserving what has been written, it is the policy of
William Morrow and Company, Inc., and its imprints and affiliates to have
the books it publishes printed on acid-free paper, and we exert our best efforts to
that end.

Library of Congress Cataloging-in-Publication Data

Jeal, Tim.
    The boy-man / Tim Jeal.
      p.   cm.
    ISBN 0-688-04899-4
    1. Baden-Powell of Gilwell, Robert Stephenson Smyth Baden-Powell,
Baron, 1857–1941. 2. Boy Scouts—Great Britain—Biography.
I. Title.
HS3268.2.B33J43   1990
369.43'092—dc20
[B]   89-13452
                                                                            CIP

Printed in the United States of America

First U.S. Edition

1 2 3 4 5 6 7 8 9 10

TO JOYCE JEAL

CONTENTS

PREFACE

There have been two biographies of Lord Baden-Powell since his death in 1941, both of them entirely uncritical: *Baden-Powell: A Biography* by E. E. Reynolds (London 1942), and *Baden Powell: The Two Lives of a Hero*, by William Hillcourt with Olave Baden-Powell (London 1964). Reynolds had been associated with the Scout Movement since boyhood, and was obliged to write his book rapidly as a hagiographical tribute for publication within a year of his subject's death. Lady Baden-Powell would have preferred it if another author had been commissioned by the Scout Association, and therefore gave him little help. William Hillcourt (formerly of the Boy Scouts of America) wrote more fully and with Lady Baden-Powell's blessing. But her co-authorship prevented him expressing any criticism of his subject, or touching upon anything remotely controversial.

In the sixties, although no new biographies appeared, Baden-Powell nevertheless shared the fate of numerous imperial heroes. But unlike many casualties of that era, far from rising again, his star actually fell further during the seventies and eighties.

In 1966 *Mafeking: A Victorian Legend* appeared. Its author, Brian Gardner, argued that Baden-Powell should never have allowed himself to become entrapped at Mafeking and that the Siege was little more than a piece of clever self-promotion. Two years later Samuel Hynes, an American scholar, asserted in *The Edwardian Turn of Mind* that, despite the Scout Movement's longstanding protestations to the contrary, the Boy Scouts had been crudely militaristic from the beginning. Other scholars would soon reject Scouting's pacific and philanthropic credentials.

In 1977 Lady Baden-Powell died. Custody of the bulk of her husband's papers thereafter rested with the British Scout Association and the Boy Scouts of America. The first author, after her death, to be given access to these two enormous collections was another American academic, Michael Rosenthal. He did not write a biography but a book about the origins of the Scout Movement, containing a biographical essay. In *The Character Factory* (London 1986), Mr Rosenthal repeated earlier charges of militarism and accused Baden-Powell of being anti-semitic, a covert fascist sympathizer, and of using the Scouts to prevent the working class developing political aspirations. He treated sympathetically earlier allegations that Baden-Powell had appropriated from others without proper acknowledgement essential ideas for the Scout Movement. He agreed with Brian Gardner over Mafeking and restated Thomas Pakenham's claim, made in his book *The Boer War* (London 1979), that Baden-Powell had ruthlessly denied 2,000 Africans food during the Siege. Mr Rosenthal also repeated the surmise, first expressed by Piers Brendon in his essay on Baden-Powell in *Eminent Edwardians* (London 1979), that Baden-Powell's relationship with his friend, Major Kenneth McLaren, could have been a physical one. But like Dr Brendon, he left Baden-Powell's sexual orientation a matter for conjecture.

When I started work on my biography in 1983, I saw my task as being to disentangle the man both from the good-natured and self-less hero of Scouting legend and the ambitious, mendacious and cruel soldier of subsequent revisionist portrayals. Michael Rosenthal's accentuation of every earlier criticism, and his addition of many more, made my job more challenging and more necessary.

Because of the detailed presentation of these allegations and their gravity (any one, if true, would be disastrously damaging to the reputation of the founder of a philanthropic youth movement), I have felt compelled to answer them directly.

Since its inception in 1908, Baden-Powell's Movement has attracted approximately 500 million members (4 million of whom are currently Scouts in America). With the exception of great religions and political ideologies, no international organization has exerted a greater influence upon social behaviour than the Boy and Girl Scouts.

Among numerous wise observations about education and boy-hood, Baden-Powell also wrote much that strikes us today as comical and misguided. His views on sex are a case in point. Confronted by a vanished world, we can either laugh at the people who held such beliefs or treat them on their own terms and try to understand them. I have favoured the second option.

After consulting the American and British Scout Archives, I studied twenty-nine other major manuscript collections, many of which contain previously unassessed letters, as do the two dozen smaller private collections which I unearthed. This mass of new material has led me to conclusions about Baden-Powell and his extraordinary creation which are often at variance with those hitherto expressed.

London,   Tim Jeal
8 August 1989

ACKNOWLEDGEMENTS

I would like to thank the following:

1) Individuals and institutions whose manuscript collections proved indispensable.
2) People who knew Baden-Powell and agreed to meet me. All those listed helped me significantly.
3) People who communicated with me on the telephone or by letter, and in many instances sent me original material.
4) Scholars and authors who aided my research.
5) The staff of institutions and libraries providing me with information and/or material.

1) I am particularly indebted to Mr Francis Baden-Powell (Baden-Powell's great-nephew) who gave me unrestricted access to his unrivalled family archive. He and his cousin, the late Miss Joan Moore (who allowed me similar access to her substantial family collection), together enabled me to give a far more detailed account of Baden-Powell's youth and young manhood than has to date been possible. I am also most grateful to the British Scout Association and to the Boy Scouts of America for admitting me to their archives. In London, Mr Graham Coombe, the Scout Association's archivist, was immensely helpful during my long period of research, and subsequently assisted me with numerous queries in writing and over the telephone. My thanks to Mr J. L. Tarr (former Chief Scout Executive of the Boy Scouts of America) and to Mr K. H. Stevens (Chief Executive Commissioner, British Scout Association) for enabling me to study at Baden-Powell House the complete set of microfilms of the Boy Scouts of America's Baden-Powell Collection. I am indebted to Mr Richard H. Nicholson (whose grandfather, Major the Hon. A. Hanbury-Tracy was the Intelligence Officer at Mafeking, and whose great-uncle, Colonel J. S. Nicholson, M.P., was Baden-Powell's Chief Staff Officer in the South African Constabulary) for lending me diaries, letters and other papers from his collection, as well as the Mafeking Day Book, an outstanding historical document previously unknown to scholars, in which is recorded every message sent or received during the Siege of Mafeking. Mrs Antonia Eastman lent me numerous letters from her great-aunt, Lady Baden-Powell, to her aunt Mrs Christian

Rawson-Shaw (née Davidson) who was brought up by Lady Baden-Powell as a member of her family. These gave me fresh insights into the Baden-Powells' family life. I am most grateful to Mrs Honor Hurly for sending me copies of letters from Lord and Lady Baden-Powell to her father, Eric G. S. Walker (Baden-Powell's private secretary 1909–14), and for typing an accurate copy of her father's diaries for 1908–11. These papers enabled me to give the first full account of the range of problems facing Baden-Powell immediately after his inauguration of the Scouts. My thanks to Mr Paul C. Richards for allowing me to study his substantial collection of Baden-Powell papers (mainly letters from Lord and Lady Baden-Powell to Mrs E. K. Wade, Baden-Powell's private secretary 1914–41) at his house in Templeton, Mass. Mrs Audrey Renew, Curator of the Mafikeng Museum, kindly sent me copies of six unpublished diaries written by townspeople during the Siege and directed me towards others. She also answered a wide range of queries about different aspects of the Siege. Sir John Vyvyan Bt. and Mr F. Vyvyan kindly allowed me to study Col. Sir C. B. Vyvyan's Mafeking Papers: a most important collection since Col. Vyvyan was Base Commandant and Chief Engineer. Mr P. B. Boyden, the archivist at the National Army Museum, made available to me the extensive Baden-Powell collection in his care and answered many queries on general military matters.

2) I wish to thank Lord Baden-Powell's daughters the Hon. Mrs Gervas (Betty) Clay and the late the Hon. Mrs John (Heather) King, who talked to me at length about their father. I am also grateful to Mr Gervas Clay for his recollections. Mrs Yvonne Broome, Olave Baden-Powell's niece, talked to me about her childhood with the Baden-Powells. My series of interviews during 1983 and 1984 with the late Mrs Eileen Wade (Baden-Powell's private secretary during 1914–1941) were invaluable. There were few days when he was in England that she did not see Baden-Powell, and there were few aspects of his life and work about which she was ignorant. My meetings with the late Mrs Annie Scofield during 1984 were no less important. As Annie Court, she had first worked for Olave Baden-Powell's family in 1904 and stayed on with Olave after her marriage as her lady's maid and housekeeper for fifty years. Her memories of the Baden-Powells' home life until they left England in 1938 were exceptionally vivid. Mrs Kathleen Lessiter, who was nursemaid to the Baden-Powell children from 1919 to 1922, kindly wrote down her recollections for me and amplified them when we met. Miss Grace Browning and the Hon. Mrs Richard (Elizabeth) Coke were friends of the family during the early years of the Baden-Powells' marriage and recalled those days for me in person. All Baden-Powell's military colleagues were long dead when I started work, but two members of the 1930s' Scout Committee

were still alive and agreed to meet me. My thanks therefore to Mr Richard A. Frost, and Mr Lawrence Impey, who accompanied Baden-Powell on his last tour of India in 1937. Mr Don Potter, an Assistant Camp Chief at Gilwell Park from 1922 to 1933, knew Baden-Powell personally and was able to tell me about the battle between Scout Headquarters and Gilwell's Camp Chief during the early 1920s.

3) Mrs J. P. B. Agate, Mrs Virginia Ashton, Lord Baden-Powell, Miss M. de Beaumont, Mr William Beckwith, Mrs Margaret Bell, Mrs Y. Binning, Mr T. E. Bower, Mr Noel Brack, Mrs Pauline Bridger-Turner, Mrs J. Browne-Swinburne, Mrs Diana Cairns, Mrs Carp-Moore, Mr R. Chignell, Mr John Christie-Miller, Brigadier William Collingwood, Mrs Hope M. Chance, Mrs Mary Comber, Mr Spencer Copeland, Mrs J. Cotterell, Mrs Ann Crothers, Mr David Cuppleditch, Dr L. Davies, Mrs Pamela Davis, Mrs Kim Doig, Lord Downe, Miss Pamela Dugdale, the Countess of Dysart, Mr D. P. Eggar, Mr J. Elliott, Colonel T. B. A. Evans-Lombe, Dr W. Everett, Mrs E. Fawcus, Mr T. R. Fetherstonhaugh, the Hon. Mrs Elizabeth Field, Mrs Ursula FitzGerald, Lady Victoria Fletcher, Miss Sybilla J. Flower, Mr Anthony Gaddum, Miss Mary Gaddum, Veronica, Lady Gainford, Mrs M. Gaster, Major J. Gilman, Mr P. E. Gipps, Mr S. C. S. Godley, Mr C. Dymoke Green, Mr R. Goold-Adams, Lady Alastair Graham, Mr Kenneth Griffith, Mrs Marjorie M. Gubbins, Mrs Barbara Halsey, Lord Hardinge of Penshurst, Mrs Diana Hargrave, Miss Jean Harrap, Mr E. E. Harrison, Mr Rex Hazlewood, Mrs Sonia Heathcote-Amory, Mr A. J. C. Hewart, Miss B. Murray Hill, Mr S. Horniblow, Mr A. W. Hurll, Mrs L. Immelman, Mr David Jefferies, Mrs J. Jenkinson, Mr C. Judge-Smith, Mr S. Kekewich, the late Miss Rosemary Kerr, Mr H. King, Wing Commander John King, Mr A. Knight, Mr A. Longmate, Lord Lovat, Miss J. Loxton, Mrs Antoinette Lunn, Mrs M. McCloud, Miss Mary Mackenzie, Sir Alastair Mackie, Mrs M. Marwick, Mrs Joan Martin, Mrs P. Massey, Sir William Mather, Mrs Jennifer May, Mrs A. Maxton-Graham, Violet, Lady Merthyr, the late Sir Iain Moncreiffe of that Ilk Bt., Major T. Morley, Mr J. H. Morrison, Mr Michael Murphy, Mrs M. Nanney-Wynn, Mrs Joan Nevill, Mrs Billie Nightingale, Miss J. M. Nixon, Sir David Ogilvy Bt., Mr C. O'Ferrall, Dr N. O'Leary, Mr E. Palmer, Mrs Victoria Payne, Mr C. H. Pickford, Mr Geoffrey Pocock, Mrs Josephine Pollock, the Rev. Norman Pollock, Mr Peter Pooley, Mr Robin Pooley, Mrs M. Power, Mr David Powell, Mr Roger Powell, Mr and Mrs S. K. M. Powell, Mr B. D. Price, Miss Faith Ratcliff, Lord Renton, Lord Rodney, Miss Diana R. Rodney, Mrs Elizabeth Rogers, Anne, Countess of Rosse, Mrs Rowcliffe, Cynthia, Lady Sandys, Commander Claude Sclater R.N., Mr Geoffrey Scofield, Mrs Camilla Shoolbred, Mrs Mary

Siepmann (Mary Wesley), Miss J. Slade-Baker, Mr T. d'Arch Smith, Commodore Dacre Smyth R.A.N., Mr R. Warington Smyth, Mrs Olave Snelling, Mr P. Snyman, Mr C. G. Sowerby, Mrs Florence Thomson, Mrs R. Tilney, Mrs Fiona Turnbull, Major James Wade, Lt-Colonel John Walton, Mrs N. Wansborough, Dr M. Turner Warwick, Mr Michael Watt, Mrs Cynthia Wearing-King, Sir Osmond Williams Bt., Commander Brownlow V. Wilson R.N., Miss Margaret Wilson, Sir John Winnifrith, Mr F. Wolsey, Mr Christopher Woodford, Miss Erica Yonge, Mr J. S. Winthrop Young.

4)   I am most grateful to Dr John Springhall (of the University of Ulster) for keeping me in touch with the academic debate about the early Boy Scouts and their alleged militarism. Dr Springhall kindly lent me various papers and publications and discussed the early years with me at length. Dr Brian Willan, the author of *Sol Plaatje* (1984), and editor of *Edward Ross: Diary of the Siege of Mafeking* (1980), generously lent me his extensive research papers on the Siege of Mafeking, including an invaluable typescript copy of all the letters exchanged during the Siege between Major A. J. Godley and his wife. The Rev. Michael J. Foster has sent me highly relevant material about the earliest use of the Boy Scout name and has generously shared with me his original research into the history of the breakaway British Boy Scouts. Dr Allen Warren (of the University of York) kindly let me have photocopies of various research notes into the Movement's early years. My thanks to Professor Richard Bradford, author of a forthcoming biography of Major F. R. Burnham (Baden-Powell's scouting mentor in Matabeleland), for sending me copies of Baden-Powell's letters to Major Burnham. I am most grateful to Dr Brendan MacCarthy for many illuminating insights into Baden-Powell's psychology. Dr Edward M. Spiers (of the University of Leeds) made many useful suggestions for my research into social life in the British Army during the decades after Baden-Powell was first commissioned. My thanks to Dr J. H. Breytenbach (Archivist, Transvaal Archives) for corresponding with me in connection with President Kruger's intentions concerning Mafeking. Mr William Hillcourt (author of the last biography of Baden-Powell) was kind enough to let me have his opinion upon various points of detail connected with Baden-Powell's earliest Scouting publications. Mr Geoffrey Pocock sent me numerous documents in connection with the early history of the Legion of Frontiersmen. Mr James Moxon (editor of a forthcoming edition of Baden-Powell's illustrated Ashanti Diary) discussed the Ashanti Campaign with me, allowed me sight of his unedited typescript, and drew my attention to an invaluable account of events preceding the campaign. Lastly I would like to thank my researchers in Scotland and in South Africa respectively, Mrs Margot Butt and Miss Daphne Saul.

5) Mrs Rosemary Barbour (Scottish Record Office), Dr B. S. Benedikz (Univ. of Birmingham), Mr J. M. Berning (Rhodes Univ. Library, Grahamstown), Mr P. B. Boyden (National Army Museum), Miss M. J. Cartwright (South African Library, Cape Town), Mr Michael Chater (Toynbee Hall), Mr David C. Conzett and Ms Betty Newton (Boy Scouts of America), Mr G. A. Coombe (British Scout Assn.), Mr A. J. Crowther (Scout Assn. of New Zealand), Mrs A. Cunningham (Univ. of the Witwatersrand), Mr J. S. Dearden (The Ruskin Galleries, Bembridge Schl.), Mr J. R. Dovell (Dep. Gov., Parkhurst Prison), Ms J. F. Duggan (Univ. of Natal), Mrs Judy Duke-Wooley (Hurlingham Polo Assn.), Mr J. M. Fewster (Univ. of Durham), Miss Cynthia Forbes (Girl Guides Assn.), Mrs E. Freake and Mrs A. Wheeler (Charterhouse School Library), Maj. E. J. S. Garbutt (Sec. 13th/18th Royal Hussars, York), Ms Ellen G. Gartrell (Duke Univ., S. Carolina), Mrs Muriel D. Gibbs (Boys' Brigade), Mr D. C. Gibson (County Archivist, Kent), Major J. I. Grant (Sec., Scots Guards), Mr T. A. Griffiths (Scout Assn of Austral., NSW), Dr J. R. Hamilton (Med. Dir., Broadmoor Hospital), Mr H. A. Hanley (County Archivist, Bucks), Miss L. Hearn (Min. of Defence Archives), Mr D. J. van den Heever (Barlow Rand Ltd.), Mr Norman Higham (Univ. of Bristol), Mr Colin Inglis (Boy Scouts of South Africa), Ms K. Jacklin (Cornell Univ., Ithaca), Mr Charles Jackson (Scout Assn. of Austral., NSW), Miss L. Kennedy (City Librarian, Johannesburg), J. Osborne (Brighton Central Reference Library), Mr Peter S. H. Lawrence (Eton College Museum), Miss S. J. MacPherson (Cumbria C.C., Archives Dept.), Ms Patricia J. Methven (Liddell Hart Centre for Mil. Archives, Univ. of London, King's Coll.), Mr Richard Milne (Scout Assn. of Austral., Victoria), Miss F. P. Ntabeni (National Archives of Zimbabwe), Mr T. R. Padfield (Public Record Office, Kew), Mrs Audrey Renew (Mafikeng Museum, Bophuthatswana), Mr J. Reynecke (Transvaal Archives), Ms D. Rhodes (Dixson Library, Sydney), Mr J. M. Robertson (Scout Assn. of Austral., Tas.), Mr J. F. Russell (National Library of Scotland), Mr F. H. Shepherd (National Archives of Zimbabwe), Mr V. Waddell (Scout Assn. of Austral., Qld), Mr D. G. Wright (Victoria and Albert Museum). I also wish to thank the staff of the Bodleian Library, the British Library, the Cape Archives, Cape Town, the London Library, the Natal Archives, Pietermaritzburg, and successive adjutants of the 13th/18th Royal Hussars.

Finally, a heartfelt tribute to Tony Whittome and Harvey Ginsberg, my editors respectively at Hutchinson and at Morrow. Thanks to Tony's sympathetic and unerring advice I was able to cut a massive typescript by almost a quarter, much improving its readability, without losing anything essential. Harvey not only made many valuable suggestions on points of detail, but also suggested the subject of this book. That was over ten years ago, and I feel more grateful than I can say that he persisted in encouraging me to get started.

ILLUSTRATIONS

All the line illustrations reproduced in the text are by Baden-Powell and © SA

Abbreviations
Copyright in each illustration is held by the person or organization mentioned in brackets after it. The following abbreviations have been used:

SA   – Scout Association
BSA   – Boy Scouts of America
NAM   – National Army Museum

Maps

Illustrations

Dame Katharine Furse
Agnes Baden-Powell (*SA*)
Peter Baden-Powell (*Mr A. J. C. Hewart*)
Father and son (*Mrs Mary Comber*)
Awaiting the arrival of the Prince of Wales (*SA*)
Royal Salute (*Mr A. J. C. Hewart*)
Peter in 1932 (*Mrs Josephine Pollock*)
The family at Adelboden (*Mrs Josephine Pollock*)
Sunday Pictorial page (*Sunday Pictorial*)
Pictures of Baden-Powell:
At St James's Palace levée (*SA*)
As a Red Indian chief (*SA*)
With J. S. Wilson (*SA*)
With Scouts at Tilbury (*SA*)
With Betty on her wedding day (*Mr A. J. C. Hewart*)
On his balcony (*SA*)
With his pet hyrax (*SA*)
On his way to Treetops (*Mrs Honor Hurley*)
Treetops (*Mrs Honor Hurley*)
At Gilwell and with three Wolf Cubs (*both SA*)

THE BOY-MAN

I

THAT WONDERFUL WOMAN

'It is a well-established fact that very many of the greatest men of the world have acknowledged that they owe much of their success to the influence of their mother.'[1]

Robert Baden-Powell, 1937

'The whole secret of my getting on lay with my mother.'[2]

Robert Baden-Powell, 1933

1. Miracles and Nightmares

Of course London had seen vast crowds before: at the recent Diamond Jubilee and at the Iron Duke's funeral. But these had been sedate and unimpassioned gatherings in comparison with the wildly cheering flood of people which surged and swayed into Piccadilly Circus and Trafalgar Square on the evening of 18 May 1900. There would not be another spontaneous outburst of popular rejoicing to rival it until Armistice Day 1918.

Throughout the South African War Britain had been represented abroad as tyrannical and incompetent, only now managing to crush the Dutch farmers of two insignificant republics through resort to vast superiority of numbers. Mercifully the story of one small tin-hut town on the veldt had turned this unflattering version of events on its head. At Mafeking the British and colonial defenders had been few, and the Dutch besiegers many. To rejoice therefore at the relief of this small town was not to exult as a bully over a beaten victim, but to give thanks for the rescue of brave and resourceful men who for 217 days had defied impossible odds.

At Hyde Park Corner thankfulness and reviving national pride called forth patriotic songs and passionate cheering. In front of one particular house in nearby St George's Place the crowd was pressing forward against the railings, heads tilting to get a better view of the upstairs windows. At intervals they were rewarded by the appearance on the balcony of a stout and silver-haired old lady. From a distance she might almost have been another more famous old lady, but by now the Queen Empress and Mother of the Nation was in her bed at Windsor. Yet looking down at the waving, singing press of people, Mrs

Baden-Powell, as mother of a national hero, enjoyed sensations not far
from regal. Motherhood was after all a sacred institution, and since the
son was still at the scene of his triumph in South Africa, Henrietta
Grace Baden-Powell must needs represent him at home.

A few days later she stole the show at the Alhambra Theatre where
the outstandingly successful *Soldiers of the Queen* was playing. She had
already provided her son's first biographer[3] with enough material to
write a more readable book than all those that followed. Now she gave
a series of newspaper interviews which, while allowing proper pride of
place to Major-General Baden-Powell, left few of the journalists in any
doubt as to who had supplied the motive force behind all the family's
achievements. In a special supplement to *The Sphere*, she had described
various aspects of the 'training' she had given her children: how she
had taught the value of organization and planning, without imposing
restrictions or giving prizes; how she had fostered truthfulness and
honour by showing trust. None of her children ever took more from
the communal cash-box in the hall than they listed in their accounts.
Her children had always written to her each week when away, and did
so still though in their forties. Few academic subjects had been too
recondite for her to be able to assist them with. A journalist writing for
The Lady's Realm summed up a general feeling: 'It is impossible to
overestimate what her children owe to her.'[4]

Yet their debt was not entirely benign. In 1900 only one of Henrietta
Grace's six children had married. Three lived permanently at home
with her, and the two soldier sons did so whenever they had leave.
Thirty years earlier she had been closely questioned by an envious
schoolmistress about the uncanny influence she had with her children.
Writing to her favourite son, George, she explained that the mistress
particularly wanted 'to know by what method I have made you all so
good and so wonderfully obedient to me; she says she has been more
struck by hearing how you show *the spirit of wishing to do my will* than
by anything else. I could honestly corroborate this account.'[5]

In 1914, at the age of 57, just after his mother's death, Lieutenant-
General Sir Robert Baden-Powell corroborated it too with every
sentence of the eulogy he wrote for the Boy Scouts' official newspaper:

> There is only one pain greater than that of losing your mother, and
> that is for your mother to lose you – I do not mean by death but by
> your own misdeeds. Has it ever struck you what it means to your
> mother if you turn out a wrong 'un or a waster? She who bore you
> as a baby, and brought you up . . . and was glad when you showed
> that you could do things.
> As she saw you getting bigger and stronger and growing clever
> she had hoped in her heart of hearts that you were going to make a
> successful career and to make a good name for yourself – something

to be proud of. But if you begin to loaf about and do not show grit
and keenness, if you become a slacker, her heart grows cold with
disappointment and sorrow – all her loving work and expectation
have been thrown away, and the pain she suffers through seeing you
slide off into the wrong road is worse than if she had lost you in
death . . . Make your career a success, whatever line you take up,
and you will rejoice her heart. Try not to disappoint her but to make
her happy in any way that you can; you owe it to her . . .[6]

And if one's father was dead, and mother's 'heart grew cold', what
then? The anxieties and ambitions that drove Baden-Powell throughout his long life owe so much to his mother's influence that an account
of her background is essential.

*

Henrietta Grace had always been inordinately proud of her father. For
while Captain William Henry Smyth was a half-pay naval captain for
much of her childhood (she was born in 1824), he was also a gold
medallist of the Royal Astronomical Society, a vice-president of the
Royal Society and the author of an encyclopaedic guide to the
movements of the stars. Yet even as a girl she valued his membership
of the nation's scientific establishment more for the social kudos that
went with it than for the opportunities it gave her to mix with famous
scholars and scientists.[7] She regretted that few of her father's friends
had any connection with profitable occupations. She therefore looked
forward to the visits of the rising young lawyer, James Stephen,[8] with
whom she discussed railroad stocks, recent wills and the relative
earnings of well-known authors.[9] Industrialists she found just as
entertaining; and small wonder when Mr Wilkinson's party trick was
'to lay a thick pole across two tumblers of water and cut it through
with a sword without spilling a drop'.[10]
    Henrietta Grace felt overshadowed by her three well-educated older
brothers, all of whom were determined to succeed and did.
Warington, a geologist, rounded off his career with a knighthood and
the official position of Inspector of Crown Minerals. Charles became
Astronomer Royal for Scotland, and Henry distinguished himself as a
general in the Royal Artillery. The six Smyth girls were expected to
make marriage their career, but the fierce competitiveness of her
brothers affected Henrietta Grace deeply. One day her own boys
would be expected to vie with one another just as keenly and outdo all
their cousins.
    Her haphazard education, while better than that meted out to many
girls of her class, was nevertheless partly responsible for her tendency
to see achievement in terms more of social success than intrinsic worth.
She grew up to respect the single-minded pursuit of scholarship, but

never understood the disinterested passion which inspired so many of her father's scientific friends.

One such friendship would have a greater impact upon her than any other. Dr John Lee was a keen amateur astronomer and antiquary; he was also immensely rich and lived at Hartwell House, one of the country's finest Jacobean stately homes. What drew Henrietta Grace to Lee was not his love of science, nor even his purchase of sophisticated telescopes for her father, but Hartwell House itself with its aura of aristocratic grandeur. Lee had been a Mathematical Fellow at St John's College, Cambridge, but he was also the sole surviving kinsman of the line of baronets responsible for building and extending Hartwell over the centuries.[11]

Henrietta Grace and her father stayed as Lee's guests for many weeks at a time, year after year.[12] Nothing delighted the scholarly landowner more than to invite thirty or forty scientists to stay with him for anything up to a month, discussing their latest theories. It was ironic that he cared nothing at all for the aristocratic world which his house so vividly evoked for Henrietta Grace. He married a woman whom he described as being of 'humble station but excellent character', and invariably wore an old blue coat with brass buttons, and an antiquated old stovepipe hat.[13] Science and learning alone mattered to him. In 1851, after many years of effort, he finally persuaded Smyth to leave London and come to live in a nearby village. But although Lee helped his friend with the purchase of his new house, he nevertheless considered himself the real beneficiary of the arrangement, since he now had one of the country's foremost astronomers working at his side in Hartwell's observatory.[14] Lee and Smyth were gentlemen of a kind more often encountered in the eighteenth century. Both would have been amazed had they been able to foresee that by the end of the century most 'gentlemen' would deride as 'bad form' bookish and scholarly occupations, saving their applause for prowess in sport. *Scouting for Boys* would be published a mere forty years after these gentlemen died, yet that sensationally popular book would have been incomprehensible to them.

When Smyth expired in 1865, he was an Admiral on the retired list and a prominent figure in the worlds of astronomy, geography and hydrography. His life had been a fruitful and distinguished one, by any criteria. Yet in contributing to the various printed accounts of his life, he had been curiously reticent about his parents and his childhood. It has hitherto been accepted by all Baden-Powell's biographers that William Henry Smyth was the legitimate son of a well-respected American landowner, Joseph Brewer Palmer Smyth, of New Jersey, whose loyalty to the British Crown in the War of Independence had forced him to flee the country, consequently losing everything he had once owned. Henrietta Grace always feared the truth was less palatable.

In 1892 her second son, George, by then a recently knighted M.P., decided that it would be prudent to prepare a properly researched pedigree in case he were ever created a baronet or a peer. He contacted a cousin, G. A. Maskelyne, who was employed at the Public Record Office and was therefore an experienced researcher. After a preliminary examination of the available records he sent George a most unwelcome letter: 'I have never met with the smallest evidence that would satisfy say the College of Arms as to the parentage of your distinguished grandfather, and I do not very well see whence it is to be obtained. This is rather understating the impression left on my mind.'[15] His further researches in England and America convinced him that Joseph Smyth had been a cheat, a liar and a bigamist who was not the father of the woman whom Admiral Smyth had thought of as his sister, and possibly not of the Admiral himself. No proof could be found of a marriage between the Admiral's parents. His father's claim for compensation for the losses he alleged he had suffered during the War of Independence had been rejected by the British Treasury Commissioners on the grounds that the deeds and other papers produced by him were forgeries.[16] If he had ever returned from America, where he either died or disappeared in 1789, Joseph would have faced prosecution for fraud. Far from choosing a nautical career after deliberation, the Admiral had run away to sea as a cabin boy to escape his poverty-stricken home. He had only entered the Royal Navy as an ordinary seaman when the merchantman in which he had been serving was commandeered by the Admiralty.

This history (see Appendix I for a fuller account) made William Smyth's achievements all the more remarkable, but caused Henrietta Grace and other members of the family embarrassment and shame. She had long suspected the existence of such skeletons and therefore clung tenaciously to compensating family myths handed down by her father. Without a shred of genealogical evidence, he had adopted the arms of Captain John Smith, the nigh legendary founding father of Virginia.[17] His daughter extended this process, describing herself as great-niece to Lord Nelson.[18] This was, however, entirely fanciful. Her mother's half-brother had married an extremely distant relation of Nelson. Yet these legends were taken very seriously by Henrietta Grace's children. Baden-Powell himself would support the John Smith story until 1930, many years after it had been abandoned by his Smyth cousins; and he was still describing his mother as Nelson's great-niece when he was first listed in *Burke's Peerage and Baronetage* in 1922. Henrietta Grace used to make out that her father had been at Naples with Nelson, at a time when the great man had been dead for almost a decade. Nor can her unfounded assertions be dismissed as the kind of romantic embellishments which were commonplace in the ages of Walter Scott and Tennyson. Henrietta Grace would soon be responsible for giving her family a double-barrelled surname, for altering the family's coat of arms and for claiming that her husband's family was in direct line of descent from a Welsh prince.[19] She needed to indulge in this genealogical myth-making as compensation for a real family history she could not accept. Her sons supported her endeavours because – knowing that the rapid expansion of the middle class was making life more and more competitive – they at once saw the advantages of having an aristocratic-sounding name and an impressive pedigree. But Henrietta Grace was driven by deeper needs and ambitions.

She inherited from her father not only his gifts for factual embroidery, but his tenacious character and his capacity for action. Had her family background been merely conventionally respectable, it seems unlikely that she would ever have been driven to undertake her own great creative enterprise: the transmutation of a disaster-prone family into a success-generating cooperative, in which she would be treasurer, director of planning and supreme arbiter. Possessing all the worldly calculation essential for that task, she also owned a passionate nature; and in the matter of her own marriage, she would listen to her heart rather than her head.

★

When Henrietta Grace was 15, she visited Oxford with her parents. She had hoped to meet William Buckland, the university's first and most eccentric Professor of Geology. In his rooms at Christ Church, he kept a small menagerie which at times contained bears, monkeys, guinea pigs and lizards. In her diary Henrietta Grace mentioned her hope that the professor would introduce her to some 'lions'. Since she usually employed this term as a synonym for famous people, it seems unlikely that Buckland had made a dangerous addition to his collection. In fact he was out of town when Captain Smyth called, and he and his daughter were lucky to find another Oxford acquaintance at home when they called at his house in New College Lane. This was the Reverend Baden Powell.

Powell had been Savilian Professor of Geometry at Oxford for many years, and knew Smyth from meetings at the Royal Society where they discussed the complex mathematical formulae required in original astronomical calculation. Henrietta Grace and her parents dined with the professor and his wife, and afterwards were delighted by their host's 'beautiful experiments in polarized light'. Later he played the organ and insisted that Henrietta Grace try her hand.

Miss Smyth did not meet Professor Powell again until 1845, six years later, by which time she was 21 and he 48 and a widower now. That year the annual Visitation Dinner at Greenwich Observatory was organized by Captain Smyth. Before the gentlemen went in to dinner,

Henrietta Grace sat quietly with the professor on a little sofa, enjoying once more his 'very amiable yet clever countenance and gentlemanly bearing'. In December Baden Powell stayed with the Smyths for three days at their house in Cheyne Walk. Already powerfully drawn to him, Henrietta Grace blushed with pleasure when she saw him gaze intently at her while she warmed a foot at the fire, and then heard him sigh deeply and 'exclaim aloud, though evidently unconscious that it was heard: "Yes, perfect".'

During the course of a walk through Chelsea, Henrietta Grace chose two topics of conversation which she knew would deepen his feelings for her. She had recently been running a small Sunday school class, and now explained her system of teaching and how she had 'so gained the affection and confidence of the children that they opened their little hearts most unreservedly to me and this enabled me to give I hope really suitable advice'. For a man with no wife and four children still young enough to need parental care this could only have been wonderfully heartwarming information. Besides being a scientist Baden Powell was an ordained cleric with a reputation for holding alarmingly advanced religious views. At Oxford he was well-known for a particular obsession; hardly any of his sermons lacked a reference to the insufficiency of scriptural grounds for transforming the Jewish Sabbath into the Christian Sunday. As one old friend said, 'He had the Sabbath on the brain.' The Fourth Commandment, with its injunction to respect the Sabbath above other days, was anathema to him; so when Henrietta Grace launched into a fierce attack on the literal interpretation of the Commandment as being 'against the spirit of the New Testament', Professor Powell was deeply moved. 'He suddenly exclaimed, "You do not know how this interests me!" The great agitation of his voice instantly proved this little speech an offer.' Although Henrietta Grace claimed she had been ignorant of Professor Powell's vehemently anti-Sabbatarian views, she noted in her diary: 'He would not I believe have married any woman who differed on this subject.' What all Oxford knew so well had evidently reached her ears.[20]

Henrietta Grace feared that her parents would veto the marriage on account of Professor Powell's age and because she would be his third wife (the first two both having died). In fact Captain and Mrs Smyth needed very little winning over and the marriage took place the following March in New St Luke's Church, Chelsea.

For all her vaunted successes with children, Henrietta Grace disliked her husband's offspring from the beginning. Fortunately Professor Powell's two younger children had been adopted by an aunt immediately after their mother's death. Matters improved slightly between Henrietta Grace and her little charges after the dismissal of an unsatisfactory governess, but 7-year-old Carrie was never accepted and was soon packed off to Tunbridge Wells to join her two younger sisters in the care of their aunt. Baden Henry, then aged four, stayed on with his stepmother, who later thought him a bad influence on her children, though she never specified in what way. Physically weak, quiet and studious, the poor boy suffered from temper tantrums.[21] Quite often he too was sent away for a spell in Tunbridge Wells. Henrietta Grace's relations with her own children would be a different matter.

Her first son (christened Warington in honour of her eldest brother) was born 'after indescribable agonies' on 3 February 1847. Only ten months later George made his appearance, to be followed by Augustus in 1849 and Frank a year after that. Between pregnancies Henrietta Grace enjoyed entertaining eminent visitors. In 1847 the British Association met at Oxford and for a week she was hostess to the most famous scientists in the land: Sir John Herschel, Sir David Brewster, Sir Roderick Murchison, Sir Henry de la Beche, William Fox Talbot and Sir George Airy. On one of these social evenings Frank Buckland, son of the eccentric Professor of Geology, arrived with a bag of snakes and a bear dressed in an undergraduate's cap and gown. On another occasion the young French astronomer, Urbain Leverrier – who had taken a leading part in the discovery of the hitherto unknown planet Neptune – played the violin while Henrietta Grace accompanied him at the piano.[22]

But weeks like this one were sadly few and far between. Within Oxford itself, Baden Powell was becoming an increasingly isolated figure. As early as 1833, in his book *Revelation and Science*, he had argued that recent geological discoveries made it impossible to deny the contradictions in the Bible's account of the Creation. In the 1840s, he spoke out boldly even in letters to bishops. 'If a church offer arguments as the proofs of its infallibility, which yet to me are unsatisfactory, it has no right to condemn me for rejecting them.'[23] In September 1853 Henrietta Grace recalled her husband telling her that 'every miracle would be explained by natural means in time . . . Mesmerism has actually cured the blind and made water taste like wine.'[24] Publication of such views could lead to prosecution in the church courts. Already Professor Powell had written enough to wreck his chances of preferment. Many clergymen shared his radical views but never voiced them. When bishops and even a few fortunate rectors were paid in thousands a year and valuable sinecures were numerous, it took a man of high principles and great intellectual honesty to publish unorthodox ideas.

When in the early 1850s, Baden Powell knew that he was mistrusted by most of his clerical colleagues in Oxford, and had all but given up hope of opening the University to scientific studies, he turned his attention to London where he began to give regular summer lectures.[25] Their success suggested to him a new role as scientific pundit and popularizer, but this would be impossible unless he left Oxford. A move to the capital also made sense in other ways. Captain Smyth occupied a privileged position in metropolitan intellectual circles, and Baden Powell was himself making more and more friends among London-based radicals and intellectuals. In 1852 he took a long lease on a house in Stanhope Street, just north of Hyde Park, and on 17 May the following year he moved there permanently with his wife and children.[26]

'What a family this is!' wrote Henrietta Grace shortly after giving birth to her sixth child and first daughter, christened Henrietta in honour of herself.[27] It was only a year since her sons Warington, George, Augustus and Frank had been joined by another brother, Penrose. Nothing delighted her more than to see her learned professor 'with baby in his arms and his eight small children jumping around him'.[28] (She had included Carrie and Baden Henry in this total.) But during 1855 and 1856 Henrietta Grace lived through the nightmare of losing three children: Penrose, aged three; Henrietta, aged two and a half; and Jessie, aged only eight months. The fact that these deaths followed one another so swiftly made them very hard to bear, even in an age when so many died in infancy. Diphtheria probably accounted for two deaths and pneumonia for the third. The inadequacies of the medical profession added to the anguish of these illnesses. Unable to believe her children were truly dead, Henrietta Grace would place their corpses by the fire so that they should not grow cold.[29]

By the time Jessie died, Henrietta Grace had become pregnant again and dreaded the future. Her overriding longing was to have a child that lived, whatever its sex. Her natural preference, given the loss of her only daughters, was for a girl. But on 22 February 1857, she gave birth to a son. He was christened Robert Stephenson Smyth Powell, but from very early in his life was called Stephe (pronounced Steevie), Ste, or Stephenson. He would only become Robert to the world at large after he was knighted and chose to be Sir Robert. His first two names were in honour of Robert Stephenson, only son of the famous engineer who, like his father, had admired the works of Professor Powell. Whatever hopes of future benefit Henrietta Grace may have entertained when this rich man agreed to be Stephe's godfather were quickly dashed. The potential benefactor died when his little namesake was only two and no legacy was forthcoming.

Stephe began his life in a privileged position. Because of the recent deaths there were seven years between himself and Frank, the youngest of the other four. But Stephe's advantage did not last long enough for him to enjoy it, for he was scarcely weaned when his mother gave birth to a longed-for daughter, Agnes. Then two years later, when Stephe was three, another brother made his appearance:

Baden Fletcher Smyth Powell. As so often happens, the last son of an
ageing mother comes to occupy a special place in her affections, and in
no time at all Baden was 'darling baby', 'the precious babe' or 'sweetest
Badie', whereas Stephe remained plain Stephe, or Stephenson more
often than not. Later Stephe sometimes called Baden 'the curled
darling' in ironic mimicry of his mother's tender epithets.[30]

Apparently Stephe was able to dress himself by the age of 3 but,
in his mother's eyes, 'possessed no special disposition for mischief or
adventure'.[31] Nevertheless his artistic talent was undeniable from the
age of two and a half when he drew a picture of men leading camels and
carrying crosses in their hands. 'The Lord Jesus Christ and good men
taking up crosses to remember him by. RSSP 1859,' Henrietta Grace
wrote under it. From about the time when they were two she would
seat her children round her in a ring and tell them moral stories. The
need to take up our crosses and bear them patiently was one such, and
since all Bible stories suggested Eastern scenery Stephe had included
camels in his visual version of the sermon.[32] A few years later he went
on to illustrate classics like *The Adventures of Gil Blas* and some animal
stories of his own. He sketched seaside views when holidaying in
Cornwall or on the Kentish coast, and at home drew plants under the
microscope with great precision. But his father's skilful pen-and-ink
cartoons, drawn in the manner of Cruikshank, proved the most
enduring influence on Stephe's work; and many of the comic
illustrations he produced during his teens are indistinguishable from
his father's productions.[33]

Professor Powell was a tolerant and enthusiastic father but suffered
from a scholar's self-absorption. Carrie remembered this trait and later
described 'how he would take her with him for walks in New College
Gardens or in Christ Church Meadow, allowing her to sit silently
employed with pencil and paper, while he worked amid his books and
instruments. She learned to watch for the pauses in his work, when her
questions would please.'[34]

Stephe was allowed – as his brothers had been before him – to enter
his father's study as soon as he was able to crawl up the stairs unaided.
A note survives to the effect that on 12 April 1860, Stephe played 'this
little piggy' with his father in his study.[35] By then the Professor was
already a sick man and unable to exert himself. A few days later his
condition deteriorated alarmingly, and Stephe and Agnes were sent
away to stay with their mother's parents in the country. Stephe would
never see his father again, though he received some paper animals cut
out by him on his deathbed.[36]

His final year was the most harrowing and momentous in Professor
Powell's life. During it he published *The Order of Nature*, in which he
courageously threw his full support behind recent advances made in
the fields of biblical scholarship and social history. The intensity of the

passions and anxieties aroused by religious controversy at this time can scarcely be exaggerated. The idea that man – far from being the centre of the universe – might be only the last link in the evolutionary chain, struck terror into the hearts of most Victorians. To live in a mechanistic world without any hope of personal immortality was a prospect few people were prepared to contemplate. Baden Powell did not go that far, but in *The Order of Nature* he finally abandoned his earlier attempts to find satisfactory rational proof of the validity of Christian belief. Instead he now stressed the personal spiritual appeal of Jesus' teaching, claiming that the only 'proof' Christianity required was contained in the moral truth of the Gospels. Such arguments placed him far closer to the Unitarians and to radical theologians like Blanco White and Francis Newman than to his old colleagues in the Anglican Church.

During the 1850s, many clerics explained away evolutionary theories by arguing that the gaps in the fossil record and the apparent suddenness of changes in species could only be explained by God's decision to create anew every time conditions became unfavourable for existing species. In *The Order of Nature* Baden Powell poured scorn on such last-ditch arguments. In the October issue of the influential *Quarterly Review* his book was savaged by the Archbishop of Dublin and others. Far from recanting, Professor Powell sent off a still more trenchant essay – in which he demolished the historical authenticity of the miracles – for inclusion in a collection provisionally entitled *Essays and Reviews*. Benjamin Jowett, of Balliol, was another contributor and wrote of their intentions: 'We are determined not to submit to this abominable system of terrorism, which prevents the statement of the plainest facts, and makes true theology or theological education impossible.'[37] Baden Powell had just been reported to the Bishop of London for heretical preaching, so he knew what Jowett meant.

When *Essays and Reviews* was published in late March 1860, Baden Powell was suffering from breathlessness and chest pains, and his health grew suddenly worse in mid-April.[38] This was cruelly frustrating for him. The British Association would be meeting in Oxford in June and Darwin's theory had been scheduled for debate. With theological conservatives like 'Soapy' Sam Wilberforce, the Bishop of Oxford, now declaring against Darwin, an historic confrontation was inevitable. Baden Powell supported Darwin, and Darwin admired Powell's writings as he indicated very clearly in his introduction to the third edition of *The Origin of Species*. Professor Powell thus seemed set to play a decisive part in the proceedings at Oxford, as the first eminent cleric to declare publicly for Darwin. Nor could he hope for a better forum in which to outmanoeuvre his Anglican traducers.

But he did not get better. Professor Powell died on 11 June 1860 with Henrietta Grace and three of his sons at his side. Several of his enemies were callous enough to suggest that his death was an example of that divine intervention in human affairs which he had so often ridiculed.

At 3, Stephe was too young to understand the finality of death but, brought up in a close-knit family in which his father was idolized by his mother and had often been available to him, he must have found the loss very distressing. Augustus had adored his father, and Stephe was upset by his favourite brother's grief. Professor Powell died just too soon to see *Essays and Reviews* become one of the most famous books of the nineteenth century. Along with two other contributors he would have been prosecuted in the church courts for the heretical contents of his essay.[39] When, ten years later, Canon Pusey crowed over his death as 'his removal to a higher tribunal' and publicly suggested that he had died without the consolation of religious faith, Stephe was old enough to understand the attack. He grew up with a distrust of clergymen and theology which he would never lose.

Baden Powell had been admired by some of the nation's intellectual leaders – Darwin, Babbage, George Eliot, G.H. Lewes, and James and Harriet Martineau. But after his death most of these intellectual friends distanced themselves. Henrietta Grace had admired well-known scholars but had never shared her husband's passion for scientific truth. Her love for him had led her to suppress her own social ambitions which had been simmering since her girlhood days at Hartwell House. Yet even while his struggle against his ideological enemies had been approaching its climax, she had been venturing into a glittering milieu entirely ignored by liberal intellectuals. In May 1858 she had achieved her long-standing ambition to be presented at Court, and for some years prior to that had been striving to cultivate various aristocrats. Just before the family had moved to London, Henrietta Grace had admitted her ambitions. 'By moving there we shall probably secure a position for our darling children in Society, which as far as earthly things are worth consideration, will be very desirable . . . We will not throw it away.'[40]

In his letter of condolence to Henrietta Grace, Benjamin Jowett described Professor Powell as 'one of the very small class of really original minds and perhaps one of the still smaller class who venture to say what they think'; he then went on to exhort the widow: 'I cannot regard it as an aggravation of this calamity that you are left with a large family of children. It is a trust which may almost be regarded as a glorious one. When children like yours have good natural abilities and dispositions, there is nothing that may not be done with them and for them.'[41]

Henrietta Grace heartily agreed. She was not overawed by the magnitude of her responsibilities.

2. 'Poor Little Stephe' (1857–68)

Of all Lord Baden-Powell's biographers only the earliest, Harold Begbie, did not give the impression that Stephe was his mother's favourite son. Often the idea that he was uniquely adored by her has been conveyed indirectly: the intensity of his affection seeming to imply an equally profound reciprocal emotion in her. Francis Aitken, writing like Begbie in 1900, described Baden-Powell's love for his mother as 'passionate devotion'[1] and assumed an especially privileged relationship. But Henrietta Grace's diaries and her letters to her other children[2] show that in boyhood Stephe ranked lower than George and Baden in his mother's affections and enjoyed fewer opportunities than Agnes to be with her.

Of course children in large families always have to learn that they will never have more than a part of their parents' time and love. But when the father is dying and the mother is not only looking after him but also caring for a newly-born baby, the other children will be lucky to get any attention at all. A child of 3 or 4 can hardly be expected to be logical about the sudden removal of loving parents and having to endure a two-month exile with grandparents in the country. When this happened to Stephe he missed his mother very much, nor did he see her for long when he came home to London after his father's death. Henrietta Grace was physically and emotionally exhausted after her ordeal and went to stay with her Powell cousins at Speldhurst in Kent to recuperate. Only baby Baden went with her; he had been born just three weeks before his father's death. When away again early the following year, Henrietta Grace confessed to her mother that she felt guilty about 'poor little Stephe' and added, 'I do not feel as if I was (sic) doing my duty to him whilst so long away – though he is so well taken care of.'[3] Stephe was just 4 when his mother wrote this letter, and he would again be separated from her for several months that summer.[4]

During the latter part of 1860, and throughout 1861, Stephe suffered from weeping fits and tantrums. 'Strange fits of passion' his mother called them, but she seemed not to connect them with his thwarted longing to be with her.[5] If she was to be away, though, her parents' house was probably the best place for the children. Stephe played most often with Agnes, who was closest to him in age. He had a little cart in which he enjoyed pushing his dolls.[6] Like Agnes, he made dolls' clothes and delighted in discussing them with her.[7] He would later say that he learned the art of 'skirt dancing' – as he called dancing in a girl's skirt – in his early childhood years. When he was not with Agnes, he was with 12-year-old Augustus who, in spite of the six-year age difference, enjoyed drawing with him in the garden and showing him the birds' eggs he had found in the woods.

In January 1862 Augustus began to display symptoms of tuberculosis, losing weight and strength rapidly. Henrietta Grace decided that he might do better if given the benefit of country air. The boy's aunt and uncle, Charles and Susan Powell, offered to have him at Speldhurst where his spinster aunts, Eleanor and Emily, would have more time to devote to nursing him than would his hard-pressed mother in London. From the point of view of Stephe and the other children, however, the arrangement seemed less than ideal. For the whole of 1862 and for the first three months of 1863, Henrietta Grace was travelling backwards and forwards between London and Speldhurst – sometimes spending a few days there, sometimes a few weeks.

By March Augustus was an invalid, needing to sleep every afternoon and only able to get out in a wheelchair. He sent home patient and courageous letters, giving details of his life: the bitter taste of the quinine he was obliged to drink, the difficulties he was experiencing in stuffing a viper, and the progress he was making in rearing young sparrows and blackbirds.[8] Augustus included special messages for Stephe, and quite often wrote to him directly, telling his mother that nobody but Stephe himself should open these letters.[9] Henrietta Grace wrote back: 'Stephenson has made a drawing for you quite by himself, and then he asked me to tell him how to spell the words he wanted to write on the back. He draws away by himself all kinds of subjects, without anything to copy from. He looks very pale and thin.'[10]

All Augustus's letters to her were read aloud by Henrietta Grace to her other children. Since she told them that there was little chance of his recovery, it must have been heart-rending for them to learn how much their brother wanted to come home. 'Please will you draw me a plan of the garden?' he asked, so that in a reallocation of plots he should get the bed facing south. In the same letter he requested: 'Thank dear Stephenson for his nice picture and tell him that it was very well drawn indeed . . . I send him this picture of me with Mama's badge.'[11] As Henrietta Grace assured Augustus, Stephe often spoke about him and 'looks through the window of the library every day to Mr Heathcote's weathercock and says "the wind is not good for children today".'[12]

In late March, after spending a month with Augustus, Henrietta Grace came home with bronchitis; she was ill enough to need a nurse. The youngest children were again sent to their grandparents, and soon their mother heard that 'Stephenson is constantly talking about his Mama and wishing to come home to her.'[13] In May the whole family stayed with Augustus at Speldhurst and the sick boy enjoyed watching Stephe ride a pony called Sandy, showing no fear at all. The following February Henrietta Grace left London to be 'constantly with my darling boy'. Although apparently close to death, Augustus lingered on through March and into April. 'I have explained to him,' declared his mother, 'as nearly as I can his exact state, and it makes him quite happy to know that all must now be left to God's will, whether he may live or die.'[14]

'This world is such an endless trial now,' wrote Henrietta Grace in March. She faced a new quandary. 'Augustus still dwells so much on having Stephe to stay with him but we cannot attempt it at present for he is too weak to bear more than one person at a time with him.'[15] Augustus would never see his favourite brother again. For whatever reason, his mother did not let Stephe go with Frank and George when they went to say goodbye to the dying boy on 1 April.

By then Augustus had written his last letter to his brothers. In a shaky hand he thanked them for all their letters and asked them to pray for him. Letters like this one, read aloud to 'the little ones' by George, must have had a profound effect, as must the will which Augustus had composed with his mother's help. While his 'money and microscope' were left to his mother to hold 'for the general use of all', Augustus bequeathed his next most valuable possession to Stephe. This was his telescope. Stephe also inherited his brother's stamps, his scrapbooks and compasses. Augustus died on 3 April 1863 aged 13.[16]

Only two months later Henrietta Grace's favourite son, George, showed definite signs of having the same illness. But fortunately for George – and for Stephe as it turned out – Speldhurst was not to be used as a sanatorium again. After consulting the country's most eminent physician, Henrietta Grace decided to follow the advice of those recommending a long sea voyage to Australia. George would stay briefly in Madras and return via the Cape.[17] He was then 16, and would spend four more winters abroad during the next six years: two in India, one in Portugal and one more in Australia. With 'my own most precious and most darling Georgie' far beyond the range of visiting, with Warington now serving in the Merchant Navy and Frank recently sent away to Marlborough, the autumn of 1863 was to be a very special time for Stephe, Agnes and Baden. At long last, after almost continuous disruptions of their home life, their mother was able to devote the greater part of her time to them.

In a letter beginning typically 'my sweetest darling George',[18] Henrietta Grace described for her absent son how the three youngest children sat with her drawing every evening after their tea, 'until my dinner bell rings, and then we all go to the library and they & Miss Groffel [their German governess] sit at work at the round table whilst I have my sad solitary supper'. Stephe, Henrietta Grace explained, was so thin that he was being given as much milk and cream as he would drink. But although Stephe was sharing a room with Fraulein Groffel, his mother did not let him have Augustus's old bedroom; that was being kept for George.[19]

Perhaps it was the realization that he would never in any ordinary

way be able to win as privileged a position in his mother's heart as that
enjoyed by George and 'the precious babe' that drew Stephe to acting
and clowning at a very early age. Few activities could rival it for
attracting attention. Occasionally though, he disappointed his mother
by being 'too shy to act'.[20] But within a few years he had become the
'prime comedian' and leader in all family theatricals. All the children
tried hard to please their mother and he was no exception. Holidaying
in Cornwall when he was 7, he delighted her by presenting her with a
large bunch of wild flowers on her birthday.[21] 'Remember to help
others,' she told him. 'We cannot be good ourselves unless we are always
helping others.'[22] That this sank into Stephe's mind was evident 40 years
later when he wrote the Scout Law and dreamed up the daily good turn.

On the whole the children responded well to Henrietta Grace's
constant stream of exhortations and behaved as their mother wished
them to do. Stephe's picture of the good men carrying crosses pleased
Henrietta Grace, just as Warington had pleased her by drawing
machines decorated with crosses and actually presenting her with a
couple of crude wooden crucifixes.[23] Every biographer of Baden-
Powell, writing after the foundation of the Scouts, has mentioned
Stephe's 'Laws for me when I am old', written in February 1865 just
after his eighth birthday, and has seen them as early evidence of a
flawless character. In fact, as will be seen, Henrietta Grace had
Christian Socialist contacts and encouraged some of their beliefs in her
children. When George was 6, his mother reported him as saying:
'You will not see many poor people when I am a man; they will all have
money and be able to buy things. For I shall give it to them and build
some houses for them.'[24] Stephe's version is longer than this and, apart
from its clearly having been written by an older boy, incorporates
more of the religious sentiment which usually found a place in
Henrietta Grace's letters at this date.

LAWS FOR ME WHEN I AM OLD
I will have the poor people to be as rich as we are, [wrote Stephe] and
they ought by rights to be as happy as we are, and all who go across
the crossings shall give the poor crossing sweeper some money and
you ought to thank God for what he has given us and he made the
poor people to be poor and the rich people to be rich and I can tell
you how to be good. Now I will tell you. You must pray to God
whenever you can but you cannot be good with only praying but
you must try very hard to be good.

by R.S.S. Powell, Feb. 26th 1865.[25]

Undoubtedly Stephe himself was trying to be 'good' and had made
great progress. Two years before he penned these lines, Henrietta
Grace had pronounced him 'wonderfully improved . . . So good, and

as sweet as can be. Indeed all three little dears show the effect of the last
4 or 5 months training.'[26] She often talked about her 'training' but
without ever being very precise about it. Certainly the boys had to
keep accurate accounts of their expenditure, they had to write
regularly if away and were constantly encouraged to make the most of
their abilities. But there was nothing unusual about this. Her
encouragement of outdoor exercise was certainly interesting at this
date, and very likely had a lasting influence on Stephe. But her real
'training' had less to do with specific activities than with her emotional
relationship with each child. When asked by a headmistress to explain
'by what method I have made you [her children] so good', Henrietta
Grace suggested that she had succeeded because each child had within
himself or herself 'the spirit of wishing to do my will'.[27]

Her enthusiastic praise for all forms of pleasing behaviour obviously
played a part, but less perhaps than her frequent depiction of herself as a
poor widow struggling on their behalf without any real help or
understanding. 'So many plans for your dear futures I am gradually
carrying out,' she wrote to them all in late 1869. 'Will my dear sons
ever feel gratitude or any sympathy for their poor mother, working on
alone for your benefit? But what comfort you all give me in being
good.'[28] And being 'good' also meant displaying 'thorough openness'
with her and never, like Frank, being devious, or falling victim to
'peculiar modes of retiring within himself;[29] nor, like Stephe,
surrendering to 'strange fits of passion'. When Stephe became famous,
Henrietta Grace would tell reporters that he had never cried as a boy.[30]
That he kept his feelings hidden would be noted by many people down
the years.

The crucial lesson that Stephe learned in the months after his
favourite brother's death was that in a cruelly uncertain world his
mother was all important and yet might at any moment absent herself
or become remote. His safety would therefore have to lie in striving to
please her enough to keep her with him. To feel good, it was going to
be necessary to *be* good in Henrietta Grace's sense of the word. Only
by acting up to his mother's expectations could he keep at bay that
horrifying spectre of a self-sacrificing mother's heart 'grown cold with
disappointment'.[31]

3. Clinging Together

In the eighteenth century there had been a relatively stable social
hierarchy. Aristocracy and gentry were at the top, closely followed by
an upper middle class of army and naval officers, clergy, lawyers and
bankers; then the commercial classes, and beneath them a ragbag of
shopkeepers, skilled craftsmen, clerks, small farmers and so forth.

Lowest of all was the vast labouring class. But by the time Professor Powell died the central strata were beginning to blur and overlap, as more and more professions were recognized and a greater and greater variety of goods and services generated wealth for an increasingly large proportion of the population. The old upper middle class became acutely vulnerable to the commercial class below and, throughout the whole middle class, uncertainty of demarcation created a minefield of defensive snobberies.

The idea of losing the social position into which one had been born was the private nightmare of all but the most securely insulated Victorians. Henrietta Grace was tormented by it. 'My nerves have almost gone beyond my control – sleep is barely possible. I have felt nearly out of my mind with anxiety – fear, terror for those I love so dearly. My sweet good children, if only I could do more for you . . . I feel daily that I must try harder still to keep up our precious children to the high position and standard they would have taken had their dearest Father lived. I know the advantage for them of good cultured society . . .'[1] Like many prosperous merchants, the Powells had left the City in the late eighteenth century and opted for the ownership of land. Professor Powell's father had owned estates in Kent; but they were divided in a manner more beneficial to the professor's two brothers than to himself.[2] As an Oxford professor and an Anglican clergyman, Baden Powell would unquestionably have been a gentleman, and the fact that his father had been High Sheriff of Kent would have given him additional cachet. Given the essential base of enough money, the social position of a boy's parents could lift him in manhood above a crowd of financial equals. But money – taboo subject though it was – remained the solid bedrock upon which all social pretensions had to be firmly grounded.

One way to appear to have more of the stuff than one actually had was to live in the kind of house which prosperous people inhabited. Then one could clandestinely engage fewer servants than the number usually thought necessary, and even let the place for part of the year. In reality Henrietta Grace's financial position was not as precarious as it has usually been represented. The professor left £2,000 in 3% Great Western Debentures, and land in Kent which she sold in 1863 for £6,300. Although the lease on the family house in Stanhope Street was in trust for the children, she had marriage settlement investments worth £5,000. One of her husband's sisters decided to give her £200 a year, and she would soon receive a Civil List pension of £150 per annum. With all her capital invested, her total income was between £700 and £800 a year, about the sum which a young lawyer or physician might have expected to earn, but well below what successful members of either profession would have commanded.[3]

Henrietta Grace's decision to leave the vast house in Stanhope Street would have made more sense if she had chosen to move into a considerably smaller one, but her choice of an only marginally less imposing house in an exclusive neighbourhood just to the south of Kensington Gardens meant that part of her living expenses would have to be met out of capital. 'I suffer fearfully,' she confessed, 'from the dread of leading my darling boys to the most dangerous idea that they may safely meddle with capital.'[4] But by 1869, with George now 22 and Frank 19, she suffered even more from the thought that her boys would soon be boys no longer and that their whole lives might be blighted unless she were able to provide for them 'a gentlemanly home' and attract to it 'good society'.[5] Though 'in the midst of great poverty' – as she chose to describe circumstances which would have struck the majority of her fellow citizens as more than comfortable – Henrietta Grace was determined to 'rise to the occasion and spend out for them'.[6] She comforted herself with the thought that the 'inductive powers of reasoning' passed on to her by her husband made it safe for her to abandon the 'tight laws of prudence, which tend to mediocrity in all things'.[7] Prudence was fine for unadventurous people, but not for *her* family. All her children were going to excel.

Henrietta Grace already knew the Earl and Countess of Rosse, Lord and Lady Stanley of Alderley, Lord Brassey of railway contracting fame and assorted members of the Baring family. Her house in Hyde Park Gate would certainly be sufficiently distinguished for grand entertaining, but she would not be happy with it until she had rebuilt the dining room and replaced virtually all the furniture. To do this she was prepared to borrow £1,500 from her lawyer at 6%, which was then an exorbitant rate.[8] Many years later Hilda – who married Warington shortly before Henrietta Grace died – would accuse her mother-in-law of being ridiculously naïve to suppose that 'living in a great house and entertaining was the way to get her family on'.[9] Hilda was both right and wrong. Henrietta Grace's actions undoubtedly helped George to get on, and probably had some beneficial effects upon Stephe's early career. But for Warington, Agnes and Baden there would be no benefit at all, in fact the reverse, for the capital which they would otherwise have inherited was dissipated in the decades after their father's death. Moving in exalted circles can certainly help a family to get on if the great folk encountered have jobs or patronage in their gift. So, in the crucial matter of jobs and marriages, did Henrietta Grace's social efforts have any discernible effect?

She *did* contrive to get offers of jobs for her boys, but these came through contacts which would have been available to her if she had gone to live in a modest suburb. One friend of her father promised employment in the Post Office,[10] another advised her about obtaining clerkships at the House of Commons. Her brother-in-law, William Flower, offered secretaryships at the Royal College of Surgeons to both George and Frank.[11] A more exotic offer came from Benjamin Jowett, who recommended George as tutor to the children of the Hungarian royal family.[12] That nothing came of any of these possibilities was largely due to Henrietta Grace's loftier ambitions. Two vital offers would nevertheless be accepted; these were made to Stephe by Henrietta Grace's brother Henry Smyth and they would outweigh all her entertaining as will be seen. Her later invitations to Lord Wolseley, when he was Adjutant-General, would, however, also have favourable repercussions.

Henrietta Grace's luncheon parties and soirées might well have helped her children to make advantageous marriages if she herself had not discouraged this manner of 'getting on'. She wanted to keep her children with her not only for emotionally selfish reasons but because she foresaw that the large house and lavish entertaining, which she adored, would have to be financed with the help of her sons' incomes. If they formed separate families, these vital funds would be lost. Not only that: her plans to subsidize the careers of some of her sons from the earnings of the others would have been thwarted if any got married.

'Do, dear sons, cherish this home feeling amongst you: that all your hearts may cling to your mutual home, and to each other,' wrote Henrietta Grace in 1869, and in the same year: 'Talking of families, do let us cling together through life, as we were in your sweet youth.'[13] 'Clinging together' also required each son, on coming of age, to hand over to his mother the 1,000 guineas of capital that he had inherited from his father, so that she could use it on behalf of whichever member of the family she decided needed it most. Warington handed over his money to his mother in May 1869, when George was in Australia for his health. Henrietta Grace told George that Warington 'is generous enough to want me to keep all his money, and to send out any amount for you'.[14] Warington had been put into the Merchant Navy by his mother, rather than the Royal Navy, on financial grounds. The grandson of an admiral and the nephew of a serving captain in the Royal Navy, Warington could easily have been nominated as a midshipman.[15] For a fraction of what she spent on her dining room, Henrietta Grace could have seen her son a naval lieutenant instead of a 4th Officer on a P.&O. steamship earning £4 per month.[16] A system of communal sharing could have been fairly operated, but in practice it was not. The expenses which Stephe and Baden inevitably incurred after joining exclusive regiments could not be met out of their pay. And George, when opting for a political career, would receive no pay as a Member of Parliament, and would therefore have to rely on his family until ministerial rank might come his way. Frank was called to the Bar, but preferred the hazardous life of an artist. Believing in his talent, his mother supported this plan. For years the whole burden of the family's expenditure would be met out of capital and out of Warington's income.

He left the Merchant Navy at the age of 26, passed his Bar examinations and rapidly established himself in the Admiralty Court. In many ways he had been the most adventurous son, in boyhood being the skipper of various small boats in which his brothers had acted as crew. His love of swimming, shooting and exploration had seemed to mark him out for an independent life. But eldest sons whose fathers die often try, out of love for mother, to take their father's place in the family. After thirteen years at sea, Warington came home again and did not leave for another 40 years. In 1913, aged 66, he finally considered his duty done and married the woman to whom he had been secretly engaged for over two decades. By then Hilda Farmer was too old to bear children. When he died in 1921 after only nine years of married life, his widow wrote bitterly. 'My Warington gave all his money, all paid to his mother's a/c, and [inherited] no capital at all except a few hundred pounds . . . He became first K.C. of the Admiralty and made a great deal of money. He was not allowed one penny of it by her [Henrietta Grace] or any member of his family for his lifelong toil. The family slogan was "Warington can do it!" '[17] When, during the First World War, Stephe told Scoutmasters that they should be like 'elder brothers' to boys in their troops who had lost fathers, he was paying his belated tribute to Warington.

At Warington's expense the 'curled darling', Baden, would become an officer in the Guards, but in the end the family system would work to his disadvantage too. His real gifts were scientific. When at last, aged 44, he plucked up sufficient courage to leave the army and buy an ailing scientific journal, there was no capital left to advertise it. In spite of the journal's undoubted merits, he never achieved a viable circulation. Agnes would also suffer from lack of capital. After her mother's death, she was obliged for many years to live with her brother Frank, whom she detested.[18]

Of course any family producing in a single generation one exceptionally famous man and another who would probably have won fame unless robbed by early death, can hardly be set down as a failure in a competitive society. Nor can it be denied that their desire to please and fear to disappoint their mother ranked as a vital motivating factor in the lives of both Stephe and George. But Henrietta Grace's system, which she claimed required brother to help brother, also required brother to vie with brother and, in the case of Warington, to be exploited by brother. The successes in the family bred a sense of failure in the rest. Frank, for example, whose paintings were exhibited at the Royal Academy and the Paris Salon, suffered almost as much as Baden from a feeling of having failed to achieve his potential. Unlike Baden, however, he had the resolution to break free emotionally. He advised his mother firmly to learn the wisdom of 'condescending not to aim too high too long . . . and after a reasonable time to cave in and enjoy ordinary luck.'[19]

In 1869 – the year in which Henrietta Grace refurbished her house – she also did something more far-reaching. Being well aware of the way in which a socially mobile and money-making society idealized symbols of aristocracy, she decided to improve upon the family name. Among middle-class families jockeying for advantage, any aristocratic connections, however remote, were flaunted to excellent effect. The contemporary fascination with genealogy and heraldry was all but universal and explains the enormous sales of Walter Scott's novels and Tennyson's *Idylls of the King*. There were many other symptoms of this obsessive interest in an aristocratic past: the revival of Gothic architecture, the medieval subjects of so many Pre-Raphaelite paintings and the revival of archaic customs.

Henrietta Grace had long been interested in genealogy and family legends, as witness the Nelson connection and John Smith, but the Powells had interested her even more. Her husband's curious Germanic-sounding Christian name, Baden, had been his father's too.

Professor Powell's great-grandfather had married a Miss Susannah Thistlethwayte, whose grandfather on her mother's side had been a certain Andrew Baden born in 1637.[20]

There was of course no valid genealogical reason for yoking this distant ancestor's name together with that of Powell as an equal partner in a double surname. But Henrietta Grace was sure that three good things could be achieved if she were to change her family's surname to Baden-Powell. In the first place, by linking her husband's Christian and surname together in a permanent combination she would create a lasting memorial to him. Secondly, to be a Baden-Powell sounded much more distinguished than to be a mere Powell among thousands of others. Even within the narrower limits of her husband's branch, she liked the idea of setting her own children apart from their Powell cousins – and even from their own half-brother and half-sisters whom she wished to exclude.[21] The logic for both exclusions was non-existent. The Powell cousins were also descended from Andrew Baden, and to exclude any of Professor Baden Powell's children was even more illogical. Thirdly, at a time when the royal family's German origins and multiplicity of marital connections was no source of embarrassment in England, to have a Germanic-sounding name – vaguely implying kinship with the Grand Duke of Baden's family – was a definite social asset. In fact Henrietta Grace decided to quarter the Powell coat of arms with those of the Grand Duke. This took many years to achieve, but at last she was able to tell a relative: 'I am thankful that at last the "Garter" [Garter King of Arms at the Royal College of Heralds] has sent the proper coat of arms here to combine the Baden and the Powell arms – he had to be very careful lest the Duke of Baden should attack us if we adopted his entire coat.'[22]

Although only 12 when his name was altered, Stephe became its most ardent supporter and shared his mother's determination to deny it to their cousins. 'I object strongly to Wilfred [a first cousin] being a Baden-Powell, and if some of you bloaters don't stop him, I will write to him myself – and this I say in jolly good earnest.'[23] Stephe had to battle hard to get everyone to use the new name and did so right through school and his early years in the army, until at last able to tell his mother in 1886 that a letter addressed to him as Captain Powell had been returned to the sender marked 'not known'.[24] It is not recorded whether his younger brother, Baden, enjoyed being Baden Baden-Powell, but it seems doubtful that *he* would have pressed his schoolfellows to adopt it.

When Henrietta Grace changed the family name, the Anglo-Saxons – and indeed the entire 'Teutonic race' – were in high favour. In 1867 the historian E.A. Freeman had published the first volume of his *History of the Norman Conquest*, which was an extended elegy for 'Teutonic England'. The year 1866 had seen the publication of Charles Kingsley's *Hereward the Wake*, and 1864 his *The Roman and the Teuton*, in which the Teutons were represented as a young, strong and morally pure race unlike the corrupt and effeminate Romans. Without 'the muscle of the Teuton' and his moral purity, the British Empire might share the fate of the Roman. The idea of the Romans being an over-civilized people who had lost touch with primitive survival skills, would be one taken up by Stephe in later life. Kingsley's Teutons were 'forest children', living naturally, unlike the former denizens of Rome and the nineteenth-century inhabitants of large cities. Many of the ideas contained in *The Roman and the Teuton* would be expressed by Stephe 40 years later, especially the dangers of too much civilization and too much education. The particular form which English national-ism was taking in the late 1860s, must have added to the family's satisfaction with their splendid new double name.

But in the late 1880s, when fear, rather than admiration, was the usual response to increasing German strength, Henrietta Grace placed more emphasis upon the Powell element in the family's name and laboured hard to prove descent from Athelystan Glodrydd, Prince of Fferlys. In fact there was no historical evidence for connecting her husband's branch of the family with the Welsh Powells. The earliest-known Powells in the professor's line came from Suffolk and could be traced to the late fifteenth century.[25]

In his early teens, Stephe lived under the shadow of his elder brothers and learned a lot from the way in which his mother was grooming them. No detail was small enough to escape her attention. Her boys were not using suitable writing paper, so she ordered from

Waterman's 'beautiful rough surfaced, yellowish tinged, square paper' which would be 'nice and gentlemanly for my dear sons'. For unimportant correspondence, though, she had a cupboard full of cheap French paper bought for half-a-crown.[26] She told her sons that each one 'must be a true gentleman in dress, as well as mind', and therefore bought for the older boys gold watch-chains with real gold pens and pencils attached. Less easily visible accoutrements could be of baser metal. In brushes, ivory-backed ones were as gentlemanly as silver, and would also last indefinitely if the bristles were replaced. Silver-plated mugs were 'vulgar in the common patterns', but if made to order and embossed with a coat of arms they might be mistaken for silver. Similarly the Broadwood grand piano and 7-foot billiard table, with its shaded lamp, would be thought to be their own rather than merely rented for a few weeks each year.[27] Curiously, although Henrietta Grace was obsessed with keeping up appearances, she sometimes found her success too complete, as when Warington went abroad with a rich young man who, thinking him anything but a pauper, flatly refused to pay more than half their expenses.[28]

For Henrietta Grace, friendships had to be useful or they were pointless. 'I am determined,' she resolved, 'not to make any new friends unless very choice people indeed.'[29] But 'very choice people' could not always be persuaded to be useful, while sometimes slightly less choice people could. The Huths were a case in point; they did not have much real knowledge of society but they did have a lot of land in Sussex and were kind enough to invite the entire Baden-Powell family to stay with them on numerous occasions. Thus the boys gained their first experience of gentlemanly country pursuits like hunting and shooting.[30] A year or two later the Huths were dropped in favour of the Bayleys who had estates in Scotland, then becoming increasingly fashionable. The arts were viewed in the same utilitarian light. Henrietta Grace considered music to be 'the best outside means of polish'. It delighted her to see less talented Powell cousins playing handfuls of wrong notes while her own George and Frank dazzled everyone on the piano and violin.[31] Stephe would benefit, since the rendition of comic songs would earn him initial popularity in his regiment, but this was not quite the elegant repertoire which his mother had originally had in mind for him.

Henrietta Grace's absolute faith in herself as the family's infallible strategist had an immense impact on Stephe and the others. 'First,' she told them, 'devise a plan of action and work up to it as closely as possible. Second, always get in advance of business & engagements . . . Not even great talents and great ambitions will have the effect their owners may wish unless they overcome the general shortsighted looking to the present, and plan forward.'[32] Both Stephe and George took her advice very seriously, making their plans of action and listing the various phases in meticulous detail. They always made sure they planned forward beyond immediate aims to more distant ones. The present was very rarely their principal concern.

In one important respect, though, Henrietta Grace was unable to practise what she preached. Her social life in the present could only be continued at the expense of certain future plans. During the middle 1870s, she seriously considered borrowing money to buy and sell property on the largest scale her credit would permit. In the end, although she looked at numerous building plots and houses, her only investment was the purchase of another lease in the road in which she lived. She had never been able to keep her current expenditure low enough to free adequate funds to meet interest payments on invest-ment properties. Given the huge rise in prices in the South Kensington area during that decade, it was unfortunate for her entire family that she never pressed ahead.[33] She was not the only down-to-earth Victorian to become interested in spiritualism, but probably there were not many others who used séances to guide them in investment decisions. Once she was saved from disaster, when discouraged by spirit voices from buying a house which subsequently burned down.[34]

Henrietta Grace made mistakes, and her sacrifice of capital on the altar of 'appearances' was one of them, but her force of character, and her overwhelming enthusiasm for all her decisions and for whatever surroundings or circumstances she had created, swept her family along with her. 'Can you picture us here at this moment?' she asked an absent son. '9 p.m. in our pretty sitting room. I at my writing table with the shaded candle, the bright red silk curtains drawn . . . Tea just taken away from the little green velvet table, and standing against the walls three magnificent paintings purchased by me . . .'[35] Stephe too was swept along, although he knew that the price of that 'pretty sitting room' and the hired grand piano and exclusive luncheons was a winter of exile in lodgings on the South Coast while their smart London house was let. Sometimes Henrietta Grace rented country houses and later, when Stephe and Baden were away at boarding school, she and Agnes set out sadly on protracted visits to the houses of rich but tedious friends.[36] It was typical of her, while enduring such periods of exile, to be wondering whether to take a house in Cowes for the week of the regatta, or whether all her financial sinews ought to be devoted to the extra rooms she hoped to build on to her London home.[37]

For Stephe, home was not so much a place in which to feel secure as a card to be played in the all-important game of getting on. Happiness would lie in striving to achieve what his mother wanted. It would have been strange if a child brought up in a home where so much was not as it seemed had not been influenced to feel that appearances were all important. Stephe, as the family's most gifted actor, became better than any of them at putting across whatever persona seemed best suited to a given situation. This would extend to what he wrote. While in the army he earned extra money by working as a special correspondent for various newspapers. 'Instead of taking my powers to be original my business was to write what at the moment the public wanted to believe . . . It does not in the long run pay to kick against the pricks.'[38] Of course when he later advised the nation's youth that success did not lie in the acquisition of wealth and power but in selflessness, truthfulness and helping others, this was again what the public wanted to hear. What he had learned in his childhood and still secretly believed at the height of his fame was that 'the desire for self-advancement and the fear of failure' were together responsible for most human achievements.[39]

But if an almost cynical realism was one legacy of his childhood, another was a need to fantasize. A boy encouraged to dream of future grandeur while being obliged to leave a smart house and live in winter lodgings, was compelled to develop compensatory imaginative powers. Many novelists have had similar childhoods. The Boy Scout Movement has been described as 'a major act of creative fantasy' and the definition seems apt.[40] When a boy who grew up without a father creates an army of substitutes as a man, the connection hardly seems fortuitous. A lifetime's obsessive concern with manhood, manliness and how to acquire its attributes began for Stephe with childhood anxieties about what information his father might have passed on to him if he had lived. He would write for his own children numerous notes to be opened if he died before they grew up. The boys left fatherless by the First World War distressed him greatly. 'Except where the scoutmasters take his [the father's] place, the boys have no-one to consult on intimate subjects.'[41] Stephe felt this same lack acutely in his early years; a boy could not talk to his mother about 'intimate subjects'. But Henrietta Grace liked an open forthright manner, so Stephe could not disappoint her. Later he would often point out the value of being able to conceal true feelings.[42] By the time he went away to school he was already a puzzling person, extremely reserved and yet apparently bold and free of shyness; soon he would combine popularity with a perplexing absence of close friends.

4. Stephe at School (1868–76)

All Henrietta Grace's children began their formal education at home. Stephe, Agnes and Baden were given lessons together in reading, writing and singing by their mother and by their governess, Fraulein Groffel. Drill, dance and exercise were also part of the daily routine. Henrietta Grace believed that 'children should be reprimanded lovingly' and that their obedience was 'largely owing to their mother'.[1] When Stephe was 7 he was sent to a dame school in Kensington Square, and walked there each day along respectable streets, past private gates and railings set across the roadway, attended by uniformed gatekeepers in cockaded hats. London was a city of crinolines and horses, and on his daily walk he would have noticed the young crossing-sweepers (mentioned by him in his 'Laws for Me') – boys often no more than a couple of years older than himself – working in all weathers, sweeping away the mud and horse dung, saving gentlemen's shoes and ladies' dresses.

In 1868, when he was 11, Stephe was sent to Rose Hill, the Tunbridge Wells preparatory school where his father had been educated. Here, diligence in the classroom and good behaviour outside it were the norm in a school where the masters, rather than the boys, set the moral tone. Stephe did not find it difficult to conform. His first report was typical: 'Conduct in school: painstaking and industrious. Conduct out of school: very good.'[2]

Ever since 1860, when two boys had died at St Paul's School, Henrietta Grace had worried about George and Frank who were pupils there; so in 1863 she sent them to Marlborough, a relatively new but by now popular school in the country offering reduced fees to the sons of clergymen. *Tom Brown's Schooldays* was one of the most widely read and influential books of the age. In it there is a young master who rhapsodizes about the discipline and unselfishness to be learned on the games field. This young master was based on G.E.L. Cotton, who taught at Rugby and subsequently became headmaster of Marlborough. There he pioneered the introduction of organized compulsory sport, partly to canalize energies which might otherwise have been expressed in rebelliousness, and partly to train the boys' characters. It would not be long before the altruistic team spirit of the football field came to be contrasted favourably with the selfishness of classroom work undertaken for personal benefit.

At Marlborough George rowed and played cricket for the school, but Frank was the real athlete, playing rugby football for Marlborough and later winning a Blue at Oxford; he also excelled as a cross-country runner and became excellent at tennis, golf and billiards. After he left school, he was so far behind in academic subjects that he had to live with a tutor for over a year before he was able to satisfy the examiners at Balliol.[3] Stephe admired his elder brothers and was impressed by reports of their sporting triumphs at Marlborough.

In deciding not to send Stephe and Baden there, Henrietta Grace was influenced by Frank's academic difficulties, but money played a greater part. 'Computed what was best for us,' she recorded in March 1870. 'Charterhouse seems the best.'[4] This was because she hoped to see Stephe and Baden among the 60 'Gownboys' who received a free education on the Charterhouse Foundation. There was no competition by examination, and places went to the sons of poor people of good family. The Gownboys therefore did not consider themselves inferior charity boys but members of an élite more exclusive than those who were in the school simply by virtue of their parents' ability to pay. Gownboys had to be nominated by governors of the school, so Henrietta Grace 'made endless journeys and inquiries' about the best way to proceed. She succeeded first with Baden who, being three years younger than Stephe, had much less need of an immediate place. Three months were to pass before she received the Duke of Marlborough's nomination for Stephe; it arrived on 23 June 1870, by which time Stephe had sat an examination at Fettes College in Edinburgh. A few days after the Duke's letter arrived, Stephe learned that he had won a scholarship at Fettes.[5] Nevertheless Charterhouse was preferred as better known and more exclusive.

However, like most of the other leading public schools, with the possible exception of Rugby and Eton, Charterhouse was at a low ebb in its fortunes.[6] Forty years earlier there had been nearly 500 boys in the school; in 1870 there were only 120 pupils. But Henrietta Grace knew that in two years the school would be moving to the country, away from its cramped site near St Paul's Cathedral. Charterhouse was even closer to Smithfield cattle market, with all its inevitable smells and noises. Along with the other ancient public schools, the atmosphere of Charterhouse belonged more to the eighteenth than to the nineteenth century. 'Big School', in which all but the two top forms were taken, had no gas lights, and on foggy mornings or winter afternoons boys had to bring candles. Such work as was done had to be achieved amid a hubbub worthy of the nearby cattle market.

For two centuries pitched battles had been fought between members of the school and the Smithfield butchers' boys. Soon after his arrival at Charterhouse, in November 1870, Stephe was on the school's football ground watching a game when, from the other side of some hoardings, the butchers' boys 'attacked with showers of stones and brickbats . . . This was responded to from our side in like manner, with occasional sorties by strong bodies over the wall.' Stephe was one of a small group of spectators too young to take part in the fray. Suddenly he was aware of his clerical headmaster standing next to him and saying:

'I think if you boys went through that door in the side wall, you might attack the cads in the flank.'

'Yes, Sir,' one of us replied, 'but the door is locked.'

The worthy doctor fumbled in his gown and said: 'That is so, but here is the key.'

And he sent us on our way rejoicing, and our attack was a complete success.[7]

The sixty Gownboys lived in a single house. Their 26-year-old housemaster, Frederic Girdlestone, left discipline almost entirely in the hands of senior boys – the monitors and uppers, all of whom were allowed to inflict corporal punishment. As well as suffering regular 'swishings', the junior boys also had to cope with ordinary bullying.[8] Decades later in New Zealand, Stephe met the headmaster of a well-known local school. At Charterhouse 'he had been known as the "pig" on account of the blows he dealt us and the cruelties practised upon myself and others'. Stephe would show no surprise that this particular Carthusian had gained a great reputation for 'character training'.[9] After all, he considered the ability to endure physical hardships an essential prerequisite for 'manliness'.

Junior boys spent much of their time in one vast room, 'Writing School', with its carved heraldic ceiling supported on massive oak pillars. The uppers would call boys from this room to go on fagging errands for them or to make their toast or porridge. Each upper had his own fag, and for almost three years Stephe's upper was Edward H. Parry. Many junior boys stayed away from the fires, preferring to be cold rather than to make themselves so easily available for fagging duties, but Stephe did not hide away to gain a few moments to himself. He enjoyed pleasing Parry and did all he could to obtain 'extra delicacies' for him; thus he became expert in the most difficult techniques of toasting, preparing for him 'frits' (a round of bread buttered and then toasted) and 'splits' (a round toasted on both sides, then divided and re-toasted). Parry would one day pay tribute to 'the most amusing attentions' lavished upon him. On one occasion Stephe gave him 'a very nice copy of Dryden with the inscription: "From his affectionate fag RSSBP".'[10]

Stephe wrote many years later, with approbation, of boys being 'very apt to make a hero for themselves of a fellow who is older than them'. And hero-worship would play an important part in Scouting. Parry was Stephe's hero at school and a brilliant footballer. Stephe later explained how it was only admiration for his idol that induced him to take up the game with real determination. This was the more touching since Parry considered his young fag 'not very skilful at either cricket or football'. On leaving school Parry played for the Old Carthusian team that won the F.A. Cup in 1880, and went on to play for England. Stephe remembered at school having 'the honour of holding his overcoat while he played, and of cleaning his boots and his muddy garments, and giving him his hot water after the game was over . . . It was thanks to him that a good deal of my life at school was fashioned.' Although Stephe wrote this eulogy in old age, he did not mention his friend's name.[11] Parry would display the same reticence.

In the middle of Stephe's Charterhouse career, he and various others were instrumental in founding a social club called the Druids. Each member was known by a nickname, Stephe's being predictably (and prophetically) Lord Bathing-Towel. Parry's was Captain Perrywinkle. Stephe decorated the club's minute book with delightful sketches, drawing for a frontispiece the word 'Druids' in letters formed from pictorial representations of the various soubriquets of club members.[12] The final 'S' of DRUIDS is made with a curving towel resting upon a small periwinkle shell. When Mrs Eileen Wade, Stephe's secretary, was writing her short biography of her employer in 1921, Parry responded to her request for recollections. Among much straightforward information, he mentioned as an aside the Druids' minute book and the proximity of the towel and the shell to one another. Since he omitted to mention who or what the periwinkle represented, Mrs Wade would have found the reference incomprehensible.[13] It would seem that, even after 50 years, he had only been prepared to hint at his real affection for his erstwhile fag. If this seems baffling, the fact that Parry became a schoolmaster, and later the chairman of the Private Schools' Association, may in part explain his caution. At Charterhouse by the turn of the century there was a rule forbidding boys of different ages from different boarding houses to meet one another in their own time; and at other schools there were still more draconian rules by which even masters were forbidden to be alone with a boy if the door to the room were closed. Even the most innocent relationships ran the risk of being labelled homosexual. When G. H. Rendall, who followed Haig Brown as headmaster of Charterhouse, described his boys as 'amorous but seldom erotic', many of his staff thought him over-optimistic. Against a background of suspicion and innuendo (which had never existed in his own schooldays), Parry would have been careful to see that nothing written by him could be construed by the cynical as evidence of physical or emotional attachment between himself and the future Chief Scout. His inclusion of a reference, certain to baffle Mrs Wade, can only have been due to a desire to let Stephe himself know that their friendship had not been forgotten. The reminder surely found its mark, for Stephe included his complimentary recollections about his footballing friend (albeit without naming him) in the book which he was writing at the very time when Parry sent his piece about their schooldays.[14]

Baden-Powell never wrote about the sexual atmosphere of Charterhouse in his time, but Francis Vane – an exact contemporary – did. The conclusion Vane drew from his experiences at school was that 'young boys (it must be some mistake in the creation) are not attracted by girls; rather the contrary by other boys'. He thought this natural, and opposed 'spying and detection as altogether repellent'. He nevertheless doubted the wisdom of boarding education for boys and noted how some used almost feminine wiles to attract other boys. When 'a remarkably pretty boy' told him he loved him, he considered the remark innocent because he had saved him from a bully.[15] 'Emotional friendships of that kind are not necessarily harmful, and sometimes they are useful to both the bigger and the smaller boy – calling forth the chivalrous and protective instincts of the former, and providing the latter with a kindly instructor.'[16] This was certainly the view taken by Baden-Powell. When starting the 'Rovers' (or Senior Scouts), he encouraged them to become heroes to the younger Scouts, but never indicated that there could be any effects of hero-worship other than the normal transitional part it plays in the development of growing boys. Unlike Vane, who later worked with him in the Scouts, Stephe never seemed troubled by the common consequences of a hero-worship that persisted beyond boyhood.

Old boys of schools where they have been exceptionally happy are rarely able to be dispassionate about their alma mater's failings. Academic standards at Charterhouse when Stephe was there were lamentable. He was listed two places from the bottom of the lowest form on entry but, as Edward Parry related ironically, 'through not gaining unpopularity by undue attention to his studies, he got up the school quickly'.[17] But Stephe, though critical of the emphasis placed upon the classics, hardly seemed to notice the other inadequacies: History, English and Geography hardly taught at all; French and German entrusted to hapless foreigners ragged beyond endurance; Science taught by a master laughed at by the other staff for bringing his apparatus in a green bag, and for teaching a utilitarian subject fit only for lower middle-class technicians. Later Stephe would insist that a public school education was 'good not so much for what is taught in the class-room as for what is learnt on the playing-field and out of school'. This made the boys more important than the masters. A boy's 'comrades discipline him', Baden-Powell wrote approvingly. 'Until he has earned the right to make his voice heard, he gets very definitely put in his place. In other words, he is "licked into shape". There is a considerable hardening process about it which is all good for him in the end. In the old days the Spartans put their boys through a very rigorous training in hardness and endurance before they were allowed to count themselves as men, and so do many savage tribes of the present day.'[18]

Stephe was at Charterhouse 40 years after Dr Arnold had told his praeposters at Rugby that they should look first for moral principles in a boy, then gentlemanly conduct, and only after that for intellectual ability. In the 1860s and 1870s, the cult of manliness associated with athleticism – which spread like wildfire through the public schools, demoting intellect still further at the expense of 'character' owed more to Arnold's associates and pupils than to the Doctor himself. Men like Cotton of Marlborough, Percival of Clifton and Thomas Hughes, the author of *Tom Brown's Schooldays*, were key figures. Their message reached Charterhouse in the very decade when Stephe was

there, and was all the more influential on account of the move to the
countryside. A school with broad acres around it could accommodate
far more football pitches and cricket fields than could an ancient
London school in cramped quarters. But the move would have a
deeper effect, removing the boys from their old proximity to the
commercial heart of the greatest city of the world. Stephe had until
then been content with his life in London, but afterwards he began to
develop a contempt for towns which would intensify over the years.
His new world on the heights of Godalming, in leafy Surrey, would be
more evocative of the life of the old landed gentry. The school would
scorn commerce, exalting careers coloured by aristocratic ideals: the
military, politics, the civil service and the law. When a pompous
prospective parent said to Dr Haig Brown, Stephe's headmaster, 'I
want you, sir, to assure me that the boys who come to your school are
the sons of gentlemen,' he received the answer, 'Well, they always
leave gentlemen."'[19]

The school moved to its new site on a windswept spur of the Surrey
Downs on 18 June 1872. The new buildings, which the headmaster's
son described as 'a noble block in domestic Gothic with high-pitched
roofs and stately towers',[20] were later condemned by Osbert Lancaster
as 'an extensive concentration camp' only aesthetically pleasing at a
distance. 'When seen from the Godalming-Guildford road, silhouetted
against a sunset sky, this extraordinary cluster of spires and pinnacles
momentarily achieved the romantic aspect of a rural version of St
Pancras Station.'[21] The fact that, though newly built, the school had
no piped water on the same floor as the dormitories and that no fixed
baths had been installed stands as a striking tribute to the determination
of the headmaster to foster the 'manliness' which most parents wanted
him to instil. British plumbing was the most advanced in the world,
yet Carthusians were obliged for several decades more to excrete like
men in earth closets. For the first few months in the new buildings the
boys were so badly troubled by rats that they were allowed to keep
ferrets in their quarters. Within their new boarding houses, most boys
still lived in hideously overcrowded common rooms, and the more
civilized small bedrooms of the old Charterhouse were done away
with in favour of vast barrack-like dormitories. There were fires in the
common rooms, but in their studies boys had to sit in their overcoats in
winter. Another indication of the new ethos was the abolition of house
libraries.[22] Nevertheless the first summer term was pleasant enough,
resembling, it was said: 'One long picnic or camping out; a huge
holiday, encompassed with all the special providences of "the Swiss
Family Robinson".'[23]

It was a hot summer, the cricket field was not yet ready for use, and
young Stephe had not yet learned to swim, so the River Wey was
barred to him, but he was able to explore the neighbouring woods. In

his autobiography, which was written to 'be helpful to young fellows in aiming their lives', he would make much of his adventures in 'The Copse' below the playing fields. 'It was here that I used to imagine myself a backwoodsman trapper and Scout. I used to creep about warily looking for "sign" and getting "close up" observation of rabbits . . .'[24] These recollections, however, seem to have been tailored as the right sort of schoolboy memories for a later Chief Scout. He describes being stalked by masters, whom he thought of as Redskins, and eluding them by hiding above their eye-level in the branches of trees. This bears too neat a resemblance to an identical incident in his extravagantly fanciful book *My Adventures as a Spy* published fifteen years earlier during the First World War. After that war Red Indians became extremely popular in Scouting, which may explain his comparing the masters looking for him with Redskins. Unfortunately he left little indication of the books he read as a boy. But in *Scouting for Boys* (2nd ed. p. 181), he does mention having read the works of George Catlin, the American author of the *Manners, Customs and Condition of the North American Indians*. He may also have read Fenimore Cooper's novels. During Baden-Powell's boyhood, adventure fiction for boys was becoming increasingly popular, with Ballantyne, Kingston, Kingsley and Mayne Reid satisfying the thirst for accounts of daring deeds in distant parts of the world. Such books exalted the brave and active hero and largely ignored – except for purposes of ridicule – characters of a contemplative disposition. The outposts of Empire, the American Frontier and exploration in general were favoured themes. In the year when Stephe moved to the new Charterhouse, Mark Twain wrote his vivid account of his days as a Californian gold miner. This was *Roughing It*, which became a best seller, and brilliantly expresses the way in which the whole White Anglo-Saxon Protestant world was gripped by the idea of manhood and manliness. In California there had been

> . . . an assemblage of two hundred thousand young men – not simpering , dainty, kid-gloved weaklings, but stalwart, muscular, dauntless young braves, brimful of push and energy, and royally endowed with every attribute that goes to make up a peerless and magnificent manhood . . . No women, no children, no grey and stooping veterans . . . It was a wild, free disorderly, grotesque society: *Men* – only swarming hosts of stalwart *men* – nothing juvenile, nothing feminine visible anywhere.

In America young men went west, and from Britain they were already streaming abroad to hold and administer the growing Empire. Stephe loved Twain's books, and quoted from his *Life on the Mississippi* in his first published work on Scouting.[25]

A young man who was thrilled by thoughts of adventure had little

time for his studies. Stephe's reports at Charterhouse were outstandingly poor but, since it was 'bad form' to work hard, would have been
rated outstandingly good by the boys. He slept in French, paid 'not the
slightest attention' in science, had 'to all intents given up the study of
mathematics', and in classics seemed 'to take very little interest in his
work'. Apart from continuing to persevere at football, Stephe was one
of the first to join the newly formed Band and Rifle Corps and became
a keen member of each. He played the bugle and the flugel horn, and
for three consecutive years was in the school's shooting team.[26]

Stephe's need to please his mother affected his behaviour at
Charterhouse where he worked hard to make himself admired and
popular. He found that what had been a small boy's conscious charm
could be converted into clowning and mimicry. He also relied upon
slapstick. 'I invented for myself a sort of diving slide . . . I used to take
a run at a table, slither across it on my tummy, dive and roll over on to
the floor and come up standing. It was very effective.'[27] His
buffoonery in mathematics became more and more daring, until he
was sent to the headmaster for swearing and gesticulating while
working on a problem. By then well-known for his acting skills,
Stephe told Haig Brown that he had been rehearsing a scene from
Macbeth and quoted, 'The devil damn thee black, thou cream-faced
loon.' He got away with it.[28]

Edward Parry had no doubt that 'the prestige he gradually acquired
arose from his good-humour, his powers of mimicry and wonder at
his many quaint antics which to the ordinary boy marked him out as
being gifted with an admirable species of madness.'[29]

His artistic talent also won him admirers. His sketches in the Druids'
Club's facetious minute book perfectly complement the dotty rules
and comic speeches. Stephe was generous with his drawings and gave
many to friends. An album in the library at Charterhouse, which once
belonged to a contemporary, Edward F. Brown, contains a wonderful
selection of vignettes sketched by Stephe in 1872 while waiting outside
St Paul's Cathedral on the morning of a service of thanksgiving for the
recovery of the Prince of Wales from a serious illness. Policemen push
back crowds, a man climbs a lamp-post, dogs scavenge in the gutter
and a coach with a wonderfully pompous coachman arrives. Stephe's
gift excited particular interest because he could draw equally well with
either hand.

His first great success as an actor at Charterhouse came when he
played the part of Bob Nettles, an attractive and troublesome boy, in
Tom Taylor's *To Parents and Guardians*. The 15-year-old Stephe was
singled out for praise by the press and, in his own words, 'developed a
perfectly noxious swollen head'.[30] He appeared in various other plays,
including an operatic version of *Cox and Box*, in which he played the
landlady 'with a vivacity and animation which elicited deservedly

frequent tributes of applause'.[31] In the army he would make a speciality of female roles. When he left Charterhouse, the butler in his house 'saved a part of the dress he wore in his last theatrical performance'.[32] This was in *The Waterman*, a ballad opera in which Stephe played the waterman's wife, Mrs Bundle. His singing won him as much acclaim as his acting, since he could take any part from baritone to soprano. He shared this gift with the music master, John Hullah. 'It was rather startling,' Stephe recalled, 'to come into a room, and, hearing a lady's voice singing with intense feeling, to find a particularly manly man performing.'[33]

In later years Stephe felt slightly uneasy about his passion for acting:

> There is a joy in acting which cannot well be accounted for by one who is not a professional psychologist or hypnotist. The power to move his fellow creatures, whether to laughter or to tears, is one which certainly gives to the actor a subtle sense of power and elation . . . Whether the elation comes of admiration excited in the breasts of the audience or from the feeling that you are bringing happiness to others, is a matter of some question.[34]

He sensed that the popularity he gained as a performer had its darker side. 'Getting a laugh is somehow an attractive pursuit to most men, and a boy who has made himself popular as a buffoon at school often strives hard in later life to keep up his reputation as a wit, and sometimes the struggle is a very hard one. I suffered that way myself . . . Somebody gave me a copy of *Joe Miller's Jest Book*, and I kept this secretly on tap for use when occasion arose for me to be funny.'[35]

When at the very end of his school career Stephe became goalkeeper of the school's football XI, his reputation as a wit went with him to the playing fields. To impress the opposition he was never without two pairs of boots, and he would change them over at half-time with much ceremony.[36] From time to time he would shin up the posts and walk along the crossbar.[37] Harold Begbie, Stephe's first biographer, found out from masters at Charterhouse that whenever Stephe had kept goal 'there was always a knot of grinning boys round the posts listening with huge delight to their hero's facetiae. He also had the habit, such were his animal spirits, of giving the most nerve-fluttering war-whoop imaginable when rushing the ball forward.'[38] In spite of the histrionics, Stephe turned out to be an excellent goalkeeper in a team below the standard of those that followed. Against a stronger Westminster XI, Charterhouse lost, and were saved from a drubbing solely by Stephe's keeping: 'Powell in goal was exceedingly useful.'[39] So Stephe at last became a hero, well-known – according to his headmaster – 'for the considerable help he gave to young and inexperienced boys in their early trials'. 'It was a pleasure to fag for

B-P,' recalled a younger schoolfellow writing to the *Daily Telegraph* after the Relief of Mafeking.[40]

But Edward Parry was right to describe Stephe as a boy who was 'generally popular but never seemed to make any close friends'. This view was shared by Frederic Girdlestone, Stephe's young house-master, who thought him too reserved for close friendships. He contrasted this reserve with the boy's apparent absence of timidity in his dealings with masters.[41] Stephe had already developed the jovial public manner that would serve to keep others at a distance and, by masking his emotions, make him feel secure. Parry considered Stephe unlike other boys, 'who were often puzzled by him & never quite knew when he was joking and when he was serious'. Boys who are unsure of this often suspect mockery, and fear that the laughter provoked by a brilliant mimic may one day be at their expense. Perhaps this explains why, instead of being called 'Bathing-Towel' – his own preferred nickname – Stephe was more often known by the unattractive 'Bowel' or its shorter synonym, 'Guts'. Since this last was in general use long before his successful footballing exploits, its meaning is most unlikely to have had any connection with courage.[42] The licence that all jesters enjoy, and must have, can leave a measure of resentment in the hearts of those not similarly privileged. But though he was allowed his 'many quaint antics', the others knew that they were only marginal non-conformities not in any way threatening the deeper assumptions of their world, in which originality was suspect and social qualities were prized more than individual ones. Indeed, all his life Stephe prized the virtues which he would later group under the heading 'Public School Spirit': self-reliance, responsibility, fortitude, loyalty and respect for tradition.

The strength of the public schools lay in their ability to teach boys to respect communities and how to get on in them. In the army and the colonial service, the lessons learned would prove invaluable. The isolation from women, the hardships, the shared values, the self-control were not only a preparation but a shared experience that created close bonds between men similarly educated, even if at different schools. Rules might have been silly or cruel, but they had been suffered by all; and to have endured them created pride, just as a young African took pride in his initiation scars. But the public schools did not remove a boy from his family and from women merely for a brief period of initiation: in the nineteenth century a boy was there for three-quarters of the year and school became a substitute for family. Affection for contemporaries could easily be transferred to the place itself.[43] To Stephe, new Charterhouse at Godalming was a second home: much more important than it was for those whose parents did not let their houses for long periods and live elsewhere.

At Mafeking Stephe would advertise in the local paper for an Old

Carthusian with whom to celebrate Founder's Day. Before the Siege he had written to his old housemaster asking for a list of the school's forthcoming events. He would regularly attend a dining club for boys who had been pupils at old *and* new Charterhouse. He would delight in meeting Carthusians in places as far afield as Matabeleland. As an old man he would be President of the Old Carthusian Club and would often watch school football matches. He performed in Charterhouse theatricals, laid the foundation stone of the Memorial Cloisters, and continued a friendship with his housemaster that only ended with the latter's death. He also sent regular pieces to the *Greyfriar* (Charterhouse's magazine inviting contributions from old boys). Stephe's narratives invariably cast him in an adventurous light, as if he were once more appealing for the admiration of his schoolfellows.

The supposed innocence of boyhood, and nostalgia for it, would one day become an obsession with many male Edwardians. One of Stephe's favourite paintings was by a south London Scoutmaster called Ernest S. Carlos. Painted in 1911 and entitled 'If I Were a Boy Again', it depicts an attractive optimistic boy in Scout uniform about to go out and enjoy a day of healthy outdoor pursuits, and after it a purposeful life. Not so the boy's broken-looking father, who is slumped at a table and is plainly not going outside or anywhere else. As he gazes at his son, he seems to be mouthing the words of the painting's title.

Such sentiments, essential in motivating Stephe's greatest work, owed much to his boyhood happiness at Charterhouse and his consequent nostalgia for days when he was, as Parry described him, 'a boy of medium size, with curly red hair, decidedly freckled, with a pair of twinkling eyes.'[44]

5. Choosing a Career (1876)

Throughout his life Stephe would work with tireless energy at whatever project or objective he had in hand. At school his ambition had been to be admired and popular. Yet to be popular, one had to appear not to be trying too hard. Tradesmen's sons might need to work at improving themselves, but born gentlemen already had a status which required no improvement. Of course there was a staggering amount of hypocrisy and wishful thinking in this idea, and few people knew this better than Stephe; but, along with thousands of other middle-class boys, he was influenced by the idea that gentlemen and aristocrats should not strive to assert themselves or seek advancement. An air of nonchalant ease should be affected rather than one of purposeful industry. The idea that it was unattractive to push one's own interests also had a lot to do with sport and the belief that the interests of the individual ought always to be subordinated to those of the team.

In his brief autobiography, Stephe would frequently stress his 'extraordinary luck', and how he had thought of calling his book *Bombshells of My Life*. 'My reason for doing so was that most of the important steps in my career have been unexpectedly sprung upon me by fortune or outside agencies.'[1] To be lucky is, like the privilege of exalted birth, an aristocratic virtue. One does not have to push oneself or work hard to be lucky. The claim that important events in his life had been determined by chance was, in part, intended to mask the immense amount of calculation and effort which he and his family had put into his career.

In line with the 'bombshell theory', the author of the most detailed biography to date accepted Stephe's happy-go-lucky account of how he chose a military career. 'One morning,' wrote William Hillcourt, 'he came upon the announcement of an Open Competitive Examination for commissions . . . He had not previously given much thought to a military career. But why not? There was no tradition on his father's side of the family of anyone having chosen the service life. But there was ample precedent on his mother's side.'[2] This was also the impression Stephe gave to his secretary, Mrs Wade, when she was writing her short authorized life.[3]

In fact in January 1875, 18 months before that 'one morning' when 'he came upon the announcement', Henrietta Grace discussed with her brother, Colonel Henry Smyth – then commandant of the Royal Military Academy at Woolwich – the possibility of Stephe going there to train for the Royal Artillery. She was disappointed to be told that at almost 18 he was too old to apply for entry. A month later, on Stephe's birthday, she consulted a professional careers adviser, a Mr Scoons. Not long afterwards she wrote to the Duke of Cambridge 'to put down Badie's name for the Guards'. She did not make the same representation on behalf of Stephe, but on 20 April she invited Lieutenant-Colonel John Miller and his wife to dinner. Miller was then Colonel of the 13th Hussars, and Henrietta Grace had met his wife socially the previous summer. Since Stephe was eventually gazetted to the 13th Hussars, it seems unlikely that his mother's acquaintance with the Millers had nothing to do with this.[4]

The truth was that Henrietta Grace had a firm plan for Stephe. This was that he should spend several years at Oxford and then enter the army as a university candidate.[5] In choosing the army for her two youngest sons, their mother would have been influenced by her brother, by Stephe's enjoyment of the Rifle Corps at school and possibly by Mr Scoons. But she would never have considered a military career unless the social kudos of army officers had been steadily rising since her husband's death. With the establishment of the Volunteers in 1859, soldiering became an acceptable part-time occupation for gentlemen with manly instincts. A decade later fear of

Germany, after the Franco–Prussian War, intensified popular military fervour. Victorians of an earlier generation would have been astonished by the runaway success of a book like G. T. Chesney's *Battle of Dorking*, which in 1871 described a successful invasion of Britain. In the same year the purchase of commissions was abolished, and Edward Cardwell's army reforms promised to make the army not just a casual hobby for the rich but a proper profession for men with larger capabilities and smaller private incomes. Germany was not seen as the only threat. Russian intentions on the North West Frontier and in the eastern Mediterranean also caused alarm. American industrial growth presented a different kind of challenge.

The response was a self-assertive pride in Britain's overseas possessions and a feeling that national greatness would only be retained if Imperial ties were strengthened. A cohesive Empire would best be administered and garrisoned, it was thought, by men knowing more about self-reliance and leadership than about science and the classics. Writing of a time only slightly earlier, G. M. Young declared: 'Public opinion did not want knowledge. It wanted the sort of man whom Wellington had said could go straight from school with two N.C.O.s and fifteen privates and get a shipload of convicts to Australia.'[6]

Yet, while recognizing the spirit of the times, Henrietta Grace had continued to think a university education very desirable. After she became a widow, Benjamin Jowett wrote: 'If you think I can be of any use to you about their education [her sons] I shall be most glad to be so.'[7] As Master of Balliol, Jowett had accepted George without demur, though the boy's education had been hopelessly disrupted by illness. Frank was accepted at the third attempt, after spending a year with a tutor recommended by Jowett. 'He deserves to be made the most of,' the Master of Balliol had told Henrietta Grace, 'if he can only be stirred up to greater industry.'[8] And 'stirred up' he had been, so he should, as his mother put it, 'have for the rest of his life the distinction of having been "a Balliol man".'[9] She poured scorn on the suggestion that he should go to Trinity, and pitied the son of a friend who had been sent to Exeter College.[10]

Stephe then was to have the best of both worlds: a couple of years at Balliol, 'the very first and best college',[11] and then a career in a socially desirable regiment. Henrietta Grace intended the same for Baden, and wrote to Jowett about him six months after making her first inquiries concerning the Brigade of Guards.[11]

When Stephe failed his examination at Balliol in April 1876 it was a very bitter blow, given all the family's connections; not only were George and Frank still in residence, but their elder half-brother had gained a First in Mathematics while a member of the college. Nor, as in Frank's case, was there talk of stirring Stephe up. He was simply 'not quite up to Balliol form'. Balliol was intellectually pre-eminent, but

Christ Church led the field socially so it was there that Henrietta Grace next directed her attentions. Stephe went up to be examined a few weeks later and saw, among others, the mathematics tutor Lutwidge Dodgson, the author of *Alice in Wonderland*. 'He very soon found out what I could have told him from the first, that my knowledge of mathematics was beneath con——, well, was below what was needed for Christ Church, and that wasn't much.'[13] Stephe wrote this in the draft version of his autobiography, but it was not in the published book, where no mention of his Oxford failures appeared. It is a telling indication of how much Henrietta Grace cared that, 25 years later when her son was one of the most famous men in the Empire, she should have told the biographers Begbie and Aitken and numerous journalists that Stephe would have gone to Christ Church if he had not decided to go straight into the army.[14] The same untruth appeared at the time of Stephe's wedding in 1912 when he himself was almost certainly responsible for it. The *Westminster Gazette* was typical. 'It may not be generally known that it was almost by chance that "BP" became a soldier. When he left Charterhouse it was intended that he should go straight to Oxford, and his name was therefore entered on the books at Christ Church. Before he went up, however, an army examination was held, and "just for fun" he entered for it.'[15]

In case it be thought that the Dean of Christ Church overruled his mathematics tutor, it should be recorded that he wrote to Henrietta Grace in October 1876 explaining that Stephe's work had been so bad that he had been unable to do that. Mrs Baden-Powell wrote a crowing letter to Dean Liddell after Stephe had passed into the army, to make sure that he realized how mistaken he had been. Liddell replied, expressing regret 'that we have not Stephenson's name on the books of our House'.[16] Both Henrietta and Stephe were to develop an entirely utilitarian attitude towards the press, and clearly considered it reasonable – given Liddell's regret – to alter his decision retrospectively. Nor, since he died in 1898, was he going to object in 1900 or 1912.

Only in 1915, after his mother's death, did Stephe publicly admit what had happened at Oxford. This was in his best book, *Indian Memories*; and even then, he employed a consoling distortion. 'I had for the time,' he wrote, 'to take up my position as an unattached member (of the university). Within a few days of my joining, I went up for the army examination.'[17] In fact nobody could join the university without going through the ceremony of matriculation. Stephe is not listed as having done so, nor is his name among the unattached students admitted in 1876. It is however possible that he would have matriculated the following October and become an unattached member at the start of the new university year, had he not succeeded in the army examination.[18] It is a curious fact that, according to his mother's extremely sketchy diary for 1875, he was in Oxford for a few days almost exactly a year earlier than the Christ Church fiasco of 1876. On 15 May 1875 he had returned to London from Oxford in a state of nervous and physical collapse. It may be relevant that in 1884 and 1886, he would use in the first instance an accident, and in the second an illness, to explain his inability to get through the Staff College examination.[19]

Since his mother was still unable to acknowledge his rejection 25 years after the event, Stephe can hardly have been anything but agonizingly aware of her disappointment at the time. Since he had longed to please her since early childhood, it is hardly surprising that the result of his Oxford experience deepened his dislike of academic work. He chose not to argue that his success in the army examination proved Oxford wrong, but rather that all examinations were non-sense. 'I practically got into the army by fraud,' he wrote in the manuscript draft of his autobiography, but cut this from the published version, which he revealingly called Lessons from the 'Varsity of Life – the implication being that life was the only real university able to teach anything worth learning. He attributed his success in the army's Latin examination entirely to the chance of his knowing that the key word 'plumbum' meant lead. He claimed he owed his pass in the preliminary mathematics paper to his having memorized word for word 'the several books of Euclid required'. Success in the French paper was explained away because his examiner had known the French master at Charterhouse, and he asserted that because Herbert Plumer – who ultimately became a Field Marshal – came lower than he, 'it just shows the valuelessness of examinations.'

In November 1906 Stephe told the boys of the Mercers' School, in an entirely typical speech, that 'the whole secret of success in life was to "play the game" of life in the same spirit as that in which they played on the football field . . . I only obtained one prize while at school. It was called Hallam's Constitutional History, and some day I am going to read it. Even stupid fellows like myself can get on by hard work.'[20] In fact Stephe's success in the army examination was so striking that his later attempts to downgrade his achievement appear almost perverse. He was lucky to be able to drop mathematics after a fairly simple preliminary examination; but in the four subjects he took, his marks in Latin and Greek were outstanding and in English composition and French he also did well. In none of his published works did he ever mention having won the French Prize. It is also noteworthy that he never gave much emphasis to the fact that Thomas Page – who taught the Sixth Form classics and was by any yardstick the school's most gifted master – had pronounced his work 'satisfactory in every respect'.[21] Baden-Powell later attributed his success to 'a dose of special cramming in good hands'.[22] A total of 718 candidates sat the examination for commissions in both infantry and cavalry; Stephe asked to be considered for both 'on the principle that if one missed the pigeon there was still a chance of hitting the crow'.[23] He hit both with devastating effect, coming second in the cavalry list and fifth in the infantry.

While the philistinism of the public schools undoubtedly led him to make light of his own academic gifts, Stephe was not unresponsive to intellectual ideas. In most biographies of Baden-Powell, three exceptionally famous men are claimed as close friends of the family; Thackeray, Browning and Ruskin. While Thackeray was a casual acquaintance who died when Stephe was 6, and Browning was known to the Baden-Powells only because his son Robert Wiedemann was a friend of Frank at Oxford, John Ruskin made a great impression on Henrietta Grace and through her on Stephe.

In 1867 Stephe had briefly been sent to a small private school in Cheshire, run by a clergyman. His mother and sister had stayed at nearby Winnington Hall, then housing an unusual girls' school. (Henrietta Grace was fascinated by female education and would later sit on the Council of the Girls' Public Day School Trust.) A frequent visitor to Winnington was John Ruskin, who lectured the girls in drawing and history of art. He also loaned to the school many fine paintings and a magnificent collection of minerals. His interest in the pupils owed much to his need for solace after the ending of his pitiful infatuation with the teenage Rose La Touche, but his concern for the school, both educational and financial, was genuine. Henrietta Grace met Ruskin through the headmistress Miss Margaret Bell, and for a time he seemed drawn to Agnes, writing to her and even inviting her to visit him at Denmark Hill.[24] Ruskin probably met Stephe only once, when Mrs Baden-Powell asked him to watch her ambidextrous boy drawing. The critic assured Henrietta Grace that no harm would come of the habit. Ruskin's real influence on Stephe was indirect and lay in the field of ideas.

For a time Ruskin confided in Miss Bell, who relayed many of the great man's utterances to Henrietta Grace. Occasionally she met him in person to discuss new educational theories and controversial matters such as women's rights. Although she found him extremely con- servative in his view of women, Ruskin placated her by praising Professor Powell's writings.[25] Henrietta Grace then heard at first hand of Ruskin's hatred of city life and the industrial society. At the time of their acquaintance, Ruskin was becoming ever more convinced of the predatory evils of commerce, and was urging businessmen to model their conduct on the ethical codes of the professions. He believed that the ideal of 'service' ought to be exalted above the desire for personal gain.[26] His call to the nation to seek 'not greater wealth, but simpler pleasures' would influence William Morris, Arnold Toynbee and a host of others; but in no other instance would the impact of his ideas be responsible for anything as tangible as the chivalrous idealism and anti-urban sentiments of Baden-Powell's great movement.

Another frequent visitor to Winnington was F. D. Maurice, founder of Queen's College, Harley Street, and the Great Ormond Street Working Men's College at which Ruskin lectured. So did that epitome of Christian manliness, Thomas Hughes, who taught boxing and gymnastics. 'Round shoulders, narrow chests, and stiff limbs,' he contended, 'were as bad as defective grammar and arithmetic.'[27] Henrietta Grace must have become familiar with most of the ideas current among the Christian Socialists; their glorying in physical toughness, their revival of knightly virtues, and their desire to be 'knight-errants' fighting sin and social injustice. Nor is she likely to have been unaware of their faith in cold baths and manly sports as antidotes to fornication, masturbation and sexual 'impurity'. (On this delicate subject Stephe would consult his mother when he wrote the warnings against masturbation in Scouting for Boys.)[28] Henrietta Grace had long considered it to be her duty to talk to her family about contemporary ideas. 'I cannot talk enough,' she wrote, 'for all are so ready to listen and be influenced by what I say.'[29]

The Christian Socialists entertained a variety of political beliefs, ranging from views close to Communism to an advocacy of a return to paternalistic relationships, in which class differences would persist but gentlemen be ready to accept their responsibilities to the poor, rendering service in exchange for the privilege of leadership. This combination of emotional conservatism with progressive practical aims would one day be repeated within the Scouts – enabling the movement to embrace, at rank and file Scoutmaster level, a wide spectrum of political views.

In 1870, in his famous Oxford lecture, John Ruskin called upon the youth of England to 'make your country again a throne of kings; a sceptred isle, for all the world a source of light, a centre of peace'. England, to achieve this, 'must found colonies as fast as she is able, formed of her most energetic and worthiest men; seizing every piece of fruitful waste ground she can set her foot on, and there teaching her colonists that their chief virtue is to be fidelity to their country, and that their first aim is to be to advance the power of England by land and sea.'[30] During the 1870s Oxford was galvanized not only by a fascination with Imperial duty but by the ideal of serving the poor at home. In 1874 Ruskin began his symbolic act of local service: the improvement of a muddy track on the outskirts of Oxford. Most of the undergraduates who worked on Ruskin's road were at Balliol. They included Alfred Milner, the future arch Imperialist; Arnold Toynbee, the social reformer; and very likely George Baden-Powell, who was an exact contemporary. Balliol was then dominated by Liberal Imperialists, many of whom would make their mark: Curzon,

Asquith and George Parkin were three such. George Baden-Powell would have been another unless robbed by an early death.

George's influence on Stephe was second only to that of Henrietta Grace. Stephe became George's favourite brother, and reciprocated by describing George as his mentor.[31] During the protracted Antipodean visit, which turned out to be the last of the many voyages undertaken by George to cure his tuberculosis, he wrote a book called *New Homes for the Old Country*. In it he advocated emigration to the colonies and closer Imperial links. Publication was in 1872, and Stephe read it attentively.[32]

Almost as influential as Ruskin with George's Balliol generation was the Oxford historian J. A. Froude, who idealized the white settlers of distant colonies. Froude hoped to create in these far-flung places a simpler state of society and a nobler form of life than that pertaining in England. For him, too, urban life was a cancer sapping the physical and moral health of the nation. He favoured state-aided emigration and saw the emergence of a colonial population of healthy, clean-cut, sunburned farmers as some kind of compensation to England for the degeneration of city dwellers at home. When George was at Balliol, Cecil Rhodes was an undergraduate at Oriel, Froude's former college. It is significant that in later life when Stephe wrote about Rhodes he frequently mentioned how much Rhodes had been affected by Ruskin's famous speech.[33] Although Stephe failed to get in to Balliol, his brother George made sure that he was aware of many social and political ideas then forming which would dominate the late Victorian era.

The overwhelmingly Edwardian character of the Scouts has been argued in recent years, and certainly many underlying ideas do belong to that era, but many others of equal importance can be traced to Stephe's teens, when he had not yet entered the intellectually stultifying world of the army and was still exposed, through his mother and elder brothers, to new developments in contemporary thought. There can be no doubt that he owed his first suspicions of soft urban living and his initial interest in chivalrous manliness to his mother's friendships with Miss Bell, Ruskin and their Christian Socialist friends. Nor is it less certain that he owed to George his early interest in the Empire and the idea that the rugged self-reliant life of colonial farmers was the ideal existence which British men and boys were denied by over-population and industrialization.

Stephe, as it happened, was not denied adventurous outdoor pursuits. 'I do love to see them quite free to swim and play wherever they like,' Henrietta Grace wrote of her children during a stay in the country.[34] When he was 15, Stephe was allowed to accompany his brothers on an ambitious river journey. They paddled up the Thames almost to its source in Gloucestershire, carried their collapsible boat across country to the Avon, and eventually came to the Llandogo Falls via the rivers Severn and Wye. At night they slept in tents and cooked their evening meal over a fire. In 1873 Warington left the Merchant Navy and settled down at home again. He designed and supervised the building of a 5-ton yacht, the *Diamond*, and for the next three years took George, Frank, Stephe and Baden on extended summer cruises along the South Coast. When writing about these trips in later years, Stephe would give the impression that he and Warington had been much younger than they were. In fact Warington was an experienced yachtsman of 26 and Stephe, at 16, was no child. To appeal to his Boy Scout readership Stephe would exaggerate the scrapes and dangers, but these yachting trips undoubtedly gave him an early taste for roughing it.[35]

In the years when the Baden-Powell brothers sailed together, the most famous authors of boys' fiction were glorifying adventurous lads who took the sporting camaraderie of the games field to distant countries, where they rescued injured friends from the jaws of crocodiles and saved grateful natives from hordes of cannibals. The ideal servants of Empire overseas would be young men who had not outgrown the boyhood ideals of their leisure reading and their schooldays. For many, Imperial service in India, Africa and the Far East offered the best chance of escaping a society in which a man had to forget his youth if he wanted to grow up. But in strange and curious lands, the romance of heroism, self-sacrifice and the mastery of others could continue to exist as in a perpetual boyhood. If Stephe was not a sworn devotee of this conception when he joined the army in 1876, he would become so within half-a-dozen years.

On 11 September 1876 Stephe was gazetted as Sub-Lieutenant in the 13th Hussars, then stationed at Lucknow in India. The cavalry was more expensive than the infantry, but because the 13th was in India, Stephe's membership would cost no more than living in an infantry regiment stationed in England. Successful candidates in the army examination were usually sent to the Royal Military College, Sandhurst, for two years. 'But in my case,' wrote Stephe, 'war with Russia was on the tapis, officers were wanted at once; and therefore the first six who passed for Cavalry were gazetted direct to regiments instead of going to Sandhurst.'[36]

War with Russia did not materialize, but by the time it was evident that the Tsar would not use the massacre of Bulgarian Christians by the Turks as a pretext for threatening British interests in the region, Stephe had already sailed for India on the troopship *Serapis*. He left Portsmouth on 30 October 1876, on the eve of Disraeli's proclamation of Queen Victoria as Empress of India.

2

SERVANT OF THE RAJ

1. Heat and Dust (1876–79)

The *Serapis* was one of five identical troopships used on the Indian run to carry up to two thousand souls in the trooping season. With the wind astern, her sails supplemented the power of her small engines. She rolled unpleasantly in heavy seas; there was no ice aboard and no fans. Junior officers were accommodated on the lower troop deck in an area known as 'Pandemonium' because of its proximity to the engines. On all the lower decks the heat was terrible during the later stages of the five-week voyage.

'Lights out' was at ten, and at that time the First Lieutenant – accompanied by the Field Officer of the day and the Subaltern of the day – made a circuit of the ship. Stephe could not have escaped this duty but, to spare his sister's and his mother's feelings, did not describe the conditions on the deck where the wives and children of N.C.O.s and enlisted men were quartered. George Noble, a subaltern in the 13th who later became a friend, was more forthcoming. 'In hot weather, most of the women and children would be lying about in their berths "in puris naturalibus" so that other senses besides that of smell were offended, and our procession was generally greeted with jeers and abuse, couched in filthy language.'[1]

As usual on long voyages, an entertainments committee was formed and Baden-Powell overwhelmed them with his boxful of plays. He was soon performing most of the old Charterhouse favourites: *Cox and Box, Whitebait at Greenwich* and the *Area Belle*.[2] In the Red Sea the temperature rose steadily as the ship steamed south. 'Four or five children died and several ladies were ill, continually fainting. Worst of all, all the cooks got so ill they had to go to hospital.'[3] Baden-Powell would often affect this kind of callous jocularity, in emulation of the laconic unemotional style then favoured by military men. In some ways it was a form of self-defence against the omnipresence of death; a close relation to the gallows humour of men at war. In India the enemies would be typhoid and cholera, which still made the sub-continent one of the most dangerous parts of the Empire in which to serve. Frederick Stevens Dimond, who had been one place behind Stephe on the Cavalry List and was on the *Serapis* with him, also gazetted to the 13th Hussars, would die of cholera before he was thirty.

But in the last days of November 1876, heat or no heat, the junior officers were irrepressible. While *Serapis* was negotiating the Suez Canal most of them went ashore. 'Some fellows played "Hi Cocka-lorum"; others, myself amongst them, set fire to some of the bushes that grow in the sand every few yards, then one of us started off with a great fog-horn belonging to the ship and led the rest of us a chase all about in the desert.' When *Serapis* docked at Bombay, Stephe and Dimond had great difficulty in getting their baggage loaded on to a bullock wagon. 'We had donned our best uniforms and were not a little proud of ourselves in the early part of the day; but as hour followed hour in that soggy heat we seemed to melt into the thick-bound cloth . . . By nightfall our pride had all leaked out, and under the cover of darkness we willingly climbed up on to the pile of baggage on our bullock-cart and allowed ourselves to be ignominiously carried through the back streets of Bombay to our hotel.'[4] (Illustration p. 73.)

During the long train journey to Lucknow, the young officers spent a night in a small rest house, keeping their loaded pistols handy in case assassins came to cut their throats. Twenty years had elapsed since the Mutiny, but their knowledge of the country was chiefly derived from reading accounts of atrocities. Yet within days of his arrival in Lucknow, Baden-Powell was thoroughly reassured by his brother officers' habitual condescension towards all Indians. When the adjutant showed him his bungalow it was surrounded by a large crowd of would-be servants, who were whipped away by the bearer and servants to the former occupant. Not yet appreciating that in times of food scarcity employment by Europeans offered the best hope of survival, Stephe found this scene amusing. 'I like my native servants,' he told his mother, 'but as a rule the niggers seem to me cringing villains.' The way in which 'every native, as he passes, gives a salute', irritated him. 'If he has an umbrella up he takes it down, if he is riding a horse he gets off. . . . If you meet a man in the road and tell him to dust your boots, he does it.'[5] Although such servility did not seem right to Stephe, he would very soon take it for granted. The continuance of the British Raj depended in large part upon the ability of its executives to believe themselves innately superior to those they ruled. For a brief period Baden-Powell was influenced by his step-brother's view that India could and should develop, 'making use of modern things'.[6] But soon, like most civil servants and army officers in India, he would support the princes and maharajahs and would ridicule educated Indians: 'a crowd of clerks, lawyers, and agitators', and would conclude, 'for these people our modern efforts are not required, their old style is more in keeping with their character and country'.[7]

It is always difficult for one age to understand another, and with hindsight Victorian army officers look to have been remarkably

insensitive to other races. When a brother officer's syce (groom) was
kicked to death by one of Baden-Powell's horses, 'it was agreed by all
that the syce must have done something extraordinary to frighten the
horse'. In fact the animal in question had been temperamental since
fracturing his skull on a stable wall. Nevertheless, nearly 40 years later
Baden-Powell would still term this incident 'justifiable homicide'.[8]
Stephe shared a bungalow with Captain T. G. Cuthell, 'who shot a
coolie when firing at a deer'. About £10 in the money of the day was
paid over to the man's family, and no more was said. 'And so the world
wags on,' commented Baden-Powell, adding bleakly that not everyone was so lucky, since 'some fellows have got into a row at Meerut for
shooting coolies'. On another occasion Stephe overheard a snatch of
conversation: '"I say, Dick, I hear your bearer died this morning."
"Did he? Confound it. I wish someone would let a fellow know. There
have I been yelling for him the whole afternoon."'[9] But that was at a
time when many men in the regiment were also dying of cholera.

Stephe disliked Lucknow from the first. The Indian quarter he
considered 'no regular town, except where you come on a bazaar, and
that is an arrangement of mud hovels'.[10] The scarred bullet-pitted
ruins around the Residency were interesting as relics of the famous
siege, but did not make up for the drabness of the military cantonments
with their identical bungalows and miles of dusty roads. But as at
Charterhouse, although his situation seemed unpromising Stephe
quickly worked out who did what, and how matters were organized.
The regiment, he found, was not run by the Colonel and the troop
officers, but by the Adjutant and the senior NCOs.[11] He therefore
rapidly made friends with the Adjutant, who fortunately ran the
regiment's theatricals. Stephe's troop captain told him that it would be
vital for him to know 'how to drink three glasses of port at the same
time, and that midday stables were not merely a time for watching
men stroking their horses, but mainly for watching one dog against
another at rat killing'. Stephe was soon impressed to find that when the
Colonel was reported to be coming round, 'the chairs on which we sat
around the rat-pit, were, by a system of ropes and pulleys, quickly and
quietly hoisted into the roof of the stables'.[12]

To give his family an idea of life in Lucknow, Stephe recommended
to them The Dilemma, a novel by G. T. Chesney. The British civil
population were represented as a dull lot, obsessed with etiquette and
resenting the superior status accorded to army officers, particularly in
the cavalry. The cultural shock of Indian life had led most British wives
to retire into the safe routines of small-station Anglo India. And since it
was impossible to bring out many possessions, a luxuriant snobbery
based on minor social distinctions restricted more generous
impulses.[13]

The hero of The Dilemma was a young subaltern, who chafed at the tedium of his life. Conversation in the mess was utterly threadbare since 'the different members had completely thrashed out each other's ideas'. The routine weekly dances and cricket matches, and the absence of real military work had Chesney's young subaltern crying out, 'Is this life? Is this to last for ever?'[14] At times Stephe wondered the same. But even at 19 he was averse to introspection and did his best to be outward-looking. In all the weekly letters he wrote home, he managed to find matters of interest to report. Even snakes – which caused considerable anxiety – could furnish an entertainingly told anecdote. 'The other day 3 or 4 fellows were standing in a circle talking at the race course when suddenly, out of a little hole hopped a frog – then a second which was quickly followed by a snake's head, who, when he saw all these fellows looking at him, modestly retired. But they got buckets of water and filled his hole – so that he came at them, but they killed him and found he was a cobra, 53 inches long.'[15]

The simple cantonment bungalow was an unvarying block of rooms, each leading into the next. Concrete floors, wire-netted windows and battered second-hand furniture were not attractive, but Stephe stressed his bungalow's better points. Between his bedroom and the bathroom there was, for excellent sanitary reasons, an ante-room. 'This,' he wrote, 'is really a fernery and makes the bedroom beautifully cool and pretty; and on the verandah outside my window there are ferns and flowers too oh it's very fine. We have got a monkey and a deer in the garden and lots of doves, parrots etc. in cages.'[16]

During his first tour of duty in India, Stephe made no friends. He shared his bungalow with Dimond, whom he liked but to whom he never became close, and with Captain Cuthell, a considerably older man with a wife in England. William Christie, the Adjutant, was also much older, but from the beginning Stephe got on well with him and spent a lot of his time with him and his wife. They were not socially hidebound and Christie, although from a middle-class background, had risen from the ranks. Mrs Christie would look after Stephe when he was ill, and in some ways she and her husband were like parents to him. Like Baden-Powell, Christie drew well and was an accomplished actor, but perhaps the greatest attraction his home had to offer was the company of his young daughters.[17] As he grew older, Stephe would continue to prefer the companionship of girls in their early teens to that of mature women. As his secretary wrote many years later, they 'gave him their fullest confidence and with them he felt completely at home'.[18] He particularly took to two of the four Christie girls as one of them recalled:

My elder sister and I always 'inspected' the new young officers who came out from England, and in the evening of his arrival we walked up to the bungalow where he was to live with two others, and found them all reclining in their long chairs in the verandah. We immediately demanded the new subaltern's name. 'Charlie,' he said, laughing at the two funny little girls with their bushy brown hair and inquisitive eyes. And 'Charlie' he has been to us ever since. He was a great pal to us. Most evenings he would come over to our bungalow with his ocarina, and with one child hanging on each side of him, he would take us out into the quieter roads, playing tunes to us and teaching us to be observant. He sometimes had to be reprimanded for waking up my small sister with his cat-calls and jackal noises. On wet evenings we would sit in his room and he would draw, paint or sing for us.

When, several years later, he was sent north to Afghanistan, 'he immediately collected us to help him to pack,' the same sister recorded. 'We sat and watched the operation with tears and smiles, B-P singing most of the time, "Oh, yes, I must away, I can no longer stay." Before we said goodnight, we kissed his sword and laid it under his pillow for luck, and he left early the next day . . . Gradually we got letters from him, one of them wishing we would cut off our hair and send it to him to stuff his pillow . . .'[19]

Baden-Powell's first two biographers, Begbie and Aitken, reported that shortly after his arrival in Lucknow, he 'assembled all the European children he could find in the station to march at their head through the streets'. All the while he played the ocarina, a simple whistle-like instrument, and performed 'The Girl I Left Behind Me' with great feeling, 'which suffered however a little from his comprehensive grin'.[20] If this story had been published after the formation of the Scouts it would have looked suspiciously like an invented anecdote intended to convey the early development of his rapport with boys and girls. But both authors published eight years earlier, and clearly had the story directly from Henrietta Grace. It would have required not only a strong streak of exhibitionism but also considerable daring for a young subaltern to draw attention to himself in this way. That Stephe possessed both these qualities in abundance he would prove conclusively during his first tour. But as at Charterhouse, his theatrical performances in women's clothes, his falsetto comic songs and other eccentricities did not undermine his fundamental acceptance of the values of the new community in which he found himself. A telling example is the way in which he would subscribe to the prevailing snobbery directed against technical branches of the service and would accept that 'a fellow in the Artillery or Engineers worth knowing seems from all accounts to be a rarity'. This was in spite of his own uncle then being a colonel in the Royal Artillery. Stephe scorned the man who had come top on both lists in the Army Examination because he had 'no money, or wit and had not yet bought a pony'. He also had 'a thin white face, thin long whiskers and wore spectacles . . . Not quite Cavalry, is he?' Baden-Powell solemnly told his sister, who spent almost all her time in London, that 'a young woman who cannot ride counts for very little I find'.[21] He became obsessed with the right place to buy certain articles of clothing. Boots had to come from 'Bartley's of Oxford Street . . . You could not appear in native boots.' Nothing pleased him more than to have the handiwork of his tailor admired.[22]

Coping with the Indian climate turned out to be a more formidable proposition than mastering regimental mores. Between April and November the temperature soared on the Plains, making life in Lucknow an ordeal. To get any work done at all during the day, officers and men had to rise at 4.30 am. Within two hours it would be too hot outside to do anything until late afternoon. Even before dawn officers would return from parading with their shirts and jackets wringing wet, and Stephe's servants would rub him down with rough towels and give him cold coffee while he lay on his bed under the punkah. Between seven and eight he attended stables and then inspected his troop's bungalow before going to orderly room. Clothes soaked once more, he would breakfast in the mess and then return to his bungalow to be dried again. He then slept until three in the afternoon with his feet tied up in handkerchiefs to protect them from mosquitoes. In the early evening he would 'ride out in the stifling hot air along baked roads' and return soaking yet again. Another bath, another rub, and he would dine in the mess, only to return to his bungalow wet through for the last bath of the day.

> Oh it's awful . . . When I go into the stables the poor old horses look as though they had just come in from a long gallop, all dripping with perspiration. All the birds in the trees sit still with mouths open to catch the air. Three men gone mad in the last week. One in the 65th [an infantry regiment] tried to cut his throat. One of our men was caught loading his carbine for the third time during the week . . . Two or three men have been taken with apoplexy.[23]

Unfortunately Stephe had to endure more than the heat. At dawn, along with the parades and drills, he and 'Tommy' Dimond attended Riding School. Military Riding Masters were stern disciplinarians, more interested in achieving the regulation parade-ground posture by strapping boards to their pupils' backs than in teaching the value of gentle hands and a delicate understanding between horse and rider. Getting novices to grip with their knees by putting them over a substantial jump without the benefit of reins or stirrups was effective, but caused unnecessary accidents. Stephe referred to his 'early miseries' in the Riding School and to numerous painful falls. He was wounded in the hand during sword drill and, more seriously, was beginning to suffer from fever, weight loss, toothache and loss of appetite. As if this were not enough, he would also suffer from rheumatism, boils and cracked lips.[24]

Stephe had to undergo an eight-month course of military instruction at Lucknow. He worked hard at his drill books and was awarded a First Class in the end-of-course examination. His best marks were in surveying and in fortification. In tactics he did noticeably less well. For his success he was promoted lieutenant and gained two years seniority. Working hard for examinations was frowned on in cavalry regiments, so Stephe had shown considerable independence of mind in displaying such keenness. As an indication of the average cavalry officer's mistrust of 'clever' soldiers, no officer in the Household Cavalry had been through the Staff College by 1900.[25]

The impression usually given of Stephe's first two years in India is one of resolute determination to stick it out in the subcontinent, and a similar eagerness to remain with the 13th Hussars. In fact after only three months in Lucknow, and well before his health started to give way, he wrote to his brother George to inquire 'whether you people are doing anything more about getting me into the Guards'. A year later he wrote to his mother suggesting she try to get him a job as an A.D.C. to the military governor of a colony. Although he would later scorn such jobs as having nothing to do with proper soldiering, the idea appealed to him in 1878. 'An A.D.C. generally gets good pay with lots to do. Has all the domestic work of the general's house, arranges the dinner parties and who is to take who in etc., and escorts the general's daughter in her rides.'[26] This was a far cry from the tough outdoor 'flannel shirt' life he would be advocating a decade later.

Ill-health was not the only reason why, from the middle of 1878, Baden Powell became increasingly desperate to come home. In spite of his friendship with the Adjutant, Stephe was still liable to be bullied by the older subalterns, who ruled the younger ones with autocratic insensitivity, 'wheeling us into line pretty sharply'. The senior subaltern was a well-known polo player and sportsman 'with an iron will and a flow of language above average'. John Watson laid fiendishly demanding paper-chases for the freshly arrived officers to ride over, with 'parallel water-courses liable to catch your horse tripping, or "Absalom" jumps, where you took a fence under overhanging boughs. Watson himself was always there behind the pack with a hunting crop to see that none missed their opportunities.'[27] George Noble described Watson as a sadist and most of his brother officers as unfriendly and only interested in talking about horses.[28] It was 'bad form' to talk in the mess about sex, women, religion, politics and regimental 'shop'. But because new subalterns were not allowed to speak unless spoken to, there was little room for such mistakes. There were, however, plenty of other petty rules which cost a fine if infringed. The moral values of the mess were confusing. Gambling debts had to be paid at once, but tradesmen should be kept waiting. Stephe was soon writing jocular notes along with the rest of them, explaining why he could not pay this or that Indian trader for the time being.[29]

While aristocratic connections could mitigate the sin of having only a small private income, a man from an ordinary middle-class family could not hope to survive in the cavalry without means. Being the grandson of a duke saved Winston Churchill in the 4th Hussars, when several other lieutenants with incomes slightly larger than his own were driven out for being too poor. In India it was just possible for a subaltern to live on his pay, provided he received occasional payments of about £200 a year. This was roughly Stephe's position; but it was an unenviable one, and he showed considerable courage in not being ashamed of regularly recording the lowest mess bill. Instead of ordering expensive clarets at dinner, as did most of his brother officers, he would content himself with a little sherry mixed with soda water. In the hot weather he would often sit all day in the mess, thus benefiting from the work of the mess punkah wallahs and saving himself the expense of engaging a man at his bungalow.[30]

George Noble found that his popularity increased when his fellows discovered that he had 'a fair baritone voice and could strum a little on the banjo'.[31] Stephe owed his friendship with William Christie, the Adjutant, to his ability to act and paint scenery. Very few professional companies could afford the expense of journeying through India to relatively small stations; so dramatic and comic talent within the regiment was fostered. Concerts and theatricals took place almost every other week and played an important part in keeping up morale.[32] As early as February 1877 Stephe was appearing in *Whitebait at Greenwich* and his description of his performance captures the spirit of such enterprises:

I acted the part of a waiter at a hotel. He had been deserted by his parents, but he had in his pocket a police handbill giving a description of his father: 'Deserted his child; a man surname unknown; christian name Benjamin; had on when last seen corduroy breeches; height 5 ft 10 in his shoes.' So whenever a man came into the hotel I inquired whether his name happened to be Benjamin, and when it wasn't I was fairly disappointed. At last a couple arrived and I heard her call him Benjamin. I got out my tape measure and in pretending to dust him down I secretly and eagerly took his measure: 5 ft 8 inches. In a fury of excitement I jerked up his foot to measure the thickness of his boot. In spite of his indignation and struggles, I found it 2 inches thick, I immediately claimed him affectionately as my father and her as my mother. Their indignation was great as they were only cousins and not married.[33]

In November 1877 he made his first appearance dressed as a woman. This was as Lady Allcash, 'a lady making her first tour', in H. J. Byron's farce *Fra Diavolo*. In years to come he would play numerous female roles and would often make his own dresses.[34] Lieutenant Arthur Brookfield, who later became an MP, and who played Pantaloon to Stephe's clown in a regimental pantomime, found his 'merry disposition' slightly disconcerting – coexisting as it did with an iron resolve to get on. Brookfield recalled that when Baden-Powell started to distinguish himself 'it was rather the fashion to criticize his work on the ground that he seemed too inclined to court the approval of the gallery.'[35]

In June 1878 Stephe was granted leave and travelled to Simla in the Hills to stay with his half-brother, Baden Henry, who was now an Indian High Court Judge. Simla was the summer headquarters of the Viceroy, and most of the Government departments moved there in the hot season. Baden-Powell aptly described it as 'a sort of Cowes in the mountains'. Among wooded hills, 'all the houses are perched about on the edge of precipices, roofed in with wood and have large verandahs running round them'.[36] Stephe's attitude towards Baden Henry was extremely condescending. After meeting some of his half-brother's friends, Stephe told his mother that he had felt thankful that he had not gone into the Civil Service. 'I suppose at this moment I know more people in Simla than BH does, and of a much better class. If I want to call on anybody I just have to call there and introduce myself and we are friends immediately . . . But if BH calls in that way, people are more chary about receiving him till they have found out all about him, as "Civil Servant" is no recommendation seeing that half are niggers or cads.'[37]

Baden Henry had then been working on what would be the standard legal work on landownership in India. Stephe referred airily to this work as 'his manual on forest law, whatever that may be'. Baden Henry had also written a magisterial two-volume work on *The Manufactures and Arts of the Punjab*. But Stephe could not take his scholarly half-brother seriously. Like many bachelors Baden Henry had become rather set in his ways, reading the newspapers each morning at exactly the same time 'with occasional ejaculations. "Och! This is *too* silly – no – no – my dear man!" Then swallowing down his food with awful sniffs and sighs.' To Stephe's disgust he only took one walk a week, 'wandering down the mountainside with measured steps and slow'.[38] In one respect, however, Stephe vowed to emulate his half-brother. Baden Henry had entered for the Simla Academy Exhibition two pictures which had been highly commended. Stephe resolved to enter some work the following October 'to see if I can get a prize over his head'.[39] Unlike other Powell relatives, Baden Henry made regular contributions towards Stephe's expenses; and the 1500 rupees he produced that year were indispensable.[40]

Baden-Powell's fame as an actor had preceded him to Simla, so when the town's Amateur Dramatic Club needed a replacement at short notice for the part of a Jacobite lord in Bulwer Lytton's *Walpole*, they called upon him. What made this particular production exceptional was the fact that the Viceroy of India was the playwright's son. Lord Lytton attended several rehearsals and was there on the first night. When Baden-Powell's colonel refused to extend his leave, the Commander-in-Chief told the Adjutant-General to see if he could bring about a change of heart. Thus Stephe was granted two extensions of leave and received invitations to some very select functions, at one of which he met 'a small but very polite officer' in the refreshment room. When he was unable to make the waiter understand what he wanted, the stranger came to his aid – suggesting, as an afterthought, that Stephe would get more out of India if he learned Hindustani.[41] This 'polite' officer was Major-General Frederick Roberts, who within half-a-dozen years would be Commander-in-Chief in India, and would go on to command all Britain's forces in the most crucial phase of the Boer War. Stephe neither mastered Hindustani, nor managed to ingratiate himself with Roberts.

But if Baden-Powell made no impression on Roberts, he was far from inactive in pressing his mother to seek out and entertain those in England who might push on his career. Colonel Baker Russell, who within three years would be Colonel of the 13th Hussars, was one officer to whom Stephe asked his mother to make herself particularly agreeable. Stephe knew that Baker Russell was one of Sir Garnet Wolseley's favoured officers – a member of the future Field Marshal's so-called 'Garnet Ring'. Henrietta Grace was also instructed to invite any other well-connected 'swells' to dinner if the opportunity ever arose.[42] Mixing with the élite of Simla and feeling his health improving by the day, Stephe dreaded returning to the dusty inferno of Lucknow where deaths from heat apoplexy and cholera were commonplace. But there was no help for it and in late August he was back with his regiment again, experiencing what he described as 'existence not life'.

Within days he was suffering from diarrhoea, and wrote begging his mother to 'get hold of some fellow at Horse Guards . . . the right man can do a great deal more than simply advise'. It says a lot for his confidence in his mother that he could suppose her able to influence key officers on the Commander-in-Chief's staff. His one hope was to exchange into another regiment as soon as possible and to this end Henrietta Grace was to investigate the relative expenses of the

Dragoon Guards and the Foot Guards.[44] By late September Stephe
was sure he could never go through another hot season in India. His
liver hurt, he was plagued by boils, headaches, giddy spells and weak
knees. In mid-November he wrote telling his mother that 'both
doctors say I am not a likely fellow to get acclimatized . . . I long to get
a letter from you telling me to come home – I don't care what I get into
as long as it is not in India.' He longed for a year's leave and then an
exchange. On 28 November, to his great joy, the Medical Board
pronounced him 'ill and wanting a change to England at public
expense'. The symptoms listed included enlargement of the spleen,
dyspepsia, diarrhoea and 'a general malaise'.[45] He boarded the *Serapis*
in Bombay on 6 December 1878, two years to the day after he landed in
India for the first time.

2. Home to Mother (1879–80)

For several years Henrietta Grace had been determined to move to a
larger and grander house. A few months before Stephe's return she
acquired a long lease on 8 St George's Place, a very substantial but
architecturally undistinguished house at Hyde Park Corner, only a
stone's throw from the Duke of Wellington's Apsley House and
directly opposite the famous 'Row', where fashionable 'Society'
disported itself on horseback and in carriages. The Baden-Powells
could now count as their immediate neighbours the Earl and Countess
of Lovelace and the Marquess of Aylesbury. Stephe was convinced
that the extra expenditure involved would yield magnificent social and
professional dividends. 'I yelled with delight when I received your
letter saying you had No. 8,' he told his mother. 'Now all is really well.
Ask any 13th lads you can. . .'[1] While still in India he scanned the social
journals to see that Henrietta Grace was making the maximum use of
her new social asset. 'I see again in the *Court Journal*, "Mrs BP's small
and early dance". Make them mention it in *Vanity Fair* as well.'[2] Since
the house would have to be let for the major part of the year, he was
determined that the most should be made of it while the family was in
residence.

In his honour Henrietta Grace gave a dinner for 24 guests, few of
whom had been chosen for their entertainment value. Two generals,
both on the point of retirement, could conceivably have been useful to
Stephe. An Oxford friend of George had been asked because he
worked in the political department of the India Office. A Lord Chief
Justice had been invited for the benefit of Warington, now practising as
a barrister, and for Frank, who hoped to be called to the Bar. Another
guest was Lady Westbury, whose son was a lieutenant in the Scots
Guards, which was the regiment Henrietta Grace had earmarked for

Baden. The Bishop of London, a friend of the late Professor, gave the occasion gravitas.[3]

But though he might merit a dinner, the hopes Stephe had entertained for exchanging into the Guards were quickly dashed by his mother. As George had suggested to her several months earlier, 'exchanging into an English regiment would be a lot of *present* expense'. Instead George felt that Stephe should follow his sick leave with a year of ordinary leave and then rejoin the 13th Hussars, unless he had in the meantime passed into the Staff College.[4] Only 'precious Badie' was going to enjoy the social glory of being an officer in the Guards. Nevertheless George would give much thought to Stephe's career in years to come. In 1877 George had managed by sheer nerve to persuade Sir George Bowen, the Governor of Victoria in Australia, to employ him as his private secretary. He had thus brought himself to the attention of 'Mr Herbert, the Finger of the Colonial Office', and also to the notice of Herbert's cousin, Lord Carnarvon, who had been Colonial Secretary in 1878. George would stick to Sir George Bowen like a leech and, although despising him, would ultimately owe his knighthood to the connection. 'The great way to get on with him is to give him something about you to boast about . . . His opinions are just those that have been last driven into him by anybody.'[5] George wrote regularly to *The Times*, sent articles for publication in *Fraser's Magazine* and was working on two books of political economy which, when published, he meant to send – along with favourable reviews – to a large number of influential people. On his own initiative he began to investigate and write about the effects of the sugar bounty system on West Indian trade. This strategy cannily anticipated Sir William Crossman's West Indian Commission a year later, and secured from Gladstone's government an offer of the post of Joint Commissioner.[6] Stephe knew he could not emulate his astonishing brother for the present, but the way in which George used a combination of patronage and enterprise to get on was not lost on him.

For the moment there was not a lot Stephe could do to further his career. He would need the nomination of his colonel before he could hope to get into the Staff College, but there were more prosaic courses he could attend in the meantime. One was run by the School of Musketry at Hythe in Kent, and those gaining a certificate qualified for employment as regimental Musketry Instructors, which in India carried an extra 100 rupees a month in pay. George Noble passed through Hythe a couple of years after Stephe and described the course as 'a most useless one'. The Army Drill Book was frequently altered, but much time was spent learning it by heart. The theory of musketry was crammed into four lectures, which also had to be remembered to the last sentence.[7] In the group photograph of Baden-Powell's course, while most of the young officers posed straightforwardly Stephe played his ocarina. Hythe was close to the regional garrison camp at Shorncliffe, where Stephe did his best to mix with 'swells'. One such was the Brigade-Major, Francis Grenfell (later Lord Grenfell) who ran the garrison's entertainments. He persuaded Stephe to give a series of comic lectures on subjects such as 'Ancient Roman Barrel Organs' and 'Steam Engines of All Sorts'.[8] Apart from making him known to every senior officer at the camp, these lectures had the virtue of being repeatable to different audiences in the future.

Practical jokes were the order of the day at Hythe and Stephe, being addicted to this form of humour, lost no time in joining a group known as 'the fire brigade'. 'As soon as we saw a party of officers comfortably settled to whist in the ante-room after mess, a cry of "Fire!" was raised, and immediately one party detailed for catching the victim rushed out and took up position below the mess-room window, while the second party of rescuers shouting, "Smith's on fire!" would rush and seize Smith from amongst his friends and carry him to the window and throw him out to be caught by those below.' Baden-Powell's reward for participating in numerous 'rescues' was to be gagged, roped securely to a plank and then dumped in the guard-room with a note to the effect that he had fallen from a window and broken his neck.[9]

To his credit Stephe enjoyed occasional jokes against himself. During his two years in England he was invited to take part in various private theatricals. One invitation came from Lord and Lady Wolverton who lived near Blandford. Stephe did not know the family but had been introduced by a friend as an excellent actor.

> I arrived about tea-time and was ushered into a large house party by the footman. I was a stranger to them all and they had not heard my name announced so they merely invited me hospitably to sit down and have some tea. Presently, finding that I had come by train, they asked whether I had seen anything of a small hunchbacked man with red hair, who was expected by that train . . . They said that for one thing he was very bad-tempered, and very conscious of his deformity and had to be treated with the greatest tact, but had otherwise been recommended to them as a suitable actor, and his name was Baden-Powell.

Stephe was left wondering whether the friend who had introduced him was responsible, or whether he owed his embarrassment to his aristocratic host.[10]

In later years Baden-Powell would write more about one production than any other. This was a performance of Robertson's *Caste* mounted on two evenings during February 1880. Stephe invariably neglected to mention that these performances took place at his own home in St George's Place. On both occasions the family's genius for self-promotion was evident. The *Court Journal* published a full account.

> Last Tuesday evening, and again on Wednesday, Mrs Baden-Powell gave two superb entertainments at her residence near Hyde Park Corner, on both of which occasions private theatricals were provided for the diversion of the guests. At nine o'clock the fair hostess threw open her salons, and assisted by her daughter, Miss Agnes Baden-Powell, received the guests on the landing of the principal staircase.

After the play, supper was served at one in the morning, when 'the hostess, with her indefatigable sons, led the way to the dining room where a most recherché repast was served to the visitors'.[11] In the play Stephe took the part of the cockney plumber, Sam Gerridge.

As the title implies, *Caste* is a satire on class, which was a subject of intense fascination to Stephe. In preparing himself for his part, he dressed up in clothes suitable for a plumber and sallied forth 'to study my models in the workshops and bars of the neighbourhood of the Commercial Road'. He mingled with the crowds outside Buckingham Palace as they watched fashionable people arriving for a royal function. When a drunk pestered a couple of girls standing near him, he got rid of the man. Through these girls he met a young carpenter called Jim Bates, and soon became his 'constant companion at his work and in his amusements . . . Under his able and unsuspecting instruction I soon picked up the desired knowledge of the manners and customs of his kind and through a method far pleasanter than I had ever anticipated . . . When the play came off my visits to Jim naturally ceased.' Presumably it was 'natural' for him to stop seeing Bates because he could not have gone on indefinitely pretending to belong to the same class. Nor would he have wanted to admit that he had been using him. Yet seven or eight years later, dressed in his magnificent Hussar uniform, Baden-Powell spotted Bates at an Aldershot Review toiling along in the crowd. He promptly told him who he was and then, as if in recompense, gave him a pass for a special enclosure. There is something unconvincing about this anecdote as told by Stephe.[12] Although he was a formidable actor, it would have been an astonishing feat to be the 'constant companion' to a man from another class without ever arousing his suspicion. In Baden-Powell's journalistic pieces fact and fiction often blur as he presents the version of events he would have liked to happen, rather than the one which actually did.[13] In view of his later enjoyment of the company of enlisted men, it is easy to believe that he sought out working-class men during this visit to England. He might well have *wished* to bridge the class gulf and to be accepted by a carpenter as his companion, but whether he actually succeeded in the way he described seems doubtful.

Amateur theatricals brought him in touch with young women for the first time. His only references to them when writing home from India had been facetious.[4] Nor did he have any interest in the daughters of his mother's neighbours; in one case he ridiculed the affectionate notes sent to him, and could not bring himself to look at 'the de Stern lumps', daughters of an immensely rich man.[15] For a while Stephe attached himself to Sir Charles Young's travelling company of amateur actors and played the part of Sir Claude Beville, a young baronet, in *Faustine*, a melodrama written by Young. In a scrapbook, Baden-Powell preserved a letter written to him by a female member of the cast: 'Dear Sir Claude, You shouldn't try to make jokes. You shouldn't indeed . . . Why are you so polite to [illegible] and so rude to *me*. Entre nous (oh! I forgot you don't understand French) between you and me I hear rumours of Faustine in June . . .' The letter is pasted into an album in a way that makes several lines impossible to decipher. It goes on: '. . . because I won't have it. Of course you are as bad as possible, but then one is accustomed to it . . . Marguerite.'[16] Marguerite was in fact a *Mrs* King, who was then staying at Albert Mansions, Victoria.[17] No other letters from her survive, but this one suggests that Stephe's jocular, rather detached attitude towards women attracted as many as it repelled, although – as he would later explain to his family – if close relations seemed imminent he would quickly dispel any romantic expectation.[18]

Henrietta Grace herself was in no doubt about the undesirability of any of her sons forming relationships which might lead them to abandon the magnificent house that could only be financed with the aid of those sons who were earning. The 1880s marked the culmination of her system of communal sharing and her control over her children's lives. She wrote to them all, charging them always to remember their mutual dependence:

> When you are old you will boast of it and so remarkable a distinction will it be that men will then scarce believe it. They will deem it impossible that you and we – seven of us living in the world, not shutting ourselves up, five young men at the very ages to be tempted to spend on yachts and horses and books and pictures and wines and dinners and carriages and clubs – should yet all join in one purse that all can cheerfully agree to arrange expenditure . . . that each and all as they earn add it to the public purse, without one murmur . . . I really think one of you should keep this letter to remind you of it in old age. For alas! I suppose we must stop this purity and virtue when any one of you marries and ties each one down to the selfish ordinary life of earning and spending for himself alone.[19]

In the summer of 1880, well into Stephe's second year at home, a

British force about 2,500 strong was surrounded and defeated with heavy loss at Maiwand near Kandahar in Afghanistan. Over 1,000 officers and men were reported killed or missing. On 1 September Major-General Sir Frederick Roberts and an army of 10,000 men avenged this defeat. The 13th Hussars had been ordered to Kandahar, but arrived too late to take part in the fighting. This made Stephe feel better about not being there. Any officer able to boast the experience of 'service in the field' had better prospects of promotion, and in some cases might get into the Staff College without passing the examination.

But as Stephe's leave came to an end, he had the consolation of knowing that it would not be the hot season when he arrived, and that in any case he would be stationed in the hills of Afghanistan on his return.

After a farewell dinner for fourteen people given by his Uncle Colonel Smyth, Stephe boarded the *Serapis* once more, and the following day wrote to George displaying an almost parodied absence of regret to be returning to India: 'Woke at 5 this-morning and played ocarina to Shreiber's banjo and Burn's penny whistle (the 2 other blokes in my cabin) till we had aroused everybody . . . I'm going to have a whisky and hot water, and then turn in. Shreiber pays for the drink. Goodbye ducky. (Shreiber wrote that).'[20]

At Plymouth Major Seymour Lacy, who had also acted in *Caste*, 'came on board and stayed some time'.[21] Ten years earlier when Stephe had been a schoolboy, he and the major had both acted in *To Parents and Guardians*. Lacy was twenty years Stephe's senior and had played in many other school productions. In 1883 he was abruptly dismissed from the army, 'Her Majesty no longer requiring his services'. No record of the nature of his offence survives.[22] In the register of Old Carthusians he is described as *spurcissimus*, or very wicked, and 'unworthy of the name of Carthusian'. When such misfortunes overtake middle-aged bachelors who are fond of associating with boys, the obvious conclusion is usually correct.

Two days out of Plymouth a storm started to rage, and while 'saloon furniture was smashed', and 'a lot of men were awfully terrified', Stephe was giving his lecture on barrel organs. Anyone guessing that he was returning to a country upon which he had vowed never again to set eyes, would have had to be gifted with second sight.[23]

3. Blood and Friendship (1880–82)

Shortly after his return to detestable Lucknow, Baden-Powell was thankful to receive orders to join his regiment in Kandahar. He began

his northward journey by train, travelling with a recently arrived
subaltern, a vet and two doctors. The railway ended at Sibi in
Baluchistan; from there the little party had a six-day march to Quetta
with their retinue of servants and laden pack animals.

> It's a jolly life [enthused Stephe], the scenery is generally beastly –
> one march the road was perfectly straight for 18 miles – a low ridge
> of mountains 5 miles on each side, not a speck of vegetation – all
> white boulders and glaring sun. It was fun at Sibi, for the first time
> seeing everybody walking about with a revolver on. We always
> carry one. At the first camp some friendly natives came in covered
> with wounds, they had got from Afghans.[1]

Beyond Quetta, which was twelve days' march from Kandahar, no
small British detachments were allowed to travel without an escort of
native cavalry. With four troopers, two sergeants and an apothecary
now added to his party, Baden-Powell journeyed on. As they climbed
higher it grew colder but he enjoyed camping out each night in mud
forts. Wearing a chamois leather waistcoat and a long quilted coat for
extra warmth, he felt comfortable and relaxed. The outdoor cooking
reminded him of the trip he had made up the Avon with his brothers
years before.

A formidable range of hills divided Quetta from Kandahar, and the
precipitous track was extremely hazardous for baggage animals.
Stephe's powers of jocular understatement would one day make him
famous but he started early. 'The consequence,' of the sloping track, he
told his mother, 'was dead camels on either side of the road all along
and a splendid aroma.'[2] George Noble, his friend, had gone by a few
days earlier and was less restrained in his description.

> We passed between walls of dead animals. Some of the beasts still
> alive and being devoured by vultures. I do not think I ever saw such
> a ghastly sight. Elephants, camels, donkeys, and even dead men
> were lying there. And every form of carrion-eating bird, from the
> stately lammergeier to the hill crow, seemed to have collected
> round. The whole scene might have been taken from some picture
> of Dante's inferno.[3]

Kandahar, with its flat-roofed houses, narrow alleys and imposing
domed mosque, was girdled by massive grey walls. All British officers
and men visiting the town itself went about armed with hog spears,
sticks and revolvers. After Roberts' decisive victory over the Afghans,
individual *ghazis* – religious zealots – started murdering British
soldiers in the belief that they would go straight to paradise if caught
and hanged. Although Baden-Powell joked about the hangings merely
offering an incentive, Noble was probably right in guessing that even
the Afghans lost their desire for resistance when they saw how ruthless

the British were prepared to be.[4] At any rate, the murders became less frequent.

The 13th Hussars had quarters at a place called Korkoran, seven miles outside Kandahar. Senior officers occupied the house and gardens of an Afghan prince while the majority, Stephe included, found themselves in tents. The temperature was mild in the day if the sun shone, and always bitterly cold at night, but Baden-Powell found this preferable to summer in the Plains. 'I am now sitting outside my tent in a warm sun,' he told his family on Christmas Eve. 'Some fox terriers of the regiment are playing and a nigger is getting a dozen with the cat of ninetails on the other side of me . . .'[5] For somebody who had been educated at a school where beatings had been frequent and at times savage, and who was an officer in an army that had not long abandoned flogging men almost to death, the sight of Indians or Afghans receiving 'a dozen' would not have caused much concern. Nor were public hangings in England abolished till Stephe was 10 years old. Yet these facts granted, there is a chilling detachment about Baden-Powell's description of executions in Afghanistan which does not for example strike one on reading George Noble's account of the same events. On his very first day at Kandahar, Stephe had noticed 'a rough gallows outside the main gate where they string up Afghans every few days'.

'Rough' was the right word, as he would see a few days later, when the scaffold collapsed during a double execution, leaving the two wretched men to wait while the structure was rebuilt. Noble found another botched execution 'a ghastly sight' which haunted him years later. This time the drops had fallen away slowly, leaving the men to face death by slow strangulation, a fate made worse by the failure to pinion their arms properly. Hence one of the men was able to raise himself up by holding on to the rope, thus doubling the length of his agony.[6] Many other bungled hangings were recorded by Stephe.

When the three criminals were placed ready with the nooses around their necks the Commissioner directed that the drops should be pulled simultaneously when he gave the signal by cracking his hunting crop. Two of the executioners watched him, the other only listened for the crack. The Commissioner slung the lash round his head but failed to make the required noise, consequently two malefactors were at once dangling in the air, while the third, with the listening executioner, still waited.[7]

Against this background of hangings, floggings and murders, Baden-Powell and the men of the 13th Hussars mounted a production of *The Pirates of Penzance*, sticking their swords in the ground to mark the limits of their stage, and keeping loaded revolvers close to hand.[8] An unpleasant feature of life at Korkoran was the speed with which the regiment's Indian servants disappeared, never again to be seen alive. Stephe recalled the exasperation felt when the head cook to the mess vanished. 'We suspected a village near here of murdering him, for he went to buy eggs, so we sent a squadron out there with the political officer and they searched the place, but of course found no signs of the old boy; if they had they would have killed the villagers and burned the place.'[9] He wrote this account at the time, but when mentioning the incident in his autobiographical *Indian Memories*, published in 1915, suggested that 'they would have hanged some of the villagers'.[10] All or 'some', this action would still have meant killing innocent people. But his attitude to the Afghans remained ambiguous. In spite of the bloodshed, he still felt that 'there was a certain amount of good feeling' between these 'awful looking sportsmen' and the British Army. 'They looked on a good fight almost as we would regard a good football match.'[11] Since Baden-Powell would one day take part in a pageant based upon Sir Henry Newbolt's *Vitaï Lampada*, he did not think this analogy between sport and warfare fanciful.

> The sand of the desert is sodden red,
> Red with the wreck of a square that broke;
> The gatling's jammed and the colonel dead,
> And the regiment blind with dust and smoke.
> The river of death has brimmed its banks
> And England's far and honour a name,
> But the voice of a schoolboy rallies the ranks:
> 'Play up! play up! and play the game!'

It would, however, be a mistake to suppose that such sentiments sprang from lack of first-hand knowledge of the consequences of war. While at Kandahar, he was sent to the field of Maiwand with a squadron ordered to investigate the causes of the disaster. Stephe's job was to draw maps for use at the courts martial of officers.

He found that the sand was worse than 'sodden red'. Over a thousand Britons had died and not a few Afghans, and many had been dug up by dogs and jackals. The ground was littered with decaying half-eaten corpses of men and horses. Although Baden-Powell was unable to eat meat for a week, he found the battlefield, for all its stench and horror, a fascinating place. There had been no rain and very little wind since the battle, and the footsteps and wheel-tracks were still clear in every direction. Piles of empty cartridge cases showed where the fighting had been heaviest, and the movement of guns was equally easy to deduce. The force had been too small, and had made matters worse by poor reconnaissance and bad shooting. Following the marks on the ground, recording their position accurately and deducing what had happened, were activities which Stephe thoroughly enjoyed. They marked the start of his lifelong interest in tracking. The Berkshire

Regiment had defended the rear of the retreating guns and had made their last stand by a mud wall. 'They were all killed there,' wrote Stephe, 'and the shortest way of burying them was to throw down the wall on top of them.'

Maiwand would have discouraged many men from ever wishing to visit another battlefield, but for Stephe it had the opposite effect. He would travel a long way, and on occasions make special trips abroad to examine particularly interesting fields. The expedition had also been professionally useful, making him known to General H. C. Wilkinson, commanding the Cavalry at Kandahar, and Colonel O. B. C. St John, the Chief Political Officer. Best of all, a set of Baden-Powell's maps was sent by his new colonel to Sir Garnet Wolseley, now Adjutant-General to the Forces.[12].

Thoughts of blood and death preoccupied Stephe after his return to Korkoran and are at the centre of a piece he sent home for publication in the Carthusian magazine *The Greyfriar*. Called 'The Afghanistan Helmet', it reads like straightforward autobiography without any indication that it was in fact fiction. Writing in the first person, Baden-Powell described a small action against hill tribesmen, in which the youngest subaltern in the regiment was shot through the head while crouching next to the narrator. This young man, with the appropriately sanguinary soubriquet of 'Jam', lay twitching and bleeding to the horror of all around, 'but my acting propensity at once stood by me, and in spite of my own feelings, I was able in my everyday voice to give orders'. This 'story' prefigures another in which an officer shoots his wounded comrade to save him from mutilation at the hands of the Matabele.[13]

In Afghanistan the only human target Stephe hit with a bullet was himself. He blamed his Indian servant for leaving his revolver loaded after borrowing it, so that when he rushed out into the night after a horse thief it went off, sending a bullet down through his calf into his heel. In describing the incident, George Noble said nothing about horse thieves or careless servants; merely that 'Baden-Powell managed in playing with a revolver to shoot himself in the leg.'[14] The accident happened just before the regiment was ordered to leave Kandahar for Quetta, and, although he travelled on a covered litter, he still suffered agonies on the journey over a range of precipitous hills.

Quetta was small and nondescript, consisting of a few bungalows, a barracks, a small native bazaar and a couple of streets of mud huts. Stephe was invited to stay in a tent pitched on the lawn of Colonel St John's bungalow. He was served 'the best of light food' and whiled away his time executing delicate drawings to enclose in letters to some of the aristocrats he had met in England. Eventually the day came when the surgeon arrived to cut out the bullet. 'I felt inclined to say, like I do at the dentist, "Well now, the pain has gone . . ."' The operation, which he endured without anaesthetic, was agonizing. Afterwards, enhancing his reputation as a wit, he would hold up the bullet lovingly for the inspection of visitors, just as if he had given birth. 'Is it not quite too distinctly precious?' he would stammer.[15]

Quetta turned out to be a death-trap. Two officers and half-a-dozen men died of enteric fever, with many more (George Noble included) lucky to survive. 'It was depressing to lie in hospital,' wrote Noble, 'and see one man after another carried away. So numerous were the funerals that it was forbidden to play the "Dead March" as it had such a depressing effect on the other patients.'[16] Baden-Powell's obsessive belief in the beneficial effects of fresh air began in Quetta. 'Constant fresh air in my tent has kept me well, while other fellows living in awful little brick hovels . . . get seedy.'[17] Two months after his arrival in Quetta, he was well enough to appear on mounted parade.

In August and September Stephe organized no fewer than four plays, two of which were to be of great importance to him. The cast consisted almost entirely of N.C.O.s and men, with the exception of one officer who took the female leads in *The Area Belle* and *Rosebud of Stinging Nettle Farm*. As a subaltern noted, 'One of our fellows made a very pretty girl.'[18] Stephe had known this 'young cornet', who he too thought 'made a wonderfully good lady', since the beginning of the year. Shortly before he had left Lucknow, a new doctor had arrived 'accompanied by a lad of apparently about fourteen'. The doctor was coming on to Kandahar, so Stephe asked, '"What will you do with your son?" "My son? This is not my son. This is an officer who has come to join the 13th . . ."' In reality Kenneth McLaren was 20, and after leaving Harrow had passed through Sandhurst. On account of his appearance, Stephe would call McLaren 'Boy', or 'the Boy'.[19]

In *The Area Belle*, a farce by William Brough, Baden-Powell played 'Tosser', a Guardsman infatuated with Penelope (the Area Belle) played by McLaren. When Penelope entered she was singing, 'I'd choose to be a daisy if I might be a flower,' which must have caused plenty of merriment. 'Everybody says I *am* a flower. Pitcher says I'm like a rose. Tosser calls me his tulip. Chalk says my breath is like buttercups . . . Oh, it's very nice to be universally adored.' 'Where can Penelope be?' blurts out a distraught Tosser on another occasion. 'I am longing to embrace her.' In H. J. Byron's melodrama, *Rosebud of Stinging Nettle Farm*, Stephe played the father of Rose, 'an accomplished, beautiful only child', played by McLaren.

The deaths continued and Quetta became no less vile, but after these two plays Stephe's letters grew increasingly lighthearted. 'Ah! here we are again – the "Dead March" has just struck up outside my window – that's the fifth day running a funeral has come past at this time of evening . . . This would be a splendid place for an undertaker.'[20] He went straight on to describe the first of his many picnics with McLaren;

this one at a spot in the hills outside Quetta which they called 'Rosherville', after London's famous pleasure gardens. Their routine would usually be the same: after shooting pigeons or black buck, they would spread out rugs under the trees and have 'a quiet sleep and read'.[21]

By late September, when Stephe was delighting the regiment with his triumph as the contralto Ruth in *The Pirates of Penzance*, he was living in the hut next to McLaren's and was instructing his brothers to 'drop in at the Kyles of Bute at a place called Taniburroch [Tighnabruaich]. Here you will find MacLaren's [sic] people who are a very jolly family I believe. MacLaren's brother is Capt. in the Royal Dragoons.'[22] Sometimes Stephe would return to his hut to find McLaren, 'the little imp', fast asleep on his bed with his dog 'Beetle', who had helped him to consume a large tin of Baden-Powell's biscuits.[23] At the beginning of October, something happened that brought the two men much closer.

> That poor little chap McLaren . . . last night when I went to bed I was awfully thirsty and there was no water in my bottle, so I sent my man to ask him for some. He presently sent me back a glassful – but I held it up to the light and saw 2 inches of castor oil floating on top. Of course at that I had to turn out of bed and go to give the boy a good walloping. This morning I went into his room and found him on his bed crying, with a telegram, which he handed to me, saying his mother had died yesterday. Poor little chap! I've been trying to comfort him as well as I can – but I break down more than he does almost – he's so awfully cut up.[24]

After the murders at Kandahar, the corpses at Maiwand and the funerals at Quetta, no human suffering seemed poignant enough to touch Stephe or release the emotions he had striven so hard to master from his childhood onwards. But when that worst fate in the world, the loss of a young man's mother, had actually happened to his dearest friend, Stephe was overwhelmed. Loss and hardship seemed best coped with by those with the thickest shells, and few carapaces seemed harder than Stephe's. Yet the tenderness he lavished on children like the Christie girls showed the underlying tension – the need to express the loving side of his nature. The relief of finding a real friend, with whom he could discuss whatever he wanted without reserve, was immense. In fact what made the difference between the unhappiness of his first two years in India and his euphoric second tour was his friendship with Kenneth McLaren.

At the end of October the regiment moved to Muttra which, like Lucknow, was in the Plains. Yet not once in his three years there did his occasional bouts of fever and diarrhoea lead him to ask for leave in the Hills. Many years later he wrote that if anyone wanted to contact him in paradise they should ring 'Koila Jheel Number One. Muttra Exchange, India Trunk Line'.[25] The telephone was only one of the novelties and delights of his life in Muttra. On arrival Stephe took a bungalow with McLaren, and his every letter home included some snippet about his new friend: how he took tins of Stephe's shrimp paste; how he flicked ink at the pages of Stephe's letters when he wanted him to ride with him; how 'the boy's laugh was like a railway whistle'; and how it amused him to cram 'poor Bloater [Baden-Powell's new puppy] right down one of my top boots'.

Occasional remarks show his growing awareness of his family's irritation with endless paragraphs about a young man they had never met. Henrietta Grace's displeasure became patent when her son informed her that he meant to spend his next leave in Australia with McLaren, rather than in England with her. Stephe would finally be forced to abandon his plan when he was made Adjutant of the regiment. He responded to his mother's pique with his usual jocularity: 'The Boy is very fit – (Oh you don't know him – I forgot) – he gave me some beautiful English silk handkerchiefs.' Asked by his mother whether the Boy's 'railway whistle laugh is a nuisance', he replied, 'Bloater's sharp teeth are worse.' Since none of McLaren's brothers were invited to dine at 8 St George's Place, Stephe rebuked his mother, who then sent him no letter for five weeks. But if his new friendship caused a brief cooling of his relations with his family, it enabled him to be more objective about his mother's power over her children.[26]

> You just leave your children alone now, Ma – they can get on all right – only you never will trust them to fly by themselves – you tie a string to each of them, and directly he flutters out of the nest he doesn't try to fly 'cos he knows he's supported by the string – someday when you do take the string off he'll have got so used to it that when he does try to flutter off the nest he'll fall to the ground. Cut the string now, ma, and kick them out to fly alone and find worms for themselves.[27]

Stephe rather spoiled the effect of this letter by ending with a request to his mother to pay his Naval and Military Club subscription of £36.

Baden-Powell's new-found happiness even enabled him to look favourably upon an Indian town. 'I and the Boy rode all through Muttra this afternoon,' he told his sister, 'it is the best native city I have seen – all built of real stone – paved and very clean (for India) – and crammed with temples and praying places – and very picturesque especially where it overhangs the Jumna.'[28] Officers in the 13th sometimes received invitations from neighbouring princes and maharajahs to stay with them and then go pig-sticking. At the Maharajah of Deeg's palace, Stephe and McLaren shared the same magnificent room. 'As we had one large marble hall as our joint room, the Boy read a novel to me as we lay in bed till breakfast time.'[29]

The two friends adored pigsticking.

> I see now the sunny yellow grass jungle, [wrote a nostalgic Stephe near the end of the century] and the brown, strong-shadowed coolies beating through it with their discordant jangle of cries and drums . . . their shouts drawing slowly nearer and nearer, and our horses' hearts beating quick and tremulous between our knees. Suddenly both horses fling round their heads, they are trembling in every limb with excitement. There he stands – not thirty yards from us – a grand grey boar with yellow curling tushes, and his cunning savage little eye glistening in the broad morning sunlight . . . He swings round, trots for a few paces, and then breaks into a rough tumbling canter across the yellow grass . . . Our horses are mad keen for the fray, and as one tears through the fresh cool air all bodily weight seems to leave one's extremities and to be concentrated into a great heartful of emotion.[30]

The boar's tushes were razor-sharp and could disembowel horses and inflict serious wounds on men, although most injuries were caused by falls. By general consensus at the time, pigsticking was the most dangerous and exciting blood sport. Years later Baden-Powell tried unconvincingly to justify his pleasure by claiming that the pigs had endangered native lives and crops. At other times he was wise enough to admit that the wild exhilaration he had felt had far outweighed the sport's undoubted cruelty.

Often it would take many spear wounds to kill a boar and before that he would retreat into thick jungle. If the beaters then failed to drive him out, Stephe and McLaren dismounted with their spears and plunged in. 'Then we had awful fun – one of us would go near the pig and when the beast came at him, he would receive him on his spear, and the other fellow would dash in and give the pig a fair broadside wound: after two or three repetitions of this manoeuvre we got him down and killed him.' Occasionally the two of them would kill as many as four boars in a single day. Stephe would often fight on foot, stripped to the waist, wearing his shirt as a turban.[31]

During 1882 Baden-Powell wrote a short story called 'The Ordeal of the Spear', in which two officers who were 'an unusually good pair of friends', decided that they would like to marry the same girl. To solve the problem of which one of them should be allowed to propose to her, they agreed to give that honour to whomsoever could first inflict a wound upon the pig. 'Calvert smiled curiously at this new idea of the boy's, while his eyes sparkled at the sporting smack of it.' So they go after a pig, and 'the boy' draws first blood with his spear. However, he never has a chance to propose. The last two paragraphs of the story

see the girl tossed from the back of an elephant and trampled underfoot, leaving the two young men to return to the mess together no less
'an unusually good pair of friends' than they were at the start of the
story.[32] As far as Stephe was concerned, there was not the slightest
danger of any woman upsetting his relations with McLaren. Although
he occasionally received unsolicited letters from women who had seen
him act, and was even proposed to by one enthusiast, he greeted these
attentions with ironic amusement. One admirer was informed that she
could ride with him on an elephant (she could not have read his short
story) if she could 'get Mrs A to chaperone me; and I warned her that if
she attemped to make love to me I should immediately get off the
elephant and walk home with Mrs A.'[33] The fair proposer was treated
to 'a quiet talk and some advice, and I have made her smile on a chap
who likes her better than I do – so it's all right.'[34] When Baden-Powell
stayed briefly in the hill town of Naini Tal, he liked the place but could
not stand the women: 'Och such cards, I mean the ladies – of course
there are lots of good men – but those women, ain't I just becoming a
misogynist . . .'[35] In May McLaren went on leave to Kashmir. 'My
boy went away yesterday for 3 months, and I am all alone in Bloater
Park [McLaren's name for their bungalow]. It's beastly melancholy
here. I shall get used to it before he gets back I suppose – and as we
have got 19 horses and ponies between us I find lots to do . . .'[36] A few
days later Stephe wrote home asking his mother to purchase 'a nice
little present for the Boy – I think a pair of ivory brushes – good ones
with K. McL. on the backs would be rather nailing'.[37] He tried hard to
get his colonel's permission to join his friend in Kashmir, but failed.[38]

Both men were proud of their home, Bloater Park, and took pains to
fit it out becomingly with bearskins, buck's heads, arrays of crossed
hog spears and polo sticks, and gun racks on each side of the fireplace.
They hung the walls in the saddle room with blue cloth, and took
immense pains with the stables, painting them white inside with a
fawn-coloured dado defined by a red line, 'the first stables I have ever
seen painted in India'. They had a large compound, a flower garden
and plenty of beds for vegetables. They had four dogs, their favourite
being McLaren's Beetle, who came with them whenever they went
pigsticking. They jointly owned 'a very neat and light trap' and would
drive out in it whenever going to shoot. Of their numerous horses,
Stephe's mare, Hagarene, which cost him a thousand rupees, was the
most expensive. But while he and McLaren both owned a few valuable
horses, they also tried to buy cheaply from Indians and then train these
animals to sell them as polo ponies to newly arrived officers. 'My
ponies were at all times pets and companions . . . going out for walks
with me, running with me, stopping and turning as I did, and coming
to hand when whistled for.'[39] Their most unusual pet was a pig called
Algernon.

When Baden-Powell was chosen for the regiment's polo team to take part in a large inter-regimental tournament, he was genuinely surprised. He knew he was not in the same class as McLaren, who would lead the 13th Hussars to three victories in the final of the tournament for the entire army in Hurlingham. Known by the men as 'the little prince', McLaren became the best back in the army, worth two men to his side.[40]

Evenings in the mess, after the senior officers had returned to their quarters, were regularly interrupted by high-spirited ragging which often ended with subalterns racing their polo ponies over jumps of piled-up furniture. Another favourite was called 'Bounding Brothers of the Bosphorus', in which the players, after a ludicrously formal approach, suddenly turned a somersault on to a pile of upturned chairs – a painful business, demanding a good deal of nerve, even when drunk. Occasionally a plate of money was awarded to the first officer to return to the mess carrying a sheep.[41]

While he had been at Kandahar, Stephe had played an enterprising practical joke on his new commanding officer, Colonel Sir Baker Russell. Somehow he had persuaded the A.D.C. to the General for the District to lend him one of his master's uniforms. Decked out as a general, with a whitened moustache, Stephe stalked into the hall where a regimental concert was being held and, as he walked up the aisle from the back, called out 'in a genially considerate tone, "Sit down men, sit down." This of course made them all look round and stand up in salute.' Baker Russell greeted the supposed general, who astonished him by nimbly hopping up onto the stage and starting to sing the Major-General's song from *The Pirates of Penzance*.[42]

Stephe later attributed the favour his colonel was to show him to two incidents. In the first he successfully tracked down a sergeant-major's horse which had strayed many miles, after most of the regiment's horses had stampeded during a storm. In the second he pointed out a short cut on the march from Kandahar to Quetta that enabled Russell to make fools of several self-important staff officers. In fact, since 1877, the whole Baden-Powell family had been actively engaged in wooing Baker Russell.[43] When Russell was on leave in England, Stephe wrote to his mother gratefully: 'Sir Baker has written to me every mail of late and is full of your invitations, etc. I think they will bear good fruit.'[44]

In March 1882 Stephe was appointed Adjutant by Russell, who would have known how much the extra pay would mean to him, just as he would have known that many of his richer officers would not have considered the money adequate compensation for the quantity of administrative work involved. For Stephe the appointment would have many consequences which far outweighed the merely financial.

4. 'A Scout Must Be . . .' (1882–86)

As Adjutant, Stephe's entire day from morning until early evening was taken up with parades, drills, musketry instruction, office work and orderly room. At weekends he went pigsticking with McLaren as before. The two friends also organized regimental gymkhanas and continued to play for the first polo team. Baden-Powell was the busiest officer in the regiment.

Although most Adjutants concentrated on their regiments' discipline and efficiency on the parade ground, Stephe devoted most of his energies to the training and welfare of his men. Apart from a few senior officers in the army's hierarchy, most officers at regimental level intended, unless religiously motivated, to have as little to do with their men as possible. So when Stephe decided to deliver a series of twenty lectures to his men and, in addition, to instruct them in the field in subjects like map-work and tracking, he was doing something most unusual. His impulse for spending so much time with his men sprang as much from his enjoyment of their company as from any Christian Socialist desire to 'improve' them. By the early 1880s the liberalism he had imbibed from his mother had not been destroyed so much as overlaid with the reactionary attitudes common to most army officers. A full four years before his brother George became a Conservative M.P. in 1885, Stephe had been vociferously urging him to abandon the Liberal Party.[1] But as Stephe's earliest books would show, he had a surprising ability for juxtaposing reactionary and radical ideas.

Baden-Powell published an aide memoire for men on outpost duty in 1883, and in the following year his first significant work, *Reconnaissance and Scouting*. This had started life as the twenty lectures delivered to his men. 'Success in modern warfare depends on accurate knowledge of the enemy,' Stephe began his preface, continuing with a eulogy to the men who brought that knowledge. 'Scouts are the eyes and ears of the army and on their intelligence and smartness mainly depends the success of all operations . . . A scout must be a man of intelligence and pluck, and a good horseman, with confidence in himself, that is to say, one who will not lose his head in a sudden emergency, but can trust to himself to get out of all difficulties, and who is full of "dodges" to meet every kind of incident or accident that may occur.'[2] Baden-Powell insisted that men could be trained 'to notice what would escape an ordinary man's eye'[3], and hinted at educative possibilities in observation when he described how Houdini had 'taught his son to notice at one glance every article in a shop window, and to carry them in his mind'.[4] The originality of *Reconnaissance and Scouting* lay in its author's rejection of the slavishly obedient soldier in favour of a thinking individual, suitable for employment in small tactical groups.

Just as at school, where Baden-Powell's mimetic talents and inventiveness had run counter to his desire to be a conforming member of the community, so in the army his delight in the capabilities of individuals was at variance with his wish to be seen as an efficient and yet unexceptionable cavalry officer. His earliest books illustrate this same tension between originality and conformity, which would characterize his entire career until finding triumphant fusion in the Scout Movement.

Stephe stated in *Reconnaissance and Scouting* that 'no soldier on service has such a good chance of distinguishing himself as a scout'.[5] For a man fascinated by acting and the impression he was making on others, there was a strong romantic appeal in imagining himself a scout in enemy territory, surviving by stealth and deception. That most of his actual scouting exploits would involve him in little danger would not stop him writing them up as if they had done. This mingling of reality with make-believe in accounts of his early adventures would make them of lasting imaginative importance to him.

By 1883 Stephe had every reason to feel satisfied with life. He had found a field of activity which not only entertained his young soldiers and brought them closer to him, but also gave new scope to his creative gifts. That he should simultaneously have formed the first, and only, close male friendship of his life made Muttra the heaven on earth he thought it.

3

MEN'S MAN

1. 'My Best Friend in the World'

In recent years two authors have suggested that Baden-Powell may
have been a homosexual. Neither offered any evidence, and both based
their supposition entirely upon a shared suspicion that his relationship
with Kenneth McLaren might have been a physical one.[1] Yet by
confining their attention to one friendship, and by making physical
relations the acid test of a homosexual orientation, they missed a more
important point. Whether a man acts upon a homosexual inclination or
not (or even acknowledges his tendency), is not more significant than
the effect such a tendency will have upon his life if it is denied. Indeed, a
repressed instinct may well affect behaviour and thoughts more
dramatically than a proclivity actively pursued. Nevertheless, since the
suggestion of homosexuality has been made specifically in connection
with McLaren, I intend first to determine whether any evidence exists
that can substantiate that allegation; then I will take a broader, more
discursive view of Baden-Powell's other relationships, and his
thoughts about men and women.

In 1901, when Baden-Powell described McLaren as 'my best friend
in the world',[2] 'the Boy' had been exactly that for twenty years. From
the time when Baden-Powell had comforted McLaren after the death
of his mother, they had been devoted. Stephe had stopped wanting to
return to England; his complaints to his mother about India, and his
pleas to her to help him to transfer to another regiment had abruptly
ceased. He and McLaren always made sure that they were allocated a
shared bungalow whenever the regiment was ordered to a new station.
They exchanged presents frequently, and missed one another when
separated. Years later Baden-Powell would write in relation to
marriage that two men could be just as happy living together as any
man and woman.[3] Even the most ideally matched marriage partners
could never have held as many pleasures and mutual interests in
common as did Baden-Powell and McLaren, with their love of every
kind of sport and their numerous shared animals.

When the 13th Hussars at last returned to England in 1886, Baden-
Powell spent the first weeks of his leave in Scotland with 'the Boy',
rather than in London with his mother.[4] Whenever Stephe made a brief
excursion abroad – which he did in January 1887, to see the Franco-
Prussian battlefields – the only two people to whom he wrote regular

letters were his mother and McLaren.[5] 'The Boy' and Stephe treasured gifts they received from one another and when, soon after the regiment moved to Colchester in 1886, Stephe lost a gold pencil given to him by 'the Boy', he was sufficiently upset to consult the Chief Constable of the town and to have 'Notices of Reward' specially printed and distributed throughout Colchester.[6]

By 1888 it was clear that Stephe's family could not afford to keep him with the regiment while it remained in England; so he was obliged, much against his wishes, to go out to South Africa as A.D.C. to his uncle, Lieutenant-General Henry Smyth, who had been appointed military Commander-in-Chief at the Cape. The very first letter Baden-Powell wrote to his mother after sailing was one reminding her on no account to forget to post the picture which he had painted as a Christmas present for 'the Boy'. For the next five years the two friends wrote regularly to one another. Between 1893 and 1895 they were together again briefly, in Ireland, and although McLaren was now far too skilful at polo to play in the same team with his old friend, they acted together in the same plays. A photograph of McLaren playing a judge, and Baden-Powell a burglar, recalls one such performance [see first photo section]. On the same evening, Baden-Powell gave a particularly convincing exhibition of skirt-dancing in the persona of Miss Daisy Bell.[7]

Later that year (1895), McLaren was appointed A.D.C. to Sir Baker Russell, by then a major-general commanding the North West District of England with his headquarters at Chester. Six months later Sir Baker and 'the Boy' were at the dockside bearing gifts, to say adieu to Baden-Powell, who was sailing from Liverpool for a spell of active service in West Africa. The following year, when Russell was given the Bengal command and Baden-Powell the colonelcy of the 5th Dragoon Guards, also in India, the two friends were able to go on occasional expeditions together, whether sharing the same tent on a tiger shoot or buying antique curios.[8] But, for McLaren, their reunions were tinged with sadness. Their happy life at Muttra lay far in the past, and he was now nearly 40 years of age. Separated from all his companions in the 13th Hussars, and with no prospect of a regiment of his own, McLaren faced a bleak future. His periods of leave in Scotland were no better. 'Spent one happy day out of 60 days here,' he wrote in his sister's visitors' book in July 1897.[9]

In the autumn of 1898 Sir Baker and 'the Boy' returned to Britain, and within three months McLaren had married Leila Evelyn Landon, an army officer's daughter. Stephe could not get leave from India to be his friend's best man.[10] Nine months after his wedding McLaren received an invitation from Stephe to join one of the two regiments of irregulars which he was raising for active service in South Africa, in what promised to develop into an all-out war against the Boer republics. Although his wife was six months pregnant, McLaren agreed to go.

When 'the Boy' was a prisoner in Boer hands and lying gravely wounded outside Mafeking, Baden-Powell had to be restrained by his staff officers from rushing through the lines under a flag of truce. After his repeated pleas to Commandant Snyman, the local Boer Commander, to release McLaren had been rejected, Stephe sent personal telegrams to President Kruger urging him to overrule Snyman.[11] 'It is so horrible to sit here within sight of his hospital and yet not be able to see him and help to soothe him,' Stephe told his mother.[12]

During the six remaining weeks of the Siege, he wrote to McLaren almost every day. 'How I do wish I could be with you,' he wrote typically; varying the formula slightly in succeeding letters: 'I only wish I could be there to look after you.' He thought of his wounded friend all the time. 'Your two photos are the only ornaments on my table as I write,' he told 'the Boy'.[13] During the following weeks he sent across the lines, under flags of truce, cocoa, wine, a soft mattress, hairbrushes, books, mosquito curtains, eau de cologne, soup, lemonade, stamps, stationery and money. Baden-Powell knew that the Boers read these letters attentively, therefore it is not surprising that none is very intimate. Each begins 'My dear Boy,' and ends either 'Yours ever, James' (McLaren's nickname for him, which Baden-Powell would adopt as his secret code-name in Ashanti and Matabeleland) or 'Yours ever, R.S.S.B.P.'. In the past he had written to Commandant Snyman with peremptory condescension; now he thanked him effusively for the care and kindness which was being lavished upon Captain McLaren.[14]

After Mafeking was relieved, McLaren returned to Britain to convalesce. Baden-Powell remained in South Africa for a further year and a half before taking six months' leave. The first person with whom he stayed on arrival in Britain was McLaren, and when he left for the Cape his last letter to be posted before his ship sailed was an instruction to his mother not to forget 'to send to McLaren his Xmas present'.[15] *Plus ça change!*

McLaren's wife had given birth to a daughter in October 1899. Baden-Powell was naturally asked to be Eilean's godfather, and took his duties seriously enough to ask his mother to visit the child on his behalf while he was in South Africa.[16] Eilean was always 'Ulti' to him, since she had been born on the day of Kruger's ultimatum to Great Britain.

In March 1903 Stephe returned home permanently and, after a couple of days with his mother, went to stay with McLaren and his wife. He was with him again on 17 May, the first anniversary of the Relief of Mafeking to be celebrated by him in England.[17]

From 1901, when he was Inspector General of the South African

Constabulary, Baden-Powell employed McLaren as his London-based recruiting officer. Stephe was often exasperated with his senior colleagues in the S.A.C. but never with 'the Boy' whose advice he sought constantly.[18] From his correspondence with McLaren at this time, he learnt that his wife was ill with disseminated sclerosis. Leila's death at the age of 29, in November 1904, was not therefore unexpected. Baden-Powell found his friend's grief very affecting and was moved to tears by his courage at the funeral. For several weeks afterwards, little Eilean stayed with Baden-Powell and his mother, and 'has quite adopted us as relations'.[19] It was Stephe's hope that Kenneth would come and stay with him until adjusting to his new situation, or longer; he was therefore dismayed to discover that 'the Boy' had found another comforter in the shape of his wife's former nurse, Ethel Mary Wilson, whom he intended to keep on as 'Ulti's' governess. Baden-Powell and Henrietta Grace, who had enjoyed having Eilean McLaren in the house, were both worried that 'the nurse' would use Kenneth's grief to wheedle her way into his heart, and perhaps lure him into a second marriage.[20]

Baden-Powell's hostility to Ethel Wilson may have had as much to do with snobbery as jealousy. She was a younger daughter of a struggling south Yorkshire farmer and, having no money, was not a 'lady' in his understanding of the word. Nevertheless Stephe managed to contain his indignation when McLaren retained the woman's services. They saw one another less often but their friendship remained intact; so much so that in 1907, Stephe asked 'the Boy' to help him organize the first Scout Camp on Brownsea Island. Then in December, he persuaded his friend to become the first manager of the Boy Scouts. However, this arrangement did not last long as McLaren resigned in mid-March of 1908.[21] The explanation given in both official histories of the Scouts is ill-health, but since at this date McLaren was fit enough to be assistant manager of polo at Hurlingham and to be the umpire at many international polo matches, this must be wrong. He resigned his job at Hurlingham at the end of March 1909 after a disagreement over his salary, no mention being made of illness.[21] In his letter of resignation from the managership of the Scouts, McLaren said that he had been unable to get on with Peter Keary, the managing director of Pearson's, the Scouts' publisher and principal backer.[22] Since Baden-Powell also disliked Keary, these difficulties would probably have been overcome had not McLaren recently announced his intention of marrying.

On 28 September 1910, Major Kenneth McLaren married Miss Ethel Mary Wilson at the parish church of Garton-in-the-Wolds in Yorkshire. The ceremony was attended only by relatives and local people and the best man was Kenneth's youngest nephew. Stephe was then crossing the Atlantic at the end of a Scouting tour of North

America, but he had not intended to come. He did not see McLaren
again that year, and saw him only once in the year that followed. Then
in 1912, he himself married, asking his brother Baden to be his best
man. McLaren was not invited even as a guest. Since Stephe's bride
would turn out to be jealous of his former friendships, and particularly
of his friendship with 'the Boy', the two men did not meet again.

When war broke out in 1914 Major McLaren, by now 54, offered his
services and was sent to France with the Casualty Records Department. A year later the first symptoms of what was described, on his
death certificate nine years later, as 'softening of the brain' became
apparent. In addition he suffered from what Baden-Powell called
'melancholia', but which would be classified today as clinical
depression. 'The Boy' spent the last half dozen years of his life either
confined in Camberwell House Asylum, or in a smaller private mental
hospital in Hertfordshire.[23] Stephe did not attend his friend's funeral in
1924, but he invited Eilean to stay with him for a few days a month
later, and thereafter sent her birthday greetings each year on Kruger's
Ultimatum Day.

At its height Stephe's friendship with McLaren made a considerable
impression upon other people. A. H. Brink, Commandant Snyman's
secretary at Mafeking, welcomed Baden-Powell to Pretoria 26 years
later, as mayor of that city, clutching like holy relics three letters in
which McLaren thanked him for his kindness in 1900.[24] He had not the
slightest doubt but that Baden-Powell would be entranced to see them.
In the same month Stephe sought out in the Cape a Major Miller, who
had been in McLaren's squadron in the Boer War, and visited him on
two consecutive days in order to talk about his dead friend.[25] Another
person who recalled their friendship was Major-General Sir John
Moore, who had been veterinary surgeon to Baden-Powell's two
regiments in 1899. After attending the 1933 Mafeking Reunion
Dinner, he posted to Baden-Powell a photograph of McLaren with his
favourite charger taken shortly before he was wounded.[26]

Two years after the Relief of Mafeking, Baden-Powell had written
to McLaren mentioning that he had passed through Pinetown in Natal,
where they had been stationed in 1886, but had not had time either to
visit their old house or the grave of Beetle, McLaren's beloved
terrier.[27] On visits to South Africa in 1926 and 1936, Baden-Powell
made up for this and photographed both house and grave on each
occasion.[28]

When Stephe was in Muttra with 'the Boy' in the 1880s, he wrote a
short story for *The Greyfriar* called 'The Polo Cap'.[29] It was about an
officer who died as a result of falling on his head during a polo match.
On the way to the maidan before the game, he had told the first person
narrator that he had seen so many men die unexpectedly that he kept all
his personal letters in an envelope on which he had written: 'PRIVATE

– In the event of my death, please burn this bag with its contents, without further examination.'

Baden-Powell himself certainly shared an enthusiasm for burning papers. 'The whole idea of journalistic battening on one's intimate relationships is repugnant to me,' he wrote in 1933.[30] Five years later, shortly before sailing for Kenya where he would live out his final years, Stephe spent the best part of three days burning 'old papers etc. So much waste paper goes into our furnace for heating the wing that there is always hot water there.'[31] That so many 'old papers' were finally saved was due to salvage work by Baden-Powell's secretary, Eileen Wade. She sent her husband, Major Wade, to cart away 'wheelbarrow loads of stuff'. 'I saved everything,' he claimed later with excusable hyperbole.[32] What the Wades saved did not, however, include many personal letters, wonderful though it was that they should have preserved so many revealing first drafts of articles and other writings. The rest of the Baden-Powell papers, which Stephe preserved, included his scrapbooks, his personal and his staff diaries, over two thousand letters to his mother, journals of individual campaigns and trips, and accounts of Scouting tours and inspections. All these, with several hundred other letters, were deposited at the Army and Navy Stores, where they would remain until Lady Baden-Powell returned to England as a widow during the Second World War.

In 1944 she undertook a major 'resorting' of her late husband's papers, almost certainly destroying any letters which she found distasteful. She also sent to some favoured individuals letters, either originally written by Baden-Powell to them or written by others to him, but which she nevertheless thought would be of interest to them personally.[33] Because she revered her husband's writings, she would only have destroyed material which she found personally threatening. The daughter of Mrs James G. Dugdale (who as Miss Ellen M. Turner was the only woman in whom Baden-Powell had shown any interest during the 1890s) told me that she visited Pax Hill during the 1930s and was inadvertently shown a number of photographs of her mother, which had been defaced by Lady Baden-Powell.[34] Since Stephe wrote frequently to Miss Turner (and these letters have survived) *she* must have written back to *him*, but as might be expected none of her replies exists. According to the present (and third) Lord Baden-Powell, his grandmother Olave 'was very possessive' and was 'very jealous of that particular friendship [the one with McLaren].'[35] Since McLaren had been very much closer to Baden-Powell than Miss Turner ever was, 'the Boy's' letters would have had an even slimmer chance of surviving Lady Baden-Powell's 're-sorting'.

It is therefore hardly surprising that apart from a brief message congratulating Stephe on winning the Kadir Cup for pigsticking, a letter of resignation from the managership of the Scouts, and three

notes written when the sender had recently been wounded, no other
letters out of the hundreds sent by McLaren to Baden-Powell over the
years have survived. Of course every correspondence is two-sided. If
'the Boy' had preserved some of the hundreds of letters written to him
by Baden-Powell, they would have passed on his death either to his
25-year-old daughter, Eilean, or to his second wife, Ethel. These two
were the only beneficiaries of his will. Although 'the Boy' died in
Camberwell House Asylum in south London, his house in Scotland
was kept on by his wife and daughter for several years after his death.
When it was finally sold Ethel retained a smaller house in the same
village, so McLaren's death did not bring about the kind of upheaval
which often leads to the wholesale destruction of papers. A likelier
possibility is that after Kenneth's insanity had become serious enough
to make his confinement necessary, Ethel went through his papers,
destroying whatever she thought unimportant or unpleasant. In this
latter category would have been letters written by people she had
reason to believe despised or disliked her. Stephe had given her ample
reason to suppose that he disapproved of her by never inviting *her*
when he asked Eilean to stay. He used to call her Mrs 'Royal' McLaren
when mentioning her in his diary – although her hauteur in his
presence must have been caused by insecurity rather than arrogance.[36]

Ethel died in 1967, having spent the last years of her life in Horsham
in a home for elderly vegetarians of a religious disposition. It is hard to
imagine her in such a place leafing through letters describing pigsticking and tiger shoots in the great days of the Raj. When she died,
everything she possessed passed to one of her many nieces, Miss Enid
Blackith, a Canterbury schoolmistress. Miss Blackith died soon
afterwards, leaving her flat and its contents to her sister Marjorie, who
survived her by only a year. Marjorie had been married to Mr Alfred
Longmate of Chesterfield, who is now the owner of a black tin chest
with 'Captain K. McLaren' painted on the front. The chest contains
neither letters, nor anything else once owned by 'the Boy'.[37]

McLaren's daughter Eilean, little 'Ulti', left Scotland in the late
1920s and returned to the Northamptonshire village of Creaton,
where her mother had been born and brought-up. She lived partly
there and partly in the New Forest at East Boldre near the port of
Lymington on the Solent. Her childhood had not been happy. 'The
Boy' treated her harshly after her mother's death, subjecting her to
beatings and long periods in solitary confinement, punishments which
would have been severe if meted out to a cavalry trooper. A succession
of English boarding schools was followed by a Swiss finishing
school.[38] In the mid-1930s she met Walter Woodford, a Lymington
pleasure-boat skipper, whom she secretly married in 1942, coyly
describing him as a 'marine artist' on her marriage certificate.[39] This
union did not thrive, although the couple had a son. By the early 1950s

Eilean Woodford was back in Creaton separated from her boatman husband, who had gone to live on the Norfolk coast where he was plying his trade once more. The last years of Eilean's life were wretched and she began to drink heavily; she died of cancer in 1957. Her only son, Christopher, found no letters, no photographs – in fact nothing at all connected with his grandfather.[40]

A couple of years earlier Christopher's aunt, Mabel Landon – the only surviving member of McLaren's first wife's family – had died in Creaton House, where McLaren had often stayed and where Baden-Powell had visited him on a number of occasions. Eilean had lived for several years in her aunt's house after leaving Scotland, and the place was stuffed with family papers. All these were burned by Mabel Landon's executors. Two photograph albums survived the fire, but one has disappeared. The sole survivor is still at Creaton House and contains photographs of McLaren and his first wife on their wedding day, press reports of the ceremony and various sporting photographs.[41]

Thinking it just possible that McLaren's second wife, Ethel, might have had a confidante among her brothers and sisters, I endeavoured to trace their descendants. All her brothers and one of her sisters had emigrated to Canada, while another sister had settled in New Zealand. But with the help of three of Ethel's nieces – Mrs Victoria M. Payne, Mrs Elizabeth Rogers and Mrs Florence Thomson – I managed to contact every branch of this scattered family. Nobody owned any letters, but the photograph of Eilean, Kenneth and Ethel, taken on the day of McLaren's second marriage [see first photo section] was the best of about half a dozen pictures brought to light. Efforts to trace letters written by Kenneth to his four brothers and two sisters proved even less successful. Nevertheless, more photographs [see first photo section] were found; most of them the property of Mrs Jennifer May, Kenneth McLaren's great-niece, without whose help I would have been unable to trace enough descendants of 'the Boy's' immediate family to feel sure that no letters sent by him to his brothers and sisters had survived.

In 1965 a tea chest of assorted books and bric-à-brac was bought at a Glasgow auction. At the bottom was a battered Edwardian soap-box containing old papers; the disappointed purchaser threw these away, but later had second thoughts and retrieved them. Finding references to Baden-Powell, he gave the papers to a Scoutmaster friend. They turned out to be the daily letters which Baden-Powell had written to 'the Boy' when he was wounded and a prisoner. The box had once been the property of Mr B. W. Cowan, who had died shortly after the Second World War and at Mafeking had commanded the Bechuanaland Rifles. When the relieving forces finally drove away the besieging Boers, the hospital tent in the Boers' principal laager was inadvertently shelled.[42] In the the ensuing chaos, Baden-Powell's letters were found

by Cowan in the debris and appropriated by him.[43] The only other
record of letters written by Baden-Powell to McLaren is in the form of
a letter-book, containing eight carbon-duplicates written during the
last quarter of 1902. All are semi-official communications on the
subject of recruitment to the South African Constabulary, with a few
personal messages appended.[44]

My final attempt to locate papers shedding additional light on
Baden-Powell's only close friendship involved me in tracing the
descendants of some of his and 'the Boy's' regimental friends. When
Baden-Powell was unable to return from India to be best man at
McLaren's first wedding, Walter Charles Smithson, another officer in
the 13th Hussars, stood in for him. Unfortunately Smithson married
late in life and had no children. A great-niece whom I traced had several
photographs, but no letters.[45] Although I contacted the descendants of
a dozen other officers in the 13th Hussars, none was able to help me.[46]

Of course, it is possible that another soap-box miracle will occur and
other letters come to light, but, given Stephe's and Olave's sorting
sessions, 'the Boy's' first wife's early death, his second wife's dislike of
Baden-Powell and his only daughter's alcoholism, the odds seem
heavily stacked against new finds being made.

A sad footnote to the friendship came in 1933 when Baden-Powell,
in his autobiography, described 'Ginger' Gordon of the 15th Hussars
as 'my best friend'.[47] The officer in question was Major James
Redmond Patrick Gordon, who served under Baden-Powell as
second-in-command of the Native Levy in Ashanti in 1895. Given
Baden-Powell's spartan personal habits and way of life, it would have
been curious if Gordon had really been his best friend. 'Ginger' was
married, but nevertheless enjoyed gambling, womanizing and spending a great deal more money than he could afford on clothes, carriages
and horses.[48] Between 1896 and 1903, Baden-Powell could not have
seen Gordon at all because the places in which they were stationed were
far apart. They saw each other from time to time between 1903 and
1907, in which year Gordon took up an appointment with the
Egyptian Army, which he held until shortly before his death in 1910.
By claiming close friendship with an officer he had seen so rarely, and
in the same book only devoting one neutral sentence to the man who
had once mattered to him more than any other human being, Baden-
Powell seems to have been trying to direct the eyes of posterity away
from his great friendship, which he once said had 'made the sun shine
once more for me'.[49]

The facts I have assembled point to a close and long-standing
friendship, which ended after 30 years with a second marriage which
Baden-Powell could not accept. There is no evidence to justify the
claim that the friendship between Baden-Powell and McLaren was
physical.

Strong emotional relationships were thought perfectly normal and acceptable between men during the nineteenth century, and there are many examples of writers celebrating one man's love for another without fear of being thought improper. Tennyson's *In Memoriam*, published in 1850, contains passionate invocations which aroused no adverse comment at the time. In the 1880s Lord Selborne,[50] who became Lord Chancellor in 1872, could write of his friendship with Frederick Faber, the virtuous founder of Brompton Oratory, in a way which ten years later (after the Labouchere Amendment to the Criminal Law Amendment Act, the Cleveland Street homosexual brothel scandal and the trials of Oscar Wilde), would have been looked upon with acute suspicion. 'Our affection,' declared the Lord Chancellor, 'became not only strong but passionate. There is a place for passion, even in friendship; it was so among the Greeks; and the love of Jonathan for David was "wonderful, passing the love of women".'[51]

The Victorian concept of manly love has its roots in a tradition stretching back to ancient Greece, and to the chivalric love between medieval knights. Its revival in nineteenth-century England met the needs of a society in which most 'gentlemen' married late for economic reasons, and in which many clergymen, schoolmasters, dons and army officers remained bachelors all their lives. Inevitably their friendships with other men became emotionally vital to them. Close and 'pure' friendships were encouraged as deliberate policy in the public schools until the mid-1880s as an antidote to homosexual 'beastliness'; and among mature men the idea was commonplace that because such 'comradeships' were free from the 'grossly carnal' reproductive acts associated with the love of women, they were superior. The inadequacies of female education, and the way in which women were excluded from virtually all the leisure activities enjoyed by men, also played an important part in their demotion. Yet in spite of the undoubted existence of very large numbers of emotionally intense but physically chaste male friendships, such as that between Baden-Powell and 'the Boy' almost undoubtedly was, we are perfectly entitled to question today whether the attempt to deny the undoubted link between love and sexual desire could have succeeded as well as it did without repression, sublimation, and in many instances massive doses of self-deception.[52]

2. 'The Finest Creature'

'A clean young man in his prime of health and strength is the finest creature God has made in the world.'[1]

Robert Baden-Powell, 1922

At the start of the previous chapter I contended that a repressed homosexual tendency can affect a man's thoughts and behaviour just as powerfully as a proclivity actively pursued. It is wrong to suppose that because a man remains sexually chaste, he cannot therefore be a homosexual. A repressed instinct, far from disappearing because it is denied, will manifest itself, consciously or unconsciously, in many other areas of a man's life.

Recently it has become fashionable to rebuke biographers for a post-Freudian disinclination to lay sufficient emphasis upon the influence exerted by vanished social conditions when attributing particular sexual orientations to their subjects.[2] Plainly a balance must be struck which enables the historian to acknowledge the complexities and ambiguities of bygone cultural behaviour (and romantic male friendships offer excellent examples), and yet does not require him to jettison the insights which psychologists, psychoanalysts and students of sexual behaviour have made possible during this century. Not the least of these insights has been the discovery that very few people are entirely homosexual or heterosexual, but incline towards one or other with varying degrees of intensity. It is also common knowledge now that members of one sex, denied the company of the other – either in single-sex schools, prisons, warships, or regiments posted overseas – are more likely to form homosexual relationships than men or women in ordinary civil society.[3]

After his all-male education at Charterhouse, Baden-Powell went straight to India, where the men and N.C.O.s in British regiments were expected to patronize 'native' brothels, but the officers were expected to remain chaste. In the subcontinent there were very few unmarried white women of their own class and, as in England, pre-marital sexual relations would have been absolutely unthinkable. Late marriage was the norm for cavalry officers, so a period of ten or even twenty years of celibacy was considered normal. It would be hard to imagine a worse preparation for understanding women, or for em-barking upon married life. Indeed, until the early 1890s, there is abundant evidence to show that Baden-Powell had no intention of getting sufficiently close emotionally to any woman to make marriage even a remote possibility.

When he met the daughters of senior officers, or of civil servants in India, he made a habit of telling them at the outset that marriage was not on the agenda, and he was 'simply there as a friend'. 'That's what I do and matters being thus defined, the girl confides in you and you have much more fun. I chaperone my girls and they look upon me as a brother.'[4] With every hint of sex removed from a relationship he could get on reasonably well with women. In spite of his obsession with 'manly' sports, he also enjoyed many feminine pastimes such as choosing fabrics and furnishings, and designing embroidery patterns for regimental wives.[5]

Baden-Powell's attitude to women ranged from companionable neutrality to outright hostility. His remark to his sister about becoming a misogynist had been jocularly stated, but was perfectly true. When writing home to his mother about the few women he had found agreeable, he would never describe them as beautiful. 'Plain but pleasing' was praise indeed, conferred upon the only woman whose company he enjoyed during his three years on Malta in the early 1890s. 'Big and handsome' and 'nice and heavyish' were compliments bestowed upon potential marriage partners shortly after the Boer War.[6] The problem, as he explained to his mother, was that he could not tell when women were good-looking. Henrietta Grace had mentioned, in a letter, a girl whom she had heard 'is said to be pretty'.[7] He told her wearily in reply that she might be right but he could not say. 'I'm no judge,' he explained.

Yet he was not so inhibited about pronouncing women ugly. In 1893, when describing a French consul's wife whom he had met in Tunisia as 'charming . . . with such eyes and smiles', he hastened to confide to his diary that he had 'just managed not to bolt straight away, but I got my knapsack and gun from her and sniggled out as soon as I could'.[8] On the same day he wrote: 'Another beautiful lady at déjeuner – great porpoise of a woman . . . got up to look like a young doll.' When he described meeting 'a beautiful French officer' also in Tunisia, there was nothing ironic about his use of the adjective 'beautiful'.[9] Feminine beauty was not the quality which drew him to the woman he eventually married when he was 55, although she was in fact most attractive. Olave Soames's purposeful walk and sporting prowess were what struck him most favourably.[10] It has been noted in several books that Edwardian adventure writers like Buchan and Sapper make their only sympathetically presented women indistinguishable from young men, slim-hipped, athletically minded, and so forth.[11] Miss Soames would add to these qualities a dislike of feminine clothes.[12]

The women who particularly alarmed him were those whose sex appeal was obvious. 'When a girl tries to attract she at once repels,' he warned young men. 'A loud vulgar girl may lower the standard of innate character that was in the man, and put him on a lower level, possibly for life.'[13] Yet when the overt sexual threat was removed he could be playfully flirtatious, as with Mrs King who acted with him in *Faustine*, and as he would be with Miss Ellen Turner in India in 1897. Of course there could be no threat at all with very young girls and for the first 50 years of his life Baden-Powell was rarely without such correspondents. As soon as the Christie girls became young women, they were replaced with others such as the daughters of Lord and Lady Downe; Winifred and Lesley Winter in Mafeking; and Miss Dulce Wroughton, daughter of a friend of Kenneth McLaren.[14] In Dulce's case the correspondence was prolonged by the McLaren connection and lasted until she was almost 20. Stephe was exceptionally good at amusing his young ladies with jokes about their pets and their governesses, and stories about his own doings. Occasionally there would be a hint of closer affection, but it would be quickly turned into a joke. 'As if I could call you a *beast*, even in play . . . I'm longing for lunch time on Monday to come round. Ain't I greedy?' Or another letter to Dulce, who had been upset by an erroneous report that he was engaged to one of the daughters of the fabulously rich American businessman, Levi Leiter. 'My dear Dulce, So I hear you are going to kill Miss D—.L—. How very naughty of you!' Although Dulce became a successful actress, Stephe did not continue their correspondence on a regular basis. After 1907 when her brother went to the first Scout Camp on Brownsea, Stephe wrote more often to *him*. Her age and her sex were both against Dulce, as Baden-Powell revealed to her when he told her he wanted her to be 'a sort of Pete – (h'm that's odd; there is no feminine for Peter) a sort of girl Peter Pan, the boy who couldn't grow up. And long may you be so.'[15]

Perhaps it was not surprising that when Baden-Powell did finally propose for the first time, when he was 47, it was to a girl who was then 18. Miss Rose Gough was his undoubted favourite but, as will be seen, he would consider many other women as potential brides. On the whole they fell into two groups – either very young in their late teens or early twenties, or in their fifties.[16] Stephe shared this reluctance to court women in the prime of life with Robert Louis Stevenson and J. M. Barrie, whose hero in *The Little White Bird* explains matters well. 'Just as I was about to fall in love, I suddenly found I preferred the mother.' In a similar vein, Stephe would write to his mother asking whether she could find somebody for him like Lady Downe, who was in her forties. Stephe had then been 27.[17]

Baden-Powell's fear of women stemmed from his difficulties in breaking free from his mother, who created particular problems for all her sons by openly opposing any relationships likely to lead to marriage. All children experience guilty feelings about their awakening sexuality, and Victorian children were made to feel considerably worse by contemporary attitudes towards sex, but few of them could have been told, as were Stephe and his brothers, that breaking away from home and marrying was morally wrong.

When reading about the feelings of devotion which many Victorian men felt for their mothers, even when they themselves were middle-aged, it becomes clear that Henrietta Grace's hold over her sons was an exaggeration of a widespread phenomenon. Today, with the commercial exploitation of sex and the cultivation of physical beauty as an end in itself, it ill-behoves us to patronize Victorian men for separating women into opposing categories, seeing them either as angel mothers and innocent girls or as degraded whores. The all but universal guilt about sexual impulses made this attitude inevitable, which is not to say that many strictly brought-up men did not make satisfactory marriages; rather that those whose emotional links with their mothers had been especially close, and whose sexual guilt consequently remained overwhelming, found it well-nigh impossible to form relationships with women.[18]

In 1893, Henrietta Grace's favourite son George married, and not long afterwards her anti-matrimonial views began to soften. The lease on 8 St George's Place would soon be up, the family's finances were still precarious and George's defection had shattered the myth of perpetual family loyalty. It had also given her an inkling of the immense advantages which could accrue if other sons married women as rich as George's bride. Stephe, however, was badly shaken by his brother's decision. 'I'm so glad, and yet – I shall feel your gap in our ring more than anybody else 'cos I seem, to myself, to be the one whose hand you hold. However . . . I suppose I must make up my mind to it.' For himself, he explained, he would have to wait until he had 'investigated the earth, and gone deeper into it, in a wooden box'.[19] When Stephe heard about his brother Frank's engagement in 1902, he commented sombrely, 'now it only remains for Warington to marry himself, and it will then be my turn – and I shall have no excuse for evading it.' With his mother soon actively encouraging her sons to settle down, marriage became a duty.

In 1905, the year in which Baden-Powell screwed up his courage to make his first (and as it turned out unsuccessful) proposal of marriage, he was mesmerized by *Peter Pan*, which he saw twice during its first month. He probably knew the famous *cri de coeur* in Barrie's *Tommy and Grizel*: 'She knew that despite all he had gone through, he was still a boy. And boys cannot love. Oh, is it not cruel to ask a boy to love?' When men remain boyish well into middle age, continuing to love pranks and practical jokes, to enjoy making animal noises with children and to seek attention by singing falsetto songs in public, it seems reasonable to interpret this immaturity as symptomatic – in part at least – of a reluctance to grow up. To this list should be added Stephe's lifelong addiction to macabre tales and adventure stories, and his frequent use of schoolboyish expletives in his letters: 'Te, he!', 'Hoo!', 'My wig!', and so forth. Very often the best Scoutmasters, the 'boy men' as he called them, feared growing up too and never entirely succeeded. Consequently they were capable of deep insights into the minds of their boys and of showing an intense sympathy with their interests.

The idea of the Scout Movement being a safe haven for boys and young men was in his mind from the beginning. Adult life was full of dangers – women could deprave them, politicians mislead them and gambling and drunkenness wreck their lives – but in his 'boys only' world, he would counteract these dangers with hiking, camping, cheery singsongs and other 'safe' activities. John Hargrave, a future Commissioner for Woodcraft in the Scout Movement, was sure that Baden-Powell's protective attitude towards young men 'had the tendency to prolong adolescence . . . and to retard their natural growing to manhood'. 'Baden-Powell's use of the term "girlitis", as a kind of sneering at (if not a smear upon) any Scout who showed a tendency to pair off with a girl – making normal sex attraction appear as some rather ridiculous disease – was of course linked with his own exaggerated "mother worship".'[20] It is unlikely to have been fortuitous that Baden-Powell's mission to protect young men from women should have started when he himself felt intensely threatened in that direction.

So what was it that boys (and by inference he himself) had to fear from women? At times Baden-Powell's distaste for female sexuality seemed to confuse him by its intensity, as when he ended an unfinished pencil note in this fashion: 'Young fellows are apt to excite their lust by talking about love or toying about with girls – but this is all bad for you because you get to think too much on . . .'[21] Had he continued he might have been brought face to face with the inconsistency of his entire drift, which was that a 'manly man' should neither desire nor even think of women sexually.

This was of course what his mother had once dinned into him. A common problem for Victorian men who had been dominated by their mothers was the fear that other people would share their mothers' disapproval of their sexual desires. Women to be 'good' therefore had to be totally lacking in sexuality. No other kind of woman would be acceptable to mother. There is a famous Baden-Powell cartoon in *Rovering to Success*: 'There are Women and Women', which perfectly illustrates this idea. 'You will be on the right side,' he told his young readers, 'if you take on with a girl whom you can bring to your home without shame, among your mother and sisters. Remember that whoever she is, she is someone else's sister; think of him and behave to her as you would wish him to behave to your sister.'[22] This revealing injunction to boys to consider the feelings of a girl's brother rather than the girl herself when deciding how to treat her, shows how unreal women were to him. To 'think of him' while with her was quite literally what many Victorian men did when they married the sisters of close male friends.

In an undated and unfinished note about sexual reproduction, written in about 1930, Stephe described marriage as 'the coming together of a man and a woman not only to help each other as comrades, two men could do that, but to carry out the Creator's law of making children to replace you'.[23] The suggestion that a woman's only advantage over a man as a close companion lay in her repro-

THERE ARE WOMEN AND
WOMEN.

ductive capabilities could only have been made by a man who had
never been strongly drawn to women, either physically or emotionally. It is noteworthy that in writing about the sexual attraction of
adolescent males to women, he dismissed it as the 'rutting season', a
phase 'that troubles some fellows to an alarming amount of depression
or excitement, which often lasts for several months. Indeed in
occasional cases it goes on for a few years. I get lots of letters from
young fellows who have never been told what to expect when they are
growing into manhood . . . I have been able to reassure them and help
them to take it calmly and to get over it just as they would get over the
measles . . .'[24] This astonishing passage was published in *Rovering to
Success* in 1922, by which time Stephe was already a baronet, Chief
Scout of the World and the recipient of numerous foreign honours.
Presumably nobody who knew better dared to contradict him on such
a potentially embarrassing matter. Yet the preposterous idea that
sexual attraction to women virtually ceases after a year or two could
have been contradicted by any heterosexual man of his acquaintance.

That sex was sinful was a Victorian and Edwardian commonplace,
but the particular way in which Baden-Powell expressed this loaded all
the odium for the 'dirtiness' of sex on to women. He warned boys and
young men against the dangers of letting their thoughts 'run on dirty
things' and becoming 'dirty minded little beasts'. 'Keep yourself clean
and don't let yourself give in to any temptation to make a beast of
yourself.'[25] Boys were particularly prone to acts of 'beastliness' when
the 'rutting season' coincided with an attack of 'calf love'. 'In that calf
love period don't forget that you are a man and not a beast.'[26] The fact
that Baden-Powell was railing against possible acts of fornication
might seem to justify the extreme disapproval, but since the act itself

would remain the same after marriage, the animal metaphors merely confirm the deep disapproval Baden-Powell felt for boys and young men developing sexual feelings towards women. If they did so, they at once became 'beasts'. And 'the manliest man has the least of the beast'.[27] When boys talked 'dirt' they were talking about women. 'We want clean manliness not sniggered smuttiness among our rising generation,' he remarked at the end of an unpublished draft article entitled 'A Dirty Age'. This was principally devoted to attacking paintings of 'female anatomy – awful at that', which he had seen at the Royal Academy Summer Show, probably in 1928.[28] In 1923 and 1925 he was also offended by the number of nudes. If female nudity was a sign of 'a dirty age', it was clearly a phenomenon which any exemplar of 'clean manliness' would want to avoid. 'Clean' is an adjective Baden-Powell frequently used in connection with men and boys but never with women. 'A clean young man in his prime of health is the finest creature God has made in this world.'[29]

When Baden-Powell visited the Paris Salon in 1893, his favourite picture was of a group of fencers, but he deplored the numerous 'naked women lying about, some face up, others face down'.[30] His hatred of female nudity went further than mere prudishness, since he felt that men could be contaminated simply by looking. In an undated draft of a letter intended for the press, he complained about 'the exhibition of naked girls on the public stage . . . the continuance of such shows cannot fail to have a deteriorative effect, moral and physical, on our lads'.[31] The same thought even entered his dreams. On 16 January 1915 he dreamed he visited the kitchens of a barracks. 'I saw cooks and maids at work. I gave a special look at them to see if they were likely to be dangerous to the morals of the young officers, but . . . I classed them at once under the terms we used at school as "Hags and Heifers".[32]

Other notable advocates of the great outdoors and of adventure, largely masculine preserves, shared Stephe's love of 'the clean'. Walt Whitman often used to describe his young soldier friends as 'clean', as did T. E. Lawrence his Arab boys. 'Our youths began to slake one another's few needs in their own clean bodies.'[33] General Gordon used to wash boys who were the objects of his philanthropy, and Baden-Powell praised those clubs where a boy on arrival 'took off all his clothes' before 'going into a big warm plunge bath'. In fact at a club in Hull, which he had singled out for special praise, the secretary discovered that 'at a very early age the youngsters objected to be looked upon as something in the nature of performing animals by too curious visitors'.[34] In the days of rudimentary plumbing, when some Scouts found it difficult to take regular baths at home, Baden-Powell's commendation of proceedings, which today would cause consternation, would have aroused no opposition. But the frequency of his exhortations to Scouts to keep their minds and bodies 'clean' indicates how anxious he was on the subject. He considered the tenth Scout Law: 'A Scout is clean in thought and word and deed' to be the most important. He advised that particular attention be given to 'keeping the racial member clean'.[35]

Baden-Powell's battle to protect clean young men from contamination made him adopt some extremely uncommon attitudes for a soldier. Until the Contagious Diseases Acts were repealed in 1886, the army had run its own brothels at every major military cantonment in India, with the girls being inspected several times a week. Within the army it was generally maintained that the existence of these brothels was essential for the morale and the physical well-being of the troops. By providing prostitutes it was also hoped that homosexuality in the ranks would be curbed.[36] The army continued on a local ad hoc basis to supervise brothels, even after Parliament had outlawed them. When Baden-Powell became Colonel of the 5th Dragoon Guards, he showed himself unusually hostile to prostitutes and although he was not foolhardy enough to try to place the brothels out of bounds, he did from time to time suggest that the men should voluntarily cease visiting them. The high incidence of venereal disease was his ostensible reason. Baden-Powell told his N.C.O.s that if they wanted to beat men who decided to go into the bazaar, he would turn a blind eye to it.[37] On one occasion Stephe 'consulted the Provost Sergeant and told him to do what he could to prevent these women [prostitutes] coming into our camp . . . He and his myrmidons captured a few of the women and taking them to the guard-tent, turned them up and gave them a good spanking'.[38] Baden-Powell's social club founded on Malta during the early 1890s was named 'The Poultice' because he hoped to cover over the sore caused by prostitution in Valetta.

It might be thought that Baden-Powell's attitude to women of gentle birth underwent a change during the years in which he was trying to find a wife, but Eric Walker, who was then his secretary, did not think so. Recalling an incident in April 1910 when 'a charming lady' had greeted him warmly, only to be rewarded by a mumbled '**** the woman', Walker wrote: 'What an extraordinary attraction he has for the fair sex, although he seems to think very little of them.'[39] This did not require great perspicacity, since occasionally in his speeches at public meetings in aid of the Boy Scouts, he would joke about this very subject. At Birkenhead in 1906, when the mayor said he would step down and leave the platform for Baden-Powell, Stephe replied: 'I think that is a little cowardly of you, because you can talk and I can't. I can get on with boys but not with ladies.' This was an allusion to the large number of women in the hall.[40]

Antipathy or indifference to women is not alone enough to establish a homosexual inclination. If, however, these co-exist with a corresponding attraction to men and everything masculine, the case would seem to be proved.

Baden-Powell's enthusiasm for far-flung places would be closely linked not just with his love of what he called 'the flannel shirt life' but with the emotional and aesthetic affinity he felt for the well-muscled males who were taming nature in these remote places. Shortly after returning from a trip to Canada in 1910, he wrote of the pleasure he had taken in 'the comradeship of men who are men . . . It is good merely to watch their movements, their handiness and resource, they are so patient and quiet in all they do . . . I see in my mind's eye my friend Jack, a great strapping lumberman, who can carry his 300 lb. load, and skip his 6 foot 6 inch height and his weight of 15 stone into a birch-bark canoe. I could watch him by the hour . . .'[41] During 1910 and 1912 Baden-Powell went fishing in Norway where he admired the physique of the country people, one of whom 'seeing that I was fishing from a rock which did not give me the best advantage, waded in, and putting his arm around my waist carried me off to a more advantageous position.'[42] The way of life and appearance of Australian stockmen and South African farmers also appealed to him. 'It is hard work there – hard sweaty work, with arms tanned, sunbrowned faces with cheekbones showing . . . riding after stray cattle, ploughing a straight furrow . . . Drinking in life with the breath of the veldt . . . There's joy in it. It's a man's life.'[43] For the same manly qualities he admired the hillsmen of Kashmir, 'who left their legs all bare to be admired, for they are splendidly made'.[44]

Whereas female nudity, even in the sanitized context of art, smacked of 'dirtiness', male nudity was quite different. During the Great War, in one of Stephe's many visits to France, he watched the men 'trooping in to be washed in nature's garb, with their strong well-built naked wonderfully made bodies' and took nothing but pleasure in this 'happy brave family laughing together'.[45] Society certainly took a more relaxed view of men swimming naked than it would have done had women shown the temerity to do the same. But it is not so much the fact that Baden-Powell took male nudity for granted that is note-worthy, but that he consistently praised the male body when naked and denigrated the female. At Gilwell Park, the Scouts' camping ground in Epping Forest, he always enjoyed watching the boys swimming naked, and would sometimes chat with them after they 'had just stripped off'.[46] When public censoriousness finally turned against male nudity, treating it in the same way as female nakedness, Baden-Powell was appalled. In 1934, commenting on the police banning boys from swimming nude in the Serpentine, he suggested that Scoutmasters should 'educate the boy by encouraging his self-*ex*pression, instead of disciplining him by police methods of *re*-pression'.[47] It is entertaining to speculate what he might have written if it had been suggested that girls should be allowed to swim naked in a public place.

Another incident illustrative of Baden-Powell's appreciation of naked boys occurred at Charterhouse, when he was staying overnight at the school with his old friend A. H. Tod, who had been in the Rifle Corps and in the football 1st XI with him. In November 1919 Tod was over the retirement age but still teaching because it was wartime and all the younger staff had joined up. 'Stayed with Tod,' Stephe wrote in his diary. 'Tod's photos of naked boys and trees etc. Excellent.'[48] That a bachelor housemaster should have taken large numbers of nude photographs of his boys evidently did not strike Baden-Powell as undesirable. A few days later he wrote to Tod about starting a Scout troop at the school and added that he would soon be visiting Charterhouse again, 'which will give me the opportunity of seeing the football; and possibly I might get a further look at those wonderful photographs of yours?'[49]

This album of 'figure studies', as Tod described it, was still in the library at Charterhouse in the mid-1960s, but by the end of that permissive decade had been destroyed. This appalling act was undertaken 'to protect Tod's reputation' and out of deference to the feelings of the sons and grandsons of the boys depicted.[50] Fortunately the rest of Tod's albums were spared and they comprise what must be the finest single photographic record in existence of public school life in the late nineteenth and early twentieth centuries. So what were the missing album's contents?

According to one source the nude figures were 'contrived and artificial as regards poses',[51] which makes them sound like those late Victorian pseudo-classical nude photographs which were really pornography but were sold under the guise of art. In the same way an artistic publication like *The Artist and Journal of Home Culture* appealed to homosexuals with its illustrations and its homoerotic poetry.[52] The Grecian and athletic context was all important, allowing emotions which contemporaries normally reprehended to seem respectable. Tod was a classicist and a keen sportsman and his nude boys may well have been throwing javelins or posing as Myron's Discobolus, although the 'trees' Stephe mentioned suggest that the boys were clambering among branches like dryads. But whatever the contents, the Charterhouse authorities in the late 1960s clearly construed them to be damaging to Tod's reputation. Probably they did not know that when Tod was taking his photographs, large paintings of naked boys by the artist Henry Scott Tuke were being hung in the Royal Academy each year and causing no particular stir, although today their erotic intention seems clear.[53] Tuke was a homosexual, as were many of his customers, but his pictures were art and therefore safe from censure. It is an irony of history that in the inhibited days before the First World

War Tod's photographs had been far safer than they were in a decade normally associated with permissiveness.

There is little doubt that Tod was a repressed homosexual; as indeed were many public school masters. The majority managed to follow Plato's prescription glorifying the love of man for man, or man for boy, while remaining physically chaste. Others – and there were plenty of them – persuaded themselves that the desires which they struggled against so manfully were not carnal. The literature of this kind of self-deception is vast,[54] but one example will suffice. The Reverend Edward C. Lefroy wrote widely admired poems about sporting boys during the 1880s and 1890s. 'I have inborn admiration for beauty of form and figure. It amounts almost to a passion and in most football teams I can find one Antinous . . . some folk would say it is sentimentalism to admire any but feminine flesh. But that only proves how base is the carnality, which is now reckoned the only legitimate form. The other is far nobler . . . Platonic passion in any relationship is better than animalism.'[55] Often such passages were written without conscious hypocrisy. But when Oscar Wilde wrote of Lord Henry Wotton's desire to merge souls with Dorian Gray as 'the most satisfying joy left . . . in an age . . . of grossly carnal pleasures' it is clear that he was satirizing writers of the Lefroy school.

The relevance of such writings to an understanding of Baden-Powell lies in the way in which he too uses words as a kind of code. Lefroy's 'animalism' seems first cousin to Baden-Powell's 'beastliness' with women. A boy should know, wrote Stephe, that 'the higher he raises himself above the animal instinct the less he is of the beast and the more he is of the man'.[56] Lefroy's 'sentimentalism' is another euphemism for platonic homoerotic feelings, and is frequently employed by Baden-Powell. Scoutmasters were asked to guard against it, since experience taught that displays of overt affection could easily lead to direct physical approaches.[57] Stephe adopted an understanding, almost sympathetic attitude to the problem. After finding the atmosphere at Pennant Hills, the principal Australian training camp, 'too sentimental', he wrote confidentially to the Chief Commissioner for New South Wales:

> You may be puzzled to know what I mean by 'sentimentalism' – but I trace it to Macallister, the camp chief, who is a genius in his way but emotional. He has great influence over the boys who go through the training under his hands, and the danger that I see is that his emotionalism may communicate itself to them (in fact it has evidently done so in some cases that I came across). Romance and sentiment are excellent qualities and should be encouraged; but within limits.[58]

Macallister remained at his post, in spite of his 'emotionalism', another code word.

Lawrence Impey, who at the time of writing is one of the only two survivors of the Scout Association's Committee of the Council during the 1930s, recalls Baden-Powell's extreme reluctance to discuss the perennial problem posed by homosexual Scoutmasters.[59] Indeed when mentioning in his diary that individual Scoutmasters had been accused of homosexual misbehaviour, Stephe would often resort to euphemisms about them being 'in trouble'.[60] He must have known that he could never be the man to clamp down in the way that his colleagues would have wished. The nude swimming and sun-bathing at Gilwell Park undoubtedly proved an added temptation to homosexually inclined Scoutmasters, but could he, who had attacked the police 'repression' at the Serpentine, deny his boys 'self-expression' at Gilwell? He himself enjoyed seeing 'the fine athletic sunbrowned bodies' at the poolside, and commented in his diary on 'the delightful sights – esp. at the swimming pool'.[61] He may not have connected the sacking of two Assistant Camp Chiefs in succession at Gilwell with the free and easy atmosphere of the place.[62] He certainly believed that sex and 'sentimentalism' could be 'kept within limits' if men exercised self-control. But his idea that a man could be a suitable Scoutmaster if he needed to make constant efforts to do so would not have been shared by most members of the Committee.

So, returning to Mr Tod and his famous friend, as they sit perusing 'those wonderful photographs' after having had the satisfaction of watching the boys of Charterhouse thrash Lancing by five goals, is it reasonable to imagine that they thought what they were doing had as little to do with sexual feelings as examining fine porcelain? It seems most unlikely that Baden-Powell could have written requesting a second sight of the album, so soon after his first, without consciously recognizing as he wrote that his interest was not simply aesthetic. His excuse was that he would be coming to Charterhouse anyway to discuss starting Scouting at the school, and this true cover story would have enabled him to present his interest to Tod as more casual than it was. He may also have been testing Tod to see whether he might offer a glimpse of other albums and photographs. I do not though for a moment believe that Baden-Powell's interest in such material meant that he ever contemplated making sexual advances to boys. The fact that he had not found it in him to condemn 'sentimentalism' (providing no sexual overtures were made) should be weighed against occasional harsh remarks about erring Scoutmasters. 'Had the Law allowed it,' he wrote, after a Scoutmaster had been sentenced to three years' imprisonment for sexual assaults, 'one would have been glad to see a flogging inflicted . . . as a deterrent against the crime of spreading such sin among the boys.'[63] Although 'glad to see' was an unfortunate expression, given Baden-Powell's interest in corporal punishment, his hatred of paederasty was genuine. Like Lord Esher, the *éminence grise* of the Edwardian establishment, who also enjoyed nude photographs and in addition wrote clandestine erotic verse, Baden-Powell was in a position of public trust which made watching, at one remove, almost the only way for him to satisfy his interest. The other was to seek the company of men like Tod, who lived in close contact with young males. Through their shared memories of Charterhouse and their undoubted 'sentimentalism', which in both their cases found no physical fulfilment, they would have felt a close understanding that required no words of explanation.

In 1917, two years before Stephe admired Tod's photographs, his reaction to a contemporary novel gives another indication of the strong emotional hold which the public school world still exercised over him. The author of this novel was a 17-year-old boy who had recently been expelled from Sherborne for having a homosexual liaison. Alec Waugh's account of public school life was widely construed as a damning attack since it included scenes in which boys lied and cheated, were irreligious and obsessed with sport, and indulged in homosexual practices. When Arnold Bennett read *The Loom of Youth*, he prophesied the demise of the public schools. Other critics were no less pessimistic and the governors of Sherborne struck Waugh's name from the list of old boys. But when Sir Robert Baden-Powell first expressed his opinion of this notorious book in a personal aside incorporated into a draft memorandum – probably sent for comment to Lionel Helbert, the recently appointed Commissioner for Public and Preparatory Schools – his opinion was quite different. 'By the way, have you read that wonderful book *The Loom of Youth* by Alec Waugh? It will be an eye-opener to many who are not well up in the psychology of the boy or in what goes on in a public school of today.'[64] Indeed it was. But what was it about it that appealed to Baden-Powell so much? The novel's principal target was the public school mania for sport, which stultified all mental subtlety. Salvation, Waugh argued, lay in work with aesthetic value, such as poetry and art.[65] This was hardly a message to find favour with Stephe. In fact Waugh himself, in writing about his novel and his frame of mind at the time he was working on it, provides the key to why Baden-Powell enjoyed it so much. 'It is in such a mood,' wrote Waugh, 'that a man at the end of a long and intense affair writes to the mistress whom he still adores, but nonetheless holds largely responsible for the rupture . . . In the last analysis . . . *The Loom of Youth* is a love letter to Sherborne.'[66] Baden Powell, who had loved his schooldays too, must have been delighted by the way in which the author makes his reader feel that he or she is really there at Sherborne with him – so lovingly is the place recreated. Facts like the prevalence of homosexuality in the sports teams, and the observation that 'there are jolly few of us any better',[67] were neutralized by the book's passionate nostalgia. But Baden-

Powell could not have missed them. When expelled for a sexual offence, one of the boys takes it like a sportsman: 'Oh well, it's no use grousing. I suppose if one hits length balls on the middle stump over square leg's head, one must run the risk of being bowled . . .'[68] As Baden-Powell would have wished, they played the game.

The subject of the memorandum into which Baden-Powell inserted his parenthetic praise for 'that wonderful book' was the way in which the Scout Movement offered to all boys the character training which many of them had missed out on through not having been to a public school. That it was possible for Stephe simultaneously to applaud a novel exposing public schools as seed-beds of hypocrisy and to praise these same institutions as nurseries for good character seems very remarkable. Yet Baden-Powell's note about *The Loom* had not been meant for mass consumption but only for the eyes of friends in the Movement like Lionel Helbert and Arthur Gaddum, both public school men. Baden-Powell could afford to be unbuttoned with them in a way he would have thought inappropriate with ordinary acquaintances. Tod, who had been an exact contemporary at school, would have been in a still more privileged position. These men had all been at their public schools before homosexuality had been described as a definite condition in works like Edward Carpenter's *Homogenic Love* and Havelock Ellis's *Sexual Inversion*. The Wilde trials, and other homosexual scandals during the following decade, meant that the days of naïve homoerotic friendships were replaced by an age of guilt and suspicion. If accused of homosexuality, a man in public life fled the country or – like the Boer War Commander, General Sir Hector MacDonald – blew out his brains. Wilde appealed to the Home Secretary to be released on the grounds that continental criminologists considered homosexuality akin to lunacy.[69] Small wonder then that books like *The Loom of Youth* produced such anger and evasion. Those reacting in that way had not exactly forgotten their past, but had buried their memories of it. When homosexuality was publicly condemned as an appalling evil, not surprisingly the majority of homosexually inclined men fought their tendency through denial, sublimation, marriage, or all three. When moments of self-awareness occurred, they were swiftly 'forgotten' again; unless, as in the case of Baden-Powell's spontaneous reaction to Waugh's book, and his interest in Tod's photographs, there was a failure to recognize the implications.

His reaction to the way of life of the homosexual commander of a sail-training ship is an example of partial recognition. In March 1928 Stephe visited the West Country, hoping to learn whether it would be feasible to acquire the old Napoleonic man-of-war, *Implacable*, for the Sea Scouts. This vessel was part-owned by Mr George Wheatley Cobb, who owned and skippered a similar ship, the *Foudroyant*, which

he ran as a sail-training ship in Falmouth Harbour. Baden-Powell went
aboard and recorded in his diary: 'He trains about 40 boys at his own
expense for the sea living on board. His wife lives ashore!'[70] Although
Cobb chose only the best-looking boys for his ship, it is quite possible
that Baden-Powell detected nothing untoward about the
Foudroyant and her crew. But if his diary comment ('His wife lives
ashore!') was meant merely as a statement of fact, why that exclamation mark? The obvious interpretation must be that he knew very
well what other people would have thought about Cobb's living
arrangements if they had known about them; they would have thought
him up to no good, hence that exclamation mark. If this is right, the
absence of any note of disapproval (and his diary contains plenty of that
commodity in other places) may seem very reprehensible in a public
figure who ought to have been uniquely sensitive to the welfare of
boys. But Baden-Powell probably assumed that men like Tod and
Cobb were able to keep 'their sentimentalism within limits'. After all,
he too enjoyed the company of older boys and young men and
understood the emotional enjoyment derived from their proximity.*[71]

    The army had once furnished Stephe with just such an emotionally
fulfilling milieu, with the vast majority of his 'men' being between 17
and 20. When Baden-Powell failed to regain control of his old
regiment during the Boer War, he accused the War Office of failing to
understand the 'sentiment attaching to it', which made him view
another man in command as someone 'rogering his wife'.[72] He was of
course unmarried at the time. On another occasion he described his
regiment as 'more than a wife to me'.[73] By spending the greater part of
his free time with his men, Stephe was doing something considered
extremely unusual even by philanthropically inclined officers. Apart
from taking groups of men out on overnight scouting expeditions, he
would quite often be the only officer taking part in regimental
theatricals. He was undoubtedly the only one (when he ran his social
club on Malta) who joined in gymnastic displays which involved
physical contact with N.C.O.s and privates.[74] When he was considering a transfer from the 13th Hussars, his principal regret had been the
impending loss of 'his many pals amongst the sergeants and
privates'.[75] One sergeant used to knit him pairs of socks, and several
privates came to him for individual drawing lessons.[76]

    To recognize exactly how remarkable Baden-Powell's interest in his
men was, it is only necessary to read accounts of how his contemporaries – men like Haig, Kitchener and Smith-Dorrien – seemed scarcely
aware of their men being human.[77] Kitchener, it was commonly
believed, had never during his entire career addressed a single word to

* Unknown to Baden-Powell, Cobb used his ship for orgies during which he
photographed the boys.[71]

a soldier unless it had been an order. Sir William Robertson, who achieved the near miracle of becoming a Field Marshal after enlisting in the ranks, recalled that very few officers had even known his name. Baden-Powell was fascinated by this unbridgeable gulf and sent home from India for the anonymously written *Through the Ranks to a Commission* (1881).[78] A 'Gentleman Private', writing in 1883, attributed this gulf to 'offensive snobbism' on the part of officers.[79] Baden-Powell could be fiercely snobbish too. He was disgusted that his publisher should employ 'very common managers', and he even condemned a full-blown colonel who came to live in his home village as 'very common'.[80] But these men were all middle-aged. His snobbery, however, was never aimed at young men. On the troopships going out to India and returning, he had always made friends with individual bluejackets, particularly, on one voyage the signalman and the captain of the mizzen-top [81] There had never been any question of finding the sailors 'common'. The men with whom he spent months at a time in the Rhodesian bush were no gentlemen, but they 'were fit and hard . . . and we were good tried comrades all'.[82]

To be young and male was to be exempt, in Baden-Powell's canon, from the usual tyranny of social distinctions. The anonymous author of a book called *Social Life in the British Army* (1900) painted a very different picture of the norm. Officers, he stated, might 'lead their men in their games, yet any further intimacy would be regarded as a very serious offence indeed. When the match was over, no officer would dream of walking up to barracks with one of his cricket playmates of a few minutes before. Indeed, should he do so, I fancy very serious notice would be taken of such a breach of discipline.'[83]

The reasons for such 'very serious notice' were twofold. In the first place, it was feared that familiarity between officers and other ranks would undermine the men's obedience – the supposition being that only if officers appeared to be remote and god-like beings would their authority remain unquestioned. The second reason was quite simply fear of homosexuality.

In 1875 the Liberal M.P. John Holms wrote a book about conditions of service in the army, and claimed that homosexuality was widespread.[84] He was ably supported by other authors with inside knowledge. Anyone who visited Aldershot, or Shorncliffe, would have been unobservant to have missed the astonishing number of soldier prostitutes touting for business. In the Guards homosexual officers were numerous, and the guardsmen who obliged them were picturesquely known as 'fitters' and 'twisters'.[85] They also 'rented' themselves to 'the best gentlemen in London', according to one of their number. An earl, a duke's son, two colonels and a major were all implicated in the Cleveland Street homosexual brothel scandal in 1889, along with the Prince of Wales's equerry.[86]

Regular scandals created an atmosphere in which young officers could be ruined by unsubstantiated rumours. In 1885 an officer in Winston Churchill's 4th Hussars was forced out for having 'improperly associated with non-commissioned officers'.[87] Baden-Powell well knew that the 'quiet and cheery chats' which he had with individual men in his quarters were 'quite contrary to regulations'. Nevertheless he recalled having 'kept a confidential report of each man for my own information. At my tea-table was forged a link which never broke.'[88] He would talk to them about their homes, their morals, their feelings, and their prospects. His objective was to make each man feel 'he is my particular friend . . . I have found it easier to do it with the worst characters'. Intimate chats would often follow an earlier session at which Baden-Powell had thumped the table and shouted at the 'bad' man in question.[89] 'The biggest blackguard' in the regiment particularly appealed to him. 'Something in the twinkle in his eye had prepossessed me. I had a private talk with him, and from that day to this he never gave a moment's trouble.' This same man's mother died, and Baden-Powell gave him some money as well as the routine permit to attend her funeral. When 'the blackguard' started to weep, Baden-Powell 'sent him out with a "don't-be-a-fool" pat on the shoulder, but my right hand was richer for a hot and grimy tear-splash'.[90] Although not a few officers would have sympathized with a bereaved trooper, only those with an emotional attachment to young men would ever have felt themselves the 'richer' for a 'grimy tear-splash' or have been willing, as Baden-Powell was at this time, to sleep in a railway hut full of private soldiers during some manoeuvres.[91]

Baden-Powell continued his private chats with 'the men' even after he left the army in 1910. During the Great War he spent several months 'in close touch with our young soldiers' and found that 'very many of my young friends opened their hearts to me to an extent to which they confessed they would not go with their parson'.[92] At the same time he was carrying on a vast correspondence with Boy Scouts, principally about their struggles not to masturbate. He was still doing so in 1937, when aged 80. 'My correspondence is largely a confidential one with Rovers and young men in this stage [late adolescence] anxiously seeking advice or comfort in the chaotic state of their minds.'[93] He would also advise boys in person on sexual matters, as he explained to a Cambridge college chaplain. 'My own way is simply the straightest of straight talking to the boys individually.'[94] One boy was worried because he had taken 'such a particular fancy' to another boy, whom he was helping not to start 'that rotten habit of self-abuse'.[95] Baden-Powell considered chaste romanticism perfectly in order, but absolutely nothing else. He expressed this view to the clergyman who wrote from St Augustine's College, Canterbury, to ask whether it was advisable for Scoutmasters to 'fondle' a boy in order to show him 'that it is not only possible but natural for an embrace to be pure'.[95] 'Self-control', Baden-Powell always argued, was of overriding importance in Scouting and in life. What had to be achieved was 'that deeper form of subordination of one's own desires'. 'Ruling one's self' was another favoured synonym for self-control.[97]

Psychoanalysts connect a strong need to advise others how to combat particular desires with a strong disposition on the part of the advice-giver to succumb to them. A man entertaining desires he cannot acknowledge, and therefore denies, often deals with them by 'projection'. If the unwanted desires are attributed to other people (in Baden-Powell's case to young men), his attempts to reform *them* enable him to control his own urges. Advice-giving helps in another way. 'Bad' desires engender guilt, and when parents (or a parent) have insisted upon 'goodness' and unquestioning conformity to their wishes at all costs, as Henrietta Grace had, the guilt is all the greater. Renunciation of instinct, through fear of loss of love, is followed by what Freud called the creation of 'an internal authority, and renunciation of instinct owing to fear of conscience'.[98] Often renunciation is not enough, and then guilt can only be assuaged by reparation through a sublimated activity such as reforming others. The worse the personal struggle against instinctual feelings, the more intense will be the desire to save potential sinners. Baden-Powell's advice-giving was at its height during the Great War shortly after his marriage.

When, just before that war, he at last found a young woman not only prepared to marry him but ruthlessly determined to prevent him back-tracking, he took fright at the last moment. He failed to escape, and shortly after his marriage he started to suffer from agonizing headaches. Two years later when they were still no better, he consulted Dr F. D. S. Jackson of Harley Street.[99] Although Jackson was a medical doctor, he must also have had an interest in psychoanalysis. At any rate, shortly after visiting him Baden-Powell began to keep a record of his dreams.[100] Whether he returned to Jackson after his first consultation is unknown, but he continued to write down his dreams during the years in which his three children were conceived and born.

In 1919, two years after the birth of his third and last child, he began to sleep out on a balcony instead of with his wife.[101] From that date his headaches left him and he recorded fewer and fewer dreams, until virtually ceasing to record any by the end of the following year. Jackson had evidently thought his famous patient's headaches were psychological in origin; and, in line with the theories of Freud and his followers, had expected repressed wishes to emerge in his dreams. If Jackson hoped that insights gained in the process would help Baden-Powell to resolve the conflict causing his tension headaches, there is no evidence to show that they did. The ending of his reproductive duties and his departure to a separate bedroom appear to have been what brought relief.

On 3 April 1917 Baden-Powell dreamed that he was in a country town looking in at a shop window. Several men were standing beside him. 'One, on my left, whom I took to be a soldier without looking at him, pressed rather closely to me. As I turned away, suddenly I found his hand in my pocket . . . I thought of a ju-jitsu grip for holding him but finally put my arm around his neck to make it look as if we were good friends and yet to have a hold on him as we marched to the police station . . . Through his coat I could feel that he had little on under his coat and a sort of lump on his chest and I felt a great pity for him.' This double-image of an erection, which is also a deformity, seems to condemn any homosexual desire to touch. And Baden-Powell, when he touches, does so innocently. His pity for the man fits the psychoanalytical theory of 'projection' – whereby the reprehensible action or desire is attributed to someone else. The soldier, rather than Baden-Powell, is the evil-doer, committing a crime and having an erection as he places his hand in Baden-Powell's pocket. The insight into his own condition came with Baden-Powell's sudden feeling of warmth towards the man. A few months earlier Baden-Powell had dreamed that he himself had been arrested for an unspecified crime.[102]

This confusion about who was virtuous and who needed to be disciplined or controlled lies at the heart of another dream. Baden-Powell found himself sitting on top of a step-ladder with a whip in his hand, lecturing a group of guardsmen. Suddenly one came towards him menacingly. 'I flicked my whip about in order to keep him at a distance but he caught the lash and came towards me, dragging the whip so that I had to come from off the ladder. I pretended I was going for him but he only asked if I had ever been "disciplined".'[103] Normally Baden-Powell told boys and young men to control themselves, and spoke to them from his exalted position as a national figure. The guardsman in the dream had not accepted his elevated advice-giving status and, after refusing to be 'disciplined', had forced Baden-Powell down on to his own level and asked him whether *he* had ever been 'disciplined'.

In his waking life, shortly after his marriage, Stephe was excessively eager to assure friends and family that he was happy in his new state. Several of his dreams are on this theme. In one he forgets he is married and feels he must make up for it with a display of hideously self-conscious enthusiasm 'in order that B[aden] should see how happy we were though married, and might feel the inducement to get married himself'.[104] An eagerness to persuade unmarried men to marry (probably as a defence against homosexuality) forms part of an earlier dream, which highlights his sexual confusion. He and his wife, Olave, were driving together over open moorland in a four-wheel dog cart. Unexpectedly they passed a well-dressed young man in London clothes.

O[lave] remarked that it was odd. I slipped my arm around her waist and kissed her. She said that this was not very proper before the young man, and I retorted that it would do him good and probably encourage him to go and get married . . . [Shortly, they arrived at an hotel.] Olave went up to her room and I followed with wraps a few minutes later. I arrived on the landing and forgot which of two doors was ours. 644 or 646 . . . so I gave our whistle which was answered from 644. I walked in and found a young officer there in shirtsleeves, breeches, and gaiters, shaving. So I begged his pardon . . . and excused my mistake by explaining that he had answered me with the same whistle that she would have used. I came out puzzled and awoke.[105]

Men who are not physically or emotionally attracted to women inevitably marry reluctantly and suffer acute conflict when they do. The causes of homosexuality are complex and controversial. But research into the family backgrounds of male homosexuals has yielded results which show that certain family patterns are frequently repeated. The classic situation is one in which the father is either absent or hostile to the son, while the mother is possessive, over-emotional and controls the entire process of upbringing, punishing and rewarding. The early death of Professor Powell, coupled with Henrietta Grace's policy of making her sons dread causing her heart to 'grow cold', clearly fit the commonest pattern.

The available evidence points inexorably to the conclusion that Baden-Powell was a repressed homosexual. I suspect that far more men of his generation who had been similarly conditioned and educated were homosexually inclined than is generally supposed today. Robert Graves, another famous old Carthusian, writing some decades later, blamed the public schools for making boys treat the opposite sex as obscene. 'Many boys never recover from this perversion. For every one born a homosexual, at least ten permanent pseudo-homosexuals are made by the public school system: nine of these ten as honourably chaste and sentimental as I was.'[106] A dependable informant quoted by Jonathan Gathorne-Hardy in his book The Public School Phenomenon, spoke of 'British upper-class males [of the pre-Great War generation] being homosexual in everything but their sex lives'.[107]

In the public schools there was usually a clear-cut division between love and lust. Older boys loved younger ones but seldom made sexual advances. Boys of a similar age frequently used one another as convenient sex-instruments.[100] In adult life homosexual gentlemen tended to preserve the distinction, keeping sentiment and lust apart by having romantic friendships with members of their own class and sexual relations with working-class men. This preference was also due to the fact that such men were, as a rule, less inhibited and therefore more willing. Moreover, they could be bought. Baden-Powell's enjoyment of the company of enlisted men was never in doubt; nor was his appreciation of their physique and his desire to speak to them about intimate subjects. But is it likely that actual sexual contact took place?

Baden-Powell's admiration for muscular men made him a frequent visitor to the Aldershot Army Physical Training School during the 1920s. From 1927 to 1929, Robert Musk, an 18-year-old lance-corporal in the Duke of Cornwall's Light Infantry, was at Aldershot training to be a regimental physical training instructor. He was in India for five years and then returned to England, where he left the army and came to live in Baden-Powell's village of Bentley. In 1936 Musk took an unskilled job with the Post Office, which he kept until his retirement. He died in 1980, leaving an impressive collection of Mafeking memorabilia including a selection of valuable Mafeking bank notes printed from Baden-Powell's original drawings, historically important signals in cypher regarding De Wet's movements and a complete set of the *Mafeking Mail*, which would have been valuable even before the Boer War ended. Musk never worked for Baden-Powell and he could hardly have known him socially, so the great man's gift of these papers (for such it must have been) is curious.[109] But it does not prove a physical relationship. A propos of physical training instructors, Baden-Powell attributed to a party of African chiefs who had visited Britain during the 1890s an admiration for 'the gymnastic instructors at Aldershot', which sounds uncommonly like his own. 'When they saw these men performing their various exercises they were tremendously taken with them, but they were not fully satisfied until they had had the men stripped and had examined for themselves their muscular development. And I must say these gymnasts were magnificent specimens . . .'[110] (Baden-Powell's drawing of this incident is reproduced on page 109.)

There are numerous references in Baden-Powell's diary to vets, butlers, waiters, soldiers, servants, plate-layers, signallers, railway clerks, hairdressers and other working-class men, whom he had remembered after a considerable lapse of time.[111] Considering his simultaneous concern to cultivate socially useful officers, and his remarks about people being 'common' or 'nobodies', it is strange to find him writing down the address of 'a very friendly' Greek commercial traveller with whom he slept in the deck-house of a ship bound from Malta to Brindisi one night in July 1892.[112] Eighteen months later he 'made friends with one A. Minghetti, a railway clerk in Taranto', and saw him on two more evenings before leaving town.[113] I do not know how he first made the acquaintance of some firemen at Fire Brigade Headquarters in Clerkenwell during the 1880s, but he already knew them before he asked their advice about a design for a machine-gun pulling harness in 1887.[114] Nor can I explain how he came to write a letter with 'a romantic commencement' to a soldier called Macdonald in South Africa. This letter, which probably no longer exists, miscarried and was opened in error by an unknown officer, whom Baden-Powell addressed as 'Dear Sir', when assuring him that 'the rather romantic commencement may have made it [the letter] appear more interesting than it was'.[115]

In the army, during his years as a regimental officer, Baden-Powell was never without a soldier servant. One, who served him during the early and mid-1880s, had first appeared with him in theatricals when he was a boy trumpeter of 16. Taylor had progressed to the rank of corporal before Baden-Powell took on another young soldier, called Bain, whom he described as 'a boy'. As well as serving Baden-Powell, Bain rode in his élite machine-gun driving team in military displays and tournaments.[116] There is, however, nothing strange about officers having soldier servants, except perhaps, in this case, for the youth of Baden-Powell's pair. A soldier servant would also accompany him on expeditions into the African bush, or on campaigns. An illustration in the first photo section shows Baden-Powell gun-cleaning with a young man called Galloway in the wilds of Swaziland in 1889. This picture, and the preceding facts, suggest nothing in themselves except that Baden-Powell had abundant opportunity for clandestine sexual encounters.

The four trips he made to North Africa, when stationed on Malta between 1890 and 1893, provided the best opportunities of all. He normally stayed out in the country between Tunis and Bizerta with a pig farmer called Smith who had been educated at Wellington College. There could not have been many Old Wellingtonians in the 1890s who chose to farm in a country as remote and arid as Tunisia. Pigs also seem an odd choice, as pork does not keep well in a hot climate.[117] Baden-Powell never dignified Smith with a Christian name, and since there were seven Smiths at Wellington at about the time when the pig farmer must have been there, I have not been able to trace his family. A bachelor, he lived with a servant-cum-companion whom he called Hadj Amor. Possibly a schoolboy knowledge of Latin was responsible for making him into 'the Pilgrim of Love', but Amor could equally well have been an Anglicization of the Arabic A'mur. Baden-Powell also gave the man's name as Ben Ali Sed Kaoui. Stephe was grateful to Ben Ali for enabling him to make 'many friends among the Bedouins, whose hospitality and sportsmanship I much enjoyed'. Ben Ali was in Baden-Powell's words, 'a very superior kind of Arab', who spoke excellent French and English, and had been to Mecca. Stephe was surprised, on first staying with Smith, to find that Ben Ali waited at table as a servant but joined in the conversation as an equal and often wore European clothes. Baden-Powell was also taken aback to discover that Ben Ali had committed a murder and for several years had been protected by Smith from the French authorities. The Arab was later caught by the French, and transported to Cayenne from whence he escaped, only to be hunted down and shot. On one occasion Baden-Powell spent 'a delightful night' in the desert with Ben Ali at a place called Sidi Salem El Owain. He does not date this event, but according to his diary it must have been in late December 1890 or November 1891. The Arab had prepared supper for Stephe with his own hands: 'a bowl of rice and chicken and kid stewed together . . . Then we sat round a blazing log fire for the nights were cold, in the brilliant starlight . . . And when we coiled down to sleep we did so together, under his one blanket.'[118] In August 1895 Baden-Powell began to contribute a number of travel articles to the *Badminton Magazine*. These included one about Ben Ali, whom Baden-Powell now called Hadj Ano. The dative or ablative of the Latin noun anus is ano, meaning to or for, from or in the anus.[119]

Other officers in the 13th Hussars enjoyed visiting North Africa, and a few years before Baden-Powell became the Military Secretary on Malta, Walter C. Smithson had asked him to visit the region with him. Smithson would be 'Boy' McLaren's best man in 1898. He and George Noble were both friends of Walter Burton Harris, *The Times*'s correspondent in North Africa. The journalist married briefly in the same year as McLaren, but his marriage was soon annulled on the grounds of non-consummation. Harris was an excellent correspondent, who understood North Africa well and spent most of his time in the society of Arabs.[120] He is reputed to have been a homosexual. North Africa and the Levant offered homosexuals the kind of opportunities which the risks of blackmail and public revulsion made hazardous in England. Baden-Powell later stated that the principal purpose of his Tunisian and Algerian visits had been to collect intelligence material on the French port of Bizerta and a new French field gun being tested in Algeria. I examine the factual basis for these claims in Chapter 4.7 and find them unconvincing. Quite simply he enjoyed being in North Africa.

Baden-Powell's view of sex (not just his attitude towards female sexuality) was intensely fearful. His ferocious lifelong battle against masturbation furnishes the best example of his general horror. He had been born in the year in which William Acton's notorious diatribe, *Functions and Disorders of the Re-Productive Organs*, had appeared; and until the turn of the century most experts still agreed with Acton that masturbation led to insanity, blindness and suicide. But in the early years of the present century doctors of the eminence of Henry Maudsley disowned their earlier views. Not so Baden-Powell, whose antipathy towards masturbation seemed to increase.

In 1908 he had a furious argument with Pearson's, the publisher, and

Horace Cox, the printer, of *Scouting for Boys* about the inclusion in the
body of the book of his attack on 'self-abuse'. Pearson's prevaricated,
Baden-Powell fulminated and Cox simply stopped his presses and
won the day. He considered Baden-Powell's explicit material obscene.
A watered-down version of Baden-Powell's views finally appeared in
the 'Notes to Instructors' section of the book, which was not designed
to be read by boys.[121] The original typescript of the book contained a
far more alarming warning than the one eventually published, of
which the following gives the flavour: 'The result of self-abuse is
always – mind you, always – that the boy after a time becomes weak
and nervous and shy, he gets headaches and probably palpitations of
the heart, and if he carries it on too far he very often goes out of his
mind and becomes an idiot. A very large number of the lunatics in our
asylums have made themselves mad by indulging in this vice although
at one time they were sensible cheery boys like any one of you.'
Furthermore, if a boy 'misused his parts' he would 'not be able to use
them when a man; they will not work then. Remember too that several
awful diseases come from indulgence – one especially that rots away
the insides of men's mouths, their noses, and eyes, etc . . . The next
time you feel the desire coming on, don't give way to it. If you have the
chance, just wash your parts in cold water and cool them down. Wet
dreams come from it especially after eating rich food or too much
meat, or from sleeping with too warm a blanket over your body or in
too soft a bed, or from sleeping on your back. Therefore avoid all
these. Avoid listening to stories or reading or thinking about dirty
subjects . . . Be strong and don't give way to it.'[122]

Today we find it exceptionally puzzling how men who had been to
public schools where masturbation was commonplace could have
subsequently held forth so confidently about the awful dangers of a
process which had clearly left the majority of their schoolfellows
unscathed. Simple hypocrisy is not an adequate explanation. Baden-
Powell called masturbation 'the most dangerous of all vices', and told
Scoutmasters that if they remained silent out of prudishness, it 'would
be little short of a crime'.[123] He genuinely believed in the arguments
put forward by the school of medical opinion which held that 'the
semen not used for propagating the species is naturally absorbed and
transmuted and becomes the parent of many qualities that make a
man'. This meant that a boy 'practising self-abuse is absolutely giving
away his future manhood'. This is how Dr Schofield, sexual adviser to
the Movement, explained matters to those attending the Scoutmasters'
Conference in Manchester in 1911. Baden-Powell fully endorsed his
final infelicitously worded peroration, in which he urged Scoutmasters
'to push prudery on one side, and to take their boys in hand . . .'[124]

Such statements said more about those voicing them than the boys
who were their targets. Only intense fear of sex, and of women, could

have led to this concerted attempt to suppress every manifestation of sexual desire. The fervour of Baden-Powell's lifelong campaign did not weaken even when, in 1930, Dr F. W. W. Griffin, then editor of *The Scouter*, wrote in a book for Rover Scouts of the temptation to masturbate as 'a quite natural stage in development' and suggested that boys should read H. Havelock Ellis's *Little Essays of Love and Virtue*. Ellis's final conclusion was that 'the effort to achieve complete abstinence was a very serious error'.[125]

Baden-Powell's resolute opposition to all attempts to persuade him to relax or qualify his total ban on 'self-abuse' owed a lot to his connection of the habit with 'dirty' talk about women.[126] If boys began to associate girls with sexual pleasure through masturbation, 'the rutting season' would quickly be upon them, swiftly followed by premature 'girlitis'. The male comradeship of the Scouts would thus be threatened. Even the comparatively free-thinking Dr Griffin dreaded the day when 'across the charming prospect of comradeship falls a dreadful shadow – the girl'. Inevitably Baden-Powell's own sexual anxieties were responsible for the intensity of his attack on masturbation. Since he found young men beautiful and women often the reverse, he must himself, when tempted to masturbate, have fantasized about 'clean young men', rather than 'pinkish, whitish, dollish women'.[127] Since interest in sex either seemed likely to lead boys to 'beastliness' with women, or to a propensity for 'the love that dare not speak its name', it had to be curbed and crushed by iron will-power. This was once again a case of Baden-Powell fighting his own battle at one remove. His fury with Pearson's, after their cowardly surrender to the printer over the exclusion of the 'continence' section from the main body of *Scouting for Boys*, had been all the greater because his mother had approved his words on the subject.[128]

When Stephe had been a child, his mother's wishes had become inseparable from his own conscience, which still, in adulthood, demanded 'good behaviour'. Anyone obliged to fight his inclinations as hard as Baden-Powell was, would only have lapsed from strict 'purity' in exceptional circumstances, afterwards working obsessionally to repair the damage by warning others. Even in his dreams, Baden-Powell advised marriage, and tried to whip down the men who might pull him from his high place into their midst, if he let them. Yet, how dangerously he lived. The railway hut and the desert blanket were tightrope temptations only to be dared by a moral gymnast with absolute faith in his will-power and balance.

Havelock Ellis, in those essays sensibly recommended by Dr Griffin of *The Scouter*, argued that sublimation could not 'be carried out easily, completely, or even with unmixed advantage. It is with sexual energy (well observes Freud, who attaches great importance to sublimation) as it is with machines: only a certain proportion can be transformed

into work.' This is extremely well put. It must however be conceded
that his years of advice-giving to soldiers, followed by the invention of
the world's greatest youth movement, offered Baden-Powell scope for
sublimation which Freud himself would have marvelled at.

4

IN THE BALANCE

1. The Ambitious Adjutant (1882–84)

Sir Baker Russell K.C.M.G., K.C.B., Colonel of the 13th Hussars (inevitably known as 'The Baker's Dozen'), believed in giving considerable reponsibility to his officers, not excluding the youngest subalterns. Baden-Powell was deeply impressed by Russell's method of leadership, and would one day profit by following his example. Sir Baker was a passionate but kindly man, at one moment capable of riding down an officer who had annoyed him, at the next of apologizing tearfully for hurting him. A great favourite with Sir Garnet Wolseley, Russell had served under him in Ashanti, in Zululand and most recently in Egypt. He owed his present rank and his two orders of knighthood to these campaigns and to Sir Garnet's influence. Yet Baker Russell was no Staff College military expert. He knew hardly any words of command and despised the drill book, but, in Baden-Powell's judgment, 'had a soldier's eye for the country and for where his men ought to be in a fight'.[1] With his black moustache, thick black eyebrows, booming voice and towering height, Russell was impressively manly. Stephe was captivated:

> I know that if he had ordered me to walk over a cliff or into a fire I
> would have done so without any hesitation . . . He had a magnetic
> attraction which would have led men to do anything that he
> commanded.

Baden-Powell was particularly intrigued by a quality which he described to his brother Frank as Baker Russell's 'humbug'. Frank had had the temerity to speak belittlingly about Sir Baker, whom he had met at one of Henrietta Grace's grand dinners. Baden-Powell was most indignant when Frank called Russell 'a man of small ideas' and pointed to a leader in the St James's Gazette in which 'a humbug' was defined as 'an objectionable and trifling hypocrite'. For Frank's benefit Stephe attempted his own definition of a humbug as 'a man who "groups" various catch-penny "events" to conceal and further some main design'. Lord Palmerston, he explained to Frank, had been a humbug in exactly this sense. Stephe mentioned that he had been reading Voltaire simply in order to appear more cultivated. And what was wrong with that? 'A man may be a bit of a fool, but his main

design is to be thought clever and to get in to good berths in
consequence – therefore he groups a lot of smatterings of various kinds
which catch the public eye in all directions.'[2]

'Grouping' was in fact invented by George and Henrietta Grace, and
would be energetically espoused by Stephe. 'I told you last week,' he
informed his family, 'that I had a tiny little event grouped – but still an
event – and here it is. I drew some little ink and white sketches on the
back of some old menu cards and sent them to the secretary of the
Simla exhibition – telling him I had never learned drawing but merely
sent these to show how easily "effect" could be got by a "beginner"
simply by using ink and white . . .' Not unnaturally the secretary was
bowled over and hung the pictures in a prominent position. 'I wrote a
note presenting them to Bill Beresford [Lord William Beresford,
Military Secretary to the Viceroy of India] but something stayed my
hand, and I tore up the note, for the thought occurred to me – oh well,
never mind what it was – only perhaps Connaught would like
something of the sort to decorate his new home with when he is at
Meerut.'[3] Prince Arthur, Duke of Connaught and Strathearn, was
Queen Victoria's third and favourite son. In the autumn of 1883 he was
appointed Divisional General at Meerut and came out to India with his
shy and awkward young wife, Princess Louise of Prussia.

In 1883 Stephe (or to be more precise one of his *horses*, ridden by a
brother officer) won the Kadir Cup, one of India's two most sought-
after pigsticking trophies. The cup itself remained in the hands of the
Meerut Tent Club, but Baden-Powell instructed his mother to 'look
sharp and have a copy made to put on the mess table when Connaught
comes'.[4] Henrietta Grace went one better and had handles added so
that it could be used as a loving cup and passed from hand to hand to be
admired, as indeed it was, when the Duke dined with the 13th Hussars.
The artless intensity of Stephe's desire to impress the Duke and his
retinue was a demonstration of the art of social climbing on an epic
scale, but his self-mocking awareness of this makes it hard to dislike
him for it.

> The 'events' are slowly developing [he told George, the master-
> tactician, gleefully]. The Duke dined with us the night before last –
> my string band played at dinner and *my* glee club sang after it – and
> *my* Kadir Cup was brought up for his inspection and after dinner he
> and I had a long talk.[5]

Since Stephe had killed roughly twice as many boars as any other
officer in the regiment that year, it fell to him and his friends, McLaren
and Dimond, to take the Duke out on his first pigsticking expedition.[6]
Baden-Powell and McLaren were often asked to dine with the
Connaughts, and Stephe dazzled them with his acting in those hardy
perennials *Whitebait at Greenwich* and *Box and Cox*. This was at Meerut,

and he obtained special leave to stay on there when the regiment returned to Muttra. The Duke's A.D.C., Lord Downe, offered to put him up, and the Duke invited Baden-Powell to dine each evening: 'Last night after dinner en famille we all went off to a dance in the royal carriage, Duke, Duchess, Downe, Lady Fitzgerald, self. Received at the entrance with all honours etc . . . One man in the course of the evening asked me in good faith whether I got much extra pay as extra A.D.C.'[7]

In March the following year, Stephe returned to Meerut for a month's probationary training in the Adjutant-General's office. Lady Downe, who thought 'Mr Baden-Powell such a nice fellow and so clever', asked him to stay again.[8] In comparison with most young officers in India, Stephe was a rare 'find', and the Downes and Connaughts were lucky to have secured such an entertaining guest. He was overwhelmed by his good fortune: 'Here I am close to HRH seeing him every day (he was sitting in my room talking to me while I dressed this-morning) and I am saving money by it! – I don't pay house rent! And I get breakfast provided every day and dinner every night at this house.'[9] For any son of Henrietta Grace, there could have been no greater joy than to live with royalty and to save money at the same time.

His social successes became self-sustaining and soon he was in receipt of regular invitations from no less a person than Lord William Beresford, the Viceroy's Military Secretary. To make sure that his host realized what a talented family he belonged to, Baden-Powell presented him with copies of a recent pamphlet on ballooning by Baden, and George's latest political work, State Aid and State Interference.[10]To be Beresford's guest at Government House in Simla was a heady experience:

> My wig, he did do me well; he has a beautiful complete house . . . furnished like an English home, and everything regardless of expense . . . Do you know, Ma – I find I am getting known in India. Everybody I have been introduced to at Simla has said, 'How are you getting on . . . I suppose you have just come up from the Duke, haven't you? Are you going to send any more of those little sketches to the exhibition this year?' . . . Even the Adjutant-General came up to me . . . and me with a pair of trousers on that I wore at Charterhouse . . .

And Stephe had every reason to be pleased with himself. Not through the 'right connections' but through his own talents, he was mixing on equal terms with the most important officers in India. Although he never lost his sense of humour about his social triumphs, the game he was playing was in earnest. 'These little events that I group, you *must keep quiet,*' he warned his mother, 'and these pages must be burned in which they appear. Yours I tear up religiously.'[11]

Stephe was regularly selling sketches of Indian life to *The Graphic*, and he was also writing a few short stories. In December 1883 he was appointed Brigade-Major at Meerut by Baker Russell for the month's military manoeuvres, thus cutting out six senior officers. This temporary appointment would look impressive in future applications for staff work. Sir Baker was tipped to become the next Inspector General of Cavalry in Britain, or else to get the Cavalry Brigade at Aldershot. If he could then manage to become his A.D.C., Stephe knew that he would be ideally placed for rapid promotion. Such reflections made him tolerant of Sir Baker's foibles; normally a foe to regular drinking, he professed to admire the colonel's habit of downing a bottle of champagne with breakfast and to be amused by his 'preventive' for chills caused by sitting around in sweat-drenched clothes. Russell used to send a butler round the ante-room with a tray crowded with glasses of claret mixed with stout, announcing 'with the colonel's compliments'. 'Think of it – on an empty stomach at about 10 a.m., we were ordered to drink it.'[13]

Stephe did not possess Baker Russell's piercing eyes and commanding good looks, but he shared his love of guile and quick-thinking. As inspecting general at the Meerut cavalry manoeuvres, the Duke of Connaught spotted some of Baker Russell's guns going off in the wrong direction, doubling the distance they should have had to travel. When asked why his guns were being misdirected, Russell smiled imperturbably. '"You will find, Sir, that by the shorter way they would come across heavy ploughland, and in the middle of it a stream eight feet wide and five deep, and they are now going for a crossing a mile higher up where there is a house and in which they will post a look-out with signalling apparatus." "Dear me," replied the Duke, "do you know all the country as well?" "Well, Sir, Mr Baden-Powell has been over it with his scouts, and made a map of it, which I am using now."'[14] This was pure invention.

Baker Russell taught Stephe that whether he was right or wrong, if he could only assume a confident and masterful demeanour triumph could usually be wrested from disaster. Had Baker Russell ever been shut up in Mafeking, he would doubtless have bluffed the Boers as convincingly as his brilliant young subaltern was destined to do. It must have occurred to Baden-Powell that someone as adept at deception as Baker Russell might not always prove a dependable patron. At any rate, in spite of his habitual optimism, he made up his mind during the mid-1880s never to be without a 'second string to his bow'. In India this 'second string' would be the lectures which he first began to deliver to his men during the early summer of 1882, and which he decided to get published a year later.[15] Given the good use to which George had put his various publications, Stephe's ambitions for his book – which he had decided to call *Reconnaissance and Scouting* – were not surprising. In April 1884, after several setbacks, he confessed to George that he was desperate to get it published. 'If it did not sell to the extent of 20 copies – it would be a grand advertisement for me – because I could send copies to all the boss Quarter-Master-Generals, Wolseleys, etc., asking if they approve of it.'[16] George rapidly clinched a publishing deal and then encouraged Stephe to start work on a book about pigsticking, which would appeal to most high-ranking officers and could be dedicated to the Duke of Connaught. Not to be outdone, Henrietta Grace ordered 10,000 handbills which she intended to ask the publisher of *Reconnaissance and Scouting* to mail to all the officers on the Army List, drawing her son's book to their attention.[17] 'How much does it cost to get F.R.G.S. [Fellow of the Royal Geographical Society] or some such bundle of initials put after one's name?' Stephe asked his mother, with the title page in mind.[18] He remained constantly on the look-out for foreign cavalry manuals. 'Material for a book can of course be obtained from the many other existing books on the subject.'[19] Although, from the context, it is fairly clear that Baden-Powell did not intend to acknowledge his 'borrowings', there is an ingenuous almost schoolboyish glee in this, as in all his 'dodges' for getting on, which disarms ridicule.

In the first week of January 1884, Stephe celebrated his optimistic hopes by sending his mother a curious drawing. It was of an octopus with six rather than eight arms, five of them representing Henrietta Grace's sons, with Baden Henry making up the sixth. Henrietta Grace herself was depicted as 'the eyes directing the whole' as the octopus, propelled by its achievement-conscious arms, clambered up the ladder of fame.[20]

Several months later Stephe told his mother that all she would need to do from now onwards would be 'to sit down with folded hands and . . . watch us racing for honours. We are all started fair and all doing well . . . Only give a man a standard and he can always work up to it – tell W[arington] he has got to pay the house rent and I bet he does it.'[21] With the extra pay he derived from his positions as adjutant and musketry instructor, and with money earned by his books and the drawings he was regularly sending to *The Graphic*, Stephe was almost managing to live within his means, but he still needed occasional infusions of cash from his family. Recognition of his dependence did not however prevent him from handing out advice to his brothers; Baden was his favourite target, with Frank a close second. 'One thing I can do,' he told his mother in March 1881, 'is see the faults of others – so while they are occupied in their different lines, I'll look on, and correct or encourage as I see it may be necessary.'[22]

He rebuked Baden for dressing badly, for getting a second class in the Hythe Musketry Course and for buying a cheap 'Davis' saddle for his horse. He ought at once to pull out the rivet-heads with 'Davis' stamped on them and hammer in plain ones instead. Baden might think snobbery absurd when it concerned itself with saddles, but he ought to realize that he could blight his chances of promotion by failing to appreciate the importance attached to such trivia.[23] Frank, meanwhile, stood accused of spending too much money on luxuries and of failing to recognize that beggars should not presume to be choosers. 'If he gets a commission he [Frank] shouldn't chuck away the chance whatever the subject. Woodcuts pay well, are instructive and not below a good artist.' And on the same theme: 'He ought to stoop to "low" art till he can pay his way.'[24] By setting himself up as mentor to Frank and Baden, Stephe would have known that he was winning his mother's approval. On a deeper level, he was mitigating the feelings of inferiority caused by her neglect after Baden's birth and during Augustus's long illness.

Nobody could fault Henrietta Grace for being lacking in energy; but Stephe was sometimes horrified to hear that she had not been careful enough of her own dignity – for example, driving in a landau drawn by a single horse. There were only 'two decent possibilities for a lady's one-horse-carriage,' he told her, 'a miniature brougham or a Victoria'.[25] Stephe was not always consistent. Too great an interest in social good form and 'society' matters was the principal fault he found in his brother officer, Captain T. G. Cuthell, and his wife: 'She is an *awful* woman and he is an *awful ass.*' Cuthell on one occasion read out a passage from one of his wife's letters about Mrs Spilling, another officer's wife. 'She sports a Victoria and pair, which is rather handsome – I think she must have come into some money lately . . .' Many years later Baden-Powell, who admired people with acute deductive powers, would have had to admit that he had underestimated Mrs Cuthell. When the same Mrs Spilling died she left a substantial sum of money, much of which passed on her husband's death to Stephe's two daughters. Mrs Cuthell, awful woman or not, wrote successful books about Indian life; and her husband gained immortality, of a sort, through his stomach-turning articles on taxidermy in *The Boy's Own Paper.*[26]

By appearing to be more brilliant and capable than everyone around him, Stephe managed to convey an impression of supreme self-confidence. During the summer of 1883 he had turned down an offer to be A.D.C. to his uncle Henry Smyth, now a Lieutenant-General. 'If I were an ordinary subaltern I might take it,' he had told his mother regally.[27] But a year later, he was having to face up to the consequences of his pride. With no stepping-stone appointment in sight, he seemed on the point of returning to an England so much more expensive than India that he would be obliged to live on hand-outs from his family.

Then on 13 November 1884, the 13th Hussars received orders to sail for South Africa rather than England as expected. Against all expectations this extra duty in Natal would last ten months during which time Stephe's sustaining faith that talent and drive alone would be enough to bring success was to be severely tested.

2. Marking Time (1885)

The 13th Hussars had been ordered to the British colony of Natal as a warning to the leaders of the Boer republics of the Transvaal and the Orange Free State. Ever since the 1830s, when the abolition of slavery throughout the British Empire had encouraged thousands of the descendants of the original Dutch settlers to 'trek' away eastwards from the Cape Colony with their wagons and oxen, the relations of Great Britain with the Boer republics (which owed their origins to this exodus) had been calamitous. The Transvaal and the Orange Free State were annexed by Britain in 1877, a quarter of a century after being granted their independence. Four years later this led to war. After an incompetently conducted campaign on the British side, Gladstone decided not to embark upon a major conflict. Instead, his Government granted to the Transvaalers 'complete self-government, subject to the suzerainty of Her Majesty'.[1] Unfortunately the Boers would one day mistake this magnanimity for inherent weakness, with disastrous consequences. Before that, however, in 1884 (the year of Stephe's arrival in Natal), the Boers threatened to intensify their long-standing attempts to expand to the north and west, carving up the lands of the Bechuana tribes.

General Sir Charles Warren was sent to Bechuanaland with 5,000 men to call a final halt to this process. The 13th Hussars had been ordered to Natal so as to be there – in readiness to support Warren – should the Boers decide to fight. From the moment of landing, Stephe's prayer was for war. He knew that to gain promotion to the highest positions in the army he would either have to pass the Staff College exam (which his weakness in mathematics made unlikely) or distinguish himself on 'active service'.[2] In April 1884, while still in India, he had been relieved to have an excuse for getting out of sitting for the Staff College. Whether the concussion he suffered after a riding fall could really have set him back sufficiently to justify pulling out seems very doubtful, since he only lost a week; so his old fear of examinations – dating back to the Oxford débâcle – was the real culprit. With the Staff College closed to him, a war was vital. But the Boers churlishly decided to negotiate with Warren.

Baden-Powell's friend George Noble shared a house with him and McLaren for part of their time in Natal, and his description of the

regiment's arrival conveys a mood of despondency which set the tone
for the future. It was raining hard, they had no horses, and were in a
place neither near enough to a decent-sized town to be entertaining
from a social point of view, nor sufficiently far out in the wilds to offer
good shooting.[3] Pinetown was a straggling settlement fifteen miles
from Durban, boasting a general store, a church and a few tin-roofed
clapboard houses. With the prospects for war growing daily less
promising and McLaren despatched to Cape Town for a garrison
course, Stephe soon felt depressed and lonely. He did not even have the
pleasure of pigsticking to console him; nor could the place provide a
polo ground, since the countryside was too rough and hilly.[4]

Yet dreary and depressing though his brief South African interlude
undoubtedly was, it was significant in several ways. Exactly why
George Baden-Powell became interested in South Africa remains
uncertain, but it seems likely that after his successes in Australia and, in
1882, in the West Indies, he needed to stake out a new arena for his
talents in colonial diplomacy. Henrietta Grace may well have
suggested South Africa, since in the autumn of 1883 she had held a
dinner for the Prime Minister of the Cape Colony when he visited
London. Other guests had been the editor of *The Times*; Sir Robert
Herbert, Permanent Under-Secretary at the Colonial Office; the Earl
of Kimberley, Secretary of State for India, and the Financial Secretary
to the Treasury. Although George had no official position of any kind,
Henrietta Grace had somehow managed to lure these exalted men to
her table – and very impressive their names looked when listed in the
newspapers. George's ultimate ambition was to be appointed High
Commissioner at the Cape. In pursuit of this distant objective, he
sailed for South Africa in February 1885, recognizing that first-hand
knowledge of the situation in the Transvaal in the meantime offered
other opportunities for government employment, especially if – as
seemed likely – he was to be chosen as a Conservative parliamentary
candidate. The expenses for George's trip were to be met by a series of
articles which he had been commissioned to write for *The Times*. After
staying with the Governor at the Cape, George pressed on to
Kimberley where he stayed with Cecil Rhodes. These contacts, he
assured Henrietta Grace, would soon secure 'something for Stephe to
do here'.[5]

At the time Stephe was trying to join a regiment of irregulars which
seemed sure to be sent to Egypt – another potential battle-ground.
George urged him to drop this plan, since he mistakenly believed that
the 13th Hussars would themselves soon be sent to Egypt. While
staying with Rhodes, George had followed his usual procedure of
informing the local press of his movements; a newspaper reporting his
sojourn with the diamond king thus chanced to reach Sir Charles
Warren's breakfast table in Bechuanaland. The General, who had been

worried about having to write a lengthy official report on the Bechuanaland crisis in relation to the region's future economic prospects, was overjoyed to learn that a man possessing the ideal qualities to produce such a report was not only close at hand but apparently lacking other occupation. He telegraphed at once asking George to join him at Mafeking. George did so poste haste, and from that small town wrote to his mother in early April asking her to inform as many British newspapers as possible that: 'George Baden-Powell C.M.G. is with General Sir Charles Warren in northern Bechuanaland visiting the great native chiefs of our new Protectorate in the interior of Africa.'[6]

Had Bechuanaland been allowed to fall into the hands of the Boers, British expansion in southern Africa would have been at an end. Cecil Rhodes had known this all too well, and his representations had played a major role in persuading the British Government to proclaim a protectorate over Bechuanaland. George Baden-Powell therefore arrived at a key moment in South Africa's history and, with his usual knack of falling on his feet, had met all the principal participants and managed to write himself into the action. 'I have just sent a capital letter to Lord Stanley,' he told his admiring mother. George was never afraid to knock on the door, nor to buttonhole any potentially useful individual. Joseph Chamberlain, who had been waylaid in just this fashion, described George as 'the most conceited young man I have ever met in the whole course of my life'.[7] Fortunately Rhodes and Warren thought differently.

By the end of June, George was staying with Stephe in Pinetown and telling him that Sir Charles Warren was sure to need the services of the military members of the Baden-Powell family for his next 'little war'. For Stephe, rotting in Pinetown in his glorified tin shed, the arrival of his all-conquering elder brother was an apocalyptic experience.[8] How could he have worried so much about trifles like the Staff College when George, who had come out with nothing to do, had nevertheless ended up rendering services which might yet be rewarded with a knighthood? George brought news that the family had bought a celebrated old sailing yawl, the *Pearl*, which had been built for the Marquess of Anglesey in 1820. Warington was already winning races and the yacht not only promised to be a significant social asset but was large enough to accommodate the family in the winter when their house was let. Moreover, George told Stephe that when he was in Parliament, as he was sure he soon would be, he meant to use his influence to forward both his younger brothers' careers. Stephe naturally did what he could to impress George and succeeded. 'I rode out with Stephe yesterday,' George informed his mother, 'he having charge of a parade of the regiment. He looked a long way the smartest of the lot; spoke the loudest and clearest, and was as calm as could be. He has piles of office

work which all melt away in double-quick time; and he is evidently the
Colonel's right-hand man in every way."[9]

Just before George's arrival, Stephe had telegraphed to Lord Downe
and Lord William Beresford begging for employment in Afghanistan.
But these requests, like his pleas to be sent to Egypt, fell upon deaf
ears.[10] Therefore George's presence provided a much-needed tonic. 'I
am awfully surprised to hear in detail how well the family is getting
on,' he told Henrietta Grace, admitting in another letter that he was
'afraid of being left behind'.[11]

At Pinetown, with time on his hands, Stephe wrote a manual
entitled *Cavalry Instruction*, which was published to excellent specialist
reviews later in the year. He also undertook a scouting and surveying
expedition which he deliberately surrounded in mystery, describing it
as a secret mission to establish the number of passes through the
Drakensberg Mountains on the border with the Transvaal. He grew a
beard and wore rough clothes, but never kept his presence a secret
from Boer farmers. They were expected to believe that he was a
newspaper correspondent 'writing up the country from an emigration
point of view' – an occupation which, if true, would hardly have won
him friends.[12] 'Keep it dark,' he ordered George dramatically, 'not a
word to a soul.'[13] Since George was moving about, it was extremely
naïve of Baden-Powell to send him 'secret' information without any
guarantee that it would actually reach him. Many years later Stephe
told his secretary, Mrs Wade, that Sir George White would not have
made such a disastrous start to the Boer War if he had seen the maps
which he himself had made in 1885.[14] Baden-Powell dreamed up this
secret mission himself, without any orders, his aim being to send in a
report to the War Office and thus draw attention to himself as a suitable
candidate for intelligence missions. To this end he also sent a copy of
Reconnaissance and Scouting to the Quarter-Master-General.

Another trip made by Stephe in 1885 would deepen his interest in
scouting and the open-air life. He went on safari with four officers and
an experienced Durban-based big-game hunter, Reuben Beningfield.
They travelled by steamship to the old Arab slave port of Inhambane,
near Lourenço Marques in Portuguese Mozambique, and then
proceeded inland. Between July and September they shot numerous
hippopotami, koodoos, wildebeeste and impala. Stephe kept a bushcraft diary for the benefit of his young soldiers, filled with numerous
hints about tracking. 'I found my way back by sun and landmarks . . .
all diverging tracks having been marked with a few strokes in the sand
to show that they were not to be followed (tip for advanced Scouts).'
He was already planning an 'Instruction Book' for Scouts, which
would be published fourteen years later as *Aids to Scouting for N.C.O.s
and Men*. The most famous 'yarn' arising from this trip (Baden-Powell
would tell it again and again) was how he acquired the African

nickname of M'hlalapanzi: 'the man who lies down to shoot'.[15] Since the hippopotami often stayed submerged with just their nostrils, eyes and ears above water, Baden-Powell lay on his back 'in order to get a steadier aim', with his rifle cradled between his thighs and the barrel resting on his genitals. The impression he gave in his autobiography was that the nickname was a compliment since the word had the subsidiary meaning of 'the man who lays his plans carefully before putting them into practice'.[16] In fact his interpretation of African expressions was notoriously unreliable. In his diary he reported that many Africans 'shrieked with laughter' when mentioning his nickname, and would beg him to enact it, whereupon they would laugh even louder.[17] And who could blame them? He looked exactly like a man whose penis was a gun (see drawing in first photo–section). I cannot imagine any more striking illustration of Baden-Powell's long quest for virile confirmation than this self-portrait with his gun between his legs. The wish-fulfilling aspects of the 'yarn' are underlined by the fact that it was a partial fabrication. He was actually first called M'hlalapanzi not while aiming at a hippopotamus but when he lay down to fire at a paper target, while still in the town of Inhambane.[18]

The 13th Hussars sailed for England in the first week of October 1885. Just as had happened in Lucknow when Stephe parted with the Christie girls, here in Pinetown he left behind several sad young girls – among them the vicar's daughter, Nancy Robinson, who half a century later remembered Stephe playing leapfrog on the verandah of his house with McLaren and Noble, and entertaining her 'in our wilderness of a garden, with tracking games among the fruit trees and the tall grass'.[19]

3. 'A Fresh Start' (1885–87)

'So we have all to make a fresh start in life, trusting now solely to our own energies to organize victory.'[1]

Henrietta Grace Baden-Powell, 1887

The 13th Hussars landed at Portsmouth on 4 November 1885, and entrained for Norwich the following day. After the bright sunlight of India and the steamy humidity of Natal, Stephe quite enjoyed the rain and fog of an English winter.[2] The cost of living was less pleasing. At home he would never be able to afford a single polo pony, let alone a string. Worse still, unless he was able to sell a constant stream of articles and sketches he would soon have to ask his mother for financial help. Since she was already obliged to live for six months at a time in Shoreham Basin aboard the Pearl, while her house was let, the idea of asking for cash was not an appealing one. 'I am miserable,' he told her, 'on account of your loneliness on that yacht in spite of all of us being in England.'[3]

As in the past, most of Henrietta Grace's attention was focused upon George, who had been selected as Tory candidate for a Liverpool parliamentary seat. In the run-up to polling day in this by-election, George was for several days the house guest of Lord Stanley, the Colonial Secretary. He wrote to his mother joyfully: 'At last one of your sons is staying with a Secretary of State on most friendly terms . . . a great success scored for the whole family.'[4] But George had still not been paid by the Government for his work in Bechuanaland and, more seriously for the family's finances, an economic recession had affected Warington's income by reducing the amount of litigation in the Admiralty Court.[5] The by-election cost George all the money he had made in the previous six months. Henrietta Grace wrote appealing to her brothers and sisters for minimum donations of £50 each, but to her disgust none gave more than £25.[6] On 25 November George was elected to Parliament, but since members were not paid a salary he would still have to be made a junior minister if the family's precarious finances were to improve.

Only a week after her son's triumph, Henrietta Grace learned that the substantial inheritance which she had hoped would pass to her children on the death of Professor Powell's spinster sisters would in fact remain with the Speldhurst branch of the family. George counselled courage: 'We never have got much from dead people – we must make it for ourselves and will.'[7] This was all very well for George to say after costing the family more than anyone else. He would again require money when a General Election was called during the following summer. In the meantime Frank had sold a marine painting for the genuinely magnificent sum of £400 and, instead of giving the lion's share to his mother, had taken himself off to Venice. Henrietta Grace wrote explaining to him how important it was for them all that he should finish at least two large Venetian subjects before he returned home. She also rebuked him for turning down commissions from steamship companies, which Warington had laboured hard to secure for him.[8] She appealed to Frank, as the son with the highest earning potential, to save the family. After reminding him of the lost inheritance, she penned her memorable rallying call about 'trusting now solely to our own energies to organize victory'. Frank did not reply. The Venetian paintings were not completed, and when they finally were ten years later, it was Henrietta Grace herself who bought them.[9]

Meanwhile Stephe faced a nightmarish dilemma. In order to work on his weak mathematics and French for the Staff College examination, now only six months away, he would have to give up the adjutancy. This would briefly oblige him to leave the regiment, since all eight regimental troops already had captains. Until one of these eight officers left the regiment there would be no troop for him, and in the meantime he would only receive half-pay of £10 per month. 'Will that pay my share of expenses at No. 8?' he asked his mother anxiously. 'I can get clothes etc. out of reviews, sketches in *The Graphic* etc . . .'[10] He begged George to ask Sir Charles Warren to take him on to his staff when he left for the Sudan. Warren obliged George and offered Stephe a post. But would this amount to genuine 'active service' – the only alternative to the Staff College for rapid promotion? Stephe thought Warren's appointment looked more like a Resident Commissioner's job than a campaigning general's. In the meantime George and Stephe believed that Sir Baker Russell was on the point of being given command of the Cavalry Brigade at Aldershot. If this happened, Stephe would be sure to become his A.D.C. But alas for him, Russell was only appointed to the Aldershot command three years later and in the interval, in spite of Stephe's despatch of photographs of himself, and other ploys to remind his patron of his existence, Sir Baker did not make him an offer even when he took command of the Cavalry Brigade at Shorncliffe. Because Stephe had been so confident that his old colonel would help him, he had instructed George to 'tell Warren that I have as good as got a good thing at Aldershot (so I have, for Lady Russell has asked me to go and stay there from Saturday to Monday next).' He could not have been more wrong.[11]

Then six months later he failed the Staff College examination, blaming a bout of fever.[12] If this sounds suspiciously like the convenient concussion which he had suffered just before his last attempt in India, it should be recorded that Baden-Powell had definitely contracted malaria in Mozambique during the previous summer. How he must have cursed himself for rejecting Warren! His position had now become desperate. He managed to get back into the regiment as a captain commanding a squadron but was unable to avoid sliding into debt. In February 1887 he had to ask his mother to settle his mess bill. 'How I do hate this begging and borrowing . . . I keep on the look-out for ADCships or anything to pay.'[13] In July Stephe tried every trick he knew to get himself chosen as A.D.C. to the Duke of Connaught. But in vain.

With his career apparently doomed to prolonged stagnation, he reactivated a plan which had first occurred to him in 1883. He had hoped then that, by sending to the Quarter-Master-General a published version of his reconnaissance lectures, he would be marked down as a likely candidate for the Intelligence Branch 'to send out suddenly to any country, with whom we may be on bad terms, to sketch and report on from a military point of view'.[14] Within a month of returning to England from South Africa, he told his mother that he had hopes that the War Office might send him to the Prussian manoeuvres as an official British observer.[15] He wrote to General H. Brackenbury, the new Director of Military Intelligence, but failed to persuade the man to place him on his 'list of eligible young men'.[16] Stephe therefore decided to visit the Continent in a private capacity. International relations in Europe were tense during the 1880s. A Franco-Russian *entente* had been the inevitable response to the secret Austro-German alliance of 1879. British relations with France were vitiated by conflicting interests in Africa, and Russia's ambitions in Afghanistan and the Levant made friendly relations with the Tsar impossible. The decade was a highly significant one in the history of repeating weapons. Machine-guns like the Nordenfeld marked an enormous advance from the earlier Gatling guns. In 1884 Hiram J. Maxim invented a machine-gun in which the energy of discharge furnished the operating power. The Maxim and its Vickers modification – both of them British – were to spawn an entire new generation of competing weapons. Adventure writers would soon be weaving plots involving stolen plans and secret weapons.[17]

Romantic enthusiasm and the hope of being favourably noticed were together responsible for Baden-Powell's decision to attend the German and the Russian manoeuvres in the summer of 1886. Thanks to a friend whose family owned a shipping company, Stephe and his brother Baden sailed from Hull to Hamburg without having to pay. Baden, who was still in the Scots Guards, was an expert on military observation balloons, and was therefore known as 'the balloonatic' within the family.[18]

Whatever image Stephe and Baden had of themselves as they set out, it would not have been as spies. Both men took their full dress and undress uniforms with them, as well as their own passports. Neither of them spoke more than a few words of Russian, and their mastery of German was not impressive. On arrival in Germany, far from attempting to conceal their nationality they went to see the British Military Attaché in Berlin, and on arrival in Russia sought out the British Ambassador in St Petersburg. On 18 August Stephe wrote to George telling him that the Ambassador had been 'gracious but no help', and that A. J. Herbert, the second secretary, was 'an ass not knowing anything nor able to help in any way'.[19] From Herbert's point of view the Baden-Powell brothers were an embarrassment. The British War Office had only obtained clearance for three officers to attend the Russian manoeuvres, and the Ambassador thought it would arouse unnecessary suspicions if the Foreign Office were now to seek clearance for two more 'official' observers at such a late stage. Stephe and Baden had counted on paying for their trip by writing about the manoeuvres on their return, which would be impossible if they were barred.

Fortunately hordes of civilians flocked to get a good view of the proceedings in both Germany and Russia. Since manoeuvres by their nature took place in vast areas extending over many square miles, it was beyond the capabilities of the military authorities to exclude unauthorized observers, or to pick out foreigners from the mass of local camp-followers.

From Berlin Stephe wrote telling George that Baden had managed to get a good view of the German ballooning experiments, while he himself had visited Spandau before dawn for the purpose of 'timing the firing experiments with repeating rifles, which we could not get to see'.[20] He said nothing in this letter about being questioned by a sentry close to the scene of these firing trials, nor of being obliged to feign drunkenness in order to escape arrest. This more colourful version of events appeared later, in 1915, in *My Adventures as a Spy*, and in the manuscript (but not the published version) of his autobiography.[21] Since he had risked telling his brother that he had been timing rifle trials, he must have thought his letters safe from scrutiny and would surely have mentioned his adventure with the sentry if it had indeed taken place. The only reliable account of their exploits is contained in a letter to George written by Stephe during the sea journey back to England.

> During our 10 days we were run in 3 times! The police and officials all knew us and we presumed that our letters were being opened so we daren't write much for you or for the papers. But we have done well – we saw *everything*: much more than our official officers saw – because one day was set apart for secret experiments from which they were requested to keep away – and needless to say we were there and saw everything. The last night of all just as I was returning homewards, somehow I got caught about midnight, and was sent back there and then under charge of an officer to St Petersburg: but by extraordinary good luck B[aden] was not with me at that moment, so he was able to go on and see what there was to be seen next morning. However complaints had come against us – one on account of Baden drawing a caricature of an old gentleman in the train – and we found ourselves known to the police and everybody; and Herbert [second secretary British Legation St Petersburg] advised us to make our way out of the country, so we found out when the steamer sailed and then gave out in the hearing of the hotel detective that we were going by train and off we went to Cronstadt and nipped on board and got passed out by the police officer there.[22]

To have attracted the attention of the police so many times in so short a visit was remarkably careless, and Stephe must have found it very galling to have to take advice from 'the ass' Herbert.

He made an exciting narrative of these events in the published version of his autobiography, in which he described his capture. He and Baden had gone separately to witness some searchlight experiments on the last night of the manoeuvres at Krasnoe Selo outside St Petersburg. Since the Tsar was going to be present, Stephe must have known – given the contemporary terror of anarchists – that the Russian secret police would be sure to be particularly vigilant. Leaving after the trials, Baden-Powell recalled seeing the carriage lights of the Tsar's entourage approaching a fort against which there was to be a mock attack.

> As the first carriage passed me I did a stupid thing; I bowed my head to avoid being recognised. This made the occupants of the carriage suspicious. They were Staff Officers. They stopped the carriage, promptly seized me and hustled me into it and drove on without a word . . . Then they questioned me as to who I was and why I was there and finally handed me over on arrival at the fort to some officers in the garrison. I truthfully told them that I was an Englishman, that I'd been looking on at the manoeuvres as a spectator and had lost my way to the station, and I should be glad if they would direct me how to get there. They did that by sending me back in charge of an officer to be handed over to the police and to be removed to the capital . . . There I was placed in open arrest, that is allowed to live in an hotel, but not allowed to leave the town. I was there befriended by a German officer who was acting as waiter in the hotel for reasons of his own, and he kindly told me which of the hotel frequenters was the detective specially charged with watching me. I received warning that I had better get away without delay as the charges against me would mean five years imprisonment without trial, but that arrangements had been made with the captain of an English ship, sailing from a neighbouring port, to take my brother and myself as members of his crew. I evaded the attentions of the watchful detective, and we made our way devious so as to put any follower off the scent, and succeeded in getting on board ship, where we passed muster, when passports were examined, by lining up with the crew.[23]

A striking difference between these two accounts (the latter written nearly 50 years after the events described) is the way in which Mr Herbert's all-important role is eliminated in the published narrative. The claim that Stephe and his brother had needed to line up with the crew when passports were examined is clearly false, since in the letter to George Stephe had stated that he and Baden had been 'passed out by the police officer there' (i.e. at Cronstadt where they boarded ship). If the Russian authorities had thought Stephe anything more than a nuisance, they would have imprisoned him. By leaving him under partial observation and then dropping a hint to the British Ambassador

that the brothers should be advised to leave, the Russians rid
themselves of two inquisitive foreigners without having to face the
diplomatic consequences of charging them. Since the brothers had
been kept as virtual prisoners, Herbert could only have learned about
their predicament from the Russian police. This embarrassing fact
explains Baden-Powell's decision to omit all mention of Herbert's
help.

Because the report that Stephe sent to the War Office describing
what he and Baden had observed no longer exists in the War Office
records, it is impossible to estimate the military value of the
brothers' observations – although the Adjutant-General, Lord
Wolseley, would soon thank them warmly for their 'creditable and
interesting report on the Russian manoeuvres'.[24] In November Stephe
wrote to his mother telling her that 'an order has come out that all
officers attending foreign manoeuvres on leave are to do so in
uniform!'[25] If Stephe's and Baden's adventures were in part responsible for this order (as Stephe obviously suspected) Wolseley
would soon show that he was undismayed. If the blunders are
forgotten, along with Stephe's subsequent distortions, the trip to
Germany and Russia gave evidence of considerable daring.

Stephe betrayed no embarrassment over his brief detention; and
only a week after his return to England he wrote to General Sir Evelyn
Wood, his divisional G.O.C., suggesting that he be sent to the next
German manoeuvres.[26] Wood decided not to forward the request to
General Brackenbury, but Baden-Powell took the decision philo-
sophically. The manoeuvres had after all given him an excellent excuse
to bring himself once more to Wood's attention. Sir Evelyn was a close
friend of Sir Garnet Wolseley and had served under him in Ashanti and
Zululand. By gaining Wood's favour, he could hope to gain
Wolseley's.

Several months earlier Wood had inspected the regiment at
Colchester; and Baden-Powell had successfully demonstrated that, in
situations where silence was essential, hand signals could be employed
as effectively as trumpet calls to direct cavalry. In November Stephe
managed to sell to Sir Evelyn a scheme for teaching private soldiers
mapwork and reconnaissance.[27] Three months later Henrietta Grace
informed Frank that, 'Stephe is back at Colchester to carry out his new
plan, which Sir Evelyn Wood consented to . . . and about which he has
sent news to Lord Wolseley.'[28] Both Stephe and his mother had been
trying to attract the recently ennobled Wolseley's attention for the best
part of four years.

Chance had given him George Noble as a brother officer and a close
friend; and in February 1886 Stephe stayed at the Nobles' mansion just
outside Newcastle. George's father Sir Andrew was a director of
Armstrong's, which was already second only to Krupp in the

manufacture of armaments. Baden-Powell was taken round Armstrong's works twice during his stay with the Nobles, and on both occasions was shown 'the whole manufacture of machine-guns'.[29] Then in 1887, when his squadron was stationed at Seaforth outside Liverpool, Stephe became involved in preparations for a military tournament to celebrate Queen Victoria's Golden Jubilee. In view of his skills as an organizer of amateur theatricals, it was hardly surprising that his major contribution to the tournament should be a dramatized 'military entertainment'. With machine-guns very much in mind after his time in Newcastle, he now sought out Mr Torsten Nordenfeld, the inventor of the gun which bore his name. Stephe thought that a 'Nordenfeld' mounted on a 'galloping carriage' would add spice and drama to his tournament entertainment. Mr Nordenfeld agreed and lent him a gun.[30] Before the tournament, Baden-Powell practised driving this gun 'over the rough country and sand-dunes' along the coast at Seaforth.

At the tournament the machine gun stole the show. Baden-Powell's dramatic entertainment opened with scouts advancing cautiously in search of the enemy and reached its climax with a mock fight involving the Nordenfeld. After displays of wrestling and swordsmanship, there was an exhibition of 'gun driving'. A few days later Stephe was in barracks when his sergeant burst into his quarters and blurted out that Lord Wolseley was outside on the barrack square asking for Captain Baden-Powell. Stephe went out imagining himself to be the victim of a practical joke, but he was not. Wolseley, who had heard about the 'gun driving' at the tournament, wanted to know whether Nordenfeld guns could be drawn by horses across rough country. Baden-Powell immediately had the gun brought out and the horses harnessed. Minutes later they were rumbling out of the barracks together, 'Lord Wolseley sitting on the gun and I on the rear-wheeler . . . I took him straight up over the dunes, a real up and down switchback performance, which made him hang on tight to the handstraps . . .' Not long afterwards an ecstatic Stephe wrote to George: 'I have had a great event: a private letter from Wolseley.'[31]

Dear Captain Baden-Powell,
    A recent inspection of the handling of the machine-guns attached to the several regiments of Cavalry at Aldershot was anything but a success, attributable apparently to the defective training of the detachments. I am anxious that this defect be remedied, and I wish you, as one of the few officers of the Army who have the requisite knowledge, to do so. It will be necessary for you to be at Aldershot for about a fortnight, and I want you to let me know when it will be convenient for you to go there.

Yours truly,
Wolseley.[32]

Stephe duly went to Aldershot in late November. He spent a fortnight working with Mr Nordenfeld and the officers and men of the 5th Lancers and 18th Hussars on the best way to use Nordenfeld machine-guns, which had just been adopted for the British cavalry. A major problem was how to release the gun quickly if it was attacked while being driven. Stephe's response illustrates his capacity for ingenuity and occasional unscrupulousness. He himself thought of the basic principles for 'a quick-release harness', but could not work out the detail nor the kind of couplings required. However, through his earlier acquaintance with the men of the Clerkenwell Fire Brigade he was able to solve the problem. He took out one of the senior firemen, who was an expert in harnessing horses to equipment, and bought him a stiff drink in a local public house. 'In a few minutes he had grasped what I wanted and had suggested with a rough explanatory drawing, a very practical form of attachment which exactly met the case. I was then able to design a completely new form of harness which was ultimately adopted; and I received £100 for it.'[33]

By the time Stephe left Aldershot he had carved himself a niche in Lord Wolseley's memory, but it remained impossible to calculate when the Adjutant-General might decide to offer him specific employment. That might still depend upon his passing the wretched Staff College exam or managing to gain experience of 'active service'. But it now looked most unlikely that he would be able to afford to stay in the regiment long enough to do either.

When George was appointed British Arbitrator in the Behring Sea fisheries dispute, Stephe wrote asking his brother to take him to Canada as his secretary. He hoped to combine the work with some money-making travel journalism and as much reading for the Staff College as he could fit in. Unfortunately George had already engaged everyone he needed.[34]

At this moment of crisis Uncle Henry Smyth's job as Commandant of the Royal Military Academy, Woolwich, came to an end. Like his mother, Stephe had always been dismissive of his uncle, who had remained a colonel for over a decade. In the years before her brother's marriage when he was nearly 50, Henrietta Grace had often joked about his inability to find a wife.[35] Apart from thinking him humourless and slow-witted, the Baden-Powells also considered him pathologically mean.[36] It therefore astounded Henrietta Grace and her clever sons when Uncle Henry suddenly announced that he had landed the plum appointment of Commander-in-Chief in the Cape Colony.

They had no means of knowing it but Stephe, George and Henrietta Grace, by their joint endeavours with Lord Wolseley and Sir Evelyn Wood, had already secured for Stephe interest which would bear spectacular fruit when these two men came together as Commander-in-Chief of the British Army and Adjutant-General in 1895. But they had lit an extremely slow-burning fuse and in the meantime Stephe would have to remain in the army. Neither he nor his family saw any way of achieving this without the kind of increase in pay that an A.D.C.'s job would bring. Uncle Henry must have struck them as an improbable *deus ex machina*, but that is what he turned out to be.

On 30 December 1887, two weeks after gratefully accepting his uncle's offer, Captain R. S. S. Baden-Powell A.D.C. sailed from Portsmouth aboard the S.S. *Pretoria* bound for South Africa. That a young man of such prodigious energy and ambition should have required this straightforward piece of nepotism to survive in the service says much about the difficulties of rising solely by merit in the late Victorian army.

Less than a month after Stephe sailed, George was appointed Joint Commissioner in Malta, his brief being to make recommendations for a new Maltese constitution. He received a knighthood before he left the island. 'So all has come as it should,' he wrote to Henrietta Grace, 'the grand result of many grouped events . . . Years of work have now come to their first harvest.'[37] Within weeks the new knight was cannily putting together an anti-Home Rule book from the speeches and essays of the great, coupling his own name as editor with theirs. On publication Lord Wolseley would be the first to receive a copy. In this way, George worked in Stephe's absence to ensure that the future Field-Marshal kept Captain Baden-Powell's name in mind.[38]

4. With Uncle Henry and the Zulus (1888)

Baden-Powell had the good fortune to arrive at the Cape at a significant period in South Africa's history. In all external respects Cape Town still seemed to be the same quiet Dutch colonial town it had been twenty years earlier, with its pleasant gabled houses, avenues of oaks and lumbering bullock-carts. Yet all this was on the point of changing, as Great Britain at last began to see South Africa and the Cape as places in their own right and not just as strategic bases for the defence of India.

The event primarily responsible for ringing this change had been the discovery of the Kimberley diamond fields in 1870. Ten years later the whole region had been incorporated into the Cape Colony and in the year of Stephe's arrival diamonds furnished half the value of the Colony's exports. If this new wealth was staggering, the extent of the gold reefs discovered on the Witwatersrand in 1886 was almost beyond comprehension. Two years earlier Britain had agreed to Germany's occupation of the territory on the Atlantic coast later known as German South-West Africa, and in the same year Germany had extended her influence into Central East Africa (Tanganyika Terri-

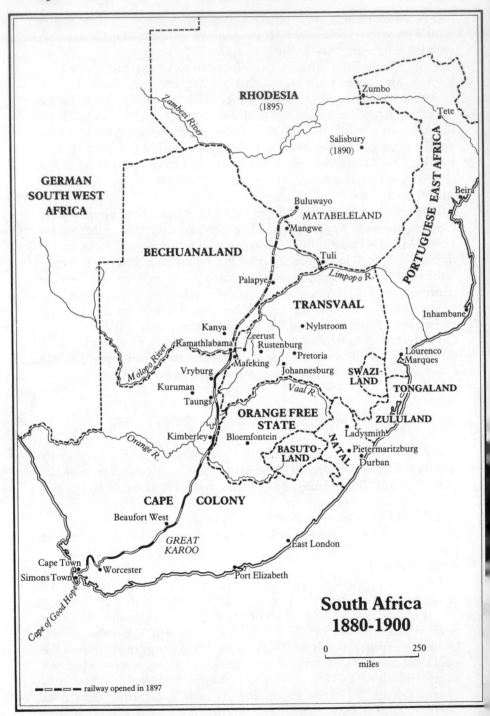

RHODESIA
(1895)

Zambezi River

Zumbo

Tete

GERMAN
SOUTH WEST
AFRICA

Salisbury
(1890)

PORTUGUESE EAST AFRICA

Beira

Buluwayo

MATABELELAND

Mangwe

BECHUANALAND

Tuli

Limpopo R.

Palapye

Inhambane

TRANSVAAL

Nylstroom

Kanya

Zeerust

Ramathlabama   Rustenburg

Molopo River

Vryburg

Mafeking

Pretoria

Lourenco
Marques

Johannesburg

SWAZI
LAND

Kuruman

TONGALAND

Taungs

Vaal R.

Orange R.

ORANGE FREE
STATE

ZULULAND

Ladysmith

Kimberley

Bloemfontein

BASUTO-
LAND

Pietermaritzburg

NATAL

Durban

CAPE   COLONY

Beaufort West

GREAT
KAROO

East London

Cape Town

Simons Town

Worcester

Port Elizabeth

Cape of Good Hope

**South Africa
1880-1900**

0   250

miles

━ ━ ━ ━ ━ railway opened in 1897

tory). With Britain also bent on making new acquisitions in Africa, and with the gold-rich Transvaal eager to acquire an outlet to the sea, South Africa's days as an international backwater were over.

★

To start with, however, none of this excitement came Stephe's way. 'I have *no work,*' he told George two months after his arrival. 'Look out on my behalf wherever there is a chance of war, and get me recalled by Lord Wolseley for machine-gun duty.'[1] While waiting to be summoned by his uncle (a rare event), he sat correcting the proofs of his recently completed compendium of pigsticking. From his office in Cape Town Castle, he could see through open windows 'dense green trees, and brilliant sunshine, and Old Table Mountain peeping down at one here and there between the branches'. McLaren wrote regularly, and his soldier servant from Seaforth offered to come out at his own expense if Stephe would have him.[2] Though bored, he loved apricots, grapes and sleeping in a tent which he was able to do while his uncle and aunt chose to live outside Cape Town among the foothills at the back of Table Mountain.[3] Baden-Powell used to come in to his office from Wynberg each morning along a pleasant country road, alternately running and walking (a mode of locomotion later widely known as 'Scout's Pace'). Sometimes he glimpsed wildebeeste and buck during his 8-mile journey.

Uncle Henry was a rather peppery, humourless man of 62, bald, with a long thin nose, thick sandy-coloured eyebrows and small suspicious eyes. He was exceedingly cautious, thinking things through in advance in meticulous detail and never making impulsive decisions. Aunt Constance, or Connie, was by contrast a mercurial, warm-hearted woman. The daughter of a rich Welsh quarry owner, she had always been something of a tomboy – even as a girl walking with long quick strides, shooting and swimming well, and always at her happiest wearing old tweeds. She married Henry Smyth when she was 29 and he nearly 50 years of age. Stephe rode with her for an hour or so each day, played chess with her and shared her interest in painting and embroidery. She showed great compassion for tramps and the mentally ill, but could be brutally scathing about members of her husband's family.[4] Stephe was very upset when she made it clear that she had no intention of asking Henrietta Grace out to the Cape.[5]

In spite of its new wealth, Cape Town was still provincial in atmosphere in the 1880s. Baden-Powell was amused by the quantity of teashops and the way in which 'all Cape Town knocks off business at eleven o'clock for tea'. As A.D.C. to the Commander-in-Chief, he was much sought-after socially and soon knew most of the leading citizens, both Dutch and English. He became Secretary of the Polo Club, second whip of the Cape Foxhounds and a member of the exclusive Tandem Club. His acting performances in the ballroom at the Castle earned him admiration in the press and from local ladies, as cartoons in *Cape Punch*[6] made clear, depicting him surrounded by numerous admirers offering him strawberries and cream. He also continued his female impersonations, both as a dancer and as a singer.

Lady Rosmead, the High Commissioner's wife, embarrassed him when he came to tea with her by demanding that he sing, in the manner of a 'prima donna', without his wig and female clothing. While she scrutinized him through her lorgnette, her butler looked on impassively. When her ladyship grilled Stephe about the women he found attractive, she was disappointed by an attitude she mistook for excessive circumspection.[7]

When George Baden-Powell had first met Lord Rosmead he had told Henrietta Grace: 'I *must* be a success if he is.'[8] The quality which neither George nor Stephe was able to fathom was Rosmead's diplomat's capacity for refusing to commit himself. When George was in Bechuanaland with Sir Charles Warren, he had observed the telegraphic messages passing between Rosmead and Warren, the former accountable to the Colonial Office and the latter to the War Office. Rosmead, as High Commissioner, had asserted his supremacy in all civil matters and had done his utmost to restrict Warren's scope for action.[9] Baden-Powell would soon learn a lot more about colonial politics and the delicate balance of power which existed between the civil and military authorities.

During the first week of June General Smyth received a telegram from Sir Arthur Havelock, the Governor of Natal, asking for military assistance to suppress a Zulu insurrection. 'If only the Boers or the Zulus would kick up a row I should be happy,' Stephe had confided to his mother three months earlier.[10] Now it seemed that he would have his wish.

The 2,000-strong army which General Smyth eventually commanded in Zululand was a hotchpotch force consisting of men drawn from four British regiments, the local mounted volunteers and a native levy. In addition he had under his orders an equal number of Zulus, whose 'chief' was a white adventurer. Throughout his life Stephe was fascinated by maverick pioneers who outraged the rules of ordinary white society and yet secured an unassailable position for themselves beyond the civilized pale. John Dunn was a Scot who began his career in Zululand as a hunter. He became King Cetewayo's chief advisor and closest friend. Through the Zulu ruler's patronage he gained control of the coastal region of the country from the Tugela to Ngoye, and with it the ownership of thousands of head of cattle. When relations between Cetewayo and the British deteriorated, Dunn advised the King not to fight. But Cetewayo rejected this advice and so Dunn deserted him, siding with the British and rendering them invaluable service. As a

Below: Professor Baden Powell shortly after his marriage to Henrietta Grace Smyth; and Henrietta Grace at the time of her marriage.

Bottom: Stephe at the age of three; and at the age of five.

Stephe aged sixteen.

Title page lettering from Druids' Minute Book, each letter representing the soubriquet of an individual member. Baden-Powell was Lord Bathing Towel (the curving 'S') and his friend Edward Parry was Captain Perrywinkle (the periwinkle shell), see p. 30.

see p. 30.

The new Charterhouse,
Godalming, Surrey.

Left: Baden-Powell's quarters in Lucknow drawn by himself in 1877.

Below: Lieutenant R.S.S. Baden-Powell aged 21.

Bottom left: Baden-Powell playing the ocarina at School of Musketry Hythe, 1880.

Above: 13th Hussars Pantomime at Lucknow May 1877. Baden-Powell is the clown on right.

Lieutenant Kenneth McLaren in 1880 aged 20.

Baden-Powell and McLaren in 13th Hussars' Polo Team, Muttra, 1883.

Baden-Powell and McLaren with their servants outside 'Bloater Park', Muttra, 1882.

Top: 13th Hussars Pigsticking Group. Seated on left Colonel Baker Russell, also seated Baden-Powell and next to him standing, in dark coat, McLaren. George Noble is second from right in back row.

Above: Baden-Powell and McLaren pigsticking with H.R.H. the Duke of Connaught at Delhi, 1884.

McLaren's terrier 'Beetle'.

Above left: Baden-Powell as 'Joe the Burglar' and McLaren as 'the Judge' in regimental theatricals, Dundalk, 1895. *Inset*: Kenneth McLaren in Ireland, 1895. *Below left*: McLaren in Bulawayo, 1899, five months before he was wounded outside Mafeking.

McLaren on his wedding day in 1910 with his second wife Ethel Mary Wilson and his only daughter Eilean.

Right: Baden-Powell drawn by himself shooting hippopotami in southern Africa in 1885.

Below: A self-confident Baden-Powell, standing in centre, on the voyage out to the Cape, 1888. His uncle General Henry Smyth and his aunt Constance are seated.

Above right: Baden-Powell gun-cleaning in Swaziland with his servant Galloway in 1889.

A deeply-depressed Baden-Powell (second from right back row) in 1893 on his brother George's yacht off the Albanian coast. George is on extreme left standing. (See p. 156).

This sketch of a butterfly contains the outline of a fortress, and marks both the position and power of the guns. The marks on the wings between the lines mean nothing, but those on the lines show the nature and size of the guns, according to the keys below.

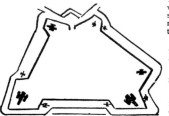

The marks on the wings reveal the shape of the fortress shown here and the size of the guns.

FORTRESS GUNS.

FIELD GUNS.

MACHINE GUNS.

The position of each gun is at the place inside the outline of the fort on the butterfly where the line marked with the spot ends. The head of the butterfly points towards the north.

Page from *My Adventures as a Spy* (1915) in which Baden-Powell described spying activities, most of which allegedly took place in various countries bordering the Mediterranean between 1890 and 1893.

Below: Miss Caroline Heap 1891.

Above left: Baden-Powell (standing, extreme left) in the garrison's gymnasium on Malta, taking part in a display circ 1892. *Above right*: Caricature of Baden-Powell 'skirt dancing' by Marcel Pic 1893.

reward for his betrayal of his patron Dunn received about a third of the country.[11] Now, in 1888, he was ready to fight against Cetewayo's son, Dinuzulu, who had in his turn rebelled against British rule. Dunn had 48 Zulu wives and over 100 children and seemed, when Stephe met him, 'a fine broad-shouldered bearded man of middle-age wearing a cowboy hat and an Inverness cloak and carrying a rifle.'[12] Dunn's 2,000 Zulus left an abiding impression upon Baden-Powell.

> When we topped the rise, we saw moving up towards us from the valley below three long lines of men marching in single file and singing a wonderful anthem as they marched. Both the sight and the sound were intensely impressive. Every now and then one man would sing a few notes of a solo which were then responded to by an immense roar of sound from the whole impi [regiment] of deep bass voices and higher tones singing in harmony. Then in the midst of their song there would be a sudden break and a shrill whistle would go up or a crash as they struck simultaneously their great hide shields with their assegais. The timekeeping and rhythm of these warriors in their singing was marvellous, accompanied as it was with stamping of the feet and booming and rattling at given periods . . . a glorious sound. The men themselves looked so splendid . . . very smartly decked out with feathers and furs and cows' tails. They wore little in the way of clothing and their brown bodies were polished with oil and looked like bronze statues.[13]

Their spears, assegais, axes and clubs intrigued him, as did the 'black polished rings' made from blood and wax and worn on the heads of all 'élite soldiers'. Stephe was thrilled by the sights and sounds of African militarism, not as an idea but as a vital and exuberant way of life. When he one day wrote choruses for the Boy Scouts and dreamed up camp-fire rituals, John Dunn's Zulus would be in the forefront of his mind. Although he sometimes descended to sentimental inanities about the Zulus' 'dog-like fidelity',[14] he had great respect for their discipline and physical prowess.

Before General Smyth and his staff arrived on 20 June at their base camp, at a place called Eshow, a mixed force under Major A. C. McKean, including 200 'loyal' Basutos,* had defeated one of Dinuzulu's four impis [regiments] in the field against the British. Given the inequality of weaponry, it was not very surprising that only six British lives had been lost in this defeat of several thousand Zulus. Smyth's next objective was to relieve the besieged Resident Magistrate; and McKean was given command of a flying column, with Stephe as his staff officer. Dunn's 2,000 Zulus would accompany the column, which included 400 mounted infantry and Dragoons and 200

* From neighbouring Basutoland.

Basutos. The European officers soon found themselves powerless to stop the Zulus and Basutos burning 'enemy' kraals along the route. Up to 80 a day were going up in smoke by 11 July – a day on which they also killed four men and mortally wounded a young woman. McKean and Baden-Powell did what they could for the girl, but she died during the night. On the following day the looting and burning continued, but the Magistrate was duly relieved and his fort's defences strengthened. Forty members of the garrison had died; almost all of them black policemen.[15]

By the middle of July it was clear that General Smyth's force had acquired a reputation ludicrously more formidable than its actual deeds warranted. The morale of Dinuzulu's followers was already close to collapse by the time he retired to his stronghold in the Ceza bush in early August. Much of his following fragmented into small marauding groups. The Ceza was a mountain plateau only approachable via 'an almost perpendicular rocky scarp overgrown with thick bush and huge boulders'. Before Baden-Powell and his troop of Inniskilling Dragoons set out for the stronghold on a reconnoitring mission, he already knew that most of Dinuzulu's warriors had slipped away into the neighbouring Transvaal. On the morning of 12 August when he clambered on to the plateau, he was not very surprised to find it deserted.

In 1919, when Baden-Powell started his woodcraft training courses for Scoutmasters at Gilwell, he awarded candidates their 'Wood Badge', which consisted of several wooden necklace beads on a leather thong. The first badges were formed from beads belonging to an African necklace, which Baden-Powell suggested he had found in Dinuzulu's hut in the Ceza. There is, however, no record of this find in his diary or in letters written at the time, though he does mention appropriating the necklace of the dead African girl.[16] Stephe had a keen love of the absurd, and it may well have amused him that many of his Scoutmasters firmly believed that beads from an African girl's necklace were relics of a Zulu king. After the Second World War the origins of the 'Wood Badge' started to cause embarrassment. To have stolen a Zulu ruler's property was thought underhand and unpleasant, as was the idea of the founder of a worldwide multiracial brotherhood fighting against Africans. So it became policy within the Movement to claim that Baden-Powell had been given the necklace by Dinuzulu. 'This change,' wrote the Deputy Chief Scout in 1959, 'was made first in *The Gilwell Book* and gradually in all our literature.'[17]

The conflict which benefited Stephe most was fought out after the real fighting was over; it sprang from the customary antipathy between the military and civil authorities during all colonial uprisings. General Smyth had wanted to inflict a crushing defeat on 'the enemy'. The Governor of Natal, Sir Arthur Havelock, looked upon the rebels as misguided subjects rather than as an enemy, and therefore wanted to hold back Smyth's forces once Dinuzulu was on the run. He hoped to use local levies and police after the turning point had been reached, keeping the soldiers in reserve in case of a new upsurge of violence.[18] While Havelock complained to the Colonial Secretary that Smyth's force had been absurdly large for so trifling an insurrection, the General himself argued that the rebellion had only collapsed because its leaders had felt so thoroughly overawed.

Soon after Dinuzulu had fled from the Ceza bush, both General Smyth and Baden-Powell began to blame Havelock for delaying the attack on the Ceza stronghold and thus allowing the Zulu ruler to escape. The Governor furiously denied this, and said that Smyth would have been too late anyway; this was probably correct, since in mid-June Stephe had admitted to George that it seemed probable that Dinuzulu would have fled before they reached his stronghold.[19] But whatever the rights and wrongs of the arguments, there was no doubt as to who won the row which followed, and whose arguments were presented more effectively in the British press. From the very beginning Stephe had been sending material home to George to get into the newspapers. 'Of course I cannot write myself direct to Times, Broad Arrow, or Pall Mall, but if you receive long letters describing what is going on you will know how best to utilize them.'[20] George certainly did know best.

On 13 September *The Morning Post* published a long article chronicling General Smyth's virtues and Sir Arthur Havelock's shortcomings. There were many complimentary mentions of Captain R. S. S. Baden-Powell, the General's A.D.C.. *The Times* had carried a similar piece the day before, and specialist papers like the *Army and Navy Gazette* – which were taken seriously by serving officers – printed full accounts expressing fury that General Smyth had been 'interfered with'. In this particular newspaper Stephe was credited with commanding 'a picked force' chosen to make the 'final dash' on the Ceza, rather than with being the commander of a more modest reconnaissance party.[21] It was fortunate for Baden-Powell's prospects that Zululand fascinated the Adjutant-General, Lord Wolseley, whose destruction of the Zulu dynasty in 1879 was the root cause of the present troubles. Wolseley exchanged letters with Smyth and Baden-Powell, expressing his sympathy over Sir Arthur Havelock's supposedly disgraceful behaviour.[22]

For many years Wolseley had been disgusted by the way in which governors of colonies, and their masters in the Colonial Office, habitually tried to restrict the powers of generals commanding troops in the field by insisting upon respect for natives' rights. The Adjutant-General was convinced that tribes like the Zulus, who massacred their enemies, always interpreted forbearance on the part of British troops as a sign of weakness.[23] Therefore he was delighted to be able to use the public quarrel between Smyth and Havelock over Dinuzulu's 'escape' to force upon the Colonial Secretary a small but significant addition to the regulations governing the control of troops in colonial insurrections. A Colony's Governor would still keep his supreme authority, but 'he would incur special responsibility if he should direct the troops to be stationed or employed in a manner which their commander shall consider open to military objection'.[24]

These events brought Stephe indirectly to Wolseley's attention again, but an incident in which he was directly involved earned him the Adjutant-General's personal sympathy. On 10 August, on his way to the Ceza, Stephe had come upon a looted trading store where the European trader and his son had been murdered by a band of Dinuzulu's Usutus.* Whether the twenty or so Usutus, whose tracks were followed by Baden-Powell's Zulu scouts the following morning, were the murderers is uncertain. In the manuscript of his autobiography,[25] Baden-Powell stated that they were, but gave no reason for thinking so. He and his men were certainly aroused by prowling Usutus during the night of the 10th, and the next day tracked them to some caves a few miles away. What orders Stephe gave cannot be determined, and in any case even if, as he claimed later, he had given orders that the prisoners' lives were to be spared, his Zulus would still very likely have done as they wished.[26] At a distance of half a mile, the Zulus were beyond his or anyone else's control. His Zulus charged into the caves and stabbed to death two men and a woman, then took 26 prisoners and 110 head of cattle.[27]

The Governor of Natal at once wrote to General Smyth deploring the deaths caused by Baden-Powell's column and pointing out that, because the Usutus had been just across the border in the Boers' New Republic,† their killing amounted to murder. Smyth was curtly ordered 'to prevent a re-occurrence of the lamentable mistake that appears to have been made'.[28] Baden-Powell's diary suggests that he had not known until two days later that he had been near the border; but years later he let slip that the Usutus had tried to save themselves by crossing into the New Republic. 'However we disregarded the border and followed them up, attacked, and got them.'[29] At the time Baden-Powell was able to show that there were inconsistencies in the Government map of the border issued to troops, and so Havelock decided not to bring actual charges.[30] Needless to say, an action which shocked Havelock struck Lord Wolseley as an example of commendable zeal. He felt that cross-border raids ought to be severely punished, and the perpetrators pursued. It is ironic that by losing control of his

* The name which Baden-Powell always gave Dinuzulu's warriors.
† Part of Zululand ceded by Cetewayo to the Boers in 1884.

native followers, Baden-Powell inadvertently impressed Wolseley as an officer who knew how to get Africans to exert themselves. This would have far-reaching consequences.

Also important for the future was Baden-Powell's meeting with Colonel Sir Frederick Carrington, who had overall command of Natal's Native Levies in Zululand. Carrington had been Commandant of the Bechuanaland Border Police in 1885 when George had been with Sir Charles Warren's party, and the two men had met and got on well. Carrington now saw the recently knighted George as a potential source of patronage and was therefore extremely attentive to Stephe.[31] 'He [Carrington] has almost promised me command if there is a row between Khama [King of Bechuanaland] and Lobenguela [King of the Matabele] which seems to be likely.' Carrington's offer when it came would be far more dramatic.

While most settlers in Natal had been in favour of the campaign against Dinuzulu, there were vociferous critics among the whites who thought the resort to military force brutal and unjust. Among these critics were Harriette and Frances Colenso, the daughters of the late Bishop of Natal, whose unswerving support for Cetewayo had lasted until his death in 1883. Now the bishop's daughters had taken up the cause of Cetewayo's son, Dinuzulu, with the same fervour. Their father had been a close friend of Professor Powell and had shared his moral courage, being ready to risk ostracism by subjecting the Bible to historical analysis. For several years the bishop's son had shared a house with Frank Baden-Powell. So very naturally, when the sisters learned in the mid-1880s that George was interested in southern Africa, they appealed to him to help. He at once told them that he supported the stand they were making against Britain's policy of divide and rule in Zululand. 'I have determined to write something putting the Zulu claims before the British public,' George had told Harriette in 1885. 'They would find me sympathizing with the natives' rights fully.'[32]

When Harriette and Frances read the press accounts praising General Smyth's proceedings in Zululand and noted the frequent references to Captain Baden-Powell, they at once laid the blame on George. 'That self-seeking cad of a Baden-Powell,' they called him. That any son of Professor Powell could have behaved in such an unprincipled manner in order to advance his brother's and his uncle's careers shocked them deeply.[33]

Three months after leaving the Ceza bush, Dinuzulu walked quietly into the Colenso sisters' house outside Ladysmith and told them he meant to give himself up.[34] He was sentenced to ten years' detention on the island of St Helena, where Harriette Colenso would often visit him. Stephe met Harriette in 1890 on board ship when she was on her way to England to petition Parliament on behalf of Dinuzulu;[35] they found little to say to one another.

On the march back to Durban from Zululand, Baden-Powell entertained himself by reading a life of Joe Grimaldi, the famous clown. During the campaign, this gifted cleric's son had surmised that 'the veriest parson' could not have been more obtusely mistaken in adopting a lenient attitude towards rebellious Africans than the humanitarian Governor of Natal.[36] Stephe delivered another jab at clergymen during the voyage from Durban to the Cape. 'We landed a parson at Port Elizabeth and immediately the wind changed and blew in our favour and we sped along at 13 knots all night.'[37] But the events in Zululand may have had a deeper impact on him than he admitted. Six months later he wrote to his mother, asking her to send him some of his father's theological works. One of these books, which had played an important part in his father's disgrace, was *The Order of Nature*. Stephe would pronounce it the most remarkable book he had ever read.[38]

5. The Lure of the Dark Interior (1888–90)

Back at the Cape, congratulations were showered upon General Smyth and his nephew for the success of their campaign. Baden-Powell was officially appointed his uncle's Military Secretary, and *The Cape Argus* celebrated the appointment with a lengthy biographical portrait. When Stephe heard that his mother had ordered 300 copies, this was too much even for him: 'I believe it is the surest way to damn one's prospects to let people know you are advertising yourself . . . We are inclined to do this in the family a little too much.' Given the way in which she and George had laboured to make sure that his not always judicious deeds in Zululand had received favourable attention, Henrietta Grace was very angry and Stephe had to write a tactful and conciliatory reply to her indignant blast. 'When I talk of steering clear of advertising, I only mean that we are quite on our proper pedestal now – at least I know *I* am.'[1]

Yet 'on his pedestal' or not, Stephe was still given no work of any significance by his uncle, and had to resume his morning rides with his aunt and their afternoon sketching expeditions. He wrote for her a mocking little verse, in the style of Longfellow, that sums up his own feelings about the tedium of life at the Cape.

> Tell me not in accents dreary
> That you find bazaars a bore,
> That of crewel-work you're weary
> And that raffles you abhor.[2]

In March 1889, he met a man whose dramatic life and personality told him exactly what was wrong with his present existence. Frederick

Courtenay Selous was then laying plans with Cecil Rhodes to open up 'Rhodesia' for white settlers. Rhodes had just 'bought' all the mineral rights in Matabeleland from King Lobenguela in consideration of £1,200 a year, 1,000 cartridges and a steamboat. In June 1890 Selous would lead his 700 pioneers on their epoch-making trip into Mashonaland. Although the settlement of Rhodesia was still a year away, Baden-Powell sensed the excitement of great events whenever he was with Selous. 'He is,' he told his mother, 'the most wonderful man of this century.'[3]

After leaving Rugby, Selous had sailed for Africa to become a hunter and explorer. In his best-seller, *A Hunter's Wanderings in Africa* (1881), he had recorded his many adventures and travels which had taken him as far into the interior as the Zambezi. To meet Selous, with his piercing cornflower-blue eyes and handsome bearded face, was an experience which few people forgot. Rider Haggard would base the character of Allan Quatermain, the hero of *King Solomon's Mines*, on him. Stephe would never forget the way in which, in conversation, Selous almost acted out his narrow escapes from hostile men and beasts. He would include several of these adventures in *Scouting for Boys* nearly twenty years later.[4]

Between April and July 1889, his dealings with Selous made Baden-Powell determined to do some exploring in the region of the Zambezi.[5] At the same time he used to chat with Captain Graham Bower R.N., the High Commissioner's well-informed Imperial Secretary. The Captain told him in detail about the way in which the destiny of southern Africa was being decided while they kicked their heels at the Cape. Sir Charles Warren's closure of Bechuanaland to the Transvaal Boers had been part of the deliberate encircling of the Transvaal, which Rhodes and Selous now planned to carry further by settling Mashonaland and Matabeleland. Warren's expedition had also prevented Germany from expanding eastwards from her recently acquired colony of South-West Africa; and General Smyth's expedition to Zululand had been mounted on a grand scale, in part to persuade the Boers and their German allies not to attempt any further expansion.

The area to which Bower drew Baden-Powell's particular attention lay to the east of the region in which Rhodes and Selous would soon be making history. Germany, said Bower, was planning to snatch part of Portugal's decaying colony of Mozambique. The British Government would therefore welcome accurate information about the navigability of the Zambezi and the real extent of Portuguese settlement in the more remote parts of the ailing colony.[6]

Once Bower had suggested the idea, Stephe was so gripped by it that he at once acquired copies of the four existing maps of the region, including the one Livingstone had made during the disastrous

government-sponsored Zambezi Expedition of 1858–1864. An extraordinary stroke of fate made him even more determined to chart the
river. Sir John Kirk, who had been Livingstone's botanist and right-
hand man during the ill-fated expedition, unexpectedly turned up at
the Cape. By then Baden-Powell had instructed Warington to buy him
a collapsible boat. Although Kirk had narrowly escaped being
drowned in the Zambezi, he inspected Baden-Powell's boat when it
arrived and instead of urging caution encouraged him to press on with
his enterprise. Selous did the same.[7] With his excitement mounting by
the day, Baden-Powell sent home for more and more impedimenta: an
air mattress with waterproofed pockets for the preservation of maps
and diaries in the event of a capsize, life-jackets of various designs and a
formidable stock of medicines.[8]

Just as Baden-Powell was beginning to think that he might yet rival
the great explorers, Uncle Henry announced that the High Commissioner was about to return to England and that he, General Smyth,
would have to act in his place until the arrival of his successor. In these
circumstances he would need the help of his staff as never before,
particularly that of his Military Secretary.[9] Stephe would therefore
have to forget the 'Dark Interior', which in his uncle's opinion had
little to do with soldiering and would almost certainly have laid him
low with malaria and other dangerous tropical diseases.[10] As if to
confirm the wisdom of Uncle Henry's cautious nature, Stephe
suddenly fell ill. A gigantic boil appeared on his neck; it was so painful
and protuberant that he had to take to his bed for several weeks and
after that to convalesce for two months, during which time he returned
to England for a brief period of home leave.

Incredibly, this ill wind almost immediately started to blow him
good. In England, thanks to George, Stephe met a future Pro-Consul,
Sir Francis de Winton, who was about to sail for Africa as Special
Commissioner to Swaziland. As a result of this meeting de Winton
invited Baden-Powell to be his secretary for a month, subject to
General Smyth's approval. During his three weeks' leave Stephe went
to Edinburgh in order to see McLaren and the 13th Hussars, stayed
with the Nobles, went to the War Office to try to accelerate payment
for his machine-gun harness and spent time with George. His mother
and Agnes had received no advance warning of his sick leave and were
unable to return from a holiday on the Continent in time to see him.[11]
Baden-Powell was back in Cape Town only two months after his
departure. Since General Smyth had been told that his nephew would
be in Swaziland for little more than three weeks, he allowed himself to
be persuaded by Sir Francis de Winton to let Stephe go.

Wedged between Mozambique to the east, the Transvaal to the
north and west and Zululand to the south, the small upland kingdom
of Swaziland perfectly illustrated the disaster of unrestrained European

encroachment. The Transvaal Boers had employed their usual mode of expansion. After a series of hunting expeditions, they had sent their cattle across the border to graze. A foothold thus secured, they had wrung concessions from the native chiefs, sometimes in return for aid in their quarrels and sometimes after gifts of guns, alcohol and other goods. The Boers blamed the British settlers for setting up the liquor stores and, given their own religious scruples about alcohol, there was probably some justice in the accusation. The situation was dire. King Mbandeni had become an alcoholic, along with many of his leading subjects. British and German gold prospectors and concession-seekers were pouring into the country, most of them totally unprincipled and only too eager to take advantage of Swaziland's drink-sodden ruler.[12]

Before setting sail, Baden-Powell prepared a confidential report on Swaziland for de Winton, in which he argued against annexing the territory. As a British Crown Colony it would, like Zululand, cause nothing but trouble and expense. The best solution would be to let the Boers have it, and to use this apparently generous act as a lever for prizing from them vital concessions such as a customs union and improved rail links between the Transvaal and the Cape Colony. The Boers would be sure to take the bait since they were desperate to secure an Indian Ocean port and would consider Swaziland a crucial step towards the sea – an entirely useless one, argued Stephe, since Britain controlled intervening Tongaland. The people totally ignored in Baden-Powell's analysis were the Swazis themselves who had actually asked for British protection.[13] But in fairness to Stephe the officials in the Colonial Office and at the Cape also saw the situation only in terms of the continuing struggle between the Boer republics and British interests in southern Africa.

The behaviour of the Queen-Regent Labotsibeni, who in following the custom of her ancestors had just executed all the recently deceased king's counsellors, would have earned the censure of every missionary in southern Africa. But Baden-Powell, far from being shocked, persuaded the Queen-Regent to tell him how she chose the ordinary people who were to accompany the dead king. His question surprised her. The only way to be fair, she explained patiently, was to select people entirely at random 'without favour or affection; and in that way everybody has the same chance'.[14] Baden-Powell met the executioner, Jokilobovu, and 'struck up a great friendship with him', learning how he killed his victims with a single blow from a short knobkerry at the base of the skull.[15] It is to Stephe's credit that he made no hypocritical attempt to use the violence and 'savagery' of Africans to excuse the violence and rapacity of Europeans. He would quote the Queen-Regent as saying of the white traders: 'They steal our cattle and women and enslave our children . . . We have asked them to go back to their own country but they only curse and beat and shoot us.' The missionaries had told her that she could trust 'Christian traders', but as Baden-Powell commented, 'the teaching of the missionaries has been absolutely let down by Christianity as seen in practice.'[16]

Baden-Powell's most memorable experience during the Swaziland mission was a meeting in Pretoria with Paul Kruger, the President of the Transvaal. Sitting in the President's modest single-storeyed house, Stephe thought this flabby-faced, big-nosed man 'a great hero, and second Cromwell'.[17] Kruger's ability to summon tears to underline his sincerity made a considerable impression upon Stephe. After several sessions together, de Winton and Kruger agreed that a Joint Commission representing Great Britain and the Transvaal should return to Swaziland to determine whether the basis for a settlement existed. Baden-Powell did not realize it, but long before their meeting Kruger had decided to stall de Winton over Swaziland because he hoped to acquire the territory unconditionally in a year or two, in return for stopping a mass trek into Rhodesia by Transvaalers, whom he intended in the first place to encourage. Swaziland would eventually become a British Protectorate in 1906.

The Swaziland mission left Baden-Powell with no enthusiasm for high diplomacy, although he had liked Vice-President Smit and General Joubert. He recognized that the 'outwardly slow' manner of the Boers was a mask concealing great practicality and determination. They were also, he noted, 'quick enough to see and recognize any display of English hauteur or attempt to patronize. They have simply to be treated as equals and friends.'[18] He paid Smit and Joubert the rare compliment of suggesting that they call upon his mother when next in London.

Neither Stephe's boil – which had led to his meeting with de Winton – nor the High Commissioner's decision to leave the Cape – which had led General Smyth to stop him going to the Zambezi – had made Baden-Powell lose faith in his ability to shape his own destiny. But while Stephe continued to exchange friendly letters with Lord Wolseley and Sir Evelyn Wood – telling them about Zululand and Swaziland – the reality of his day-to-day existence, in spite of all his 'grouping', was his continuing dependence upon Henry Smyth. This was forcibly brought home to him shortly after his return from Swaziland to the Cape. His head was full of dreams of what 'that most useful man de Winton' might do for him when his uncle suddenly announced that he had been offered the Governorship of Malta and had accepted. Stephe, he said, could come with him as his A.D.C. and Military Secretary, but he warned: 'If you come, you will have to look to my work only for your employment . . . and you will have to give up the expectation for extraneous objects, whether political, sporting or exploratory.' General Smyth particularly resented the way in which George thought that he 'should be always ready to push you [Stephe] into any external occupation that promises to lead to advancement of any kind'. He told his nephew to choose between a life dedicated to 'the development of South Africa's progress', or the more conventional military career which would follow on from a spell as Military Secretary on Malta.[19] Stephe wrote to George and told him that he had reluctantly accepted his uncle's offer and terms. 'Of course,' he added, 'if something better falls in my way I should ask to chuck up my billet and take it.'[20] But when Francis de Winton wrote asking for Stephe's services on an expedition to Uganda, Uncle Henry stuck to his guns.[21] If his nephew decided to go, he should not expect to return to Malta. So Stephe had to refuse; and the officer sent to Uganda in his place, Captain Frederick Lugard – after defeating the French faction in that country in fierce fighting – would justly be given the credit for securing Uganda for Britain.

Baden-Powell was horribly depressed as he packed for the voyage to Malta. He felt in his bones that his future lay in Africa and not on a small Mediterranean island, but his poverty obliged him to cling to his uncle's patronage. He had come very close to great events and great opportunities without quite being able to grasp them. There could scarcely be another captain in the British Army receiving regular letters from Lord Wolseley, but what good had this been?[22] Sir Frederick Carrington had promised future employment, but Stephe doubted whether anything from that quarter would ever prove sufficiently auspicious to justify abandoning his present security. There seemed no escape from years and years of social duties, which threatened to be more formidable now that Uncle Henry was to be both Commander-in-Chief and Governor of Malta.

6. The Prisoner of Malta (1890–93)

On 27 February 1890 Baden-Powell, now a Brevet-Major and still acting as Military Secretary and senior A.D.C. to his recently knighted uncle, took up residence in the San Antonio Palace in Valetta. Stephe was nothing if not adaptable and Malta, with its garrison of five battalions and its massive naval presence, would provide him with far better opportunities for theatrical and philanthropic projects than anything at the Cape.

As senior A.D.C. Baden-Powell was in charge of the Governor's social arrangements such as balls, dinners and hospitality dispensed to the officers of foreign flotillas and the socially exalted owners of yachts. He never had anything to do with his uncle's real work as Governor, which involved placating members of the Italian-speaking party on the island's Executive Council and defusing highly charged issues concerning language, culture and education. Nevertheless, the formality of Stephe's position and the deference with which he was treated by local socialites offered some compensation. The classic complaint addressed to him by those disappointed not to have been invited to a function was the supposition that 'some mistake had been made'. Baden-Powell's reply was always brief. 'Dear Madam, There has been no mistake. Yours sincerely . . .'[1] The Palace provided a setting for his theatricals more imposing than any heretofore and made local society still more eager to see him act. Gilded ceilings and marble floors did nothing to inhibit his performances. 'I remember how naughty you were when you were the hatter in "Box and Cox" and made the girls go into hysterics,' wrote one of his admirers 40 years later. 'I wonder if you remember little me!'[2]

Stephe's most memorable performances on Malta were those given in another part of town, in the Valetta gymnasium, at smoking concerts which he organized each week to pay for a social club for the men of the garrison. A favourite device was to have a private soldier come on and announce that Major Baden-Powell was indisposed and that he had therefore been told to take his part. The man would then 'sing a song caricaturing a foppish officer inspecting the guard', and follow this with a rendering of 'You should see me dance the Polka', with the performer 'imitating how everybody danced from Tommy Atkins up to the Governor'.[3] At some stage in the proceedings the audience would tumble to the fact that the supposed private soldier was in fact the Governor's Military Secretary. Baden-Powell also enjoyed giving dancing displays with a dummy partner, while another speciality was his impersonation of a barrack-room lawyer. 'While the audience is waiting for the next singer, there is a noise heard in the wings, and then a loud voice cries, "I tell you I *will* go on. It's no use of you a'stopping of me, I'm a' goin' to tell 'em all about it, I am," and then with a great clatter a private comes stumbling on to the stage with tunic open, hair all over the place, and cap at the back of his head. "Beg parding, sir," he says to the officer in the front row, "but these here manoeuvres has been all conducted wrong. . .".[4] The gymnasium was always packed, with sailors perched up in the rafters and on the wall-bars almost as densely as on the floor below. 'The cheer set up by this splendid audience when "B-P" appeared was, even without the crowd on the rafters, enough to bring down the house.'[5] His female impersonations were as ever a particular draw and his aunt described how on one occasion 'when a lady failed to do her part of the dance on the programme, he donned a lady's dress and, amid roars of laughter, gave a most attractive skirt dance.'

Sir Henry Smyth disliked his nephew's performances but Aunt Connie was more relaxed. Sometimes Stephe would 'appear to write a note during an official dinner party, and hand it to a footman to be given to her ladyship. She would open it in anticipation that some social mishap had befallen, only to be confronted with a lively caricature of a guest sketched on the back of a menu – a trick that proved almost too much for her very merry ladyship's composure.'[7] Baden-Powell used to keep an eye on her to prevent embarrassment, such as could have been caused by the easily detectable bootlace with which she sometimes secured her diamond necklace.

Although Stephe was in his middle thirties he had lost none of his fondness for practical jokes, some of them quite mean, enjoying for example sending expert sportsmen with their numerous dogs and guns to parts of the island renowned for their lack of game birds.[8] When the Round the Island Yacht Race was held, he and several others hired a small steamer for the day to 'kidnap' a friend's yacht. But the plan went disastrously wrong and they ended up aground, having put a hole through a Maltese nobleman's mainsail with their pop-gun cannon.[9]

Malta was much less provincial than Cape Town, having an active opera house, resident aristocracy and a cultural diversity reflecting the island's Norman, Italian and Spanish heritage. Among the English community, however, social tittle-tattle dominated all else. Since this generally consisted of talk of love affairs, engagements and marriages, Stephe disliked it: 'Whenever people come hinting at various engagements and asking my opinion, I first let them know that I think it, if not caddish, at least uncharitable to pass on rumours, and then I remark that as it is a matter that entirely concerns the two people engaged, I don't see why *I* should be called upon to express an opinion.'[10] This attitude had less to do with priggishness than with his personal view of marriage as a threatening business. In many ways Malta was an excellent place for finding a wife, and Baden-Powell's position as Military Secretary gave him plenty of advantages. The best catches were the daughters of the rich owners of yachts, like Lady Sybil Erskine, the Earl of Rosslyn's daughter, whom Stephe described as: 'Great friends with me (even more so than I am with her)'.[11] A few months later, when his mother inquired how Lady Sybil was, Baden-Powell told her: 'I fear she is not at all what I want.'[12] As usual his closest friendships were with much younger girls – children in fact. One such was 'a little girl who used to live not far from the Palace'. Later she recalled for a journalist, 'What an awful tease the Military Secretary used to be . . . When one of the Palace peacocks was found defunct in the gardens, he accused me and my sister of having shot it with a catapult from one of our top windows. We were capital signallers, and Baden-Powell engaged us to flag-wag to him every morning.'[13]

Nevertheless, on Malta, Baden-Powell seems to have formed his first close friendship with a woman of marriageable age. Her name was Caroline Heap and she was the daughter of an American engineer, Mr Gwyn H. Heap, who lived in Valetta from 1890 to 1892 in which year he left to take up the post of American Consul in Constantinople. Caroline was nineteen, with bright blue eyes, a striking rather than a strictly pretty face and an ebullient, forceful personality.[14] The first indication that Stephe had met her came in a letter to his mother written in October 1890: 'There is a nice old electrical engineer and his daughter here and I've a good mind to tell them to call at No. 8. *She's* a good sort of girl – plain but pleasing . . .'[15] Caroline [see first photo section] was not plain, so Baden-Powell's self-confessed inability to judge the quality of feminine looks was to blame for this misconception. But he liked her outward-going, energetic American manner enough to suggest a meeting with his mother, the first time he had ever thought of conferring such a privilege on a girl. It seems likely that he saw Caroline regularly, but unfortunately only a fragment of the diary he kept on Malta still exists. It was preserved by his secretary Mrs Wade and is in the form of a typed copy of the original apparently made by Olave Baden-Powell after her husband's death. The copy covers only the month of January 1891 and a few days of February.[16] The diary itself would seem to have been destroyed, so Lady Baden-Powell probably found the references to Caroline too complimentary to permit the document's survival. Even in the fragment Caroline is mentioned eight times, and Baden-Powell must have seen her more often than that since she took part in various of the country dance groups which he organized.[17]

Shortly after he arrived in Malta he won a pony and cart in a raffle and drove it as a troika, with one wheeler and two leaders. He often invited Miss Heap out for drives, taking her to the races, on shopping expeditions and on sight-seeing trips. Stephe probably felt relaxed with Caroline because he never considered her to be socially or financially qualified to be his wife. He visited her once when she moved to Constantinople in August 1891,[18] but their friendship effectively ended when she left Malta. Two years later she married Captain Arthur Slade-Baker of the Royal Artillery; that was in 1893, the year in which Stephe was so shocked to learn that George intended to marry.[19]

Marriage, he told his mother, was fine 'for the rest of the family (always excepting me – I'm too young yet)'.[20] A light verse written by him at this time was not entirely facetious:

> I ne'er shall forget her
> That girl of Valetta.
> The first time I met her
> I thought she was prime.
> But I managed to get a
> Peep through her faldetta,★
> And thought that I'd better
> Get out while I'd time.[21]

★ Head-shawl worn on Malta

Some years later Stephe told the second young woman for whom he ever felt affection that on Malta he was supposed to have been a terrible rake and gambler which, he added, was entirely untrue. 'There was certainly a disposition to match-make, if not to love-make, but it was all on one side (because of reports of my fabulous wealth), but the other side was so extremely numerous that therein lay my safety. I had all the same to give out that I was already secretly married in S. Africa!'[22]

At least there was 'safety' during the many hours he spent in the Valetta gymnasium with the soldiers of the garrison and the blue-jackets of the Mediterranean Fleet. But not even the hero-worship of so many men compensated Baden-Powell for his uncle's refusal to let him go to Uganda. Even six months after he had been forced to turn down de Winton's invitation, he could not come to terms with the situation. 'This is awful,' he told his mother, 'I thought that once Sir F. de Winton had gone I should have got rid of the longing to be with him, but I feel more and more anxious to be there. I can't think of anything else . . . You can't picture that "camp sickness" (as I should call it) that gets hold of one – a sort of hunger to be out in the wilds and away from all this easy-going mixture of office, and drawing room, clerk and butler . . .'[23] Worse for Stephe was his certainty that through not bravely accepting de Winton's offer, he had lost the one absolutely vital opportunity that fate would ever offer him.

Yet the risks would have been very great. Back in Britain again he would have been unable to afford to live in his regiment, and his position would have been more perilous than ever. Baker Russell now commanded the Cavalry Brigade at Aldershot, but he had still not offered Stephe the Brigade-Major's job. And although Stephe had sent crates of Maltese oranges (then a great luxury) to Lord Downe, the Duke of Connaught and Lord Wolseley, the results had been a few polite letters and nothing else.[24] Baden-Powell was depressed enough to consider transferring into a regiment in Egypt, where he would at least be able to live cheaply.

In May 1892 Sir Frederick Carrington at last came through with an offer, but sadly it was only the command of a troop in the Bechuanaland Police. 'I don't think it is quite good enough to accept, is it?' Stephe asked George.[25] Indeed it was not. But worse was to come. The War Office refused to recognize his time in Zululand as the kind of 'active service' required to qualify him for staff appointments without his having been to the Staff College. With a heavy heart he wrote home asking for 'arithmetic, algebra, and Euclid books', since he proposed 'to work for the Staff College again' [26] Deep down he knew that at the age of 34 he was too old to go back to school. It would have to be 'active service' such as de Winton had offered (and he had foolishly refused) or nothing. 'I have got such a beastly desire to be up and doing, out of this stagnation,' he told George.[27] But what, and how?

Stephe's one solace during this miserable period was the opportunity which his service on Malta gave him to make brief trips to Sicily, Italy and North Africa. During his first summer in Valetta, he persuaded his uncle to appoint him his Intelligence Officer. Baden-Powell was thus able to confer upon his travels away from Malta a respectable veneer of utility. An Intelligence Officer's duties were not demanding, merely requiring him to collect general information on the topography, fortifications and superficial military dispositions in neighbouring countries. He told his entire family that if any of them chanced to meet the new Director of Military Intelligence, they were not to neglect to mention his name.[28] With his other irons in the fire so obviously cold, Stephe hoped that this intelligence gathering might end his 'stagnation'. If it did not, nothing else seemed likely to.

Between 1890 and 1893, Baden-Powell made seven trips to countries in the Eastern Mediterranean. He would be disappointed by the actual impact these missions would have upon his career, but the effect they would have upon his image of himself would be profound.

7. Spies and Butterflies (1890–93)

Few of the reports sent in during the 1880s and the 1890s by officers working either for the Director of Military Intelligence or as interested outsiders have been preserved. This has meant that, even in scholarly histories of the British Intelligence Services, Baden-Powell's best-seller, *My Adventures as a Spy* (1916), has been quoted as an important and authentic source. It would make tedious reading if I were to compile a comprehensive list of the ways in which Stephe's published text is contradicted by his contemporary diary entries and letters. There can be no doubt that he later 'improved' and amplified his accounts of many of his intelligence-gathering journeys, all of which had been undertaken with sight-seeing and meeting old friends equally in mind. He always enjoyed staying with French cavalry officers stationed in Tunisia and Algeria and was evidently trusted by them. So there is something rather theatrical about the way in which he sometimes represented his activities in the French North African colonies as dangerous. A good example occurs in *My Adventures as a Spy*:

A foreign country had recently manufactured a new field gun which was undergoing extensive secret trials, which were being conducted in one of her colonies in order to avoid being watched. I was sent to find out particulars . . . On arrival in the colony I found that a battery of new guns was carrying out experiments at a distant point along the railway. The place was by all description merely a roadside station, with not even a village near it, so it would be difficult to go and stay there without being noticed at once. The timetable, however, showed that the ordinary day train stopped there for half an hour for change of engines, so I resolved to see what I could do in the space of time allowed.[1]

He went on to describe how he saw the guns parked in the station yard and managed to get a look at them until sent away by a sentry. Later on, as the train left the station with Baden-Powell aboard, a corporal saw him using binoculars to make a final scrutiny of the guns. Several hours later a passenger who had become friendly with him warned him that he would be arrested when he reached the next station. By getting out at an earlier stop, Baden-Powell claimed that he managed to avoid this fate.[2] The unnamed foreign country was of course France, the colony Algeria and the incident, *if* it occurred, did so on 7 May 1893. On that day Baden-Powell was in Biskra, a small Algerian village on the railway line connecting Setif with Constantine. The War Office undoubtedly paid for this visit to Algeria but issued no specific instructions; Stephe undertook the trip on his own initiative, conveniently combining it with his final return journey from Malta to England.[3] Many small details given by Baden-Powell in his book do not accord with the account in his diary. For example, he actually stayed overnight at Biskra, which he stated in his published account would have given away his real intentions.

In fact, if he ever carried out any espionage in the place, he did so in the early hours of the morning and it could have had nothing to do with the station yard. His diary makes this clear:

> Got up at 4 – and went for a stroll around. To get to a rising ground on which stands one of the three blockhouses guarding the town, and from which I hoped to get a view, I had to wade across three strips of the river. Made my sketch – wandered back in time to get coffee, pack up, and leave by the 7.35 train for Setif. Only one thing marred my pleasure – and that was I have not been able to get some information I wanted, though I had tried one or two people – viz whether there were any wild boar in the neighbourhood. [The following two italicized passages were added by Baden-Powell, presumably later, in a different-coloured ink.] *Alias mil. intelligence of the place.* I booked my place in the train and then attempted to make one last attempt in the crowd – but in vain *and finally persuaded the Zouave, whom I had my eye on, to journey in my carriage, and most intelligent, well-informed and communicative I found him.*

Of course – regardless of the later addition of the italicized words –* 'wild boar' may genuinely have been a synonym for military equipment, even though he had been pigsticking with French officers two weeks earlier,[4] and more recently had been told by other French cavalrymen exactly where wild boar could be found in central Tunisia.[5] In his book *Pigsticking or Hoghunting* (1889), Baden-Powell had included information on the whereabouts of boar in a large number of countries and the subject of their distribution continued to interest him. But, assuming that 'wild boar' on this occasion was a code-word for guns, there are still plenty of inconsistencies between the published account and the unpublished diary entry. For example, the Zouave in the carriage does not appear in *My Adventures as a Spy*, and there is no friendly passenger in the diary. Baden-Powell described in his diary the buildings and the landscape seen from the train, and then wrote the following – the italicized words again being added later in a different ink: 'In the evening feeling rather unwell – *in other words some soldiers from my questions suspected me and telegraphed to that effect to Setif*. I left the train at a station an hour short of Setif to go to an inn and to bed. It would make no difference to my journey – as the train only went as far as Setif and I should have had to sleep there.' Quite possibly he really did leave the train as described, and some soldiers may have been suspicious of him, although it is impossible to believe that he could have been foolhardy enough to have used his binoculars from the train window after being warned by a sentry in the station yard. If there had really been a Zouave in the carriage with him, as the latter diary entry would suggest, the binoculars incident becomes totally unbelievable.

The large number of inconsistencies seemed due to Baden-Powell's desire to 'improve' the prosaic original incident and to make it into a dramatic adventure story. Yet even the diary on its own is highly suspect. Given his schoolboy French, and his English clothes, how could he have expected not to arouse suspicion by poking about in a small place like Biskra, where there were military installations? Nor would his decision to leave the train before Setif have availed him if the French authorities had really been eager to apprehend him. He travelled on to Algiers via Setif on the very same railway line the following day, so it would hardly have been difficult to arrest him. If he had genuinely feared arrest, he would have left the country as soon as possible; but four days after the incident he was happily socializing with the officers of the 1st Chasseurs d'Afrique in Algiers and Blida. They entertained him royally with luncheons, dinners, visits to barracks and, for good measure, a tour of 'some of the most curious streets in the Arab quarter' of Algiers.[6] In fact, so little apprehension did he feel that he returned to England via Marseilles and Paris.

The best-known pages in *My Adventures as a Spy* (which Baden-Powell wrote during the Great War when spying was a subject which aroused intense interest), were those on which he ingeniously purported to have concealed detailed plans of fortifications within the patterns of a butterfly's wings and the veins of a leaf[7] (see first photo section). In the introduction to his selection of true and fictional spy stories, *The Spy's Bedside Book,* Graham Greene stated that he found it hard to believe in 'Colonel [sic] Baden-Powell, on a butterfly hunt in Dalmatia, incorporating the plans for fortifications into the pattern of his butterfly's wings'.[8] Greene mistrusted the fantastic ingenuity of the idea. The details, which generally convinced him of the narrator's veracity in such accounts, were invariably mundane. The excerpt Graham Greene chose to quote[9] shows Stephe's strength as a writer: his down-to-earth tone and deceptively simple style (which he would later use to such excellent effect in his 'yarns' for Boy Scouts).

> Once I went 'butterfly-hunting' in Dalmatia. I went armed with most effective weapons for the purpose, which have served me well in many a similar campaign. I took a sketch-book, in which were numerous pictures – some finished, others only partly done – of butterflies of every degree and rank, from a 'Red Admiral' to a 'Painted Lady'. Carrying this book and a colour-box, and a butterfly net in my hand, I was above all suspicion to anyone who met me on the lonely mountain side, even in the neighbourhood of the forts. I was hunting butterflies, and it was always a good introduction with which to go to anyone who was watching me with suspicion. Quite frankly, with my sketch-book in hand, I would ask innocently whether he had seen such-and-such a butterfly in the neighbourhood, as I was anxious to catch one.[10]

Baden-Powell was in Dalmatia during the second week of August 1892; and although he mentioned in his diary that the British Consul-General in Sarajevo, Mr E. B. Freeman, was out butterfly-hunting when he called on him, there is no other reference to this pursuit either for its own sake or as a cover for espionage. Baden-Powell in fact spent his time bicycling through Bosnia. Since a Croatian baron was the only other man in the region who owned a bicycle, Stephe could not have chosen a more eye-catching mode of transport. He made himself even more conspicuous when he lost his pump and conducted an exhaustive search for the baron in order to borrow his.[11]

Nevertheless Baden-Powell *did* go out sketching forts on the western shore of the Straits of Messina, and on that occasion he did conceal his real activity under the guise of being an entomologist. Crossing the Straits he recorded having a delightful run – observing butterflies all the time. Since the Straits were five miles wide at the point where he crossed, his mention of butterflies would seem much more likely to indicate seaward-facing forts than winged insects. On many other occasions when he mentions capturing butterflies he means just that, as when on 25 April 1893 he went in pursuit of butterflies with some French army officer friends.[12]

Another example of Baden-Powell's story-telling at its best was also culled by Graham Greene for his selection:

The game of hide-and-seek is really one of the best games for a boy, and can be elaborated until it becomes scouting in the field. It teaches you a lot. I was strongly addicted to it as a child, and the craft learned in that innocent field of sport has stood me in good stead in many a critical time since. To lie flat in a furrow among the currant bushes when I had not time to reach the neighbouring box bushes before the pursuer came in sight taught me the value of not using the most obvious cover, since it would at once be searched. The hunters went at once to the box bushes as the likely spot, while I could watch their doings from among the stems of the currant bushes . . . This I found of value when I came to be pursued by mounted military police, who suspected me of being a spy at some manoeuvres abroad . . . After a rare chase I scrambled over a wall and dropped into an orchard of low fruit trees. Here squatting in a ditch I watched the legs of the gendarmes' horses while they quartered the plantation.[13]

In his diary Baden-Powell described the same incident, which took place at some Austrian military manoeuvres on 30 August 1892. 'I watched the reconnoitring – then the artillery – then the cavalry. Here I was spotted by a staff officer who sent a mounted gendarme for me but he never found me. He wasn't a gendarme – he was a fool . . . It was in a kind of orchard country. I could see his legs only, trotting about among the trees; if he had dismounted he would have seen me. I wasn't going to shout to him, so we never met.'[14] For this incident then, there had been a solid basis in fact (although there had been but one gendarme who had signally failed to 'quarter' the plantation). But for many of the events described in *My Adventures as a Spy,* I have found no evidence at all.

In the manuscript of his autobiography Baden-Powell claimed to have 'caught' four spies in his time, one of them 'a coal merchant in Hull'. In Stephe's Staff Diaries, the entry for 1 May 1909 reads: 'Spies – I received a private letter from Major Wilson D.S.O. E[ast] Y[orks] Yeomanry, enclosing a report of Sergt. Lee-Smith (which was corroborated by his own clerk) of a man suspected of being a German officer who has been living for six months at Hornsea – nominally as a coal dealer – but hiring horses and riding out all day making maps etc., communicating apparently with another at Flamboro.'[15] These then were two of the 'four spies', for whose capture the credit should have gone to Major Wilson and Sergeant Lee-Smith. The remaining two of the four were 'caught' by Stephe in Valetta on 2 February 1891: 'On my way back from parade I caught and stopped 2 foreigners photographing French Creek.'[16] Nothing further exists to show whether they were simply over-enthusiastic sight-seers or whether they were detained.

When the German invasion scare was at its height in Britain between 1906 and 1910, Baden-Powell was sold a bogus invasion plan by an enterprising group of German-American forgers who had set up a 'spy-bureau' in Belgium. They contrived to sell similar material to Major-General J.S. Ewart, the Director of Military Operations, and to William Le Queux, the espionage writer.[17] Stephe believed in this plan implicitly and gave a series of lectures on the subject, finally obliging the Secretary of State for War, R. B. Haldane, to answer questions in the House about the advisability of permitting generals to make speeches likely to heighten international tension.[18] Baden-Powell never lost faith in his German invasion blueprint and wrote to Lord Grey in 1916 re-affirming his belief in its authenticity.[19]

Because espionage is an activity founded upon duplicity, it is probably naïve to expect too much veracity from its practitioners, but Baden-Powell's exaggerations and distortions arose from deeper causes. His longing to be a romantic hero derived from his childhood need to attract his mother's attention away from the more favoured George, the more talented Frank and 'darling Badie'. Stephe, however, had additional less personal reasons for needing to elevate minor incidents from his life into major dramas. By the time he wrote *My Adventures as a Spy*, he was already having to supply his Boy Scouts with adventure 'yarns' in a wide variety of publications and could therefore hope to recycle individual chapters from his spying book over again in *The Scout, The Wolf-Cub* and *Yarns for Boy Scouts*. This repetition of his spying stories in time had the effect of making Baden-Powell's reputation as a spy almost equal to his fame as the Defender of Mafeking.

The book itself was reissued under a new title in 1924, eight years (and many editions) after its first publication. It became *The Adventures of a Spy*, rather than *My Adventures as a Spy*. By then the book had started to embarrass him, particularly when construed as auto-biography. In early 1924 Baden-Powell was under pressure from the Scouts' Committee to sanction a biography. 'I am hesitating,' he wrote back to Percy W. Everett, who was a director of Arthur Pearson & Co. as well as a key member of the Committee. 'There are pros and there are cons – especially cons from *my* point of view.'[20] One of those cons was his fear that various supposedly authentic happenings in his life, about which he had written many times, would be found to be invented. This was probably the moment when he decided to make additions to his Tunisian and Algerian diaries.

If Stephe's life had offered him less scope for action, he might well have become a writer of adventure fiction. Indeed, when compelled to be relatively inactive during his Indian years, he had written many 'stories', always presented neither quite as fact nor quite as fiction.[21] *My Adventures as a Spy* was in that tradition. The same desire to invent, embroider and resort to 'make belief' would make *Scouting for Boys* a creative triumph and one of the most popular books ever written, but it also made his book on spying a most unreliable record of his actual experiences in that field. He needed to believe the world was an essentially malleable place, in which invention could transform reality.

8. Lord Wolseley's Man at Last (1893–95)

During the summer of 1892, Sir Henry Smyth had told Baden-Powell that he did not intend to stay on as Governor of Malta beyond the end of 1893. This faced Stephe with the old predicament which had originally led him to accept his uncle's offer to be his A.D.C. – namely that he could not afford to live as an ordinary officer in his regiment while it was stationed in the British Isles. His pay would be £300 per annum, his expenses £700, and the most he could realistically expect to earn from the sale of occasional sketches and articles would be no more than say £50 a year.[1]

Instead of waiting until the very end of his uncle's term, Stephe decided to return to England in the spring of 1893. He did so principally because Sir Baker Russell had advised him against further delay. Since Russell's command at Aldershot was drawing to a close, and since Stephe expected his old colonel to land the important post of Inspector General of Cavalry, he felt confident that Sir Baker's influence would never again be more useful to him.[2] Another reason why Baden-Powell felt confident about returning to England at the earliest opportunity was George's engagement, announced on 12 February 1893, to the heiress daughter of an Australian landowner. Frances Wilson already possessed a fortune of £100,000 which provided an annual income of £5,000. Just over a year earlier George had written to his mother describing marriage as the only investment likely to yield 'a lasting form of income' – an understandable opinion given his recent loss of £1,500 (all borrowed) on the stock market. 'There are numerous girls about with at least two or three thousand [a year],' he pointed out to Henrietta Grace. 'If we could each pick up one, the family would be able to spend £15,000 a year, or more, instead of £2,000, which would mean greatly improved comfort all round.'[3] Very soon after their marriage George's wife agreed that, in view of all the money spent by Henrietta Grace on George's political career, she ought to pay her mother-in-law £2,000 at once. This enabled Henrietta Grace to help Stephe; and a year later George himself guaranteed to see his younger brother through the following two years.[4]

Although Stephe's immediate financial fears were eased, he was now ignominiously dependent upon a triumvirate of benefactors: George, his mother, and above all his sister-in-law, who was probably only helping him because she felt obliged to. As anxious as ever to get a job enabling him to stand on his own feet, it seemed an answer to a prayer when, in October 1893, Sir Frederick Carrington sent Stephe a telegram inviting him to go out to Matabeleland as his Staff Officer. He was therefore devastated to be told a few days later that the Colonial Office had refused to pay for imperial officers to be sent out to reinforce Cecil Rhodes's company employees and the local volunteers. When Baden-Powell eventually heard that Lobenguela's army of 5,000 warriors had been defeated by Rhodes's men, he knew he had missed another 'little war' which – like Uganda – could have proved the open sesame to a command of his own in southern Africa.[5]

This blow was swiftly followed by a worse one. Far from being appointed Inspector General of Cavalry, Sir Baker Russell was offered the inferior post of G.O.C. of the North-West District of the United Kingdom, with his headquarters at Chester. This was effectively a demotion, making it plain that Sir Baker would never win promotion to any of the army's top jobs. Two hundred miles from Whitehall, he would have no influence at all.[6] The appointment also came as a severe shock to Kenneth McLaren, who was a great favourite with Russell and could have expected, as one of the Inspector General of Cavalry's two A.D.C.s (Stephe being the other), to have been in daily touch with the most influential officers in the army. He was still listed six places below the regiment's most senior captain, and knew that without obtaining a strategically useful job he would never rise above the rank of major. 'The Boy' reluctantly agreed to go to Chester as Sir Baker's A.D.C., although it would once again mean separation from Stephe. But since he would have damned his career by remaining in the regiment, McLaren had no real choice. This was sad for both men, since they had been happy to be together again in the regiment for the first time in six years. In Ireland, where the 13th Hussars were stationed, McLaren had bought horses for Baden-Powell before his arrival, and the two old friends had soon been acting in plays together, riding across country and visiting mutual friends.

With the Staff College no longer a possibility, a 'little war' within the next couple of years was absolutely vital for Stephe if he were ever to command a regiment, let alone aspire to greater things.[7] Nor were George's heavy-handed hints to him about the desirability of getting married what he wanted to hear.[8] Through Agnes he had recently met an heiress, Edith Christie Miller whose parents, Stephe told Henrietta Grace, were 'very kind, very rich, but – as the Duke of Cambridge would say – very common'.[9] Baden-Powell could not bring himself to propose to Edith until 1905, by which time she would have other plans.[10] He still felt, as he had done when reacting to the news of

George's engagement, unwilling to consider marriage for himself. It is symptomatic of Baden-Powell's loneliness that on his return from Malta he should have written to William Christie's girls, who were now grown-up and living in England, asking them to make him 'very glad indeed' by writing.[11] Between 1876 and 1893 he had spent only three years in England – and none of these consecutively. The Christie girls reminded him of happier more settled days in India when he and McLaren had been young officers with the whole world apparently before them.

In January 1894, sailing along the Albanian coast in his brother's magnificently appointed yacht, Stephe inevitably reflected upon the contrast between Sir George Baden-Powell's worldly achievements and his own. After such prodigious efforts it was heartbreaking to consider that he might end his career as a major (his present rank), or at best a colonel. This was hardly what his mother had set her heart upon. Stephe appears in a group photograph [see first photo section] taken on board the *Otaria* that January. Normally the life and soul of the party, he is standing in the back row almost squeezed out of the picture, behind George and Frances, Frances's brother and sister-in-law and other guests, including an African and an English clergyman whose company Stephe would not normally have endured. But Frances was religiously inclined and so, with her money ultimately underpinning his career, Baden-Powell had the sense to bite his tongue. There is a sadness about his expression which the soft-focus enhances rather than obscures. 'Until I too can succeed,' he seems to be saying, 'I will not exist.' Compared with his self-confident face photographed seven years earlier, when Stephe had been with his aunt and uncle on their way to the Cape [see first photo section] the resignation and misery of the later expression seems even more striking.[12]

Baden-Powell returned from the Mediterranean to Ireland. During the course of the next two years the 13th Hussars moved from Ballingcollig, near Cork, to Dundalk, and Belfast in the North. According to George Noble the new commanding officer, Colonel E. R. H. Torin, was 'a pompous ignorant ass' under whom the regiment had deteriorated on account of his 'bullying way of sitting on those officers who did not please him'.[13] Stephe escaped briefly when he acted as Brigade-Major to Colonel French (later Field-Marshal Lord French of Ypres) at some manoeuvres in Berkshire; but no staff appointment followed.[14]

Then four months later, Baden-Powell received a telegram from Lord Wolseley which he knew, as soon as he had read it, marked the turning point in his life. Later he recalled the ecstasy of the moment: 'The pink "flimsy" bearing the magic words, "You are selected to proceed on active service," gives to the recipient a gush of elation . . . He treads on air, he becomes an object of interest to all, and especially to himself.'[15] The Staff College would be irrelevant now, if he took full advantage of this opportunity. 'Well My Dearest Mother,' he wrote joyfully, 'Would you believe it – I've got my orders for going on service at last! I'm to go to Ashanti as one of the staff . . . I needn't tell *you* it is a great thing for me.'[16] A few days later he crossed the Irish Sea for an interview with Lord Wolseley, who had been appointed Commander-in-Chief only weeks earlier. On arrival he found the passages of the War Office 'blocked with fellows longing to go'. Three hundred officers had made representations about their suitability for his job alone. Wolseley welcomed Stephe warmly, and told him he was to command a Native Levy which would act as the advance guard for the whole party. Baden-Powell wrote at once to his mother, who was out of town: 'I've been given *the* one very duty that I had hoped for but had not dared to ask – viz to have charge of the Reconnaissance work. It is a grand thing for me – and will be even grander if the enemy will only attempt to stand against us.'[17] He had now succeeded in gaining entry to Wolseley's famous 'Garnet Ring' – his hand-picked group of favoured officers, also known as his 'Africans' (as opposed to Lord Roberts's favoured 'Indians'). General Sir Redvers Buller and General Sir Evelyn Wood had both served in Africa under Wolseley. Now it was Stephe's turn to go to the Field-Marshal's continent at his behest. His career was no longer in the balance as it had been for thirteen long years; he would now rightly be looked upon as a coming man.

To have gained the personal favour of the Commander-in-Chief and his Adjutant-General (Wood) during a decade in which the aristocracy and the rich considered that a career in the army offered their sons more kudos than any other activity was a great achievement. It is therefore ironic that almost 40 years later, when Baden-Powell wrote his autobiography, he should have sought to attribute his selection for the Ashanti campaign to chance and good luck. In August 1893 he had taken part in cavalry manoeuvres at the Curragh, and during a mock battle captured a battery of guns by a simple ruse. By ordering some of his men to tow branches behind their horses along a dusty road, he raised enough dust to suggest that a large force was attacking from the front. Under cover of this diversion, the greater part of his squadron crept unobserved into the battery from the rear. This incident, Stephe claimed, had so impressed Lord Wolseley that he chose him for Ashanti.[18] This of course was nonsense. There is no mention of the 'branches ruse' in any of his letters, although he did tell George that there had been a mock battle during some enjoyable manoeuvres.[19] But this was *two years* before Wolseley became Commander-in-Chief and it is wildly improbable – even supposing the incident took place – that the then Adjutant-General would have been more than marginally influenced by it. That earlier history of dinners with Mrs Baden-

Powell, a machine-gun harness, intelligence reports, George's brilliantly angled Zululand press reports, Stephe's brief command of a native contingent against Dinuzulu and his publications on scouting and reconnaissance would all have weighed more with the Field-Marshal than a clever idea at some manoeuvres. Yet Stephe had never wanted to admit how hard he and his family had worked to secure his advancement. Just as at Charterhouse he had considered hard work to be bad form, even in old age he would prefer to associate himself with aristocratic good fortune rather than with middle-class effort and application. He consequently robbed his family of the credit for a great triumph of their 'grouping' method. If George's knighthood had been 'the first harvest' for so much endeavour, Stephe's selection as one of Lord Wolseley's favoured 'Africans' deserves to be considered the second.

5

THE COMING MAN

1. 'A Grand Thing for Me': The Ashanti Campaign (1895–96)

The country to which Lord Wolseley was sending Baden-Powell was one in which he himself had served with characteristically crushing impact. In 1873, just after enduring the seventh full-scale invasion of the Gold Coast by the Ashanti in as many decades, the British Government decided to send Sir Garnet Wolseley to punish them. He did so the following year with his usual thoroughness, and by the Treaty of Fomena required the Ashanti ruler to pay a massive indemnity of 50,000 ounces of gold and to renounce all claims to sovereignty over half-a-dozen neighbouring tribes. The Ashanti would also have to abandon 'human sacrifices' and keep open the road linking their capital of Kumasi with the Gold Coast.

A year later the Governor of the Gold Coast, Mr G. C. Strahan, sent a despatch to his masters in the Colonial Office in which he lucidly spelled out their dilemma. Because Wolseley and his 2,000 soldiers had broken the power of the Asantehene (or ruler of Ashanti), he had no control over tribes which had formerly been his vassals and consequently could not stop the inter-tribal raids which were already damaging trade. But if the British were to allow the ruler of Ashanti to grow strong again, in time he would once more wage war on the Gold Coast.[1]

For a decade the Colonial Office pursued a policy defined by an astute Under-Secretary as 'masterly inactivity'.[2] Then in the mid-1880s the Colonial Office began to receive warnings from British traders about French and German ambitions in the region. The London and the Manchester Chambers of Commerce urged a more energetic policy in West Africa, not only to keep out foreign competition but also to revive stagnating trade. They felt that the presence of a British Resident in Kumasi would prove a stabilizing influence. Believing that such a move would simply hasten the incorporation of Ashanti into the Gold Coast Colony, the British Government preferred to do nothing. By 1893, however, the acting Governor of the Gold Coast had been converted to the view that 'the Ashanti have exercised such a baneful influence on the English settlements of the Gold Coast in years past . . . and have so constantly interfered with trade that it should be a settled policy of H.M.

Government to expedite the annexation of Ashanti with all reasonable and proper means.'[3]

It only awaited the arrival of a Colonial Secretary in favour of Imperial expansion in Africa to set the ball rolling. With the appointment of Joseph Chamberlain in June 1895, the moment had come.

Chamberlain lost no time in elaborating his doctrine. 'I regard many of our colonies,' he declared in August 1895, 'as being in the condition of undeveloped estates, and estates which can never be developed without Imperial assistance.'[4] The new Colonial Secretary saw at once that, if the Gold Coast was ever to prosper, Ashanti would have to be annexed. So early in September he told the new Governor, Mr W. E. Maxwell, to send an ultimatum to the Asantehene Agyeman Prempeh. In December 1893 a Permanent Secretary in the Colonial Office had proposed that: 'If we decide for protection [declaring Ashanti a British Protectorate], we should begin by demanding a large sum for indemnity in respect of recent events [Ashanti raids on the Gold Coast] to be withdrawn if Prempeh asks for protection.'[5] This was power politics at its most cynical.

In Maxwell's ultimatum, Prempeh was declared not to have observed the terms of Wolseley's Treaty of Fomena. He had failed to pay the whole of the financial indemnity (which he must now remit in full), had attacked tribes friendly to the British Government, had checked trade and had permitted the continuance of human sacrifice. Prempeh was also informed that he would have to accept a British Resident at Kumasi forthwith. For the Governor suddenly to invoke a 22-year-old treaty without immediate grounds for complaint struck Prempeh as extraordinarily unjust. Full payment of the absurdly large indemnity had never been expected or there would have been agitation for it years ago; nor was it reasonable to blame him for having failed to establish peaceful conditions in Ashanti (conducive to the growth of trade) without first having permitted him to impose his authority upon subject tribes. But since the chiefs of these tribes were endlessly seeking sanctuary in the Gold Coast and appealing to the Governor for protection, Prempeh had often been thwarted. Nor did he think it fair to describe as 'human sacrifices' death sentences required by the Ashanti legal system for a range of crimes no more extensive than that obtaining in England 100 years earlier.

Believing that an appeal to Queen Victoria – over the heads of Governor Maxwell and his colleagues – would secure justice for him, Prempeh sent an embassy to England and ignored the ultimatum. This was a serious mistake. His ambassadors were refused an audience with the Queen; nor were they received by the Colonial Secretary, who believed that Prempeh had only sent these envoys as a delaying tactic and would disown on their return whatever they negotiated in

England. Chamberlain therefore asked the War Office for assistance, and in due course Lord Wolseley prepared an expeditionary force. Ashanti would receive British 'protection' whether its ruler and its people wanted it or not.

In the House of Commons Chamberlain chose to represent himself and the Government as acting solely in the interests of Ashanti and the Gold Coast. For decades, he said: 'This district of Africa, which is rich in natural resources, has been devastated, destroyed and ruined by inter-tribal disputes, and especially by the evil Government of the authorities of Ashanti.'[6] Wolseley's 1874 expedition had created a power vacuum and consequent chaos. In 1896 the intention was to fill the vacuum with British rule.

★

Most Victorian army officers longed to fight, considering with Lord Wolseley that the sentiment ' "war is a horrible thing", is a nice heading, but only for a schoolgirl's copy book'.[7] 'It is only through experience of the sensation,' wrote the Commander-in-Chief, 'that we learn how intense, even in anticipation, is the rapture-giving delight which the attack upon an enemy affords . . . All other sensations are but as the tinkling of a doorbell in comparison with the throbbing of Big Ben.'[8] Stephe's only fear as he prepared for departure was 'that the enemy will give in altogether'. The same sentiments were echoed by the vast majority of his brother officers. Like them, he wanted to go not simply for the sake of a fight but to gain promotion. Thanks to their superior weapons, few white soldiers were likely to die at the hands of their enemies during campaigns against Africans. Such 'little wars' were often viewed almost as a superior kind of sport – 'man-hunting', as Baden-Powell described tracking down enemy patrols. Nevertheless the reputation of West Africa as the white man's grave-yard had earned that region real respect – principally, but not by any means entirely, on account of disease. In 1824 the Governor of the Gold Coast and most of his 500-strong force were killed by 10,000 Ashanti. Sir Charles McCarthy's gold-rimmed skull had been the drinking cup of Ashanti rulers until Lord Wolseley's arrival half a century later.

When Stephe boarded the train at Euston, bound for Liverpool, he was seen off by his brothers Frank and Baden, and by 'about a million of the public . . . although it was past midnight, cheering and singing patriotic songs as if we were off to fight the French'.[9] Baden-Powell would have known that Wolseley's triumph of 1874 had been bought at the expense of 300 British casualties, the majority from disease. He was warned about malaria by Wolseley himself, who recommended him to 'take a double set of mosquito curtains to rig over my bed at night, to keep out the malaria'. Once inside the curtains Baden-Powell was advised to smoke a pipe of tobacco. Since insects dislike smoke this was excellent advice – given, incidentally, before the Anopheles mosquito had been identified as the culprit.[10] Baden-Powell dutifully smoked until the damp climate rotted his tobacco.[11]

Sir Baker Russell and Kenneth McLaren came aboard the transport at Liverpool to say farewell. Sir Baker gave Stephe a short sword-bayonet which he had found effective in hand-to-hand fighting against the Ashanti in 1874. 'The Boy' handed over a compass – an indispensable aid in the tropical forests which covered much of West Africa. During the voyage Baden-Powell read Sir William Butler's *The Story of a Failure*, an account of the author's inability in 1874 to stop the Native Levy from melting away into the forest after the Ashanti capital had been taken. Butler's force had come from a single tribe, and Baden-Powell determined not to make the same mistake in recruiting his own men.

'The job for my force,' Baden-Powell wrote, 'was to go ahead of the main body which was composed of white and West Indian troops, to scout in the bush some days ahead, and to ascertain the moves and whereabouts of the enemy. Also we had to act as pioneers in cutting a path and making a roadway through the jungle for the troops to follow . . .'[12]

On arrival at Cape Coast Baden-Powell and his subaltern, Captain H. W. Graham, recruited their 800 men from six tribes, the largest contingent being furnished by King Matikoli of the Krobos. It amused Baden-Powell that these local chiefs were known as kings, and it appealed to his sense of humour to fine them a few shillings for some paltry irregularity.[13] Actually assembling the Levy was far harder than obtaining promises of men from the various chiefs. Noon on 16 December was the time ordained for the Levy to parade for the first time outside Cape Coast Castle.

> The parade-ground outside the castle lies like an arid desert in the midday sun, and the sea-breeze wanders where it listeth. Not a man is there. It is a matter then for a hammock-ride through the slums of the slum that forms the town. Kings are forked out of the hovels where they are lodging, at the end of a stick; they in their turn rouse out their captains, and by two o'clock the army is assembled. Then it is a sight for the gods to see 'The Sutler' putting each man in his place. The stupid inertness of the puzzled negro is duller than that of an ox; a dog would grasp your meaning in one-half the time. Men and brothers! They may be brothers, but they certainly are not men.[14]

The last two sentences of this passage, which appeared in Baden-Powell's published account of the Campaign, have been quoted by both his recent detractors, Piers Brendon and Michael Rosenthal, to show that he was an unrepentant racist. In fact, passages almost as critical of Africans were written by two of the nineteenth century's greatest missionaries, Robert Moffat and David Livingstone, both of whom developed close and affectionate relationships with individual Africans. Livingstone wrote of a tribe that he esteemed more than many as being 'totally lacking in all self-respect, savage and cruel under success, but easily cowed and devoid of all moral courage'.[15] From the Africans' point of view, Baden-Powell's arrival presented them with an interesting opportunity for earning money and trade goods. Naturally they hoped to secure whatever advantage they could without endangering their lives or exhausting themselves unduly. Being accustomed to having his orders promptly obeyed and his prearranged appointments kept, Stephe made the common European mistake of supposing that Africans whose way of life did not require the punctuality demanded of factory workers were too stupid to run their affairs in an organized fashion. By his statement 'they may be brothers, but they certainly are not men', he did not mean to relegate them to membership of some sub-species. His preoccupation with 'making men' out of his raw young soldiers gives an indication of what he really meant. Somebody who was 'not a man', in the sense of being self-reliant and hardy, was 'a waster' or 'a jellyfish' in Baden-Powell's argot, but he would not have intended to imply that an African 'jellyfish' was not a human being. The fact that he wrote openly about Africans in this way, for publication, shows that he expected most of his readers to share his views, as indeed they did. He called Africans 'niggers' or 'savages', as did most Britains of all classes during the 1890s.

From Stephe's point of view he was paying his Africans a generous wage to serve in the Levy (they were being paid as much as the privates among the expedition's 2,000 British soldiers), but they saw no reason why they should not try to extract more from him and find out how little they could get away with doing. Although Baden-Powell misunderstood his recruits en masse, he developed excellent relationships with individuals and relied very heavily upon one man in particular, Chief Andoh of the Elmina tribe, to whom he dedicated his book *The Downfall of Prempeh*, calling the chief, 'My Guide, Adviser and Friend'. In writing to Lord Wolseley, who considered that the negro would have remained 'more useful if we had never emancipated him',[16] Baden-Powell never pandered to his Commander-in-Chief's prejudices. Instead, he described Chief Andoh as 'one of the very best and nicest natives I ever met'.[17]

Baden-Powell ruled out the possibility of a serious mutiny by enrolling numerous different tribal contingents, but this presented him with severe linguistic and organizational difficulties. Nevertheless the various groups worked well at different tasks. Building bridges was one of the Levy's most important jobs and Baden-Powell was impressed by the coastal tribesmen's mastery of knots which they used in making fishing nets. By knotting lengths of creeper they could bind substantial wooden structures together. Yet these same men caused an early crisis by refusing to march because they had insufficient salt in their ration. Not having enough salt to grant their request, he tried to reason with them; having wasted several hours in fruitless negotiation, he 'called out to the King to warn his men that I was now going to fetch out our old friend "the whip that talks" and that the last man in camp would be the one he would talk to. I moved with a joyous step to my tent, and when I came out a minute later and gave one resounding crack with my hunting crop, the whole party had scrambled to their feet and were already humping their packs up on to their shoulders.'[18]

Stephe adopted as his personal catch-phrase: 'A smile and a stick will carry you through any difficulty.' If smiling persuasion failed, the stick or whip remained in reserve. Whether he ever used either is uncertain.[19] He himself denied it; but Harold Begbie, his first biographer, contradicts him – although no evidence exists, and when Begbie's book was in preparation Stephe himself was in Mafeking and therefore unable to comment. Floggings undoubtedly took place in Baden-Powell's column, as in the main force, with the number of lashes limited to twelve in general orders, and these only to be delivered in the presence of a commissioned officer.[20] One such punishment was sketched by Baden-Powell, and a slightly altered version of this was later published in *The Graphic* [see second photo section].[21] Most nineteenth-century European travellers, in command of hundreds of African porters, had resorted to floggings and threats of summary execution when placed in circumstances often much less dangerous than those in which Baden-Powell and his subaltern regularly found themselves.[22] Had they ever capitulated to malingerers, it would have doomed the further progress of the Levy, and very likely of the whole expedition, which relied upon the advance party to clear the ground and give warning of the enemy's presence. In dense forests men who knew the terrain, even if armed with spears, could easily surprise and even annihilate a better equipped force. Their 500 Africans were armed with primitive flintlocks and issued with red fezes, but these accoutrements did not make them any less indisciplined. Most of the tribal groups were unable even to communicate with one another, except through interpreters.

'In addition to the "whip that talks" I had also another moral persuader in the shape of Isiqwi-qwa, a Colt repeating carbine. This weapon could bang away from its magazine a dozen rounds if need be as fast as a man could fire.' By means of a demonstration on some paw-paw fruit, Baden-Powell usually managed to defuse potentially explosive situations.[23] But since he and Graham could have been murdered in their sleep with the greatest of ease, Baden-Powell engaged a 'special body-guard of eight hammock men from Sierra Leone. Their country manners and customs and language, being entirely alien to those of my larger contingent, would keep them as a corps d'élite, a thing apart, a reliable guard.'[24] He faced a real crisis when these very men turned against him, but again his Colt repeater saved him. He had been confronted on a deserted path by all eight hammock men, whose demeanour left him in no doubt that they meant trouble. Raising his Colt and releasing the safety-catch, Baden-Powell ordered them back to camp and to his great relief, they obeyed. Stephe's African factotum (a member of the Hausa tribe) punished the miscreants in local style.

> He cut down a small tree so that it lay about a foot above the ground, and he made the whole lot of eight men sit on the ground and put their legs under the tree with their feet projecting on the far side; then each man had to lean over and touch his toes with his fingers; the Hausa then came along and tied every thumb to every great toe. This was his idea of a stocks and there he left them for the night. The prisoners, however, devised a method of obtaining release – or thought they did. One of them started to yowl in a miserable way at the top of his voice and as soon as his breath ran out, the yowl was taken up by the next, and so it went on in succession. This they hoped would disturb me to such an extent that I should order their release. But before I could suggest a remedy the Hausa himself had devised one. He cut a thin whippy cane and went to the singer and smote him across the back, and then stood up by the next man ready to smite the moment he began his song. The singing stopped like magic and was not resumed.[25]

There are many accounts of the predicament of whites in remote parts of Africa, and all confirm the importance of maintaining a bold front and behaving as if invulnerable. In *The Flame Trees of Thika*, Elspeth Huxley wrote about white settlers in Kenya at a later date, but her thesis applies equally to isolated white officers leading large numbers of Africans three decades earlier.

> Respect [wrote Mrs Huxley] was the only protection available to Europeans who lived singly, or in scattered families among thousands of Africans accustomed to constant warfare and armed with spears and poisoned arrows . . . This respect preserved them like an invisible coat of mail or a form of magic, and seldom failed; but it had to be very carefully guarded. The least rent or puncture might, if not immediately checked, split the whole garment asunder and expose the wearer in all his human vulnerability . . . Challenged, it could be brushed aside like a spider's web.[26]

On this expedition Baden-Powell constantly demonstrated his canniness in dealing with his men. They constructed their bridges carefully because, on completion, he obliged the builders to jump vigorously upon them. But canny or not, it took all Baden-Powell's skill to persuade his men to cross the river Prah after some of his Adansi scouts returned with intelligence that Prempeh and the Ashanti meant to lure them all forward and then fall upon the column's rear. News that some of the Ashanti were armed with modern Snider rifles proved very damaging to morale, since the Levy had nothing better than antiquated flintlocks.[27] The Gold Coast proverb: 'Softly, softly, catchee monkey,' proved extremely helpful to Baden-Powell.[28] He divided the Levy into small companies of about twenty men under a 'Captain' responsible for their conduct.[29] Stephe was not helped when Graham was laid low by malaria, and the two officers sent to replace him suffered the same fate. 'As for me,' Baden-Powell told Wolseley, 'I have not yet had time to get anything worse than a healthy appetite.'[30]

On 27 December 1895 the Levy crossed the river Prah – the huge dug-out ferry making numerous journeys before the whole force and its equipment were deposited on the far side. During the next few days the forest became thicker, and the path narrower. If the scouts were bringing in accurate information, the Ashanti king was assembling an army of 8,000 warriors. In early January, as Baden-Powell's men drew closer to Kumasi, the Ashanti capital, he gave orders to move only by night.

It was as dark as pitch, one's only guide to the path was the white rag or package on the next man in front. With stick in hand, one groped one's way through the deep, dense gloom . . . Now a jerk down as one stepped off a hummock, now a stumble over a root, now caught in a prickly creeper, now ploughing through the holding swamp; and all around the deep silence of the forest, only broken by the rare crack of a trodden stick. One could scarcely believe that several hundred people were with one, moving – slowly, it was true, but still moving – ever forward. The carriers carried, in addition to their loads, their own packages of food and furniture – the furniture consisting of a mat, the food of plantains and dried fish . . . Fallen trees were frequent and tangled bush and streams combined to check and break the column. Each man took his several seconds to negotiate the obstacles, and lost a few yards of distance in doing so, thus every minute saw the column growing longer. This could only be remedied by frequent halts and slow marching at the head . . . Then the whisper passed that the scouts had discovered the enemy. Suddenly a flicker and a flare of light in the bush well to our right. Enemy? No, it is the advanced scouts on our road, who think they have discovered an ambush. They creep round the particular thicket they suspect, then suddenly lighting

brands, they hurl them into the hiding place to light up the hoped-
for target. This time they draw blank . . . The march does not
appear so tedious or so slow when one moves among the scouts.
These fellows are on the *qui vive* all the time – now stopping to
listen, now diving into the bush, with scarce a rustle, to search the
flanks, nor is their watchfulness too great for the occasion, for twice
we came upon the glowing logs of outpost fires that have hastily
been quitted; but those are the only signs of men.[31]

In the early stages of the march the British troops had liked to chant
their song:

> Oh Prempeh, Prempeh,
> You'd better mind your eye;
> You'd better far be civil,
> Or else you'll have to die,
> And your kingdom of Ashanti,
> You'll never see it more,
> If you fight the old West Yorks
> And the Special Service Corps.[32]

In fact from the very beginning Prempeh gave every sign of wishing to
be 'civil'. The first evidence of his unwillingness to fight came on 8
January, but his envoys were not trusted. On 11 January Major
Gordon, who had taken over from Graham as second-in-command of
the Levy, sent a note to Baden-Powell: 'Had great palaver . . . The
King had sent his two little sons as hostages covered with golden
ornaments. I coveted the latter but would have nothing to do with the
former, and repeated my message that nothing could be done except at
Kumasi, and there in Prempeh's presence . . .'[33] Since Prempeh had
sent his sons in person, their message ought to have been considered
trustworthy. It is not clear whether Gordon or Baden-Powell relayed
everything they knew to Sir Francis Scott, the commander of the
expedition. They may have prevented intelligence getting back to the
main body in an effort to deny Prempeh a peaceful conclusion.
Certainly they both wanted proper 'active service' but so too did Sir
Francis, who must have feared being made to look foolish, with his
gigantic force, if Prempeh refused to fight. By his determination to
march into Kumasi, Sir Francis and his staff may well have been
hoping to provoke resistance.

On 15 January the Levy arrived at the village of Ordasu, a mere two
days' march from Kumasi, to be greeted by another embassy, this time
offering complete and unconditional submission. Yet even now
Baden-Powell and Gordon affected to be unconvinced. 'In spite of all
assurances we cannot trust to what the Ashantis say,' wrote Stephe.[34]
But two days later in Kumasi as the main body of British troops

marched in, Prempeh told General Sir Francis Scott that it had always been his intention to submit to the Governor of the Gold Coast as soon as he entered the town. But Stephe still doubted his good faith and during the night, he and some of his Adansi scouts lay in hiding close to Prempeh's residence in case he tried to escape under cover of darkness. Prempeh stayed where he was, and Baden-Powell and his men only succeeded in scaring a number of the King's counsellors on their way back to their huts. His men also pounced on several of their armed servants, and he himself wrestled one of these men to the ground. As with so many of Baden-Powell's accounts of his adventures, this incident was later inflated to such an extent that the servant became 'Prempeh's Chief Scout'. For Mrs Wade's biography, Stephe obligingly drew a sketch of this incident, writing under it: 'Capture of Prempeh's Chief Scout 1895.' (The date should have been 1896.) In *The Downfall of Prempeh* (Baden-Powell's published account of the campaign) he entitled one of the drawings: 'Capture of one of Prempeh's scouts by the author.'[35] The text, however (p. 121), makes it clear that the man was merely a servant who had done no harm to anyone. Robbed of his weapon, he was at once released.

The following day the whole of Sir Francis Scott's force paraded in a closed square on the open space in the centre of Kumasi. Prempeh, who had obviously hoped for better terms because of his offer to submit, was outraged to be ordered to kneel down in the presence of his people and hug the knees of Governor Maxwell, who was seated next to Sir Francis Scott and his staff officer, Colonel Kempster, on a daïs made of biscuit tins. The Governor announced that, since the terms of the Treaty of Fomena had not been observed, he would not conclude another treaty unless the expense of the present expedition were met at once. When asked to pay 50,000 ounces of gold, Prempeh was astounded; the most he could manage immediately, he said, was 700 ounces. Whereupon Maxwell arrested not only him but his mother and father, his brother, his uncles, and a dozen of his advisers. The detention of Prempeh, whom Maxwell wished to deport to a remote island, came as a great shock to the Ashanti and to the Colonial Secretary. 'Remind Maxwell,' minuted an exasperated Chamberlain, 'that if Prempeh agreed to ultimatum and paid indemnity no further steps would be taken against him. He has submitted, and as to the indemnity if he has no money he cannot pay . . . Mr Maxwell must give us much better reasons [for his action] than any adduced at present.'[36]

Maxwell justified himself by saying that, since Prempeh had neither been defeated in the field nor even suffered the destruction of his principal towns, it would be impossible to convince his people that British authority had to be respected in future unless something dramatic were done. 'To have been satisfied by mere words, whether the verbal supplication of a frightened but unpunished savage, or written promises, would have been folly.'[37] Chamberlain was probably more influenced by the reflection that, since the British Government could claim legitimacy neither through a treaty with the lawful government of Ashanti nor by right of conquest, Prempeh, if left at liberty, would have been entitled under international law to sign a treaty with France or Germany.[38]

The rank and file members of the British force might have felt more sympathy for Prempeh had they not discovered large numbers of decapitated bodies and skeletons in the town. As indicated earlier, these corpses did not as they supposed belong to hapless victims of 'human sacrifice', but were the bodies of condemned criminals who had been brought to Kumasi from all over Ashanti for execution. Death was not dealt out arbitrarily for the amusement of the King and the executioners, as claimed by Baden-Powell.[39] Nevertheless the skeletons put paid to any sympathy the British might otherwise have felt for Prempeh. Stephe, however, expressed no disgust. 'If you want a few hundred fresh skulls,' he informed his artist brother, Frank, 'I can send them to you with very little difficulty.'[40] Frank declined this offer. When Baden-Powell was despatched to nearby Bantama with orders to find the royal treasure, he found instead a large brass bowl about the size of a hip-bath and as deep. He was delighted to learn that this container was the very one used to collect the blood which regularly flowed from the necks of those executed. As he told Frank, this was a souvenir which he would certainly be bringing home.[41] He later presented it to the Royal United Services Institution. The discovery of the 'blood bowl', as he called it, made up for the disappointment of not being able to bring back a gold snake and gold sword, both of which he had been obliged to give up to the Colonial Office along with other golden artifacts. Nevertheless he kept back, illicitly, some gold jewellery which he would one day have made into earrings for his wife.

Prempeh would live in exile for 25 years in the Seychelles, where he became a Christian and attended church wearing a top hat and frock-coat. By then his son was a Boy Scout. Baden-Powell would later claim that the Scouts' staff originated in Ashanti as the forked stick with which Captain R. S. Curtis, of the Royal Engineers, had lifted up the telegraph wire to hang it out of harm's way in the branches above the track.[42] The Krobo fishermen's knots and their skill at bridge-building had suggested knots (and indeed bridge-building) as important elements in the Boy Scout programme.

At the start of the wearying 150-mile march back to the coast, Baden-Powell wrote to Lord Wolseley, bemoaning the fact that 'the Ashanti have caved in without a fight . . . We are a very sad camp in consequence . . . '[43] By the time Cape Coast Castle had been reached, half the force was suffering from dysentery and malaria. Over three-quarters of the officers were laid up, and two senior members of the staff were mortally ill. One of these – Prince Henry of Battenburg, a son-in-law of Queen Victoria – died during the voyage home.

By contrast, Stephe, after a week of non-stop marching through the tropical rain forest, was in excellent health. To have kept control over nearly 1,000 untrained Africans for six weeks, and to have kept them together through some of the most difficult terrain in Africa, was a great achievement. To have kept fit, too, also had nothing to do with luck. Apart from sleeping inside double mosquito curtains, he had taken great care of his feet and had always had a dry change of clothes to put on. Baden-Powell, aged 39, was a very different proposition from the young man who had begged to come home from India. His slight build now belied his toughness.[44]

On his return to England, Baden-Powell was immediately promoted to the rank of Brevet Lieutenant-Colonel. He had also achieved a lucrative journalistic scoop when, through pure good fortune, he had got his copy through to the *Daily Chronicle* (which retained his services), predicting the imminent surrender of Kumasi just before a tree fell on the telegraph wire and stopped all communication for several days. He was paid five guineas a column by the *Daily Chronicle*, and a lump sum of £170 from *The Graphic* for his sketches. He was also offered an advance of £100 by Mr Methuen to turn his diary into a book. 'Did I tell you,' he wrote uneasily to his aunt, Lady Smyth, 'I've given in to pressure and agreed to become an author. I am very much ashamed of myself – and the publishers would not take the book if, as I proposed, it was to be anonymous. But the lure was offered, my debts stared at me, and I fell.'[45] Given Stephe's inclusion of the picture of himself capturing the 'Chief Scout', his efforts to persuade Methuen to publish anonymously are unlikely to have been vigorous.

Sir George Baden-Powell set the final seal of success on the expedition when he hosted a celebratory dinner at the House of Commons. Guests included Lord Wolseley, Mr W. St. John Brodrick, soon to be Secretary of State for War, Viscount Goschen, the former Chancellor of the Exchequer, George Curzon, Under-Secretary of State for Foreign Affairs, and General Sir Reginald Gipps, the Military Secretary at Headquarters.[46] The expedition itself ended in a curious way which eerily anticipated Stephe's next appointment.

On arrival at the London docks, a big ship entered the dock just ahead of us and as she did so a band on the wharf struck up 'See the Conquering Hero comes', and a large posse of generals and staff officers from the War Office formed up on a red carpet to receive her as she moored at the quay. As our ship was then warped in to the opposite side of the dock the band suddenly ceased playing and the bandsmen, together with generals and staff, were observed scuttling round the dock, hastily leaving the first ship in order to come round and welcome us. There had been a slight mistake. The first ship proved to be the transport bringing from South Africa as prisoners the officers and men implicated in the Jameson Raid,★ for trial and punishment at home.[47]

The Jameson Raiders included in their number almost the entire police force of Rhodesia, and their removal had not gone unremarked by the Matabele. In any future emergency in Matabeleland, or anywhere else in Africa, Lord Wolseley would know that in Lieutenant-Colonel Baden-Powell he had one officer upon whom he could call with unreserved confidence.

2. Mistake in Matabeleland (1896–97)

After much wining and dining in London, since 8 St George's Place was let, Stephe accepted an invitation from George and Frances to join them at Coryton Park, their country house in Devonshire. There he got on with his book and his commissioned articles. He also played with his baby niece and listened politely to George's arguments in favour of what he now called 'double blessedness'.[1] By the middle of March he was back with his regiment in very different surroundings: a barracks at the end of the Falls Road in Belfast.

There he and his subaltern shared a small house 'bearing the romantic name of Eno Villa', ('romantic' because even then Eno's Liver Salts were famous). His squadron's horses were stabled with the nags which pulled the city's trams; and the regimental drill ground was nothing better than a boggy field. 'I had in consequence to carry out riding instruction on the main road, which was hard on the horses' legs and considerably interfered with the traffic.' It was also dangerous for inexperienced riders; in the last week of April a trooper fell from his horse and fatally fractured his skull. Baden-Powell was officiating at his funeral when an urgent telegram was handed to him. The sender was General Sir Frederick Carrington, who informed Stephe that in three days' time he was sailing for South Africa, en route for Rhodesia, and wanted to take him as his Chief Staff Officer. Baden-Powell thrust the order of service into the hands of his subaltern and rushed out of the graveyard. It would take him two days to get to London, leaving him 24 hours in which to assemble his kit, see his family, get leave from his colonel and travel to Southampton for embarkation. A letter of confirmation from the War Office was already on its way.[2] Carrington had offered Stephe the same job three years earlier, but this time the

★ See also pp 174, 207 and 209.

position was much graver. When the Secretary of State for the Colonies had asked Lord Wolseley to nominate a suitable officer to command the British forces likely to be required, the Commander-in-Chief had named Carrington.[3] Rhodes and the directors of the British South Africa Company, which administered Rhodesia, would have preferred Colonel H. C. O. Plumer.[4] Luckily for Baden-Powell, brother George had been able to influence the course of events.

Through good luck or contrivance, Lord Wolseley visited George at his house in Eaton Square on 14 April, and George was able to press him to appoint Carrington instead of Plumer.[5] Three days later Sir Frederick Carrington had been nominated to command the Imperial forces earmarked for Rhodesia. Stephe's appointment as Chief Staff Officer had then been a foregone conclusion.

In West Africa the skulls and skeletons had satisfied the British troops that their cause was just and that, freed from what George Baden-Powell described as 'barbaric despotism', the Ashanti would lead healthier and more prosperous lives under the British flag.[6] In Rhodesia the same comfortable belief had been entertained by the settlers in 1893 on the eve of Dr Leander Starr Jameson's invasion of Matabeleland. King Lobenguela, so the argument ran, was an arbitrary tyrant whose people would welcome the overthrow of a repressive military system and a new era of peace and progress. But, as events would shortly show, this was wishful thinking. The subjects of Lobenguela, like those of Prempeh and of the Khalifa in the Sudan, had no desire to be liberated and showed themselves willing to die in tens of thousands in order to avoid British 'protection'. 'It does not seem within the bounds of common sense,' a perceptive white Rhodesian policeman told his men, 'to suppose that a nation of ferocious savages will allow us quietly to take possession of a country which is virtually theirs by right of conquest without in any way resenting it. To imagine it even is a direct insult.'[7]

At this date Rhodes saw the country primarily as a base from which to launch further acquisitive forays and to thwart any similar northward movements by the Portuguese or the Transvaal Boers. Consequently he left the administration of the country almost entirely in the hands of his friend and associate Dr Jameson. Unfortunately the flamboyant doctor was surrounded by a group of young aristocrats described by the later Administrator, Lord Grey, as having 'the jolly reckless spirit of adventure aimed at making a million in half-an-hour and then clearing off home to Piccadilly'.[8] Jameson granted his favourites vast tracts of the country, setting aside for the Matabele wholly unsuitable reserves. The Matabele's herds were disposed of in the same cavalier way.

The Matabeleland Native Police raised in 1894 (although Matabele themselves) soon gained a reputation among their own people for

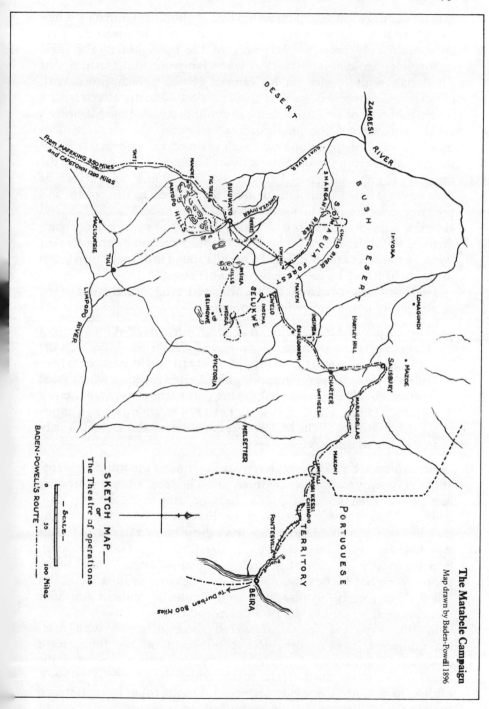

The Matabele Campaign

Map drawn by Baden-Powell 1896

brutality and lawlessness. Terrorized by the police, exploited by white Commissioners and squeezed out by adventurers, the Matabele knew they could only preserve their way of life by fighting. The ideal opportunity arose in January 1896 when Jameson led the majority of Rhodesia's white police on his famous 'Raid', which ended with inglorious defeat and capture in the Transvaal. Shortly afterwards, a severe outbreak of rinderpest and a drought decimated the Matabele's cattle. This proved the final goad which stung them into violent insurrection. Their rebellion was well planned and coordinated, but the premature slaughter of some outlying farmers lost the Matabele the impact of total surprise. Forewarned, the white inhabitants of Bulawayo, Gwelo and Tuli armed themselves to the teeth and prepared defences. The first murders took place on 24 March 1896, and six days later there was not a white man left alive in the outlying districts of Matabeleland. The rebels would eventually murder 314 white settlers. As a proportion of a population of little more than 3,000 in southern Rhodesia the statistic was horrifying.

These killings occurred before Baden-Powell's arrival, but he subsequently heard harrowing accounts.

A bride, just out from home, had her dream wrecked by a rush of savages into the farmstead. Her husband was struck down, but she managed to escape to the next farm – only to find its occupants fled. Ignorant of the country, the poor girl gathered together what tinned food she could carry, and, making her way to the river, made herself a grassy nest among the rocks . . . For a few terrible days and nights she existed there, till the Matabele came upon her tracks, and shortly stoned her to death.[9]

Other whites who had been present at the time of the murders wrote about tiny groups of men, women and children, outnumbered by hundreds or even thousands of Matabele, fighting to the last cartridge, and then being speared, burned or bludgeoned to death.[10] The murders which aroused most fury were those perpetrated by Africans who knew their victims personally. Many of the people killed had been popular locally. As one of the rebels explained later, 'These white people were our friends . . . We had no grievance against them, but killed them merely because they were whites.'[11] Violent emotions were aroused by the murder of women and children.

In Bulawayo the whites answered these atrocities with mass executions of 'spies', who were condemned on the flimsiest of evidence. 'There is a tree,' wrote Frank Sykes, a settler, 'known as the hanging tree to the north of the town, which did service as gallows. Hither the doomed men were conveyed. On the ropes being fastened to their necks, they were made to climb along an overhanging branch, and thence were pushed or compelled to jump into space . . .'[12] Olive

Schreiner published a photograph of this tree, with three men hanging from its branches, in her book *Trooper Peter Halket of Mashonaland* (1897). A group of white settlers look on with satisfaction or indifference. According to Miss Schreiner, the condemned men had been forced to jump from the branches by the firing of repeated volleys of buckshot.[13] Baden-Powell acquired a copy of this photograph and pasted it into his scrapbook of campaign memorabilia. He wrote above the picture, 'The Christmas Tree', which was the name the locals used.[14]

Baden-Powell arrived in Bulawayo on 3 June; he had left Cape Town on 19 May and completed the last ten days of the journey in a memorable coach – 'a regular Buffalo-Bill-Wild-West-Deadwood affair hung by huge leather springs'.[15] A week earlier Captain Michael MacFarlane, ex-9th lancers, had led 200 men of the Bulawayo garrison against an enemy force eight times larger. Although there were said to be 10,000 Matabele in the district, those facing MacFarlane had broken and fled. A few days later Bulawayo was reinforced by Colonel Plumer's Matabele Relief Force of 600 men recruited in Kimberley and Mafeking. Two hundred and fifty men came in from Salisbury and Gwelo under Colonel Beale, and a further 200 half-castes, or Cape Boys, arrived from the Cape Colony.[16]

As Chief Staff Officer to Sir Frederick Carrington, Baden-Powell was expected to take charge of the office work connected with commissariat, transport, ordnance, remounts and medical supplies for all these men, as well as for the troops in transit from Britain. From a small tin-roofed shed, Stephe struggled to cope with insoluble problems. Supplies throughout the country were nearly exhausted, and because the rinderpest had killed most of the transport animals he found it hard to keep the troops in food, let alone build up a reserve for the rainy season.[17] But he loved the atmosphere of the place. 'Streets filled with crowds of the most theatrical looking swashbucklers and cowboys . . . All men dressed in Boer hats and puggree, flannel shirt, breeches and puttees; so sunburnt it is hard to tell at first sight, whether a man is English, half-caste, or light Kaffir.'[18]

Late on the evening of 5 June, just as Baden-Powell was closing up his office, Sir Charles Metcalfe (consulting engineer of the British South Africa Company) burst in, followed by Frederick Russell Burnham, an American scout also employed by the Company. They had been visiting Colonel Beale's camp seven miles out of town when they had almost stumbled into a large enemy impi. At 3.00 a.m. Baden-Powell crept out to look at the Matabele; and later that morning, accompanying Beale's 250 men, he took part in his first and only cavalry charge against an enemy.

As we came up close, the niggers let us have an irregular, rackety

volley, and in another moment we were among them. They did not
wait, but one and all they turned to fly, dodging in among the
bushes, loading as they ran. And we were close upon their heels,
zigzagging through the thorns, jumping up now and then, or
pulling up, to fire a shot (we have not a sword among us, worse
luck!), and on again . . . Everywhere one found the Kaffirs creeping
in to bushes, where they lay low until some of us came by, and then
they loosed off their guns at us after we had passed . . . Presently I
came on an open stretch of ground, and about eight yards before me
was a Kaffir with a Martini-Henry. I felt so indignant at this that I
rode at him as hard as I could go, calling him every name under the
sun; he aimed – for an hour, it seemed to me – and it was quite a relief
when at last he fired, at about ten yards distance, and still more of a
relief when I realised that he had clean missed me. Then he jumped
up and turned to run, but he had not gone two paces when he
cringed as if someone had slapped him hard on the back, then his
head dropped and his heels flew up and he fell smack on his face,
shot by one of our men behind me . . . I had one close shave. I went
to help two men who were fighting a Kaffir at the foot of a tree, but
they killed him just as I got there. I was under the tree when
something moving over my head caught my attention. It was a gun
barrel taking aim down at me, the firer jammed so close to the tree-
stem as to look like part of it. Before I could move he fired, and just
ploughed into the ground at my feet.[19]

The whites suffered only four men seriously wounded and four horses
killed. In his report for Carrington Baden-Powell put the Matabele
dead at 200 men.[20] He admitted afterwards that 'this was a very one-
sided fight, and it sounds rather brutal to anyone reading in cold blood
how we hunted them without giving them a chance – but it must be
remembered we were but 250 against at least 1,200. Lord Wolseley
says "When you get niggers on the run, keep them on the run," this we
did . . . '[21] In comparison with much that appeared in the local press,
Baden-Powell's remarks seem quite mild. The Matabele had tried to
wipe out all the whites in Rhodesia and might even have succeeded.
Their intended victims inevitably felt resentful.
    After his first fight against the Matabele, Baden-Powell reflected
uneasily upon the blood-lust of the settlers who had fought with him.

    I did not at the time fully realize the extraordinary bloodthirsty rage
    of some of our men when they got hand to hand with the Kaffirs,
    but I not only understood it, but felt it to the full later on, when I too
    had seen those English girls lying horribly mutilated and the little
    white children with the life smashed and beaten out of them . . .
    Don't think from these remarks that I am a regular nigger-hater, for

I am not. I have met lots of good friends among them – especially among the Zulus.[22]

The battle of 6 June turned out to be a turning point in the campaign. The Matabele now withdrew from the Bulawayo area, splitting into two separate groupings, one centred at Taba Zi Ka Mambo 59 miles north-east of Bulawayo, and the other, commanded by half a dozen chiefs, in the Matopo Hills 20 miles south-west of the town. This region of granite hills was honeycombed with caves and hidden fissures which offered the Matabele an ideal headquarters from which to continue a guerrilla war.

Now that offensive operations against the Matabele had to be undertaken many miles away from Bulawayo, the problems of transport and supply became even more acute, causing an unwelcome increase in Baden-Powell's work-load. Nevertheless on 12 June, he managed to get away for a couple of days and nights with the American scout, Burnham, on an expedition to the Matopo Hills. The Matopos were justly described by one Rhodesian old-stager as 'a ghastly country for fighting. One ought to be a goat or a mountain sheep to climb about the granite kopjes.'[23] But Baden-Powell found it immensely exhilarating clambering over the great boulders seeking to establish the precise whereabouts of a Matabele impi. During the following months he managed to make six more excursions to the Matopos, generally with two or three companions. He was delighted to discover that some Matabele had been heard calling him 'Impeesa': the hyena or creature that skulks by night. Thinking it sounded more complimentary, Baden-Powell changed the hyena into a wolf, producing 'the wolf that never sleeps' as his own translation. The best-known and most resourceful scout on the whites' side was Jan Grootboom, a Cape Boy, who would soon make the dangerous initial contacts with the Matabele which preceded Rhodes's first indaba (meeting) with the Matopo chiefs. On several occasions Baden-Powell went out scouting with Grootboom, who had a high opinion of Stephe's bushcraft, praising his skill in avoiding detection. 'If they [the Matabele] want to shoot him, they must go after him, and catch him out where he hides.'[24]

On 16 July, when Colonel Plumer opened his all-out campaign to defeat the Matabele in the Matopos, he chose Baden-Powell as guide to his entire force of over 1,000 men and put him in command of the 300-strong advance guard. Morale was high since ten days earlier, at the cost of ten lives, Plumer had knocked out the only other centre of Matabele resistance at Taba Zi Ka Mamba. But within a week of the troops' arrival in the Matopos it was clear that no such early success would be achieved in this broken country against an enemy well supplied with firearms (mainly provided by deserting native policemen). The strongholds of individual chiefs were attacked in succession. On each occasion the rebels were compelled to evacuate their kopjes, but they simply moved on to similar defensible hills. Now it was the turn of the whites to suffer losses and by 24 July twenty whites had been killed, even though the Cape Boys invariably formed the first wave in each scrambling attack on a hill stronghold.[25] During this period Baden-Powell went on a number of intelligence-gathering patrols, trying to discover positions from which the Matabele might be surprised. He had little success.

On 5 August Plumer's force attacked the hill stronghold of an important rebel chief called Sikhombo. This onslaught was a failure since the Matabele remained in possession, although attacked by Plumer's entire force. Seven whites died, all but one of them either officers or N.C.O.s. These casualties drove home to all involved that if every stronghold cost as many lives, a much larger force would be required to crush the enemy in the Matopos. Two of Plumer's most popular officers had been killed, and the entire force was demoralized. 'It is a sad shock,' Stephe wrote next day, 'to sit in one's little mess of half a dozen comrades once more, and to find two of them are missing.'[26] He also reflected upon the arbitrary suddenness of death. He had attended the burial of a sergeant-major during a lull in the fighting. 'Curious – within an hour of being as full of life and energy as any of us, he was dead and buried and had a cross up over his grave.' At one stage during the fighting Baden-Powell talked at some length to a trooper. 'Next time I saw him he was hanging across a horse's back with some of his brains bulging from his short-cropped hair.'[27]

The day after the bloody stalemate at Sikhombo's stronghold, Cecil Rhodes joined Colonel Plumer and Sir Frederick Carrington at their camp. The British troops already in Rhodesia were costing his British South Africa Company £4,000 a day, and Carrington was now convinced that many more men would be needed to clear the Matopos. Rhodes therefore decided to abandon his idea of total victory, and instead elected to try negotiating with the Matabele.

The Colonial Office's representative, Sir Richard Martin, supported a policy of dealing severely with the chiefs but granting an amnesty to their followers if they laid down their arms. Rhodes considered this a recipe for prolonging the fighting; the chiefs would never give up while the threat of imprisonment or execution hung over them.[28] He admired strong leaders and had much less sympathy with their followers.

The day before Plumer's failure, Baden-Powell had unwittingly stumbled upon the means of opening negotiations with the Matabele chiefs. On that day he had been scouting with Grootboom, Richardson (the Native Commissioner in the Matopos) and three native boys when they caught an old Matabele woman who turned out to be a niece of M'zilikatze, King Lobenguela's predecessor, and the mother of a leading chief in the Matopos.[29] On 10 August, before he left the Matopos for Bulawayo, Baden-Powell took the old woman back to where her kraal had been before it had been burned down. 'There we built her a new hut, hoisted a white flag, gave her two cows and some corn, and an old woman prisoner to look after her. We told her all our conditions for peace and left her there.'[30] Baden-Powell had hoped to play a part in actually assembling the opposing parties for their first session of negotiations. Instead Carrington gave him command of a squadron of the recently arrived 7th Hussars with orders to complete the pacification of the north-east of the region. After Stephe's departure, the old woman relayed the terms which he had left with her to the leaders of the rebellion. As a direct result Jan Grootboom and John Colenbrander, a prominent settler, managed to organize the first series of meetings between Cecil Rhodes and the eight principal chiefs in the Matopos.

Baden-Powell later noted down in his diary the Matabele's grievances, as expressed to Rhodes, and after this list added Rhodes's pledges to them. He accepted that the Native Police had been brutal and promised to disband them. He promised to reform the company's Native Administration and to dismiss corrupt white Native Commissioners. He made a promise, which he honoured, that none of the Matopo chiefs would ever be put on trial if they laid down their arms. Baden-Powell recorded the answer made by Sikhombo, spokesman for the Matabele, and acknowledged its truthfulness. 'When asked why the rebels had not stuck to legitimate war instead of murdering women and children, Sikhombo replied that the whites had begun that game – (this afterwards appears to be true. Some women were killed by Crewe on Arthur Rhodes's farm)'.[21]

Baden-Powell admired Rhodes's bravery in going with three unarmed men to meet the Matopo chiefs. He was 'captivated' by the millionaire's energy and ambition. 'I am a barbarian,' wrote Rhodes. 'I believe with Ruskin that all healthy men love to fight, and all women love to hear of such fighting . . . I love the big and the simple . . . Expansion is everything . . . I would annex the planets if I could.'[32] Rhodes agreed with Kipling that: 'England is a stuffy little place, mentally, morally, and physically.'[33] For many years Baden-Powell would express an identical opinion. He felt very privileged to be taken aside by Rhodes one day and given the answer to the question that had puzzled so many people about the Jameson Raid. Had Rhodes warned Jameson before the Raid, or given him direct instructions? Rhodes told Baden-Powell that he had telegraphed shortly before Jameson set out: 'Read Luke Chap XIV, verse 31–32 (What king going to make war against another does not first see whether he can meet 20,000 with 10,000, or whether it is better to send an "ambassage" while the other is yet a great way off.)'. Baden-Powell did not say whether or not he found this retrospective wisdom convincing.[34]

The area to which Stephe had been ordered to proceed was the Somabula Forest, 100 miles north-east of Bulawayo – a place apparently teeming with rebels. After being defeated by Plumer at Taba Zi Ka Mambo, Mkwati, the single most important chief in this part of the country, had rallied his followers in the forest. These men, like their leaders, were either of the Makalaka or Maholi tribes; they were *not* Matabele. In fact, Mkwati and his father-in-law, Uwini, were enraged by news of negotiations in the Matopos. They expected the Matabele chiefs to make favourable terms with the whites, who would then be free to crush all the non-Matabele tribes in the country. Consequently Mkwati and Uwini created their private police force to prevent any Matabele resident in their area from surrendering.[35]

Quite early on during his time in Matabeleland, Baden-Powell had learned that the rebellion was being underpinned by the priests of the Mlimo, an unseen deity of the Makalaka people. This religious system had been adopted by the Matabele, although most of the Mlimo's priests and warrior-chiefs were Makalakas. Baden-Powell thought there were three priests and four chiefs serving the cult. Since the priests were not Matabele, the messages they received from their god in their cave shrines were not in favour of negotiation. Baden-Powell knew that the priests often told their followers that the white men's bullets would be turned to water if they attacked bravely.[36]

Earlier in the campaign, Burnham and a Native Commissioner called Armstrong had shot a priest of the Mlimo in the south-west of the country, but had persuaded Lord Grey, the company's Administrator, and many others in Bulawayo that they had killed *the* Mlimo. Baden-Powell was always better informed about the cult, and almost from his first week in the country knew that the god was not believed to inhabit any single priest.[37]

When Stephe arrived in the Somabula Forest and took command of his column of 356 men that had preceded him there, Chief Uwini had just been captured during an attack on his stronghold. 'He was badly wounded in the shoulder, but, enraged at being a prisoner, he would allow nothing to be done for him; no sooner had the surgeon bandaged him than he tore the dressings off again. He was a fine, truculent-looking savage, and boasted that he had always been able to hold his own against any enemies in this stronghold of his, but now that he was captured he only wished to die.'[38]

With the help of an interpreter Baden-Powell asked Uwini to order his people to surrender, but the chief refused. 'He is,' Baden-Powell conceded, 'a plucky and stubborn old villain.'[39] But Uwini's capture posed an awkward problem for him. The chief could not realistically be taken on with the troops for a two-week patrol. Alternatively, if he were sent back on the five-day journey to Bulawayo a rescue might be attempted and a sizeable force would therefore have to accompany him. Gwelo was a possibility since it was considerably closer, and Baden-Powell was planning to convey the wounded Hussars there. Uwini could have been held at Gwelo until an opportunity arose for moving him to Bulawayo where he could have been tried in a civil court.

Sir Frederick Carrington had given his officers printed orders requiring them to hand over all prisoners to the Native Commissioner for the region in which they were captured, so that they could be brought before a civil court.[40] Instead Baden-Powell decided to try Uwini at once by court-martial and then execute him as a warning to his followers. Unless Uwini's men could be persuaded to leave their cave strongholds and lay down their arms, the Hussars would have to go in and force them out, the result would be more deaths on both sides. But if Uwini's claims to be invulnerable to bullets (as a priest of the Mlimo) were shown to be moonshine, his followers might well decide to surrender without a fight. Baden-Powell discussed the situation with Val Gielgud, the local Native Commissioner, who thought Uwini's refusal to order his men to surrender justified making an example of him. N. D. Fynn, the other Commissioner for the area, had interviewed a large number of local Maholi and Matabele and was convinced that Uwini and his son-in-law, Mkwati, were entirely responsible for keeping the rebellion going. According to Fynn, Uwini had already murdered a neighbouring chief and a number of his people when they had tried to hand over their firearms to the Native Commissioner. There was some evidence, based upon unsubstantiated testimony, that pointed to Uwini's having ordered the murder of some white miners who had been prospecting on the river Gwelo.

Since Baden-Powell's treatment of Uwini would soon become a matter of official and public controversy, even threatening to destroy his career, the background is important. Baden-Powell asked Major H. M. Ridley of the 7th Hussars to be President of the Court. He thought Ridley incompetent but, since the major was next in seniority to himself, he had no choice.[41] Ridley, who had himself intended to send Uwini to Bulawayo when his wound had healed – and would have done so had he remained in command – was surprised to be asked by his superior officer to preside at a court-martial. He asked Baden-Powell if he had the power to convene such a court and was assured by him that he had. Because Baden-Powell was Carrington's Chief Staff Officer, Ridley accepted this; but he did mention to Baden-Powell that he had been cautioned by Carrington not to shoot any prisoners.[42] Uwini was court-martialled on 13 September and arraigned on three charges: with being a rebel in armed resistance to constituted authority; with sending his men to attack 'friendly' natives; and with sending men to kill white people near the Gwelo river. The last two charges Uwini vigorously denied. The evidence for his direct involvement in the murders of the white prospectors was flimsy. From the chief's point of view, the proceedings were a farce; he considered that the white men had never had any right to come to his country in the first place.

The Hussars had spent the two days before his capture searching for his grain stores and either stealing or burning them. Anyone offering opposition had been shot. Uwini felt that he was fighting in defence of his people, his possessions and his land, and so saw no reason either to deny that he had fired on the white men who had entered his cave or that he had refused to lay down his weapons. He explained that he had fired at the intruders because he had been sure that they meant to kill him. Indeed the shot which wounded him in the shoulder could easily have proved mortal had it struck him in the chest. The prosecution made much of Uwini's having fired at his adversaries in order to prove that he was 'a rebel *captured* while in armed resistance to constituted authority'. Baden-Powell altered his diary in conformity with this idea. He wrote at first: 'Uweena fired a second time at Halifax [the trooper who wounded him] and eventually gave himself up,' but then changed it to: 'Uweena fired a second time at Halifax, before he was at length cornered and captured.'[43]

An account of Uwini's capture furnished by an officer in the 8th Hussars was published in the *Bulawayo Chronicle* on 19 September. The author stated that Uwini had been wounded during the morning in one cave without the trooper who had shot him knowing that his victim was Chief Uwini. When the wounded man's identity was discovered later in the day, five soldiers tracked him down, following a spoor of blood into another cave. After token resistance, Uwini gave himself up. Baden-Powell's subsequent claim that he had been captured 'offering determined resistance and firing on his captors' was not factually correct.

Baden-Powell had intended the court to find Uwini guilty on three charges, and obligingly it did so. Two troopers confirmed that Uwini had fired two separate shots, and Gielgud swore that he had refused to surrender and to ask his men to hand in their guns. Two Africans testified that Uwini had sent men to kill the white prospectors, while another claimed that the chief had murdered natives who had been neutral or friendly to the whites. The African witnesses may well have been motivated by fear or the hope of a reward. Uwini declined to call any witnesses in his defence. On finding him guilty on all three counts, the court sentenced him to be shot. The warrant was signed by Ridley as President of the Court and was confirmed by Baden-Powell.

At sunset Baden-Powell paraded all the 'friendlies', refugees and prisoners to witness the execution. He expected 'the moral effect to be very good among the natives as Uweena had a great reputation with them'.[44] Chief Uwini was shot by a firing-party of six men, one of whom afterwards pulled a cheap iron-wire bracelet from the dead man's wrist.[45] Four years later the same man gave this trinket to Baden-Powell as a memento. After the execution, Uwini's wives took his body back to his cave for burial. Three weeks later N. D. Fynn, the local Native Commissioner, minuted: 'There can be no doubt that the death of Uwinya has had the very best results in ridding the country of the chief obstacle to a peaceful settlement.' Gielgud confirmed this: 'Many Maholi headmen surrendered during the next two or three days . . . These rapid results could not have been hoped for if the prisoner had been tried and executed at a distant time and place.' Baden-Powell's action therefore seemed to have saved lives on both sides.

When Lord Rosmead, the High Commissioner at the Cape, heard about the shooting, he was less interested in the military consequences than in the moral and legal propriety of the execution. He telegraphed at once to Sir Frederick Carrington:

I must point out that the ordinary courts of the country are still in existence and that martial law has not been proclaimed; the execution of Uwini appears therefore prima facie illegal and I must therefore request that as soon as possible, without prejudice to the military operations, you will place Colonel Baden-Powell under open arrest and order a Court of Inquiry.

Viewing this telegram as one more link in the endless chain of interfering complaints with which the Colonial Office had long sought to immobilize all military operations in the colonies, Sir Frederick declined to arrest his Chief Staff Officer, and asked Rosmead to defer any arrest until the Court of Inquiry had sat.[46]

When the news of Rosmead's decision to order Baden-Powell's arrest began to appear in British newspapers, there was considerable puzzlement. How was it, people asked, that martial law was not in force in a country where fighting had been raging for six months? Was it sensible for a civilian High Commissioner to issue arbitrary orders to a general in the field over 1,000 miles away? Rosemead's anger owed a lot to a similar execution in Mashonaland only a week earlier, on which occasion a Major Watts had tried and shot a chief called Makoni. As a direct result of this incident, Rosmead had telegraphed an un-ambiguous order to all officers in Rhodesia, entitled 'Trial of Prisoners', prohibiting the trial of prisoners by military courts in all circumstances. This order had reached Bulawayo on 8 September, the day after Baden-Powell had left.[47]

Rosmead maintained that prisoners-of-war should never be shot 'unless guilty of some violation of the customs of war, as would of itself expose them to the penalty of death . . . I do not think that rebellion, or instigation of rebellion, is a violation of the customs of war.' Men fighting for their country and the interests of their people should not be executed like war criminals. Rosmead did not change his mind after the Court of Inquiry – convened on 30 October to look into Uwini's execution – had exonerated Baden-Powell. He acknowledged that there had been extenuating circumstances and that the execution had yielded practical results, but he still insisted that it had been illegal and immoral.[48]

Had this incident destroyed Stephe's career, as it might well have done, he would have had cause to feel aggrieved. Before he took command of Ridley's column, these men of the 7th Hussars had been killing any 'rebels' who tried to prevent the 'confiscation' of their grain supplies. Even attempts to resist the burning of their kraals was punished by volleys of shots. The behaviour of officers who sanctioned the killing of many dozens of such men was far worse than Baden-Powell's conduct when he sanctioned the execution of a single man.[49] A letter that Carrington wrote to Baden-Powell on 28 September highlights the absurdity of reserving censure for incidents like Uwini's death. Baden-Powell was told that in future he 'should not kill any unless they showed fight since they are on the surrender'.[50] But what constituted 'showing fight'? Being armed with a spear, or actually firing a well directed shot?

Henrietta Grace was distressed by accounts of the war, both in Stephe's letters and in the press. She was particularly upset by stories of women and children being taken prisoner. Her son explained the purpose of this as best he could.

> The advantage of capturing the women and children is that we thereby capture the transport train of the enemy. They cannot get their food carried from place to place without them so we can then come up with them more easily . . . I had over 900 of them [women] at one time – and as soon as we capture a stronghold we send in our army of ladies to bring down the grain from the inaccessible rocks and crags in which it is generally stored.[51]

One service that women were rendering to the rebels, Baden-Powell considered fit only for George's ears. Certain prostitutes in Bulawayo were refusing intercourse unless paid in ammunition.[52]

The Liberal periodical *Truth* had published a number of articles deploring the shelling and burning of kraals and suggesting that the war was being fought 'in order that prospectors may have an opportunity of wandering about in search of traces of gold on which to base some rotten company, by means of which investors at home are to be cozened out of their money'. When *Truth* attacked Baden-Powell for seeking to please 'the gold seeking scum of Bulawayo' by executing Uwini, he professed amusement.

Funny to see what a lot of fuss over so little a matter! Funny old Labby! [Henry D. Labouchere, editor/proprietor of Truth] I love to see him rush into print . . . I suppose I am described as a mercenary swashbuckler . . . murdering brother-men simply because their skin is darker than my own . . . But I don't think that the swashbuckler's trade is quite as paying as that of the ink-slinger.[53]

This was rather rich coming from a man who was sending back material to The Graphic.

Truth accused Rhodes and the Colonial Office of 'tricking the Matabele out of their country and independence, massacring them by the hundred with machine-guns, robbing them of whatever they possessed worth stealing, driving them into revolt from sheer despair, and finally subduing them after a bloody war'.[54] Although the Matabele themselves enjoyed possession of their country through conquest, a century has done nothing to weaken this judgment. Of course Baden-Powell was not to blame for the wider situation in Rhodesia, but there was a side to his nature knowledge of which inevitably causes misgivings in connection with Uwini's execution.

During his years on Malta, Baden-Powell had travelled extensively in North Africa, spending weeks at a time with French officers. On 7 April 1891, he noted in his diary: 'We passed the rifle range where C. [Carbonais, a Tunisian trader, who often acted as Baden-Powell's guide] told me they occasionally shoot soldiers condemned to death by court martial. He himself saw a Zouave shot a short time ago for striking an N.C.O. and there is another now under sentence for desertion . . .'[55] A couple of years later Baden-Powell narrowly missed witnessing an execution by firing squad. Staying with a French regiment at Tlemcen in Algeria, where the execution was to take place, he was unable to see it because he would have missed the fortnightly steamer when it called at the nearby port of Nemours. The following morning when the Zouave was due to die, Baden-Powell had been up at dawn to catch the coach to the port.

As we passed the barracks and camp 'boots and saddles' was sounding, and the infantry were falling in, and a string of men and boys were hurrying along the roads to see the fun. But my coach lumbered along away from it all along the dusty high road and for a time I was immersed in reading up the country we were to pass through – when suddenly it occurred to me why was I not at this execution? A sight that would not occur again probably – it came on me like a cold shudder – looked at my watch, it was getting on for 6.30. If I jumped down now and happened to find a horse I could not possibly get back in time. Then followed a day of rage for myself, and absolute misery at what I had missed just from having my plans well-laid beforehand: a thing I am always deprecating – Ouf! I couldn't do anything, nor think of anything. We passed through some beautiful scenery . . . but it had no interest whatever for me. Then to add to my annoyance the coach got into Nemours soon after 5 p.m. instead of in the night and then I was told the ship was not expected till next afternoon – not in the morning. So I could easily have stayed that day in Tlemcen and seen everything – Ooh! It will take a long time before I get over that catastrophe . . . [56]

The disappointment remained with him after his return to England – where, perhaps to make up for what he had missed, he painted several water-colours of firing squads in action (see second photo section) and wrote an extraordinarily authentic-sounding account of a French execution:

A thrill seems to go through the crowd. The young Tirailleur is marched forwards towards the wall, to where there stands a post: a stout post some six feet high, with a cross-bar through it near the top. For a few moments the escort are round him at the post. Then they shamble hurriedly away, leaving him there alone, his arms pinioned over the cross-bar and his eyes bandaged. So helpless he looks – one almost expects to hear him cry for mercy. Can no help come for him? Must he really die, here, at the hands of comrades and officers? And as we gaze, bound by the horror of the situation, his features seem to blur; a whiff of smoke! – he is puffing one last cigarette! A sudden flash of an officer's sword and the firing party come sharply to the present. There is a breathless, sickening pause. It seems an age before 'PRRR–AH'! the volley flies: and through the light-brown wisp of smoke one sees him hanging limply from his arms, head down, and knees all loose and swaying. Dead . . . A young soldier clatters to the ground, fainting; and behind me a spectator turns away quite sick. Now as they cut the cords, the corpse crumples down at the foot of the post. A sergeant steps up to it from the firing party and places the muzzle of his rifle to the ear of the poor dead thing. [57]

Stephe's fascination with executions does not alter the fact that the arguments he used to justify executing Uwini were more convincing than those subsequently put forward by Burnham, Watts and another young officer, Lieutenant Gibbs, seeking to explain why they had felt compelled to authorize similar shootings. [58] It would, however, be ridiculous to suppose that Baden-Powell's obsessive interest in executions and the ritual surrounding them played no part in his decision to shoot Uwini.

After despatching Uwini, Baden-Powell continued northwards on the heels of Mkwati, Uwini's son-in-law, but failed to catch him. Nevertheless Stephe loved patrolling with his column. 'We all sleep in the open – and it is perfectly divine – fire at feet – saddle backed by a few

bits of bush at your head to keep off the wind. Any amount of blankets
and a nightcap – and fine bright sky overhead. If the Prince of Wales
went down on his bended knees I wouldn't change with him.' Baden-
Powell slept with his pistol lanyard round his neck and claimed that if
anyone came within ten yards of him, he would wake up 'however
softly he may tread'.[59] He found the business of survival in the wild not
just a necessity but an intriguing science. Once, when desperately
short of water, he had seen a buck scratching in the sand and, by
digging at the same spot, had found water. Sudden movements of
game he usually associated with the presence of humans, and he
rapidly discovered how skilful the Matabele were at hiding even
without cover, just by keeping absolutely still and paying careful
attention to the colour of their background.[60]

A year later in Dublin, lecturing on the campaign, Baden-Powell
would say that 'the best lesson that I personally learnt was the art of
scouting'.[61] In the same lecture he told an anecdote that he liked
sufficiently to repeat in his autobiography:

I was out scouting with my native boy in the neighbourhood of the
Matopos. Presently we noticed some grass-blades freshly trodden
down. This led us to find some foot-prints on a patch of sand; they
were those of women or boys, because they were small; they were
on a long march, because they wore sandals; they were pretty fresh,
because the sharp edges of the foot-prints were still well defined,
and they were heading towards the Matopos. Then my nigger, who
was examining the ground a short distance away from the track,
suddenly started, as Robinson Crusoe must have done when he
came on Friday's foot-mark. But in this case the boy had found not a
foot-mark, but a single leaf. But that leaf meant a good deal; it
belonged to a tree that did not grow in this neighbourhood, though
we knew of such trees ten or fifteen miles away. It was damp, and
smelt of Kaffir beer. From these two signs then, the foot-prints and
the beery leaf, we were able to read a good deal. A party of women
had passed this way, coming from a distance of 10 miles back, going
towards the Matopos, and carrying beer (for they carry beer in pots
upon their heads, the mouth of the pot being stoppered with a
bunch of leaves). They had passed this spot at about 4 o'clock that
morning, because at that hour there had been a strong wind
blowing, such as would carry the leaf some yards off their track, as
we had found it. They would probably have taken another hour to
reach the Matopos, and the men for whom they were bringing the
refreshment would, in all probability, start work on it at once, while
the beer was yet fresh. So that if we now went on following this
spoor up to the stronghold we should probably find the men in too
sleepy a state to take much notice of us, and we could do our
reconnaissance with comparative safety.[62]

Apart from learning a lot about scouting from Grootboom, Baden-Powell also learned much from Burnham, the American scout, whom he described as 'a sort of better class Buffalo Bill'.[63] He had not, however, been introduced by Burnham to the folk-lore surrounding cowboys. He went with George Noble to see Bill Cody's [Buffalo Bill] Wild West Show during the summer of 1887; and that autumn had incorporated into his own dramatic entertainment in Liverpool spectacular riding and shooting scenes very similar to those in Cody's show. The cowboy influence came out clearly in Matabeleland where he first wore the species of broad-brimmed cowboy or Stetson hat which twelve years later would reappear as the Boy Scouts' official headgear. The Scout neckerchief also started life here as 'a grey coloured handkerchief loosely tied round the neck to prevent sunburn'.[65] 'What was it made me go to the extravagance of subscribing to *Harper*'s, but Remington's sketches of Cowboy Life?'[66] he remarked in his diary in September 1896, adding that 'the trappings of camp life' were 'his toys', which would never fail him.[67] So life in the Wild West and on the veldt had more in common than Stetson hats.

Frederick Remington drew the illustrations for the stories of Owen Wister, the well-connected young Philadelphian who had removed the cowboy from the dime novel, romanticized his rougher qualities and recast him as a chivalrous hero. The equation of the outdoor life with clean living and moral virtue would form an essential strand in the thinking behind the Boy Scouts. In Wister's famous story *The Evolution of the Cow-Puncher* (1895), a young English peer goes to Texas to live as a cowboy. He soon feels a close kinship with the Texans. 'Deep in him lay virtues and vices as coarse and elemental as theirs . . . directly the English nobleman smelled Texas, the slumbering untamed Saxon awoke in him . . . Sir Francis Drake was such a one . . . conqueror, invader, navigator, buccaneer, explorer, colonist . . .'[68] Baden-Powell enjoyed the same social mix in Rhodesia, where the younger sons of aristocrats sought their fortunes alongside hardened adventurers. Stephe liked men such as Val Gielgud, the Native Commissioner, 'American by birth, cowboy by education and gentleman by nature,' who might have stepped straight out of one of Wister's stories. Like Wister Baden-Powell admired the physique of outdoor men and wrote warmly about 'comradeship' with them.[69]

Burnham had been a scout with the U.S. Army in the Apache Wars, and, according to Stephe, because of his service with the Red Indians, 'brought quite a new experience to bear on scouting work . . .' Before meeting the American, Baden-Powell had never used the word 'woodcraft', which was to become such an important part of his scheme of *Scouting for Boys*. In his published account of the Matabele Campaign (1897), he called the art of noticing small details on the veldt 'the science of woodcraft'. It is therefore quite incorrect to attribute all his enthusiasm for woodcraft to another American, the author and naturalist Ernest Thompson Seton, whom he met in 1906. 'We English,' wrote Baden-Powell in 1896, 'have the talent of woodcraft and the spirit of adventure and independence already born in our blood.' [70] He was not using the word in its original English sense of woodland skills connected with forestry and the chase; by the mid-nineteenth century, this meaning was obsolete outside the works of Sir Walter Scott. In fact it was in the American sense that Baden-Powell used and understood the word. In the novels of Fenimore Cooper and Mark Twain, woodcraft meant a knowledge of forest conditions which would enable a man to support himself in the wilderness and to thrive there without help from the civilized world of towns and cities. To foster this kind of self-reliance would one day become a central aim for Baden-Powell's Boy Scouts. In *Cavalry Instruction* (1888) he had written at length about tracking; but Burnham's familiarity with Indian methods of finding water, trapping, observing game and travelling without either compass or maps in wild country, added a new dimension to Baden-Powell's understanding of the subject. [71]

On his return to London, Stephe would find himself day-dreaming while an old dowager was handing him a cup of tea at a smart 'At Home'. As she chatted, he was overwhelmed by his longing for the freedom of Africa's open spaces. 'I used to think that these visions of the veldt would fade away as civilized life grew upon me. But they didn't. They came again at most inopportune moments: just when I ought to be talking *The World*, or *Truth*, or *Modern Society*, and making my reputation as a "sensible well-informed man, my dear".' [72] The romantic and dramatic aspects of tribal life appealed to him as much as they did to writers like Rider Haggard.

Today, when out scouting by myself, [wrote Stephe] I lay for a quiet look-out among some rocks and grass overlooking a little stream . . . Presently there was a slight rattle of trinkets, and a swish of the tall yellow grass, followed by the sudden apparition of a naked Matabele warrior standing glistening among the rocks within thirty yards of me. His white war ornaments – the feathers on his brow, and the long white cow's-tail plumes which depended from his arms and knees – contrasted strongly with his rich brown skin. His kilt of wild cat-skins and monkeys' tails swayed round his loins. His left hand bore his assegai beneath the great dappled ox-hide shield; and, in his right, a yellow walking-staff. He stood for almost a minute perfectly motionless, like a statue cast in bronze, his head turned from me, listening for any suspicious sound. Then, with a swift and easy movement, he laid his arms noiselessly upon the rocks, and, dropping on all fours beside a pool, he dipped his muzzle down and drank just like an animal. I could hear the thirsty sucking of his lips from where I lay. He drank and drank as though he never meant to stop, and when at last his frame could hold no more, he rose with evident reluctance. He picked his weapons up, and then stood again to listen. Hearing nothing, he turned and sharply moved away . . . I had been so taken with the spectacle that I felt no desire to shoot at him. [73]

This description highlights the dilemma faced by the white adventurer who came to Africa as an agent of industrial forces. He thought tribal virtues praiseworthy and yet for economic and political reasons was helping to sweep them away along with the African warriors who embodied them. Many years later, Baden-Powell would write deploring the destruction of 'the tribal system of training and discipline [in Africa],' admitting that, 'we have given nothing in return beyond a few spasmodic schools and missions on the one hand, and the widespread provision of cash wages, bad temptations, and such teachings of civilization as they can gain from low class American cinema on the other.'[74] One way out of the dilemma was employed by Baden-Powell in India, a year after the Matabele Campaign, when he decided to train his young city-bred soldiers to harden themselves and learn self-reliance as practised by tribal people. His chosen method was to give them experience of scouting and surviving in the open.

So while men like Burnham and Baden-Powell knew themselves to be the destroyers of warrior societies, in which they saw many merits, they could console themselves with the thought that by cultivating in their fellow whites the tribal virtues of bravery, endurance and skill in woodcraft, they were counteracting the softness and inertia of American and European city life. This, when extended to urban boys, would become a central objective of the Boy Scouts.

In Matabeleland Baden-Powell began to articulate ideas that would find permanent expression in *Scouting for Boys*. Besides dwelling upon the character-forming attributes of the outdoor life, he began to lay down ideal behaviour patterns for his young military scouts – such as 'what the Americans call "jump" and "push"'. These he translated as 'alertness, wide-awakeness, readiness to seize your opportunity'.[75] The 'be prepared' alertness demanded of Boy Scouts a decade later would not be so different. Reflecting on what gave the English and the British colonial troops their 'spirit of practical discipline, which is deeper than the surface veneer discipline of Continental armies', Baden-Powell attributed it to school football and 'stern though kindly parents'.

Football demanded that a boy ' "keep in his place" and "play not for himself, but for his side" '. Without team spirit, Baden-Powell felt that the Matabele Campaign might have dragged on indefinitely. The troops showed eagerness to do their best 'not because they are "– well

ordered to" (as I heard a Tommy express it), nor because it may bring
them crosses and rewards, but simply – *because it is the game*.[76] Boy
Scouts would later be expected to be active games-players rather than
onlookers at professional football matches. They would also be
enjoined to keep in their places, and put the good of their nation before
their own advancement.

Such matters pointed to a still distant future. For the present,
Baden-Powell's service in Rhodesia gave him a reputation for
efficiency, toughness and mild eccentricity. Colonel Alderson, who
commanded the Mashonaland Field Force, praised the brevity of his
orders which in a few lines 'told all one wanted to know, and, in other
things, left one a free hand'.[77] Another officer described the vast
volume of work Baden-Powell got through. 'He never seemed to be in
a hurry, or to be overworked, or have a care on his mind.'[78] Baden-
Powell's eccentricities included wearing 'a peculiar pair of riding
breeches . . . like those affected by stage inn-keepers or Tyrolean
hunters. The upper part was of dark velveteen, or velvet cord, to
which were laced long, drab-coloured, skintight stockings or gaiters,
extending from the middle of the thigh to the ankle, and ornamented
with numerous round pearl buttons.' The old soldier who recalled this
costume used to spend hours wondering 'how "B-P" got in and out of
these complicated breeches. Once seeing him preparing for a tub in the
collapsible bath, which accompanied him everywhere, I lay in wait,
but just at the critical moment I was called away.'[79] Another trooper
remembered Stephe wearing a cowboy hat and holsters for two
revolvers. In view of his sporting such virile accoutrements, it
surprised him that Baden-Powell used scented soap out on the veldt.
But nobody could argue with his determination. He forbade his men
to take off their boots at night and used to creep around the sleeping
forms under their horse blankets, rapping at the soles of their feet with
his cane. 'We got cunning eventually,' one man recalled, 'and used to
take off our boots and put them at the bottom of our blanket.'[80]

In spite of Uwini, Baden-Powell came through the Matabele
Campaign with an enhanced reputation for staff work and for
commanding mobile columns. Already marked down as a man who
knew about African warfare, he would in future also be seen as an
officer who could get on with colonials – in short the ideal commander
to be sent out to raise irregulars in southern Africa should the need ever
arise.[81]

Stephe returned to England on the same steamship as Cecil Rhodes
and Olive Schreiner, who refused to talk to either of them. The
manuscript of her passionately anti-Imperial novel *Trooper Peter Halket
of Mashonaland* was locked in her cabin. Rhodes was returning to
England to face interrogation by a House of Commons Select
Committee for his part in the Jameson Raid. But even at this nadir of

his fortunes, he had abandoned neither his determination to thwart
Paul Kruger's ambitions for the Transvaal nor his own ambition to
unify South Africa under the British flag. Stephe, who had returned
from one African expedition to see the Jameson Raiders step ashore
and was now returning from another with Cecil Rhodes by his side,
could have been forgiven for supposing that his destiny lay in southern
Africa. In the short term, however, matters would not run quite to
plan.

3. Indian Interlude (1897–99)

The deep competitiveness which had burned in Stephe since childhood
would not be assuaged unless given greater satisfaction than the Brevet
Colonelcy now conferred upon him. Since he was still only a major in
his own regiment but senior in army rank to the commanding officer
and the second-in-command, he would have to seek the colonelcy of
another regiment. Then he could expect four years in command, and
after that either half-pay or promotion. Thanks to his 'little wars'
Baden-Powell, at 40, had become the youngest colonel in the British
Army, but this still might not be enough to save him from being
prematurely shelved.

    Henrietta Grace had been ill and was convalescing in a country hotel
when Stephe returned from Rhodesia in January 1897. He therefore
took rooms at reduced terms in a hotel in suburban Richmond where,
away from the distractions of life with Warington, Frank and Agnes at
Hyde Park Corner, he hoped to convert his Matabele diary into a
book.[1] Methuen had already offered £200, so it was a shock to him
when General Sir Redvers Buller, the new Adjutant-General, refused
to sanction publication on the grounds that Baden-Powell would be
'profiting at the Government's expense'. Stephe replied disingenuously that 'it had not struck him that he was likely to make any
money'. All he had wanted was 'to give his experiences in ordinary
language so they might be of use to young officers'. In the end Buller
grudgingly withdrew his objections.[2] When George sent Lord
Wolseley a copy of Stephe's *Matabele Campaign*, the Commander-
in-Chief told him that his brother 'writes as well as he fights; indeed
there are few in the army who are as good *all round* as he is.'[3]

    Stephe lunched at George's house in Eaton Square the day after his
return to England. He found Doctor Fridtjof Nansen, the Norwegian
explorer, staying there. Nansen was the most sought-after man in
London, having recently completed a daring walk on the Polar ice
to the most northerly latitude ever reached. With an unerring
nose for publicity, George had sailed into the Varangar Fjord in
Norway and on managing to intercept the returning Nansen, had

invited him to sail south from Vardo in his yacht. In London George gave a splendid dinner in the explorer's honour – guests included Colonel R. S. S. Baden-Powell, the Chancellor of the Exchequer, the Leader of the House of Commons, the former Colonial Secretary and Sir Henry Morton Stanley, the world's most famous living explorer.[4]

When Nansen departed, Stephe spent a couple of nights with George, who explained that when the lease on 8 St George's Place came up for renewal in four years' time, the house would have to be abandoned. He was doing his best to persuade Henrietta Grace to find 'a haven of rest' in Bournemouth or Cowes. If that huge house were no longer draining away such a large proportion of the family's available cash, Warington and Frank would be able to live in a smaller shared house in London and thus keep most of their income. Stephe would also be spared having to pay much of his steadily improving salary into the family's exchequer. As Stephe well knew, only George had any chance of persuading their mother to leave the scene of her social triumphs. But George had recently been troubled by liver pains, which Stephe thought more alarming than his brother seemed prepared to admit. In other ways, too, George had at last suffered disappointments. He had twice failed to secure his election to the exclusive Royal Yacht Squadron, being blackballed at the second attempt by no fewer than 25 members.[5] Nor had Lord Salisbury offered him the long-awaited junior ministry.

At the end of February Stephe left his Richmond hotel, having completed his book, and rejoined the 13th Hussars in Dublin. A week later the War Office ordered him to take command of the 5th Dragoon Guards, then stationed in India. Baden-Powell described leaving the regiment in which he had served for 21 years as 'one of the bitterest moments of my life'.[6] When he told his servant, Martin Dillon, that he was going, the man wept openly and penned a heartfelt note: 'I give you my word no matter how good my place is I will give it up and go to you as soon as ever you get back to England. I hope we will live together.' Dillon predicted that Stephe would receive 'a great welcome' from the regiment on his return from Rhodesia. 'Just like myself they are longing to see you.'[7] Stephe's first biographer talked to a group of sergeants in the 13th, asking whether the men 'liked' Stephe. 'There was a silence for a second or two, and at last one of the sergeants replied hesitatingly: "Well no, I shouldn't say they *like* him," and then in a burst – "Why, they worship him!"'[8] Nothing illustrates his success as a regimental officer better than his relationship with Edward Sargeaunt, who had been his troop sergeant-major in India in the 1880s and afterwards in Colchester and Liverpool. When Sargeaunt died in 1929, although his wife survived him he left all his regimental cups, presentation salvers and other mementoes to Stephe, who had been consistently kind to him after he retired and had been instrumental in getting him a cottage in Speldhurst where his Powell cousins were the largest local landowners.[9]

On the day he left the 13th Hussars for ever, Stephe planned to slip away unnoticed in the early morning before breakfast. He therefore asked Dillon to have a cab ready at the back of his quarters.

> When all was ready [he recalled] I sneaked out of the back door, there to find my cab, with the Regimental Sergeant-Major sitting on the box conducting the band, which was also in attendance, every man of my squadron harnessed in on long ropes, and the whole regiment there to see me out of the barrack gate. And off we went, the most choky experience I have ever had. My last glimpse of the barracks showed blankets being waved from every window, and all through the slums and streets of Dublin went this mad procession which finally landed me at the station with a farewell cheer.[10]

*

Before Baden-Powell's arrival in India, the 5th Dragoon Guards had been proficient at drill and smart on the parade ground. A slavish obedience to orders was still widely supposed to be the hallmark of a good cavalry officer. The senior officers had been horrified to learn that a young Brevet-Colonel with more experience of African campaigning than parade-ground ceremonial had been appointed to command them. Baden-Powell, however, was tactful but firm, and some of the older officers who could not accept this youthful new broom retired.[11] Baden-Powell disliked what he called 'kid-gloved high-collared officers', who were snobbish towards colonials and officers from less exclusive regiments. Nor was he keen on 'highly trained staff officers who were bound hard and fast by rules'. He preferred a man able 'to fall in with the ways of the country where he is, and ready to cast off the Red Books'.[12]

He at once reduced all drill and ceremonial, and discouraged formality. He was always approachable, and broke the old custom that a subaltern could never address anyone above the rank of the senior subaltern unless first spoken to. He took junior officers into his confidence and showed them his campaign mementoes.[13] But his private chats with the rank and file were considered even more eccentric. To improve his men's health, Baden-Powell built a bakery, a dairy, a soda water factory, a temperance club and supper rooms where alcohol was served. He tried without success to persuade the men to forgo their visits to the 'rag', or brothel, in the bazaar, though the best he ever achieved was a semi-voluntary ban lasting a couple of weeks. He spoke to all ranks about the dangers of venereal disease and felt disgusted enough by its prevalence to order his Provost Sergeant to whip away prostitutes following the troops when the regiment was on the march.[14]

Despite the long interval since Stephe had last been in Meerut, the place itself was utterly unchanged, although not one of the people he remembered was still there. A dozen years earlier he had hero-worshipped Baker Russell with his manly bearing and chestful of medals. Now, as colonel of a regiment of his own, he wanted *his* young officers to look up to him. When a group of them asked him to come pigsticking, he knew he was being tested. 'It was an anxious moment. I wasn't sure whether my nerve had survived the years of abstinence from the sport.' The pigs proved elusive that day and after several hours he dismounted to search a likely-looking thicket. Suddenly a huge boar hove into view and, before Stephe could reach his horse, charged him. 'I had just time to lower my spear as he rushed onto it and it went deep into his chest. But the shock of the impact threw me over on my back, and, while I held tight to the spear-shaft, he was there just over me, trying to reach me with his tusks but held off sufficiently by the spear.' When Baden-Powell's young companions found him in this position, they killed the pig and asked admiringly: ' "Do you always go in on foot, sir?" "Of course," ' he replied. [15]

Being Colonel brought home his age to him as never before. His mother was staying in Bournemouth where he jokingly promised to join her. 'Just the place for a decrepit old colonel from India to come and pick up his health.'[16] Henrietta Grace, who since George's wedding had executed a complete volte face, kept pressing him about his plans for marriage. 'Yes,' he replied with slight exasperation, 'I *shall* be very pleased when I find myself married and settled, and in the meantime I am at least not wasting my time as I am now working up for a pension.'[17] Early in 1898 Henrietta Grace broke her leg while staying in Scotland. Just as he had pretended to have a wife in South Africa while he had been on Malta, he now decided to use his mother's accident to keep the more blatant husband-seekers at arm's length. He therefore sent a Scottish press report about 'Mrs Baden-Powell's accident' to the editor of Meerut's newspaper. The result was: 'Mrs Baden-Powell, wife of the popular Colonel of the 5th Dragoon Guards, who broke her leg while walking on the mountain above Inverary, has now completely recovered from her injuries. It is not, however, expected that she will come out to Meerut this year.' Although Stephe claimed to have had a lot of 'fun' over this incident, his mother was not amused.[18] He had seemed very depressed before sailing. Was there something on his mind? 'I thoroughly inquired into it,' he reassured her, 'and I can't find the slightest shadow of any kind of trouble, above the surface of money troubles . . . I am not in love (only wish I were!).'[19]

The problem identified by George was that the Baden-Powell family was at long last breaking up, and so each member owed it to himself or herself to develop an independent life. And if, like Stephe, one did not feel attracted by the opposite sex and yet was being pressed to marry by the one person whose opinion mattered most to one, life became fraught. Suddenly Stephe found himself looking at married couples with a new eye. Major-General Edward Locke Elliot, the Inspector-General of Cavalry in India, was seven years older than he and had recently married a young and forceful wife. Baden-Powell stayed with him in Simla for a couple of days in June 1898, and 'enjoyed every minute of it'. He pronounced Elliot 'the only man I have ever felt that I wouldn't mind changing places with. Young, smart, keen soldier, good swordsman, first-rate race rider and across country, plays polo, pigsticks, plays the piano beautifully; charming wife plays the violin; jolly little daughter . . . Mrs Elliot won the jumping competition (open to men as well as ladies), and even the baby's pony took a prize . . . Among many good books in the house I read one of Le Gallienne's . . .'[20] Elliot was plainly a man of intellectual discrimination. A mere two years after Oscar Wilde's downfall very few soldiers would have dreamed of buying anything by the decadent *fin-de-siècle* writer, Richard Le Gallienne, who in deference to Wilde always affected velvet jackets and shoulder-length hair.

During his first summer back in India, Stephe accepted an invitation from the Simla Amateur Dramatic Club to play the part of Wun-Hi, the Chinese tea-house owner in *The Geisha* – an operetta which was at the time still playing in London after a year's run. This brought him face to face with a number of single women of marriageable age, among whom was the actress playing the part of Molly Seamore, the English heroine of the piece. Molly, out of pure mischief, becomes a geisha at the tea house and is soon pursued by an unscrupulous Japanese nobleman. The operetta tells the story of her rescue from the consequences of her folly. 'Miss Turner,' wrote the *Simla Times*'s reviewer on 1 September 1897, 'made Molly exactly what the author intended her to be, a sprightly, thoughtless girl, full of fun and adventure without counting the cost either to herself or others . . . The character [of Molly] is worked out to perfection and with abundance of *chic* by Miss Turner.'[21]

Baden-Powell's job, as the pidgin-English-speaking tea house owner, was to provide the evening's humour. His grasping nature and inarticulate sobbing whenever misfortune befell him convulsed the audience. There were rumours in the Green Room that Colonel Baden-Powell was interested in Miss Turner. The two were seen riding outside Simla on Jakko Hill, which was a favourite spot for lovers and would-be betrotheds.[22] It seems unlikely that Stephe fell in love with Ellen Turner; his letters to her are affectionate, but no more than were his earlier letters to child correspondents. He seems to have been fond of her much as he had been fond of Caroline Heap.[23] Nevertheless he admired Ellen's vivacity and, rare for him, took the trouble to write to her mother from time to time. He also made himself agreeable to her father, a colonel in the Royal Engineers who liked him enough to give him occasional presents such as a portable camping-chair. Stephe and Ellen went cycling together, and he used to amuse her by employing one of Meerut's professional letter-writers to send her nonsensical communications, as if from the firm of Wun-Hi & Co. 'Our representative will call on you at three o'clock, or soon after it if he is then sober, which, however, is unusual for him at that hour . . .'[24] Baden-Powell gave a dinner party for *The Geisha*'s cast and organized a picnic for the cast, largely to please Ellen.[25]

When six years later Ellen was engaged to be married to a rich young captain in the 18th Hussars, Stephe wrote her the thoroughly decent letter convention required. But a hint of pathos crept in with the humour: 'I *do* congratulate you. He is an excellent chap and you will have a very good time. So much so that you will go and forget your old friends . . . Do you remember when you used to treat me like a dog! Well – I've a good deal of the dog in me: he doesn't *say* much but *he's all right*! is poor old Wun-Hi.'[26] This was written on 6 September 1903, and at the very top just under the date, Baden Powell wrote: 'Tomorrow is an anniversary with me!' 7 September 1897 marked neither the opening of *The Geisha* nor the last night, but fell in the middle of its run. There is no mention in other surviving letters and diaries of any significant event occurring on 7 September in any of the years between 1897 and 1903. So it is hard to imagine what else the 'anniversary' could have been unless Stephe was referring to an unsuccessful proposal of marriage. He had then been under considerable pressure from George and his mother.

In his courtship Baden-Powell had often represented himself as a staid and rather avuncular figure, yet during these final years in India he could be as mischievous as ever he had been. Stephe's most celebrated hoax took place in October 1897. He and Captain Quentin Agnew, A.D.C. to the Commander-in-Chief, returned to Simla from Agnew's country retreat to find that a theatrical performance was going on that evening. They therefore took a box at the theatre for a party of friends and booked a table at the Club for later in the evening. While they were dressing, Agnew suggested that they disguise themselves to see if they could carry off the pretence of being a couple of newspaper correspondents – one from Rome and the other from London, both sent to India to report on the anticipated Afghan War. Agnew persuaded another A.D.C. to accompany them in their disguises to the theatre, to introduce them to their friends and to explain that Colonel Baden-Powell and Captain Agnew had been detained by the Commander-in-Chief. They had expected to be found out almost at once, but they were still being taken seriously as newspapermen at the end of the play. They therefore decided to go on to their own supper party as guests instead of hosts. Baden-Powell recalled what happened next:

> I sent a hurried note to a young officer in my Regiment who was there on leave and asked him to go to the Club and act as host on my behalf and to receive our guests, as I had been detained . . . In a P.S. I added that among the guests were two war correspondents who were strangers to the place and who were to receive special attention, one of them being an Italian count. When we arrived at the Club there was my faithful subaltern waiting to receive us but, when in default of any Italian he started to talk to me in most indifferent French, I nearly broke down with laughter. As it was, though I held my facial muscles under control, the tears welled out of my eyes, and he anxiously asked: 'Est-ce-que vous êtes malade aux yeux?' to which I replied in broken accents: 'I am a leetle sick in ze eyes.' This phrase became a memorable one in Simla for months afterwards.
>   Towards the end of supper . . . out of the tail of my eye I saw one of the guests pass behind Agnew and, recognising his back view, go to speak to him. To her surprise she found herself confronted by a bearded man with a Cockney accent. She whispered her suspicions to a friend. Something desperate had to be done. Accordingly I showed signs of having had more wine than was good for me, which caused the ladies in my neighbourhood to feel that the time had come to withdraw; and as I got up insistent on following them I was promptly tripped up and thrown down by the nearest man. But I struggled on, following the hurrying ladies into the next room, till they appeared to be really alarmed, when I pulled off my wig and showed them that it was all right . . . I was promptly pounced upon and rolled up in the carpet and sat upon.[28]

Colonel and Mrs Turner and Ellen were among those dinner guests entirely taken in by Baden-Powell and Agnew. A couple of weeks later Ellen told Stephe – whom she knew to be inordinately proud of his regiment's dairy – that a cousin of hers was arriving from England with her children. They would be passing through Meerut on a certain day, so could Stephe kindly go to the train and give her a few bottles of his regiment's wonderful milk? On the appointed day Baden-Powell had some of the best sterilized milk prepared and put in bottles which he attached to the handlebars of his bicycle, and then he rode off whistling merrily to meet the mail train. It was only then that he recollected that he only knew the lady's christian name: Rosie.

I met the train and walked all down it, looking at every likely looking woman, and finally, summoning all my courage, I went and asked each in turn if her name was Rosie. It was quite strange the different ways in which they received my question. The worst of it was that not one of them seemed pleased . . . The consequence was that I came away without discovering Rosie and without delivering my milk, as, by the time I had done with them, they would not accept my milk as an apology. As I re-passed my friends' house they were all sitting on the wall waiting for me. They gave me three cheers and asked how Rosie was looking and then I knew that I had been had. But it is a silly game, that of practical jokes, and I never indulged in it myself – except of course when necessary to pay out other people.[29]

Neither in his *Indian Memories*, published in 1922, nor in his autobiography did Baden-Powell admit who had 'paid *him* out' by playing this joke. The identity of the joker is only to be found in Ellen Turner's unpublished reminiscences of her Indian days.[30] Stephe's claim never to have played practical jokes except to settle old scores is another example of his disconcerting ability to be ingeniously mischievous and primly censorious more or less at the same time.

Another of Baden-Powell's enduring contradictions was his passion for manly hardships and his simultaneous interest in homemaking skills. 'The place is gradually getting furnished,' he told his mother of his house in Meerut, 'and I have struck on such a lovely colour for covers and curtains viz. salmon colour and dark pink.' Later he enthused about how 'pretty' the interior had become now that he had hung his carefully chosen curtains and his Indian embroideries.[31] Yet when war broke out on the North-West Frontier, Baden-Powell was desperate to get there, regardless of whether the Commander-in-Chief decided to send for the 5th Dragoon Guards. After three months of constant trying, he finally succeeded in getting leave for long enough to travel to Malakand to 'see the ground over which so much of the fighting has taken place – and possibly to see a skirmish'.[32]

His keenness to be directly involved in the fighting was shared by the majority of officers in India, but whether most of them would have been as eager to go simply as an observer seems doubtful. General Sir Bindon Blood, who had commanded the 8,000 men of the Malakand Field Force in a hard-fought campaign and was now mopping up, did not need additional regiments. He was, however, perfectly happy to satisfy Baden-Powell's longing to be fighting and sent him a telegram: 'We are having a pheasant shoot on the 7th [January]. Hope you will join us.'[33] In the course of this fighting Baden-Powell witnessed what he would always consider the bravest action he had ever seen. A solitary Afghan tribesman came charging down from a mountain ridge that was being shelled by the British and, on his own, attacked an entire battalion of infantry.

> He came on . . . with his blue clothes flying out behind him and a big glittering sword in his hand . . . One could see spits of dust jumping up around him, but they did not deter him, till suddenly he stumbled and fell . . . he was evidently hit but was binding up a wound in his leg. Then he picked up his sword and shaking it at us came on again limping, but determined to get there. It was a grand and pathetic sight to see this one plucky chap advancing single-handed against the whole crowd. Our men in front ceased firing at him, whether out of admiration or under orders I don't know, but a minute or two later he suddenly tumbled forward and rolled over and lay in a huddled heap − dead. As we went up the heights afterwards I passed him as he lay, and was glad to see that some of the Indian troops had, out of admiration for him, laid him straight and covered him over.[34]

As usual, everything about the seat of war pleased Baden-Powell. A harrowing night journey over a bumpy mountain pass, in a 'rotten cart with a half-dead pony . . . and a good chance of attack by Ghazis', was ideal. 'The sun set and the moon rose and we toilfully bumped along, but I liked it. At last, close under the mountains we sighted the layer of smoke from our camp, and, at the same time, the bivouac fires of the enemy twinkling all along the heights, which gave me a throb of pleasure.'[35]

During the course of 1897, Baden-Powell took his interest in scouting and reconnaissance a significant step further. In the mid-1880s when he had lectured on these subjects, he had thought scouting an important military activity but had not considered training individual men as members of a special unit exclusively devoted to scouting duties. On 2 August he told his mother that he had recently had 'a lot of men specially trained as scouts'.[36] When thieves broke into the guardroom of an infantry regiment stationed in Meerut, the native police could make no headway at all. 'But when we heard of it later in the day,' recorded Stephe, 'I laid on some of my new scouts and we soon found some more foot tracks that had escaped notice.'[37] The three sets of footprints were followed over a wall, through a shrubbery and eventually to a main road, 'where a two-wheeled cart, with a single pony harnessed to it, had stood for some time (hoof marks and droppings) and then had driven off in a northerly direction'. The police in the next town were telegraphed and the thieves were subsequently arrested while still on their journey.[38]

When Baden-Powell wrote his *Report on the Scouting System of the 5th Dragoon Guards*[39], he mentioned that his scouts were trained to deduce information from tracks and that they were encouraged to study

Sherlock Holmes. One of Baden-Powell's subalterns recalled that Stephe was an admirer of Conan Doyle. 'In my view,' he wrote, 'this started his great interest in deduction.'[40] In *Scouting for Boys* there would be half a dozen references to Sherlock Holmes and one to Dr Joseph Bell, the Edinburgh professor upon whom Conan Doyle had based his legendary detective. Scoutmasters would be invited to set up mystery crimes, either taken from one of Doyle's stories or of their own invention, and to ask their boys to study the clues and to solve the crime using their deductive powers. But even before Sherlock Holmes's appearance, Baden-Powell had written in *Cavalry Instruction* (1886) about the importance of studying every kind of evidence and then 'putting things together'.

Other elements from the 5th Dragoon Guards' scouting system which would one day find their way into *Scouting for Boys* were map reading, recording details of a recently visited locality, finding the way using a compass, the stars and remembered landmarks; tracking, improving the quickness of eye and ear, estimating heights and distances, keeping fit, avoiding alcohol and remaining continent (i.e. avoiding venereal disease – Baden-Powell would later use this term to mean avoiding masturbation). Stephe would also list some of the scouting games played by his dragoons in *Scouting for Boys*. There is however no evidence that he had any idea of starting an organization for boys at this time in his life. H. G. Kennard, his adjutant in India, was convinced of this, as was Ellen Turner.[41]

Six men under an officer made up each scout training group, and 6–8 would one day be the number of boys in each Boy Scout patrol under their patrol leader. Ever since 1883 Baden-Powell had entertained a secret dream of one day founding a specialist body of hand-picked men.[42] In the following year he had told his mother he would 'happily spend 5 years' organizing a regiment of gentlemen rankers. Stephe had envisaged this regiment as becoming 'an intelligent body of scouts such as no other army could ever hope to possess'.[43] Until 1897–98, when he trained his regimental scouts in the 5th Dragoon Guards, he had been unable to organize anything resembling this ideal grouping.

From June 1898 Baden-Powell found himself an acting Major-General in the absence of his divisional general, Sir Bindon Blood. In April the following year, he thought that he was about to be promoted to the rank of Brigadier-General. Military Headquarters in Simla approved the appointment and asked for London's confirmation. Lord Wolseley, however, promptly refused the request. This was unlikely to have been because of Baden-Powell's comparative youth. During this very month (April 1899) Sir Alfred Milner, the High Commissioner at the Cape, began to send back to London a series of flamboyant and alarmist despatches, intended to jolt the Cabinet into threatening military intervention in South Africa. So Wolseley would already have formed an idea of the type of African employment he might soon wish to offer to Baden-Powell. A secret War Office memorandum shows that he had definitely made up his mind about this in early May, less than a month later.[44] The Commander-in-Chief would have known that if he authorized his protégé's promotion to an Indian command, he would then be committed to employing him in any future South African war as commander of the Brigade he had been given in India, thus ruling out the far less conventional role Wolseley had in mind.

In spite of his many successes as colonel of his regiment and his popularity with the civil population of Meerut, there were times when the ease of his social conquests and the intensity of the demands upon him made Stephe long to escape his admirers and those aspects of his own personality which made him court them. When he was staying at Mussoori, between Simla and Naini Tal, he found his fame as an entertainer had preceded him and that he was 'expected to attend a grand masonic banquet that night . . . and afterwards to be funny till 1 a.m.' Suddenly he had known that he had to get out of the place and so bolted during a storm with his Arab pony, his groom and four porters.[45]

> There are times in every man's life [he wrote] when his whole being cries out for a steady spell of doing nothing in particular . . . Nowhere is this more acutely felt than in India. A feeling of staleness comes over you, and instinctively you look around for an antidote. If the call of the wild then makes itself heard, the right thing is to yield to it.[46]

In the summer of 1898 Baden-Powell took a trip to Kashmir which convinced him that the outdoor life, enjoyed purely for its own sake without any military objective, was immensely valuable. Before setting out, he paid considerable attention to his equipment. 'Roughing it,' he insisted, 'does not exist for any but the ignorant. The experienced camper knows what to take and he also knows that the necessaries are sometimes luxuries.' Stephe's equipment included old kid gloves to protect his hands from mosquito bites, a Kodak camera, quinine, Bologna sausage, soup, dog biscuits, candles, whisky, waterproof sheets, lanterns, a tin-opener and a corkscrew.[47] On this trip he adopted clothes that he would occasionally claim as the inspiration for the Boy Scout uniform; these included the Stetson he had worn in Rhodesia and a flannel shirt, but not the famous shorts [see second photo section]. Yet in spite of all the planning, Baden-Powell viewed camping and walking in wild places as an experience which transcended practical considerations.

Going over these immense hills – especially when alone – and looking almost sheer down into the deep valleys between – one feels like a parasite on the shoulders of the world. There is such a bigness about it all, that opens and freshens up the mind. It's as good as a cold tub for the soul.[48]

With a collapsible bath in his luggage, Stephe was equipped to cleanse his body as well as his soul. His father's pantheistic book, *The Order of Nature*, was a significant influence upon him, as a sub-heading in *Rovering to Success* makes plain: 'Nature Knowledge as a Step Towards Realising God'. Baden-Powell also used to quote Bacon's aphorism: 'The study of the Book of Nature is the true key to that of Revelation.'[49] In a bizarre way he managed to combine camping equipment, adventure and religious sensations in a remarkable synthesis. In his published *Matabele Campaign* he described his camping impedimenta as his 'toys' and then went on: 'May it not be that our toys are the various media adapted to individual tastes through which men may know their God?'[50] Quite literally Stephe worshipped what he called the 'flannel shirt life' and everything that went with it. 'Not being able to go to my usual church (the jungle) on Sunday, I went to the garrison church instead,' he wrote to Ellen Turner, more in earnest than tongue in cheek.[51]

In Kashmir Baden-Powell's attitude towards wild life betrayed no signs of softening. Bears were particular objects of his blood-lust. 'I could see his head and shoulders above the bank – and I plugged him with a nice steady shot which sent him back with a yowl head-over-heels backwards . . .' Later Baden-Powell gazed down at the dead bear, which he thought 'looked like a respectable old gentleman who had once imbibed too freely – and was lying in the gutter in his glossy black clothes . . .'[52] Stephe was still a long way from adopting the advice which he would one day give to Boy Scouts: to stalk wild animals with a camera, rather than a gun. Strangely his bear hunts have a unique place in the history of Scouting. While waiting for his beaters to drive bears in his direction, he had time to begin writing 'a book about scouting' and to 'jot down . . . first heads for chapters, and finally subjects of paragraphs'. By early September 1898, the scouting book had progressed sufficiently for him to dictate it to the regimental shorthand clerk on his return to Meerut.[53] He tentatively entitled this new work *Cavalry Aids to Scouting*. Incorporated within the text were most of the lectures he had given to his regimental scouts and a lot of suggestions for practical work, as well as numerous personal anecdotes and adventures. The basic assumption underlying the whole book was the author's conviction that scouting bred self-reliance by making men use their intelligence and act upon their own judgements without needing to wait for advice from an officer or an N.C.O..[54]

Shortly after returning to Meerut, Baden-Powell was shocked to

hear that George had died.* 'Poor George,' Stephe commiserated with
his mother, 'he always took me under his wing and I cannot yet realize
that he is gone.' He consoled himself with the thought that his brother
had 'tasted of the best of this world'.[55] From a purely practical and
material point of view, the loss of George was not the disaster it would
have been for Stephe four or five years earlier. His position with
Wolseley was now established and intervention from George would
not be needed again. He acknowledged that it was 'an awful blow' to
his mother – as indeed it was, not only in personal but in financial
terms, since Frances would not prove as responsive as her late husband
to Henrietta Grace's unashamed requests for cash. On 30 October,
three weeks before George's death, he had agreed to leave his mother
£10,000. It therefore came as a devastating blow to learn that although
George had signed a will benefiting her as promised, it would have no
legal effect. He had understood that £10,000 had been gifted to him
absolutely as part of his wife's marriage settlement, whereas in fact he
had only been granted the income from that sum for his lifetime.
George's estate barely provided token legacies for his brothers and £500
each for Henrietta Grace and Agnes.

From Stephe's point of view the least desirable consequence of
George's death – his personal loss apart – was the fact that from now on
he would be expected to provide a much higher level of financial help
for his mother.[57] This would make Henrietta Grace keener than ever to
see him profitably married.

In the first week of May 1899, Baden-Powell left India for what he
believed would be four months' leave. 'I am sitting in front of my tent
taking tea,' he wrote shortly before embarking, 'a rich glowing sunset
lighting up the horses being groomed at evening stables, while the
band is playing a lively selection to the camp.'[58] He would undoubtedly have written a lengthier valediction if he had known that he was
bidding farewell not only to India but to his life as a regimental officer.

* He had been suffering from cancer of the liver since the late summer.

6

THE HERO

1. A Visit to the War Office (May to July 1899)

Baden-Powell reached England on 21 May 1899 without any presentiment of great events in the offing. His principal concern was to see all the members of his family, and in particular his brother's widow and her children – 3-year-old Maud and 1-year-old Donald. He found morale at St George's Place at a low ebb. His mother was again at the seaside, recuperating from a nervous collapse which had followed George's death.[1] Agnes was in an equally depressed state. She had briefly been courted by Guglielmo Marconi, the inventor of wireless telegraphy, but nothing had come of it. They had met because of the inventor's interest in the possible usefulness of Baden's military kites in ship-to-shore wireless experiments. Nothing had come of that either.[2] More recently Agnes had been strongly drawn to a Captain Hawley, an amateur archaeologist, whom she had recently met in Wiltshire. The captain had loved sitting up 'late at night over her tricks and games', but Agnes's cause was harmed when Henrietta Grace forbade her to travel anywhere alone with Hawley, who had suggested that they visit various museums in Salisbury together.[3] Agnes at the age of 39 did not dare ask her mother whether Captain Hawley could be invited to stay. Instead she persuaded Warington to ask on her behalf, but whatever Henrietta Grace's response it would appear that Hawley never came. So after all the excitement of having archaeological books 'modestly laid on her bedroom doormat' by the gallant captain, Agnes returned once more to bicycle rides around the Serpentine and teaching tricks to her eleven tame sparrows.[4]

Nevertheless Stephe learned from his sister that she had gone as a spectator to a county field day and had met Lord Wolseley, who had at once treated her to a ten-minute eulogy of Colonel R. S. S. Baden-Powell.[5] By way of compensation for her disappointments, Stephe took Agnes to the Trooping of the Colour. He also visited the Royal Academy, went to the Derby with Baden and watched McLaren lead the 13th Hussars polo team in the final of the Hurlingham Inter-Regimental Tournament.[6]

On 3 July Baden-Powell lunched at his London club, the Naval and Military. Major George Gough, Lord Wolseley's A.D.C., came across from another table and said: '"I thought you were in India. I have just cabled for you to come home as the Commander-in-Chief wants to see you." With such coolness as I could command I said: "Well, here I am"; and after lunch we went down together to the War Office and I was once more shown into Lord Wolseley's room. He had a knack of trying to spring surprises on you and was all the better pleased if you were not bowled out by them . . . On this occasion he said: "I want you to go to South Africa." With the air of a well trained butler I said: "Yes, sir." "Well, can you go on Saturday next?" (This was Monday.) "No, Sir." "Why not?" Knowing well the sailings of the South African steamers, I replied: "There's no ship on Saturday, but I can go on Friday." '[7]

In this matter-of-fact way Baden-Powell learned of the appointment destined to make him a household name. As he was leaving, Wolseley asked him what his address would be before sailing. 'I said that if he didn't want me in London I would be at Henley for the boat races.'[8] Some years later several journalists suggested that Baden-Powell had been staying with a woman at Henley.[9] The truth was rather different.

In spite of his mother's new-found enthusiasm for him to marry, Stephe had made precious few efforts in that direction. One concession to his mother's feelings had been his acceptance of an invitation from a rich family living at Henley to attend their ball during the Regatta Week and to join their house party. Mr and Mrs William Dalziel Mackenzie owned a substantial house called Fawley Court, where they lived with four unmarried daughters. Yet in spite of these young ladies' wealth, as soon as Stephe left Lord Wolseley's office he sent a telegram to his would-be hostess to excuse himself. Mrs Mackenzie, a formidable matriarch, was unimpressed to hear that her backsliding guest would be leaving the country that very Friday. In her opinion this was no excuse for crying off at such short notice. Colonel Baden-Powell had accepted her invitation over three weeks earlier and ought to honour his obligation. He tried to propitiate her by suggesting that Baden go in his place, but this only made matters worse. After a heated exchange of telegrams, the man who would soon be Britain's most famous soldier meekly agreed to go to Henley.[10] Since he could not expect to be home until Wednesday afternoon this would only leave him two full days before he sailed.

2. Mission Impossible (July to September 1899)

Thirteen years before Wolseley informed Baden-Powell that he was about to leave for South Africa, the discovery of the world's richest gold reefs on the Rand had made it extremely desirable from Britain's point of view for the Transvaal to be drawn permanently into the British Empire. Desirable or not, what actually happened was that their new wealth encouraged the Boers to affirm their independence with ambitious schemes for expansion. The British Government believed that closer ties between the 'Mother Country' and her white-settled colonies were essential for the nation's survival as a great power, and therefore viewed the possible emergence of an independent South Africa as a grave threat. There was an ominous international dimension since France and Germany were encouraging the Boers.

Relations between Great Britain and the Boer republics had deteriorated significantly after the disastrous raid on the Transvaal led by Dr Jameson in December 1895. Although Cecil Rhodes had played a leading part in this drama, until the previous year he had hoped to bring about a peaceful federation within which the Transvaal, the Orange Free State, Natal and the Cape Colony would move towards ultimate integration. This would be brought closer by improved rail links and the abolition of trade barriers. But President Kruger's resistance to all measures that he feared might undermine his country's independence had finally led Rhodes to abandon caution. With Jameson, he had planned an armed raid on the Transvaal timed to coincide with an uprising in Johannesburg. With as many Uitlanders (foreign prospectors, traders and businessmen) as Boers living in the Transvaal and paying the major part of the country's taxes without receiving any democratic rights in return, there was plenty of local resentment against Kruger. The Raid, however, was disastrously botched, and the rising never materialized. Rhodes's dream of a united South Africa was wrecked; and the mutual mistrust of Boer and Briton seemed certain to lead to war.

Before the Raid the British Colonial Secretary had tacitly encouraged Rhodes and Jameson. Afterwards he naturally kept his own counsel, but Chamberlain's ultimate aim was still to gain control over the Boer republics. By obliging Kruger to give the vote to the Uitlanders, he hoped to retain the loyalty of these formerly disenfranchized Britons when they finally ran the country. In May 1897 he appointed as his High Commissioner at the Cape a man as determined as was Rhodes to establish British supremacy in South Africa. Sir Alfred Milner was convinced that Kruger would only make real concessions if forced to the very brink of war, or even to war itself. From the spring of 1899, the initiative in South Africa passed from Chamberlain and his Cabinet colleagues to Milner.

On 5 June Sir Alfred abruptly broke off direct talks when Kruger refused to enfranchize all those Uitlanders who had lived in the republic for five years. Instead Kruger insisted upon the naturalization of the Uitlanders well before they qualified for the vote. Believing that Kruger had conceded enough to justify further negotiations, Chamberlain deplored Milner's action. The Boers, imagining that Chamberlain and Milner held identical views, speeded up their military plans (including the purchase of the most up-to-date field guns manufactured by Krupp and Creusot).

In London the Cabinet was left with two choices: either to recall Milner, which would have meant giving up the idea of a British South Africa; or to make firm demands on the Boers in the knowledge that these would probably have to be enforced by the British Army. In reality dismissing Milner was unthinkable, since it would be seen internationally as a humiliation for Great Britain. The Cabinet was therefore left hoping and praying that the Boers would give way as soon as serious threats were made. But in early September the Cabinet's requests for various safeguards convinced Kruger that the British would not be satisfied until they owned his country. He therefore withdrew all his offers and war became a certainty.

*

On 3 July, when Baden-Powell had been summoned to the War Office, this grim situation had not quite developed. Nevertheless Lord Wolseley was a worried and frustrated man. Believing that war could not be avoided, he had advised the Cabinet in the first week of June to permit the mobilization of an army corps, a division of cavalry, a battalion of mounted infantry and four infantry battalions. Lord Lansdowne, the Secretary of State for War, with whom Wolseley was scarcely on speaking terms, had refused to act. A month later, Wolseley's suggestion that 10,000 men be sent at once to South Africa was also flatly rejected. Such was the state of Britain's unpreparedness that the despatch of even 10,000 men would have meant calling out the Reserves and applying to Parliament for a vote of funds. This would have been interpreted as a declaration of war, and was thought to be not only in advance of public opinion but to constitute an open invitation to the Boers to make a pre-emptive strike against Natal. The Cabinet therefore merely authorized a few additions to the artillery at the Cape, and the despatch of twenty 'Special Service Officers' to organize the defence of the frontiers and to impress the Boers with an idea of British determination.[1] Baden-Powell learned that he was to be in command of these hand-picked Special Service Officers.

Since there has been considerable confusion among historians about what Baden-Powell was sent to South Africa to do, and what Lord Wolseley really had in mind, it is worth trying to find out what led the Commander-in-Chief to issue Baden-Powell with some extremely surprising instructions.

Wolseley had been contemplating sending Baden-Powell to South Africa since mid-May, when the Intelligence Division had submitted various proposals to him in connection with South Africa.[2] The central idea had not originally been dreamed up by intelligence officers at all but by Colonel John Sanctuary Nicholson, whom Baden-Powell had met in Matabeleland and who was now Commandant General of the Rhodesian Police. In correspondence with Colonel John Hanbury-Williams (Sir Alfred Milner's Military Secretary), Nicholson had outlined a plan for a raid on the northern Transvaal by about 250 Rhodesian volunteers, the object being 'to "contain" a considerable force of Boers' in the event of war. On 1 July Colonel William Everett, the Assistant Adjutant-General at Headquarters, wrote a long memorandum on Nicholson's proposal for the benefit of the Secretary of State for War. He headed this document: 'Secret Memorandum on the project of a raid from Southern Rhodesia on the Northern Districts of the Transvaal.'[3] Colonel Everett believed that Nicholson could 'by a combination of audacity and wariness, do much in detaining a Boer force in the North; but the risk would be considerable'. Everett (the assistant to Sir Evelyn Wood who was in turn Wolseley's right-hand man) discussed Nicholson's plan with his two masters. They decided that a plan like Nicholson's could only go ahead if under the direction of an experienced Special Service Officer commanding more men than Nicholson had thought necessary. 'The officer who undoubtedly would be looked upon in Rhodesia as the right man in the right place if sent out to command their forces is Colonel Baden-Powell,' wrote Everett, speaking for Wood and Wolseley. He believed furthermore that the arrival of Baden-Powell and other Special Service Officers 'would in itself have a moral effect on the Transvaal'. A force of 1,000 men was thought adequate for the task of 'continually menacing the back door of the Transvaal and by rapid feints detaining a much larger number of Boers from concentration in the South'.[4]

In retrospect it seems extraordinary, after the shambles of the Jameson Raid, that Wolseley was prepared to consider a similar enterprise even if commanded by an officer in whom he had total confidence. In his attempt on Johannesburg Jameson had tried to raise 1,500 men but had only succeeded in recruiting half that number. The Boers had surrounded his men and forced their surrender with the utmost ease. Even supposing that Baden-Powell were to demonstrate superior tactical skills and to achieve a large measure of surprise, his mission would still be impossible.

During the last twenty years only one historian, Thomas Pakenham, has shown any understanding of Baden-Powell's predicament.[5] More recently the American historian, Michael Rosenthal, has accused Baden-Powell of failing to carry out the task assigned to him, and having quite unnecessarily 'permitted himself to be entrapped' in Mafeking, 'a tin-roofed town with nothing particular to recommend it'.[6] Rosenthal's claims owe much to a more substantial attack mounted twenty years earlier by the historian Brian Gardner in his *Mafeking: A Victorian Legend*. The idea that the Siege of Mafeking was one long music-hall turn, during which suffering was minimal, is largely Gardner's creation. Apart from blaming the press and Baden-Powell for transforming a minor event into a major feat of arms, Gardner also accused Baden-Powell of tactical naïvety in having unwittingly allowed himself to be entrapped. These arguments were repeated not just by Rosenthal in 1986 but by Piers Brendon in 1980.[7] All three critics have self-contradictorily implied that Baden-Powell welcomed a siege as an easier option than the more useful and demanding mobile role which had actually been assigned to him. The injustice of these strictures becomes apparent when Wolseley's reasons for issuing his desperate instructions are understood, and when Baden-Powell's first two months in South Africa are examined in detail.

The Commander-in-Chief was obsessed with the nightmarish imbalance of forces in South Africa. Remembering only too well the superiority in tactical thinking and marksmanship demonstrated by the Boers twenty years earlier at Majuba Hill, Wolseley had considerable respect for them. He was therefore appalled to know that until British reinforcements could be shipped from India a mere 7,000 British regulars would be guarding the Cape Colony; and the whole of Natal south of Ladysmith would be defended by 3,000 troops. At the same time 20,000 Boers lay in wait around the northern apex of Natal and, further south, the Cape Colony was menaced by a further 20,000.[8] If Kruger declared war before Britain could mobilize an army corps and additional colonial troops, Wolseley hardly dared think of the consequences. A Boer push through Natal could very well end with the loss of the port of Durban and the colony itself.

Such horrifying possibilities explained Wolseley's willingness to see Baden-Powell run colossal risks. If Stephe could occupy 5–6,000 Boers in Bechuanaland and the Northern Transvaal, even for a month, the pressure on Natal might be sufficiently reduced to save the colony until the arrival of Britain's army corps.

At the Cape in late May Sir Alfred Milner's Military Secretary, Colonel Hanbury-Williams, still supposed that Colonel Nicholson would be authorized to carry out his own plan. He told Colonel E. A. Altham of the Intelligence Division: 'I think his [Nicholson's] metier should be to contain as many Boers away from the South as possible . . . But we must not risk any "escapades".'[9] By escapades Hanbury-Williams meant 'raids' or 'demonstrations', as they would coyly be described in Sir Evelyn Wood's written instructions to Baden-Powell. How then was Baden-Powell supposed to 'contain' Boers and keep them away from the South without any 'escapades'? Fortunately for Stephe, the inexorable demands of a steadily worsening situation would suggest the perfect way; but on 3 July 1899 when Lord Wolseley took him in to see Lord Lansdowne, the army's youngest colonel was overwhelmed. His Commander-in-Chief had just confided to him his fears that war was inevitable, and had moreover accorded him the privilege of commanding the very first party of British officers to be sent out to South Africa on special service. Baden-Powell had waited all his professional life for just such an occasion and was not now going to tell Wolseley to his face that his orders were dangerous and impracticable. He sensibly decided to keep quiet and do the best he could in whatever circumstances he might find himself.

Sir Evelyn Wood sent Baden-Powell a written version of Wolseley's verbal orders on 7 July. Stephe was instructed 'to endeavour to demonstrate with the largest force at your disposal, in a southerly direction from Tuli, as if making towards Pretoria'. For this purpose he was to raise a regiment of 590 irregulars. Before the end of the month this order had been amended and he had been told to raise not one regiment but two.[10] Apart from detaining 'a considerable number of Boers', Baden-Powell's regiments were expected to protect Rhodesia, to convince the Boers that this small British force was an indication of greater things to come and to discourage the natives from supposing that it would be in their interest to support the Boers.[11] Wood concluded his orders by giving Baden-Powell 'full discretion as to your action on the above lines'. Mafeking, Stephe was told, would be held by local forces under the command of the Resident Commissioner. Before he left the rambling War Office building in Pall Mall, the Secretary of State had accorded him the high-sounding title of 'Commander-in-Chief, North-West Frontier Forces'.

'As I walked home,' he wrote later, 'I landed on a street refuge, held up by passing traffic, where I found that my neighbour was Sergeant-Major Manning of my regiment, home on leave.' When Baden-Powell blurted out that he was bound for South Africa, Manning begged to come too. True to his enlightened attitude towards N.C.O.s, Baden-Powell not only agreed but later recommended Manning for a commission and made him Adjutant of one of his regiments.[12] But Stephe found that he was given less liberty in the choice of his staff officers.

Wolseley appointed as his Chief Staff Officer Major Lord Edward Cecil, who was the fourth son of the Prime Minister, Lord Salisbury. When Wolseley had been Commander-in-Chief in Ireland Cecil had been his A.D.C.. He had distinguished himself in the Sudan in 1898 as Kitchener's A.D.C. and had won the D.S.O.. However, for all his advantages of birth, Lord Edward was not the kind of man Baden-Powell liked. He was a most unusual soldier, being introverted and literary and, although gifted with a keen sense of humour, not really a sociable man. He would be extremely unhappy while serving under Baden-Powell, but his mother's death, his wife's probable infidelity and his own ill-health were more to blame for his misery than anything done by his commanding officer. Another officer pressed upon Baden-Powell was Lieutenant the Hon. Algernon Hanbury-Tracy, Royal Horse Guards, the second son of Lord Sudeley.[13] Hanbury-Tracy would be Baden-Powell's Intelligence Officer and Press Censor.

Baden-Powell met Cecil and Hanbury-Tracy before leaving England. Another fifteen officers were chosen by Wolseley after Baden-Powell had embarked; they would join him later in South Africa. Of these he already knew several such as Colonel Herbert C. O. Plumer, who had commanded the Matabele Relief Force when Bulawayo was attacked in 1896. Major Alick J. Godley, a tall, good-humoured and exceptionally capable Anglo-Irishman, had served with distinction in Mashonaland. Lieutenant-Colonel Charles O. Hore, whom Baden-Powell had never met, had fought in Egypt in the 1880s and again in 1898. Nor did Stephe know Captain Charles FitzClarence, a descendant of William IV and the Irish actress Dorothea Jordan. FitzClarence would display outstanding bravery, for which he would be awarded the Victoria Cross. Lieutenant-Colonel Courtenay B. Vyvyan had been in Matabeleland, where he had stood in for Baden-Powell as Chief Staff Officer when Stephe was away commanding a mobile column.

Baden-Powell would have preferred to be given a free hand to choose his own staff, but apart from an inability to get on with Colonel Hore he would ultimately have little cause for complaint. He himself chose Kenneth McLaren. 'The Boy' sailed with the party which left Southampton on 15 July, a week after Baden-Powell and Cecil. Several officers would be recruited locally in Rhodesia and South Africa, among them Captain Gordon Wilson who was big-game shooting in Rhodesia when Baden-Powell met him. Wilson's wife, Lady Sarah, was a daughter of the Duke of Marlborough and one of Winston Churchill's aunts. She was destined to have a more adventurous campaign than her husband. Lieutenant Lord Charles Cavendish-Bentinck, a half-brother of the Duke of Portland, was holidaying at the Cape with his wife when he learned that Baden-Powell was looking for officers. A less satisfactory volunteer was Lieutenant Ronald Moncreiffe, a friend of the Princess of Wales and a celebrated gambler and bon viveur. To start with Moncreiffe would serve Baden-Powell well, but later he began to drink heavily and suffered a mental collapse.[14] The overwhelmingly aristocratic complexion of Baden-Powell's staff, although delighting Henrietta Grace, owed more to chance and to Lord Wolseley than to Stephe's choosing.

After saying goodbye to his family, Baden-Powell went to Charterhouse and told Dr Haig Brown lightly that he hoped the military authorities would find 'a warm corner' for him in South Africa.[15] Knowing exactly how warm the 'corner' already chosen for him was likely to be, he took the precaution of visiting his solicitor to make a new will before he sailed.[16]

On the voyage out Baden-Powell drafted the Standing Orders for his force. Since these were published on 28 July (when the continuance of peace was still a remote possibility), he could mention neither the 'raids' into the Transvaal which Wolseley expected him to make nor the objective of occupying large numbers of Boers and keeping them away from the vulnerable defences of Natal. 'This force has been raised for the duty of defending the border,' he began, 'but should it become necessary to practise the "essence of defence", viz to take the offensive, the following points should be borne in mind . . . We have failed before when opposed to the Boers by walking into positions prepared by them as traps for us, and by using infantry only, and thus being very slow in our moves. Our principle should be . . . to turn up unexpectedly by fast moving . . .' These were excellent intentions; and in view of the way in which British generals would shortly blunder into the Boers' prepared positions on the Modder River, as well as at Magersfontein and Colenso, it is tempting to suppose that in similar circumstances Baden-Powell might have done better. He ended his Standing Orders with an exhortation to everyone to 'pull together' and 'play the game to the very best of his ability'.[17]

When Baden-Powell stepped ashore at the Cape he expected to be warmly welcomed by the High Commissioner, Sir Alfred Milner, and the G.O.C. Sir William Butler. After all, he came with Lord Wolseley's instructions in his pocket (albeit signed by the Adjutant- General). Stephe was therefore shocked by the unconcealed hostility shown him by Butler when he reported to the office in the Castle where Uncle Henry used to sit. Sir William glanced through Baden-Powell's list of requirements – which included arms, ammunition, boots, horses and transport vehicles – and then lectured him on the political situation at the Cape. After Rhodes's downfall the new Prime Minister, W. P. Schreiner, would not allow anything to be done which might prevent an eleventh-hour compromise with the Transvaal. If Colonel Baden-Powell thought he was going to recruit men for his regiments in the Cape Colony, then he had better think again. Nor need he imagine that he would be able to recruit in Bechuanaland. Sir William clearly thought that Baden-Powell had been sent by the Commander-in-Chief to provoke a border incident which would give the war-mongers in England a chance to railroad the country into an unnecessary war. Butler agreed to let Baden-Powell have guns and ammunition but declined to allow him horses or transport from the Remount Department. He could therefore claim not to have sent the young colonel away empty-handed, although guns without transport were useless. Stephe left Butler's office feeling badly shaken. His 'pretty big enterprise' seemed to be starting, as he put it, 'under a cold douche of discouragement'.[18]

Nevertheless, given Sir Alfred Milner's abrupt termination of talks with President Kruger Baden-Powell felt confident that he could at least rely upon the High Commissioner for his support. He was therefore appalled to be treated almost as coldly by Sir Alfred. Unknown to Baden-Powell, Milner had not been consulted about his mission and therefore felt resentful.

It has not hitherto been appreciated that Sir Alfred knew Colonel Nicholson well and was privy to his plans for raiding the Transvaal in the event of war. Since Nicholson was Commandant of the Police in Rhodesia, Milner felt that he could rely upon him not to mobilize too many policemen and white volunteers for service against the Boers. Milner thought there would be another Matabele Rebellion if more than 400 men were withdrawn from the white civil population. On 10 June Milner confided his misgivings to the Hon. Arthur Lawley, the new Administrator in Rhodesia: 'Matters are much complicated by the fact that the War Office are sending out special service officers – Baden-Powell etc., etc. to "organize" a fighting force in the Protectorate [of Bechuanaland] and Rhodesia. I hate this, and would much rather leave it all to Nicholson.'[19] Lawley wrote back saying that 'if Baden-Powell is sent up to "boss" them [Nicholson, the police and the Rhodesian volunteers] they will be very loath to lend a hand. He is very unpopular here.' Milner received a similar communication from Sir Walter Hely-Hutchinson, the Governor of Natal, who had been told by the commander of the colony's volunteers that they would only serve under their own colonial officers and would deeply resent being placed under Imperial officers like Baden-Powell.[20]

The day after his frosty interview with Sir William Butler, Stephe was ushered into the high-ceilinged office in Government House where he had occasionally visited the late and unlamented Lord Rosmead. Now Sir Alfred Milner sat in Rosmead's chair. As a young man Sir Alfred, unlike Baden-Powell, had been joyfully accepted by Dr Jowett at Balliol where he had enjoyed a distinguished academic career. Milner often seemed aloof and intellectually arrogant to strangers, reserving his geniality for friends. Ignorant of the complaints pouring in from men like Lawley, Stephe could not understand why Milner was so unhelpful – especially since he had a reputation for wanting to be tough with the Boers. Sir Alfred told Baden-Powell pointedly that recruiting in Johannesburg, however discreetly conducted, was absolutely out of the question.[21] Stephe remained mystified.

In fact Sir Alfred's basic objection to Baden-Powell's mission was not that it might cause war prematurely but that it might *prevent* war altogether. Milner was frightened by Wolseley's impetuosity. If this young colonel offered himself as a bait too tempting for the Boers not to try to snap up, things could easily go disastrously wrong and

Baden-Powell might end up appearing the aggressor. Milner's greatest fear was that Wolseley's despairing efforts to avoid a military débâcle could end up giving the British public the impression that Chamberlain and the Government had secretly turned their backs on a peaceful settlement. Since this revelation would arouse furious opposition to any use of force, Sir Alfred had been doing his utmost to make the Boers, rather than the British Government, seem devious and bellicose. If Baden-Powell were to charge into this delicate situation with his clod-hopping irregulars, Milner saw his hopes both for war and for a British South Africa vanishing like a puff of smokeless powder.[22]

Unaware of the diplomatic tightrope that Milner was walking, Baden-Powell listened in silence as the High Commissioner told him that the War Office, on his urging, had ordered all Special Service Officers to wear civilian clothes rather than uniforms and to travel to Bulawayo under false names. Since his mission had already been reported in the Cape newspapers, Stephe was stunned.[23] It was already distressingly clear that almost everyone would have been happier if he had stayed at home. The G.O.C. did not want his force; Sir Alfred Milner viewed it as a potential embarrassment, and had vetoed recruiting; and it would soon be apparent that no government department wanted to admit that it was his paymaster.

In view of what Milner told them about the need for secrecy, officials at the War Office decided that it would be politically inept to place Baden-Powell's regiments on the Army List. To avoid publicity the Colonial Office would have to finance and take responsibility for Baden-Powell's force. So although Sir Alfred Milner was not keen to be connected with Baden-Powell and, unlike Lord Wolseley, had no vested interest in his future success, he found himself willy-nilly having to act as the little colonel's superior officer. This change of master did not help Baden-Powell with supplies. Later he told Wolseley that he had been obliged to raise and supply his regiments 'without any assistance from the Army beyond a few officers (and, I think, 23 pairs of boots)'.[24] Although his horses were eventually supplied by the Army, the bulk of his supplies and equipment was bought privately or provided by the British South Africa Police in Bulawayo.[25]

Baden-Powell left Cape Town for Bulawayo on 28 July, only three days after his arrival. Lord Edward Cecil remained behind to try to wrest some guns and ammunition from General Butler, who now seemed to be going back on his earlier promise of limited assistance. Cecil got nowhere, so he sought out Mr Ben Weil whose wholesale business, based in Mafeking, dominated all others in Bechuanaland and the northern Cape. Weil himself was then in Cape Town cannily 'laying in heavy stocks of food stuffs, fodder, grain, clothing and equipment such as are used as a rule by troops'.[26] The trader did not tell

Cecil that Mafeking was already well supplied and would be supplied still better when he returned there. A new tax was expected shortly on all goods entering Rhodesia and to beat the deadline tons of merchandise had been rushed up by rail to Mafeking.[27] When Cecil offered Weil a promissory note for £500,000 to buy supplies for Baden-Powell's regiments, the trader knew that Lord Edward had neither the backing of the authorities nor a personal fortune approaching the value of the order. But knowing who his aristocratic client's father was, Weil felt entirely secure. His decision to give credit on this scale was the single most important reason why Mafeking was able to face a prolonged siege.[28] Cecil left Cape Town on 14 August without having extracted any artillery from Butler.

On his arrival in Bulawayo on 1 August, Baden-Powell was met at the station by Colonel Nicholson, who managed to conceal his indignation at having his plans appropriated by the War Office and handed over to this dapper slouch-hatted little colonel. As Commandant of the Police, Nicholson knew everyone who was anyone in Rhodesia, and would be responsible for initiating much of the gossip which later tarnished Baden-Powell's reputation.[29] The two most senior officers under Nicholson, Colonel G. L. Holdsworth and Lieutenant-Colonel William Bodle, also felt bitter to have been upstaged by this outsider.[30]

Nevertheless in August 1899, Nicholson and his colleagues promised to supply Stephe with rifles, but their pessimism about the immediate prospects for recruiting men shook Baden-Powell. Nicholson said that he would allow 100 policemen to join the new frontier force, but warned Stephe that he doubted whether more than 300 civilians would be prepared to volunteer.[31] The following day he learned that two-thirds of the 300 men ready to join him were 'loafers and wasters'. 'Good men' did not want to abandon their jobs on the off-chance of war.[32] He therefore decided for the present only to take on enough men to train the horses, while he worked to get clearance to recruit in Durban and in the Cape. Eleven days after his arrival, he had still recruited only 50 men for one of his regiments, and even fewer for the other.[33]

Baden-Powell hit upon a partial solution when he decided to organize a squadron of young men who would be allowed to retain their jobs until hostilities became certain. In the meantime they would train at weekends.[34] Knowing this could be only a *faute de mieux* measure, he decided to recruit secretly whatever Milner might say. By 16 August three officers were recruiting for him *sub rosa* in Natal and the Cape.[35] He naïvely formed the opinion that Milner's handsome Military Secretary, Colonel Hanbury-Williams, was a man he could trust; so he told him in confidence of his secret recruiting. Hanbury-Williams replied angrily: 'I warned all the officers against this [recruiting in the Cape] before they left Cape Town, and about the immense difficulties of the political position.' The last thing Milner wanted was a public rupture with the Cape Ministry before he was sure that Chamberlain and the British public were safely in favour of war.

During the next few weeks Hanbury-Williams gave little comfort to Baden-Powell as his difficulties multiplied. When Stephe suggested that he would need 150 more men than originally sanctioned by the War Office, Hanbury-Williams warned him not to press for extra funding. 'It might make difficulties for us as to other matters. Twig?'[36] Baden-Powell did twig, but went on recruiting in secret. Even so, he ended up with many recruits who could not ride a horse and 'who had never seen a rifle'.[37] Major Alick Godley listed the professions of many of the 447 members of one of the two regiments (the Protectorate Regiment): 29 labourers, 26 farmworkers, 16 carpenters, 16 decorators, 18 diggers, 12 engine drivers, 11 storemen, 12 masons, 10 electrical engineers; and among the others 2 jockeys, 2 vets, 1 tripe-dresser, 1 male nurse, 1 florist, 1 hairdresser, 1 riding master and several musicians, policemen, cooks, chemists, stewards and waiters.[38] On one occasion, while inspecting some recruits, Baden-Powell was very nearly shot by them. 'They were put through the actions of "Ready", "Present", and "Fire". Two or three did more than merely go through the action, they actually did fire, having forgotten to unload their rifles after a previous lesson on how to load.'[39] The recruits' progress in the saddle was as disappointing as their handling of firearms.[40]

A man more stupid than Baden-Powell might have imagined that, by some miracle of patriotism, his incompetent 'loafers' might prove a match in open country for farmers who had learned to ride and shoot as children, and knew the region intimately. But Baden-Powell shared Winston Churchill's conviction that 'the individual Boer, mounted in suitable country, is worth from three to five regular soldiers.'[41] If that were true of trained regulars, Stephe could have been forgiven for thinking that he ought to outnumber the enemy by at least ten to one to be sure of the outcome. But this of course was never going to happen.

Baden-Powell called his two regiments the Rhodesia Regiment and the Protectorate Regiment – the first being intended to defend Rhodesia and keep open a line of communication and supply for the Protectorate Regiment, which had been raised to defend Bechuanaland. The last-mentioned regiment would also be expected to make the 'feints and demonstrations' described in Baden-Powell's famous War Office instructions.[42] He appointed Colonel Herbert Plumer to command the Rhodesia Regiment and Colonel Hore to command the Protectorate Regiment. The Rhodesia Regiment was trained and raised in Bulawayo, while the Protectorate Regiment was based in Bechuanaland, eighteen miles north of the small town of Mafeking.

During August and September Baden-Powell spent much of his time shuttling back and forth between the two places. By 17 August Plumer had 140 men in training and Hore 110. A dozen days later, thanks to Baden-Powell's secret recruiting, Hore's tally had increased to 337 and Plumer's to 250, with the promise of 160 more when the local Volunteers came in. By mid-September both regiments were approximately up to strength (i.e. 450 men each).[43]

On 19 August Baden-Powell was flabbergasted to be informed by Hanbury-Williams that his Natal and Cape Colony recruits could not be sworn in anywhere in the Cape, but should first be moved across the border into Bechuanaland.[44] For a man facing what looked like certain annihilation, instructions like this were hard to endure. Estimates of Boer numbers fluctuated wildly from week to week. On 21 August Baden-Powell thought they numbered about 5,000. A month later reports indicated that there were between 7,000 and 10,000 Boers in the area.[45] The senior Intelligence Officer on the border was Colonel Raymond N. R. Reade, who travelled freely in the Transvaal in the guise of a mining engineer. He provided Baden-Powell with reliable information about Boer intentions and numbers. Incredibly he was recalled to Cape Town in late September precisely when Baden-Powell needed him most.[46]

It is obvious that men who shoot and ride badly must stand a better chance of survival against men who do both well if they are placed behind barricades, or in trenches, rather than on horseback on the open veldt. The refusal of historians like Brian Gardner and Michael Rosenthal to recognize this fact seems to stem from their ignorance of the calibre of the men Baden-Powell recruited with such difficulty. His two regiments were also grievously disadvantaged in respect of field guns: the Protectorate Regiment having only a single 7-pounder fit for field work.[47] Out-gunned and out-ridden in open country, Baden-Powell knew his men would be wiped out within hours if he allowed them to tangle even with one of the five enemy commandos* now known to be gathering twenty miles away.

In mid-August Baden-Powell had chosen a forward base at Ramathlabama in Bechuanaland conveniently close to the town of Mafeking, which he already feared would be attacked as soon as war was declared. On 18 August he made a detailed analysis of Mafeking's defences and indicated numerous ways in which these could be improved. Since the town was across the border from Bechuanaland just inside the Cape Colony, these works would have to be carried out in secret. Although well aware of the odds he faced, Baden-Powell was still hoping to make his 'raids and feints to draw more troops to the scene', but he was becoming increasingly worried about his ability

* Groups of Boers, usually about 1,000 strong, raised in particular districts for mobile warfare.

both to raid the Transvaal and to guard his 'baggage laager' and prevent his 'line of supply being cut in the face of at least two if not three commandos of strong numbers'.[48] On 27 August he redefined the offensive role of the Rhodesia Regiment, limiting its attacks to 'the delivery of blows at small forces of the enemy'. 'Big engagements' were ruled out.[49]

In the dying days of August Colonel Hanbury-Williams, whose grasp of the Boers' dispositions in the northern Transvaal (thanks to Colonel Reade) had always been superior to Wolseley's, conceded that Baden-Powell was going to have to change his 'system of tactics in fighting the Boers'.[50] Lieutenant Hanbury-Tracy who, as Baden-Powell's Intelligence Officer, was better informed than most, described Wolseley's original orders as 'faulty, for our force could not have cut itself adrift from its base unless superior in numbers to the enemy in the country in which it was to operate. we could not raid the Transvaal without the certain knowledge that we were in sufficient strength to be able, when we wished, to fall back on our base for supplies.' Hanbury-Tracy considered that 'the disparity of forces' made 'raids like those performed in the American Civil War quite impossible'. He concluded that 'Baden-Powell's only course was to occupy Mafeking and play a game of bluff'.[51]

On the last day of August Baden-Powell received warnings from two separate sources that the Boers were planning an incendiary attack on his stores at Mafeking.[52] The same day Colonel Hore sent in fourteen men from Ramathlabama to guard the vast accumulation of supplies which was growing with the arrival of every train from the south. On 9 September Baden-Powell recorded that much of these stores had arrived 'without being asked for and without notice'. Apart from the build-up caused by tradesmen's efforts to beat the anticipated tax on goods bound for Rhodesia, and Weil's nose for the profits to be made from holding large stocks in the event of war, there were the purchases made at Lord Edward Cecil's behest. General Butler had been recalled, and many of the orders placed by Stephe with his department were now suddenly being acted upon (long after alternative arrangements had been made). Faced with this ever-increasing mountain of goods, Baden-Powell hired a large storage shed, which was filled to the rafters by early September. New consignments had to be covered with tarpaulins and 'stacked in great piles near the railway station'. Baden-Powell had the whole area brightly lit and armed his watchmen with shot-guns. Although 'this valuable stock was soon the talk of the neighbourhood',[53] Stephe could see advantages. The stores might be vulnerable, but they would attract more Boers to the region. 'They believe our force to be a large one and liable to increase owing to the large amount of stores collected here.'[54] On 9 September Baden-Powell telegraphed Hanbury-Williams asking if he could order a squadron of the Protectorate Regiment into Mafeking to guard the stores.

It is entirely mistaken to argue as Gardner and Rosenthal have done that Baden-Powell 'committed a classic military blunder' in allowing 'the guardianship of stores to dictate the immobility of all those for whom the stores were intended'.[55] Baden-Powell had never wanted his base to be at Ramathlabama, and had only been prevented from making Mafeking his headquarters by Milner's deference to the wishes of the Cape Ministry. Far from dictating an unwanted change of plan, the stores actually gave him a providentially convincing argument for doing precisely what he wanted. The inferior quality of his recruits, the unexpectedly large number of Boers and his lack of field artillery made a move to the relative security of Mafeking absolutely essential. That the vast surplus of supplies had attracted and would detain more Boers than had ever been anticipated was a bonus rather than a demerit, given his instructions.

It is ironic that Baden-Powell himself must bear part of the responsibility for misleading historians.[56] In his autobiography he was unable to resist the temptation of making out that he had outwitted Milner and the Cape Ministry. He claimed that he had only received permission for putting an armed guard into Mafeking – but, because the size of this guard had not been specified, he had cleverly 'moved the whole regiment into the place without delay'.[57] This was totally untrue and unfortunately led historians to imagine that the need to protect his stores had compelled the move. In reality Milner had known for over a month that Baden-Powell wanted to make the town his headquarters, and on 12 September – to Stephe's immense relief – Hanbury-Williams at last sent a telegram indicating that, if he were now to ask formal permission to move the whole regiment, it would be granted. Hanbury-Williams ended his telegram: 'I consider it very desirable to have the regiment at Mafeking to guard its base and the railway works . . . The Boers are within 8 miles of Mafeking while the regiment [at Ramathlabama] is 18 miles distant.'[58] Hanbury-Williams also warned Baden-Powell that he had just received information that the Boers intended to attack Mafeking and cut the railway.

Baden-Powell lost no time in appointing Colonel C. B. Vyvyan his Base Commandant at Mafeking, and in placing the stores under an Army Service Corps captain. But no appointments could conceal the fact that without more men the Protectorate Regiment's role would have to be entirely defensive. On 15 September Baden-Powell finally admitted to Hanbury-Williams that his men were really nothing more than 'an organized crowd of recruits mounted on ponies . . . They are bad riders and bad shots.' He then steeled himself to ask Hanbury-Williams to convince Milner of the need to request the despatch of a British cavalry regiment to Mafeking. Otherwise no 'real blows' could be dealt to the Boers, since the Protectorate Regiment on its own (even if it were an efficient force) would be too small to go on a raid and simultaneously protect its base at Mafeking. But with a regiment of cavalry in the town, the Boers would feel obliged to deploy a very large force to prevent a raid on Pretoria.[59]

On 19 September, after receiving Milner's permission, Stephe moved the Protectorate Regiment into Mafeking. He then telegraphed to the new Commander-in-Chief at the Cape – Lieutenant-General Sir F. W. Forestier-Walker, under whose orders he had just been placed – urgently requesting two more guns and the immediate despatch of 100 Cape Police to Mafeking. With these additions he thought he might just survive a determined attack. But he went on to repeat his earlier request for cavalry, without which, he warned Forestier-Walker, his men would be 'tied to the place in order to protect it, which is not at all in accordance with the object of the force – viz extreme mobility . . . and ability . . . to inflict blows sufficient to draw a strong force of the enemy against it'.[60] Forestier-Walker telegraphed a curt refusal to his plea for cavalry, but approved the despatch of 100 Cape Police and two guns. These last, through an unfortunate mix-up over the code word, turned out to be obsolete 7-pounders rather than modern 5-inch howitzers.[61] Colonel Reade had supported Baden-Powell's request for extra police, but he had really thought an addition of 400 infantry essential for the defence of the town. He believed that the Boers would invest Mafeking in force and that any cavalry in the town would be unlikely to escape the surrounding cordon.[62] By 12 September a siege looked inevitable and on that day Baden-Powell asked Colonel Vyvyan to consider all preparations for the defence of the town his special responsibility.[63]

Baden-Powell was later entirely unrepentant about allowing his mounted irregulars to be besieged, and argued that if the garrison had consisted solely of infantry the Boers would have known that foot soldiers could not deliver a rapid thrust at Pretoria. The force at Mafeking could therefore have been safely watched from a distance and largely ignored. But horsemen, on the other hand, could threaten a break-out unless the Boers were to besiege the town in large numbers.[64] Even now Stephe tried to persuade himself that if the Boers' numbers were ever to drop dramatically, a mobile role might still be possible one day. But in the short term, he felt obliged to tell Forestier-Walker on 30 September that since there was no effective garrison at Mafeking, the Protectorate Regiment would have to remain there permanently, although this ran counter to Wolseley's instructions. He therefore asked the G.O.C. directly 'if this departure from instructions is approved'. Forestier-Walker telegraphed back saying that he and Sir Alfred Milner knew that 'the present employment of the Protectorate Regiment as garrison for Mafeking was not in accord with the object for which it has been raised', but since no other force could be found for the job, they saw no alternative to Baden-Powell's men being used to defend the place.[65] Baden-Powell undoubtedly departed from his original instructions but with the knowledge and consent of the most senior military officer in South Africa and of the High Commissioner.

Not many years later Baden-Powell was mocked for having acted out 'the strangest role ever played by a cavalry leader': to have 'burrowed underground at the very first shot being fired . . . and commenced to eat his horses'.[66] Recently Michael Rosenthal has claimed that after the Siege Baden-Powell lied about his original instructions in order to furnish himself with 'a retroactive defence' for having departed from them.[67] Baden-Powell's War Office instructions required him to preserve his mobility and 'by bold feints to render valuable service by containing in the [border] district a considerable force of Boers' and 'detaining' them away from their 'concentration' [area] in the South'.[68] He later defined his most important duty as being 'to draw as large a force as possible from opposing the British on their southern borders'.[69] But was that so different from the one great imperative in his original instructions? While 'drawing Boers' is not exactly the same as 'containing' them, the effect would be identical – i.e. for a month or two a smaller number of Boers would be free to attack the hard-pressed British troops in Natal than would otherwise have been the case. And if from within Mafeking Baden-Powell could 'draw' and 'detain' as many Boers as he could hope to keep occupied if he were out on the veldt (where he would have been speedily defeated), his departure from the military method laid down by Wolseley was entirely justified. Michael Rosenthal's strongly implied suggestion that Baden-Powell was cowardly to have avoided 'actively engaging the enemy in the field', preferring the 'rather less dangerous enterprise of enduring a siege within a fortified town',[70] is equally unjust, given his circumstances. In September he twice begged Sir Alfred Milner to relieve him of the command of the Frontier Force as soon as his two regiments were up to strength, so that he could command the 5th Dragoon Guards when they came out to South Africa. He *longed* to be able to 'engage the enemy in the field'. Milner and the War Office declined his request.[71]

Of course Baden-Powell would never have been so vulnerable to criticism if he had taken the easy way out and publicly said that he had been given impossible orders. Lord Wolseley was replaced by Lord Roberts in December 1900; so after that Baden-Powell could easily have disowned his orders without harming his future career. Instead he sidestepped the whole question by claiming to have had verbal rather than written instructions. His motive for doing this was not, as has been suggested, to conceal his failure to act as directed (he did after all achieve the principal objective required of him), but to avoid biting the hand that had fed him.

On 14 November 1900 he wrote to Lord Wolseley thanking him for everything he had done for him 'from the time when you talked so encouragingly to me at Liverpool, and afterwards sent me to conduct machine-gun trials at Aldershot thirteen years ago . . . I have to thank you for every step in my very rapid promotion – and I am deeply sensible of my indebtedness.'[72] Baden-Powell would prove a formidable adversary to people who crossed him, but he was loyal to his friends. In this revealing letter he also mentioned another reason why he had never criticized his written instructions. Wolseley had given him *verbal* orders too. As Baden-Powell was leaving the Commander-in-Chief's room, Lord Wolseley said, 'Prepare at Mafeking for being cut off.'[73] In late September Baden-Powell made sure that these 'preparations for being cut off' (which had been vetoed for so long by Milner), were prosecuted with vigour.

Baden-Powell's recent critics have assumed with the benefit of hindsight that a siege had always looked a safe bet – rather as if Baden-Powell had been gifted with a psychic ability to read the future. The coming siege, wrote Brian Gardner, 'brought to him the chance of a lifetime . . .'[74] It is, however, preposterous to suppose that he saw his situation as an enviable one as he waited for between 6,000 and 7,000 Boers, commanded by a famous general, to appear in front of his rapidly-dug defences which were manned by fewer than 1,000 part-timers and two dozen regular soldiers. Within days the Mafeking garrison could easily have shared the fate of the defenders of nearby Vryburg, who had been contemptuously brushed aside. Baden-Powell had no guarantee that the townspeople would support him if the approaching siege should happen to bring loss of life and damage to property. The British Government had given the citizens of Mafeking little cause for loyalty. Betrayal from within or defeat from without looked far likelier outcomes for Stephe than the achievement of lasting fame.

3. Preparing for the Worst (September to October 1899)

The town of Mafeking was small, having only 1,700 white and 5,000 black inhabitants; but, as in many pioneering outposts, civic pride had grown up along with the brand-new buildings. In 1899, fourteen years after its foundation, Mafeking could boast a market square, government offices, a convent, a hospital and extensive railway workshops. There were several hotels, a Masonic Hall, a gaol, a library, a courthouse and a branch of the Standard Bank. Residents could read

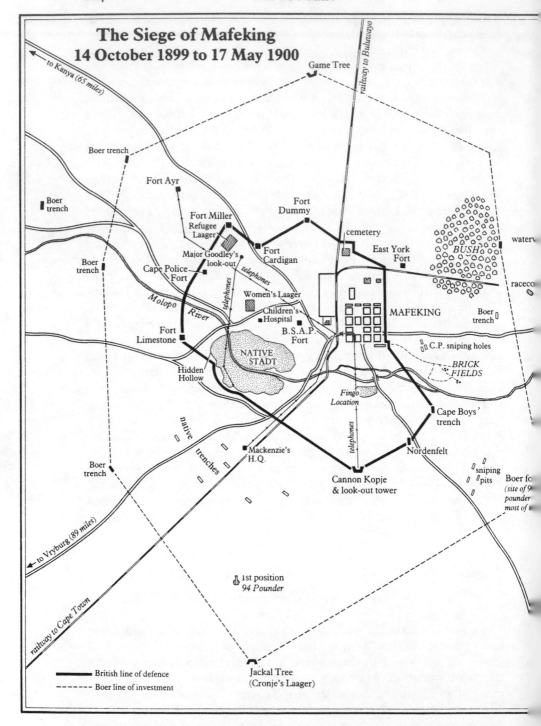

The Siege of Mafeking
14 October 1899 to 17 May 1900

to Kanya (65 miles)

railway to Bulawayo

Game Tree

Boer trench

Boer trench

Fort Ayr

Fort Miller

Fort Dummy

cemetery

East York Fort

BUSH

water

raceco

Refugee Laager

Major Goodley's look-out

Fort Cardigan

Cape Police Fort

Boer trench

telephones

telephones

Women's Laager

Children's Hospital

B.S.A.P. Fort

MAFEKING

Boer trench

Molopo River

Fort Limestone

NATIVE STADT

Hidden Hollow

C.P. sniping holes

BRICK FIELDS

Fingo Location

Cape Boys' trench

native trenches

Mackenzie's H.Q.

telephones

Nordenfelt

sniping pits

Boer fo

Boer trench

Cannon Kopje & look-out tower

(site of 9 pounder most of t

to Vryburg (89 miles)

railway to Cape Town

1st position
94 Pounder

Jackal Tree
(Cronje's Laager)

British line of defence
Boer line of investment

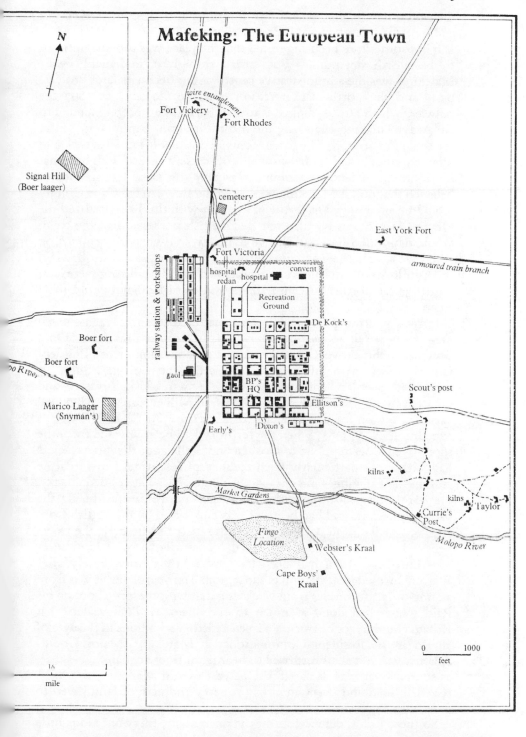

Mafeking: The European Town

N

Fort Vickery
wire entanglement
Fort Rhodes

Signal Hill
(Boer laager)

cemetery

East York Fort

Fort Victoria
railway station & workshops
hospital   convent
redan   hospital
Recreation
Ground

Boer fort   armoured train branch

De Kock's

Boer fort

gaol

o River

BP's
HQ

Marico Laager
(Snyman's)   Ellitson's

Early's   Dixon's

Scout's post

kilns

kilns   Taylor

Currie's
Post

Market Gardens

Molopo River

Fingo
Location   Webster's Kraal

Cape Boys' ■
Kraal

0   1000
feet

1/6   1
mile

their own newspaper, attend race meetings at their own race-course and worship at any one of four churches.

It has sometimes been suggested that the place was too insignificant to be worth defending. But, small though it undeniably was, Mafeking was the administrative centre of the Bechuanaland Protect-orate and the north-eastern region of Cape Colony. In 1897 the railway, which already linked it to Kimberley, had been extended to Bulawayo, making Mafeking the most important commercial centre for 100 miles around. The town 'contained valuable railway stock and other supplies',[1] and Baden-Powell's officers all agreed with him that it had to be defended. Colonel Vyvyan, the Base Commandant, believed that unless Mafeking were held the Boers in the Cape Colony would be encouraged to throw in their lot with the Transvaal and the Orange Free State. He also felt that British possession of the town would deny the Boers any chance of making a diversionary attack on Rhodesia later in the war.[2] Furthermore, the Hon. Sir Arthur Lawley, the Administrator in Rhodesia, maintained that if Mafeking were lost, the tribes of northern Bechuanaland and the Matabele would rebel again.[3]

In reality, strategic considerations mattered less to Baden-Powell than the heartfelt appeals he received daily from the residents. On 5 September the Town Council had sent a deputation to the Resident Commissioner demanding protection in the event of war. Since his reply had been, in the words of the Town Clerk, 'evasive and unsatisfactory', they appealed to Sir Alfred Milner himself. They had excellent reason for feeling alarmed. Ever since Sir Charles Warren's expedition of 1884–85, when the territory had been wrested from the short-lived Boer republic of Goshen and Stellaland, the Transvaalers had harboured particularly keen feelings of resentment towards the citizens of Mafeking – and not just the white ones. The resident blacks, the Barolongs, had fought the Boers half-a-dozen times during the past four decades and had been actively supported by the British from 1870 onwards. If the Barolongs had not resisted so fiercely, the Boers believed they might have expanded westwards without hindrance. The European town had been laid out in 1885 immediately after Warren's armed intervention in the region. Ten years later, it was from a camp only a few miles from Mafeking that Dr Jameson set out on his Raid which had done so much to convince the Transvaalers that Britain could never be trusted. Given a history so odious in the eyes of all Boers the Resident Commissioner at Mafeking, Major Goold-Adams, was not at all surprised to hear from Boer acquaintances that, as soon as war was declared, the hated town of Mafeking would be seized, looted and every item of property and acre of land given to deserving Transvaalers.

So there it lay, defenceless on the open veldt, this obnoxious little town only eight miles from the border, stuffed full of valuable supplies and garrisoned by a mere 400 irregulars and a rapidly assembled Town Guard. The Boers were well aware that it had never been built as a military post, and so believed it could not be properly defended. Historians eager to belittle Baden-Powell's defence of the place usually criticize the Boers for never having cared enough about the town to make any serious effort to take it. But a little history, a lot of stores and the same strategic considerations that had made Baden-Powell and his officers think the town worth holding had made the Boers consider it well worth taking.

Major Alick Godley, whom Baden-Powell appointed Adjutant of the Protectorate Regiment and commander of the western defences, understood the garrison's job to be 'to act as a bait for the Boers', and to 'bluff' them into thinking the defences far more formidable than they actually were.[4] Godley brought the Protectorate Regiment into Mafeking on 19 September and at once started to plan a system of trenches and fortified emplacements to defend the western approaches to the town. Two days later Colonel Vyvyan handed to Baden-Powell a document entitled 'Outlines of Scheme for Defence of Mafeking', in which the town was divided into an Interior and an Exterior area. By 'Interior' Vyvyan meant the European town and the railway works which together, he proposed, should be divided into five wards, each under a separate commander and each having its own point of assembly in case of alarm. There was to be a Special Reserve to make a last-ditch defence of the central Market Square, and also to be rushed to any gravely threatened point. Certain locations within the town were to be strengthened by breastworks and obstacles, but the major defence works were to be constructed in the Exterior area which, Vyvyan suggested, should be divided into a north and a south zone. Having read his Base Commandant's proposal, Baden-Powell placed him in command of the Interior area and approved his arrangements for its defence.[5] Since it was suggested after the Siege that Vyvyan was entirely reponsible for planning the defences of the town,[6] it is worth noting that Baden-Powell rejected his entire scheme for the vital Exterior area and divided the command of it among five officers instead of the two Vyvyan had recommended.

Baden-Powell was away in Bulawayo when Colonel Vyvyan and Major F. W. Panzera (formerly of the Royal Artillery), his second-in-command, started working in earnest on the defences. Both men were well-known in Rhodesia and Bechuanaland and were popular with the townspeople of Mafeking. They became a familiar sight walking together – Vyvyan small, grey-haired, and softly spoken; and Panzera tall, burly, absolutely fearless and rather gruff in manner. On 21 September a local Defence Committee was formed and its members 'agreed to place themselves under the orders of the Base Command-

ant'. Rifles were distributed and north-east of the town a start was
made at clearing the bush and scrub, which it was feared might be used
as cover by the enemy. Vyvyan also began to fortify Cannon Kopje, an
old siege-work built by Sir Charles Warren's men in a key position
2,500 yards south of the town. The ground was very rocky there,
which made excavation virtually impossible, so Vyvyan had to
transport tons of earth out to the fort in order to raise its ramparts. He
sited a 7-pounder in the work and manned it with a strong detachment
of British South Africa Police.[7] A week earlier all the townsmen had
been enrolled as special constables, and on 28 September they took the
oath of allegiance. The 300-strong Town Guard thus formed was not a
trained body but would be expected to defend the inner perimeter.

With Baden-Powell's permanent return to Mafeking on 30
September, an even greater sense of urgency was felt everywhere.
That day reports were received that the largest force of Boers in the
area, numbering about 5,000 men, was under the orders of General
Piet Cronje, whom Alick Godley called 'their great fighting general'.[8]
Cronje had defeated a British force at Potchefstroom in 1881, and in
1896 had rounded up Jameson's men with insulting ease. He was
accompanied by the Boers' great strategist General J. H. De la Rey.
Another Boer general, J. P. Snyman, who was reputed to be 'very
anti-English', was also inspanned not far from the border with a large
commando. The Boers' numbers in the immediate vicinity were
thought to be anything between 6,000 and 8,000.[9] Colonel Vyvyan
noted in his diary on 1 October 'common report through district is that
this force is intended to attack Mafeking'.[10] Cronje was reported to
have thirteen guns, most of them of modern design. On the British
side, the total number of white men under arms in Mafeking was
1,183.[11] (Baden-Powell placed his own figure slightly lower.[12]) An
accurate figure for blacks and people of mixed race under arms is
harder to arrive at. The total of 300 given by Baden-Powell in his
official report is wildly misleading. The real number of Africans under
arms in Mafeking was at least 750, with a further 300 contributing to
the town's defence by labouring to build the siege works and dig the
trenches.[13] Baden-Powell therefore faced the Boers with almost 2,000
armed men; and although three-quarters of them were entirely
untrained, he could never have attempted to defend a perimeter of six
miles without the active help of all of them – whatever their colour.

Even in August Baden-Powell had recognized the strategic
importance of Mafeking's native stadt with its population of 5,500
(swollen to 7,500 by refugees). Situated only half-a-mile from the
small European town, the stadt sprawled on both banks of the Molopo
river, which flowed on past the southern side of white Mafeking at a
distance of only 400 yards. Because the river ran in a shallow valley it
offered the Boers a chance to creep up between its banks to within

striking distance of the European town. Baden-Powell knew that since the valley was full of huts, he could prevent the enemy from using it simply by providing the Barolongs with arms and ammunition.[14] By keeping the Barolongs' village within the outer defensive perimeter, he was able to free many whites for the defence of other sectors. Some of his officers, however, thought the stadt 'a menace blocking the line of fire'.[15]

The European town was smaller than the stadt, occupying an area of only 1,000 square yards. Most of the houses were mudbrick bungalows roofed with corrugated iron, fanning out from a central market square. The railway workshops which provided employment for much of the population lay immediately to the west of the European area, at a point where the railway line passed through Mafeking running from north to south. Just to the north of the built-up part of the town, across a dusty recreation ground, were the most substantial buildings: the new Victoria Hospital and the two-storey convent occupied by Irish Sisters of Mercy. To the south-west, the Barolong stadt straggled across an area almost twice as large as that occupied by the European town. To the east of this concentration of huts, and immediately south of the European sector, was the Fingo Location, and next to it the Cape Boys' 'kraal'. The defended area, measured from the north-eastern corner of the town to the south-western extremity of the stadt, was just over two miles across. The most southerly point was the old fort at Cannon Kopje, which was over a mile from the town and, being 200 feet high, commanded the whole place and would therefore have to be held at all costs. From this fort a deep defence trench was excavated, running away both to the east and west and ultimately encircling the entire town and the native stadt, and connecting about a dozen forts and gun emplacements (later there would be over twenty). Inside these outer forts other redoubts and trenches were dug, from which an enemy successfully penetrating the first line could be taken in the flank. Many of these forts were connected by telephone to the central headquarters' bombproof shelter. The only area which could not be contained within the defences was the site of some old brickfields, which stretched for half-a-mile to the east of Mafeking. This jumble of ruined chimneys and crumbling kilns could only be defended by judiciously placed riflemen.

On all sides of the town the sunbaked treeless veldt stretched away into the shimmering distance, dipping slightly as it went. The ground only began to rise again some 1,000 yards away. Mafeking was therefore perched on a little rise in the centre of a vast far-reaching depression, rimmed with low hills. While the garrison's four 7-pounder guns, two smaller-calibre pieces and seven .303 Maxim machine-guns would not be able to hit the enemy's longer-range guns on those distant hills, they would be able to give any advancing men a very difficult time. On 5 October with the Boers' forces assembling only eight miles away, Baden-Powell issued an order that nobody would be allowed through the outposts without a pass. The following day he advised all women and children to leave the town; free tickets could be obtained from the Civil Commissioner, Charles Bell. Those women and children who were staying were obliged to leave their homes and take up residence in the 'Women's Laager' on Mr Rowlands's farm just to the north of the stadt, where they were expected to be safe from shell-fire.

All through the first two weeks of October Colonel Vyvyan and Major Panzera were to be seen supervising their African labour gangs as they strove to build new defences. The Protectorate Regiment was now on duty day and night. 'The alarms are incessant now,' Major Godley told his wife on 6 October.[16] Displaying a glimmer of that gift for understatement which would soon help to make him famous, Baden-Powell told his mother that, 'with 6,000 or 7,000 Boers camped within 10 miles of us, I have just a little bit of responsibility'.[17]

During the night of 7 October Baden-Powell and Lieutenant Ronald Moncreiffe rode out to the border and crept up close to two large enemy laagers which they reckoned contained 200 wagons. Seeing these large concentrations of armed men with his own eyes left Stephe with no illusions about the dangers ahead.[18] A few days earlier he had conducted a field day for the Protectorate Regiment during which they had been ordered to come out to attack an enemy squadron represented by the British South Africa Police.[19] Afterwards Godley noticed how 'fussed and worried' Baden-Powell was. 'We have all worked our best and he is rather crabbing our show – says the horses do not look well – how on earth could they? And that the Regiment is not fit to take the field. He appears to expect us to work like a trained cavalry regiment.'

Baden-Powell considered that Colonel Hore, who had been ill for several weeks, was unequal to the onerous task ahead of him; but he could hardly replace him at this eleventh hour. Captain F. C. Marsh, one of the regiment's troop commanders, had struck Stephe as particularly slow in the field. Because he was an infantry officer, this was understandable. Since Marsh later commanded not only the armed Barolongs in the stadt and a squadron of the Protectorate Regiment with equal success, it was just as well that Baden-Powell did not – as he had initially intended – relegate Marsh to the non-combatant role of quarter-master. 'Hore's incompetence' upset Godley less than the way in which Baden-Powell 'got his knife into him'. 'It is absurd and unpractical [sic] of him to ballyrag Hore. It would be much better if he would make the best of him and try to encourage him instead of frightening him. As it is he has made him afraid to take the smallest responsibility, and more hopeless than ever, and he is driving the rest of us to distraction.'[20] Hore, in Godley's opinion, was 'a nice old thing who mistook his vocation and ought to be a comfortable old farmer'.

Cronje's reputation and the Boers' dislike of Mafeking made everyone in the regiment feel tense and fearful – particularly when they remembered that the whole town looked to them as their saviours. If the regiment could only manage to charge out and give the enemy 'a good kick' when his forces arrived, Baden-Powell believed that the Boers would treat the place with circumspection and delay their all-out attempt to storm it. Each day gained would enable Vyvyan and Panzera to improve the defences. 'We are in such a jumpy state,' wrote Godley, 'that whenever anybody shuts the lid of a box, we think it is a Boer.' The recently arrived J. Angus Hamilton of *The Times* noticed that jumpiness was not confined to Baden-Powell's irregulars and their officers. The male residents of the town were in a quandary. 'They are uncertain whether to face the music or to skip with their women and children. Ostensibly they wish to bear the brunt of an attack upon their town, but as the numbers of the Boer force concentrated upon the border increases, the number of men available for actual volunteer service grows beautifully less.'[21]

Men who were leaving presented one kind of problem; men who were arriving as refugees presented another. Apart from several hundred Fingoes and Barolongs coming in from the immediate vicinity, almost 2,000 'foreign' blacks – mainly migrants from the Johannesburg area – also arrived in Mafeking.[22] Baden-Powell knew he would have to feed these people or drive them away. Later he was not sorry to have let them stay, since many had worked in the mines on the Rand and were expert at excavating bombproof dug-outs. The whites who arrived as refugees, roughly 100 in all, were mainly of Dutch extraction.[23] Even after they had taken an oath of loyalty, Baden-Powell and his officers mistrusted them. The white male refugees were therefore placed in a laager to the west of the town and virtually confined there in case any were spies.

An early example of the cunning that would in time gain Baden-Powell a psychological advantage over his adversaries was his published order on the subject of spies. Dated 7 October, it ran:

SPIES
There are in town today nine known spies.
They are hereby warned to leave before 12 noon
tomorrow or they will be apprehended.[24]

Of course he had no idea how many spies there were in the town, but by naming a precise number he gave an impression of omniscience. Of greater importance was his instruction to Major Panzera to assemble hundreds of 'mines'. In due course scores of black wooden boxes (in reality filled with sand) were carried out beyond the outer perimeter with a great pantomine of excessive caution and buried on the veldt. The following day, recalled Baden-Powell, people were warned to stay away from the east front during a trial of these 'mines'. 'With everybody safely indoors, Major Panzera and I went out and stuck a stick of dynamite into an ant-bear hole.' After a gratifying explosion, both Baden-Powell and his commander of artillery 'saw a man bicycling away as fast as he could go towards the Transvaal.'[25]

Chance, as well as guile, played an important part in giving the Boers an exaggerated notion of the impregnability of Mafeking's defences. On 13 October, the day on which the Boers first appeared close to the town, two trucks filled with dynamite were still in the station yard and not, as had been thought, on their way to Bulawayo. Orders were immediately given for them to be shunted up the line before any chance shell caused a disaster. The engine-driver had steamed five miles when he saw a party of Boers 1,000 yards ahead of him; he uncoupled the trucks and, having shunted them towards the Boers, returned in the direction of Mafeking. He had steamed less than a mile when he heard the Boers firing at the truck and a few moments later a massive explosion boomed out across the veldt. It rattled every window in Mafeking and terrified the hapless Boers who had been its unwitting cause.[26] They believed the trucks had been deliberately detonated by some mysterious contrivance and this belief increased their fear of mines.[27] In an early exchange of letters, General Cronje rebuked Baden-Powell for using mines in contravention of the Geneva Convention. 'Defence mines,' Baden-Powell replied, 'are a recognized adjunct of civilized warfare both by land and sea, and are in no way forbidden by the Geneva Convention.'[28]

On 9 October the first train carrying women and children left for the Cape, and two days later another departed. Wives who left behind husbands wondered whether they would ever see them alive again. In public Baden-Powell appeared entirely confident that the Boers could be kept at bay, but he knew perfectly well that a determined attack on two or more fronts would be more than his inexperienced men and improvised defences could withstand. Lady Sarah Wilson, the wife of Baden-Powell's A.D.C., Captain Gordon Wilson, had been in Mafeking ever since her husband's arrival there. On 12 October Baden-Powell sent a staff officer to tell her confidentially that when the Boers arrived the following day 'they would probably try to rush the town; and that the garrison would be obliged to fight its way out'. Lady Sarah remembered the officer 'begging me to leave at once by road for the nearest point of safety. Naturally I had to obey.'[29] Baden-Powell was not alone in feeling that the Boers would take the town swiftly if they acted with decision. Major Godley shared this view.[30]

Far away in Cape Town, Sir Alfred Milner anticipated that Kimberley with its garrison of regular troops might just survive the coming onslaught. But he held out little hope for Mafeking, in spite of its garrison of 'plucky officers'.[31] Joseph Chamberlain was equally pessimistic about Baden-Powell's chances.[32]

Baden-Powell now published a notice headed 'Alarms'. If an attack were imminent, a red flag would be flown at Dixon's Hotel. 'The "Alert" will be blown and the town bell rung. All buglers will take up the call and all the bells in the town rung furiously. After their men have fallen into their respective posts, all commanders of sections and armed forces will send a man to report to Colonel Baden-Powell at Dixon's Hotel.' On 9 October, President Kruger had issued an ultimatum demanding that Britain should agree to arbitration on 'all points of mutual difference' and that the troops 'on the borders of the Republic shall be instantly withdrawn'. A time limit of 48 hours was set.

Next morning Godley told his wife that the Boers were expected to attack at 2.00 p.m. 'Baden-Powell has just sent up to say we are to go to meet them and surprise them, so we are off.'[33] While Godley and his men were mounting their horses, a final train laden with passengers left for the Cape. It returned four and a half hours later, having been obliged to turn back because of damage to the track.[34] That afternoon Baden-Powell led out three squadrons of the Protectorate Regiment and a troop each from the B.S.A.P. and the Cape Police to the heights south-east of the town. He concealed his men in the scrub below the brow of the hill, hoping to take the Boers by surprise if they tried to dig in their guns on the heights. But no Boers came and late in the afternoon Baden-Powell returned to the town, where he inspected the Town Guard whose members cheered him, the Queen and old England. 'It was an extremely enthusiastic scene,' thought the journalist J. E. Neilly, 'and had a pathos of its own. Who knew how many of those brave fellows would come through the fire unscathed?'[35]

A ganger came in on a trolley during the evening with news that the Boers had ripped up the railway lines at Kraipan, 35 miles to the south. For days now Baden-Powell had been expecting two modern guns to be sent from Vryburg, and had eventually despatched one of his two precious armoured trains to collect them. In fact both the guns and the train were destined to fall into enemy hands. Surrounded and hopelessly outnumbered by a large force under General J. H. De la Rey, the train's crew of fifteen had fought bravely for an hour before surrendering, by which time their commander Lieutenant R. H. Nesbit had been shot through the jaw and nine of his men seriously wounded. This skirmish would go down in history as the first action in the Boer War. To have had six 7-pounders instead of four would have been a considerable advantage to Baden-Powell. The only recent bonus had been the unexpected arrival of four Maxims, bringing his total to seven. He was shocked to learn at this time that while he had been vainly appealing for guns, the Cape Government had been sitting on a spare battery of 12-pounders. Even two of these pieces would have spared the town from the heavy shelling which now seemed inevitable.

Thinking of this, and the two 5-inch howitzers which he would have had if the right code word had been used, he felt bitterly let down. One more reminder of the penny-pinching unhelpful Alfred Milner and the Cape Ministry arrived that very day in the shape of a telegram from the handsome Hanbury-Williams. Instead of wishing him good luck, Milner's Military Secretary informed Stephe curtly that the British Government would not pay for the evacuation of the women and children.[36] Imagining the likely effect this slap in the face would have on the morale of the townspeople, Baden-Powell kept the information to himself for the time being.

With Britain and the Boer republics now at war, Baden-Powell declared a state of martial law. Later that evening the telegraph line linking Mafeking with the south went dead; it had been cut by Boers crossing the border near Maritzani twenty miles away.[37] By dawn the following day, communication with the north had also been lost. Shortly before this happened Reuter's man at the Cape sent Baden-Powell a telegram very different from Hanbury-Williams's last communication: 'Whole of England watching you, admiring splendid spirit of yourself and garrison.'

At 6.30 a.m. on the 13th the men posted at Cannon Kopje reported by telephone that a force of Boers was moving across their front 3,000 yards distant. Baden-Powell despatched the Protectorate Regiment to their old position just below the crest of the south-eastern heights, but the Boers were approaching with great circumspection, outspanning eight miles away and sending forward smaller bodies of 400 or 500 men to probe the outer limits of the town's defences. When Stephe heard that the railway line had been pulled up five miles north of the town, he ordered out the armoured train to try to stop them destroying the track closer in to the south. He wanted to make sure that he was not prevented from making tactical use of his steel-plated engine and its armoured trucks with their loopholes for rifles and machine guns. (So that these specimens of the ingenuity of Mafeking's railway work-shops might play their full part in the defence of the town, 1½ miles of new track had been laid across the northern face.) The train caught up with the Boers three miles south of the town and dispersed them with machine-gun fire, without (as far as could be seen) inflicting any casualties. The train also fired on another party of Boers, and this time a man was mortally wounded; he turned out to be one of Baden-Powell's native scouts.[38]

Many times during the previous month Baden-Powell had reflected that the first proper fight with the Boers would be all important – not so much in terms of the numbers engaged or even the casualties suffered, but from the point of view of the impression it would give to the Boers of the fighting spirit of the defenders. The enemy, he was sure, would realize that men who fought bravely in the field would be extraordinarily difficult to dislodge from entrenched positions.

At 5.30 a.m. on the 14th, Baden-Powell sent out Lord Charles Cavendish-Bentinck with 'A' Squadron of the Protectorate Regiment to 'try to get a chance at the enemy'. According to Godley 'this was B-P's characteristic way of putting it, and showed the mode in which he had undertaken the task of bluffing the Boers'.[39] As matters fell out, Bentinck suddenly encountered more of the enemy than he wanted to 'get a chance at'. He had split his squadron into several patrols, and had only 60 men with him when he was spotted by about 500 Boers. Bentinck was four miles north of Mafeking and therefore in very grave danger of being cut off and surrounded. Fortunately for him, the corporal of the squadron's right flank patrol observed his officer's predicament from half-a-mile away, and on his own initiative galloped towards the town to summon the armoured train. Half an hour later this mobile fortress was steaming to Bentinck's aid and within minutes opened fire on the Boers with rifles, two Maxims and a 1-pounder Hotchkiss. Although the Boers soon found the train's range, they failed to hit it and the driver and his crew managed to keep them occupied until the break in the line six miles out brought him to a halt. The firing had been heard with great anxiety in the town, and its sudden cessation led Baden-Powell to believe that his train was about to share the fate of the one wrecked near Vryburg. He therefore decided to risk sending his precious reserve force ('D' Squadron) under Captain FitzClarence 'to assist and if necessary draw off the enemy and relieve the crew of the armoured train'. Baden-Powell knew what a gamble he was taking to commit almost half his trained men several miles outside Mafeking, against a superior force. If the Boers possessed accurate intelligence of his numbers, they might judge this to be the perfect moment to launch an attack on the vulnerable north-eastern defences which had been weakened by the departure of FitzClarence's men. Major Baillie, the correspondent of The Morning Post, a retired cavalry officer, recognized the gravity of the situation. 'The strain on Colonel Baden-Powell and the headquarters' staff must indeed have been great. For four hours they were anxiously waiting. Reports were not favourable, and they knew that a disaster to this small force risked the whole defence as there was literally not another man to send to their support. Indeed one squadron engaged was actually a part of the defence of the northern portion of the town.'[40] This was 'bluffing' with a vengeance.

When Captain FitzClarence arrived and engaged the Boers, they were already withdrawing, and cleverly accelerated this movement in order to place their entire force beyond FitzClarence's right flank. This manoeuvre left FitzClarence's men sandwiched between the Boers and the train, effectively preventing the train's crew from firing without risk of hitting their compatriots. The Boers continued to fall back, enticing the intrepid Captain to a point not far from a place in which they hoped to surround his squadron: a low ridge, covered with scrub and heaped masses of crumbling rock, which they meant to hide behind in order to pick off the foolishly pursuing British. The ridge also hid a larger body of Boers and their artillery.

At 7.30 a.m. Baden-Powell was very alarmed to receive a message stating that FitzClarence was pressing back the enemy. He at once sent a despatch cyclist and a horseman (Major Baillie, who volunteered for the duty) with orders to FitzClarence to retire at once. Hearing what sounded like 9-pounder guns in action, he also sent a 7-pounder field gun and a troop to cover the withdrawal. This timely action saved 'D' Squadron. As soon as FitzClarence's men came within 800 yards of the ridge, they ran into a well-directed fire from Boer snipers positioned behind rocks and in the branches of trees. Denied such cover themselves, the hapless British were pinned to the ground. Two cousins, Corporal Parland and Corporal Walshe, were both shot in the head and killed within moments of the start of the engagement, thus becoming the first Britons to die in action during the war. The man who shot them from a tree, Ockert J. Oosthuizen, became the first Boer to lose his life when he inadvisedly dropped a scrap of paper which fluttered to the ground. This was spotted by Trooper Wormald, who 'picked him off like a rook'.[41]

When the Boers began to shell the approaching British, Lieutenant Hubert Swinburne (one of only two other officers with FitzClarence that day) was in charge of the horses. The only cover he had been able to find for them had been a couple of deserted African huts. The first two 9-pounder shells, he recorded, 'burst right in the middle of us' killing two horses and wounding one man. Then I knew it was all up with us unless a miracle happened, and I bade a mental farewell to my friends.'[42] Then, inexplicably, the shelling stopped. J. Angus Hamilton was another journalist who, like Baillie, managed to get himself involved in the thick of the fighting. He considered this cessation of firing 'an extraordinary blunder' on the Boers' part, since 'they might have wiped Squadron "D" out of existence'.[43] Probably the Boers had spotted the 7-pounder coming to FitzClarence's aid and had decided that other reinforcements could not be far behind. At any rate, by the time FitzClarence had been able to retire they too were seen abandoning their position and heading back towards their laager some eight miles in the rear. FitzClarence's men were under fire for three hours but showed no inclination to turn tail when facing such frightening odds.[44]

Afterwards Baden-Powell had mixed feelings about the morning's work. Two men were dead, two more were dying, one was missing, eleven were wounded and fifteen horses had been killed.[45] All this had happened because FitzClarence had allowed himself 'to get too far out without orders', endangering the lives of his own men and those sent in support.[46] According to Hamilton, FitzClarence had displayed 'inopportune gallantry'.[47] But while the casualties had been unacceptably heavy for such a small force on its very first day of fighting, Baden-Powell warmly congratulated all those involved. He told Swinburne that the dash and daring shown by the Protectorate Regiment would have 'disheartened the enemy a good deal'. Looking back, Godley was sure it had. 'The effect of this fight was far reaching. The Boers held off, and did not molest the town until eleven days later, during which valuable time the defences were greatly strengthened.'[48]

As part of his case for denying Baden-Powell any credit for the Boers' failure to take decisive action during their first weeks outside Mafeking, Brian Gardner claimed that President Kruger had ordered Cronje not to try to take the town if it seemed likely to cost him more than 50 lives.[49] His only evidence was a hearsay report by a member of the force which eventually relieved Mafeking, to the effect that 'an American writer' (presumably resident in Pretoria during the war) had heard that Kruger 'used to fly into a passion whenever an attack on Mafeking was suggested'. Dr J. H. Breytenbach, the Transvaal State Archivist and a distinguished historian, has stated categorically that President Kruger did not issue Cronje with any specific orders in relation to Mafeking. In fact when Kruger intervened directly over the town early the following year, it was to order Commandant Sarel Eloff to storm the place. Cronje's eventual decision to begin a siege was his own and his officers' and was arrived at against the advice of his military adviser, General J. H. De la Rey, who advocated leaving 'a strong vigilant commando' of no more than 1,000 Boers to deal with any raids which Baden-Powell might try to launch. Cronje, he said, ought to head south at once with the bulk of his force.[50]

It is unlikely that Cronje made up his mind in favour of a siege before the end of the month. While he was probably impressed by the spirit of FitzClarence's men, their foolhardiness must have given him cause to hope that he might yet entice the greater part of Baden-Powell's mounted force out into the field. This would be worth waiting several weeks to accomplish and, if successful, would save many lives which would be lost in any full-scale assault on the place. In the meantime he could shell the town to see whether a few deaths would persuade the townspeople to urge Baden-Powell to surrender. And if 12-pounders were to prove insufficiently alarming, he could send for a heavy-calibre siege gun. Of course if he could take Cannon Kopje, the place would be his within days.

In Cronje's opinion De la Rey's advice was premature. Because of his own well-earned reputation for cunning, Cronje was known as the 'old fox'. He was sure that with a little patience, Mafeking could be his at very little cost. On the evening of 14 October as the shadows lengthened on the veldt, the old fox would have been surprised had he been told that the Siege of Mafeking had already started. But it had. Three miles away from Cronje's tents and wagons, the defenders in the trenches outside Mafeking could see the distant camp-fires of the encircling enemy glowing against the black land. They knew even less what the future held.

4. The Siege of Mafeking: First Phase (October to December 1899)

Throughout the day that followed FitzClarence's action, the towns-people braced themselves for an attack or a bombardment; but nothing happened. Emerson Neilly, the *Pall Mall Gazette*'s correspondent, thought the position 'hopeless' and found it 'impossible to avoid pitying the women and children who had been left behind [in the town]'.[1] Ada Cock was one of these women, and she shared the journalist's pessimism. 'There seems but small chance for us,' she wrote.[2] With over 6,000 Boers encamped in four massive laagers only two miles from the town, this gloom was easy to understand. A large town might withstand prolonged shelling, but how could a tiny place like Mafeking possibly escape total destruction within a few hours? The sight of men clambering on to the roofs of the convent and the hospital to deck them with huge red crosses brought home to everyone watching exactly what was going to happen. A red cross was also flown above the main marquee in the Women's Laager.

The shelling began shortly after 9.00 a.m. on 16 October. There was nothing Baden-Powell could do about it since the two Boer 12-pounders operating from the north-eastern heights were out of range of the garrison's artillery. Baden-Powell was outside the hospital chatting with Nurse A. M. Craufurd and the Matron, Miss Hill, as the shells began to fall. He had just been visiting the men wounded in FitzClarence's escapade. 'There was a bang,' recorded Miss Craufurd, 'and a nurse came out with a scared face. It was the first shell in Mafeking.'[3]

Because Baden-Powell had expected his red crosses to be respected, he had not ordered the excavation of shelters for the hospital and the convent, both of which were hit in the first bombardment. In other parts of the town trenches and bombproof shelters had been dug, but not nearly enough. All had been occupied with great rapidity as soon as the shells started to fall. The Town Clerk, J. R. Algie, had a wry sense

of humour and noted how the N.C.O. in charge of the police office
'bolted across to Riesle's cellar'. 'Old Bell [the Civil Commissioner]
was also missing, and it was rumoured he took refuge in a well. Ben
Weil [the general merchant] lay under the railway bridge fixed up with
bags of lime. Two of our men [in the Town Guard] bolted to the bed of
the river and Miss Becker was hysterical laughing and crying all day
long.' Not long afterwards Algie related how people were 'going
about town telling . . . how they dodged the shells and how brave they
were'. At Dixon's Hotel, where Baden-Powell had his Staff Headquarters, Algie noticed that the ordinary Union Jack had been taken
down and a smaller flag 'about six inches square put in its place'. This
he was sure meant that the commanding officer considered this shelling a mere prelude.[4]

Baden-Powell himself carried on throughout the shelling as if
oblivious to the explosions. Godley thought it 'splendid to see him,
just as one or two shells burst in the market square, sitting in a chair
with his staff all round him dictating messages as cool as a cucumber'.[5]
Although it was unwise in one way to encourage people to treat shells
cavalierly, Baden-Powell's calmness under fire steadied their nerves.
One of Stephe's ruses also helped. Several days earlier he had ordered
the erection of a dummy fort with dummy guns and two huge
flagstaffs. This position was subjected to 'a perfect hurricane of shells'
for most of the morning.[6]

When there was a lull in the shelling towards midday, the
townspeople ventured out of their hiding places. After hearing so
many earth-shaking explosions they expected to see most of the town
level with the ground. Instead they were amazed to discover that
thanks to the flimsy mudbrick construction of their buildings, shells
had passed straight through whole houses, only detonating when
hitting the ground anything up to 100 yards away. Under shell-fire the
collapse of upper storeys is a major cause of death. Since the convent
was the only building in town with two floors, only the nuns ran much
risk of being buried alive. Direct hits, or injuries inflicted by shrapnel,
were real dangers, but the sandy soil helped absorb the shock of
explosions. This first bombardment showed that people were
relatively safe, provided they took shelter. Nobody had been killed.

During the rest of October immense energy went into the construction of bombproof shelters for the town's white population. In
most cases these were five to six feet deep and three or four feet wide.
Railway rails were laid across the trench, with sheets of galvanized iron
covering them and four or five feet of earth placed overall and covered
with tarpaulins. While offering no defence against a direct hit, these
shelters were effective against blast, shell splinters and shrapnel.
Before long an effective warning system was devised. A given number
of bells (so many for whatever part of the town was threatened) would

be rung to prepare the inhabitants and as soon as the flash of the gun was seen the final alarm bell would be sounded giving people just enough time to dive for cover.

At 2.15 p.m. on this first day of shelling, the Boers sent in an emissary under a white flag. This man, whose name was Everitt, was that rarity: a pro-Boer Briton living in the Transvaal. When he invited Baden-Powell to surrender 'to avoid further bloodshed', Baden-Powell listened 'with polite astonishment', and asked him to what bloodshed he referred, since to date only a chicken had died and a donkey been wounded.[7] He was angry to learn that Everitt had not been blindfolded immediately on reaching the perimeter and had thus been allowed to note the armoured train's position.[8]

If the results of their bombardment disappointed the Boers, so too did their efforts to lure out the defenders. At dawn on the 17th they pulled back from the north-eastern heights, as if returning to the Transvaal, but at noon they returned – far too soon to convince Baden-Powell that they had really gone. Next day he admitted how tempting it would be 'to go out and attack one laager hoping to get it smashed before the others could arrive; but it is more than likely that this is part of their scheme in the hope of being able to cut us off'.[9] Young Lieutenant Swinburne shared this view, being certain the Boers were trying 'to exhaust our patience'.[10]

On the 19th the Boers sent forward about 150 men to dig trenches near the waterworks 4,300 yards north-east of the town. Baden-Powell considered that these Boers were 'the bit of cheese to lure us out'. His scouts later found 'all the other neighbouring bodies of Boers still in their places, and well concealed and alert. Four camps of them within 1½ to 2 miles of each other – their artillery at a central camp'. By 20 October a state of stalemate seemed to exist, but during the afternoon a native messenger from Zeerust in the Transvaal slipped past the Boers' laagers and brought in news of 'the big gun that is coming from Pretoria to blow Mafeking to bits. It is drawn by 16 black oxen: its shell takes 4 men to lift.' This report was confirmed by a letter from Cronje to Baden-Powell brought in under a white flag a few hours later.[11]

HONOURED SIR, Since it appears to me that there is no other chance of taking Mafeking than by means of a bombardment, I have to adopt that course with regret. I have to allow for forty-eight hours to prepare your people, black and white . . . The time allowed to you I reckon from Saturday 21st, at 6 a.m., till Monday morning, the 23rd, at the same hour.

I am, &c.,
J.P. Cronje,
Commanding, &c.[12]

The 'big gun', a French Creusot 94-pounder, began to shell the town on the morning of 24 October, but in spite of the massive size of its projectiles inflicted only minor injuries on three people during its first day.

On the morning of the 25th, the Boers shelled the town heavily from 6.30 a.m. until noon and then advanced against the native stadt, not realizing that there were at least 400 armed Barolongs waiting for them under the orders of Captain Marsh. A successful move against the stadt was to have been the prelude to their 'real attack from the north'.[13] But Baden-Powell sent Godley in support of the Barolongs with two squadrons of the Protectorate Regiment and 40 Cape Boys, so that when the Boers were still 2,000 yards away they came under such heavy fire that they faltered and turned back. This was a very significant moment in the Siege since the stadt and the Molopo valley offered the attackers their best opening. Their repulse discouraged them from attempting to use this route again until six months had passed.

The following day Baden-Powell decided he would have to counter the threat posed by the Boers' determination to run out trenches ever closer to the town. Some were already approaching to within 1,500 yards, which meant that many streets in the town were within range of the enemy's rifles. Any closer approach would place the town in jeopardy.[14] To halt the process Baden-Powell ordered a night attack by 'D' Squadron on the closest Boer trenches, which were to the north-east.

After their efforts on the 14th, 'D' Squadron could only muster 63 men fit for duty out of 100. The attack did not go smoothly. Sergeant R. V. Hoskings said that the Boers had anticipated it and were ready, whereas the attackers were ill-prepared:

> Ahead of us was the Captain [FitzClarence] striding along with us in close column behind him. Suddenly I saw the trench loom up and I said to the S.M. [Sergeant-Major] 'For Christ's sake, tell the skipper he's right in front of it.' As he started to run to him I saw two men loom up bending over the trench. Crack! Crack! and then a rousing volley and before I knew where I was, everyone was lying down letting the volleys go over. 'Charge' came the order and we were into it . . .[15]

The British party had orders not to fire but only to use their bayonets, which Baden-Powell hoped would terrify the Boers. It certainly would have done if surprise had been achieved, but as things turned out they would have done better to have used their firearms. In the darkness they only stabbed a few Boers and probably killed three of them. At any rate the following day Baden-Powell recorded that three burials were witnessed outside one of the laagers. British casualties were six killed, nine wounded and two missing.[16]

Lieutenant Swinburne described how he was hit in the shoulder 'directly the Boers began to fire'. On their way back to the town FitzClarence's men were caught not just by the Boers' volleys but by cross-fire from the Cape Police's trenches. The lamp which was supposed to guide the men back was dim enough to be invisible. Swinburne thought the whole attack 'a mistake for a little force like ours, as we cannot afford to lose the men . . .' The Squadron had now lost 57 of its 100 men through death, wounds or illness. All the officers were either wounded or missing.[17]

The purpose of the attack had been to stop the further advance of the enemy's closest trenches and in this respect it was successful, since the Boers did not attempt to dig nearer to the town. By exaggerating the Boers' casualties and repeatedly praising the achievement of his own men, Baden-Powell raised morale. The young nurses at the hospital were less impressed. But they saw the state of the corpses. There were some with heads or limbs missing, and on dead faces expressions of pain and terror had been fixed by *rigor mortis*.[18]

On 31 October the Boers attacked Cannon Kopje, the vital fort to the south of the town. For several days past they had bombarded the kopje, and did so again with five guns from dawn on the morning of the attack. Owing to the rocky ground Colonel Vyvyan had been obliged to build up ramparts, but had not been able to construct any sort of shell-proof cover for the men in the fort itself. Somehow Colonel Walford, who commanded the 45 British South Africa Police[19] manning the fort, had managed to scratch a shallow hole between two rocks measuring about 8 feet long, 3 feet high and 3 feet wide in which he lived throughout the Siege. About 40 yards from the fort, it had been possible to dig a slit-trench for the men. The look-out man, the colonel and one or two others were therefore the only regular occupants of the fort. It was so vulnerable to shell-fire that much of the time the 7-pounder had to be dismounted and dragged down to the men's trench.

About 700 Boers attacked on a broad front, and even when they were a mere 400 yards from the fort their compatriots continued to shell the kopje. In spite of this the Boers came on across the veldt and when they were 300 yards away Walford felt he could no longer risk leaving his men in their trench. By the time they were crouching behind the fort's sandbagged parapet, the foremost line of Boers had hastily dug themselves a shallow trench from which they were able to direct well-aimed volleys whenever the defenders showed themselves. But in spite of continued shelling and very accurate rifle fire from the Boers' attacking line, the kopje's garrison responded energetically with their single 7-pounder, their two Maxims and their rifles. Baden-Powell had anxiously watched the Boers approaching 'in a great half moon' with plentiful reliefs behind them. As Walford's men fired back, Baden-Powell saw another body of Boers advancing over to the south-west, aiming to take the fort in the flank. At once he ordered his most skilful gunnery officer to open fire on this second assault force, using two 7-pounders sited just to the south of the town. It took only five minutes of brilliantly accurate shooting by Lieutenant Murchison to check and disperse this new threat. The other attackers, who had never expected the garrison of the fort to stand up to such an horrendous shelling, now found themselves the object of Murchison's inspired attention. 'The Boers rose en masse out of the long grass, appeared for an instant to hesitate . . . and then turned and fled towards their horses.'[20] Of the 45 men who had opposed them, 4 were dead, 4 dying and a further 5 gravely wounded.

Men advancing against Maxim fire suffer fearful casualties, even if as expert as the Boers at using every available scrap of cover. Angus Hamilton was always sceptical about 'official' calculations of enemy losses, but on this occasion the numerous Boer stretcher parties persuaded him that at least 40 men had been hit. Sergeant Hoskings was usually just as sceptical and his estimate was identical. Lady Sarah Wilson later said that the Boers had only admitted to her the loss of 15 killed when she had been a prisoner in their hands.[21] But given the careful planning, the numbers involved and Cronje's preparation of a larger force close to the Molopo valley for a final assault on the town when the kopje fell, it is inconceivable that such an action would have been broken off unless the Boers had sustained heavy casualties.

Among the British dead at Cannon Kopje was Captain the Hon. Douglas H. Marsham, an extremely popular man and, like Baden-Powell, an Old Carthusian. Sol Plaatje, the Resident Commissioner's black interpreter and secretary, mourned him as 'one of my closest friends in the place'. Major Baillie felt the same.[22] Captain Charles A. K. Pechell, another popular officer, also died. Baden-Powell first heard about the casualties from 'a young officer who rode in to tell us with sobs in his throat, how two of his comrade-officers and four of his men were done for, and half-a-dozen more were badly hit'.[23] The bravery of the defenders of Cannon Kopje was rightly praised but, in the Government's official History of the War in South Africa, Baden-Powell was criticized for not having built a stronger fort on the kopje. The problem had been the solid rock beneath a thin layer of soil. Perhaps he ought to have ordered Panzera to use dynamite; but since Vyvyan had not used explosives when he had built up the parapet, this may not have been practicable. Baden-Powell has also been blamed for the erection at the fort of a tall tripod-shaped look-out complete with ladder. This, it was argued, had helped the Boers' gunners to get the range of the fort. Blame for this must also attach to Vyvyan who gave specifications of this look-out in his plans.[24]

On the day of the Cannon Kopje affair, Sergeant Hoskings surmised in his diary that: 'Cronje is not fool enough to be caught napping round a tinpot show like this.'[25] The wonder was that Baden-Powell and his motley crew of defenders had managed even this long to detain a force equivalent to a fifth of the Transvaal's armies then in the field. It would be another nineteen days before Cronje finally decided that Mafeking was not worth the attentions of so large a force, nor the kind of casualties which its capture would entail. Sometimes, in order to minimize Baden-Powell's achievement, Cronje's generalship is assailed; and it is difficult not to feel that he showed too great a fear of risking lives in frontal attacks. This said, it should be recalled that Baden-Powell had seven machine guns, and his system of trenches and gun emplacements produced a defensive barrier almost as effective as a section of 'The Front' during the Great War. In the Boer War, the full impact of the revolutionary increase in the power of rifles and automatic weapons was seen for the first time. Cronje's men were not cowards as has been suggested. A month later, at Magersfontein, they fought with great skill and determination, inflicting a terrible humiliation upon Lord Methuen's division and killing almost 1,000 men of the Highland Brigade. When trapped at Paardeberg the following year, the same 4,000 Boers held off a force seven times their number for ten days before surrendering. Baden-Powell's achievement was that *he* had held off a force seven times his size not for ten days but for five weeks. Altogether, since the last week of September when Cronje had arrived in the region, Stephe and his part-timers had kept over 6,000 Boers occupied for nearly eight weeks. If these men had been in Natal during October, the war might well have been lost before Wolseley's army corps arrived.

When Cronje finally left Mafeking, taking 4,000 men with him bound for the more important operations in the neighbourhood of Kimberley, the Siege of Mafeking ceased to have any wider strategic importance. When taken up by the British press, it would of course acquire great significance of a psychological kind, but from a military point of view it became a sideshow after 19 November.

Various historians, following Brian Gardner's lead, have pointed to inconsistencies in the figures which Baden-Powell gave for the number of Boers besieging Mafeking, both before and after Cronje's departure. It is certainly true that he tended to increase the numbers as he grew older, feeling perhaps – after the stupefying statistics of the Great War – that Mafeking needed the dignity of slightly larger numbers in order to justify recollection three decades later. The exaggeration in this context seems apologetic rather than self-glorifying. In 1933, in his autobiography, he raised the Boers' initial numbers to 10,000 from the 8,000 he had claimed in his report to Lord Roberts in 1900. In 1937, in a radio broadcast, he upped the figure to 12,000, at the same time volunteering that the Siege had been 'only an

incident' and 'much over-advertised'. In fact he had issued three
similar downgradings, the first as early as 1907 when he had written
about Mafeking's 'exaggerated reputation',[26] and the others in 1933
and 1934.[27] In both these later versions, he had called the Siege 'a very
minor operation'. Given the frenzied over-reaction of the press and
public at the time, he can surely be forgiven for occasionally trying to
make the Siege more closely resemble its formidable reputation. These
exaggerations, made during his seventies, give us no right to suppose
that the Siege itself was a kind of confidence trick. Unlike his spying
expeditions, Mafeking required no imaginative embroidery to make it
a significant event.

Some inconsistency over the figures was inevitable. In his Staff
Diary on 9 October he estimated the Boers in the border area at 9,900,
and two days later hazarded a figure of 'at least 7,000, maybe 9,900'.[28]
The word 'maybe' is the key to the problem. Baden-Powell never
knew how many Boers closed in around the town on the evening of 13
October 1899. His genuine belief during much of October was that
between 6,000 and 8,000 men had besieged him. In letters to his
mother (8 October) and to Cecil Rhodes (16 November), he kept the
base figure of 6,000 but reduced the upper figure to 7,000.[29] Colonel
Vyvyan, his first Intelligence Officer, supposed that Cronje alone had
5,000 men and that the Boers also had two more substantial laagers.[30]
Hanbury-Tracy, the next Intelligence Officer, confirmed the figure of
8,000 which Baden-Powell gave in his report to Lord Roberts.[31]
Godley plumped for 9,000 at the start of the Siege.[32] In looking at all
the available estimates, and the guesses made by other diarists, a figure
of slightly over 6,000 outside Mafeking at the outset seems about
right.[33] In 1903 Baden-Powell told the Royal Commission on the War
in South Africa that 11,000 Boers had been spread over the entire
border region. It may have been his recollection of this which led him
later to come up with figures of 10–12,000. Since Plumer's force faced
1,500 Boers to the north of Mafeking, Baden-Powell's *whole* force
detained at least 7,500 Boers during October and the first half of
November 1899.

Baden-Powell's critics are on firmer ground when suggesting that in
later years he rarely gave the impression that most of the besiegers left
after five weeks. In his autobiography he conceded that there were
'later smaller numbers under Sneyman [sic]'.[34] The figure he usually
claimed after Cronje's departure was 3,000.[35] Godley and Hanbury-
Tracy agreed.[36] Certainly the Boers' numbers approached 3,000 in
early May 1900, as the Staff Day Book makes clear.[37] But more often
in the Day Book the Boers' estimated strength is set at about 2,000, and
quite often as low as 1,400. From time to time Commandant Snyman
sent men up north to cooperate with commandos facing Plumer's
force. When Plumer moved south to within fifteen miles of Mafeking

in mid–March 1900, Baden-Powell estimated that the Boers had left only 800 white men and 200 blacks around the town.[38] But since at that date he himself could only muster 188 men of the Protectorate Regiment fit for duty and had barely 100 horses strong enough to take the field, he could not risk offensive action even against such low numbers.[39] He was having trouble manning his defences adequately, and had he taken out most of his men it would have been an open invitation to the more mobile enemy to slip past him into the town. Four days later the Boers' numbers were back to 1,600.[40] Baden-Powell and his officers were never very forthcoming about the Boers' numbers after Cronje's departure because the situation was so complex. The health of the garrison, their casualties and the slow starvation of all their horses meant that, whereas Baden-Powell might justifiably have risked going out to fight 1,000 besiegers in November (when they were in fact more numerous than that), by early February, when the Boers' numbers actually fell to 1,200 for the first time, his force was too weak sensibly to attempt such a course.[41]

*

Brian Gardner, who has done most to give the Siege of Mafeking its reputation as a non-event, stated in his preface that he was particularly indebted to Angus Hamilton's account of the Siege and to the papers of Benjamin Weil. But Baden-Powell's relations with both men were far from cordial. In early October he had had a serious contretemps with Hamilton. Not satisfied that the journalist was, as he claimed, a *bona fide Times* correspondent, Stephe telegraphed Moberley Bell, the editor, eliciting from him the information that Hamilton had been employed on the supposition that he had been accepted as a volunteer in Baden-Powell's force. Believing this to be the case, Bell had agreed to print letters from him. But on learning from Baden-Powell that Hamilton had not volunteered, Bell disowned him. Only after a series of desperate telegrams from Hamilton did Bell agree to ask Baden-Powell to restore his press pass.[42] Baden-Powell acquiesced, but his relations with Hamilton remained strained. Stephe was particularly angered by a despatch Hamilton submitted to the censor in which he credited Ben Weil with being the only man in the town to have had the foresight to see what was coming. Given the tussles which Baden-Powell had had with General Butler over supplies and his problems with Milner over fortifying the town, he felt insulted by Hamilton's account. 'I told Mr. Hamilton,' he recorded in his diary, 'that there was nothing of military importance in this because it was all unfounded nonsense – but if he liked he could send it.'[43]

Benjamin Weil was very keen to secure plaudits in the press and gave six bottles of brandy to Reuter's correspondent Vere Stent. When it became apparent that Stent was not going to send the interview to

London (his reason being that the Chief Staff Officer objected to its contents), Weil asked for his brandy.[44] Baden-Powell mistrusted Weil even in mid-September when he had an 'unvarnished talk with Weil on the subject of supplies generally . . . and explained to him that his methods were not fully satisfactory'.[45] Weil was making excessive profits on all the items he was supplying, consistently asking more for them than merchants in Bulawayo would charge. Later Baden-Powell suspected him of involvement in black market sales of supposedly 'stolen' goods; in February he wrote: 'His [Weil's] stocks have been useful to us but his own duplicity has been a constant annoyance if not a danger.'[46] Baden-Powell was not alone in thinking that Weil engineered shortages in order to charge more,[47] but as he and everyone else knew, the town depended upon Weil's supplies. Gardner's reliance on Weil's opinions was as likely to harm Baden-Powell's reputation as was his faith in Hamilton's despatches.

But Baden-Powell's worst confrontation with a journalist was not with Hamilton but with J. Emerson Neilly, who was caught trying to smuggle out uncensored letters to the proprietor of the *Pall Mall Gazette*.[48] Although Neilly's press permit was removed for a time and he remained sure that Baden-Powell was deliberately prolonging the Siege as 'a promotion job', when the journalist published his account of the Siege, far from attempting to discredit Baden-Powell he praised him. 'We had one blessing, the Government had sent Baden-Powell to hold the place. He was a man in a thousand.'[49] Unlike the still resentful Hamilton, Major Baillie of the *Morning Post* hoped that Baden-Powell would swiftly be made a general.[49] Even the prickly Vere Stent could not help being impressed. One day when chatting to Baden-Powell outside his Headquarters, the Boers opened fire.

A shell whistled overhead and landed in the market place. I hoped the Colonel would take cover but he didn't, he only went on talking. A second shell sang a little nearer and raised clouds of dust not two hundred yards away. The Colonel closed the book which he had been reading, and, marking the place, rose quietly, whistling to himself, as is his habit, and as a third shell wrecked a couple of outstanding buildings, said, 'You had better come inside.' I needed no second invitation to seek the shelter of the Headquarters bomb-proof. [Five people died in this particular bombardment.][50]

It is, however, Hamilton's keenly observant if bleak assessment of Baden-Powell's character which, through the efforts of Gardner and his followers, has come down to us.

Colonel Baden-Powell is young, as men go in the army, with a keen appreciation of the possibilities of his career, swayed by ambition, indifferent to sentimental emotion. In stature he is short, while his

features are sharp and smooth. He is eminently a man of determination, of great physical endurance and capacity, and of extraordinary reticence. His reserve is unbending, and one would say,
quoting a phrase of Mr. Pinero's [the dramatist], that fever would
be the only heat which would permeate his body. He does not go
about freely, since he is tied to his office through the multitudinous
cares of his command, and he is chiefly happy when he can snatch
the time to escape upon one of those nocturnal, silent expeditions,
which alone calm and assuage the perpetual excitement of his
present existence. Outwardly, he maintains an impenetrable screen
of self-control, observing with a cynical smile the foibles and
caprices of those around him. He seems ever bracing himself to be
on guard against a moment in which he should be swept by some
unnatural and spontaneous enthusiasm, in which by a word, by an
expression of face, by a movement, or in the turn of a phrase, he
should betray the rigours of the self-control under which he lives.
Every passing townsman regards him with curiosity not unmixed
with awe . . . and he, as a consequence, seldom speaks without a
preternatural deliberation and an air of decisive finality. He seems to
close every argument with a snap, as though the steel manacles of
his ambition had checkmated the emotions of the man in the
instincts of the officer. He weighs each remark, before he utters it,
and suggests by his manner, as by his words, that he has considered
the different effects it might conceivably have on any mind . . . He
loves the night, and after his return from the hollows in the veldt,
where he has kept so many anxious vigils, he lies awake hour after
hour upon his camp mattress in the verandah, tracing out in his
mind, the various means and agencies by which he can forestall the
enemy's moves, which, unknown to them, he had personally
watched. He is a silent man, and it would seem that silence has
become in his heart a curious religion. In the noisy day he yearns for
the noiseless night, in which he can slip into the vistas of the
veldt . . . As he makes his way across our lines the watchful sentry
strains his eyes a little more to keep the figure of the colonel before
him . . . He goes on, never faltering, bending for a moment behind
a clump of rocks, screening himself next behind some bushes,
crawling upon his hands and knees, until his movements stirring a
few loose stones, create a thin, grating noise in the vast silence about
him. His head is low, his eyes gaze straight upon the camp of the
enemy.[51]

This chilly portrait brilliantly conveys Baden-Powell's isolation and
studied self-control. Hamilton was right too to recognize Stephe's
ambition, but although Baden-Powell was undoubtedly a self-
contained and reticent man the suggestion that he was cold to the point

of lacking any real emotion was wrong. The journalist cannot have realized how grief-stricken Baden-Powell was when McLaren was wounded outside the town, nor have heard how distressed he was whenever men were killed.[52]

Baden-Powell believed that to be successful, a commander should not just give orders and inflict punishment. 'Any ass' could do that. A true leader had 'to be fond of his men, full of sympathy and understanding'.[53] Sergeant Hoskings of the Protectorate Regiment, who was a hard-bitten campaigner, praised Baden-Powell for sending round bottles of whisky, rum or brandy on wet nights. 'The confidence the men have in Colonel B-P is marvellous and not at all to be wondered at. A small wiry looking man . . . with a thoughtful expression . . . Always in a good humour and ready to have amusements prepared for the men; always seeing personally to their comfort, and never tiring, he is the man in exactly the right place.'[54]

Hamilton rather exaggerated the extent of Baden-Powell's nocturnal daring. Stephe's Staff Diary establishes that only on half-a-dozen occasions did he venture into territory actually controlled by the Boers.[55] More often he confined his trips to the 'no-man's land' immediately beyond his own perimeter forts. In direct contrast to Hamilton's chilly apparition, Baden-Powell struck Alick Godley as a friendly presence when he came silently into his dug-out at daybreak. Just to see his commanding officer sitting on a sandbag near his bed made him feel more cheerful. When the Siege was at its nadir, Godley was sure that 'had it not been for Baden-Powell's amazing energy, personality and ubiquity, there would have been a good deal of alarm and despondency in the garrison'.[56] The quality which Godley valued most in Baden-Powell, his critics suspected did not exist at all: namely his ability to trust those under him. 'He lets people run their own show,' Godley told his wife, 'and he is so good in the way that he talks over everything he wants done, and discusses it with one, before giving a final order – and he is invariably good-tempered and resourceful.'[57] Major H. de Montmorency, who served with Baden-Powell in the three months after the Siege was raised, was one of the earliest sceptics about the value of the Siege. But when Montmorency came to know Baden-Powell personally, he felt compelled to praise 'the geniality, the lovable character, and the generosity towards his subordinates' of the man.[58] When the food situation became critical Miss Craufurd, by now Matron of the Women's and Children's Convalescent Hospital, admitted that she was depressed by the misery and hunger in the town, but added, 'the Colonel is always so cheerful himself, so we feel that we must be the same, and we all have such faith in B-P'.[59]

Of course it was in Baden-Powell's interest to do whatever he could to keep up morale by example, but the ability to exhibit unshakable composure when under great strain is not given to many. 'Luckily,' he told Lady Downe, 'my early play-acting instincts came in useful, and though my mind was in my boots at times with anxiety – I was able to maintain a grin to reassure those anxious appealing eyes that mutely asked at every turn "Is it all right?" "Are you *sure* we can go on?" I knew of course that if the Boers liked to make a bold stroke – especially by night, our small numbers could do nothing against them.'[60]

Although Hamilton never gave Baden-Powell credit for feeling anything as human as anxiety, for much of the Siege Stephe went in constant fear of assassination. In October he had arrested a Mr Quinlan, the Irish station master, and another Irishman called Whelan, who possessed a 'very good cypher giving military information'.[61] They were suspected of being Fenians,* not only because of the cypher but because they had delayed disposing of two truckloads of dynamite and had probably betrayed the schedule of the wrecked armoured train. By the end of October Baden-Powell had imprisoned 28 persons suspected of being spies. To reduce the chance of being murdered at night, he did not always sleep in the same place but secretly rented a room in the house of an Indian shopkeeper called Gumar Dada, slipping in unobtrusively through the open window after it was dark.[62]

Perhaps the most important reason why Hamilton drew Baden-Powell's character as he did was Stephe's invariable asperity towards people he mistrusted. Was it wise, he would have asked himself, to trust a journalist who had lied to the editor of his own newspaper? Shortly before Cronje abandoned the Siege, Hamilton and Baillie asked if they might attempt to escape from the town. Baden-Powell refused. 'I consider it best that they should not thus evade censorship by a staff officer and spread all the bar gossip of the place in interviews on reaching Cape Town.'[63] 'The war correspondents here do more harm than good,' wrote Swinburne, 'I don't wonder all commissioned officers hate them.'[64] Unfortunately for Baden-Powell's subsequent reputation, this feeling (at least in the case of Hamilton) was mutual.

*

After Cronje's departure the Boers still besieging Mafeking were led by Commandant J. P. Snyman, who abandoned the idea of storming the town. Snyman has been ridiculed for his poor generalship, but since Cronje had failed to achieve anything significant with over 6,000 men, it was never reasonable to expect more positive action from Snyman with only 2,000. He knew that the early relief of the town was improbable, and was therefore content to prevent the garrison escaping and to bring about their submission through the combined effects of hunger and bombardment.[65]

* Irish nationalists prepared to use violence to obtain independence from Great Britain.

On 15 November, before the Boers' bombardment had killed any white civilians and before anyone, black or white, had started to suffer from hunger, Angus Hamilton wrote:

> When we come to consider the siege of Mafeking in its more elemental details, the picture is not unlike those presented by the farcical melodrama. It is now nearly six weeks since Mafeking was proclaimed as being in a state of siege and, although there has been no single opportunity of any commerical reciprocity between ourselves and the outside world, the ruling prices are at present but very little above normal, distress is wholly absent, danger is purely incidental, and indeed it would seem as Colonel Baden-Powell said in a recent order, that 'Everything in the garden is lovely.'[66]

Both Gardner and Rosenthal quote this passage in support of their contention that the Siege was a benign and comical affair. In Rosenthal's words, Hamilton in this passage 'defined conditions that stayed essentially unchanged during the entire time.'[67] This is a remarkable distortion since in Hamilton's very next despatches, written on 22 and 30 November, a quite different note is sounded. The second of these is entitled 'Shells and Slaughter'; on one occasion, after a shell burst in the market square, Hamilton ran to the point of impact.

> As the shell rebounded from the ground leaving a hole many feet long . . . it had come in contact with a native before it wrecked the apothecary's store. Mingled with the fragments of glass and the contents of the shop were shreds of cloth and infinitesimal strips of flesh, while the entire environment was splashed with blood. The poor native had lost an arm, a foot lay a few yards from him, and his other leg was hanging by a few shreds of skin . . . When the bleeding body was put upon a stretcher, and the mangled extremities gathered together, the Hospital Orderly caught sight of the hand which was 'clinging' to a recess in the wall . . . Despite his fearful injuries, which were beyond the scope of human power to aid, he was not dead, feebly exclaiming as they put him in the stretcher, 'Boss, Boss, me hurt.' The ruin of the building had scarcely been realised, and the vapour of chemicals from the shell mingling with the scattered perfumes of the shop – when a second shell screaming its passage through the air hurled itself with a terrible velocity against the other window of the same building . . . escaping by a miracle five men who had been standing in the interior of the premises, but killing an unfortunate corporal, who had gone from the scene of the death of the native to get a 'pick-me-up' from the adjoining bar in Riesle's Hotel. In such a manner does the death roll pile itself up – with the impending slowness of a juggernaut and the haunting persistency of fate. If these were the actual numbers of

the killed upon this date, there were also two who were wounded, one of whom has since died, thus giving to one day a terrible trio . . .[68]

In case this is dismissed as one of the few occasions on which Hamilton recorded unpleasant events, the following is how he had described life in Mafeking a few days earlier:

Not a day has passed since the siege began but they have not thrown shrapnel and common shell, omitting minor projectiles, into the town. And still we live, with just sufficient spirit to jeer across our ramparts at our enemy. They Mauser us, and shell us; they cut our water off, and raid our cattle; they make life hell, and they can do so, so long as it may please them.[69]

To have any idea of how unpleasant a place Mafeking must have been during the Siege, its tiny population and size have to be borne in mind. In such a small community almost every person killed by a shell was known personally to everyone else in the town. The random deaths were deeply shocking to civilians who, before the world had experienced aerial bombing, were placed in the front line of a modern war. Nevertheless, because the town was honeycombed with 400 bomb-proofs and five miles of communication trenches, the casualties from shelling were surprisingly light – only nine whites dying as a direct result of shell-fire. But since all the women and children lived in the comparative safety of the Women's Laager, this gives a distorted picture of life in the town itself. Thanks to Baden-Powell's precautions, deaths due to the bombardment formed an infinitely smaller proportion of the total casualties than the appallingly high number of deaths and injuries suffered in action by the officers and men of the garrison. Remembering that Baden-Powell had just over 1,100 whites under arms at the start of the Siege, it is chilling to recall that 233 of these were killed or wounded. The figure for those who died (killed in action, missing or died from wounds) was 115.[70] There were 44 officers, of whom 6 were killed and 16 wounded. These were very severe casualty figures for so small a force to sustain – over ten times worse than those recorded during the Siege of Ladysmith.

It is uncertain how many Africans – out of the 7,500 in the town at the beginning of the Siege – were killed or wounded by shells – but many more than the whites who died or were injured in that way. Most diarists pointed to a kind of fatalism among the blacks, which made them negligent about taking cover. In spite of the fact that they had dug the whites' bombproofs for money, they did not provide themselves with similar shelters in the stadt.

The deaths which occurred during this long period of sporadic shelling were always arbitrary and shockingly sudden. Dr Hayes, the

Principal Medical Officer, recorded the death of one African, walking along the street one moment and the next torn apart: 'His hat with part of his head in it was on the verandah roof, whilst Kaffir dogs finished the rest of him.'[71] Death could come more gently. Mrs Poulton, who ought to have been in the Women's Laager, slipped from her chair without a word while pouring a cup of coffee for her husband. A Mauser bullet had come in at the window and passed through her neck. Captain R. Girdwood, the Assistant Commissariat Officer, was bicycling home for lunch when he seemed to lose his balance and fell from the saddle.[72] He had been shot through the stomach and would die next day.

One of the most frightening aspects of the behaviour of 94-pounder shells was the way in which they might explode on impact or might bounce, once or even twice, before going off. These bounces were sometimes gigantic. On 24 January 1900, a shell screamed down on the Market Square, then 'bumped right up in the air and singled out old Moschuchwi's hut (1½ miles away); after its decline it entered the hut from the back, decapitating two women and wounding three brothers severely.'[73] The author of this account was Mr Bell's African translator and secretary, Sol Plaatje, who had 'never before realized so keenly that he was walking on the brink of the grave'.[74] Nor were children exempt. A little white boy was playing with some marbles when he was hit. Baden-Powell visited him in hospital the day he died.[75] He was appalled by the terrible injuries he saw there: limbs missing, parts of faces and no adequate means of easing the victim's suffering. Mr Urry, the bank manager, avoided going near the hospital. 'The groans and shrieks of the dying are too terrible to hear.'[76]

When 30 or 40 94-pounder shells (not to mention three times that many smaller projectiles) descended upon the town in the course of a morning's bombardment, it must have been depressing to know that not even the best bombproof in town could withstand a direct hit. Lady Sarah Wilson wrote of 'the wear and tear on the mind' caused by the 'constant dangers of shells and stray bullets, and the knowledge that when taking leave of any friend, it might be the last farewell on earth'.[77] Lady Sarah herself lived through one of those traumatic escapes which many experienced, and which always left the survivor in deep shock. She, her husband and Major Goold-Adams were about to eat lunch in one of the rooms in the convent when a 94-pounder shell came right through the building, bursting in the very next room to theirs; and although a wall was blown in and bricks, floorboards and beams were tossed through the air, amazingly no one was hurt.[78] Lord Edward Cecil was writing at a desk in his office at Dixon's Hotel when a shell dropped down the chimney and burst behind the mantelpiece, wrecking the room and killing a waiter outside the door. Lord Edward had been in poor health before this escape, and the shock proved a further setback.[79] Major Baillie, Lieutenant Moncreiffe and Lieutenant Brady succumbed to the pressure and began to drink excessively. Others, like Colonel Hore and, to a lesser extent, Wilson and Bentinck, were frequently ill. Vere Stent, who had been noted for his courage during the Matabele Campaign, was very rarely seen above ground in Mafeking. And he was not the only one: the men of the Protectorate Regiment had a song about their colonel.

> There is an old Colonel called Hore,
> Whose dugout's the best in the Corps,
> When the shells fly about,
> We shout, 'Hell, look out!'
> And we see the old beggar no more.[80]

Baden-Powell rarely exposed himself to unnecessary risks, but on one occasion a shell exploded very close to him in the brickfields; on another, the Headquarters bombproof was hit.[81] Neither of these close shaves compared with any of the truly miraculous ones which he recorded in a special list. Pride of place went to a railwayman shot through the head, the bullet passing through just behind the forehead and exiting on the other side. The wounded man suffered no ill effects at all. Then there was the escape of the five soldiers sitting in a semi-circle around a friend who was singing to them. The singer was hit by a shell and quite literally disappeared, while not one of his five companions was touched.[82]

I have dwelled at some length upon such incidents because of the determination shown by recent historians to ignore the dangers of the Siege. To contemporaries, these were clear enough. When Filson Young of the *Manchester Guardian* entered the town with the Relief Column, he was amazed by what he saw. 'As one passed house after house, one with a gaping hole in its side, another with the chimneys overthrown, and another with a whole wall stove in, none with windows completely glazed, all bearing some mark of war – as this panorama of destruction unfolded itself one marvelled that anyone should have lived throughout the siege.'[83] A. W. A. Pollock of *The Times* was equally dismayed. 'More damage was done in a single street in Mafeking than in the whole of Kimberley.'[84]

Baden-Powell knew how much morale was harmed by the garrison's obvious inability to stop the bombardment. But lacking any guns able to touch the enemy's artillery, he could only hope to annoy the Boers from time to time. His favourite method was to advance his guns into rapidly prepared pits, dug during the preceding night well outside the defence perimeter. There his gunners would be exposed to immense danger. The most frequent candidate for this duty was the 1-pounder Nordenfeldt, which would often be advanced to within

1,400 yards of the 94-pounder.[85] To reduce the risks, Baden-Powell would move all his 7-pounders at night and place them in new positions so that the Boers would have to find their range afresh the following morning. Sometimes he would let the enemy see the guns being moved to new positions and would then surreptitiously move them back to where they had been before.[86] His artillery was marginally improved by the addition of a 5-inch howitzer made in the railway workshops, and possessing a range greater than any of his other guns. This piece was called the 'Wolf', which had been the nickname supposedly conferred upon Baden-Powell by the Matabele. The howitzer was in action for the whole of March 1900, but its breech was burst during an attempt to throw a shell more than 3,000 yards. Another addition to the garrison's arsenal came about fortuitously. Major Godley found an old ship's gun of Napoleonic vintage near the Women's Laager, where it was being used as a gatepost. When it was dug out and cleaned, Godley was amazed to make out the initials 'B.P. & Co.' engraved on the barrel; it had been cast by the firm of Baily and Pegg of Staffordshire. When mounted on a wooden carriage 'Lord Nelson', as the gun was named, could throw a solid cannon-ball 3,300 yards. Clearly the sudden appearance of round-shot, bouncing like gigantic cricket balls through their laagers, very much surprised the Boers, but did them little harm. The psychological value of being able to hit back was well-expressed by Sol Plaatje: 'No music is as thrilling and immensely captivating to listen to as the firing of the guns of your own side.'[87]

Of more practical, if less spectacular, effect was the work done by Mafeking's snipers. 'The Big Gun',* as Godley truly observed, was the garrison's 'worst trouble'.[88] But on 28 November, after Baden-Powell had personally reconnoitred the ground and supervised the digging of rifle pits, the 94-pounder's crew was harassed from dawn to dusk by a band of volunteer snipers.[89] The following day the Big Gun managed to fire only three rounds, so intimidated were the gunners. A few days later the 94-pounder was moved from the south-eastern heights.[90] But however brave and skilful these snipers were, they could do no more than give the garrison an occasional respite.

In early December Baden-Powell became increasingly aware of the feelings of hopelessness and exasperation in the town.[91] Very few people had expected to be besieged for more than a month or two and the continuing absence of news, coupled with the daily bombardment, was sapping morale. On 16 December, responding to this mood, Baden-Powell told Nurse Craufurd that 'we have been very quiet lately, but should soon let them know we have plenty of "go" in us still'.[92] He attributed some of the earlier optimism to occasional 'kicks'

* Called 'Grietje' by the Boers.

at the enemy, such as FitzClarence's trench attack. Since mid-
November he had been contemplating a sortie with the aim of
damaging their Big Gun,[93] and was therefore infuriated when 'two
amateur scouts went out at night without leave and . . . allowed
themselves to be seen. Consequently today the Boers have been busily
strengthening the position.'[94] He did not however abandon his hopes
of attacking this battery and a month later, on 22 December, he sent
out three of his best scouts to spend an entire night examining the gun's
defences. Their information convinced him that a sabotage raid was
feasible and so he decided to mount a night attack against the Big Gun.
A party of 150 volunteers under Captain FitzClarence and three
officers was to storm the battery, supported by a small party of
gunners under Major Panzera, who would 'blow up the Gun'.[95]

On the following night the entire party went through a dress
rehearsal with wire-cutters, axes and dynamite.[96] Before dawn on the
24th, Baden-Powell himself 'reconnoitred on foot round the south
flank of the battery'. Finding the work stronger than he had expected,
he decided 'to put the further examination of it in the hands of
Corporal Young, Bechuanaland Rifles'.[97] But the corporal never
went. Later the same day Baden-Powell, Godley, Goold-Adams,
Cecil and FitzClarence had a long discussion, and while Baden-Powell
and FitzClarence remained keen 'to have a go for the Big Gun', the rest
considered it too risky and converted their commanding officer to
their belief. As Godley argued: 'Our game is to sit tight and not risk
any disaster.'[98] Instead of 'sitting tight', Baden-Powell asked his
officers to consider another plan. Although the idea was his, the
decision to attack the Boers' siege-work known as Game Tree fort was
a joint one. Godley later went out of his way to praise Baden-Powell
for always seeking the advice of his officers before making important
decisions.[99] Sometimes Stephe would send written requests to them to
let him know the tactics they favoured in a given situation.

In his Staff Diary on 17 November Baden-Powell had written:
'Trenches at Game Tree being roofed with corrugated iron.' He had
much to think of, and he and his staff must have forgotten this
significant fact when they contemplated attacking the fort six weeks
later. Lieutenant Swinburne, who took part in the attack on Game
Tree fort, described the siege-work as 'the trench at Game Tree'. So
the 'trenches . . . roofed with corrugated iron' mentioned by Baden-
Powell, and Swinburne's 'trench at Game Tree', would seem to have
been one and the same.[100] On 23 November Game Tree was
reconnoitred, but Baden-Powell was then giving more attention to the
vicinity of the Big Gun. On 2 December a sniping party of three men
went out to within 700 yards of Game Tree, where they found an
advanced trench manned by natives. These three men considered the
fort no more formidable than 'a breastwork of sandbags with some

kind of shelter behind'.[101] The only evidence to show that any scouts were sent out to Game Tree after 2 December is a message Baden-Powell sent to Colonel Nicholson on 26 December, just after the attack. In it he mentioned that there had been a reconnaissance expedition on Christmas Day. Considering the pains he had taken to familiarize himself with the Big Gun's defences, it is sad and puzzling that he did not do the same with Game Tree fort.

Later he would offer as his principal reason for attempting to capture the fort an urgent need to enlarge the area in which the garrison's cattle could graze. This was certainly an objective worth some sacrifice, but Baden-Powell never mentioned it as an aim before the sortie was made. Instead, on the 24th, he wrote of the impending attack as a means of inducing the Boers 'to recall reinforcements [to Mafeking] from the direction of Crocodile Pools and so relieve the pressure on Plumer   '.[102] On that same day runners had come in with despatches from Colonel Plumer saying that the Rhodesia Regiment was moving south from Palapye, 250 miles north of Mafeking, and that Lieutenant H. Llewellyn had pressed on much farther south down the railway line towards Crocodile Pools, a mere 80 miles away.[103] Having been talked out of his attack on the Big Gun, yet still feeling impelled for psychological reasons to attack the Boers somewhere, Baden-Powell clutched at the news from Plumer as justification. A sortie at Mafeking might encourage any Boers opposing Plumer to leave for the south; this would enable the Rhodesia Regiment to advance and thus facilitate close cooperation with the Mafeking garrison. But since Plumer was not under any real pressure and Llewellyn could retreat if pressed, Baden-Powell could have delayed his sortie and prepared more thoroughly. Of course it is easy enough years later to underestimate the heavy sense of obligation which he must have felt to do something to boost the townspeople's morale.

The attack on Game Tree fort took place shortly before dawn on 26 December and was mounted by 150 men, supported by the armoured train, two Maxims and three 7-pounders, with 110 men and one gun in support.[104] The operation began disastrously with a bombardment of the Boers' position which served only to alert them. Through a misunderstanding the British covering fire ceased when the attackers were still 1,400 yards from the work and because the rails of the defence railway had been ripped up the train could not go out as far as anticipated in support. None of these problems, however, compared with the real cause of the carnage. Men had expected to attack a sandbagged trench but what they finally found, as Lieutenant Swinburne put it, was 'a sort of miniature Bastille which would take hours of shelling with big guns to get into'.[105] Half a dozen men and one of the officers were killed in the last 200 yards of their dash towards the fort, but the majority died vainly trying to force their way inside.

The work was protected by an eight-foot wall and was roofed over with corrugated iron and earth, so that even those who clambered on to the roof were unable to get in. Two officers were killed firing their revolvers into the loopholes in the wall, and many men died doing the same. Immense bravery was shown but to no purpose.[106] When half the men in 'C' Squadron at the centre of the attack had been shot down, the rest were forced to retreat. In the armoured train, Major Godley with only eighteen men realized that the situation was hopeless as soon as he saw 'C' Squadron reeling back. He refused to send forward the men held in reserve and sent a message to Baden-Powell recommending immediate withdrawal.

Meanwhile 'D' Squadron under the intrepid FitzClarence had been halted by a withering fire from the fort. Swinburne, the second-in-command, had described 'Fitz' as 'like the hero in a silly woman's novel strolling about under fire, with the bullets spitting about all around him'.[107] Already wounded twice since the start of the Siege, FitzClarence was hit again and his thigh shattered. He managed to drag himself to an ant-hill, where he propped himself up and lit a cigarette. When a Boer threatened to shoot him unless he handed over his sword and revolver, he refused so furiously that he was left in peace.[108] For his bravery in the three actions in which he took part, Captain FitzClarence was awarded the Victoria Cross. Two other Victoria Crosses were won at Game Tree: by Sergeant H. R. Martineau and Trooper H. E. Ramsden. No Victoria Crosses were won during the Siege of Kimberley and only one at Ladysmith.

The attack was nevertheless the worst blunder of the Siege: 26 men were killed, 23 wounded and 3 captured. Only 3 Boers died, and 10 were wounded.[109] Baden-Powell's claim that his plan had been betrayed to the enemy was probably true. Nurse Craufurd knew about the impending attack on Christmas Day, as did many other citizens; so information could easily have been leaked to the Boers by one of the Dutch inhabitants.[110] That very day, Baden-Powell had seen the Boers strengthening their positions; it was a grave fault, even if condoned by his brother officers, that he had allowed the attack to go ahead in such circumstances. The well-informed auctioneer Edward Ross heard that the men sent out during the night preceding the attack had been too frightened to go really close to the fort.[111] In view of the Boers' vigilance, their fear can readily be understood. The ground rose approaching the work but dipped immediately in front of it, giving the impression to anyone observing it from a distance that the breastwork wall was much lower than it actually was. Nor can the scout be blamed for failing to discover that the fort had a solid roof; he would have had to clamber on to it in order to do so. The real fault was that no one – whether Baden-Powell, his Intelligence Officer or any other member of his staff – recalled the reports noted down on 17 November to the effect that the trenches at Game Tree had been roofed over with corrugated iron

The day made a profound impression upon Baden-Powell, and it was obvious to Ross how 'terribly upset he was' when he met the armoured train returning with the dead and wounded, 'the brown blood clotted on their pallid faces and torn dusty clothes'.[112] The first and largest funeral took place the same evening. The dead were sewn into canvas shrouds which were soon discoloured by blood-stains; only the officers were buried in coffins. As Captain J. R. Vernon's body was lowered into the long trench, 'the rough hard voice of an old soldier who was holding one of the ropes was heard to cry out, "God bless you Captain!"' Vernon's mother would harbour furious resentment against Baden-Powell for causing her son's death; and although he sent her a sketch of the grave and the flag that had covered his coffin, she remained implacable. The journalists who had gone out with the stretcher parties after the ceasefire had been shocked to see wounds inflicted by explosive bullets.[113]

Godley, who had taken the lead in dissuading his commander from attacking the Big Gun, never attempted to mitigate the failure. Baden-Powell himself was determined in future to have nothing to do with frontal attacks on well-defended positions.[114] When he suspected that Plumer was planning such an operation, he ordered him not to proceed unless assured of a ten-to-one numerical advantage. At Paardeberg, Lord Kitchener sent repeated waves of men on suicidal attacks against prepared positions and never showed the least remorse. Baden-Powell was a different type of soldier, however. There would be no more sorties after Game Tree. When reporting to the Commander-in-Chief Baden-Powell wrote with almost excessive punctiliousness (excessive because commanding officers were always held responsible): 'If blame for this reverse falls on anyone it should fall on myself, as everybody concerned did their part of the work thoroughly well, and exactly in accordance with the orders I had issued.'[115] But in any realistic league table of Boer War blunders, the attack on Game Tree fort merits only a lowly position.

The bodies brought in from Game Tree that day heralded a darker phase in the Siege. Henceforth Baden-Powell would be concerned only with survival. Late December in the southern hemisphere is midsummer, a time of baking heat on the Bechuanaland border. From his rooftop vantage point, Stephe looked across the shimmering square towards the distant heights and saw through waves of heat haze the Boer laagers 'like so many "hills" at Epsom with a crowd of booths and tents and wagons huddled up together'. He heard 'the pop-pop of outlying pickets exchanging shots with the enemy' and seconds later the bullets 'rattling on the tin roofs in the town'.[116] The rifle fire did not stop all day and was always joined by the boom of the 94-pounder and the crack of smaller guns. How many months would it go on? So far morale had been sapped only by shells and casualties. But how would the townspeople and the garrison respond to hunger? And who would thank Colonel Baden-Powell for rationing supplies and restricting purchases? As 1899 drew to a close, Stephe looked to the New Year with foreboding.

5. *Starving the Blacks to Feed the Whites?*
(November 1899 to April 1900)

Baden-Powell has been accused of racism, plagiarism, having fascist sympathies, being a buffoon, a tyrant, a liar and a self-serving hypocrite, but no charge ever made against him can rival the gravity of the recent accusation levelled by Thomas Pakenham. This is that, while exercising absolute powers in Mafeking, Baden-Powell operated a food policy so heavily weighted against the black inhabitants that it amounted if not to mass murder, to a form of discriminatory rationing which effectively left 2,000 people without any food, thus forcing them to run the gauntlet of the Boers' cordon or starve.[1] Since the publication of Pakenham's *The Boer War* in 1979, when his accusation was given widespead publicity in the press under such headlines as 'BADEN-POWELL'S BLACK SECRET',[2] no author writing about Mafeking or other aspects of Baden-Powell's life and work has challenged his thesis. Because the charge is so grave, it is essential to go through Thomas Pakenham's evidence in detail.

He starts his account of what he calls 'Baden-Powell's version of the miracle of the loaves and fishes' with Stephe's rough stocktaking of 14 November. Assuming a population of 1,708 whites and 7,500 blacks (both figures including women and children), Baden-Powell estimated that he had enough cereal stocks to feed his adult whites for 134 days and his adult blacks for fifteen. He arrived at these figures by ignoring live meat and 180,000 lbs of tinned meat, and by allocating 188,100 lbs of meal and flour to the whites, and 109,100 lbs of Kaffir corn and mealies (the twin staples of the local African diet) to the blacks. He did not mean that there would be no food left for the blacks after fifteen days; nor even that there would then be no cereal food left. Baden-Powell's figures were based on the stocks which he was informed were held by the town's principal white merchants and by the Army Service Corps; they did not include food in private hands which, in the case of the Africans and the white small traders, was a great deal. According to Thomas Pakenham, these calculations show that Baden-Powell was proposing to feed the greater proportion of Mafeking's population with a scandalously small share of the available supplies. Baden-Powell managed to prevent starvation among the

Africans, Pakenham argues, only by feeding them part of the horses' grain and oats. This is extremely misleading because Baden-Powell did not actually feed any ground oats to anyone for several months.[3] So if, as Pakenham implies, they were left relying upon the 109,100 lbs of Kaffir corn and mealies listed on 14 November, very large numbers of them would have starved long before the New Year. This did not happen for three excellent reasons: first, there were other food supplies in the native stadt; second, Baden-Powell's 14 November figures massively underestimated the whole town's actual supplies; third, by 22 November he had decided not to restrict the flour *and* the meal to the whites, but to issue the flour to the whites and the meal, as well as the Kaffir corn and mealies, to the blacks.[4]

Thomas Pakenham gives little credence to Baden-Powell's firmly held belief that the Barolongs in the stadt had food supplies of their own. Yet this proved to be so in early January (over two and a half months into the Siege), when Baden-Powell decided to take over all bulk food supplies then in private hands (both black and white). Hitherto he had merely instructed merchants and shopkeepers to furnish him with details of their stocks and to sell no more than a given quantity of flour or meal at a fixed price to any one person in a single day. Whites had been able to buy 1 lb of bread, and blacks 1 lb of meal.[5] But on 2 January Baden-Powell's Commissariat Officer, Captain C. M. Ryan, published a General Order tightening these regulations and restricting the sale of any kind of grain to three stores: one in the stadt, one in the Fingo Location and one in the white town;[6] simultaneously he began collecting grain in the stadt. Ryan's officials understandably met with considerable mistrust.[7] Baden-Powell's intention was to reduce 'wastage' (such as the fermenting of grain for beer) and to slow down the rate of consumption by issuing all breadstuffs and grain as rations. People found holding back grain were taken before the local court and sentenced to a week's hard labour.[8]

Ryan's searches also extended to the white town, where he raided a number of small traders and some Indian shops. He found not only large quantities of undeclared grain, but also illicit bread being baked. His haul included an entire wagonload of meal.[9] In the stadt and the Fingo Location similar discoveries were made, but much was still held back. Sol Plaatje (who helped the Civil Commissioner explain the purpose of rationing to the Barolongs and Fingoes), noted on 5 January that when the chiefs supervised the search, as they did in the Location, the Commissariat officers deluded themselves by supposing that, 'when the chiefs search a hut they take away the last crumb they find in the possession of the owners, who would henceforth survive on what they purchase economically from the store'.[10] Nor was grain the only foodstuff to be found in the stadt. As late as 27 February, Sergeant Hoskings of the Protectorate Regiment recorded hearing that 'mealies were obtainable somewhere in the stadt'. After going through the township 'like a detective', he and another sergeant 'found the place, so secretly preserved by the cunning ones, and bought mealies at 2/- per dozen . . . Three days afterwards we did the same trick again and got another dozen and a half.'[11]

Hoskings's experience establishes something else which Pakenham did not take into account, but which Baden-Powell knew to be true, namely that a high percentage of the resident black population grew their own food. The whites on the other hand – many of whom were employed by the railway or as clerks – did not on the whole have the same direct access to their own food supplies, but depended upon what they bought on a daily basis from the town's shops.

There was another vitally important advantage (ignored by Pakenham) which the Africans had over the whites: they possessed large numbers of cattle, which to them represented not only food but wealth, status and the necessary coin with which to fulfil important social obligations such as the payment of lobola or bride price. The Civil Commissioner, Charles Bell, who in normal times was in charge of African welfare and was a humane man, was adamant that the native cattle should not be commandeered. Baden-Powell was sensible enough to take his advice.[12] As they ate their beasts, the Africans partially replenished their diminishing herds by raiding the Boers' cattle and sheep. It is impossible to say how many beasts were brought in. Direct reference to 144 can be found, but 200 is probably nearer the mark.[13] The success of cattle raiding is plain to see in Baden-Powell's records of the town's animal population. Between 18 March and 1 April, by which time live meat had long since replaced bread, meal and grain as the basic foodstuff for blacks and whites, the town's 600 oxen and calves only declined to 579. This was solely due to the African cattle raiders' brilliant exploits. At the outset Baden-Powell had made it clear that the Commissariat would not expect to purchase more than a quarter of the cattle brought in and would not commandeer any.[14] In March he began to worry about the dozen or so cattle being killed for food every day in the stadt, but still he did not do anything about it.[15] He only acted in April, a month before the Siege was raised, after a fortnight of what he justifiably called 'abnormal animal consumption' when 283 beasts of all kinds were killed. 'I therefore ordered that all animals should be registered and branded and owners should have to account for them when called upon . . .'[16] Because of the very high black market prices obtainable for cattle by this date, animals still tended to 'stray' even after this order was promulgated.

Pakenham seems to have ignored the Barolongs' cattle because he assumed that when Baden-Powell wrote on 14 November, 'Supplies: Meat plentiful live and tinned 180,000 lbs,' this figure included both live animals and tinned meat. But this was definitely not what was meant. On 4 March, four and a half months into the Siege, Baden-Powell calculated Mafeking's live meat (most of it in African ownership) at 279,320 lbs, which did not include 500 Government horses and almost 1,000 sheep. The total for live meat on 14 November would therefore have been in the region of 600,000 lbs – a very different figure from 180,000 lbs.[17] In fact the 180,000 lbs had even been a massive underestimate for tinned meat alone. After two and a half months of unrestricted purchase of tinned goods, Baden-Powell estimated tinned meat at 161,600 lbs.[18]

Benjamin Weil bore a large measure of responsibility for the confused state of affairs in connection with grain, breadstuffs and preserved foods of all sorts. 'His duplicity,' Baden-Powell wrote on 15 February, 'has been a constant annoyance if not a danger.'[19] Edward Ross thought that Weil deliberately underestimated supplies at the outset so that he could charge more for the luxuries which the whites were consequently obliged to buy to supplement their rations, which Baden-Powell had calculated on the basis of Weil's estimate of his stocks. There was also corruption in the Commissariat; and the senior N.C.O., the aptly-named Sergeant-Major Looney, sold Government supplies to his friends. He was dismissed from the service, lost his pension rights and was sentenced to five years' hard labour.[20] Apart from miscalculations caused by theft and sharp practice, inadequate stocktaking methods and negligence led to the unexpected appearance of additional supplies. Such discoveries made nonsense of earlier estimates. Baden-Powell's tally for Commissariat oats was 218,486 lbs on 20 March; two weeks later it had actually *risen* to 230,421 lbs.[21] This rise occurred shortly after he had started to issue to the entire garrison a porridge known as 'sowens', made from fermented oats. Another unexpected windfall explains a further increase in the oat tally during the third week of April. This was brought about by the discovery of 8,000 lbs in one of the British South Africa Police's store-rooms on 21 April.[22] Earlier stocktaking had somehow missed this hoard. Baden-Powell also noticed increases in the quantity of oats in store during March, which had nothing to do with unexpected finds. Captain Ryan, the Commissariat Officer, allowed for a 12 per cent level of loss through waste and deterioration, but when the actual loss was a mere one or two per cent he neglected to record this in his figures. This led to discrepancies of approximately 4,000 lbs per month. Such fluctuations made it extremely difficult for Baden-Powell to plan ahead, and they make it much harder for historians to judge the merits of his food policy.

Occasionally errors of the opposite kind occurred. On 4 March Baden-Powell was horrified to discover that Weil, who usually underestimated his stocks, had massively overestimated the quantity of oats he had in store. Since he was by then grinding oats to make flour for both whites and blacks, the news that Weil had 75,000 lbs[23] less oats than he had thought was extremely frightening. Baden-Powell felt much happier when he had taken rationing out of Weil's hands and had started to operate a more 'satisfactory and economical' system of control.[24]

After the Siege ended, the Town Council stated that in their opinion: 'The officer commanding would have done wisely had he right at the start taken over the whole of the foodstuffs and distributed the same in rations. Had this course been adopted the whole garrison would have shared equally and fairly and the stores would not have been wasted, as they were, in the first two or three months of the siege.' They blamed him for not taking all the town's cattle into Government ownership until the beginning of May, when the Siege had almost ended. However, Baden-Powell had been advised against taking this very step by the town's two most knowledgeable civil servants, Major Goold-Adams and Charles Bell. The Town Council was also hypocritical to blame him retrospectively for failing to begin rationing early enough. When, on 21 January, he had finally forbidden the stores to sell luxuries to anyone (since all supplies were to be taken over by the authorities and issued as rations),[25] many of the townspeople – including a number of councillors – had objected furiously. Baden-Powell had been obliged to arrest Mafeking's leading attorney, Mr J. W. de Kock, for telling merchants that the authorities had no right to impound stocks or to interfere with their free sale. Two deputations of outraged citizens then demanded that Baden-Powell release the lawyer.[26]

Baden-Powell behaved as most commanders would have done: he approached his problems cautiously in an ad hoc manner, only risking causing serious offence when the gravity of the supply position gave him no choice. Without the full support of the white Town Guard and the black defenders of the stadt, Mafeking would have fallen. Baden-Powell's desire to impose draconian solutions had always been limited by his dependence upon the goodwill of the people. He had never been in the happy position of a military commander of regular troops able to rely upon their unquestioning loyalty; only a dozen of his officers were regulars, and his men were volunteers or, as in the case of the Town Guard, civilians.

Thomas Pakenham is of course perfectly right in stating that Baden-Powell gave priority to the maintenance of white rations at a comfortable level, but that does *not* mean that he imposed a starvation diet on the blacks. Pakenham's belief that Baden-Powell stole the Africans' food and then sold it back to them is mistaken. On 15 November, Baden-Powell made it clear that he intended 'to buy up all Native food meal at a reasonable rate, and to resell it to the natives, thus keeping the price within their means and checking the issue'.[27]

More serious is Mr Pakenham's accusation that Baden-Powell denied many Africans any food at all, thereby killing large numbers of them. In the days before the town was surrounded, 2,000 black refugees sought refuge there and asked for British protection. These were the people Pakenham has accused Baden-Powell of starving and who, according to Angus Hamilton, ought to have been sent back to the Transvaal before the Siege started instead of being allowed to stay.[28]

The refugees have been incorrectly described by Thomas Pakenham as being mostly local Barolongs who had been driven from their kraals a few miles outside Mafeking. (The distinction is not an academic one since, as will be seen, a misconception concerning it flaws Pakenham's whole argument.) Several hundreds were indeed district Barolongs, but the vast majority, stated Sol Plaatje, were from farther afield: 'Bangwaketse, Bakwena, Zulus, Zambesians and Shangaans'.[29] (The Shangaans, who would suffer more than any other group, were members of a Tsonga people from southern Mozambique and had been migrant mine workers on the Rand before fleeing on the outbreak of hostilities.)

Before going on to describe the 'leave here or starve here' policy which Pakenham claims Baden-Powell visited upon these refugees, it is necessary to relate how he explains Baden-Powell's supposed decision to implement such a callous plan. He declares that suddenly, on 8 February 1900, Baden-Powell changed the entire basis of his rationing strategy. 'The reason was that an ingenious baker had found how to grind the horses' oats to make flour.'[30] So Baden-Powell decided, asserts Pakenham, 'to expel' part of the black population in order to secure for the whites the oats previously set aside for the blacks. He advances no other reason why he might have performed such a surprising volte face. Yet in Baden-Powell's Staff Diary the entry for 8 February contains the following: 'C.S.O. [Lord Kitchener, Chief Staff Officer to Lord Roberts] asks us to make supplies last 4 months i.e. to 21 May.' On 30 January Baden-Powell had fondly imagined that he would not have to hold out beyond early April. Kitchener's telegram had been sent on 21 January, so now Baden-Powell could not expect relief before 21 May. Given the unpredictable nature of all military operations, he had to add another couple of weeks as a margin of error. At a stroke he was faced with the near certainty that four more months, rather than two, would have to be endured in Mafeking; this then was the reason why he suddenly decided to change his feeding policy, not any discovery by an ingenious baker. Baden-Powell had known that oats could be ground into a kind of flour since 1 January.

The text of Kitchener's telegram ran: 'Endeavour to make supplies last four months. Send as many women, children and natives as possible away should opportunity offer.'[31] So Baden-Powell wrote in his Staff Diary the following words, which Pakenham quotes without mentioning Kitchener or new orders:

> February 8th: I propose therefore to try to get all the refugee and foreign natives to leave the place by laying down stock [of food] through Col. Plumer at Kanya [the British force now seventy miles away in Bechuanaland]: and stopping the sale in the town. The amount thereby saved, eked out with occasional issues of meat, should keep the local Barolongs and defence natives; the others could break out on stormy nights and make their way to Kanya.

Baden-Powell discussed the situation with Charles Bell who, as Civil Commissioner, was responsible for native welfare. Bell agreed that they now had no choice but to 'persuade a couple of thousand refugees to leave the place in order to be able to feed the legitimate native inhabitants [i.e. the Barolongs in the stadt] for a much longer period.'[32] Sol Plaatje agreed with Bell that if the refugees thought they could pass through the Boer lines unscathed many would be 'only too pleased to go to Kanya and leave this beleaguered place'.[33]

Baden-Powell had no intention of sending any Africans away from Mafeking without first establishing staging-posts where they could be fed. Two days after receiving Kitchener's order, Baden-Powell wrote to Plumer asking him to push supplies of food to Moshwane, only 45 miles from Mafeking, in order to 'encourage our natives to escape'.[34] He also wrote to Chief Bathoen at Kanya asking him to assist the refugees.[35] Baden-Powell then addressed himself to the problem of getting the refugees to leave and decided that there would have to be an element of coercion. If he gave advance warning of the closure of the town's grain shops on a specified day, he reckoned that large numbers would decide to go beforehand. They would have been fed until the date of their departure and so, he hoped, would be fit enough to walk 45 miles. On 11 February he announced that the refugees would not be served grain after the 20th. Unfortunately most of them were still there on 19 February despite Mr Bell's impassioned speeches explaining the advantages of leaving.

On 21 February 38 refugees managed to get safely past the Boers, and another 30 succeeded the following night. For the next ten days between 10 and 20 got away each night. Sadly, this was a case of too few too late. Already some refugees were very enfeebled. By the 23rd Baden-Powell had learned about the Siege's first three deaths from starvation.[36] Several cases of malnutrition had been noted before, but only now did Baden-Powell realize that one refugee group (the Shangaans) were in dire straits – not because of the recent closures, but because the resident Barolongs had ostracized them, and because the sprawling wasteland around the town had concealed their suffering.

Before closing any shop, Baden-Powell had secretly promised not to persist long with the experiment. On the 15th Charles Bell had urged him to feed the refugees on rations until the day of their departure.[37] Baden-Powell wrote: 'I don't see how we can feed them and at the same time persuade them to go. However, whatever you say, that will I do.'[38] Furthermore the very day on which he had closed the grain stores to the refugees, Baden-Powell opened a soup kitchen producing 'a very good looking mess of meal, horse and mule'. Bell noted that the most appreciative customers were the Shangaans, who made up roughly a quarter of the refugee population.[39] By 23 February Baden-Powell had decided that all women and children would be fed, whether refugees or not, and that soup should be 'free for those in need'.[40] His decision had been opposed by his Chief Commissariat Officer, Captain Ryan.[41]

By the end of February a free soup kitchen had been opened in the stadt as well, and was dispensing 'a gratis issue to the paupers and starving people'.[42] In late March J. R. Algie, the Town Clerk, recorded the numbers of paying and free tickets issued at four of the town's soup kitchens on an average day. They were as follows: 'Williams' [supervised by Captain A. P. W. Williams] Soup Kitchen, 402 paying tickets, 133 free tickets. Town Soup Kitchen, 530 paying, 1,000 free. Marsh's [supervised by Captain F. W. Marsh] 80 paying, 121 free. Massini's Soup Kitchen, 300 paying, 250 free.' Although Pakenham claimed that 'the Africans were all made to pay, and pay handsomely for their food', Algie's figures make it clear that Baden-Powell provided free soup for at least 1,500 people per day.[43] Algie thought *all* the soup should be provided free, but Baden-Powell was his mother's son in disagreeing – taught from early childhood to note down every item of expenditure. His brother George was the author of *State Aid and State Interference*, an attack on all forms of subsidy. Although Baden-Powell wished to save the British Government as much money as possible, his letters to Bell and Vyvyan show that he never acted precipitately over matters of feeding.

On 27 February, having heard from Chief Bathoen that he had sent men to Korwe – only 30 miles away – to help the refugees, Baden-Powell sanctioned the most ambitious attempt yet to guide out a party of refugees through the Boer lines. Two days earlier only half the members of a party of 60 had managed to get through; two women had been shot and several others whipped.[44] This failure shocked the authorities but did not persuade them to think again. From dawn on the 27th Sol Plaatje and Bell were out on horseback gathering together about 900 refugees. They were each given a piece of horsemeat or donkey, and were led out through the western defences by Sergeant Abrams of the stadt guard and twelve of his men. Because of an inexplicable misunderstanding, two detachments from the Protectorate Regiment did not turn up on time. This was disastrous, since twelve men would not be enough to protect the refugees and to keep them moving in a quiet and orderly group. When they passed through the Boer cordon, some distant shots frightened them and a large group started to run back, inducing the rest to panic. A second attempt later that night was also unsuccessful and Plaatje was bitterly disappointed. 'This is a matter of such sweeping importance as puts all other questions in the dark . . . and a serious blow to me particularly taking into consideration that I had been on horseback from early till late during the last two days – and all that for "niks".'[45] It is noteworthy that Plaatje, who went on to become the first Secretary of the African National Congress, was never outraged by this attempt to get rid of the refugees.

Baden-Powell learned the lesson of this failure and not only decided never again to attempt to convoy out so many people, but resolved to keep and feed any refugee who wished to stay. On 6 March he abandoned what might be called his exodus policy. 'Unable to get refugees out,' he told Plumer. 'They are now too weak from hunger, but I hope to feed all on soup till May.'[46] In fact when Africans did start to leave Mafeking again, it would have nothing to do with Baden-Powell or his staff. The numbers of the besieging Boers dropped sharply in mid-March (when several hundred of them left to oppose Plumer's southward march). Consequently many Barolong women from the stadt were able to leave the town and visit their fields beyond the defence perimeter without molestation. They brought back with them wild melons and Kaffir corn, and what they said about the thinly held Boer trenches encouraged a wave of new departures for Kanya and Moshwane. On 14 March Bell noticed natives streaming away from the stadt, and three days later Plaatje was astonished to discover that many Shangaans and Zambesians were leaving each night.[47]

An event which accelerated the process was the clandestine arrival in Mafeking of Lieutenant F. Smitheman, Colonel Plumer's Intelligence Officer. Smitheman had come in principally to confer with Baden-Powell about the most effective way in which the Rhodesia Regiment could tactically combine with the Mafeking garrison. But on 7 April he went to the stadt and during a memorable meeting 'persuaded the Barolongs' Queen Mother and consequently most of the Barolong women to leave Mafeking for Kanya immediately'.[48] A party of 200 Barolong women and children including the chief's wife and family reached Kanya on 13 April.[49] Many servant boys also left their employers without a word of warning and went to Kanya. This happened to Charles Weir, a clerk in the local Standard Bank.[50] Major Baillie's boy one day disgustedly tossed away his ration of horsemeat and oat biscuit and left the town.[51] Alick Godley's servant had gone a month earlier. On 2 May Plumer reported having received 1,210

Africans from Mafeking, and during the same week Bell observed that three quarters of the population of the stadt had gone. Many did not go to Kanya, but to other destinations.[52] Bell noticed that those remaining in Mafeking were principally refugees, while those who had gone were mainly Barolongs. 'They have greater courage and more intelligence than the others and took the earliest opportunity of getting out of this death trap.'[53] Almost all the Barolong women had gone by the end of April. The food crisis was over, solved by voluntary migration and not by forced expulsion. The Barolongs were as brave as Bell had suggested. On 8 April, 700 women from the stadt had been turned back by the Boers and some had been beaten. Ten days later, nine women were shot, but neither of these disasters stemmed the departures, which were at once resumed.[54]

Only when it is understood how well the Mafeking Barolongs coped with the privations of the Siege is it possible to form an opinion about the justice of Thomas Pakenham's claim that Baden-Powell starved the African refugees. A passage upon which Mr Pakenham places great reliance is taken from J. Emerson Neilly's book, *Besieged with Baden-Powell*. Neilly, it will be remembered, like Hamilton, had fallen foul of Baden-Powell early in the Siege. In the passage in question which is extensively quoted by Pakenham, Neilly referred to 'hundreds dying from starvation or the diseases that always accompany famine', and went on, 'certain it is that many were found dead on the veldt'.[55] The passage is not dated so cannot be checked against other sources; but the suggestion that large numbers of Africans who had been urged to leave the town were allowed to collapse and die within sight of the defence works seems improbable. When on 17 March Baden-Powell learned from the town's Principal Medical Officer that 'several natives are in a state of starvation, and a large number with dysentery', his immediate response was to send an urgent order to Bell: 'The starving ought to be collected without delay [Baden-Powell's underlining] and placed in the Cape Police stable so they can be fed.'[56]

Neilly cannot, however, be blamed for the way in which Thomas Pakenham changes the meaning of what he actually wrote. As a result of two substantial omissions from the original passage, Pakenham not only places the blame for the painful scenes described by Neilly on Baden-Powell (which Neilly had gone out of his way not to do), but also makes out that the heartrending lines of starving Africans so vividly depicted by Neilly had been Barolongs and not members of the most unfortunate sub-group within the refugee community. The first omission, although placing the blame for the death of many African male children on their parents (rather than on Baden-Powell), is not nearly as important as the second. So I intend first to give the Neilly passage exactly as quoted by Pakenham, only indicating with three asterisks where the vital second omission occurs. Then I will supply the missing sentences. Thomas Pakenham introduces the quote with a statement to the effect that Neilly 'was apparently writing of the five thousand Africans fortunate enough to be allowed rations by B-P'.[57]

> I saw them fall down on the veldt and lie where they had fallen, too weak to go on their way. The sufferers were mostly little boys – mere infants ranging from four or five upwards . . . Hunger had them in its grip, and many of them were black spectres and living skeletons . . . their ribs literally breaking their shrivelled skin – men, women and children . . . Probably hundreds died from starvation or the diseases that always accompany famine. Certain it is that many were found dead on the veldt . . . *** words could not portray the scene of misery; five or six hundred human frameworks of both sexes and all ages . . . dressed in . . . tattered rags, standing in lines, each holding an old blackened can or beef tin, awaiting turn to crawl painfully up to the soup kitchen where the food was distributed.[58]

These are the omitted words:

> [Certain it is that many were found dead on the veldt], and others succumbed to hunger in the hospital. The Barolongs proper were not so badly off; the least fortunate were the strange Kaffirs who came in from the Transvaal as refugees when the war started, and the slaves and servants of the Barolong nation. When the Colonel got to know of the state of affairs he instituted soup kitchens, where horses were boiled in huge cauldrons, and the savoury mess doled out in pints and quarts to all comers. Some of the people – those employed on works – paid for the food; the remainder, who were in the majority, obtained it free. One of those kitchens was established in the stadt, and I several times went down there to see the unfortunate fed. [Words could not . . .].[59]

The omitted material makes it clear beyond a doubt that Neilly had not been referring to the 5,000 Barolongs as claimed by Pakenham, but to the refugees (particularly those from the Transvaal: the Shangaans) who were plainly being given free soup. The sentences cut from this Neilly quotation make it absolutely plain that nobody in need was being denied food by Baden-Powell. Yet Mr Pakenham claims that 2,000 people were denied food altogether.

This may seem much ado about one historian's account of Baden-Powell's rationing policy, and indeed it would be if four other scholars in recent years had not quoted extracts from Pakenham's account without challenging his basic premises.[60] One of these historians quoted from the same pages of Neilly, omitting the same crucial passage and stating that Neilly was 'writing of the plight of those natives able to procure rations, as opposed to those excluded from food entirely'.[61] It is easy to see how a damaging falsehood acquires the appearance of unassailable truth by repetition over the years.

If Pakenham and his followers had merely claimed that Baden-Powell was not even-handed in his allocation of food to the different races in the town, I would agree. There is, however, an enormous difference between saying that and accusing him of deliberately excluding starving people from food. Two days after penning his harrowing description of the most needy refugees, Neilly (in a passage I have not seen quoted elsewhere) addressed himself to the problem facing Baden-Powell and his staff.

> When the Government free-food scheme got into swing, the distress was somewhat diminished, but it never died out. Some 'grousing' critics in town who could see no good in anything raised a how-do-you-do, and laid the blame of the famine upon the authorities, and would rightly or wrongly have the Colonel kill our few ill-fed beeves and give them to the blacks and allow them to have a daily share of the white rations, which were barely enough to keep us going. Had this intelligent idea been acted upon, the entire food supply would have given out in a few weeks, and we would have either died of starvation in the works or surrendered and been marched as prisoners of war to Pretoria . . . It is only right for me to explain in the interests of the name of the authorities that everything that was possible was done to alleviate distress as soon as it was found to exist.[62]

The 'grousers' mentioned by Neilly did not go unnoticed by Baden-Powell who remarked on 13 March:

> Some of the local agitators have now begun to charge us with neglecting our natives. There were four deaths yesterday from 'exposure and starvation'. We have between 6,000 and 7,000 natives here, of whom nearly 2,000 are refugees from outside. Of these 1,300 are paid or rationed:
> 286 cattle guards, watchmen on pay and rations
> 300 ditto on rations only
> 200 to 300 defence labourers pay and rations
> 500 private servants.[63]

This left approximately 700 refugees entirely reliant on the soup kitchens, but the day after Baden-Powell had made the above estimate Sol Plaatje reckoned that a substantial number of these refugees were setting out for Kanya. Some, however, stayed behind. As late as 21 April Charles Bell bemoaned the fact that there were still cases of starvation. 'There are people belonging to the refugee class who have been too stupid to find out where they can apply for relief, and are discovered when it is already too late. We are doing all we can for this class and those we get hold of in time are at least kept alive.'[64]

Bell was not alone in expressing exasperation that some of the refugees were failing to get sustenance. 'B-P has done everything he could to alleviate distress among the natives, none of whom need now starve,' wrote Ross, 'if they are not too lazy to walk as far as the horsemeat soup kitchens.'[65] On 15 April Major Baillie confirmed that: 'The feeding of the natives . . . is practically solved, except in the case of the Shangaans.' Almost all of the 30 people gathered to be fed in the Cape Police's stables, under Baden-Powell's orders, were Shangaans.[66] Ada Cock, a young mother living near the Women's Laager, was afraid to let her children near any of these migrant mineworkers from Johannesburg after it was rumoured that they had eaten the corpse of one of their number. The Shangaans dug up the bodies of dogs and ate them and were constantly on the look-out for any opportunity to snare an unwary pet.[67] The reason for their plight was not, however, either stupidity or any animosity towards them on the part of the Commissariat. Baillie put his finger on the real problem. 'These unfortunate devils,' he wrote, 'are detested by the other natives, and consequently it is very hard to look after them properly . . . so much is this so that on Mr Vere Stent ordering his Basuto servant to make some soup for a starving Shangaan he had picked up, the Basuto indignantly protested.'[68] Virtually every diary which deals in detail with the feeding problem confirms that starvation was almost entirely confined to the Shangaan population.[69] So less than a quarter of the 2,000 refugees* were at risk from starvation and a good many of those left Mafeking voluntarily during March and April with the Barolongs. Given the wealth of evidence confirming that the local and district Barolongs as well as all other native groups were fed, it is hard to understand how the entirely erroneous idea that 5,000 Africans were living on the brink of starvation in Mafeking during the Siege has persisted unrefuted for over a decade.

It is impossible to form an accurate estimate of how many blacks did die of starvation in Mafeking. The only statistics for African deaths lump them together for all causes including shell-fire. The largest figure quoted is 1,000 published by the Town Council;[70] the Cape Blue Book recorded a total of 478 deaths;[71] and Hanbury-Tracy, normally the most reliable staff source, estimated total deaths to have been 333.[72] I am inclined to think that the Town Council's figure was too high (it was given in an official letter complaining about Baden-Powell's failure to give the residents sufficient credit for the success of the defence). I would hazard that a figure of about 700 would be nearer the mark – with a large proportion dying of disease (rather than

* That is Plaatje's estimate.

starvation), and most of these being babies and young children. Dysentery was rife in the town from February onwards. An outbreak of diphtheria in the stadt claimed a number of young victims and there were many cases of typhoid and malaria admitted to the hospital in March and April.[73] If Baden-Powell is to be blamed for African deaths in Mafeking, by the same logic the civil authorities in British India should be censured for failing to prevent starvation in particular districts of the subcontinent. At this date deaths from malnutrition were not uncommon among children in London. Many of the whites in Mafeking were far from indifferent to the fate of the Shangaans. Charles Weir, the bank clerk, used to save a quarter of his meat ration so that he might 'be able to satisfy some poor creature'.[74] Although Bell was doing everything he could to organize a fair and effective system of rationing (issuing free passes and so forth), he felt the same guilt and impotence experienced by the average citizen when confronted with starving people. 'My yard is always filled with natives, who come in connection with their food supply: one man, a tall thin fellow, past fifty, when I was busy with other people about sunset, reclined on his back and proceeded to die of starvation. It was a beastly business and most unpleasant, but what can one do?'[75] He could imagine the queues that would form at his door if he were to feed those who called.

The Africans were not treated with deliberate cruelty; but did the whites enjoy a life of luxury as Brian Gardner has suggested, but which many white diarists contradict? Baden-Powell later gave out that the white adult male daily rations at the end of the Siege were ¾–1 lb of meat, 5 oz of bread, 6 oz of vegetables and minute quantities of tea, sugar and coffee. From April a quart of bitter porridge made with fermented oats was added.[76] He was proud of these rations and would have been surprised to learn that later critics should have held up these figures as an example of his meanness to the Africans.[77] In reality Baden-Powell's version of average white male rations greatly overstated what was available. In April, one white family with four children was receiving 6 lbs of corn beef and 6 lbs of almost inedible husk-filled oatmeal *per week* and no regular vegetables.[78] Even the privileged members of the Protectorate Regiment and the Town Guard ate fresh meat only once or twice a week, and then their measure contained a good deal of bone. Cattle and horses which had been starved of forage did not produce succulent cuts.[79] Even the resourceful Sergeant Hoskings, who had been on so many forays to the stadt in search of black market food to supplement his rations, had lost a stone in weight by early March and would lose more before the Siege ended.[80] Sol Plaatje, whose employment guaranteed him the full white ration, found that food had nevertheless become for him, as for all others on rations, 'one of the greatest desires of a man's dreams – on it he would spend all his money if he could'.[81]

The principal deficiency in the whites' diet was the absence of bread and filling vegetables like potatoes. During the Second World War in Britain, bread and vegetables were never rationed and people could fill up with them. The Mafeking garrison had no such opportunity. Mr H. Martin, a member of the local Chamber of Commerce, felt hungry all the time, 'particularly after having finished my dinner. We just get enough to make us feel hungry and that is all.'[82] After the stores had been forbidden to sell luxuries in late January, there had been only very occasional opportunities for whites to supplement their rations, as for example on 25 February when Weil was allowed to open for a few hours and sell up to 12 shillings' worth of items to members of the Protectorate Regiment.[83] Vegetables, according to Baden-Powell's figures, were supposed to be available every day, but in practice, as Charles Weir knew very well, he was lucky to get 'some marrows or green mealies once or twice a week'.[84]

On 20 April Baden-Powell received another bombshell from Lord Roberts, this one ordering him to make his supplies 'last longer than the date named [i.e. 18 May]'.[85] In replying, Baden-Powell said he would endeavour to hold out until the end of May. 'The great thing for us is to know specific dates as we can then adapt our arrangements to suit.'[86] Roberts's vagueness left Stephe wondering whether he might one day have to choose between surrender or forcing out the stadt's few remaining Africans to secure their rations. (A day later he decided that *in extremis* he would rather evacuate the garrison.)* Fortunately, for the present he was able to make sausages from the garrison's starving horses. These were added to white and black rations from 18 April.[87]

April was nevertheless a testing month for the garrison. Nurse Craufurd attributed a lot of the illness in the town to the ration bread. 'It is flat, round buns of brown husky stuff, so hard that it has to be broken with a hammer.'[88] Ada Cock called lumps of this composite bread 'dog biscuits'. 'My rations today,' she wrote on 23 April, 'were two dog biscuits and a piece of horse sausage.' She preferred these rock-hard items (which could be cooked in a horsemeat stew) to the kind of bun made out of oats which she received more often. 'It is very bad to eat as it gives some inflammation of the inside. The long spike-like husks of the oats and a lot of downy looking stuff I grind in the sausage machine and sift there. I use it to thicken the soup.'[89] After a meal of this bread, Ross had to 'pick the sharp pointed pieces out of my gums with a pair of tweezers'. He was also consuming brawn made from horses' hides and heads, and suggested that 'everything in the place has been eaten except horseshoes and barbed wire'.[90] Ada Cock, with her 6 lbs of corned beef per week and her 6 lbs of inedible oatmeal per week for herself *and* her four children, would have been surprised

* See p. 291.

by the way later historians used the Mafeking Hotel's impressive Christmas Menu to imply that such titbits were obtainable throughout the Siege.[91] She was perhaps exaggerating when stating in April that some of the whites in the town were 'on the verge of starvation';[92] but by then Angus Hamilton had reported how hunger was driving people to mix violet face powder with their oatmeal porridge to thicken it. 'If the truth be told,' he admitted on 30 April, 'our plight is quite sufficiently serious.'[93] It is puzzling to read a historian's recent statement that 'food for the whites in Mafeking was never really in short supply'.[94]

Baden-Powell's injustice to the Africans has also been said to extend to the few capital sentences imposed upon blacks by the Court of Summary Jurisdiction. Six Africans were shot for crimes committed during the Siege and these executions, according to Michael Rosenthal, show that Baden-Powell's justice was as weighted against the Africans as his food policy. Angus Hamilton, for once, fully supported the official line. In his opinion the execution of one African, who had been proved to have been on spying missions for the Boers, was entirely justified. 'His instructions had been remarkably explicit, and the sphere of his activities embraced our entire position . . . there remained no alternative but that which implied immediate execution.' Hamilton also approved of the execution of another African who had been sent by the Boers to spread false information.[95] Although Baden-Powell has been blamed for the executions, and he certainly had to confirm the warrants, the suspects were brought before a Court of Summary Jurisdiction which usually sat under the Presidency of Charles Bell, who was Resident Magistrate as well as Civil Commissioner; or of Lord Edward Cecil, the Chief Staff Officer. The other officers who sat from time to time were Colonels Vyvyan and Hore and Major Panzera.

Baden-Powell himself never presided over the court or sentenced anyone. Charles Bell was a just and conscientious man, completely uninfluenced by spy fever. 'There is very little evidence against the supposed spy,' he wrote to Cecil in a typical letter. 'I propose to send him to the stadt to be examined by the Chief's Council.'[96] Often a brief chat with a suspect would convince Bell of his innocence.[97] There was no real doubt that the three men executed for spying had been sent into Mafeking by the Boers. The three other capital sentences were for theft. When a man convicted of housebreaking went before a firing squad on 20 December, Ross noted: 'This sounds very severe, but as the whole town is left unprotected, and most places are with openings made by the enemy's shells, something must be done to stop this.'[98] According to Ross nobody was ever shot for a first conviction, but he did think 50 lashes an extraordinarily harsh punishment for first offenders given the food situation.[99] The African shot on 2 April for stealing a goat had stolen animals twice before, and had been 'turned out of the place and told not to return on pain of death'.[100] The most unfortunate condemned man was a horse thief who was caught in the act of stealing a stallion belonging to Silas Molema, the most influential Barolong headman, at a time when there had been a spate of thefts of horses including several belonging to the Protectorate Regiment.[101] Animal stealing was then so prevalent that Ada Cock always slept with a loaded revolver close to hand in order to defend her remaining cow. That such thefts were inspired by terrible hunger makes severe punishment seem barbarous. At the time, all the whites and many of the Barolongs felt that unless severe punishments were inflicted no people and no property would be safe. Colonel Hore proved himself the most merciful of the Court's Presidents when he threw out the case against a Shangaan accused of stealing a horse, accepting the man's defence which was that he had been living only on 'thepe' (a kind of spinach). Hore then delivered a scathing attack on 'the soup kitchen people' for failing to feed him.[102]

It is undoubtedly true that although there were plenty of whites suspected of being Boer sympathizers, none was executed. As in the case of the Irish station master, Quinlan, there was insufficient evidence to proceed. At the end of the Siege the Irishman was still in prison waiting to be sent back to England for further examination by the civil authorities.[103] Editions of the *Mafeking Mail* for 21, 22 and 23 November carried reports of a white man being fined for stealing from a black and mentioned the cases of six white Boer sympathizers remanded on suspicion of being spies. But whereas, when an African was caught beyond the lines without a pass his guilt seemed highly probable (especially if he was unknown in the stadt), it was much harder to establish the identity of white men secretly paying Africans to take out messages to the Boers. About 30 whites remained in custody for the whole Siege without being charged.

The one white man who should have been shot was Sergeant-Major Looney, the Commissariat Warrant Officer who was dismissed from the service for black marketeering. Michael Rosenthal rebukes Baden-Powell for failing to bring to justice Lieutenant K. Murchison, the Protectorate Regiment's brilliant gunnery officer, who murdered Mr E. G. Parslow of the *Morning Chronicle* after a drunken argument. 'Murchison was condemned to death,' writes Rosenthal, 'but was later released entirely because of his good work in the town's defence.' (This is another of Mr Rosenthal's debts to Thomas Pakenham.)[104] In fact Murchison was released only for a day, when his particular skills were badly needed by the garrison, who were facing several hundred Boers attacking from within the stadt. After the crisis had passed, Murchison was re-arrested. He had been condemned to death by the Court of Summary Jurisdiction and this sentence had been confirmed by Baden-Powell. Various members of the garrison, however, had noticed that Murchison had sometimes seemed unstable. Major

Baillie, who knew him better than most, 'did not consider him responsible for his actions'. When aware that such opinions were widespread, Baden-Powell very properly informed Lord Roberts and recommended that Murchison be shown clemency. It was subsequently discovered that he had been compulsorily retired from the army when serving in India, on account of uncontrollable fits of anger and persecution mania. Lord Roberts therefore commuted Murchison's sentence to penal servitude for life. When the Siege was raised, Murchison was repatriated and at first committed to Parkhurst Prison. On 12 August 1902 he was admitted to Broadmoor Asylum, where records show that until his death in 1917, he was a very disturbed patient.[105] Far from acting incorrectly in Murchison's case, Baden-Powell made sure that there was no miscarriage of justice.

In South Africa at the turn of the century, although black people were not discriminated against under the Cape's judicial system, they were invariably thought of by whites as inferior beings. Against this background Baden-Powell's treatment of the blacks in Mafeking does not seem particularly reprehensible, and the more extreme charges against him are unfounded.

6. Black Warriors in a White Man's War
(October 1899 to April 1900)

It is understood that you have armed Bastards, Fingoes and Barolongs against us. In this you have committeed an enormous act of wickedness . . . the end of which no man can foresee! You have created a new departure in South African history. It has hitherto been a cardinal point in South African ethics, both English and Dutch, to view with horror the idea of arming black against white, and I would ask you pause, and . . . reconsider the matter, even if it cost you the loss of Mafeking to disarm your blacks and thereby act the part of a white man in a white man's war.[1]

General Cronje writing to Colonel
Baden-Powell, 29 October 1899

Although the blacks of Mafeking were never starved or maltreated by Baden-Powell, they did have definite cause to harbour resentment against him. The whites played the leading role in all the set-piece military confrontations such as Game Tree fort and the defence of Cannon Kopje, but the blacks and coloureds and a handful of white officers waged a longer and more successful war of attrition against the Boers in the maze of broken-down walls and deserted kilns in the old Brickfields to the south-east of the town. This wasteland, which extended for almost a mile along the northern bank of the river Molopo, was also cratered with excavations from which clay for bricks had been dug. The whole area was a sniper's paradise, which the Boers could enter by creeping up the river-bed. From impregnable positions behind the old kilns or in the craters, the Boer snipers could pick out targets in the centre of the town and, by trenching forward from the Brickfields, could threaten a direct attack delivered from dangerously close proximity. The fighting in the Brickfields was therefore more important than any other action during the Siege, with the possible exception of the repulse of the two assaults on the stadt and the defence of Cannon Kopje. This dangerous daily duel in the Brickfields did not stop for months at a time, and so made extra-ordinary demands on those involved. It is therefore unjust that it was given so little attention in Baden-Powell's accounts of the Siege, and doubly unjust given that most of the participants on the British side were black or half-caste. During the first few days of November, the Boers began to press forward into the Brickfields constructing gun emplacements and rifle-pits among the kilns.[2] Consequently many hitherto peaceful parts of the town came under sniper-fire. On the evening of 2 November, Baden-Powell ordered 'Captain Goodyear [a white resident of the town] to take a party of his half-caste Cape Boys to get a footing in the Brickfields during the night and to open fire on the enemy coming there at dawn to take their usual posts for sniping'.[3] Next morning Bell was delighted to hear that the Cape Boys had 'got in amongst the old kilns and warmed up the Boers in splendid style'.[4]

On 6 November, Edward Ross observed the Boers 'hard at work making herringbone trenches towards the town'.[5] The next day, acting on orders from Baden-Powell, who considered it vital to stop the enemy occupying the Brickfields, Colonel Vyvyan sent 30 Cape Boys under Corporal H. M. B. Currie and 65 Fingoes under two Cape Police troopers to stop the Boers coming further along the river. It was a critical moment. Failure to stop the Boers would have spelled disaster. The Fingoes and Cape Boys had orders to dig themselves in to defensive positions and to hold these at all costs. 'The posts should understand,' wrote Vyvyan, 'that they must not give way to the enemy . . . They will be supported from the rear should they be attacked . . . In order to encourage the men in the performance of this duty, and to mark his appreciation of their loyalty and courage, Colonel Baden-Powell authorizes me to issue double pay to each N.C.O. and man of the two contingents for every tour of 24 hours.'[6]

By mid-November, thanks to some exceptionally accurate shooting, the two coloured contingents had stopped the Boers' advance; but the situation was still precarious enough for Vyvyan to ask Cecil to see that two troops of the Reserve Squadron were available to him at any moment. He also asked for four white volunteer snipers per day to strengthen the Brickfields defences.[7] By early December the Boers knew that they had met their match – brilliant snipers though they were.

In late November Edward Ross had gone to the Brickfields as a sniping volunteer, and had thought himself in 'the hottest place on earth'.[8] But in the first week of February 1900, he was sent back there and discovered that the second phase of the battle for the Brickfields was even hotter. It began quite literally with a bang. Major Panzera, the recently promoted Lieutenant Currie and Sergeant-Major William Ashton Taylor (a Cape Boy, and arguably the bravest man in the garrison) exploded a large charge of dynamite under a kiln used by the Boers for sniping purposes. Later that week they blew up two more kilns and the Cape Boys, who manned the two most advanced British works, managed to push forward their position to within 150 yards of the enemy's main trench – close enough to catch snatches of conversation. By late February, the hundred or so blacks and coloureds in the Brickfields had been reinforced by a troop of the Cape Police and a squad of volunteers. With the trenches now only 60 yards apart in places a deadly battle began in which gangs of black trench diggers on each side also played a vital part.

On 28 February, Hamilton saw the struggle intensify as the Boers drove a trench towards the British lines.

> So gallantly and vigorously did the enemy work that we could see them approaching yard by yard. It was impossible for us in the time at our disposal to do very much to stop them . . . It was useless to fire upon the natives working in the sap, since it was only possible to see the points of their picks . . . Still they came on, and that night we knew that before dawn they would be into us.

The Boers did indeed pierce the British line and then brought up a high-velocity Krupp gun and moved their 94-pounder so that it commanded the Brickfields. When all seemed lost, Baden-Powell put in a working party of 200 natives. 'We worked all night,' reported Hamilton, 'and carried our sap some 30 yards beyond theirs, and at such an angle that we enfiladed their sap . . .'[9] Even after this success, the position in the Brickfields remained perilous. The Boers found exactly the right position for their 94-pounder, enabling them to lob shells into the most advanced British post, making it immediately untenable. After losing five men, the Cape Boys retired with their bravest N.C.O., Sergeant-Major W. A. Taylor, mortally wounded by a shell splinter lodged in his brain. For four months Taylor had fought in the most advanced post in the Brickfields, personally shooting half-a-dozen Boer snipers and taking part in the dynamiting of all three principal kilns. G. Van Schalkwyk, another Cape Boy, was mortally wounded on the same day. Both men were so highly esteemed that they were buried side by side in the 'white' part of the town's cemetery, with Baden-Powell and his entire staff attending their funerals.[10]

The battle for the Brickfields fascinated Baden-Powell and during February and March he frequently intervened to issue orders.[11] Ross admired his expertise. 'You hear of the Colonel suddenly ordering the closing up of one trench, opening up of others, running saps here, and running saps there, building up emplacements, and cross trenches for enfilading the enemy's work etc., etc.'[12] The fighting in the Brickfields bore close similarities in miniature to the trench warfare that would characterize the Great War. The end came unexpectedly on 23 March when the Boers withdrew from their advanced fort and their main trench immediately behind it. Although it was not immediately appreciated, this marked final victory for the Cape Boys and their allies in the Brickfields. There would now be no possibility for the Boers to attack the town simultaneously at its two weakest points (i.e. through the stadt in the west, and through the Brickfields in the east). In the last act of the struggle there had been white men fighting alongside Africans, but for most of the time the 'British' fighting there had been black and coloured. Two days after the Boers had withdrawn, Baden-Powell clearly demonstrated whom he thought responsible for the Siege's greatest military success when he awarded a bounty of £50 to the Cape Boys.

During the Siege, Baden-Powell also acknowledged extraordinary acts of bravery carried out by African cattle raiders and despatch runners. If they had been white, many would have won Victoria Crosses for exploits often eclipsing ordinary bravery in the field. Cattle raiders had to control their fear not just for a few hours but for anything up to two weeks. Some veterans of the cattle raiding campaign, like the Barolong Mathakgong, on more than one occasion lived through the anguish of bringing 50 or so oxen over 30 miles to within sight of Mafeking and then having to endure a Boer attack in which beasts were either shot or driven away. But these men sometimes gave as good as they got, turning their expeditions into guerrilla attacks. On 9 March, 18 Barolongs lost 10 of their own number in allegedly killing 8 Boers. The immense risk such men took is made horribly clear by the fate of 32 out of 37 Fingoes who went cattle raiding and were led into a trap by two Barolongs bribed by the Boers. Lured into a gulley where a patch of reeds provided the only cover, they were subjected to a murderous fire from a 1-pounder Maxim and a field gun. Somehow they fought back with their rifles and killed six of their tormentors before being massacred. Only five left the reeds alive.[13]

The most remarkable of these African heroes used guile to achieve their ends. The prize must go to a despatch runner called Freddie

Manomphe; no fewer than three times did he encounter large parties of Boers on his way from Kanya into Mafeking. On each occasion he buried his documents and chatted to the Boers, giving them a plausible explanation for his journey; then, later, he retrieved his despatches and went merrily on his way. Even when betrayed by an African whom he had done his best to help, and after being obliged to witness a supposed accomplice getting four dozen lashes with a stirrup-leather for lying, Freddie still kept his composure and, in the superbly apposite words of Sol Plaatje, 'lied so classically, and with such thoroughness and serenity', that they believed him rather than his betrayer.[14] When stories about the castration of runners were widespread, sang-froid like Freddie's was evidence of no common bravery. Unless African runners had taken such astonishing risks, Baden-Powell would have had no information at all from the outside world with the exception of what was brought in by J. E. Pearson, a Reuter's correspondent who slipped through the Boers' cordon in mid-November, and Lieutenant Frank Smitheman of Plumer's regiment who did so in early April.

The debt which Baden-Powell owed to his African warriors was incalculable, yet in his official report to Lord Roberts he claimed that his only fighting blacks had been '300 armed cattle guards, watchmen and police'. To lend conviction to this colossal underestimate he described them as including a band of Zulu cattle watchmen (known as the Black Watch), Mr Daniel Webster's Fingo contingent and a group of Barolongs under Sergeant Abrams. In reality the sergeant's armed Barolongs alone numbered 400 – 100 more than all the blacks Baden-Powell was claiming had been armed. (The Black Watch was 200 strong; there were 70 armed Fingoes and 68 Cape Boys – giving a true total not far short of 750.)[15]

Baden-Powell did not simply lie about their numbers but made out that their deployment had been entirely defensive. This was an affront to the Barolongs who had captured an important enemy fort to the west of the stadt,[16] and a worse insult to the Cape Boys who had advanced to victory against the Boers in the Brickfields. While minor engagements like FitzClarence's trench attack were granted whole sections of the report, the crucial struggle in the Brickfields was accorded no section of its own. The injustice went further. In early November, Baden-Powell had renamed the Cape Boy Contingent the Colonial Contingent,[17] and this new name was the one he used in his report to Lord Roberts. It concealed the fact that the Contingent's members had been coloured.

In 1903 in his evidence to the Royal Commission on the War in South Africa, Baden-Powell's lies about his reliance upon Africans as active combatants were even more flagrant. When asked whether he had used them in military operations, he replied: 'No, we tried to make them defend their own town, but on the first attack on the town, they all ran away, so we did not rely upon them at all.'[18] This reply caused Sol Plaatje to accuse Baden-Powell of 'coolly and deliberately lying'.[19] Hanbury-Tracy supplied the editors of *The Times History of the War in South Africa* with the text for their chapter on the Siege and did his best to put the record straight in connection with the Cape Boys: 'It is quite impossible to describe the work done by these men under the most trying circumstances, but in stating that they were practically under one continuous rifle and shellfire for over six months, that they lived in the open all that time through the wet season, often with bad and insufficient food and scarcity of clothing, gives one some idea of what they suffered.'[20]

His critics have sometimes accused Baden-Powell of hogging the limelight and failing to give others the proper credit for what they had done. In general this charge is unwarranted, so the extraordinary effort he made to conceal the real part played by the blacks in the Siege was most uncharacteristic. Why then did he lie so brazenly, and thus deny so many Africans the recognition they deserved?

Baden-Powell's transformation of the Cape Boys into the Colonial Contingent had been in direct response to the letter he received from Cronje on 29 October, in which the Boer general accused him of 'an enormous act of wickedness' in arming blacks in what ought to have been 'a white man's war'.[21] One day later, on 30 October, Baden-Powell replied that the natives within Mafeking, 'had only taken up arms in defence of their homes and cattle, which you have already attempted to shell and raid'.[22] He maintained this position throughout the Siege in letters to Cronje and his successor Snyman. The natives, he repeated again and again, were only involved in 'defence'.[23] This insistence was largely due to his fear of causing offence in Whitehall. In September 1899, Joseph Chamberlain and Sir Alfred Milner had agreed that the participation of Africans in military operations would not be countenanced unless their lives or property were threatened. Chamberlain, however, rejected the suggestion that African policemen should be disbanded and minuted: 'Any offensive operations will be conducted by white troops . . . and in defensive operations the white troops will be placed in front of black police.'[24] So Whitehall took very seriously the aversion expressed by all white South Africans to the employment of armed blacks against whites. The recent Matabele Rebellion had given an indication of the kind of explosion that might take place if large numbers of Africans were armed and then decided to continue the war, for other reasons, once the whites had come to terms with one another.

During the three years between the ending of the Siege of Mafeking and the end of the war, Lord Roberts and Lord Kitchener – when the latter became Commander-in-Chief – faced a stream of accusations from the Boers that they had employed natives as fighting troops. Kitchener lied and lied again about Africans being employed only as non-combatant policemen, scouts and so forth. In August 1901 Chamberlain told the House of Commons that: 'Throughout this War we have given instructions that natives should not be employed as belligerents.'[25] There was immense hypocrisy on both sides, since each had employed blacks as combatants. Outside Mafeking, for example, the Boers were using at least 300 armed blacks in their front-line trenches in January 1900[26] and more in March and April.

Because such facts were vigorously denied, Baden-Powell was placed in a very awkward position when he appeared before the Royal Commission in 1903. If he had admitted the extent to which he had used his Africans in 'military operations', he would have been reprimanded. He had just been appointed Inspector General of Cavalry; and for a man in such an important position to have admitted violating the policy laid down by Parliament and the Commander-in-Chief would have been to hand the pro-Boer element in the Liberal Party a formidable stick with which to beat the Government. Baden-Powell would not only have embarrassed the most senior officers in the army but two cabinet ministers, one of whom was the Secretary of State for War. Not even his public fame would have saved his career after such a gaffe.

Baden-Powell's extreme caution also had its roots in a painful personal experience which had shown him how easily admissions about armed Africans could be used against him by envious associates. On 25 November 1899, a force led by the brother of Chief Linchwe (of the Bakgatla tribe) attacked the small Boer garrison at a place called Derdepoort on the Transvaal border 100 miles north-east of Mafeking. The consequences of his raid would be far-reaching and not even Stephe, behind his defences in Mafeking, would be safe from them.

Linchwe's people had previously been given 6,000 rounds of ammunition by Colonel J. S. Nicholson, the Commandant of the British South African Police, with the consent and encouragement of Arthur Lawley, the Resident Commissioner in Bulawayo. However, when news of a possible attack by Linchwe's men had reached the ears of W. H. Surmon, the local Assistant Commissioner, he had at once vetoed it on the grounds that it might endanger the lives of white women and children. Colonel G. L. Holdsworth, Plumer's second-in-command, arrived on the scene on 23 November and met Surmon's objection by saying that he would attack the Boers at Derdepoort while Linchwe's force guarded the border against possible counter-attacks. Through an extraordinary mixture of bungling and duplicity on Holdsworth's part, the intended roles of black and white were reversed and Linchwe's people crossed the border while the white force remained behind.

The attack was pressed home with ferocious determination. Twenty Boers were killed, two of them women. As if this was not bad enough, the Africans took 17 women and children prisoner. The Bakgatla lost 14 men killed and suffered 16 other casualties.

In Government House in Cape Town and in the Colonial Office in London, news of the attack and the deaths of the women was received with fury. Holdsworth's attempt to justify himself by claiming that Linchwe's men had disobeyed orders was not believed. Both Milner and Chamberlain agreed that Holdsworth had acted against Surmon's advice, and both considered the attack an act of aggression rather than self-defence. The presence of Holdsworth's force made it obvious that the Africans had been incited to deliver their attack. Chamberlain's worst fears were realized when the incident was seized upon by the anti-British press in Europe; one German periodical alleged that Boer women had been raped by the Bakgatla and by British soldiers.[27]

On 14 December Arthur Lawley, eager to extricate himself and Nicholson, wrote a grovelling letter to Milner apologizing for the embarrassment caused to the Government by the Bakgatla's attack and hypocritically placing the blame for the whole incident upon the man least responsible for it. Baden-Powell, Lawley told Milner, had written 'to say that he thought Linchwe should be given a free hand'.[28]

Baden-Powell had indeed written to that effect – but after the attack had been made, not before it. When suggesting that Linchwe be given a 'free hand', he had meant just that. He would certainly not have thought that Holdsworth's decision to accompany Linchwe to within a few miles of Derdepoort was 'giving him a free hand'. As soon as Baden-Powell heard about the attack (and long before Milner's and Chamberlain's anger became apparent), he sent an irate note to Nicholson ordering him to make absolutely sure in future that Holdsworth did as he was told by the local Assistant Commissioner. Holdsworth, he told Nicholson, had been politically naïve and militarily incompetent.[29] Official irritation about the incident was so pronounced that, when writing to Lord Kitchener over three months later, Baden-Powell felt obliged once again to trot out the lie to which he had been committed by Lawley and Nicholson – namely that the attack had been contrary to Holdsworth's orders.

So it was neither from any desire to be unfair to his African auxiliaries nor for any racial or personal reasons that Baden-Powell gave them far less credit than they deserved. He simply succumbed to the clear message emanating from the Commander-in-Chief's office, which was that commanding officers were under no circumstances to admit that they had ever depended upon armed Africans.

On 19 June, after the Siege had been raised, Baden-Powell sent a telegram to Lord Roberts seeking his permission to award the War Medal to some of the Barolongs' leaders such as Silas Molema and Paul

Monipa. Roberts replied the same day forbidding the award of medals: 'A signed parchment would probably be as much appreciated as a war medal and would avoid the suggestion that we had armed natives.' In his telegram, Baden-Powell had also sought approval for a gift of 200 oxen to the Barolongs.[30] It therefore seems a little hard that the author of a recent biography of Sol Plaatje should have contrasted Baden-Powell's 'rather less than gracious (and less than honest) attitude' towards the Barolongs with Lord Roberts's more generous despatch of a senior officer to present a framed parchment to the tribe.[31]

There is, however, no doubt that Baden-Powell owed more to black warriors than any other British commander in the war and was under a unique obligation to them. Before the end of the Siege, he would pay tribute in General Orders to the Barolongs' success in absorbing the principal shock of the Boers' most threatening attack and would name various Africans for individual acts of bravery.[32] But in the context of the whole Siege this was a woefully inadequate response. After working so hard for so long to achieve professional success, Baden-Powell had felt unable to risk offending his superiors in a matter about which they had given him abundant evidence of having strong views. The result was an act of injustice by omission. Dishonest and self-interested it certainly was, but not through malevolence or any animus against the blacks.

7. The Siege of Mafeking: Final Phase (January to May 1900)

With sorties ruled out after the Game Tree fiasco and with successes in the Brickfields obscured by long periods of stalemate, Baden-Powell had to think of other ways to prevent morale slumping as the realities of rationing came home to people. Thanks to his agreement of a Sunday ceasefire with the Boers, he was able to mount games and entertainments on at least one day of the week. Only on Sunday were the women and children able to come into the centre of town without fear.

On these communal occasions, Hamilton would observe everyone looking intently at Baden-Powell to try to read his thoughts. Stephe knew that if people saw him joining in the Sunday entertainments in a carefree manner as Gentleman Joe (Chamberlain) one moment and as a bewigged Paderewski the next, they would suppose matters were not as grave as they seemed.[1] Godley went to one concert with Lady Sarah Wilson and Algernon Hanbury-Tracy, and wrote telling his wife that, 'B-P made us die of laughing.'[2] Each Sunday there were 'Hottentot Dances', comic songs, parades of old carriages and what Baden-Powell called his '"World Wide Show" of singing and dancing and playing the fool'.[3] Competitions for the 'Best Siege Baby', best photograph, poem, bull, cow and so forth, vied with gymkhanas (while the horses were still fit enough to take part), football matches and other sports.

That Baden-Powell's performances and organizing abilities helped to keep up spirits in the town during the bleak months of February and March is well attested by many diarists.[4] Given his dependence upon civilians, morale was an all-important consideration, so it is unreasonable of two recent historians to have suggested, on account of the Sunday entertainments, that the Siege resembled 'a one-man-show' and 'a jolly party',[5] with Baden-Powell 'playing his part with consummate skill to what was clearly the largest audience ever to witness such a spectacle'.[6] Baden-Powell was indeed a showman; but not to have used his gifts when they were so badly needed would have been extraordinarily perverse. He needed all the admiration he could get, when so much else he was doing (the rationing, the censorship and the restrictions on movement) was unpopular.

Sometimes, when there was no shooting going on and he was not at Headquarters, passers-by might spot Stephe in his 'dwelling place on the verandah of a small house looking onto the Market Square'. 'The verandah is fairly screened from shells by the house itself,' wrote Baden-Powell, 'but is open to the bullets that come flitting through the town in search of billets. So, to stop them . . . I have had a traverse put up to screen my bed and chair. As sandbags now are scarce the traverse has been made of boxes filled with earth.'[7] (Baden-Powell is seen working in his 'dwelling place', see second photo–section.) Major Baillie would often catch a glimpse of him writing up his Staff Diary on the verandah or lying under his mosquito curtain, reading a book. 'I always know he is there, as I pass, when I see a pair of boots sticking out.'[8] Baillie also noticed Baden-Powell's habit of humming or whistling when he was around but the journalist, who was a heavy drinker, did not realize that these habits helped Baden-Powell suppress exasperation. The Colonel was also closely watched whenever he scaled the rickety elevated look-out platform, which he had caused to be erected on the roof of his Headquarters. From there, remarked Baillie: 'Baden-Powell looks out and can control the Mafeking defences like the Captain of a ship, shouting his instructions down a speaking tube to the Headquarters' bombproof, which are thence telephoned on to the parties whom it may concern, so that he can personally turn on the tap of any portion of the defences he may think fit.'[9]

Baden-Powell would spend hours staring through his Zeiss field-glasses trying to outguess the Boers. That he was often successful in predicting the enemy's intentions is evident from letters written by individual Boers. A man serving outside Mafeking wrote miserably to his wife in mid-April: 'Somehow or other Baden-Powell seems to get to know promptly any movement we intend to make. It is really wonderful how soon he comes to know of things. If we decide to occupy a new position the following night, he is sure to have taken it before us. If it is decided to have a general onslaught on his cattle the following morning, the cattle are sure not to come to their accustomed grazing grounds.'[10] Baden-Powell's intelligence gathering, while effective, was by its very nature invisible. 'Ruses' which could be divulged were therefore much more useful for raising morale.

Even J. R. Algie, a persistent critic, was delighted with the open letter written in Dutch which Baden-Powell sent to all the Boers on 10 December, distributing it simultaneously under eight white flags to every Boer position. 'Burghers, I address you because I have only recently learned how you have been intentionally kept in the dark by your officers and your Government newspapers as to what is really happening in other parts of South Africa.' Ultimate British victory was inevitable, he told them, since no other country would side with the Boer republics. They would therefore be well advised to lay down their arms by 14 December to save their farms from confiscation after their defeat. Snyman's indignation was an indication of the success of a ploy which met with almost universal approval in Mafeking.[11] Baden-Powell made a habit of hoisting red lamps during the night and using the speaking tubes in the trenches to give the impression that an attack was imminent.[12] He manufactured a number of dummies, one of which amazed Ross by its ability 'mechanically to shake its head, wave a flag, and put a pair of imitation opera-glasses up to its eyes'.[13] These dummies undoubtedly encouraged the Boers to waste their ammunition. Such stratagems could do little to harm the Boers; their purpose was to make the garrison feel less impotent, and in this they succeeded.

Men like Bell and Ross, who could both be witheringly sarcastic, admired Baden-Powell, sensing behind his often flippant exterior an iron determination to win. 'I try not only to win the game,' Stephe told his mother, 'but every trick.'[14] To do this he was prepared to go without regular sleep and to subject himself to many privations. His tastes became even more spartan during the Siege and he expected his officers to display the same hardihood. Although he could often be wonderfully sympathetic, writing sensitive notes to bereaved wives or parents[15] and visiting the wounded in hospital, he could be merciless to officers who failed to set the required example. One such was Ronny Moncreiffe who had a breakdown, caused as much by stress as by drink. He had worked hard for many months and even Ross – who thought him a snob and a soak – believed that Baden-Powell was unjust to imprison him.[16]

Baden-Powell undoubtedly enjoyed his awesome powers in Mafeking (although he chose to temper them through his Court of Summary Jurisdiction).

It is a most interesting experience [he told his mother] expecially as
my first act was to proclaim Martial Law, i.e. – as W[arington] will
tell you – that all laws are in abeyance and I take the responsibility
for everything. I have already got the jail full of suspected spies etc.
and I keep them there with no proof of guilt etc., I forbid public
houses to be open other than at certain hours and [for] any case of
disobedience I confiscate their whole stock. I have seized every
ounce of flour in the town – and am reselling it only a certain amount
each day – and so on; I am a regular Jack-in-Office![17]

His final humorous description of himself as a Jack-in-Office (a
conceited petty official) gives this gleeful (and at times exaggerated)
account of the extent of his powers a redeeming edge of self-mockery.

Jack-in-Office he might be, but Stephe always seemed the embodiment of brisk efficiency and miraculous neatness, not only of
appearance and dress. When shown the correspondence sent in by
Cronje and Snyman, and copies of the replies returned by Baden-
Powell, Edward Ross marvelled at: 'The neatness of B–P's typewritten
letters contrasted with the dirty, torn, smudged, ill-written, worsely
[sic] signed, scrap-paper-stationery used by the enemy.'[18] In these
letters Baden-Powell somehow managed to be both courteous and
ironical.

On 29 April it became apparent that the enemy at last possessed a
humorist worthy of Baden-Powell's attentions. On that day, the
members of a routine patrol were crossing the disused railway line to
the south-west of the town when one of them spotted an envelope tied
to a gradient marker. Inside was an astonishing letter addressed to 'Dan
Kolonel Baden-Powell' and signed by S. Eloff, Commandant of the
Johannesburg Commando.[19]

> I see in the *Bulawayo Chronicle* that your men in Mafeking play
> cricket on Sundays and give concerts and balls on Sunday evenings.
> In case you would allow my men to join in the same it would be very
> agreeable to me, as here outside Mafeking there are seldom any of
> the same sex and there can be no merriment without their being
> present . . .
>
>   Wishing you a pleasant day, I remain
>   Your obliging friend,
>   S. Eloff.[20]

Occasionally on Sundays there had been fraternizing between the
opposing sides, but on a very limited scale and only between the
members of remote outlying forts. Baden-Powell had always been
extremely careful about blindfolding any Boer emissaries who came in
under a white flag and would never have dreamed of allowing a dozen

men to look around within the defence perimeter. Nevertheless, he replied in the spirit of the original:

> Sir, I beg to thank you for your letter of yesterday, in which you propose that your men come and play cricket with us.
>
> I should like nothing better – after the match in which we are at present engaged is over. But just now we are having our innings and have so far scored 200 days, not out, against the bowling of Cronje, Snijman (sic), Botha, and Eloff: and we are having a very enjoyable game.
>
> I remain, yours truly,
> R. S. S. Baden-Powell.[21]

The real game, for which Baden-Powell was already preparing as his reply to Eloff was taken across the veldt under a white flag, was the attack on the stadt now considered imminent by Stephe's African spies. Although fire-eaters like the bibulous Major Baillie were going around cursing the Boers for not having the guts to have a go at the town, Baden-Powell himself felt less enthusiastic.[22] His misgivings owed a lot to the events of 31 March, when he had been given an inkling of what the Boers might do when they felt compelled to act.

During the last days of March Colonel Plumer, Major Bird and Captain McLaren, with 270 men, had advanced to within four miles of Mafeking to test the determination of the Boers to maintain their cordon. At a farm called Oaklands, Plumer had been attacked by a superior force of Boers commanded by Snyman himself, and had been badly mauled. This was the first time Plumer had fought the Boers in open country, and it was an experience he never wished to repeat. Within the space of a few hours on 31 March he himself had been wounded, along with 29 others, 8 of his men had been killed and 11 were missing. His flank had been turned, and his small force subjected to such accurate shell-fire that it was a tribute to the men's discipline that they fell back towards Ramathlabama in some kind of order.*[23] As Plumer miserably reported to Baden-Powell, 'From the way the Boers attacked, I do not think any attack of ours will drive the enemy off.'[24] As well as reminding Baden-Powell of the unwisdom of dismissing the surrounding enemy as incompetent and ill-led, the débâcle of Oaklands Farm was a horrible experience for him from a personal point of view.

On 1 April he heard that 'the Boy' McLaren lay dead on the veldt, with several other officers and a dozen or so men. Stephe had at once sent out two of his most dependable officers, Captain H. T. C. Singleton and Lieutenant Hanbury-Tracy, to bring in the dead for

---

* McLaren was awarded the D.S.O. for the qualities of leadership he displayed during this ordeal.

burial; but they had returned with only three corpses, none of which was McLaren's. Eloff, they explained, had already sent out burial parties and they had found a number of fresh graves.[25] Baden-Powell had to live through a day and night believing that his friend was dead, until learning from Snyman that 'the Boy' was alive but gravely wounded. (Exactly how close to death McLaren had been, Baden-Powell would only learn later. Suffering from severe wounds to his back, stomach and leg, McLaren would certainly have been killed as he lay on the ground, if the Boer who had found him had not also been a freemason and had therefore made sure that he received immediate medical attention.)[26]

The date which Baden-Powell's spies had thought most likely for Eloff's attack came and went. Stephe, however, was convinced that an attack would come soon. During the first week of May he received intelligence indicating that a relief column of 1,000 men had left Kimberley, so he assumed that similar reports would be reaching Eloff. The young commandant would know very well that he would have to take the town before the Kimberley force arrived. So Baden-Powell gazed out more intently than ever from his rooftop across the shimmering veldt to see what he could discern. Unfortunately for him, his intelligence reports almost always emanated from the north and hardly ever from the south, from whence Lord Roberts's relief force would eventually come. On 4 May he received a report suggesting that the Relief Column had reached Taungs, only 140 miles south of Mafeking, but he had no idea whether this was true. In fact, the column was still only 25 miles out of Kimberley.[27]

This was an exceptionally worrying time for Baden-Powell. Because of illness in the town, the number of men manning the front-line defence trenches was 13 per cent below the figure he considered a safe minimum. Almost all of these men were in hospital suffering from dysentery or malaria. There were also several cases of diphtheria and smallpox. Angus Hamilton noticed how the defenders were beginning to look gaunt and haggard. 'It is difficult to keep up one's spirits when from day to day there comes no news, only that curious ironical instinct, that perhaps it may be that we are not to be relieved at all.'[28]

The same thought was rarely absent from Baden-Powell's mind. What ought he to do when his food supplies would only last another week and he still had no reliable news as to the whereabouts of the southern column? Should he take out the 180 men of the Protectorate Regiment still physically capable of fighting in the open, and try to join hands with Plumer's 700–800 men in a desperate attempt to drive off more than twice that number of Boers?[29] On 2 May, Plumer estimated that the Boers outside Mafeking numbered 2,600.[30] With Plumer's defeat at Oaklands and the fate of his own men at Game Tree still fresh in his mind, Baden-Powell knew in his bones that this would lead to a much worse disaster than that suffered by Plumer after his move from Ramathlabama. He decided there could only be one realistic course if his food were on the point of running out.

He had first mooted the possibility of evacuating the garrison in a message to Plumer despatched on 21 April, but he had thought it very much a last resort. 'As we should have no horses and feeble men this might fail, and is for other reasons undesirable. Please keep evacuation idea secret.'[31] But within two weeks Baden-Powell, who was convinced that 10 June would see the final exhaustion of all his food, was ready to tell Lord Roberts that he would attempt to evacuate the garrison 'if relief fails'.[32] He placed a hand-written memorandum headed 'Secret Plan for Evacuation' in a locked tin box with other papers to be handed over, in the event of his death, to his Chief Staff Officer. 'Issue notice to inhabitants a day or two previous, to effect that supplies will last 5 weeks longer . . . Arrange with Plumer to have covering force sent out secretly the same night to meet us . . .' The five weeks figure would of course have been given out to mislead the Boers. Each man was to have two days' rations; nobody was to know that they were leaving Mafeking for good until 'after they have moved off'. Mayor F. Whitely or the Rev. W. H. Weekes was to remain behind in charge of the town, and for three days would present an impression of normality to the enemy. The Town Guards' rifles were to be buried and all guns spiked. On the third day Baden-Powell's letter of surrender was to be taken across to the Boers under a flag of truce.[33] It is as well for Baden-Powell's reputation that Brian Gardner did not come across this memorandum. Inevitably Stephe would have been accused of planning to leave the civilians in the lurch, rather than being given the credit for wishing to spare them the agony of a Siege prolonged beyond early June. Luckily, events outside Mafeking were already taking a different shape.

Colonel Mahon and the Relief Column had managed to evade a Boer force sent to cut them off and by 9 May had reached Vryburg, 94 miles from Mafeking. Eloff now knew that he could delay no longer.

On 11 May, Ross recorded that Baden-Powell was 'on the look-out all day and nearly always with his field-glasses pointing south. There is a sort of uneasy air about the place today as if something unexplained was going to happen.'[34] Shortly before 4.00 a.m. the following morning, Nurse Craufurd was woken by the sound of heavy firing which she suspected was coming from the Brickfields on the eastern side of the town. She herself lived in a cottage close to the children's hospital, which was situated to the west of white Mafeking between the stadt and the railway works. Because she had often heard firing at night, she went back to sleep.

On the last day of April the Boers had removed their 94-pounder to Pretoria, consequently many people (Lady Sarah Wilson among them) had abandoned their dug-outs. Her ladyship was asleep in Dixon's Hotel on the night of the attack and, since the hotel was closer to the Boers' diversionary antics to the north-east of the town, she (unlike Nurse Craufurd in the west) did not go back to sleep once woken.

> The moon had just set, [she recalled] and it was pitch dark . . . When I opened the door onto the stoep the din was terrific, while swish, swish came the bullets just beyond the canvas blinds . . . Now and then the boom of a small gun varied the noise . . . I dressed, by the light of a carefully shaded candle . . . In various stages of deshabille people were running round the house seeking rifles, fowling-pieces, and even sticks . . . All of a sudden the sound I had been waiting for added to the weird horror of the situation, an alarm bugle, winding out its tale, followed by our tocsin, the deep-toned Roman Catholic church bell, which was the signal that a general attack was in progress . . . I had a sort of idea that any moment a Dutchman would look in at the door.[35]

Nurse Craufurd woke again briefly at the sound of the bugle, but somehow she dozed off once more. At 5.45 a.m. she woke for the third time with her heart pounding. She could hear loud firing close to her cottage and rushing to the window, saw 'what looked to be the whole stadt in flames'. She and Elsie, her African maid, dressed as quickly as they could and rushed across to the hospital.

> Shall I *ever* forget that run? [the nurse wrote later]. Bullets seemed to come from all round, whizzing near us, and our legs seemed as if they would not move fast enough. Elsie fell, and I thought she was hit; but I helped her up . . . As we ran I saw a crowd – a black mass of people it seemed, running from the stadt towards the B.S.A.P. Fort. I thought then it was natives running there for protection. I nearly fell in at the hospital; my legs were trembling so . . . Our hospital was being pelted with bullets . . . After a little we heard cheering from the Fort, and we were afraid to think what it could mean. Presently we saw men looking in . . . As they came nearer and we saw them plainer, we said to each other they were Boers. As they passed us, we called out to them: 'Who *are you*, and where are you going?' They said: 'We are Republicans. The town is ours; your Colonel is a prisoner.' Elsie threw up her hands, and began to cry and wail.[36]

One person who had not been confused when he heard the firing from the north-east was Colonel Baden-Powell. This, he was sure, would be the precursor to the real attack from the west. He had been sleeping on his verandah in the Market Square, behind his barrier of earth-filled boxes, when a spent bullet had dropped almost on top of him. The first thing he did was telephone Lieutenant Mackenzie who commanded

A flogging during the Ashanti Campaign (1896); this drawing based on an original sketch by Baden-Powell.

Baden-Powell, drawn by himself, in the Matopo Hills in 1896 on a characteristically dramatic scouting mission pursued by Matabele.

'Spies' hanged outside Bulawayo in 1896. Baden-Powell preserved a copy of this photograph in his Matabele Scrapbook and entitled it 'The Christmas Tree'.

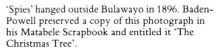

Baden-Powell's representation of the execution he longed to see but missed (see p. 185).

Baden-Powell as Wun-Hi, a Tea House owner in *The Geisha*, (1897), with Ellen Turner on the right as Molly Seamore.

Below: Baden-Powell by himself in his 'walking kit' in Kashmir in 1898.

5TH SEPTEMBER 1897.
MENU.

Olives à la Metropole.

Consommé à la Napolitaine.
Potage d'Amandes.

Truite saumonée à la Hollandaise.

Filets de boeuf à la Francaise.

Quartier d'Agneau sauce menthe.
Dinde à la Chipolata.

Tranches de Jambon au champagne.

Charlotte Russe.
Compote de Fruits à la Crème.

Glace de Vanille et Chocolat.

THE CHALET: }
Simla. }

Sir George Baden-Powell K.C.M.G
M.P., 1889

Miss Turner's menu card for *The Geisha*'s cast party, decorated by Baden-Powell with a picture of Ellen as Molly in the play.

Above: Baden-Powell and Mafeking principal officers. On ground: Lt R. Moncreiffe; seated l to r: Major A. J. Godley, Lt-Colonel C. B. Vyvyan, Mr C. G. Bell [magistrate], Colonel R. S. S. Baden-Powell, Mr F. Whitley [mayor], Lt-Colonel C. O. Hore, Dr W. Hayes; standing l to r: Major F. W. Panzera, Captain C. M. Ryan, Captain H. Greener, Major Lord Edward Cecil, Captain G. C. Wilson, Captain the Hon. A. Hanbury Tracy, Captain B. W. Cowan.

Left: The last coaches to leave Mafeking before the start of the Siege.

Below left: The War Correspondents at Mafeking outside their bomb-proof shelter, from l to r: Mr J. E. Neilly (*Pall Mall Gazette*), Mr Vere Stent (*Reuter's*), Major F. D. Baillie (*Morning Post*), Mr J. Angus Hamilton (*The Times* and *Black & White*).

The Mafeking Town Guard at Sunday prayers, on 21 January 1900, the hundredth day of the Siege.

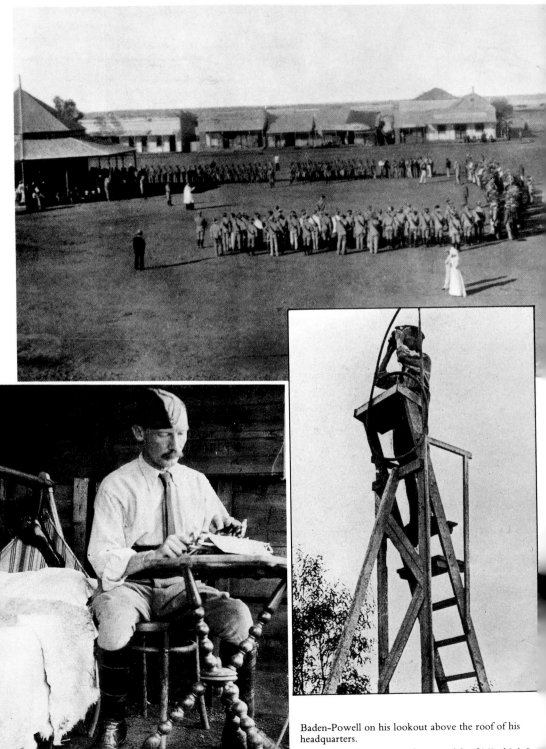

Baden-Powell on his lookout above the roof of his headquarters.

Baden-Powell typing on the verandah of Minchin's La[w] Office, where he slept, rested and often worked throughout the Siege protected by a barricade of earth filled boxes. Fear of assassination meant that he always had a revolver close to hand.

A rather theatrical portrait of Baden-Powell during the Siege with waxed moustache-ends and wearing an enormous pair of suede gauntlets.

Shell damage: Attorney J. W. de Kock's house after a direct hit. *Below*: Africans waiting to be fed at a soup kitchen.

Above: The Cape Boy
contingent in the
Brickfields. Lt H. M. B.
Currie, their commander,
is the white man near the
centre of the back row.
Next to him on the left is
Sergt-Major W. A.
Taylor.

Newsboys in London
announce the Relief of
Mafeking.

Mrs Baden-Powell waving to the crowds from the balcony of her home 8 St George's Place after the Relief of Mafeking. [Inset] Mrs Baden-Powell on her balcony.

Henrietta Grace Baden-Powell at the time of the Relief.

Baden-Powell campaigning in the western Transvaal immediately after the Relief. His almost obsessive determination to wash his entire body thoroughly each day, whatever his circumstances, would lead him to instruct Boy Scouts to do the same.

Mrs Baden-Powell breakfasting at home with her sons George and Frank and her daughter Agnes circa 1892.

Rose Kerr, a year before Baden-Powell proposed to her.

'The Worst Siege of All'. Given Baden-Powell's reluctance to marry and hi mother's eagerness that he should do so, the cartoonist of *Melbourne Punch* w being more perceptive than he probably knew. B-P was indeed pursued by women after the Siege, but not by those he thought might make possible brid

the 'Black Watch', then manning the south-western forts outside the
stadt. To his relief, Mackenzie answered; Stephe had feared he would
already have been over-run. Somewhat reassured, he telephoned Alick
Godley, the commander of all the western defences, and was still
speaking to him when a messenger burst into Staff Headquarters with
the news that a strong force of Boers had crawled up the Molopo
valley, guided by a couple of deserters, and slipped between the pickets
into the native township.[37]

Angus Hamilton, the most adventurous of all the journalists, was by
now riding towards the stadt. It was still dark, with the first hints of 'a
lemon-coloured dawn sheathed in the golden glory of the fire and
obscured by the grey-black waves of smoke'.[38] Godley, in his western
command post, had by now lost communication with Mackenzie and
with Captain F. C. Marsh (who commanded the troops, both black
and white, in the stadt). But his telephone link with Baden-Powell's
Headquarters was still functioning, and it was Baden-Powell himself
who told him that the Boers had not only occupied and burned the
stadt but had seized the B.S.A.P. Fort and had taken prisoner Colonel
Hore and most of his senior officers, who had been using the Fort as the
Protectorate Regiment's headquarters.[39] This accounted for the
remark which had so shocked Nurse Craufurd about her Colonel
being a prisoner. The Boers had meant Colonel Hore.

Baden-Powell himself was very much at liberty. He told Godley
over the telephone 'to close up the western posts so as to prevent any
Boer supports following the party that was in [the stadt]', and
explained that he would be given the Reserve Squadron of the
Protectorate Regiment for this crucial job.[40] Godley telephoned
FitzClarence requesting the immediate despatch of the Reserve
Squadron and ordered Lord Charles Cavendish-Bentinck's squadron
to reinforce the pickets to the west of the stadt, thereby preventing any
supports reaching the Boers in the stadt itself. When FitzClarence
arrived Godley positioned his squadron at the north-east corner of the
stadt, the ideal spot for preventing the Boers leaving the African village
to reinforce their compatriots now occupying the B.S.A.P. Fort.

Before these moves had been completed, Baden-Powell had withdrawn from the eastern trenches as many men as he dared and had sent
them to the threatened west side of the inner perimeter. These included
the reserve of the Bechuanaland Rifles, some men from the Railway
Division, the Cape Police and the Town Guard. So serious did the
position seem that Baden-Powell even sent for some B.S.A. Police
from the key position at Cannon Kopje.

About 270 Boers had entered the stadt, where they had divided into
three parties one of which – 150 strong, led by Eloff and including 30
Frenchmen and Germans – had rushed on beyond the African
township. Colonel Hore with 3 of his officers and 15 men had

assumed that the men running out of the smoke towards their fort were members of the Reserve Squadron falling back from the stadt. So Hore had not ordered his men to open fire. By the time he realized his mistake it was too late, and he and his men were Eloff's prisoners. Only one man, Trooper Maltuschek, refused to surrender, and he was shot dead on the spot.

Baden-Powell might have suffered a more serious reverse if he had not found out at once that Hore's headquarters was in enemy hands. He owed this discovery to an obliging Boer who, when the telephone rang, picked it up and made his nationality all too evident. To prevent the Boers from eavesdropping on British conversations with other posts, the line was cut on Baden-Powell's orders. He then sent a messenger under a white flag to ask Eloff to surrender, since he and his men were surrounded. The Commandant refused, 'thinking apparently that his men had taken Mafeking'.[41] Indeed Eloff had some reason for believing this. He was only 800 yards from Baden-Powell's Headquarters; and if he had been supported by a serious attack launched upon the eastern face of the town, as had previously been arranged with Snyman, he would have been able to squeeze the overstretched British garrison in a formidable pincer movement. The situation was deemed serious enough for the British prisoners in the gaol to be given rifles and released for the day.[42]

Baden-Powell was far from certain how many Boers were in the stadt and what number of reserves were waiting just outside the native township in the depression known as Hidden Hollow. The *Mafeking Mail* suggested that at one stage there had been 400 Boers there, who had been prevented from joining their compatriots in the stadt by the opportune arrival of Bentinck's squadron.[43] With only FitzClarence's squadron stopping the stadt Boers from reinforcing Eloff in the B.S.A.P. Fort, it is easy to understand why Baden-Powell should have sent a desperate message to Plumer during the fighting. He believed he could deal with all the Boers trapped within the perimeter but explained that, if he were to fail to force their surrender by nightfall, a further Boer attack under cover of darkness would place him in acute danger. He therefore asked Plumer to make a diversion.[44] Baden-Powell also sent a note to McLaren under a white flag, as was his daily practice, knowing full well that today the Boers would read it even more carefully than usual. 'Dear Boy,' he wrote, 'I hope you were not too disturbed by heavy firing in the night, but the Boers made an attack on us and we have scuppered the lot. Let me know if you want any clean pyjamas . . .' Since Snyman still had an American doctor (J. E. Dyer), serving with his force, translation of the colloquial 'scuppered them' would not have presented much difficulty.[45]

Whether this message had any effect in discouraging Snyman from supporting Eloff it is impossible to say. Baden-Powell thought it did.

Intelligence reports had pointed to Snyman being adamantly opposed to the offensive which Eloff had been determined to launch. Clearly if his young subordinate was to succeed in such a venture, it would expose his own tactics of investment and bombardment as pedestrian and ill-conceived.[46] But because President Kruger had ordered the storming of the town, Snyman had been obliged to promise to support Eloff should he manage to gain a foothold within Mafeking. As the afternoon progressed, however, both Baden-Powell and Eloff were left with no clear indication of what Snyman meant to do. He made some effort to support Eloff with his artillery but, being unsure of his subordinate's exact position, was afraid of sending shells right into the town.[47]

The burden of responsibility for dealing with the Boers in the stadt and for preventing more from coming in from Hidden Hollow fell upon Alick Godley. His task was made much easier by the Barolongs, who had swiftly rallied after being swept aside at the outset. By mid-morning, they had given Bentinck decisive assistance in driving back Boer reinforcements and had hemmed in two groups of the enemy: one behind the stone walls of a cattle kraal, the other in among the curious group of limestone boulders which gave the town its name. (In the Tswana or Bechuana language 'Mafikeng' meant the place of stones.) These Boers were doomed without water, and Godley already had men in the river bed with orders to shoot any enemy soldier coming down to drink. The Barolongs, if left to their own devices, would simply have waited; but Godley wanted to clear the stadt by nightfall. The 25 Boers in the kraal surrendered shortly after he had threatened to blow them to pieces with his 7-pounder. They only escaped butchery at the hands of the Barolongs because Captain F. C. Marsh, 'at fearful personal risk, jumped in amongst them and interposed himself between the cowering Boers and their would-be murderers'.[48] Two Boers had been killed and three wounded in the attack on the kraal, while two of Godley's men had sustained minor wounds. Four more Boers were killed when FitzClarence and Marsh attacked the limestone kopje. By now it was rapidly growing dark, and the Boers who had fled from the kopje were being driven towards Bentinck's men.

'I saw it would never do,' wrote Godley, 'for Bentinck and us to have the Boers between us, as we should only shoot at one another, so I sent him [Bentinck] a circuitous message by telephone and arranged for him to withdraw his men a bit and let us hunt them out.'[49] This decision, in effect to allow quite large numbers of Boers to escape, was taken by Godley after consulting Baden-Powell on the telephone.[50] Baden-Powell has been blamed by Gardner and Pakenham for inexplicably allowing this escape to occur,[51] although Hamilton, usually so critical, had thought Godley principally responsible and had considered him justified in giving the orders he did.[52] Apart from fearing that his own men might shoot one another in the dark, Godley had known that, if all the Boers were detained, he would soon have to feed, guard and accommodate not only the 30 or so already taken prisoner, but anything up to another 150 Boers, many of whom were still holding the B.S.A.P. Fort under Eloff. Baden-Powell was keenly aware that Godley's and Bentinck's men were already exhausted, but still had to accomplish the all-important recapture of the Fort.[53]

Angus Hamilton, it will be recalled, had set out intrepidly in the direction of the stadt as dawn had been breaking. He had hoped to observe the fighting from Hore's headquarters, which he thought likely to become the central position in the engagement. He had no idea when he saw men standing about outside the Fort that they were Boers; he was enlightened when a bullet struck his horse and when, seconds later, he was ordered to hold up his hands. Without even being given time to shoot his wounded horse, he was hustled into the Fort where Colonel Hore, 3 officers and 23 N.C.O.s and men were held prisoner. The Boers had been led into the town by Trooper Hayes, a British deserter with a grudge against an officer. This traitor now swaggered about wearing Colonel Hore's sword and his gold watch and chain. Hayes wanted to place the prisoners outside to stop the garrison firing on the Fort but Commandant Eloff would have none of this. Instead, for their own safety, he locked up his prisoners (eventually 32 of them) in a small storeroom adjacent to the Fort.

Later in the day, Eloff allowed Nurse Craufurd to visit the prisoners while he himself stood at the door. Like Hore and his officers, she too thought that the town had fallen. 'I felt a great lump in my throat and could hardly speak. I shall never forget their sad faces.'[54] The room stank because one of the imprisoned men was 'suffering acutely from the agonies of dysentery'. The Boers looted the stores of the regimental mess, drinking dozens of bottles of whisky. Hamilton found the French and German officers more courteous than the Boers, but could not help warming to Eloff when he came in to chat to his prisoners.

> He sat within the door upon a case of Burgundy, his legs dangling, his accoutrements jingling, and the rowels of his spurs echoing the tick-tacking of the Mauser rifles . . . Orderlies came and went, but the Commandant . . . continued to issue his instructions and his orders. He seemed to possess the complete mastery of the situation; his buoyant face was impressed with the confidence of youth.[55]

Unknown to Hamilton, many of the orderlies sent out had been shot by Bentinck's men as they vainly attempted to crawl back along the Molopo valley to summon reinforcements;[56] but Eloff rarely showed his feelings. Instead he told Hamilton and the others that when night fell they would be 'marched to the south-western laager and then conveyed to Pretoria'. The fading light comforted Hamilton since it hid from him 'the horror of being with the enemy and watching while they fired upon our own men'. All day the Fort was subjected to a constant hail of bullets. The strain on Eloff was almost unbearable, and 'at times he lost control of himself and complained querulously in Dutch about the non-appearance of his reinforcements'. When some of his men fled from the Fort to save their skins, he gave the order to shoot them down. The Boers seemed to be rallying when, to Hamilton's amazement, Eloff burst into the storeroom and announced to Colonel Hore that he would surrender to him if he could induce the surrounding British to cease firing. Hore gasped, 'What, what?' and could hardly take in what he was being told. Then Captain Singleton (known as 'Sausage' on account of a girth now much reduced) roared through a window that the Boers had surrendered.

When this news was understood and believed, it spread from fort to fort where bursts of cheering and singing of the National Anthem broke out spontaneously.[57] Between ranks of euphoric defenders, the Boer prisoners were marched to the Masonic Hall which would serve as their temporary prison. 'Singleton took Eloff in to B-P, introducing him by saying, "Commandant Eloff, Sir." In his own incomparable style, B-P held out his hand saying, "Good evening Commandant, will you come in and have some supper?" '[58]

Eloff, who had displayed exceptional courage and daring, deserved to have been supported by Snyman. If he had been, he would probably have taken Mafeking. President Kruger, when he heard of his grandson's capture, wrote furiously to Snyman asking whether he and his men had been drunk or paralysed by fear. If they admitted to having been drunk, Kruger promised to see that the whole matter was hushed up.[59] Eloff took his capture well, affecting insouciance when Hamilton came to visit him in captivity. For other Boers the misery of defeat, after their death or glory dash, proved too great to bear. When Baden-Powell allowed the Dutch Reform Church minister to preach to them in the Masonic Hall, many broke down and wept quite openly.[60]

Baillie, who had been disillusioned about everything only days before, was suddenly rhapsodic. 'It is a good thing to be an English-man. These foreigners start too quick and finish quicker. They are good men, but we are better, and have proved so for several hundred years.'[61] Unlike Baillie, Brian Gardner – while admitting that Baden-Powell had remained calm throughout the day – would give the Colonel little credit for the proceedings. He attributed 'the successful ending of the Boer resistance to the intelligent measures taken by Godley'.[62] Godley's own accounts of the day, both published and unpublished, show that he took most major decisions in consultation with Baden-Powell. Edward Ross, an alert Baden-Powell watcher, had kept his quarry in sight for much of this special day, which gave him his 'first opportunity of seeing Baden-Powell in a temporary corner, or at all hard-pressed':

> I can assure you it was indeed a lesson to all who saw him. I had that luck. He stood there at the corner of his offices, the coolest of cucumbers possible, but his orders rattled out like the rip of a Maxim. He had taken in the position without a moment's thought or hesitation, and when he knew his outposts had been passed through by the enemy, within twenty minutes he had formed an inner line of defence right across the front of the town, with men and guns in sufficient numbers to mow down any number of the enemy that would dare to attempt to cross the clear open space still remaining between where the enemy were and the town. You could not realise his commands if put down in cold black and white. It was his tone, his self-possession, his command of self, his intimate knowledge of every detail of the defences, where everything at that moment was, and where it was to be brought and put to, shewed us the ideal soldier, and what the British officer can be and is in moments of extreme peril. It was something I would not have missed seeing for anything. With only one or two with him, his officers all galloping about delivering his orders, there he stood with his hands behind his back, a living image of a being knowing himself and his own strength and fearing neither foe nor devil. Such was B.P. the soldier.[63]

Approximately 60 Boers were killed or wounded during the day, and 108 were taken prisoner. The garrison lost 12 dead and 8 wounded.[64] The British death which affected Baden-Powell most of all was that of Arthur Hazlerigg, a 20-year-old younger son of a Leicestershire baronet. Hazlerigg had failed his army examinations in England and had volunteered as a private in the Cape Police; he became one of Baden-Powell's three young men who acted as Headquarters orderlies. Over and again in the coming years, Baden-Powell would tell the story of Hazlerigg's death as an illustration of what devotion to duty should be.

> I lost my own orderly simply through his being an over-brave man [he told members of the Eton College Officers' Training Corps during the Great War]. He had got a mistaken order from a man who was drunk, I am afraid [probably Ronny Moncreiffe]. He gave him the order in my name to ride out to the Boers [at the B.S.A.P. Fort] with a message, and told him, 'never mind if they shoot, get it there.' The Boers fired heavily at him . . . After a time his horse was hit and fell; an ordinary cunning man would have laid low and

pretended he was hit too, and might have got back to safety. But he went on running until finally a shot struck him in the thigh and smashed it . . . he knew he was going to his death, but he tried to carry out the order because he had got it.[65]

Lady Sarah Wilson spent some time dabbing his brow with eau de cologne once he had been taken to the hospital and recalled: 'Just before he passed into unconsciousness, he repeated more than once: "Tell the Colonel, Lady Sarah, I did my best to give the message, but they got me first"'[66] The idea of 'doing one's best', which would be such an important element in the Boy Scout Promise, may have owed something to Hazlerigg's valiant effort. The manner of his death was not quite as Baden-Powell made out whenever he used 'my orderly' as the subject of 'pep talks' given to Scouts. After Hazlerigg was shot, not in the thigh but in the genitals, he had to lie for several hours where he fell because the firing around the Fort was so intense. He bled profusely and suffered terrible pain. Lady Sarah wrote about him lapsing into unconsciousness, having seen him many hours before his death. In reality, when the end came he was fully conscious and, according to a hospital orderly, 'shrieked in a high treble voice for about five minutes before he died'.[67] Since the story was intended to convey the message that will-power could enable a man to conquer fear and pain, Baden-Powell chose not to mention the emotional and physical agony which had finally broken poor Hazlerigg.

Eloff had launched his attack well aware that the southern relief force was then little more than 60 miles away. On 13 May a Boer commando, under Commandant Liebenberg, made a skilful interception, attacking Brigadier Mahon when he was travelling through thick bush country. On this occasion, however, the British had superior guns and drove off the enemy, but not before sustaining losses of 5 killed and 21 wounded.[68] The Boers had numbered 600 to Mahon's 1,000. But by 16 May, Liebenberg had been joined by 200 men sent from outside Mafeking by Snyman and also, more significantly, by just over 1,000 men under General J. H. De la Rey, one of the Boers' most able commanders. General Louis Botha, in overall command of the struggle to halt Lord Roberts's advance on Pretoria, had sent De la Rey post-haste to try to deny the British press their long-awaited Relief of Mafeking. On 15 May Plumer, who had recently been reinforced by a battery of Royal Canadian Artillery, joined hands with Mahon making a combined British force of roughly 2,000, almost exactly the same as the number of men available to De la Rey.

The Boers took up position astride the Molopo at a place called Israel's Farm, 8 miles north of Mafeking. The British artillery was superior, but the outcome remained uncertain. De la Rey decided to

bluff Mahon into supposing that he had a much larger force than he
really had and to convey this impression, he extended his attack around
a vast perimeter. By attacking Mahon's flanks and threatening his rear,
De la Rey believed that he could get the British to think more about
defending themselves than about attacking him. Mahon, however,
trusted his intelligence reports of Boer numbers and so, deciding that
he could not be facing more than 2,000 men, was sure that they would
be vulnerable (because so widely dispersed) if he pressed straight on.
He did just this and broke through the Boers' thinly held centre, at a
cost of 7 dead and 24 wounded. Ahead of him, the road to Mafeking
lay open.[69]

The noise of the guns was clearly audible in the town and, as Lady
Sarah Wilson recalled: 'The whole of Mafeking spent hours on the
roofs of the houses . . . '[70] As darkness came the distant firing was still
going on, apparently indicating that the Boers were holding their
ground. Unable to see anything, the townspeople left their vantage
points and returned to their homes. When Brian Gardner gave his
account of the Relief, he relied principally upon Major Baillie's gruff
matter-of-fact description, which included the brisk greeting supposedly given by a passer-by to Major W. D. 'Karri' Davies, who led
in an advanced patrol of seven men at 7.00 p.m.: 'Oh yes, I heard you
were knocking about.' Gardner omitted Baillie's sentence which
followed the passer-by's remark: 'However, when it became generally
known a crowd assembled and began to cheer, and go mad again.'[71] At
the time, Hamilton heard 'vociferous cheering about the precincts of
the Headquarter's Office' and, when he came upon Davies, found that
he and his men had been 'in a trice surrounded, besieged with
questions, clapped upon the back, shaken by the hand and generally
welcomed . . . Major Karri Davies called for three cheers for the
garrison, while the crowd took up with tremendous fervour the
National Anthem and Rule Britannia.'[72]

The main force came into the town during the night at 3.30 a.m.
Filson Young of the *Manchester Guardian* was with them. 'No art could
describe the hand shaking and the welcome on the faces of these tired-
looking men; how they looked with rapt faces at us commonplace
people from the outer world as though we were angels, how we all
tried to speak at once, and only succeeded in gazing at each other and in
saying, "By Jove!" "Well, I'm hanged!" and the like senseless
expressions that sometimes mean much to Englishmen. One man tried
to speak; then he swore; then he buried his face in his arms and
sobbed.'[73]

Baden-Powell has been accused of failing adequately to support the
Relief column on 16 May: the suggestion being that he should have
attacked De la Rey in the rear with the Field Force he had recently made
ready for a diversion.[74] This force, however, was only 180 strong and

more significantly included only 30 horses.[75] Gardner reproached
Baden-Powell for not using two or three squadrons of the Protectorate
Regiment, when he could not even raise one after all the casualties and
the bouts of illness. To have done as Gardner suggests would have
been to invite Snyman to attack the town when it was almost entirely
undefended. Baden-Powell's worst problem was his lack of battle-fit
horses, and Gardner's contention that the Protectorate Regiment's
mounts had adequate forage in April is flatly contradicted by the Staff
Diary. On 20 April Baden-Powell wrote: 'We have now come to the
end of our forage.' Two days later he observed: 'Horses are dying as
fast as they can be made into sausages.'[76]

The following day Baden-Powell's and Mahon's combined forces
attacked the Boers' laagers, but not until the enemy was already on the
move. Gardner thought it extraordinary that 'not one British soldier
followed the Boers into the Transvaal'. Since Baden-Powell was the
senior officer and in overall command, this by inference was his fault.
Lady Sarah Wilson explained why no pursuit was mounted. 'After
their exertions of the past fortnight, Colonel Mahon did not consider it
wise to pursue the retreating Boers.'[77] His horses too were in a pitiful
condition.

Filson Young was sensitive to a shift of mood after the initial
euphoria had evaporated. 'It was strange, amid the dreariness and
stagnation of this place, to think of the jubilations at home. What
cheering, what toasting, what hilarity! But here the sparkle in the wine
had died, leaving the cup, that had brimmed, flat and dull . . . Food
was scanty and of the plainest quality, there was no news from the
outside world, disease was still busy.'[78] Some members of the Relief
Column remarked upon the contrast between 'the clean, plump,
pink-and-white faces of the besieged with those of the relieving force,
haggard, gaunt and dust grimed'.[79] But they would never have felt
seriously resentful unless the Siege had caused such raptures in
England.[80]

Nobody in Britain seemed to want to know about Plumer's
regiment, or Mahon's column. The only subject that made headlines
was Mafeking and Baden-Powell. The same jealousy extended to
Rhodesia, where Nicholson and his colleagues felt neglected while
Baden-Powell's name was shouted from the rooftops.

So within a day or two of the little town's relief, understandable
envy and an instinctive feeling that the celebrations in England were
disproportionate combined to spread the first murmurs of scepticism,
which would soon be voiced by most military men who liked to think
themselves well-informed. Mafeking would survive in the public's
imagination as a great achievement until the 1960s, when every old
criticism and denigrating remark was lovingly dusted down to make
the Siege appear to have been not only farcical and insignificant but

contrived from start to finish entirely for the greater glory of Colonel
R. S. S. Baden-Powell.

Afterwards Stephe would say, on many occasions, that the Siege of
Mafeking had been 'over advertised'. But had he been to blame for
this, as his critics would later maintain?

8. Hero in a Chilly Fog (1900)

'His bright fruition of fortune and success was soon obscured by
a chilly fog.'[1]

Winston Spencer Churchill,
writing of Baden-Powell.

Eleven words launched London on five days of hysterical rejoicing:

MAFEKING HAS BEEN RELIEVED
FOOD HAS ENTERED THE GARRISON
ENEMY DISPERSED[2]

The streets of the West End of London were soon choked with
cheering, flag-waving crowds, theatrical performances were interrupted and Henrietta Grace made the first of her many appearances on
her balcony at Hyde Park Corner. A new word was added to the
English language:

Mother, may I go and 'maffick'
Tear around and hinder traffic?

ran Saki's famous couplet. Yet how on earth, given the tiny numbers
of men involved and the size of the place relieved, had it all ended like
this? Even allowing for Baden-Powell's achievement in detaining
Cronje until mid-November, the celebrations would clearly have been
excessive even for the ending of the war.

The idea that Baden-Powell and his family, skilled publicists though
they were, could somehow have engineered this astonishing outburst
of public patriotism is clearly ridiculous. It was true that Henrietta
Grace had done her best to supply eager journalists and biographers
with whatever material they wanted. Yet *she* had never sought *them*
out. Even in November 1899, with six months of the Siege still to go,
she had been bemused by the emotions which Mafeking seemed to
arouse. With her son's life in hourly danger, as she supposed, she saw
little glorious about the war which she described as 'dreadful
barbarism'.[3] By early March Frank Baden-Powell, on the way to his
studio, and Warington, bound for the Law Courts, often had to run the

gauntlet of 'crowds of hundreds and hundreds cheering, all for the welfare of the hero of Mafeking'.[1] Agnes wrote of 'being besieged and assailed on all sides' at 8 St George's Place. 'Our Boers apply for every imaginable thing – one wished to have his five children supported because he read in the papers that Colonel Baden-Powell is so noble, and another says we ought to pay his passage to Australia . . . Now I am begged to send some pictures done by the Colonel to a loan Art Exhibition.'[5]

The reason for these scenes was simple. The disasters to British arms in December's Black Week shifted the spotlight away from the big battalions to the sideshow of Mafeking. After the depressing spectacle of large British forces failing to make headway against smaller numbers of Boers, it was more than pleasant to turn to a small British garrison of volunteers holding out against a greater number of Boers. The remoteness of Mafeking from all help and its insignificant size gave it a romantic appeal that larger and more important towns like Ladysmith and Kimberley lacked. The French and German satirical cartoons representing British troops as savage louts and Queen Victoria as a bloodthirsty old witch had hurt a nation accustomed to considering itself the defender of the weak against the strong and the natural leader of great moral crusades like the fight against slavery. The nation needed 'gallant little Mafeking', and Baden-Powell happened to be in command there. That he was also a talented and unusual man was simply an unexpected journalistic bonus.

Memories of General Gordon's death in besieged Khartoum and pessimistic remarks made by men as eminent as Sir Alfred Milner and Lord Roberts gave the story tension. Was the garrison doomed? Henrietta Grace would not hear directly from her son until 17 March but in November, after reading the newspapers, she was sure that, 'if the Boers send enough men to force the place – our poor Stephe *must* surrender. Everyone calls him "the hero".'[6] From January, Agnes began to write of her brother as 'that poor martyr'.[7] Henrietta Grace took to wearing black. 'Our dear Stephe's brave Defence becomes hopeless,' she wrote early in the New Year.[8]

Stephe himself was not in any way responsible for giving this impression. All his communications with Plumer, Nicholson, Roberts and Kitchener had been cheerful and had emphasized his determination to hold out. Only in late April had he briefly mentioned the possibility of evacuation. But from a journalistic point of view, impending disaster made a better story than a Siege likely to continue for many months. The mother of Captain 'Sausage' Singleton was still terrified for her son in late March: 'No one talks of anything but Mafeking, and the air is full of rumours, one is so strung up that one feels very nervous all the time.'[9] Even Lord Wolseley feared that Roberts was sending a force which would either arrive too late or prove 'too small to effect its

object . . . I confess to a feeling of nervousness about the result.'[10] It is
a great tribute to the atmosphere of hysteria generated by the press that
the Commander-in-Chief should also have shared the sense of a nail-
biting drama reaching its uncertain climax. Certainly there *should* have
been anxiety in October and November while Cronje was still outside
Mafeking, and again in April when Eloff arrived with orders to take
the place; but the sense of constant danger played upon by the press had
little or no connection with what was actually happening.

Baden-Powell's refusal to dramatize the situation made him unpopular with many of the townspeople, who suspected that he was
minimizing the dangers in order to prolong the Siege. He was, they
thought, making the town 'a tool to gain kudos for himself' and 'had
refused assistance' for that reason.[11] Even if he had asked for
immediate aid it would not have been forthcoming. And after the
humiliating British defeats suffered in Natal that December, the
prospects for rescue became even worse. In truth Baden-Powell was
vulnerable to criticism whatever he did. Had he sent back alarming
messages, he would have been thought of as self-dramatising and
lacking in sang-froid. By sending brisk and strictly factual messages to
Roberts via Plumer, he might have thought himself beyond reproach –
but not so, he would be accused by historians of deliberately
cultivating an air of understated courage with his humorous and
laconic messages. The communication generally quoted to show that
Baden-Powell worked hard at conveying nonchalant heroism is the
famous:

All well. Four hours' bombardment. One dog killed.[12]

In fact this message (or one like it) had been sent by runner to Colonel
Plumer on 21 October, without its author having any idea that it
would be telegraphed to Cape Town and thence to London. The actual
message, which when published in the newspapers would stir so many
hearts, started life as a hurried note scribbled on tissue paper:

All is well. There was a four hours bombardment during
which a dog was killed.[13]

Rather in the way that Nelson's 'England expects . . .' message was
much improved by his Signals Lieutenant, Baden-Powell's famous
communication was given its ironic bite by the unknown telegraph
clerk who cut almost half the words and changed another.

Baden-Powell received virtually no information about public
reaction to the Siege in England from any of his regular correspondents, such as Plumer and Nicholson, who wrote only on local military
matters in their notes. As Godley wrote in late March: 'They [Plumer
and Nicholson] are really too bad and B-P is really angry about it, as

neither writes a line except on business.'[14] These 'business' messages from the north came in most weeks, but Baden-Powell received no mail from his family in England until the first week of April – the messengers being unprepared until then to risk bringing in ordinary envelopes and packets which were too bulky to be concealed in the stems of pipes, or in hollow sticks, unlike the tissue-paper 'Kaffir-grams'.[15] So until a month before the Siege was raised, Baden-Powell was largely unaware of his extraordinary celebrity in Britain. By the time he discovered exactly how famous he had become, there was nothing he could have done to change matters even supposing he had wanted to. On 12 April a runner came in with a telegram from the Queen:

> I continue watching with confidence and admiration the patient and resolute defence which is so gallantly maintained under your ever resourceful command. Victoria R.I.[16]

Of course Baden-Powell had longed to be successful and had been tormented by ambition since childhood, but the scale of the fame thrust upon him by the editors and proprietors of the halfpenny press was beyond his comprehension. He was a colonel, yet he had become as famous as the Commander-in-Chief and his Chief of Staff. As Godley later discovered:

> At all the music halls in London, the Cinematograph produces portraits of Roberts, Kitchener, Buller, Kruger, Joubert, which are cheered or hissed, and they used to include B-P, but now they have had to put him on separately at the end and exhibit him for about six encores; they have to wait for about twenty minutes or half an hour for the cheering to abate before they can play 'God Save the Queen'. He got 62 letters by this last mail, many of them containing locks of hair and asking for autographs, and 84 by the one previous![17]

This was the kind of fame that could wreck a man rather than advance his career.

Baden-Powell had always shared his ambition with his mother, yet a month after the Relief he confessed to her: 'I do wish they would not make me their hero. I don't deserve a word of it.'[18] Later he implored Henrietta Grace not to give the press any more biographical inform-ation since he was sick of 'the "gush" and "rot" about me and about you all in the papers'.[19] When his mother was about to join him at the Cape for a holiday in 1901, he warned her that there were 'two things to remember in this Colony: 1.   Everybody is equal to everybody else . . . 2.   Don't consider me a hero with the people you meet. That temporary hysteria has (thank goodness) passed off.'[20] When his name was not in the Coronation Honours, he urged his mother not to be disappointed since 'the Mafeking episode wasn't in reality anything out of the ordinary . . .'[21] Stephe had good reason to want to play down the whole episode. Two months before the Siege ended, he had had a salutary experience which had taught him that jealous individuals would use even jokes against him if he gave them the chance.

It is not known who first thought of the idea of putting Baden-Powell's head on the 3d Mafeking postage stamp used on letters delivered by boy messengers within the defence area, but it is likely to have been either Alick Godley, Lord Edward Cecil or Captain H. Greener, the Chief Paymaster and Postmaster who, earlier in the Siege, had been instrumental in manufacturing bank notes based upon original drawings taken from Stephe's sketch-books.[22] Baden-Powell thought the idea a splendid joke. 'You should see our local Siege bank-notes (drawn by me!),' he told his mother, 'also our stamps (with a portrait of myself as Queen!).'[23] In mid-April, Baden-Powell was distressed to learn that in Bulawayo 'they are furious because B-P has had a postage stamp struck with his head on it . . . They say it is just like his conceit . . .'[24] He was even more shocked to hear that the stamp was considered lese-majesty by high-ranking officers and, so rumour had it, by the Queen herself. He therefore withdrew it and began a cover-up.

The official story would be that Lord Edward Cecil and Captain Greener had decided to put his head on a stamp as a surprise, and therefore did not tell him what they meant to do. In Godley's public version the picture was taken from an existing photograph.[25] That Baden-Powell remained extremely sensitive about the matter is proved by his repetition of Godley's lie in his own autobiography published 33 years after the Siege.[26] In fact Stephe sat twice for his photograph which was taken specially for the stamp by Edward Ross, the auctioneer, who was also a competent amateur photographer.[27] That the idea for the stamp was not his own in the first place seems probable, but there can be no doubt at all that he approved of it and knew all about it from start to finish. Throughout his career Baden-Powell had difficulty in restraining himself from ridiculing the pomposity of high-ranking traditionalists. His music-hall mimicry and his practical jokes had usually provided a safety-valve, but with the stamp he had unwisely allowed 'theatrical B-P' to stray into the territory of 'military B-P'.

This incident gave warning of just how many groups resented him – not just Lord Roberts's staff, certain of Plumer's men and the people in Bulawayo. Nearer home some of the townspeople disliked him for 'keeping secret' detailed knowledge of the progress of the war in other parts of South Africa. They were wrong. Whenever Baden-Powell did acquire such information (which was very rarely), he saw that it was promptly published in the *Mafeking Mail*.[28] Yet the belief persisted that news was being denied the townspeople and the Siege needlessly prolonged. The arrest and brief imprisonment of G. N. H. Whales, the editor of the *Mafeking Mail*, for publicly expressing this fear made matters worse.[29]

No civilians enjoy being ordered around by soldiers and at times members of the Town Guard, who numbered among them some of the town's most prominent citizens, felt that they were being treated with unnecessary lack of consideration. While they had to endure living in trenches, in which flooding and baking heat alternated, they knew that Baden-Powell and his staff were living in comparative luxury in their capacious bombproof.[30] 'The town guard is unpaid which is breeding a sense of injustice,' Baden-Powell noted in his Staff Diary on 16 November. He therefore paid them an allowance of 2/6d a day, which caused further offence since it was only sixpence more than the daily wage paid to the natives digging new trenches.

Another cause of local discontent was a widespread belief that, while the rest of the town was suffering from shortages and privation, the staff enjoyed vintage wines and every kind of delicacy in their private mess. Baden-Powell was always an abstemious man, and it is inconceivable that he became a glutton during the Siege. The extra supplies ordered by Godley from Weil during December and January, before tinned goods were rationed (21 January), included tins of herrings, tongue, Ideal milk and fruit. He also bought marmalade, oaten biscuits, tea, 'Bronco' lavatory paper, bacon, cocoa, lime juice and several bottles of whisky.[31] After the sale of tinned food had been stopped for everyone, Godley put in no more orders to Weil. This does not of course prove that the staff did not eat and drink more lavishly than the rest of the population. The fact that Baden-Powell put his Staff Officers on 'reduced rations without extras of any kind for three days to try by experience to see how far we could make them go', suggests that they did normally enjoy various 'extras'. But to what extent it is hard to tell.[32]

The single most important reason why the townspeople later reviled Baden-Powell was the extent of the delay and confusion over the payment of compensation for damage inflicted during the Siege. They felt that although he set up an Assessment Board to estimate damage, he did not do enough to put pressure on the British Government to make generous awards and to pay promptly. On 20 March 1900 Baden-Powell wrote a forceful letter to the Military Secretary in Cape Town urging Sir Alfred Milner to let him know whether the Government would pay for damage to the colonists' property. 'It would be a good thing if I could have definite news on this point very soon.'[33] In a letter to Colonel Vyvyan a year after the Siege ended, Baden-Powell angrily refuted the townspeople's suggestion that he did not adequately 'represent their case [for compensation] to the Commander-in-Chief. As a matter of fact I went up to Headquarters three times about it.'[34] The councillors clearly overestimated the influence which even national heroes could wield with bureaucracies.

Because their struggle for extra payment and for war damage compensation went on for years after the Siege, the townspeople felt let down and fixed upon Baden-Powell as a convenient scapegoat. When the Siege ended, Colonel Vyvyan remained in the place for two years as Base Commandant and Major Panzera also stayed on, replacing Goold-Adams as Resident Commissioner. These officers' continuing efforts on behalf of the town were therefore self-evident to all, whereas the absent Baden-Powell could easily be accused of caring nothing for the fortunes of the little town which had made him famous. As many of the extant diaries show, he had many admirers at the time but tended to become unpopular later. When he visited Mafeking in 1912 Mrs Nelly Winter, wife of the proprietor of Dixon's Hotel where he had had his Staff Headquarters, was shocked that 'very few of the old siegeites turned up' at the Town Hall to have tea with him.[35]

Baden-Powell did his best to stifle reports of his disagreements with the townspeople. He appealed to them all in an open letter to the *Mafeking Mail*, warning them against the insidious effects of 'grousing'.[36] His efforts at keeping the grousers quiet, at least in public, were broadly successful at the time; but now that historians have discovered that there was dissent, the element of novelty has led them to give the opinions of the 'wiseacres' (as Baden-Powell called his critics) far greater emphasis than the favourable opinions which have also recently come to light.[37] In fairness much of the discontent should have been directed against the Cape Ministry and the British Government, and probably would have been if representatives of either had been conveniently to hand. Instead Baden-Powell collected the brickbats.

In May 1901 Lord Roberts wrote to Lord Kitchener: 'I gather that those who were with Baden-Powell at Mafeking do not look upon him as a great commander. So much stir was made in this country about the defence of Mafeking that some people thought B-P should have been knighted, but promotion to Major-General's rank and the C.B. seem to me quite a sufficient reward.'[38] The C.B.★ was the decoration given to all colonels who had served in South Africa, with or without distinction. If Roberts rather than Wolseley had sent Baden-Powell to South Africa in the first instance, Stephe would have been rewarded very differently.

The officers who obligingly told Roberts that Baden-Powell was not a 'great commander' may have been Vyvyan and Panzera, who were still at Mafeking in 1901 and were definitely thought of by many senior officers as the brains behind the defence – having been directly

★ Commander of the Order of the Bath; inferior to a knighthood in the same order: K.C.B.

responsible respectively for laying out the siege-works and directing the artillery.[39] They had however always been very much under Baden-Powell's directions, as his numerous notes to Vyvyan made abundantly clear.

Another officer commonly supposed to have been overshadowed and denied his proper deserts by Baden-Powell's inflated reputation was Colonel Plumer. In recent years two historians have argued that he contributed more to the military campaign in South Africa than Baden-Powell himself, and that he had brilliantly performed the mobile role which Baden-Powell had been instructed to carry out but had never dared attempt.[40] The facts, however, do not bear this out. Although Plumer is supposed successfully to have defended the vast area of the Bechuanaland Protectorate and to have stopped the Boers invading Rhodesia, no invasion was ever planned or attempted. When Plumer faced an advancing Boer commando led by Sarel Eloff on 2 November at Rhodes Drift, he was at once driven back and was only saved from annihilation when Eloff was suddenly ordered to withdraw by his superior officer in the region.[41]

It has been suggested that during March Plumer had been eager to try to defeat the Boers in the field but had been prevented from doing so by Baden-Powell's timidity.[42] Any objective appraisal of the facts points to the wisdom of Baden-Powell's decision. In mid-March Plumer and he could have matched the Boers' numbers, but the latter's superiority in field artillery (which had already cost Plumer dear) would have given them an immense advantage.[43] Nevertheless on 22 March, Baden-Powell informed Lord Kitchener that he hoped 'to join hands with Plumer at the end of the month'.[44] Plumer was also eager to link up and reported to Baden-Powell on 23 March that his scouts had found no Boers at either Ramathlabama or Jan Massibi's, both places less than ten miles from Mafeking.

By 26 March Baden-Powell knew why Plumer was encountering no resistance. The Boers were concentrating around Mafeking and their numbers had suddenly risen from about 800 to at least 2,000. Furthermore Plumer was advancing from Kanya with only 500 men. Baden-Powell therefore sent a runner with a vital message: 'Reliable native report today, young Cronje with force at Musa. If coming here, Boers combined forces against us will be too great . . . Our present wants do not justify your running great risks.'[45] Four days later he repeated this warning and told Plumer that he could help the garrison more effectively by running in cattle.[46] Plumer's continuing determination to 'join hands' and the usual difficulties and delays in communication with Mafeking led to the disaster of Oaklands Farm. All Plumer's principal engagements with the enemy ended in failure. Even his much-praised tactical decision to set up three supply bases instead of depending upon one had been because Baden-Powell had ordered him to hold a central position at Crocodile Pools and simultaneously to build up depots closer to Mafeking at Kanya and Moshwane.[47] Plumer's greatest achievement was to maintain supply lines from Bulawayo to places as remote as Kanya – to do which, his men lived rough for months at a time in humid and malarial regions like the country around Crocodile Pools on the Limpopo. But no hardships, however bravely endured, could compare with Baden-Powell's achievement in holding Mafeking.

The problem for Plumer, Nicholson, Vyvyan and all those who felt that Baden-Powell received too much attention was that he was a gift to any journalist. His many talents made good copy and he had a rare ability to make spontaneous witty remarks. His name too was a great asset, just as Henrietta Grace had guessed it would be. No mere Colonel Powell could ever have become world-famous B-P; even Emerson Neilly recognized those magic initials as heaven-sent. Two days after the Relief, a leading article by him was published in the *Pall Mall Gazette* entitled 'B-P AND THE B.P.' (the second 'B.P.' standing for the British Public).[48] 'British Pluck' was another fortuitous combination much appreciated by the press. Baden-Powell told his publisher, Mr Methuen, that a 'little lady' had simply written the initials 'B-P' on an envelope and posted it. The Post Office had done the rest.[49] Methuen offered Stephe the truly staggering sum of £5,000 to write a book about the Siege but, despite his lack of capital, he refused. Baden-Powell meant it when he said he 'wanted to let the false publicity of it all die down'.[50]

In many ways it was very unfortunate that he never did write a proper account of the Siege, since it would have pre-empted many of the criticisms later levelled at him. He would also have been able to explain the very great difficulties facing any commander needing to weld into a single, well-motivated community a population containing Chinese, Indians, Americans, Germans, British colonials and Africans. His greatest achievement had therefore been to preserve morale at a remarkably high level; the way the whole town had rallied to him during Eloff's attack had been a tribute to this communal spirit. This idea captivated Emerson Neilly, who thought that the spirit of the garrison explained why Mafeking, 'although lying remote from the main activities of the war, had yet become in a real sense its moral centre'.[51] At the height of the food crisis Angus Hamilton denied that there could be 'any possibility of a weak spirit manifesting itself at this late hour . . . since above all else the townspeople of Mafeking have devoted themselves to the work of holding this important outpost of the Empire until such moment as the Relief may come'.[52]

The Government's four-volume *History of the War in South Africa* began to appear four years after hostilities ended and would be extremely critical of the military conduct of the war. Its authors

recognized that the Siege of Mafeking had had consequences far
outreaching 'the actual military gains resulting from it'. After acknowledging Baden-Powell's lack of modern artillery, the untrained state of
his men and 'the unfortified, open, and unfavourable situation' of the
town, they continued:

> The long struggle to hold and reduce the town had been a combat of
> sentiment which bore little relation to the value of the prize itself.
> The issue was a triumph and defeat for a greater thing than arms.
> Nothing in war is more impressive than a prolonged siege . . .
> More than a heroic charge, or a pitched battle, does the long-drawn
> catalogue of the defence's perpetual resistance, disregarded danger
> and hardship, unquenchable resource and cunning, strike the
> imagination, until their mere continuance becomes a victory to the
> side of the defence and a festering sore in that of the attack. The
> leader who draws up his troops before a place of arms, tacitly
> promises them its capture; and failure entails a dangerous loss of
> confidence not only in their own power but in his. Thus so low fell
> the morale of some of Snyman's best commandos after Mafeking
> was relieved, that they openly mutinied . . .[53]

Lieutenant Hanbury-Tracy in his written account of the Siege was
often very critical of Baden-Powell, and some of his strictures were
thought too damaging for publication by the editor of *The Times
History of the War in South Africa*. Nevertheless Hanbury-Tracy (in
spite of a serious row with Baden-Powell) had no doubt that the
defence would have failed without 'B-P's ingenuity and perseverance'
and his talents as an 'organizer'.[54] A leading military authority, Major
(later Major-General Sir Henry) Thuillier, who would soon become
Commandant of the School of Military Engineering and Director of
Fortifications and Works at the War Office, considered that 'the
defence of Mafeking formed a striking example of what can be done by
able organization and good leadership. Though devoid of nearly
everything which is usually considered essential for a prolonged
defence [in particular, effective artillery and a garrison of regular
troops], Mafeking in every way fulfilled the objects required of a
defensive position.'[55]

With three exceptions (Hore, Moncreiffe and Cecil), Baden-
Powell's officers would look back upon the Siege as a great and
significant time in their lives. From the time of his return to England in
1903, Baden-Powell would hold an annual Mafeking Dinner on the
anniversary of the Relief. These occasions were well-attended and,
even during the Great War, seemed no less valuable. On 23 May 1918,
Baden-Powell wrote to Alick Godley, his closest colleague and friend
at Mafeking: 'It is wonderful how the comradeship of those days seems
to ripen as the years go on.'[56]

Looking back on the Siege from the miserable vantage point of 1918, when corpses lay unburied in the Flanders mud and there had been no ceasefire since the brief Christmas truce of 1914, it is no wonder Mafeking seemed to belong to a golden age of warfare. There each Sunday the guns had fallen silent, and Boer and Briton had helped to bury and retrieve each other's dead. After the attack on Game Tree, Baden-Powell had written to thank Commandant Snyman for the consideration his men had shown to the British wounded left on the field. After his victory over Eloff, Baden-Powell had sent back the Boer dead with a note to Snyman praising 'your Burghers for their courage'. The Mafeking veterans remembered their time together with nostalgia and affection, never with the bewildered bitterness of a later era. The distance between the outrage of poets like Wilfred Owen and the innocent patriotism of the 'loafers', whose spontaneous rendering of 'Rule Britannia' had once echoed from fort to fort, was much more than one of years.

7

THE GENERAL

1. *Commander in the Field (June to August 1900)*

During the past two decades Baden Powell's reputation as a soldier has been assailed both for his 'mistake' in allowing himself to be surrounded at Mafeking and for his 'failure' to distinguish himself in the western Transvaal during the three months which followed the Relief. This is an extremely short period upon which to base any reliable judgement of a general's performance, but since no fewer than three historians have recently castigated him for his inadequacies as a commander in the field during June, July and August of 1900, their charges must be examined.[1]

Lord Wolseley, who was still the Commander-in-Chief in Whitehall, wrote to Baden-Powell immediately after the Relief:

> You did splendidly, it was indeed one of the pleasantest things I had to do in the war when I recommended that the Queen should promote you. You now have the ball at your feet, and barring accidents greatness is in front of you. That you may win the goal is earnestly wished you, by yours very sincerely, WOLSELEY.[2]

But 'wishing' was all that Wolseley would soon be able to do for his protégé. In January 1900 Lord Roberts had arrived in Cape Town as the newly appointed Commander-in-Chief in South Africa and, before the year ended, he would replace Wolseley in overall command of the army. Roberts knew that Wolseley had always derided him as 'little Roberts' or the 'Hindoo', on account of the favour he showed to officers who had served under him in India. As Roberts's star rose, Wolseley's favour would become a liability rather than an asset.

In the weeks immediately following the Relief, Lord Roberts was advancing on Pretoria and therefore out of telegraphic contact with Mafeking. So on 25 May Baden-Powell wrote to General Sir Archibald Hunter (from whose division Colonel Mahon's Relief Column had originally been detached) on the assumption that he was now under Hunter's command. Baden-Powell explained how vital it was that Mahon's force should remain with him, for without it he could not hope to garrison Mafeking and undertake a pacification programme in the western Transvaal.[3] It was therefore very galling to be ordered by Hunter to release Mahon's entire force, which was then 1,150 strong.[4] Without these men Baden-Powell could call upon only 300 members of the Protectorate Regiment (all needed for garrison duty at Mafeking and Zeerust) and Plumer's Rhodesia Regiment.[5] Hunter seemed to be expecting him to attempt the pacification of an area of about 25,000 square miles with 850 men – only 500 of whom could be spared for a mobile role.[6]

Even with this small column, by early June Baden-Powell had confiscated over 1,000 rifles and had arrested nearly 250 Boers and rebel Britons who had refused to cooperate. He had also disarmed large numbers of Africans who had gone marauding after the Relief of Mafeking. Lord Milner reproved him for disarming his African allies; but Roberts agreed with Baden-Powell that the Boers would be unlikely to surrender their firearms if fearing African raids.[7] To those Boers who swore an oath of neutrality and handed over their weapons, Baden-Powell promised protection. The farms of men away on commando were liable to confiscation, and those who harboured the stock and other property of absentees were threatened with severe punishment.[8] Patrols would need to call regularly in case farmers had left home for the war after an earlier British visit. Such patrols would require secure local centres, so Baden-Powell posted strong detachments at places like Zeerust and Lichtenburg. He appointed magistrates and other local officials to act under Lord Edward Cecil, whom he made Civil Commissioner for the north-west Transvaal.

Baden-Powell was convinced that, unless a framework of local government and policing was left behind as the troops advanced, there would always be a tendency for areas supposedly pacified to rise again. It was therefore vexing to hear on 5 June, in his very first communication from Lord Roberts since the Relief, that while his lordship recognized 'the necessity for pacifying the country around Mafeking and for affording protection to Boers who had surrendered', he considered it 'even more important for an efficient force to move about the western part of the Transvaal to break up the commandos which still exist there'. Lord Roberts ordered Baden-Powell to use Colonel Mahon's brigade to discharge this 'more important' duty.[9] Since General Hunter had already reclaimed Mahon's force, the suggestion was not very helpful. And since all the intelligence reports reaching Baden-Powell at the beginning of June indicated that there were no commandos worth the name operating in the western Transvaal,[10] he was not amused to be told that his priority should be the destruction of these non-existent forces. In reply he pointed out that 'the establishment of a police force' ought to be considered a priority and that in the meantime he needed more troops for patrolling. Since the men of the Protectorate Regiment had now served the term for which they had

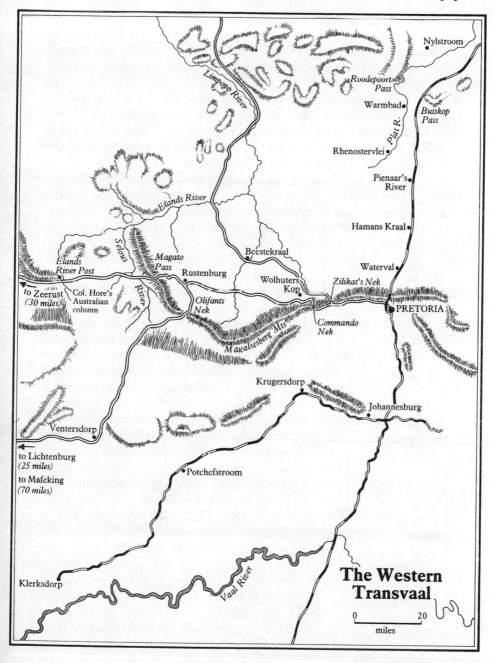

Nylstroom

Limpopo River

Roodepoort Pass

Warmbad

Buiskop Pass

Plat R.

Rhenostervlei

Pienaar's River

Elands River

Hamans Kraal

Magato Pass

Beestekraal

Elands River Post

Selous River

Waterval

Rustenburg

Wolhuters Kop

Zilikat's Nek

to Zeerust (30 miles)

Col. Hore's Australian column

Olifants Nek

Commando Nek

PRETORIA

Magaliesberg Mts

Krugersdorp

Johannesburg

Ventersdorp

to Lichtenburg (25 miles)

to Mafeking (70 miles)

Potchefstroom

Klerksdorp

Vaal River

The Western Transvaal

0   20
   miles

enrolled, Baden-Powell requested the immediate despatch to the western Transvaal of the recently arrived Australian troops, now in Rhodesia under the command of General Sir Frederick Carrington.[11]

On the day he made this appeal (14 June) his men captured Rustenburg without bloodshed. Sixty miles west of Pretoria, the town was the most important centre in the western Transvaal and, in Baden-Powell's words, 'the Mecca of the most old-fashioned and bitter of the Boers'. It had been the country home of President Kruger and his family and on entering the town Baden-Powell accepted the surrender of Piet Kruger, the President's son.

Lord Roberts had by now taken Pretoria, and on 17 June, Baden-Powell – with Godley, Hanbury-Tracy, Gordon Wilson and a small escort – rode into the Boers' capital to see the Commander-in-Chief. At the Residency, Roberts and his staff were waiting on the steps to greet the hero, while a huge crowd in the market square cheered mightily. 'It was awfully embarrassing,' Stephe told his mother. 'I felt as if I were the Queen . . . And Lord Roberts was overkind and flattering.'[12] Despite his embarrassment, Baden-Powell was relieved to learn from the Commander-in-Chief that General Carrington had been ordered to release to him 2,000 Australians from his division.[13] It was intended that Baden-Powell should eventually have a force of 3,000 men.[14] The Australians were inexperienced, but they more than doubled the few hundred men at present under his orders. Lord Roberts intended that, when Baden-Powell's force had been joined by these reinforcements, he should move eastwards to the region of Warmbad to protect Pretoria against an attack from the north, which might materialize after he (Roberts) had led most of his forces away to the east against the Boers' only remaining field army under General Botha.

Because Baden-Powell's first Australians were not due to arrive in Rustenburg until 8 July, he knew that he would not really be strong enough to move closer to Pretoria until then.[15] But when he received reports on 2 July of an impending Boer attack on Pretoria from the north through Zilikat's Nek and Commando Nek (the only two serviceable passes on the Rustenburg–Pretoria road), regardless of the risks he set out immediately with only 600 men, leaving less than 100 to garrison Rustenburg.[16] The following day, as soon as he had his men in position guarding the two passes, he learned from a Boer deserter that his compatriots had somehow assembled 2,000 men around Rustenburg, and meant to attack the town – their intention being to draw him away from the passes to enable them to launch their rumoured attack on Pretoria.[17] Baden-Powell was now in an appallingly difficult position. His first concern was for the safety of the vanguard of the Australians commanded by Colonel Hore. If they came on towards Rustenburg, they might be attacked by the 2,000

Boers outside. At this critical moment the telegraph line was cut between Rustenburg and Stephe's position at Commando Nek, making it impossible for him to communicate with the Australians.[18] He at once sent out Hanbury-Tracy with 140 men to repair the line and then 'go into Rustenburg and keep the telegraph working'.[19] Baden-Powell only wanted them to hold the town for a night, which he expected to be long enough to effect the repairs. Then, as soon as the Australians had passed through the town on the way to joining his main force at Commando Nek, Baden-Powell meant to recall Hanbury-Tracy and evacuate Rustenburg.

Unfortunately for this plan, Hanbury-Tracy arrived at Rustenburg at exactly the same time as a Boer force approaching from the west. In the heat of the moment he ordered his men to race the enemy for possession of the town. A squadron of the B.S.A.P., under Captain R. C. Nesbitt V.C., got in first and immediately took possession of the gaol, a solid stone building in an ideal defensive position. After a lengthy exchange of fire, the Boers withdrew. Hanbury-Tracy lost no time in arresting Piet Kruger and other prominent people whose motives he mistrusted. Just when Hanbury-Tracy needed new orders, he lost telephone and lamp communication with Baden-Powell, but the repaired telegraphic link with Pretoria meant that he could communicate directly with Lord Roberts.

On the evening of the day of his arrival at Rustenburg, Hanbury-Tracy received a telegram from the Commander-in-Chief who had just learned that General J. H. De la Rey was advancing on the town with 2,000 men. Lord Roberts ordered Hanbury-Tracy to retire westwards to Elands River where he should join Colonel Hore and the Australians, who could not now be expected to continue their journey to Rustenburg.[20] Hanbury-Tracy replied that he could not leave and head west because of the presence of a Boer commando on the road. His only course, if he left, would be to rejoin Baden-Powell at Commando Nek. He told the Commander-in-Chief that he personally considered it 'extremely impolitic to retire again from Rustenburg. I have great hopes,' he continued, 'that the local commando will disperse and come in, but, if the present garrison evacuates, it will, I am sure, make a large number of Boers join the commando, besides causing a great deal of unrest amongst the townspeople and loyal inhabitants.'[21] Roberts telegraphed back: 'I quite approve of your action and have directed General Baden-Powell to march back to Rustenburg tonight.'[22]

While Baden-Powell was marching back, Hanbury-Tracy received a demand to surrender from General Lemmer. During the fighting which followed, Hanbury-Tracy would have been overwhelmed if two squadrons of Australians had not providentially arrived during the battle and driven off the enemy.[23] Hanbury-Tracy issued a draconian proclamation warning the inhabitants who had taken up arms that unless they came in and surrendered by 10 July 'all their property would be confiscated, their houses burnt and destroyed, and they themselves treated as rebels,' and exiled to St Helena. The proclamation was sent out to Lemmer's commando and in Hanbury-Tracy's opinion caused 'the majority to go back to their farms'.[24] Three days later Lord Roberts reported to the Secretary of State for War that Rustenburg was 'all quiet and public confidence was entirely satisfactory due to the prompt and bold grasp of the situation taken by Major Hanbury-Tracy'.[25]

Baden-Powell arrived at Rustenburg with 450 men and eight guns on 8 July. Because the Boers were in such strength in the region, he had not been happy to be ordered to return. De la Rey could easily block the Magato Pass to prevent the greater part of the Australian force from reaching Rustenburg, which was why Baden-Powell had expressed himself in full agreement with Roberts's earlier order to Hanbury-Tracy to withdraw to the west.[26] But Baden-Powell could not help being impressed by the apparent success of Hanbury-Tracy's measures. Hanbury-Tracy was sure that the recent evacuation of Rustenburg had led directly to the recent increase in Boer activity in the western Transvaal. Inevitably it had been taken as a sign of weakness. Lord Edward Cecil, the Civil Commissioner at Zeerust, had been appalled when he thought Baden-Powell had abandoned Rustenburg. 'I suppose he had some reason or else the gods were angry with him and drove him mad!'[27] Cecil did not realize that the gods in this instance had been Lord Roberts and his staff.

Yet the situation at Rustenburg was still extremely serious; and while Baden-Powell would come to believe with Hanbury-Tracy that Roberts had been right to order him back to the town to hold it, he could see immense problems ahead if they were unable to bring in the rest of the Australians and the supply convoy now languishing at Elands River. These supplies would be badly needed if Rustenburg were ever to face a siege. Hanbury-Tracy's proclamation might sway General Lemmer's men but not the 2,000 veterans with De la Rey. Had General Carrington only parted with the Australians earlier, Baden-Powell knew that his worst problems would never have arisen. At the back of his mind was the knowledge that Lord Roberts really wanted him somewhere to the north of Pretoria and not in Rustenburg at all. But that could not be helped, since Roberts himself had ordered him back to Rustenburg.

On 10 July Baden-Powell was digging in, facing 2,000 or more Boers under the dreaded De la Rey with just over 1,000 men of his own. About 300 of these would have to be sent to hold the Magato Pass through the Magaliesberg Mountains, otherwise Hore and the Australians would never be able to leave Elands River. With an attack on the town possible at any time, Baden-Powell would always have to maintain a garrison of 300 men or more; thus only 500 men would be available for a mobile role. There was therefore no hope at all of helping Lord Roberts north of Pretoria.[28] The Commander-in-Chief himself acknowledged this on 12 July, when he warned Baden-Powell that De la Rey was moving in his direction and concluded his message: 'I quite approve of your holding on to Rustenburg and hope we shall be able to clear the district long before your month's supplies are finished.'[29]

Lord Roberts had not yet realized the strength and cohesion of the forces which the Boers were gathering together in the western Transvaal. Then on 11 July, De la Rey attacked Zilikat's Nek (which Baden-Powell had been holding until recalled to Rustenburg), and took the pass, capturing 324 British soldiers and inflicting 72 casualties. This defeat also caused the loss of adjacent Commando Nek.[30] Rustenburg, now cut off from Pretoria, was in great danger. The loss of these vital passes was principally due to Lord Roberts's failure to provide an adequate force to replace Baden-Powell's men when they had been ordered back to Rustenburg.[31] Although the Commander-in-Chief would soon joke about Baden-Powell's predilection for sieges, it was entirely Roberts's own fault that Stephe had ever been placed in this position.

Lord Roberts was sufficiently worried about Baden-Powell's position to order Major-General Smith-Dorrien to assist him from the south by driving General Lemmer out of Olifants Nek (the pass due south of Rustenburg). Smith-Dorrien's column, however, was attacked before reaching its objective and, after suffering heavy casualties, was obliged to turn back.[32] De la Rey was now ready to devote his attention to the helpless Baden-Powell cooped up in Rustenburg. Stephe estimated that De la Rey's successes had increased the number of Boers on commando in the western Transvaal to 7,000.[33] Fortunately he had seen all this before. 'If a force of enemy comes to invest us here it can do us no harm and will reduce the numbers opposing Lord Roberts [east of Pretoria],' he told the garrison.[34] Brian Gardner has pointed to the similarity between this statement and the rationale used by Baden-Powell for defending Mafeking. Mr Gardner was implying that old habits die hard and that Baden-Powell was once again cravenly avoiding the mobile role which his Commander-in-Chief had required of him.[35] In reality Baden-Powell had not chosen his position; but being in it, he sensibly laid mines (real and dummy ones), issued 'Notes for Commanders of Sections of Defences and Defence Posts', and supervised the siting of guns and the building of siege-works. He even announced a scale of rations.[36]

Having landed Baden-Powell in this predicament, Lord Roberts now became obsessively determined to move him to the east, 'to take charge of the country from Commando Nek northward and eastward'. Such a move could only end in disaster unless Baden-Powell's column were first substantially reinforced; his numbers still only amounted to half the 3,000 men promised by Roberts a month earlier.[37] Roberts therefore proposed to send Lieutenant-General Lord Methuen to a rendezvous with Baden-Powell, who would then earmark 'such of Methuen's troops as you may consider necessary'.[38] The Commander-in-Chief assured Baden-Powell that Methuen would clear the Boers from Olifants Nek and then, having left a battalion to defend the pass, would move on eastwards. 'You could then march together with a column sufficiently strong to drive everything before you,' Roberts told Baden-Powell. 'I am anxious there should be no delay in your coming this way [towards Pretoria] once Olifants Nek has been cleared.'[39] Lord Roberts sent this message on 16 July, but later that day he learned that Christiaan De Wet* had escaped from the encircling British forces in the north-east corner of the Orange Free State. Within days De Wet's movements would seem immeasurably more important to Roberts than anything happening to Baden-Powell in the western Transvaal.

Lord Methuen's arrival on 21 July with 4,000 men came as a great relief to Baden-Powell who had just heard that a Boer laager had been spotted near the Zeerust road just to the west of the Magato Pass. Relishing the freedom which Methuen's numbers gave him, Baden-Powell sent out a party of 300 Australians from Magato Pass to scatter these Boers and to reconnoitre the Zeerust road with a view to escorting Hore's convoy and the rest of the Australians from Elands River to Rustenburg. But after marching seven miles the Australians were ambushed by 1,000 Boers; and, besides suffering over 40 casualties, lost 200 of their horses.[40] Baden-Powell immediately sent out a further 200 Australians and four squadrons of the Protectorate Regiment under Captain FitzClarence. These reinforcements persuaded the Boers to withdraw. This incident convinced Methuen and his second-in-command, Smith-Dorrien, that De la Rey ought to be tackled without delay. Late on the evening of 22 July, while the Australians were still fighting for their lives, Methuen telegraphed Lord Roberts as follows: 'I have consulted with Baden-Powell. We attack De la Rey at Beestekraal Tuesday.'[41]

To Baden-Powell's horror, the following morning Methuen received orders from Lord Roberts to march 50 miles south at once with his whole force to defend the railway between Potchefstroom and Krugersdorp. Roberts was convinced that De la Rey was responsible for capturing a train on this stretch of line, but Baden-Powell knew

* De la Rey's only rival to be considered the Boers' greatest general.

perfectly well that the Boer leader was still a few miles east of Rustenburg. The railway attack was really the work of a far less formidable commander, P. J. Liebenberg, and as Baden-Powell suspected it had been carried out in order to draw Methuen away from the Rustenburg area.[42]

The removal of Methuen at this moment was not only a savage blow to Baden-Powell's hopes of regaining the initiative in the western Transvaal but also virtually condemned Hore and the Elands River garrison to death or capture. If Baden-Powell and Methuen had only been allowed to take on De la Rey they would have outnumbered him by at least 2,000 men, so it is not far-fetched to suggest that the whole course of the remainder of the war might have been different if they had followed through their plan. From this time forth, for the remaining two years of hostilities, De la Rey would exercise an independent command in the western Transvaal which neither Roberts nor his successor, Lord Kitchener, would be able to challenge. It would be De la Rey's exploits more than anything else which twenty months later would persuade Kitchener that the war must be ended by negotiation rather than outright military victory.[43] By then Lord Methuen himself would have particularly good reason for regretting that he had been called away so suddenly in July 1900. On 7 March 1902 he was decisively defeated by De la Rey at Tweebosch in the western Transvaal, his force being broken up and he himself severely wounded and taken prisoner. Although Baden-Powell has been accused of being too timid to achieve anything in the western Transvaal,[44] in reality – given his tiny numbers and Lord Roberts's contradictory orders – he did well to avoid a fate similar to Methuen's. When it is recalled that Kitchener could not defeat De la Rey with 16,000 troops, the absurdity of supposing that Baden-Powell's men could have acted against him with only 1,500 is manifest.

With the architect of the Boers' successes at Modder River and Magersfontein laagered only a few miles north-east of Rustenburg with 3,000 men and 10 guns,[45] Baden-Powell was staggered to receive a telegram from the Commander-in-Chief on the day that Methuen left, stating: 'We must break up the several small parties of Boers now opposing us in the western district and this will be better done by movable columns than by having detached small posts about the country . . . I am depending upon some assistance from you in the country north and west of Pretoria.'[46] The dismissal of De la Rey's force as one of several 'small parties of Boers' struck Baden-Powell as particularly inept given what had recently befallen his Australians. Baden-Powell must have wondered what the Commander-in-Chief had against him. The Field-Marshal had previously ordered him to hold Rustenburg and the two western Magaliesberg passes and had acknowledged that while doing so he would need more men in order

THE BOY-MAN

to send a force to the area north-west of Pretoria. For this very reason Methuen had been ordered to join him and to hand over some of his men to Baden-Powell before marching back with him towards Pretoria. In the event Methuen had drawn on Baden-Powell's already dwindling supplies, and had only left behind an under-strength battalion specifically to hold Olifants Nek. Not a man of this force would be available to Baden-Powell for his mobile column. It was out of the question for him even to consider leaving Rustenburg in present circumstances. If he did, he would endanger both the town and his wholly inadequate field force, in turn putting at risk his men at Magato Pass and Olifants Nek. And if these passes were lost, Colonel Hore and the men at Elands River would be doomed.

On 25 July Baden-Powell telegraphed to Hore warning him that: 'The Boers are gradually drifting westwards'; and that De la Rey would move with them. He enjoined Hore to dig in and 'make yourself secure against shell-fire'.[47] The following day Baden-Powell informed Roberts that, before leaving him, Methuen had undertaken to return as soon as possible to deal with De la Rey as previously agreed, and then 'to clear the country north-west and north of Pretoria'.[48] The movements of Christiaan De Wet would, however, ensure that Methuen never returned.

Lord Roberts's erratic behaviour continued. He had originally sanctioned the placing of garrisons at Zeerust and Lichtenburg, so Baden-Powell was distressed to be attacked by him on 26 July for 'scattering small detachments about the country' since their 'easy capture encourages the enemy'. Roberts ended this disagreeable telegram with a question: 'Are you still shut up in Rustenburg?' – as if, given Methuen's removal, he could be anything else.[49] Cut off from Pretoria by the loss of Zilikat's Nek, and still with 1,500 men fewer than the 3,000 promised by Roberts in mid-June, how could he move out of Rustenburg without encouraging De la Rey to attack the town? In reply to the jibe about 'small detachments', Baden-Powell pointed out that he had withdrawn one small garrison and intended to abolish the post at Elands River once Hore was rescued. He reminded Lord Roberts that on 25 June and 16 July he had asked for adequate garrisons for Lichtenburg and Zeerust which, with Rustenburg, he was still convinced ought to be retained as supply bases and refuges for loyalists.[50]. His request had never been granted. He did not bother to contradict Roberts's suggestion that patrolling was more effective than establishing small garrisons. It seemed self-evident to him that mobile columns could not operate without supply bases; both were equally important and mutually dependent. If Lord Roberts's arguments against small garrisons were taken to their logical conclusion, it would mean the abandonment of every post and town between Mafeking and Pretoria. How then would these patrolling columns be supplied and provisioned in such a vast area entirely controlled by the enemy? While 20,000 men were being thrown into the De Wet hunt and an identical number allocated for dealing with General Botha at Bergendal, Lord Roberts had decided that he could not honour his undertaking to provide Baden-Powell with a mere 3,000 men. Consequently the western Transvaal and all the Magaliesberg passes would fall into Boer hands and De la Rey would be left the undisputed ruler of an immense and virtually impregnable region.

On 29 July Roberts made his final decision to pull out of the region and sent a telegram to Baden-Powell telling him that 'beating the enemy in the field' rather than 'arranging to garrison chief towns' was the only way to win the war. Once beaten in the field 'they will see they have no chance against us . . . and we can then settle outlying districts.'[51] Baden-Powell's arguments in favour of retaining garrisons at Zeerust, Lichtenburg and Rustenburg were brushed aside. Lord Roberts had decided to send Lieutenant-General Ian Hamilton with 7,600 men to evacuate Baden-Powell and escort him to a safer position near Pretoria. The despatch of Hamilton's force would mean a delay in the preparations for what the Commander-in-Chief hoped would be his final battle against Botha; but De la Rey's presence in the area had obliged Roberts to send such a large force. The Field-Marshal's resulting unfairness to Baden-Powell is typified by a comment in a despatch of 2 August to the Secretary of State for War, Lord Lansdowne: 'Now I am obliged to send Ian Hamilton to relieve Baden-Powell, who seems to have a strange fancy for being besieged.' In another despatch to Lansdowne, dated 6 August, Roberts again represented Baden-Powell as a man who had deliberately courted entrapment. That Baden-Powell was at Rustenburg because he had been ordered back there from Commando Nek by Roberts himself was not mentioned.

Roberts's order of 29 July to evacuate Rustenburg would not be rescinded even when General Hamilton agreed with Baden-Powell that the town should be held. On 3 August Hamilton told Baden-Powell that he had telegraphed to the Commander-in-Chief saying 'that I was inclined to agree with you', but warned him that 'Lord Roberts's mind is inexorably made up and you must therefore come away with me.'[52]

Lord Roberts's hope of 'beating the Boers in the field' was no longer a realistic possibility. His final set-piece battle against Botha took place at Bergendal between 27 and 30 August and was technically a British victory; but few casualties were inflicted upon the Boers, whose forces thereafter fragmented into separate commandos. This did not bode well for the British, who could only respond by splitting their forces into groups of a similar size in order to hunt down these elusive Boer units. In December 1900 shortly before leaving South Africa for

England, Roberts described the war as 'practically over'.[53] But it was
not. The war of big battles was over, but the guerrilla war was only just
beginning. Sir Alfred Milner, the High Commissioner, exposed the
fatuity of Roberts's strategy a month before the Field-Marshal sailed:

> The fatal error is not to hold district A & make sure of it before you
> go on to district B . . . The consequence is we have a big army
> campaigning away in the front & the enemy swarming in the
> country behind it . . . The time for over-running is over . . . stage 2
> is a gradual subjugation, district by district, leaving small en-
> trenched & well-supplied garrisons behind your columns as they
> sweep the country & mounted police to patrol between these
> posts.[54]

This was exactly what Baden-Powell had attempted to do in the three
months following the Relief of Mafeking. The priority, as he had
immediately realized, was not to punish rebels but to give protection
to those prepared to swear not to take up arms. Only a policy of
garrisoning and policing could achieve this. Roberts, rather than
Baden-Powell, had been naïve in his strategic understanding of how
to win the war. The trick was not just to defeat the Boers but to stop
them rejoining guerrilla units after their commanders had abandoned
combined action in favour of lightning raids.

Although the Commander-in-Chief was as determined as ever to
abandon the western Transvaal, he knew that something would first
have to be done about Colonel Hore and the men at Elands River. On
28 July, in response to a suggestion from Baden-Powell, Lord Roberts
had ordered Sir Frederick Carrington to march to Elands River to
escort Hore and his convoy through the Magaliesberg to Rustenburg.
Baden-Powell must have found it ironic that Hore of all people, whom
he had always thought such a blunderer, should now be causing
everyone so much worry. But it was hardly Hore's fault that he was
trapped at Elands River with 307 Australians and 197 Rhodesian
volunteers. Fortunately for them all, Baden-Powell had warned them
on 25 July (when Roberts recalled Methuen) to expect a siege and to dig
defences.[55]

On the morning of 4 August De la Rey closed in on Hore's post and
opened fire with seven guns. Within hours most of the garrison's oxen
and horses were dead or dying but, thanks to Baden-Powell's
warning, the human casualties were light. Since General Hamilton and
Baden-Powell were unable to communicate with either Hore or
Carrington – but had learned on 5 August that Elands River was under
attack – they tried to discover whether the garrison had been evacuated
westwards by General Carrington, or whether he had been driven
away by De la Rey. On 6 August Baden-Powell and Colonel Mahon
(who commanded one of the three columns that Hamilton had

Far left: Olave Soames aged nine with her father Harold.

Near left: Baden-Powell and Olave on the *Arcadian* January 1912.

Below: Baden-Powell in 1910 on a fishing trip in the Canadian wilderness with backwoodsmen companions.

Olave Soames aged fourteen with her governess friend and mentor Miss Sybil ('Ba') Mounsey-Heysham. Olave appears to have turned abruptly to face the camera as if surprised during a private game.

Above: Baden-Powell and Olave, shortly after their engagement, with Hampshire Scout Commissioners.

Right: Olave Baden-Powell in Boy Scout uniform in 1914.

Below: Baden-Powell at Pax Hill, looking out from the balcony which he made his bedroom soon after buying the house in 1918.

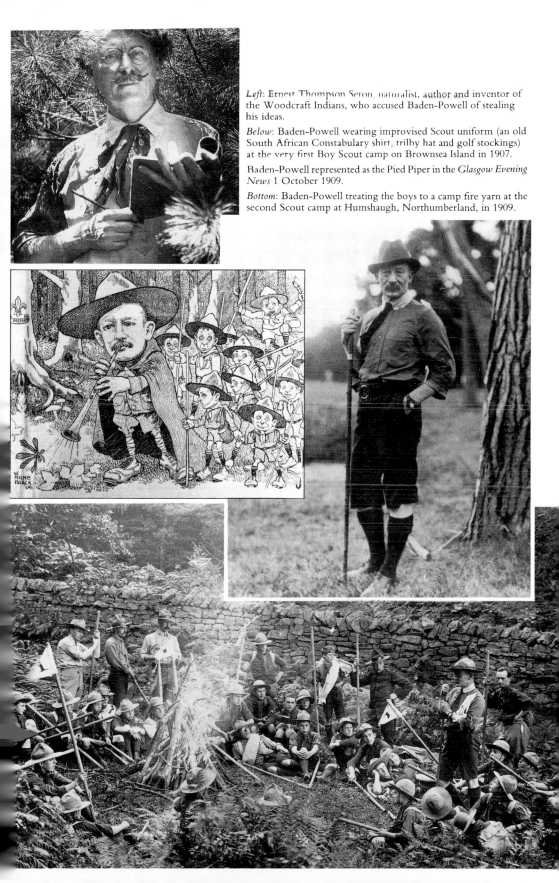

Left: Ernest Thompson Seton, naturalist, author and inventor of the Woodcraft Indians, who accused Baden-Powell of stealing his ideas.

Below: Baden-Powell wearing improvised Scout uniform (an old South African Constabulary shirt, trilby hat and golf stockings) at the very first Boy Scout camp on Brownsea Island in 1907.

Baden-Powell represented as the Pied Piper in the *Glasgow Evening News* 1 October 1909.

Bottom: Baden-Powell treating the boys to a camp fire yarn at the second Scout camp at Humshaugh, Northumberland, in 1909.

Left: Eric Walker. Baden-Powell's private secretary 1909–1914.

Right: A virtuous Boy Scout drawn by Baden-Powell, leaping over life's shortcomings.

SELFISHNESS

RACIAL JEALOUSIES

RELIGIOUS DIFFERENC

CLASS CONSCIOUSNES

GRUMPINESS

Above: Baden-Powell and J. Archibald Kyle at a Boy Scout Rally in 1909.

Right: Sir Francis Vane and one of his British Boy Scouts in 1911.

Left: 'If I were a Boy Again' by Ernest S. Carlos; a favourite painting used by Baden-Powell in campaigns to recruit Scoutmasters.

Below: Baden-Powell with Scoutmasters (his 'Boy Men') at Gilwell in 1922.

Bottom: Rousing the Scouts at Gilwell with his koodoo horn, 1922.

Below: Frank Gidney, the first Camp Chief at Gilwell.

Below: Members of the elderly Headquarters Committee circa 1922.

Lady Baden-Powell as Chief Guide 1922 (from the official programme of the 1924 World Camp).

Agnes Baden-Powell as President of the Girl Guides 1912.

Alice Behrens, the first Guider-in-Charge at Foxlease. Dame Katharine Furse, as Director of the W.R.N.S. in 1918.

Royal Salute: Sir Robert and Lady Baden-Powell with Peter and Heather in 1923.

A frightened Peter, an exasperated Olave and a resigned Chief Scout await the arrival of the Prince of Wales in 1922.

Father and son at Pax Hill 1923.

Right: This picture of 'Geordie' Lennox-Boyd and Heather Baden-Powell appeared in the *Sunday Pictorial* above a tactfully phrased notice announcing that their proposed marriage would not take place.

Below: Josephine Reddie shortly before she met Peter.

Peter in 1932.
Baden-Powell and Betty seated, with Pet and Heather on the ground. Adelboden, Switzerland 1932.

brought to Rustenburg) set out on a 'reconnaissance in strength' with 1,000 men. Baden-Powell was also accompanied by Plumer and J. S. Nicholson. He and these officers have been accused of being negligent towards Hore because they went no further than the Selous River, eight miles from Rustenburg, and only one third of the way to Elands River.[56] There they heard 'guns firing and gradually retiring westward as if the garrison were successfully withdrawing [with Carrington] in accordance with their instructions'.[57] Baden-Powell has been censured for having turned back before the return of his scouts, who would have brought definite news about what had happened at Elands River. There is some force in this criticism, but again the real fault lay with Lord Roberts.[58]

At midday on 6 August Baden-Powell sent a message to General Hamilton at Rustenburg saying that his scouts had still not reported back, but that he doubted whether Hore had surrendered, even if, as he suspected, Carrington had failed to relieve him.[59] Instead of ordering Baden-Powell and Hamilton to delay their departure from the western Transvaal until they had rescued Hore, Roberts telegraphed Hamilton telling him that, regardless of Carrington's success or failure (and failure seemed more likely), 'Baden-Powell must accompany you to Pretoria.' Lord Roberts ended by expressly refusing to give Hamilton permission to delay his departure. In this telegram the Field-Marshal indicated who would one day be the scapegoat for the whole débâcle.

> All that has occurred lately in the western Transvaal [he told Hamilton] points to the impropriety etc. of small isolated posts unable to hold their own, and the impossibility of our being able to carry on large and more important operations with our existing force when small places have to be maintained and provisioned.[60]

Roberts did not alter his decision even when, later that day, he learned that Carrington had definitely been beaten back by De la Rey. Just as Baden-Powell and Methuen together could have dealt with De la Rey, and have rescued Hore had they been allowed to do so – now Baden-Powell and Hamilton could have done the same if given an extra 48 hours. The Commander-in-Chief claimed that they did not have 'sufficient supplies' to mount a rescue.[61] But this was nonsensical, since Hore had immense stores at Elands River and in any case the country was one in which a large column could commandeer enough to live on in an emergency.[62] Roberts had been entirely wrong 'to leave Hore's garrison to their fate', as he himself put it; and his later attempts to blame Baden-Powell were unjust and dishonest. In the end Hore and his garrison would escape having to surrender; an unexpected turn of events enabled Lord Kitchener to relieve them after they had lived through twelve days of hell in the midst of the rotting carcasses of their animals. Thanks to the lessons learned at Mafeking about the construction of bombproofs, only 12 out of the 504 men were killed and 38 wounded.[63] Sir Arthur Conan Doyle rightly described 'this stand on Elands River as one of the very finest deeds of arms of the war'.[64] Unaware of the full story, Brian Gardner and Rayne Kruger (the author of *Goodbye Dolly Gray: the Story of the Boer War*) both blamed Baden-Powell for Hore's predicament.[65]

Lord Roberts had wanted Hamilton back at Pretoria by 9 August so that he could begin his campaign against Botha without further delay, but – on the very day on which he decided to abandon Hore – General Christiaan De Wet, a hundred miles to the south, duped the surrounding British and, having crossed the Vaal without being detected, began to march northwards with astonishing rapidity. The Commander-in-Chief should at once have sent back part of Hamilton's force to Rustenburg and Olifants Nek, for it was towards this pass that early intelligence reports suggested that De Wet was heading – his object presumably being to join hands with De la Rey in the western Transvaal. Yet Lord Roberts allowed De Wet's subsequent movements to deceive him, and left Olifants Nek unoccupied after Baden-Powell's evacuation. On 5 August, before leaving Rustenburg, Baden-Powell had argued that whatever else might be abandoned, this pass due south of the town *must* be retained.[66] Roberts would live to regret taking no notice.

> It is of the utmost importance [the Field-Marshal told Hamilton] that De Wet should not be allowed to get north of the Magaliesberg . . . if you can stop him the war will be practically over.[67]

Sir Ian Hamilton hurried back towards Olifants Nek when it at last became clear that De Wet meant to use it to slip through the Magaliesburg range. Hamilton has been severely criticized for arriving at Olifants Nek too late to prevent De Wet marching through the pass, but the blame for this débâcle should have been shared with Lord Roberts who had left the pass untenanted in the first place.

The one general whom Roberts blamed was virtually the only one entirely innocent: namely Major-General R. S. S. Baden-Powell. As early as 1 August, Roberts had told Stephe that: 'Had I not to send Ian Hamilton's force with supplies for you, I should have employed it . . . against De Wet, and should practically have been able to surround him.'[68] So the word would get about that Baden-Powell had been responsible for De Wet's escape, when in reality his continued presence at Rustenburg and at Olifants Nek (which he had so fervently advocated) would have guaranteed the Boer general's capture. If Roberts had ordered Baden-Powell and Hamilton to relieve Hore and then to move south, they would have arrived by 13 August in the perfect place to trap De Wet. The Rustenburg episode does not as has been suggested prove that Baden-Powell was a poor general, but that

Lord Roberts was good at blaming others for his own blunders.

When Baden-Powell left Rustenburg for the last time, he found it a chastening experience. He and his officers had undertaken to protect the families of all those who had taken the oath of neutrality; not unnaturally, these people felt betrayed and fearful for their lives. He was therefore obliged to take 239 citizens away with his column when he withdrew. It dismayed him very much that their 'loyalty' had earned them nothing better than the loss of their property and exile. Baden-Powell's personal views about the desirability of holding Rustenburg had fluctuated, but after his return there on 8 July he had become convinced that the advantages of retention outweighed the disadvantages. The authors of the British Government's *History of the War in South Africa* would later point to the speedy realization of the very fears he had entertained on leaving. 'The evacuation of this stronghold of the old Boer spirit would mean a great revival of hope amongst the despondent enemy, and would lead to the re-establishment of a new seat of government in the heart of the Transvaal, with consequent persecution of all who had sided with the British.'[69] Apart from feeling that he had betrayed the inhabitants, Baden-Powell was also wounded by a widespread rumour that he was leaving because he was afraid to face the coming onslaught.[70]

On 14 August Lord Roberts was obliged to pocket his pride and ask Baden-Powell's advice. If De Wet reached Rustenburg via Olifants Nek, 'how would he be likely to travel eastwards?'[71] Baden-Powell replied that he would head for Commando Nek, which Stephe himself had been holding since evacuating Rustenburg. And indeed, it was there three days later towards sunset that De Wet announced his presence. Stephe's force of 1,100 men was split between Commando Nek itself and a position just below the pass. He himself was in the foothills when he spotted Alick Godley riding towards his bivouac. Godley brought a note that contained a demand to him to surrender; it appeared to have been signed by the man whom 20,000 British troops had failed to catch. Godley asked what reply he should send back to De Wet, who claimed to have 2,000 men and 8 guns – almost double the number of Baden-Powell's men and exactly double the number of his guns. Stephe smiled and told Godley 'to say that my Dutch was hazy: did he mean that he wanted us to surrender, or was he offering to surrender himself to us?' Baden-Powell's note elicited an angry reply, which convinced him that the demand had not been a ruse and that De Wet himself really was at the foot of the pass with his commando.[72] If De Wet had found Commando Nek unoccupied, he would probably have risked committing part of his force to a lightning raid on Pretoria but, knowing that he was being followed by General Hamilton, he decided not to try conclusions with Baden-Powell.[73]

True to his habitual lack of consideration for Baden-Powell, Lord

Roberts ordered him to remain at Commando Nek while instructing
Colonel T. E. Hickman and Major-General A. H. Paget to pursue De
Wet northwards.[74] Baden-Powell, however, argued so forcefully for
part of Hickman's force to be left to defend Commando Nek that Lord
Roberts eventually gave in, thus freeing him to join in the pursuit.[75]
By 20 August Baden-Powell was at Waterval, where he learned that
De Wet's commando was about 15 miles away heading north. At a
place called Haman's Kraal, Baden-Powell attacked a column of about
400 Boers. This commando was not in fact De Wet's but Commandant
Grobelaar's, which was assisting De Wet's men by moving north in
parallel with them. Baden-Powell fought a mobile sniping battle in
thick bush against the Boers as they retreated in the direction of
Pienaar's River, where his men took 100 of them prisoner at a cost of
five British dead.[76]

On the following day, while General Paget appealed to Roberts for
reinforcements, Baden-Powell pressed on with 900 men towards
Warmbad, twenty miles further north.[77] He reached the small town
just ahead of De Wet's column and forced it to head westwards away
from its leader's intended junction with Louis Botha. He shelled the
convoy attached to the commando and in the ensuing confusion
managed to take 25 prisoners; at the same time he released 141 British
soldiers captured earlier in the campaign. It was now learned that De
Wet and his staff had left the commando several days earlier, and were
thought to be heading south. The enemy held the hills immediately
north of Warmbad, so Baden-Powell prepared to work round to the
rear of their position in order to cut them off. On the evening of the
24th, he made a night march which brought him up right behind them
at dawn the next day. If General Paget had then been able to attack
them, the two Boer commandos would have been forced to surrender.
But at precisely this moment, Roberts decided to withdraw Paget's
troops to Pretoria.

Undaunted, Baden-Powell, although commanding a mere 900 men
against the Boers' combined strength of 3,000, managed to persuade
Grobelaar to come in and begin surrender negotiations.[78] In the end
the Boer commander did not fall for this gigantic bluff; and lack of
supplies compelled Baden-Powell to return to Warmbad.[79] Lord
Roberts sent a telegram congratulating him on preventing 3,000 Boers
joining their main army east of Pretoria. Eight years later the author of
volume III of the Government's authoritative history of the war
concurred with this verdict.[80] This had been a great achievement,
brought about by a mixture of guts, effrontery and rapid action – the
reverse of the lack-lustre timidity which, according to his critics,
characterized Baden-Powell's military conduct during these months.
It is worth recalling that had he not complained vociferously, Roberts
would have left him in an entirely passive role at Commando Nek and

would never have given him any opportunity to show what he could do in command of a mobile column in the field. It is regrettable that Lord Roberts had only allowed Baden-Powell these ten days in which to demonstrate his talent for the mobile work which he had so often held up to him as of primary importance.

On 29 August Baden-Powell received a memorable telegram from Lord Roberts: 'I want you to see me without delay regarding formation of Police Force for Transvaal, Orange River Colony, and Swaziland.'[81] Michael Rosenthal has suggested that Roberts's nomination of Baden-Powell to head the police force may have been 'a gentle way of easing him out of the strict chain of military command' because of his supposed failure as a commander in the field.[82] Actually, Roberts had 'eased him out of the strict chain' immediately after the Relief of Mafeking by denying him enough men to show what he could do. In this context Stephe's appointment to command the new police force cannot justifiably be seen as demotion, but on the contrary as a slight thinning of that 'chilly fog' in which the Commander-in-Chief and his envious staff had deliberately enveloped him. At a conservative estimate the police would require an establishment of 5,000 men: and since Baden-Powell's force in the western Transvaal at its largest had never exceeded 2,000 men, it is easy to see why he was not cast down by this development. It seems likely that, when Roberts was finally forced to acknowledge that his hope of ending the war through set-piece battles was illusory, he cast his mind back to his earlier correspondence with Baden-Powell.

In mid-June the Field-Marshal had told Baden-Powell that, 'The arrangements which you are making for the pacification of the country, and the collection of supplies etc., seem to be excellent, and attended with most satisfactory results.'[83] A few days earlier on 9 June, Baden-Powell in one of his earliest pleas for reinforcements had explained that he needed to leave behind small posts and garrisons 'pending the establishment of a police force'.[84] A letter which Lord Roberts sent to Sir Alfred Milner on 4 July establishes beyond doubt that the Commander-in-Chief did not view the appointment as demotion. 'For head of the military police,' he told Sir Alfred, 'Baden-Powell is by far and away the best man I know. He possesses in quite an unusual degree the qualities you specify, viz: energy, organization, knowledge of the country, and a power of getting on with its people.'[85]

By 21 August Roberts had to admit to the Queen that the future lay with pacification rather than outright military victory. 'So long as the Boers kept in fairly compact bodies we knew what to do with them, but now that they have broken up into small parties . . . the advantage is all on their side.'[86] The only solution seemed to be to leave behind a network of police patrols and garrisoned posts after the army had broken up the larger forces. Roberts knew that Sir Alfred Milner shared Baden-Powell's views about area-by-area pacification, so it seems probable that his recommendation of Stephe to raise and run the police was not only a conciliatory gesture but a belated admission that the policing procedures which Baden-Powell had pioneered in the western Transvaal were the right ones for ending the war.

2. Constabulary Duty to be Done (September 1900 to March 1903)

At Rustenburg Baden-Powell had received many sackfuls of mail from admiring members of the public, but out on the veldt, where he had been for most of the three months following the Relief, he had escaped the consequences of his fame. During these winter months he found the cold sharp air at night and the warmth of the sun by day delightfully invigorating. The broad vistas across empty plain and hillside filled him with the sense of freedom he had known in Rhodesia. Away in every direction stretched the sun-bleached grasses of the veldt, glowing in great swathes of umber, orange and pale yellow.

Although such a landscape was slipping past as Stephe's train steamed westwards towards Cape Town, he found the journey far from relaxing. He was leaving the veldt and heading for the 'civilized' world from which those mail-bags had come. He chanced to share his compartment with Arthur M. Brookfield, now Colonel of a yeomanry regiment but who had once been kind to him when they had been subalterns together in the 13th Hussars during the late 1870s. While Stephe only wanted to be nostalgic about their days in India, Brookfield kept badgering him for anecdotes about Mafeking.[1] During this journey Baden-Powell understood, not just intellectually but in reality, how Mafeking had changed his life. He would always seem different to officers like Brookfield, as well as to ordinary soldiers. When the train stopped en route at two large transit camps, hundreds of men crowded around his carriage to cheer him. At one place they swarmed into his compartment in order to shake his hand. Many tried to give him things: 'a matchbox, an old knife, money, anything they happened to have about them . . . One tore from his breast his only possession, a medal ribbon.'

Given advance warning of the civic reception being arranged for him at the railway station in Cape Town and not wanting to be mobbed, Stephe telegraphed Government House announcing his intention of arriving a day later. The mayor, however, was not so easily fooled, and when Baden-Powell's train approached the platform he saw 'a swaying mass of humanity overflowing on to the roofs of neighbouring trains, all cheering and waving'. In the midst of this multitude, the mayor gave an inaudible speech and then Baden-Powell was 'bundled off on the heads of a roaring mass, out of the station into the sunlight . . .' He recalled that:

> . . . two excellent fellows seized hold of my breeches' pockets, on either side, to prevent my money from falling out, and in this way I was marched, more or less upside down, through Cape Town, all the way to Government House. There I was carried past the bewildered sentry and was at last deposited with a flop in the hall. The butler, hastily summoned from his pantry, appeared on the scene to find a dishevelled, dirty, khaki-clad figure standing there, with a roaring mob outside the door.[2]

Before coming to Cape Town, Baden-Powell had gone to see Lord Roberts briefly at Belfast in the eastern Transvaal. There they had discussed the broad structure and duties of a South African police force, which Baden-Powell would be expected to agree upon in detail with Sir Alfred Milner who, as Governor of the Transvaal and the Orange River Colony, would be his immediate superior.[3] Milner himself had been eager to secure the services of the hero of Mafeking, not least because his famous name would be a magnet to would-be recruits.[4] Stephe therefore found himself dealing with a warmer, less arrogant Milner than the aloof pro-consul who had prevented him from recruiting before the Siege. Sir Alfred seemed delighted with Baden-Powell's plans. 'His scheme,' Milner told Joseph Chamberlain, 'will admirably meet immediate requirements.' On the subject of saving money, Sir Alfred found Baden-Powell 'very ingenious'.[5] 'He is throwing himself into the work with great energy,' the High Commissioner told Roberts in a letter in which he gave notice to the Commander-in-Chief that, whether hostilities could be ended quickly or not, 'we may have to treat the war as over and so to speak recommence business before guerrilla resistance is stamped out'.[6] Although Roberts was much less optimistic about being able to end the war by a specific date, the police force would in any case be expected to be ready for duty by June 1901.

It was not long before Baden-Powell realized that in the short term Lord Roberts and Lord Kitchener – who were under constant pressure from the Cabinet to send more men home – saw the formation of a police force as a providential opportunity for reducing the number of soldiers serving in South Africa. When, on 5 October, Roberts wrote to Milner suggesting the police ought to number 10,000 rather than the 6,000 recommended by Baden-Powell, Milner and Stephe were not deceived. They wanted their police force to do police and pacification work and not to have to help get Roberts and Kitchener out of the predicament in which over-optimism and a misguided reliance upon short-term enlisted troops had placed them. Lord Roberts did not suddenly mean to make Baden-Powell's force more important; his sole concern was to save money. A War Office memorandum dated 27 October makes this very clear. 'Lord Lansdowne agrees with Lord Roberts in connection with 10,000 police, which would be cheaper than troops and enable many to go home.'[7] Being well aware of this motive, Baden-Powell insisted that his police should be called the South African Constabulary rather than the South African Rifles, the name preferred by Lord Roberts. Milner agreed, and also upheld Baden-Powell's stand against an establishment larger than 6,000 men. No lover of spending money, Sir Alfred even agreed to pay Baden-Powell's 200 officers higher salaries than their equivalents in the army in order to secure the best men available.[8] Sadly, less agreeable relations lay not far ahead.

Lord Kitchener took over as Commander-in-Chief in South Africa on 28 November 1900, and Lord Roberts returned to England to replace Lord Wolseley in Whitehall. Two days earlier, to Baden-Powell's dismay, Milner had at last given in to Roberts and agreed to the S.A.C.'s establishment being fixed at 10,000 provided that the army would pay for the extra 4,000 men. Although the Colonial Secretary, Joseph Chamberlain, had informed the War Office that members of the police could only be employed for 'the suppression of all tumults, riots, and affrays, or breaches of the peace', he had permitted a proclamation of inauguration which included the proviso that they might occasionally be called upon 'to discharge military duties'.[9] This was a role which Milner and Baden-Powell very much hoped would be avoided, but after the blistering Boer offensive launched in December 1900 it seemed likely that hostilities would still be widespread when the constabulary was ready for duty in June 1901. At the time of the Colonial Office's agreement with the War Office for there to be an extra 4,000 men, the Colonial Secretary had conceded that the S.A.C. should be placed directly under the orders of the Commander-in-Chief in South Africa rather than under those of the High Commissioner. This would inevitably create tension between Lord Kitchener and Sir Alfred Milner.

Lord Roberts had promised Baden-Powell that 20 per cent of his officers, N.C.O.s and men would be supplied by the army.[10] Stephe had also been led to believe that a similar proportion of his horses, transport, clothing, food, equipment and hospital beds would also be paid for and provided by the army. 'From the very first,' he wrote sadly, 'these undertakings began to fail.'[11] Many officers for whom he had applied were denied him, and he only managed to secure Colonel J. S. Nicholson as his Chief of Staff in December.[12] Early in the New Year he found in Colonel A. H. M. Edwards and Colonel H. L. Pilkington capable commanders for two of his four divisions. Colonel

Sam Steele, commanding the Constabulary's Canadian volunteers, was foisted upon him; risen from the ranks of the Royal Canadian North-West Mounted Police, he was a ruffian famous for his savage discipline and lack of consideration for man and beast.[13]

Baden-Powell had not wanted to recruit large numbers of Canadians and Australians, but had been obliged to do so because most of the available men in South Africa were being recruited for the army's irregular mounted corps.[14] These men, particularly the Canadians, would cause him his worst problems with drunkenness and indiscipline. Two years later he wrote to 'the Boy' McLaren (his recruiting officer in London) to inform him that, 'we are still clearing out loads of our "wasters" – mostly Canadians,' and lamenting that 'so very few colonials are sufficiently sober'.[15] Baden-Powell's own preference, as he often explained to McLaren, was for Englishmen and not 'old soldiers, but young gentlemen', just down from university or members of the Y.M.C.A., volunteer corps, or cycling and cricket clubs.[16] Stephe, however, was only allowed to recruit 1,000 Englishmen whom 'the Boy' would ensure were 'educated, well-recommended, medically fit, and good shots and riders'.[17] Unfortunately for Baden-Powell, the Australians and Canadians came with much of their own equipment and so were much cheaper and therefore more popular with the British War Office. When he received no more than a handful of officers from the army (nowhere near the 20 per cent promised), Stephe was reduced to seeking them out at the vast depot camp at Stellenbosch, described by him as 'a sort of purgatory in which officers were placed who had been responsible for any regrettable incident'.[18]

The supply of horses posed a problem almost as severe as the shortage of officers. The army's inability to honour any part of its undertaking to provide mounts for the S.A.C. was patent by mid-November, at which time Baden-Powell was obliged to send an officer to Australia to buy horses for his corps. Inevitably the army's failure to aid him plunged him into a financial and administrative nightmare; nor was it helpful that Milner should have chosen this time to start carping at him for failing to exercise sufficient financial control. In late November Baden-Powell's paymasters in London had still not authorized him to rent or purchase a central barracks.[19] Only in January was he able to establish his Headquarters at Zuurfontein and his training depot in the old dynamite factory in nearby Modderfontein, midway between Johannesburg and Pretoria. Shortages of equipment remained acute and new arrivals from England were obliged to start their training wearing bowler hats.[20]

A blunder on a par with Roberts's misguided neglect of civil pacification was the War Office's decision (based on Roberts's over-optimism) to release seasoned colonial volunteers and yeomanry after

only a year's service. In 1901 Kitchener would suffer the consequences
of this folly when his vulnerable half-trained replacements fell an easy
prey to the Boers.[21] The immense pressure on Kitchener to bring an
end to the war was at its greatest while he was awaiting the arrival of
the new troops being sent out to replace Roberts's time-expired men.
These started to arrive in March 1901, and by May 37,000 had been
landed; however, very few could be put into the field against the
Boers. The 17,000 Imperial Yeomanry and the 24,000 irregulars raised
in South Africa were, in the words of Erskine Childers (the editor of
volume V of *The Times History of the War in South Africa*) 'through no
fault of their own, as yet only the raw material for soldiers'.[22]

No wonder then that Kitchener should have cast longing eyes on the
S.A.C. whose recruitment officers, according to Childers, 'had
obtained a finer class of recruit than any other volunteer or irregular
body'.[23] Baden-Powell, however, had only undertaken to have his
corps ready by June; and although he agreed to make some men
available before then, he refused to cut short his training plans for the
majority. This exasperated Lord Kitchener who was desperate for
fresh troops. Between March and June, he wrote many despatches to
Lord Roberts expressing his frustration with Baden-Powell for not
making his police available for service in the field. The following is
typical: 'Baden-Powell does not appear to do anything with his S.A.C.
men beyond dressing them up. I am trying to get Milner to urge him
on. . . . But I fear Baden-Powell is more outside show than sterling
worth.' Michael Rosenthal quotes such criticisms without considering
matters from Baden-Powell's point of view.[24] Naturally he was not
eager for his men, who had been trained as policemen, to be used as
cut-price soldiers; and he had never undertaken to have them ready,
even for police duties, before June. Nor should the herculean task
which Baden-Powell had taken on be underestimated. He had not only
agreed to recruit and train 10,000 men and their horses in eight months
but had undertaken to create an entirely new organization with
auxiliary branches for feeding, equipment, housing, medical treatment, transport and payment. All this – along with a training in
criminal investigation – had to be achieved in a remote country while
hostilities were still in progress, without any assistance from the army.

By late May Kitchener's tone towards the S.A.C. had altered for the
better but a residue of resentment nevertheless remained. Each man
had entirely different objectives and trusted to very different methods.
Childers was one of the most astute analysts of British military
strategy during the war, and in his opinion, 'Kitchener was inclined to
think too much of propelling and too little of educating his army – to
look rather to the quantity than the quality of the work done.'[25] Many
of Kitchener's élite commanders complained bitterly about his
tendency to rush military targets so that essential work was often left

unfinished.[26] Baden-Powell, by contrast, was a man who took great pains to educate and train his men and never expected results from them before they were ready.

The S.A.C. was a civil force and only loaned by Sir Alfred Milner and the Colonial Office to the Commander-in-Chief for the duration of hostilities. Lord Kitchener's relations with Baden-Powell were inevitably affected by his (Kitchener's) worsening relations with Milner. Kitchener was sure that he could have negotiated peace with the Boers in March 1901 if Milner had not made the terms of surrender too bitter for the Dutch rebels in the Cape Colony to swallow.[27] Kitchener and Milner could not even see eye to eye over the military strategy most likely to bring the war to a speedy conclusion. The Commander-in-Chief favoured 'a sweeping and scouring system' which involved farm-burning and the removal of Boer women and children to concentration camps – his purpose being to deny their menfolk, out on commando, the supplies and intelligence furnished by a sympathetic populace. Kitchener's hope was that these ruthless measures would swiftly break the Boers' will to go on fighting. Milner, on the other hand, favoured a gentler policy of 'protection' which meant clearing a particular area of all hostile forces and then preventing their return by erecting a continuous perimeter fence within which regular patrols would operate, moving between garrisoned strong-points. Sir Alfred considered the S.A.C.'s proper role lay in garrisoning and patrolling these 'protected areas', but only after the army had first cleared them.[28]

Joseph Chamberlain and Milner thought Kitchener's methods barbarous, and this opinion became widespread after public revelations about starvation and disease within the camps. On 2 July the Cabinet told Kitchener bluntly that unless he could end the war by September, he would have to adopt Milner's 'protection' policy.[29] In May Kitchener had furtively embarked on an experiment with Milner's and Baden-Powell's preferred method around Bloemfontein, the capital of the Orange River Colony. The task of making this experimental 'protected area' effective had been entrusted to the S.A.C. as one of its first assignments. The security of Bloemfontein had soon been guaranteed by an almost impenetrable screen of perimeter fences and internal strong-points.[30] It is easy to understand why this success was not to Kitchener's liking, and why he should have continued to write unfavourable comments about Baden-Powell to Lord Roberts. Stephe was after all Milner's man in Kitchener's eyes, and Milner's desire to have Kitchener replaced as Commander-in-Chief in South Africa was widely known.

The next major move towards extending the protected areas was made in the country around Pretoria and was carried out by the S.A.C. during September. A few months earlier, great strides had been made towards mass-producing inexpensive but effective metal blockhouses. Until July blockhouses had only been used to protect the railway lines, but in that month the idea took shape of extending blockhouse lines across country and so creating fenced areas of manageable size within which the Boers could be dealt with as if inside a gigantic cage. Thus Kitchener's system of 'scouring' the countryside would form the prelude to the institution of one of Milner's and Baden-Powell's protected areas, with the perimeter fence studded with blockhouses serving as a net into which the Boers could be driven by a number of 'driving columns'.[31] This pattern of 'drives' would be the strategy which would finally achieve results. Since it depended upon elements common to Kitchener's, Milner's and Baden-Powell's schemes, it proved acceptable to all.

Unfortunately for his relations with Kitchener, Baden-Powell fell ill – through a combination of overwork, nervous stress and what he himself described as influenza (but which his younger brother called 'a general breakdown') – in June 1901, the very month in which the S.A.C. started to make its usefulness felt.[32] By the time he returned to South Africa in January the following year from his first home leave since 1895, the hard work put in on the organization of the force had paid off and the rewards been reaped by Colonels Nicholson and Edwards who had effectively run the S.A.C. during their command-ing officer's absence. On 24 May, Kitchener had told Roberts that some of Baden-Powell's officers were dissatisfied and wanted to leave.[33] Whether Nicholson orchestrated this leak of anti-Baden-Powell feeling (as he appeared to have done in Rhodesia) is uncertain, but he stood to gain most from Baden-Powell's fall. Baden-Powell's trust in the loyalty of his immediate subordinates in the S.A.C. was laudable but not very wise, given the resentment which his celebrity had caused.

Towards the end of the six months which Baden-Powell spent in England, Milner wrote to Chamberlain: 'I happen to know privately, though not directly, that without exception they [the officers immediately under Baden-Powell in the S.A.C. hierarchy] . . . all feel that they have got on better in his absence. So strong is this feeling that it has been urged on me from various quarters that I should try to dispense with his services.' Milner argued that it would be a better arrangement if Nicholson were to run the S.A.C. directly under his (Milner's) orders without there being any Inspector General. 'Questions of the actual distribution and use of the force . . . and its relations to the local government would be decided by the High Commissioner [i.e. Milner] as they ought to be, while the actual command of the men in the discharge of their duties would rest with the several heads of divisions.' Milner's motives in bringing such matters to the Colonial Secretary's attention were hardly disinterested;

he wanted to secure for himself total control over the S.A.C., without having a famous Inspector General as 'a fifth wheel of the coach'. He explained to Chamberlain that the abolition of Baden-Powell's job would have to wait until the hero of Mafeking could be 'dispensed with without the appearance of "Stellenbosching" him, always provided some other command could be found.'[34]

When Baden-Powell was in England, Milner was not alone in giving thought to his future. His other long-standing detractors were equally concerned about him. In view of Kitchener's previous remarks concerning Baden-Powell's tardiness, Roberts wrote asking his commander at the Cape whether he thought Baden-Powell ought to return to South Africa, 'or is there anyone you can name who would do better at the head of the constabulary?'[35] However, when handed the knife, Kitchener dropped it abruptly. 'I would not advise a change as he gets on well with Milner, and he is in a certain way distinctly sharp and clever. I daresay he will do better after the war is over than while it lasts.'[36] It is a measure of how bad Kitchener's relationship was with Milner that he had no inkling that the High Commissioner viewed the existence of Baden-Powell's job as an irritating brake on his own powers. But even while trying to get rid of Baden-Powell, Milner felt impelled to concede that the S.A.C. constituted 'a magnificent body of men'. 'Baden-Powell has certainly served us well in some respects,' Sir Alfred told the Colonial Secretary. 'I like him personally and I think very highly of him. He is hard-working, extraordinarily ingenious and resourceful. But for all that he is not a good organiser. He has too many "happy thoughts"; he is constantly changing his plans, and in doing so he worries and fails to win the confidence of the men immediately under him.'[37] Like Kitchener, Milner complained but at times seemed almost ashamed of doing so. In January 1902 St John Brodrick, the new Secretary of State for War, gave Lord Kitchener another chance to be rid of Baden-Powell, but once again Kitchener (never renowned for his forbearance) declined to take advantage of this final opportunity.[38]

So what of Milner's criticisms? Were Baden-Powell's subordinates really upset and confused by his 'happy thoughts'? When head of the S.A.C.'s C.I.D., Captain M. M. Hartigan thought that Baden-Powell's 'originality in many ways gave us much that we had to live down. Our uniform, the details of which were frequently altered, was unlike anything in the army or in any police force.'[39] When Baden-Powell had raised his two regiments of irregulars in the summer of 1899, he had favoured badges of rank for officers being worn on the cuffs as in the Royal Navy, rather than on the shoulder as was traditional in the army. As a full Colonel he had often worn circular rings identical in shape (though not in colour) to those worn by naval captains. When he designed a uniform for his policemen – requiring

them to wear naval rings on the cuff with a round loop in the first ring –
the Admiralty objected and he was obliged to change the loop to a
diamond shape. Unfortunately this pattern was used in the Merchant
Navy, which carried less social kudos than the Royal Navy. Such
matters were not considered trivial in 1901 and would have aroused
great indignation. Baden-Powell also caused offence by his choice of
headgear for his force. The American Stetson hat with its wide stiff
brim was more difficult to keep smart out on the veldt than the usual
soft-brimmed hat worn by irregular corps. Nor was it considered
amusing that the Stetson particularly appealed to Baden-Powell
because its trade name 'The Boss of the Plains' contained a play on his
initials. The hat was embellished with a cockade described by its
suppliers as 'Jays' Wings'; in fact it was made of dyed chickens'
feathers, but this did not stop a rumour spreading that thousands of
jays were being shot to furnish the S.A.C. with their distinctive
cockades.[40] Baden-Powell went to exceptional lengths to prevent
unauthorized people from wearing the S.A.C. hat, even threatening to
shoot any Boer found in possession of one.[41]

Although some aspects of the uniform undoubtedly caused derision,
his khaki coats with roll collars and khaki shirts with neck-ties were
later adopted by the whole army, replacing the traditional military
stand-up stock collars. Unfortunately the combination of jodhpurs,
short-sleeved shirts (with naval rings) and the Stetson hat created a
curious impression: rather as if Buffalo Bill had redesigned the Royal
Canadian Mounted Police's uniform for a Ruritanian naval brigade.
Of course many historic military uniforms were (and still are)
outlandish. That the mood during the Boer War was towards an
unostentatious conformity in uniform design made Baden-Powell's
foray into this field injudiciously idiosyncratic. After he sensed this, he
made sure he gave the impression that the men of the S.A.C. had
themselves chosen the words 'Be Prepared' for their motto; but in view of
the pleasure which he clearly derived from any play on his initials, it is
unlikely that the suggestion came from anyone but himself.[42]

Baden-Powell's decision to institute a Badge of Gallantry for his
corps provoked more serious discontent. He claimed a special award
was necessary because his men were not part of the army and so were
often considered ineligible for ordinary military decorations. Captain
Hartigan, however, felt that the existence of the S.A.C. medal made
Baden-Powell less inclined to report to the Commander-in-Chief
particular acts of bravery which, had they been reported, would
probably have resulted in the award of a D.S.O. or D.C.M.[43] To
Baden-Powell there was a special pleasure in having his own awards
and badges which resembled the pride he had once taken in designing
and awarding a special badge for his scouts in the 5th Dragoon Guards.
One of his long-standing ambitions had been to lead a body of men

who were specifically members of *his own corps*, not just under his orders but recruited by him for a force which he had invented. The S.A.C. was almost the embodiment of the 'regiment of gentlemen privates' which he had longed to raise nearly twenty years earlier.[44] In view of the later Scout Law and Promise, it is noteworthy that he issued moral guidelines for members of the S.A.C., who were urged to be 'unselfish gentlemen' whatever their origins.

Since Baden-Powell drew a large number of his officers from the ranks (thus making himself even more unpopular in high places), this should not be dismissed as humbug. Because he thought of his men as potential officers, he expected a dauntingly high standard of conduct from them.[45] His elevation of N.C.O.s to commissioned rank was attacked in the letters column of the *Pall Mall Gazette* by a correspondent who considered that many of the S.A.C.'s officers were of a type 'no gentleman would associate with in civil life'.[46] Baden-Powell's democratic impulse coexisted somewhat uneasily with his simultaneous recruitment of almost 2,000 public school men into the S.A.C.. Be that as it may, he never courted popularity with his political and military superiors by admitting many of the nominees put forward by them for commissions. In May 1902 he pointed out to Milner's irate private secretary, who had written to complain about most of his master's candidates being turned down, that he 'could not say how many promising recommendations I have had from Lord Roberts, Mr Brodrick, M.P.s by the dozen, and even Royalty, but they amount to so many that had I taken them all we should have been entirely officered by nominees.'[47] He made no exceptions for his family, telling his sister-in-law Frances that if anyone tried 'to bring interest to bear and quote high connections, it damns the candidate's chance at once. *Merit* is *all* I go by . . .'[48] Such sentiments are disconcerting when voiced by someone who had been so adept at bringing every possible form of influence to bear in his own interest.

There was, however, nothing bogus about Baden-Powell's determination to see that the rank and file were fairly treated. As with his promotion of N.C.O.s, his order that any trooper with a grievance could go over the head of his divisional commander and appeal to the Inspector General in person was anything but popular with his senior officers.[49] Nor did they like being told to treat their men 'as reasoning young Englishmen and not as mindless boys to be ordered about'.[50] When 23 men in the S.A.C.'s 'E' Division were court-martialled for refusing to march when ordered to do so, Baden-Powell thought that sentences of imprisonment were too harsh and sent a reproachful circular to all his officers telling them 'to pay proper attention to the wants of their men, and show them some encouragement and leniency when they are doing extra hard work.'[51]

Baden-Powell's view of the army as 'a university' for the working class would one day be a motive force behind the Boy Scouts. Just as he had wanted to improve his men, so he would want to improve the nation's boys. 'Here [in the army] they gain, in addition to their school knowledge, a development of physical health and stamina . . . an army officer has in his hands a valuable power as great as that of any schoolmaster or clergyman for developing his men in the attributes of good citizens.'[52] Historians who believe that militarism was all that Baden-Powell derived from the army have not taken account of the social idealism he displayed while commanding the S.A.C..

Almost every military man who witnessed the many disasters of the Boer War and who knew the percentage of men rejected for military service on account of their poor physical condition worried about the British Army's ability to hold its own against European regulars in the event of a future war. This explains a letter which Baden-Powell wrote to his publisher, Mr Methuen, in January 1901: '*Now* is the time, while enthusiasm is still warm and before we sink back into our English easy chair, for us to prepare a wise and practical organisation of the splendid material lying ready to hand.'[53] This letter has been seen as an indication of his militaristic intentions for the future Boy Scouts;[54] but since no evidence exists to suggest that he then had any premonitions about one day founding a youth movement, all that it really suggests is that he favoured better training for young recruits and possibly an organization like the as-yet-uninvented Territorials.

In later years Baden-Powell sometimes made extravagant claims for the S.A.C. as 'a peace army'.[55] This was wishful thinking, although the force did to some extent become useful to the community after the cessation of hostilities: carrying mails, diagnosing cattle disease and tracing stolen animals. After a tour of South Africa, during which he had been escorted by Baden-Powell, Joseph Chamberlain described the S.A.C in the House of Commons 'as a great civilizing and uniting influence'.[56] In reality, as Captain Hartigan admitted, 'the police had been formed to establish military outposts in a form least likely to injure the susceptibilities of a proud people. The Boers certainly looked upon us as an occupation force rather than as police.' But Hartigan also though the S.A.C. 'responsible for the success of the Treaty of Vereeniging', by which the war had finally been ended.[57]

During the four months before Colonel Nicholson joined as his Chief of Staff, Baden-Powell had been at work in his office from before dawn until seven or eight in the evening every day of the week.[58] And until he collapsed in May 1901, his hours had remained almost as demanding. When he returned to South Africa in January 1902, after his six months' sick leave in England, he decided to leave the office work to others and to enjoy a mainly peripatetic role inspecting S.A.C. posts and columns in the field. In September 1902, on a tour of inspection of small posts, he rode nearly 300 miles in eleven days; but his record was an astonishing 104 miles ridden within 24 hours.[59]

'The most convenient organization for rapid training and use in the field,' Baden-Powell told the Royal Commission on the War in South Africa, 'is the troop of about 80 to 100 men sub-divided into about 10 combatant squads of a corporal and about six men.' These six men under their corporal manned the S.A.C.'s posts and blockhouses, and 'in a sparsely populated country of great distances and poor communication represented government to the Boers and natives'.[60] The corporals had considerable responsibility and often earned promotion to the rank of sergeant and even became trainee officers. Baden-Powell was convinced that in future conflicts large bodies of men under strict discipline would be at a disadvantage when pitted against an enemy whose forces were split into smaller groups of well-motivated intelligent men.

There was never any dispute about the excellence of the S.A.C.'s personnel. Nevertheless the use to which the force was put has been rightly criticized. This, however, was beyond Baden-Powell's power to influence; Kitchener and Milner between them determined the role the S.A.C. should play. Effectively Baden-Powell was employed for eight months in organizing his force; then, after only two months of active operations, he had been sent home. On his return from sick leave the war had continued for a further five months, which meant that the S.A.C. was only employed as a police force (its intended role) for seven months under his command. It is therefore impossible to pass any meaningful judgement on his success or failure as the commanding officer of the world's largest mounted police force.

Baden-Powell was much more interested in drawing up schemes and in suggesting new methods of recruitment and training than in day-to-day administration. His money-saving ideas, as Milner had acknowledged, were ingenious, and the 'happy thoughts' which Milner claimed with some justice had confused Stephe's senior officers had also given to his new force a distinctive identity that would otherwise have taken years to establish. He depended upon the organizational skills of Nicholson and Curtis but a willingness to delegate, as Godley had truly remarked during the Siege, remained one of Baden-Powell's strengths. Like many innovators, he tended to underestimate the conviction with which reactionary views were often held.

In his correspondence with Lord Kitchener, Lord Roberts had shown little understanding of Baden-Powell's problems in inaugurating his force without significant help from the army. Nevertheless, towards the end of 1902 Roberts was responsible for Baden-Powell's selection to fill one of the most coveted posts in the British Army: that of Inspector General of Cavalry. In explaining his choice to the

Secretary of State for War, Roberts intimated that Baden-Powell had written 'quite the best book I have ever read on scouting, and is undoubtedly clever'. Failures in intelligence and in scouting, as Lord Roberts knew well, had been in large part responsible for the worst British defeats in the war. The Commander-in-Chief told the Secretary of State that he had been almost 'put off Baden-Powell by hearing he had not done as well as I had expected at the head of the South African Constabulary'; but this, Roberts assured St John Brodrick, had been because he had not been 'a great administrator'. By contrast, 'as an inspector,' Roberts continued, 'he is doing very well – very active and painstaking . . . If his health is all right I believe we could not do better.'[61]

The post of Inspector General of Cavalry was perhaps less sought after than command of a cavalry division but, a year after the end of the Boer War, the job carried great responsibility. In 1903 one of Roberts's objectives as Commander-in-Chief was to re-define the cavalry's role. After a war dominated by columns of mounted infantry, it was questionable whether cavalry could continue to exist as a separate arm in future. Because the Inspector General's job was to inspect cavalry regiments and to report on their efficiency, it inevitably involved him in drawing conclusions about the utility of cavalry in modern warfare. The suggestion that this appointment – like his job with the S.A.C. – was another sideways move is misleading. The adverse comments by Lord Kitchener and Milner would have enabled Roberts safely to send Baden-Powell home to a regional general's command had he wished to do so. His elevation seems therefore to have been another belated attempt by the Commander-in-Chief to make amends for his shabby treatment of Baden-Powell in the months after the Relief of Mafeking.

8

HOME COMES THE HERO

1. To Wed or Not to Wed

Baden-Powell's return from South Africa on 8 March 1903 was unlike any other homecoming for him. During the 37 years since his departure for India as a 19-year-old boy, he had spent only three years in England and a further three in Ireland – neither of these three-year spells being unbroken. Now at last he was returning home to take up a job which would occupy him for a minimum of four years and seemed likely to lead to further employment in the United Kingdom. There was another significant difference between this new post and all his previous home appointments – as Inspector General of Cavalry, he would be expected to live in London and work at the War Office.

His mother made it clear that she now expected him to live at home with her, along with Agnes, Warington and Baden. As long ago as the mid-1890s, George had urged Henrietta Grace to leave her large and ruinously expensive mansion at Hyde Park Corner for a country 'haven of rest'. This would have enabled Baden, Frank and Warington to buy a lease on a more modest house; and Agnes could then have divided her time between London and the country, no longer being always at her mother's beck and call.[1]

Stephe therefore regretted Henrietta Grace's recent purchase of a long lease on a house in Prince's Gate, only marginally smaller than 8 St George's Place and in the heart of fashionable South Kensington. His mother had not been persuaded to leave her old home by any concern about the burden which its upkeep was placing upon her children, but rather because of the arrival of the tube railway at Hyde Park Corner.[2]

Baden-Powell not only faced the prospect of becoming the largest contributor to his mother's expenses but also the future financial saviour of his brothers and sister. He was horrified to learn that Baden was considering leaving the army and starting a scientific journal.

Cui bono? [Stephe asked derisively] It will be the final straw against your soldiering . . . It will give you piles of work, no money return, and no thanks . . . they will pass you over. We are not rich at home and you've got to see what pay or pension you are going to get, not only for yourself – but as far as I can see to help keep F[rank] and Az [Agnes] in their old age. A major's pension won't do that – and no writing of scientific journals, or invention of small 'jins' will add much to it. Your only way is to stick to the soldiering . . . Then if you get your promotion you will be in some position to get a wife with something of her own – which you won't get if you go on poking the fire with bits of wire.[3]

But Baden left the army and bought his journal. Within three months *Knowledge* (as it was ironically called) was £400 in debt, and by its fourth issue under his ownership had lost half its initial circulation of 3,000 copies. Only the generosity of George's widow saved Baden from bankruptcy.[4]

The implications of his brother's financial failure were alarming for Stephe. The job of supporting Agnes for the rest of her life now seemed certain to fall principally upon him. Agnes and Henrietta Grace had come out to the Cape as Stephe's guests for the first four months of 1901. There, Agnes had fallen in love with the Speaker of the House of Assembly. Sir William Bisset Berry was a lively 62-year-old widower who had promptly reciprocated her interest. Sadly, some malicious gossip about their relationship appeared in the local newspapers and caused a disastrous row between Sir William and Henrietta Grace. Agnes still railed against her spinster's fate. 'I do wish you could spare a little of your thought to settle what is to become of me,' she chided her mother, 'you all seem to think I had better be a sort of general A.D.C. and I don't call that life.'[5] Baden-Powell knew that unless either he or Agnes married, after his mother's death he would probably find himself not only supporting his unhappy sister but living with her.

Stephe recognized Warington's plight as worse than Agnes's. As the solitary member of the family in gainful employment after George's death, Warington had only been able to look forward to decades more as the family's breadwinner. At 56, he was a bald and portly man with an outwardly placid demeanour who was, according to his sister, 'as happy as a king playing at a table spread all over with salmon flies' or designing one of his patented sailing canoes.[6] This was misleading. For ten years he had been devoted to a close female companion but, as Henrietta Grace often said, without a trace of shame, 'Warington and Hilda have been long attached, but neither has enough money to live upon.'[7] His income, almost all of which still went to his mother, had been lower in recent years ever since a recurrence of tuberculosis had obliged him to take an extended period of sick leave. Here too was a member of the family who might soon require assistance.

There was, however, one ray of light discernible in the year of Stephe's return: the most unlikely person had suddenly married into money. Just when Frank's artistic fortunes were at their nadir he proposed to and was accepted by a rich New Zealand girl, Florence Watt, whose father owned a flourishing engineering company. From being virtually penniless, Frank suddenly found himself living in one of the finest houses in Kensington. For Stephe this marriage was providential, since it enabled Frank to put £300 per annum towards Henrietta Grace's living expenses.[8]

Baden-Powell had been in South Africa when Frank's engagement was announced, but though far away the event had forced him to think hard about his own future. 'Now it only remains for W[arington] to get married himself, and it will then be my turn – and I shall have no excuse for evading it.'[9] During the decade after George's marriage Henrietta Grace had abandoned her veto on matrimony, and her attitude had shifted towards active support for further marriages – at least where Frank and Stephe were concerned. They had never been favourites like Baden, nor regular earners like Warington, and might when married be able to donate more than they could have afforded had they remained single. Furthermore, Stephe had lived so long abroad that she would not miss him as keenly as she would one of her homebound brood.

Baden-Powell had to face the painful fact that although he had become as famous as his mother could ever have wished, she was still dissatisfied. Her nagging at him to get married had started in the mid-1890s and had recently intensified. Shortly before returning to England he had dutifully promised 'to pick out one of those would-be daughters-in-law of yours, my dear Ma – and settle down . . .'[10] In South Africa, when asked for progress reports by Henrietta Grace, he had invariably pleaded pressure of work in explanation of his failure to find a potential bride;[11] but now that he was living with her, he could no longer hope to fob her off with excuses. And he still longed to please her. His mother was approaching her eightieth birthday, yet Stephe was as incapable of pointing out her faults as ever he had been.

Apart from his mother's keenness on the idea, there were other factors that made marriage seem more desirable than in the past. As the most successful and temporarily the richest brother (with a salary of over £3,000 per annum) he seemed destined to step straight into Warington's shoes unless he could acquire a family of his own. After his free and easy life on the veldt, he found his daily routine in London irksomely restrictive. Whether inspecting regiments or in his office, he was treated with kid-glove formality; while at home in the evenings, his dinners with his mother, Agnes, Baden and Warington – still 'clinging together' after all these years – were very different from cheerful alfresco meals with his young A.D.C.s in the Transvaal. 'I was not built for a general,' he wrote later. 'I liked being a regimental officer in personal touch with my men.'[12] He was also seeing less of old friends like McLaren and Noble. Albeit surrounded by his family, a lonelier life seemed inevitable unless he chose to marry and have children.

Since his return home he had taken great pleasure in being with Donald and Maud, George's children. 'When he came,' recalled Maud, 'he played "bears" in an inimitable way – not too appropriate in a Victorian drawing room, with me dressed up in white frills.' He used to pretend that his plumed general's hat was a chicken, and would make loud clucking noises to convince them. If either child was distressed by the sound of gunfire at a military tattoo, he 'immediately put his hands to his ears and pretended to be scared also'.[13] Stephe developed many other friendships with children at this time,[14] and the prospect of having sons and daughters of his own lent marriage an added attraction.

*

In Chapter Three I examined in detail a wide variety of evidence suggesting that Baden-Powell found men physically attractive and was sexually indifferent to women. There is, however, nothing extraordinary about his desire to marry. Since contemporary medical opinion – in the wake of the Wilde trials – maintained that homosexuality was an illness bordering on insanity, most 'sufferers' inevitably fought their desires through sublimation or marriage. As if to remind Stephe of the importance of repression, three weeks after his return to England General Sir Hector MacDonald – a war hero too – shot himself after being accused of homosexual practices. While widespread revulsion against homosexuals encouraged them to marry, public ignorance on sexual matters made this step easier for them to contemplate. Baden-Powell's belief that normal heterosexual physical attraction lasted for only a few months during adolescence must have helped him to consider marriage a feasible possibility. When he described marriage as 'the coming together of a man and a woman not only to help each other as comrades, two men could do that, but to carry out the creator's law of making children', he betrayed the predominantly utilitarian light in which he viewed the proceedings.[15] With sex indulged in only because it was a reproductive duty, there would have been no need for him to feel anxiety about not wanting it.[16] Victorian hypocrisy aided such thinking by propagating the idea that decent women had no sexual feelings. They could therefore be expected to welcome being married to a man who had no desire to have intercourse more often than was strictly necessary for purposes of procreation.

Had Baden-Powell been an out-and-out misogynist, he would have rejected the idea of marriage as altogether too frightening; but he had always enjoyed female companionship, provided he first made it clear that he was 'simply there as a friend . . . or a brother'.[17] This fear of

female sexuality led him to restrict his choice of potential brides either
to girls in their late teens or very early twenties, or to women of his
own age; his idea being that women in either of these categories were
too young or too old to be as sexually active as women in their late
twenties or their thirties. In the past he had enjoyed many friendships
with young girls, but these friendships had not survived the onset of
adulthood. Dulce Wroughton had been abandoned shortly after he
sent her that most revealing letter, in which he implored her not to
grow older but to stay for him 'a sort of Pete – (h'm that's odd; there is
no feminine for Peter) – a sort of girl Peter Pan . . .'[18] The key to
understanding Baden-Powell's lifelong onslaught on sex was his fear
of the 'contaminating' properties of sexually active women.[19]

In the past, in deference to the wishes of the late Lady Baden-Powell,
it has always been publicly maintained that she was the first and only
woman to whom her husband paid court. In reality she was neither the
first whom he courted, nor even the first to whom he proposed. His
involvement with Miss Rose Gough began in the south of France
where he met her in December 1903, and was certainly as serious as his
later courtship of the future Lady Baden-Powell. Rose was then
twenty and had a strong, slightly masculine face with thick black
eyebrows and intelligent dark eyes; and there was nothing 'dollish'
about her. She did not wear make-up or 'paint' her face as was then just
beginning to be thought acceptable for respectable women.

To start with, Stephe followed the same line that he had taken with
Caroline Heap and Dulce Wroughton, making everything jocular and
rather childish. A year after meeting Rose, he fixed up a visit to Italy
ostensibly to inspect the Italian Cavalry School at Tor di Quinto but
really in order to see her there. (Rose's mother always spent her
winters in the south of France or Italy.) As Rose recalled: 'He wrote me
that he should probably come disguised: "I'm preparing my
smuggling get-up ready for my expedition, so don't be surprised if
you don't recognise me on arrival." '[20]

Rose's father, Major Wilfred A. Gough, had been killed in action in
1885 when Rose was still an infant. A few years later his widow
Beatrice had married the Hon. Henry C. Denison, a rich man with a
taste for yachting and foreign travel. Beatrice had soon found her only
daughter's company irksomely constraining, and actively encouraged
her to marry as soon as possible. Not surprisingly Rose came to dislike
her mother and wove romantic fantasies around the memory of her
dead father. Inevitably she was drawn to men considerably older than
herself, which was why Baden-Powell was initially so well received.
She had studied music in Dresden and therefore suggested that he take
her to concerts and operas. He did so, although his own musical tastes
were limited; he enjoyed Gilbert and Sullivan, but found the most
popular of Wagner's operas difficult. *Tannhäuser* he considered 'rather

a dreary piece with plums'.[21]

At Cowes Week during the summer of 1904 he stayed with Rose and the Denisons in their house next to the Royal Yacht Squadron. As ever he enjoyed Rose's company, although the conversation on the Squadron's Lawn was not to his liking. 'I have been in a continual sea of talk,' he told his mother, 'but have not heard one sentence that did not refer either to the dress, means, or internal afflictions of one's neighbours . . . I've heard enough of those matters to last me a year.'[22]

But the following August he was back at Cowes with Rose, having again spent part of the spring in Italy with her family.[23] Stephe went on seeing Rose regularly until 9 December 1905 when his diary entries recording their meetings abruptly ceased – only being resumed on 7 April 1907. In the meantime, on 10 July 1906, Rose Gough married Captain (later Admiral) Mark E.F. Kerr R.N., a grandson of the 6th Marquess of Lothian and a man only a few years younger than Baden-Powell.

It is unknown exactly when Stephe himself proposed to Rose and was turned down, but it was probably on 9 December 1905, the date recorded as their last meeting before the long break in their relations. Both Rose's daughter, Rosemary Kerr, and her sister-in-law, Elizabeth Denison, have confirmed to me that Baden-Powell proposed.[24] In years to come Rose probably regretted rejecting him, since her marriage to Mark Kerr was loveless and unhappy. When the Admiral and Rose stayed with the Baden-Powells at Pax Hill during the 1920s, the female staff were warned in advance by Olave Baden-Powell's lady's maid to avoid being left alone with the Admiral.[25] Apart from being a womanizer, Admiral Kerr often abused his wife in public.[26]

Whereas Baden-Powell would never again see any of the other women who rejected him, he continued to meet Rose at regular intervals after her marriage. Shortly after he himself married, he introduced Rose to his wife and then invited her to help run the Guides. As the Girl Guides' Commissioner for London, Mrs Mark Kerr would later become one of the half-dozen key figures in the Movement and would write the official history of the Guides. Olave Baden-Powell undoubtedly found out that her husband had once wanted to marry Rose. Mrs Kerr's daughter showed me a copy of a letter sent by her mother to Olave, in which Rose expressed heartfelt gratitude and relief over Olave's 'understanding attitude' in connection with some unspecified but serious unpleasantness between them; this seems to have been a letter of thanks to Olave for not withdrawing her friendship after learning of the proposal.[27] Olave made sure that no word of it was ever printed in any book about her husband published during her long lifetime, and in fact no mention of it has ever been published until now. Jealousy probably explains the fact that, although

Rose Kerr stayed with the Baden-Powells more often than any other senior figure in the Guide Movement, Olave made no reference to her in her autobiography. Given Olave's exceptionally possessive attitude towards her husband's past, it is pardonable to wonder whether two Guiders who took away all Mrs Kerr's letters and other papers in 1944 were acting on Olave's instructions. A promised biography never appeared and in spite of Rosemary Kerr's later efforts to retrieve her mother's papers, they were never returned.[28]

In the summer of 1905 Baden-Powell renewed acquaintance with a family he had first come across in 1895. His sister Agnes had kept in touch with the Christie-Millers over the years and was responsible for reintroducing Stephe. In December, the month in which he was turned down by Rose Gough, Baden-Powell saw Miss Edith Christie-Miller three times. He had once described her family as 'very kind, very rich, but . . . very common'.[29] Although the family had orginally made their fortune as hatters, all Edith's four brothers were educated at Eton and had been brought up in Britwell House, a handsome country house in Buckinghamshire.

Mr John Christie-Miller, whose father was Edith's younger brother, told me that his aunt 'had a romance with Baden-Powell between 1905 and 1907, which ended when he was asked to visit Charles Christie-Miller [Edith's uncle], who had a bachelor establishment at Sonning'. Baden-Powell's diary establishes that this meeting took place at lunch-time on 5 January 1907. According to John Christie-Miller: 'Baden-Powell was warned off by Charles on behalf of the family, who thought he was after her money.'[30] After that depressing day, the Christie-Millers made no further appearance in Baden-Powell's diary.

However, Baden-Powell did not brood over this reverse for long. He had never been as fond of Miss Christie-Miller as of Miss Gough; he had also made several other overtures during 1906 (while he was still seeing Edith), the most serious of which was to a Miss Muriel Gardiner Muir, one of the four unmarried daughters of a Northamptonshire landowner. In fact Stephe made a point of lunching with Miss Muir on Rose Gough's wedding day. Early in November that year, he stayed for three days with the Muirs at their country house. According to Muriel Muir's youngest son, Mr C. G Sowerby, Baden-Powell and his mother had been 'very close friends'.[31] Mr Sowerby also told me that Baden-Powell had asked his mother to cooperate with him in writing a handbook. On 2 November, the day before he went to stay with the Muirs, Baden-Powell had started to write *Scouting for Boys*.[32] Although it seems probable that the suggestion had been made with tongue in cheek, the incident confirms the accuracy of the family's memory of the friendship. Muriel Muir married a Mr Edward Sowerby on 4 July 1907, a fact which Baden-Powell recorded in his diary without comment.

On 12 March 1907, Baden-Powell was returning from inspecting British cavalry regiments stationed in Egypt when he met aboard ship Philip L. Sclater, who had just retired from the post of Secretary to the Zoological Society and had once been a friend of his parents. Shortly after his return to England, Stephe went to stay with the elderly zoologist at Odiham Priory in Hampshire. Across the road lived Edward Chappell, the music publisher, and his attractive daughter – another Muriel. Baden-Powell was much taken with Miss Chappell, whom he sought out later in London. It might have been kinder if Philip Sclater had explained to Baden-Powell that his own son Guy, then a captain in the Royal Navy, also enjoyed Muriel Chappell's company and had recently become engaged to her. But either it had not occurred to him that a world-famous 50-year-old general might entertain thoughts of marrying a 20-year-old heiress, or if it had occurred to him, he might not have been able to think up a tactful way of discouraging him. Later that summer Baden-Powell unwittingly forced Sclater's hand. 'He received a letter from Baden-Powell asking if he could come to stay for the weekend and mentioning that he intended to ask Muriel Chappell to marry him. Philip replied, "Delighted to have you, but Muriel has just become engaged to my son Guy." Baden-Powell did not go for that weekend.'[33]

Henrietta Grace had for many years been acquainted with Lady Young, the wife of Sir George Young Bart. of Formosa Place, a pleasant house on the river at Cookham. According to her son Mr Winthrop Young, Lady Young 'half liked and half laughed at Mrs Baden-Powell's pretensions'. Agnes used to show visitors like the Youngs the 'museum room' in 8 St George's Place, which was 'devoted alone to Swords of Honour and gold caskets and the like . . . One was taken in as a matter of course, as if to a religious ceremony, to peruse the monstrosities'. (By 1905 Baden-Powell had been presented with seven Swords of Honour, six golden caskets, six gold medals, one gold chronometer, one golden diamond screen, one gold shield and two gold salvers.) 'The monstrosities' were also shown by Baden-Powell 'as a matter of course' to potential brides.

Stephe went to stay with the Youngs at Formosa during July 1905 and June 1906. On both occasions he met there Miss Olive Ilbert, daughter of Sir Courtenay Ilbert, the Clerk of the House of Commons, a radical and formerly the legal member of the Council of the Viceroy of India. Olive would later write novels under the pseudonym of Jane Dashwood and non-fiction under her own name, as well as humorous articles for the *Manchester Guardian*. Winthrop Young described Olive and Stephe 'falling into a violent flirtation. It was,' he said, 'so marked that, as happened in those days, something was expected to "come of it" . . . She was witty and clever-tongued, and they sparred admirably.'[34] Baden-Powell wrote to Lady Young after his 1905 visit: 'I did not at all like coming away from your island of delights. I hope I proved a good chaperon for that very nice young lady whom you put in my charge. I am going to call on her today.'[35] But in fact Baden-Powell and Miss Ilbert – with her intellectual interests – were poles apart and their romance was short-lived. Unknown to Stephe, Olive had been infatuated for some years with Edward Hilton Young (later Lord Kennet), Sir George Young's third son.

On Baden-Powell's return to Cookham in 1906, Winthrop Young noticed that the great man was no longer attentive to Miss Ilbert. 'I think he preferred being with me . . . He was susceptible to my looks and to the kind of activities which I was then romantically and keenly pursuing, mountaineering etc.'[36] On several occasions Winthrop took Baden-Powell out punting on the Thames and once in a Canadian canoe. They chatted about Stephe's plans for *Scouting for Boys* and he related various adventures. In order to give his hero the kind of thrill which an adventurer of his stamp deserved, Winthrop paddled him dangerously close to the weir. 'Suddenly we spun like a tee totem on a pin, and with the great wooden post sticking up through the boiling water . . . we just scraped past . . . but had shipped a quantity of water. As it swashed audibly to and fro, the General sat, gallantly immovable . . . while we shot down the rapid.'[37] Stephe did not hold this against the boy and regularly visited him at Eton, where Winthrop noticed that: 'He enjoyed being "hero'd" by the boys, and had . . . a temperamental interest in boy-life.' Winthrop found him 'fascinating for his talents and versatility which kept him restless and flickery opposite one, only really interested in one [as a means] of drawing out his ideas or memories, or gratifying his eye.'[38]

After the Christie-Miller and Gardiner Muir disappointments, and his loss of interest in Miss Ilbert, Baden-Powell at last found a family seeming to promise both matrimony and an opportunity to enjoy the company of boys. Corisande, Lady Rodney, had divorced her husband in 1902 and had four sons between the ages of 16 and 11 years. She herself was 40, which made her a very different proposition from Miss Gough and Miss Muir; but Baden-Powell may have sensed salvation in a situation where there would be no need for reproduction, since Lord Rodney had so successfully attended to this matter. In the past Baden-Powell had often admired women in their forties, like Lady Downe, and more recently – and very briefly – the widowed millionairess Mrs Assheton-Smith.[39] Although his earlier efforts had all been addressed to young girls, he had never discounted the possibility of marrying a mother-figure. Lady Rodney is first mentioned in his diary on 22 January 1907. In the preceding year, Baden-Powell had often been in touch with her former husband, Lord Rodney, who ran a boys' corps known as 'Lord Rodney's Boys'. In August 1906, Baden-Powell inspected these boys in a camp on the Isle of Wight and subsequently attempted to procure rifles for them through the War Office.[40] It seems likely that Rodney, who by then knew about Baden-Powell's plans for a boys' character-building movement, had recommended him to get in touch with his ex-wife in order to persuade her to let him give the boys some manly training. Most of the men then running boys' para-military brigades felt that their boys needed to be toughened up away from the softening influence of women.

Stephe wrote in his diary on 22 January 1907: 'Lady Rodney to see curios. Dine Lady Rodney . . .' The 'curios' were of course the swords and caskets. The following day Baden-Powell took Lady Rodney to see Shaw's *The Doctor's Dilemma*, and two days after that he sailed to Egypt from Tilbury, where he was seen off by her ladyship.[41] Within days of his return to England, he went to Wimborne in Dorset to stay with Lady Rodney and three of her boys, the fourth having just returned to Harrow for the summer term. Stephe passed three enjoyable days with Corisande and her sons, during which the spring weather was perfect for scouting games. In London the following week, he entertained Lady Rodney to dinner and soon afterwards took her to the Royal Academy Private View. Corisande lent him moral support on the day of Miss Gardiner Muir's wedding, which was on 4 July. Yet most surprisingly, after so many meetings, that day would mark their last recorded time together. And since three of the Rodney boys came to the first Boy Scout Camp on Brownsea Island between 29 July and 9 August, there would have been every excuse for further meetings. But none took place. Yet the earlier meetings were far too numerous to have been simply a utilitarian prelude to the boys' attendance at the camp. In the circumstances, and given the pattern of other sudden female disappearances from his diary, it is impossible to escape the conclusion that Baden-Powell suffered another rejection on 4 July.[42]

It is not surprising that after five years of unsuccessful efforts, Baden-Powell should have devoted markedly less of his energy to the pursuit of women during 1909 and 1910. In these years the explosive growth of the Scout Movement would keep him busier than at any other time in his life. But in May 1911, he met an admiring American widow whom he at first thought older than himself but later discovered to be four years younger.

Mrs Juliette Gordon Low was slightly deaf, extremely rich and had a passion for sculpture and travel. She was also convinced that the Boy Scouts and the Girl Guides were among the crowning achievements of the human race. She invited him to many plays and social occasions.[43] For his part, he introduced her to his mother – as always a great compliment. But Baden-Powell's relations with Mrs Low fall more naturally into that period of his life during which he would finally find a bride.

On 10 February 1905, Baden-Powell paid his first ever visit to *Peter Pan*. His companion was Mrs Bewe Leggett, another wealthy American.[44] The play made such a profound impression on Stephe that he returned on his own the following day, urging Henrietta Grace to go too without delay.[45] Afterwards he started to entertain the actress who played Mrs Darling. He had first met Sybil Carlisle in some Charterhouse theatricals in 1899,[46] but did not befriend her until she appeared as the children's mother in his favourite play.[47] And why did this famous play mean so much to Baden-Powell? 'Long after writing Peter Pan its true meaning came to me,' wrote James Barrie, 'desperate attempt to grow up, but can't.'[48] With his pranks, his acting and his gifts for entertaining children, Baden-Powell was also to some extent in that sorry plight. Not that he was ignorant of how to operate in the world of power and public affairs; his real immaturity lay in his fear that he would always be 'too young to marry'. Writing of Peter Pan himself, Barrie had conjectured: 'Perhaps he was a boy some people longed for, but who never came. It may be that these people hear him at the window more clearly than children do.'[49] People can 'long' for a son; they can mourn for their own lost boyhood; they may, if they are repressed homosexuals, 'long' for a boy, perhaps simultaneously denying their desire under the guise of a sentimental attachment to the idea of boyhood.

When Baden-Powell saw *Peter Pan* for the first time, he was moving towards a role of some kind in boys' work. He had by then undertaken to rewrite *Aids to Scouting* in a form accessible to boys, and this was also the year in which he entranced Winthrop Young with stories of his adventures. But would he one day entrance a woman who would like him enough to be his wife? Or did he even wish to grow up in that way? Interestingly, when Baden-Powell finally found his future bride he wrote in one of his earliest letters to her that he wanted to take her to see *Peter Pan*. They duly went, for the first of many visits, a few months after their wedding.[50] The part of Peter Pan is still usually played by a young woman who therefore quite literally becomes, in the words of Baden-Powell's famous letter, 'a sort of girl Peter Pan' – which was what Stephe had once wanted Dulce Wroughton, among others, to be.

Because Baden-Powell's extensive efforts to find a wife have never before been chronicled, I have thought it appropriate to describe them in isolation from his professional life, and the simultaneous development of his earliest thoughts on 'scouting' as the basis of a training scheme for boys.

2. Cavalry Chaos (1903–07)

On 7 May 1903 Baden-Powell sat at his desk in the War Office for the first time. Later he recalled 'the huge misgiving with which I faced the

ordeal of taking up the "Blue Riband" [the Inspector General's job] of
the cavalry and the yeomanry in Great Britain and Ireland, and of the
cavalry in Egypt and South Africa.'[1] He would be remarkably frank in
his autobiography about his shortcomings:

> I was fully unfitted, both physically and intellectually, for the
> position of I.G. Cavalry. Physically because I had long had a loose
> leg as a result of a shooting accident . . . and I could not supply an
> example of hard-riding horsemanship. Intellectually I was deficient
> because I had not gone through the Staff College and my knowledge
> of strategy and military history was merely scrappy.[2]

Looking back later, he wrote, 'My first step on taking over my duties
was to educate myself as far as possible in up-to-date cavalry methods –
with this intent I visited personally, first the cavalry schools of France,
Germany, Austria, Belgium, Italy and America.'[3] It was ironic that he
should have felt the need to educate himself by seeking the advice of
Continental cavalrymen, most of whom had never fought in a major
war. In 1903 no better advice could have been given than by British
officers who had learned their lessons the hard way in South Africa.
Nevertheless, Baden-Powell's foreign forays were not quite worth-
less. From visiting the French cavalry he grasped the value of having a
well-run cavalry school for training the instructors who would later
teach recruits not only riding but the care of horses, and something of
reconnaissance and billeting. In 1904 he set up the successful British
Cavalry School at Netheravon House on Salisbury Plain.[4]

In other respects, however, he contributed little to the major debates
affecting the cavalry in the decade before the Great War. In 1906 he
bought his first car, an 18 horse-power Thorneycroft fitted out with a
sleeping couch, a box for papers alongside the driver's seat and an
additional seat for an orderly. His arrival at inspections in this machine
was frowned upon by less progressive officers, but not because he told
them that the future of mobile warfare lay with the internal combustion engine. He did no such thing and never wrote one sentence
showing that he understood the implications of what it portended for
the future of the cavalry.[5] Baden-Powell had taken driving lessons a
year earlier and had been immediately impressed by the astonishing
ease with which he could reach places many miles from any railway
station which on horseback would have taken, in some instances, a
whole day longer.[6] In 1907 he jotted down this note, without apparent
consciousness of its irony: 'Transport needs great alteration to render
cavalry really mobile.'[7] It is a remarkable tribute to the conservatism of
the military spirit that an innovator like Baden-Powell should have
been incapable of recognizing the blindingly obvious shape of things to
come. Mechanization of the cavalry did not take place on a large scale
until the 1930s.

Baden-Powell's most recent biographer stated that when he became Inspector General: 'The War Office was willing to listen to new ideas. Baden-Powell was given the chance to express himself, to impose on the whole British Cavalry the methods he felt would prove most effective.'[8] But the Army Council, far from being 'willing to listen to new ideas', lost no time in putting him very firmly in his place. He had submitted a report critical of the Council's failure to reduce the ruinous expenses incurred by all cavalry officers. 'Inform General Baden-Powell,' the Council's secretary told the Inspector General for the whole army, 'that it is not within his province to criticize the action of the Army Council. The duties of Inspector of Cavalry are limited to inspection of technical training and efficiency of cavalry for war.'[9]

The saddest example of Baden-Powell's total inability to adopt an independent position was in one of the most important debates to take place in cavalry circles during the decade before 1914. The difference of opinion centred upon the extent to which cavalry training should be concerned with (a) the use of swords and lances [the *arme blanche*] on horseback, and (b) the use of the rifle when dismounted.

Baden-Powell had to treat conservative opinions seriously. Lieutenant-General Sir John French had commanded the Cavalry Division in South Africa and now held the key Aldershot Command. 'It must never be forgotten,' wrote Sir John in 1905, 'that it is only by the employment of "shock tactics" [i.e. cavalry charges] and the superior morale of the highly trained horsemen, wielding sword and lance, that success can be attained.'[10] The most influential thinker in cavalry circles during this period was Major-General Douglas Haig, who had been Chief Staff Officer to French in South Africa. When Haig was appointed Director of Military Training,[11] his views on the *arme blanche* became as dangerous to contradict as those of General French. Haig believed that 'the increased range and effectiveness of modern weapons and the greater length of battles would lead to moral exhaustion, which in turn would render cavalry attacks more likely to succeed.' He thought that modern bullets, since they were of smaller bore than older bullets, would have 'less stopping power against a horse'.[12]

Because the 5th Dragoon Guards had been involved, Baden-Powell knew that the *only* cavalry charge reputed to have been successful during the Boer War had merely been the postscript to a shooting battle won by dismounted riflemen long before the Dragoons charged an already fleeing enemy.*[13] His experience in the campaign after the Relief of Mafeking had taught him that opportunities for cavalry charges never occurred against an enemy armed with modern rifles. But for him to have come out unambiguously against French and Haig would have been tantamount to asking for early retirement.

* This incident was at Elandslaagte in October 1899.

When Lord Roberts asked him to make a report on the role of cavalry in warfare, Baden-Powell avoided pronouncing on the vexed subject of 'the value of steel arms'[14] until he had sought 'expert opinion' – by which he meant inviting Haig and French to express their already well-known views. In November 1903, at Aldershot, Sir John French told him that 'the role of cavalry was to overthrow the enemy's cavalry by shock and then to push on against other arms with the rifle or shock.'[15] This, as Baden-Powell knew all too well, was exactly the reverse of what Lord Roberts advocated: namely that cavalry should *always* use their rifles first, 'holding back the bulk of the force for shock action when the effect of fire action has produced its certain results'.[16]

It was therefore hardly surprising that Baden-Powell decided to sit on the fence when he made his report. He began his section on *Cavalry Action* by listing three ways in which cavalry could fight:

(1) Mounted by charging.
(2) Dismounted by rifle-fire.
(3) Combined action, by part firing and part charging, or preparing to charge.

It would not have taken Sherlock Holmes to deduce the flaw in his logic, but few people argued its absurdity more effectively than Sir Arthur Conan Doyle. Writing in the *Pall Mall Gazette*, Doyle pointed out that 'the tactics of the shock horseman and of the mounted rifleman are absolutely contradictory . . . The shock horsemen is always looking for good ground and someone to charge. The rifleman is looking for bad ground where he and his horse can both be concealed, with a good fire field. You can have it either way, but you cannot have it both.'[17]

Historically, cavalry officers and men had been encouraged to feel superior to foot-soldiers in order to give them the confidence to charge home against infantry squares. Sir John French dreaded the loss of this 'cavalry spirit' and argued that it could 'never be created in a body of troops whose first idea is to abandon their horses and lie down under cover in the face of a swiftly charging mass of horsemen'.[18] That such tosh could be written precisely when the Russians and Japanese were fighting a war in which cavalry had been entirely excluded by the immobilizing effects of trenches, barbed-wire and machine-guns shows how incurably romantic British cavalry officers had remained even after the disasters of the Boer War.

Baden-Powell himself considered that 'the best sensation' he had ever enjoyed was 'leading a well-trained brigade of cavalry at a gallop . . . It is the sensation that your chest is going to burst and your inside to fall out with pleasure. There is a tremendous feeling of exultation in moving that great, rushing, thundering mass of men and horses just by a wave of your hand.'[19]

As time passed, he became more rather than less reactionary in his views. When he gave his evidence to the Royal Commission on the South African War in 1903, he said that all cavalrymen should have rifles and it did not matter what else they carried. He denied that the sword or lance was of any use in a charge, and said he favoured firing from the saddle to demoralize a wavering enemy.[20] But by March 1904, he could bring himself to tell the Secretary of State: 'I fully agree with Sir John French's remarks as regards the role of the cavalry.'[21] The full extent of Baden-Powell's capitulation is evident in a diary entry several years later: 'The Adjutant-General asked my opinion about the lance for cavalry. I replied that it certainly ought to be used for its moral effect on the user and on the enemy . . . I reassured him that cavalry training was designed with a view to shock tactics being the end and aim of the whole of it.'[22] Baden-Powell had been a successful musketry instructor to the 13th Hussars in the 1880s; through his influence his regiment became one of the best at shooting in the army. He had also pioneered the introduction of the machine-gun into the cavalry. It is sad to think of such a man deferring to Haig, who would one day tell Lloyd George that 'the machine-gun is a much overrated weapon and two per battalion are more than sufficient.'[23] Even on a subject about which Baden-Powell felt passionately, he allowed Douglas Haig to thwart him. When Stephe proposed that all officers be taught a little elementary scouting at the Cavalry School, Haig countermanded him.[24]

Baden-Powell's term as Inspector General of Cavalry was not wholly without achievements. He introduced small sections within the cavalry troop to foster initiative, and instituted three months' dismounted training for all recruits. Nevertheless it is hard to escape the conclusion that professionally the years between 1903 and 1907 were among the most undistinguished in his life. If he had hoped that his accommodating attitude would result in his appointment to the Army Council, or to a more senior staff job, he was mistaken. Baden-Powell has been unfairly taken to task for his supposed failures in the campaign after Mafeking, and for failing to satisfy Kitchener and Milner when he was Inspector General of the S.A.C., but in reality the years in which he failed were those he spent at the War Office in London. Ironically the absence of criticism by senior officers has led historians to pass over this time as having been relatively successful.

3. The Nation in Peril (1903–04)

The frustrations which Baden-Powell suffered during his years as Inspector General, and the simultaneous failure of his efforts to find a bride, would have been harder to bear had he not developed a

compensating interest during this period. In 1903, he accepted
invitations to become Honorary Colonel of the Southport Cadets and
the 1st Cadet Battalion of the Liverpool Regiment.[1] He began to
inspect these and similar cadet corps because he enjoyed the company
of the boys; just as he had welcomed visiting Winthrop Young at Eton
and playing games with his nephew Donald.

But there was another side to Stephe's interest in boys' military
organizations which would result in Lord Roberts insisting that he
should make his occasional inspections a regular and formal part of his
work.[2]

Soon after his arrival at the War Office, Baden-Powell found himself
affected by the general gloom that the various post-mortems on the
Boer War were causing amongst military men. It was widely
suggested that before the war 60 per cent of would-be recruits had
failed to pass undemanding medical tests. In the autumn of 1903
the Government set up an ominously entitled 'Inter-Departmental
Committee on Physical Deterioration'. Long before this committee
announced its inconclusive findings, public men were drawing
doom-laden conclusions. Given his propensity, indeed his need, to
give advice, it was not very surprising that Baden-Powell should have
joined in.

After opening a boys' club in Salford early in 1904, he warned the
boys that the committee 'would soon give us an idea of the
deterioration there is amongst us'. But Baden-Powell did not need a
committee to tell him that the urban working class which furnished
most of the army's recruits was badly housed, badly fed and likely to
be – man for man – smaller, lighter and sicklier than his middle- or
upper-class contemporary. Frequent visits to the Midlands and the
North of England had confirmed his earlier opinion that the life led by
the average city-dweller was inherently unhealthy – not just physically, but spiritually and mentally too.

Nevertheless he thought that better health care, food and exercise
would improve matters. So too would less smoking and drinking. At
Salford he blamed the schools for ignoring such matters, but he was
delighted that the Salford Club had a gymnasium as well as a library.
'Free Libraries are, I believe, very good things in their way, and this
develops intelligence enormously,' he said sardonically, to laughter,
'but the old saying is perfectly right that there is not much use having a
big brain if a man has not a big body to carry it – (applause) – There is
no doubt that we are falling away to a lower standard than is required
for our labour and defence.'[3]

Coupled with this widespread fear of physical 'deterioration', there
was an equally prevalent horror of 'moral degeneracy'. Baden-Powell
found this idea just as disturbing. It had been forcefully articulated by
Max Nordau in Germany in 1893 and his book – appropriately entitled

Degeneration – had become a best-seller in England shortly after Oscar Wilde's conviction. Nordau had vilified not only 'decadent' poets but the realism of Zola, the mysticism of Maeterlinck, Wagner's romanticism, Nietzsche's philosophy and the decay lurking in social- ism, anarchism and the agitation for women's rights. European societies – without self-control, discipline and sexual restraint – were, he concluded, 'marching to certain ruin because too worn out and flaccid to perform great tasks'. Then there was Darwin's legacy – the disturbing belief that if the findings of *The Origin of Species* were applied to human societies, it would be seen that only the strongest nations would survive in the 'natural' conditions of international strife. Before the century had ended Houston Stewart Chamberlain, Wagner's son-in-law, had argued that Aryans had a right and a duty to extend their rule over other races; while across the Atlantic Theodore Roosevelt and Captain Mahan (the author not only of *The Interest of America in Sea Power* but of *The Moral Aspect of War*) were also obsessed with 'racial degeneracy'. Roosevelt, like Rhodes, recommended adventures in remote and dangerous terrain to keep the racial stock healthy; otherwise 'softness of fibre' might, if unchecked, 'mean the development of a cultured and refined people quite unable to hold its own in conflict'.[4]

This belief was shared by Baden-Powell. In an address given to the Patriotic Society in Liverpool on 19 February, he introduced 'loafers' and 'wasters' as a species. Typically these young working-class men drank and smoked too much and avoided playing games, preferring to watch professionals. They often gambled and spent hours of every day lounging on street corners. He would be equally scornful of public schoolboys who avoided sport in favour of academic work, later depicting a strange hybrid boy who was part school 'swot' with his cap and spectacles and part working-class 'waster' with his slouching posture, cigarette in mouth and hands in pockets (see illustration on page 362).[5] This combination of the anti-intellectual and the anti- urban dovetailed with Baden-Powell's criticism of schools for neglect- ing their boys' physical and moral development while concentrating exclusively on 'the three Rs'.

Baden-Powell's great anxiety at this time was a 'bolt from the blue' invasion, in which the Royal Navy was caught unawares and a German army enabled to land on the East Coast. Lord Roberts also took this possibility seriously. Since in wartime most of the British Army would be required overseas for the defence of the Empire, there would certainly be a disaster if an invasion ever occurred – especially if, as Baden-Powell feared, the youth of Britain was in poor shape morally and physically.

In this context he began to hold up as an example to cadets the deeds of the boy orderlies of Mafeking. Although he would later describe these cadet messengers as 'Mafeking Boy Scouts'[6] and would claim that they had been trained 'on scout lines rather than those of cadets',[7] they had in fact been members of a cadet corps founded before the Siege started.[8] They were never trained in scouting and were commanded by Lord Edward Cecil and Lieutenant Moncreiffe rather than by Baden-Powell, who took so little interest in them that he mentioned them neither in his report to Lord Roberts nor in his evidence to the Royal Commission on the War in South Africa. But while the Mafeking cadets had had nothing to do with scouting they *had* been useful during the Siege, carrying messages and thus freeing for work in the trenches many adult riflemen who would otherwise have been needed for this orderly work.[9] If members of British cadet corps and brigades could do likewise, he told the boys of Southport and Liverpool, 'there would be no reason why they should not take their place in our third line in defending our shores'.[10]

This was what he told the Boys' Brigade at their annual demonstration in the Albert Hall in May 1903. While conceding that the Brigade's 'greater virtue lay in training boys to become the best type of citizens', he urged his young audience to make themselves 'a strong force behind the Volunteers and the Army'. He ended with the story of how poor Hazlerigg had met his death at Mafeking 'in performance of his duty'.

After this Albert Hall meeting, Baden-Powell invited William (later Sir William) Smith, the founder of the Boys' Brigade, to come home with him to dine in nearby Prince's Gate. The two men 'talked to the small hours above the B[oys'] B[rigade], the Boy, the Boy-messengers of Mafeking and much else'. As a result of this meeting Baden-Powell became an honorary Vice-President of the Brigade.[11]

In April the following year Lord Roberts ordered Baden-Powell to consider inspections of local Boys' Brigades to be part of his official duties as Inspector General.[12] Roberts was gravely concerned about the shortage of army officers and discussed this problem with Baden-Powell among other senior officers. The day before he inspected nearly 7,000 members of the Boys' Brigade in Glasgow, Baden-Powell had a meeting with Colonel G.C. Kitson, the Commandant of the Royal Military College, Sandhurst.[13] Kitson, like Roberts, felt that future recruitment of officers – and for that matter men – would be much improved if organizations like the Boys' Brigade and the Church Lads' Brigade could expand their numbers. On 12 April Baden-Powell had a thought-provoking conversation with Admiral of the Fleet Sir John Fisher, who suggested that the army ought to adopt the naval practice of taking on officers in their teens as the navy did with their midshipmen.[14] Since these young officer cadets could not be plucked from the air, they would have to come from existing cadet corps and religious brigades.

Baden-Powell was ruminating on this matter as he stepped out on to

Yorkhill Drill Ground in Glasgow on 30 April 1904, dressed in his black staff officer's uniform, to inspect no fewer than 6,783 boys and 448 officers of the Boys' Brigade. This was certainly a fine turn-out, even though the Brigade had been founded in Glasgow where its strength was still greater than in any other city. Throughout the country there were said to be 54,000 boys between the ages of 12 and 18 wearing the Brigade's navy blue uniform and pill-box hats. The organization owed much to the American Temperance Cold Water Army and to the home-grown Salvation Army. Smith had been a Sunday School teacher before joining the crack 1st Lanarkshire Volunteer Rifles, thus demonstrating in his own life the way in which evangelical fervour was merging with nationalism. By putting his Sunday School boys into uniform and drilling them, he had extended the process.

What did Baden-Powell make of these young Christian soldiers as he watched them march past 'in quarter column, keeping almost perfect step, carrying their heads erect, and maintaining a well-balanced line as they crossed the field . . .'?[15] He disliked formal religion and had little sympathy for hymn-singing dissenters. Nor had he ever thought military drill served any useful purpose in training soldiers. Yet the Brigade boys *did* impress him; they marched well, their bands played excellently and they clearly took their physical exercises and everything they did seriously. They also seemed proud of their uniform and the body to which they belonged.

As William Smith had said, he meant to give his boys 'the *esprit de corps* which Public School boys acquired as a matter of course, but which was almost entirely lacking in elementary school boys'.[16] As they rode from the drill ground side by side he congratulated Smith on the boys' performance, but told him that in his opinion an organization which had been active for 21 years would have attracted more than 54,000 members 'if the work really appealed to the boys'. William Smith asked, with a hint of asperity, how Baden-Powell would set about improving its appeal if he were given the chance. 'I suggested scouting, which had proved so popular with recruits in the army. He asked me if I would not rewrite the army scouting book to suit boys.'[17]

The 'army scouting book' was *Aids to Scouting for N.C.O.s and Men* for which Baden-Powell had started collecting material in 1885, but had not actually written until August 1898 while holidaying in Kashmir. The book was accepted by Gale and Polden of Aldershot, who offered Baden-Powell the less than princely royalty of £5 per 1,000 copies, after an initial 2,000 had been sold. The corrected proofs were among the last letters and packages to be sent out of Mafeking before the Siege began; the publisher received them on 23 October 1899 and published a month later, scarcely able to believe his good fortune. Baden-Powell's unexpected celebrity turned a specialist military textbook into an instant best-seller. Within months it had sold 100,000 copies.[18] The book's message was that military scouting bred self-reliance by making men use their intelligence and act on their own initiative when away from the guidance of an officer.

Back in London, Baden-Powell wrote a tactfully phrased report of the Glasgow parade and sent it to Smith. After some remarks about the boys' marching and drill, he passed to his principal point:

> Something might, I think, also be done towards developing the Boy's mind by increasing his powers of observation, and teaching him to notice details. I believe that if some form of scout training could be devised in the Brigade it would be very popular, and could do a great amount of good. Preliminary training in this line might include practice in noting and remembering details of strangers; contents of shop windows, appearance of new streets, etc. The results would not only sharpen the wits of the Boy, but would also make him quick to read character and feelings, and thus help him to be a better sympathiser with his fellow-men.[19]

It is significant that in his very first reference to 'scout training' for boys, Baden-Powell did not mention military aims. The whole tone is closer to remarks he had made about education and morality in South Africa than to the anxious jingoism he exhibited in British towns a couple of years later. In his beloved Transvaal, far away from the strange neuroses afflicting the military establishment in Whitehall, Baden-Powell had first expressed views about observation, citizenship and good character that would only re-emerge after his 1904 Glasgow inspection as the essential motive force behind the Boy Scouts.

The boy who apes the man by smoking will never be much good.

A strong and healthy boy has the ball at his feet.

9

THE BOY-MAN TAKES HIS BOW

1. In the Beginning there was a Name: The Boy Scouts (1900–03)

In July 1900 when Baden-Powell was at Rustenburg, he received a number of letters from boys asking for his autograph as well as from the adult officials of boys' organizations requesting him to send messages to their members. His replies to two letters signed by fifteen Cheshire choirboys are historically important.

The choirboys had asked him to be the patron of their non-smoking association, to which he readily assented. Baden-Powell himself had given up smoking when he was 20 and had only resumed the habit briefly in Ashanti as a protection against fever.[1] In 1900 he had not yet attacked smoking for doing more than spoiling a scout's sense of smell, but within fewer than ten years he would write of any boy who smoked as 'a little ass . . . slobbering about with a half-smoked cigarette between his lips', damaging his heart and eyes.[2] In the 1880s, when cigars had been overtaken in popularity by milder cigarettes, the Boys' Brigade had extended their teetotal pledge to include a ban on smoking.[3] Baden-Powell told the choirboys: 'I quite agree with your principles that it is at your time of life that your habits and character are formed and remain yours during your manhood . . .' A year after his first letter (dated 23 July 1900) in which he routinely enjoined the boys to do their duty and to obey their choirmaster, he sent a more important communication. Each choirboy was to be 'active in doing good . . . By "doing good" I mean making yourselves useful and doing small kindnesses to other people – whether they are friends or strangers . . . Make up your mind to do one "good turn" to somebody every day, and you will soon get into the habit of doing "good turns" always. It does not matter how small the "good turn" may be – even if it is only to help an old woman across the street, or to say a good word for somebody who is being badly spoken of.'[4] The daily good turn would one day help persuade the public that the Boy Scouts had socially beneficial possibilities.

The old-style pledges had committed boys to forswear a few specified sins. Already, in 1900, Baden-Powell was indicating a broader, more positive form of promise – the emphasis being upon doing something good, rather than upon not doing something bad. He ended his second letter to the choirboys of the village of Weston-by-Runcorn by inviting them to write and tell him about their good turns. Instead he heard from the minister of the boys' church, the Rev. W.H. Stables, and from two local brothers – Gowan and Frederick Fryer – who proposed starting an organization which they wanted to call *The Baden-Powell League of Health and Manliness*. Members would be expected to do good turns, eschew tobacco until they were 21 and lead healthy and physically strenuous lives. Baden-Powell must have given his permission for the use of his name, since his mother was soon helping with a mass of enquiries as the Runcorn-based organization rapidly spread to other towns. A year later Stephe wrote thanking Henrietta Grace for 'all your trouble taken over the non-smoking boys'.[5] The Fryers drew up rules and a pledge form, but sadly no copies of either have survived. They also sent out a circular letter: 'Members of the League are recommended, but by no means compelled, to wear the League Badge – a Medallion bearing a photograph of Major-General Baden-Powell with the name of the League printed round it.' The League attracted more members than the Fryers and Henrietta Grace could cope with, and so its organization was handed over to the S.P.G.* in 1902.[6]

The League cannot be claimed as a prototype for the Boy Scout Movement but given its pledge, which prefigured the Scout's Promise, and the emphasis placed upon health and manliness, which would both be so prominent in *Scouting for Boys*, it is surprising that no historian of the Movement has ever mentioned its existence. If Baden-Powell learned nothing else from it, he certainly saw how effectively his name could be exploited to promote an organization even as flimsily conceived as this provincial league.

In 1901, when Baden-Powell came home to England from South Africa for six months' sick leave, he learned that three other bodies were using his name: The B-P Boys of Greenock, The B-P Brigade (attached to the Primitive Methodists' Sunday School Union) and The B-P Anti-Cigarette League.[7] In South Africa, he had already been approached by numerous boys' clubs and asked to be their patron. A Cape Town journalist, writing about him in September 1900, had described him as 'deeply interested in the future welfare of the rising generation of boys and young men'. According to this journalist 250,000 (probably a misprint for 25,000) boys had joined 'Leagues' promoting this objective and prohibiting smoking. 'His love for children is perhaps his ruling passion. He is never happier than when surrounded by them and joining in their amusements.'[8]

This reputation made Baden-Powell the obvious celebrity guest to address any large conference of schoolteachers and he was duly invited

*The Society for the Propagation of the Gospel (later the Society for Promoting Christian Knowledge).

to do just this at the Wanderers' Hall on 9 July 1902 by the Director of Education for Johannesburg. The subject on which he chose to speak was 'Cultivating Habits of Observation', which was of course what his scouts in the 13th Hussars and the 5th Dragoon Guards had been urged to do. Through looking outwards, he said, boys thought less of self and 'acquired a multitude of small interests outside themselves'. 'By personal study of the little characteristics of one's fellow-men one develops sympathy with them from the highest to the lowest, and can understand all grades much better than if one merely reads about them . . . This kind of sympathy or love . . . is the one great principle for which we ought to live.'

Baden-Powell also indicated that judging people's characters from their appearances might have rather more tangible results; and after mentioning the work of detectives, he told an anecdote about the deductive powers of the Edinburgh surgeon upon whom Conan Doyle had based Sherlock Holmes. That the equation of visual memory with intelligence was widespread at the time is apparent not only in Conan Doyle's stories but in the fiction of Jules Verne, Ballantyne and most notably in Rudyard Kipling's *Kim* (1901), in which the famous observation game made its appearance. In line with Baden-Powell's original praise of 'observation' as a tool of military scouting, Kipling made Kim's training in that art his basic qualification for Secret Service assignments. *Aids to Scouting* was a best-seller in the year in which Kipling wrote *Kim*.

In his Johannesburg lecture, Baden-Powell did not quite make the leap of telling his audience of schoolteachers that through 'scouting' education could be made romantic enough to follow a boy into his own world; but he did at least indicate that mental faculties could be as effectively exercised by means of 'adventures' outside the classroom as by formal studies within it. Then he enunciated two other ideas which would one day be articles of faith in the Boy Scout creed. First, that 'children should be brought up as cheerfully and as happily as possible', and second, that 'in this life one ought to take as much pleasure as one possibly can . . . because if one is happy, one has it in one's power to make all those around happy.'[9]

It is both strange and unfortunate that this very important lecture has never before found its way into any history of the Boy Scout Movement, since its early date would have given pause for thought to those historians[10] who have insisted upon seeing Baden-Powell's principal purpose in founding the Boy Scouts as a determination to secure for the nation generations of boys who would grow up to be dependable and self-sacrificing soldiers. Only two months after the ending of a long and bitter war, his lecture in the Wanderers' Hall was a remarkably pacific one. The abiding impression is of a man interested more in boys becoming good citizens than soldiers.

Two days before Baden-Powell delivered this lecture, the *Johannes-burg Star* had published some extracts from a circular which he had distributed to officers and men of the South African Constabulary. He urged them to be 'gentlemen' not in the sense of having money or the right background, but as men 'who could be trusted on their honour to do a thing; who are guided by a sense of what is their duty rather than by their own inclination; who are helpful and kind, especially to the weak, and who by their personal self-respect and avoidance of bad habits give themselves a manliness and dignity which no humbug can attain to.'[11] These moral guidelines pre-figure the Scout Promise (which would begin: 'On my honour I promise that . . .') and the Movement's aim of making 'unselfish gentlemen' out of all its members regardless of their origins.[12]

Nevertheless these ideas about how to improve the 'character' and education of boys did not persuade Baden-Powell to become actively involved in boys' work – despite the fact that many people involved in such activities wrote to him for advice and guidance. One such approach during 1902 was made by Mr E. P. Carter, a Government clerk in Pretoria who had founded a boys' corps called the Boy Guides' Brigade (in honour of the Queen's Corps of Guides, founded in India in 1846 to undertake scouting and pioneering work). Carter had recently come across the British-born, American-based naturalist Ernest Thompson Seton, and had been sufficiently impressed by his scheme for boy Woodcraft Indians to incorporate many of Seton's ideas into his own hitherto militaristic programme. Carter sent off an account of his improved scheme to Baden-Powell, who returned an encouraging but hardly rhapsodic response. Carter had only one troop of about fifteen boys, but managed later to increase his numbers to a point where Baden-Powell in 1912 and again in 1926 felt obliged to try to absorb them into the mainstream Scout Movement. In 1913 Carter contributed to an anonymously written article in *John Bull*, in which he suggested that Baden-Powell had stolen the basic idea for the Boy Scouts from him. Unwisely Carter also claimed that Baden-Powell's 'Be Prepared' motto was an adaptation of his own '*In Omnia Paratus*', and that his Boy Scouts' uniform was a copy of the Boy Guides' costume. The S.A.C. was already using 'Be Prepared' as its motto in 1902, and its men were wearing the Stetson hat, khaki shirt and shorts which had undoubtedly been in Baden-Powell's mind when he designed his Boy Scouts' uniform.[13] Given the idiosyncratic nature of *Scouting for Boys*, it is unlikely that Baden-Powell owed more to Carter's boys than to any other cadets. He would later meet Thompson Seton quite independently, as a result of an initiative by Seton himself.

Carter had decided to contact Baden-Powell after reading his book *Aids to Scouting*. Others had already found this little book just as fascinating. In 1900 Baden-Powell had learned that a Yorkshire vicar, the Rev. R. L. Bellamy, had brought out *Hints from Baden-Powell: A Book for Boys' Brigades*, in which he attempted to draw out moral lessons from *Aids to Scouting*. He compared the dangers faced by a solitary scout in enemy country with the problems confronting an isolated Christian boy in a sinful society. Brigade boys were urged to become 'Scouts in Christ's Army'. Later that year, *Aids to Scouting* landed on the desk of Howard (later Sir Howard) Spicer, editor of *Boys of the Empire* – arguably the most jingoistic of all the juvenile periodicals. On 27 October Spicer announced that by kind permission of Major-General Baden-Powell and his publisher, *Aids to Scouting* would be serialized in his paper in nine instalments. The first appeared under the title of 'The Boy Scout' on 3 November.[14] Spicer promised his readers a new game in the Christmas issue called 'The Game of Scout'. 'We shall furnish each boy with a full set of rules of this new and exciting game. So popular do we think the game will become that many schools will probably allot at least one day a week to the playing of it in the Easter term.' The instalments appeared but not the game. Details of 'Scouting Competitions' were scattered among the instalments, but these only involved sending in lists of newagents unable to produce copies of *Boys of the Empire* on demand. In the November issue there was a reference to 'Our *Boy Scouts*' having been 'a huge success . . . They have taken Baden-Powell's hints, and have tracked down every culprit [newsagent] who ignores *Boys of the Empire*.' A new 'competition' was then addressed to 'our army of Boy Scouts', who were offered the chance to win prizes such as a bicycle and a tool chest if they managed to send in the names of over twenty boys who wanted to join the Boys' Empire League.

This patriotic organization had been launched by Spicer earlier in the year, partly as an expression of his sincere desire to 'strengthen the true Imperial instinct in British-born boys', and partly as a circulation-boosting device. By the time *Aids to Scouting* was serialized, the Boys' Empire League had 7,000 members and a council on which sat two dukes, two earls, two barons, Sir Arthur Conan Doyle and an assortment of generals and admirals. When approached by the League, Baden-Powell sent them the kind of message expected of a national figure: 'Each member of the League must make himself into a loyal, useful, and honourable boy.'[15]

The League provided a membership badge, a life-saver's medal, a summer camp and occasional courses in physical training and swimming. It was always uninspiring and never achieved widespread popularity, but Baden-Powell must have noted that what success the Boys' Empire League achieved was entirely due to its connection with a newspaper. This would have important consequences for his own Boy Scouts.

Spicer drew Baden-Powell's attention to the name 'The Boy Scouts', but he in turn had 'borrowed' it from a successful fiction series running in a rival boys' paper, the *True Blue War Library*. In February 1900 Harry St George, a cavalry officer youthful enough to be known as the 'Boy Scout', began his series of adventures which would continue until April 1906, a year before Baden-Powell supposedly invented the all-important Boy Scout name. A few titles of the *True Blue* series give the flavour: 'The Boy Scout as Spy Tracker', 'The Boy Scout and the Invisible Boer' and of greater significance, 'The Boy Scout Joins B-P's Police'. That was in December 1900, and the following six episodes were all set in the South African Constabulary. For 6½ years the *True Blue War Library*'s 'Boy Scout' symbolized patriotic service in exotic colonial locations for thousands of boys. This long-standing use of the name 'Boy Scout' gave it a resonance by association which inevitably helped Baden-Powell's cause when he came to launch his 'Boy Scout Scheme'.[16]

Nevertheless, his awareness that the name had not been his invention would lead him to cast around for alternatives. In September 1907 his publisher, Arthur Pearson, rightly dismissed his alternative suggestion of 'The Imperial Scouts' and wisely counselled, 'I do not think you will improve upon Boy Scouts.'[17] Although Baden-Powell never acknowledged his debt to the editors of *Boys of the Empire* and the *True Blue War Library*, he remained very much aware of it – as were the compilers of a brief history of the Scouts put out by the Government's Department of Information in 1917. On 5 June 1917, he wrote to Mr G. H. Mair of the Department, strongly objecting to the statement 'that I devised the idea of the Boy Scouts from boys' publications'.[18] A year earlier he had written in answer to a direct question concerning the invention of the name: 'I had certainly never heard the title "Boy Scouts" before I applied it to boy training in Britain in 1907.'[19]

It may seem surprising – with so many ingredients of the Boy Scout formula, including the name, already in Baden-Powell's mind before he returned home – that it should have taken him another five years to unveil his great scheme. Yet there were many reasons for this. In the first place there were considerable difficulties in formulating any programme which simultaneously appealed to adults as worthwhile and to boys as entertaining. Then there would be the problem of finding a suitable financial backer, who might or might not be one and the same as the publisher of any printed material. Conflicts of interest with existing boys' organizations would also require diplomatic handling.

William Smith was certainly a much worthier advocate than Howard Spicer for the suggestion that Baden-Powell 'rewrite the army scouting book to suit boys'. But even after the Glasgow parade in 1904, it would take two more years and a great sense of personal and professional urgency to bring Baden–Powell to the point of sending Smith a paper on the subject of 'Scouting for Boys'.

2. Liberals and Frontiersmen (1904–06)

In the past Baden-Powell's books had all been written when he had time on his hands and with the ulterior motive of drawing his name to the attention of senior officers. As Inspector General of Cavalry he had very little free time, and knew that his best chance of promotion lay in not offending the likes of Sir John French rather than having 'happy thoughts' about improving boys' characters.

Within a few months of Baden-Powell's visit to Glasgow, it became apparent that no political party was going to risk the unpopularity involved in adopting compulsory military training as part of their defence policy. Lord Roberts and his National Service League supporters countered by urging that all boys be taught rifle shooting on miniature ranges. Since Baden-Powell was still inspecting cadet corps, he began to give this theme greater emphasis in his talks.

Stephe had this subject in mind when he went to Eton College on 26 November 1904 to deliver a lecture on 'Soldiering'.[1] He had been invited by Eton's militarily-minded headmaster, Dr Edmond Warre, who had established the Oxford University Rifle Volunteers and the Eton Volunteer Corps. As Headmaster he found time to be Honorary Colonel of the Oxfordshire Light Infantry.[2] The lecture was delivered to an audience including most of Eton's Corps and the meeting was chaired by Major A. A. Somerville, the master of the 'Army Class' which consisted entirely of boys intending to make the army their career.[3]

Of all the historians of the Boy Scouts, only Michael Rosenthal has mentioned the contents of this lecture. (He refers to it indirectly, concentrating exclusively on the letter which Baden-Powell subsequently wrote for publication to the editor of the *Eton Chronicle*, and which contained the substance of his original speech.) Mr Rosenthal has suggested that this letter constitutes 'the earliest version of the Boy Scout Scheme'.[4] In fact both letter and lecture, which Baden-Powell described in his diary as being about 'Soldiering', only touch upon scouting *en passant*, while the overall tone and content of both plainly link them with the efforts he was beginning to make to interest young men in rifle shooting. There is, for example, no mention of the character-forming properties of observation and scouting which would be absolutely central in the scheme Baden-Powell ultimately devised. Nor in the Eton lecture did he speak about the need to achieve broader sympathies with others and to make them happy. There are no good turns, and nothing about sharpening a boy's wits by making him remember details.

After applauding Japanese respect for their samurai ancestors, Baden-Powell reminded his audience that: 'We in England have equally good ancestors to look back to in the knights of the Middle Ages.' Preaching to the converted of the 'Army Class' and the Corps, he suggested that in their next holidays:

Each one should get together and train a squad of (say) ten boys in his village or town, just as the Knights of old used to get together their 'clump' (as they called it) of armed retainers and trained them to patriotism and use of arms. The way to set about it would be to get a few boys to come in the evening and read to them a book about the knights, such as Conan Doyle's *White Company*, etc. and go on with Fitchet's *Deeds that Won the Empire*, etc., Roberts' *Adventures of Captain John Smith*, or any other interesting accounts of the battles and self-sacrifice of our forefathers.
Then teach them:
(1) how to aim and shoot with miniature rifles;
(2) how to judge distance;
(3) how to scout;
(4) how to drill and skirmish, take cover, etc.

A form of oath was also proposed for the boys: 'I promise on my honour, to be loyal to the King and to back up my commander in carrying out our duty . . .' Baden-Powell ended with the reflection that if 200 boys each recruited their ten volunteers, there would be 10,000 under training by Christmas. 'I shall be very glad to hear from any boy who succeeds in getting together a squad as I should like to keep a register of these. And I would gladly come and inspect the one which attains the highest strength this winter.'[5] There is no evidence that any squads were formed as a result of this talk.

The Eton lecture and the subsequent letter to *The Chronicle* are historically significant but do not amount to 'the first version' of the later Boy Scout programme. The oath or promise was not a particular novelty since the Boy's Empire League had one, as did the B-P League of Health and Manliness, the Boys' Brigade and numerous other boys' organizations. On the other hand, the emphasis on chivalry and the suggestion that boys should read patriotic literature and endeavour to emulate 'the duties of the knights' do definitely prefigure passages in *Scouting for Boys*.

As if to confirm that the Eton lecture had been an attempt to encourage shooting in schools, rather than a prototype for a character-building movement, Baden-Powell sent an abbreviated version to 'Loyal Britishers' through the letters pages of the *Union Jack* boys' paper. (This was republished in *The Marvel* early in 1905.) If Britain should ever be attacked, he wrote, 'every boy in the country should be prepared to take his place and help in the defence like those Mafeking boys did'. Captains of football and cricket teams were invited to train their boys how to shoot. Like the Etonians, these young sportsmen were asked to get in touch with Baden-Powell.

In a speech at the Mansion House the following August, Roberts demanded universal rifle drill for schoolboys and a 'home defence army' guaranteed to 'render any attempt at invasion out of the question'.[6] Several months later Roberts, no longer Commander-in-Chief, began to advocate conscription. While Baden-Powell never followed suit, he did continue to support the drive to create more miniature rifle ranges. In July he opened ranges in Boothby and Louth in Lincolnshire, and later that year in Ilkley and Nottingham.[7] At not one of these places did he mention scouting, nor a general form of training based upon it.

Yet on other occasions during 1905 he showed that the spirit of Johannesburg and Glasgow was not dead. His interest in character-training and good citizenship was still developing, but not as part of his efforts to increase public interest in shooting. In June he inspected the Cardiff Boys' Brigade and delivered a speech which marked his first real attempt to follow up what he had said a year earlier in Glasgow about Scouting's potential for making boys better citizens. After describing the Boys' Brigade as 'a very important movement for the Empire because it aims at producing good citizens', he added, 'I do not mean by good citizens merely fighting men.' He told the Brigade's officers that 'they should attend to the character of the boys and foster a spirit which prompted them to help each other'. He ended by declaring that he 'would like to see all nations brought up to a high standard of brotherhood so that there would no longer be heard rumours of wars'. 'Joining the Colours,' he argued, was not the only form of patriotism, 'there should also be the patriotism of peace time.' Nor need 'self-sacrifice' be confined to the battlefield. Boys could practise 'giving up little personal pleasures in order that they may thereby give help to other people. The first and greatest step is for each boy to do at least one good turn – no matter how small – to somebody every day.'[8] What small measure of militaristic sentiment there was in this remarkable speech was entirely subordinated to Baden-Powell's civil message. This would also be true a year later, when he inspected the 2nd Volunteer Battalion of the Loyal North Lancashire Regiment and suggested that each of the regiment's volunteer scouts should 'train two or three boys of his acquaintance in scouting, because the future of the country depended so much on the character of the rising generation, and nothing forms character more than a scout's training'.[9]

Baden-Powell's lively social life during 1905 and 1906 considerably affected the direction of his thinking. For example, in June 1905 when he delivered his Cardiff speech he was staying with David A. Thomas, the philanthropically-minded Liberal M.P. for Merthyr Tydfil. During 1905 he stayed no fewer than five times at Easton Lodge, home of the socialist Countess of Warwick (Frances Evelyn Greville). 'Daisy', the best-known peeress in England, had had affairs with Edward VII as Prince of Wales, with Admiral Lord Charles Beresford and with Lord Rosebery, the former Prime Minister. But in November 1904 when Baden-Powell first went to stay with her, she was more famous for having just declared her support for the Social Democratic Federation and, as the owner of 13,000 acres, for advocating the nationalization of land. Among the inevitable Liberal and Labour politicians, her house parties also invariably boasted numbers of authors, artists and journalists.[10] Winston Churchill was a guest on at least one occasion when Baden-Powell was also at Easton. At this time Churchill was one of the Liberal Party's most determined advocates of cuts in defence spending and improvements in welfare provision.

But as it happened, his single most important acquaintanceship with a Liberal public figure was not destined to make him abandon his efforts to persuade boys to learn to shoot in favour of promoting an exclusively pacific character-building programme. Instead it encouraged him to try to combine the two objectives within a single coherent framework. The Liberal in question was the new Secretary of State for War, Mr R. B. Haldane, a brilliant philosopher and lawyer with an awe-inspiringly innovative mind. It might seem strange that Baden-Powell should have got on so well with a man who was determined to reduce expenditure on the army, but from their first meeting on 1 May 1906 he was captivated by Haldane.[11] Both men were 50 years old, and both still lived at home with formidable mothers. Haldane had recently announced the creation of the Territorial Army; this was exactly the kind of home defence force which Baden-Powell had been advocating since 1903, so its forthcoming inauguration naturally gained his approval. He met the Secretary of State twice during the key month of May 1906 and corresponded with him.

Five days after his first meeting with Haldane, Baden-Powell at long last sent off a paper on the subject of 'Scouting for Boys' to William Smith and six other eminent men (Lord Roberts; Lord Strathcona; Douglas McGarel Hogg, son of the founder of the London Polytechnic; Lord Grey, formerly the Administrator in Rhodesia and now Governor-General of Canada; Lord Rodney, founder of Lord Rodney's Boys; and H. A. Gwynne, the editor of the *Evening Standard*).[12] From December 1905 until mid-April 1906, Baden-Powell had been abroad inspecting cavalry in South Africa and Egypt, so it is most unlikely that he started work on his submission for

William Smith until the last week of April. He would therefore either have been writing it or, as I think more likely, toying with the idea of doing so just at the time when he saw Haldane on 1 May.

The Secretary of State believed that the future of his Territorials would depend upon the quantity and the patriotism of the boys now joining cadets corps or religious brigades.[13] Haldane was therefore more than intrigued to discover that Baden-Powell was convinced that 'scout training' could mould character and increase the popularity of such organizations.

Baden-Powell dined with Haldane on 20 May. Four days earlier he had noted in his diary: 'Report for Army. Boy Scouts.' No trace of this report survives in the Public Record Office; but the fact that he had written it would seem to establish that Haldane had given him the vital nudge which made him complete his paper on 'Scouting for Boys' and send it to William Smith. Stephe's split nature as innovator and conformist had always required that he entertain reasonable hopes of official blessing upon his proceedings before being prepared to commit himself to them wholeheartedly. This was exactly what Haldane provided at the perfect psychological moment.

In December 1905 Rose Kerr, the only girl Stephe had ever been keen to marry, had turned him down after a two-year courtship. His four-month tour of inspection in South Africa and Egypt had diverted him until his return to England in April – a couple of weeks before his meeting with Haldane. The emptiness of his private life, his difficulties with his mother and his thwarted desire to have children of his own all made the idea of active involvement in boys' work more attractive. And there was another thought – if he was offered no further employment by the War Office when his term as Inspector General ended in less than a year, what would he do?

But while the Secretary of State for War undoubtedly played an essential role in the genesis of the Boy Scouts, he did not see Baden-Powell's idea solely or even principally in military terms. Haldane's later description of the Scout Movement as 'a great object lesson in how to enlarge the system of our education', coupled with his belief that 'the moral element' in Scouting would help to combat hooligan-ism, show that he saw it from the beginning as more than a mere training 'for National Defence'. 'The Boy Scouts,' he said, 'attempts to lay in the boy a foundation of character upon which he may build a career in any direction.'[14] For Haldane and for Baden-Powell, learning to shoot in order to be able to defend one's country was not an end in itself as much as a single (albeit essential) ingredient in a wider good citizenship.

This would also be apparent in that long-awaited but brief paper on 'Scouting for Boys' which William Smith received early in May 1906. 'The ulterior object of the following scheme,' wrote Baden-Powell, 'is to develop among boys a power of sympathizing with others, a spirit of self-sacrifice and patriotism, and generally to prepare them to become good citizens. The method for effecting the above is to develop among boys observation of details, and to help their reasoning powers . . .' By 'a spirit of self-sacrifice and patriotism', he meant readiness if need be to die for one's country. Although important, this would be his only mention of any military intention, and the overall balance of the piece was clearly closer in spirit to his talk to the Johannesburg teachers than to his lecture to the Etonians. Boys should know 'the points of the compass by the sun, moon and stars'. They should learn to read all kinds of tracks as well as how to light fires, judge distances, give first aid, swim, write brief reports and know about the British Colonies and the Union Jack. Boys should be told that: 'Duty to their country and to their neighbours' should 'be their first guide in taking any step'. Their own 'pleasure or convenience should come second'. 'The need for good citizens' was stressed, as was the desirability of 'spotting people in everyday life who were wanting help, and helping them in however small a way'. Baden-Powell also suggested some 'Tests' for memory, tracking, fire-laying and elementary cooking. Various games were also described.

While all this was plainly taken from *Aids to Scouting*, Baden-Powell would have felt much less confident about pressing ahead unless soon after his Glasgow inspection, he had come across an organization much closer in ethos and atmosphere to the future Boy Scouts than the prayer-bashing Boys' Brigade.

In late October 1904, after inspecting a county yeomanry regiment in the north-west of England, he had been entertained by its honorary colonel Lord Lonsdale, the well-known 'sporting Earl' whose name lives on in the famous boxing trophy the 'Lonsdale Belt'. Baden-Powell found himself staying at Lowther Castle at a most propitious time, since his host was just then dreaming up a picturesque new body of patriotic volunteers.[15] The driving force was his collaborator Roger Pocock, an ex-trooper in the Canadian North-West Mounted Police and currently an idiosyncratic travel writer and journalist. Captivated by Bill Cody's touring Wild West Show, Pocock aimed to create a force giving scope to would-be rough riders, lariat men, tomahawk throwers and indeed anyone with a yen to participate in activities connected with the Wild West or the colonial frontier. The name Pocock chose for his organization was the Imperial Legion of Frontiersmen – his inspiration being Kipling's poem *The Lost Legion*.[16]

The Legion was inaugurated on New Year's Day 1905, and among its volunteers were men who had served in the remotest outposts of the Empire – honorary members included Prince Louis of Battenberg, Rider Haggard and William Le Queux. The Frontiersmen wore 'an easy shirt . . . a loose kerchief protecting the base of the skull from sunstroke . . . and a slouch hat [later a Stetson]'.[17] The similarity to the later Boy Scout uniform is obvious.

Mr Geoff Pocock, the owner of Roger Pocock's diaries and other papers relating to the Legion's early history, believes that Baden-Powell discussed the founding of the Boy Scouts with Roger Pocock in 1904 and 1905.[18] While I could find no certain evidence of this, the Legion undoubtedly made a considerable impact upon Baden-Powell. The emphasis which he would soon place upon 'frontiersmen' as role models and heroes to the boys is plainly due to the Legion. 'Besides war scouts, there are also peace scouts,' he would write on the first page of *Scouting for Boys* directed exclusively at boys rather than their Scoutmasters. 'These are the frontiersmen . . . the "trappers" of North America, hunters of Central Africa . . . the bushmen and drovers of Australia, the Constabulary of North-West Canada and of South Africa . . .'[19] He might have been listing the former avocations of typical members of the Legion of Frontiersmen. When Baden-Powell launched the Boy Scouts, many members of the Legion became Scoutmasters and named their troops 'Legion of Frontiers' Boy Scouts'.[20] Roger Pocock would be a contributor to the very first edition of the Boy Scouts' newspaper *The Scout*, in which Baden-Powell's boys were described as 'The Legion of Boy Scouts'.[21] The fact that this name was ever seriously considered is another indication of the extent to which Baden-Powell had been influenced by Pocock's creation. Nevertheless this was never acknowledged; and the only direct reference to the Legion in *Scouting for Boys* would be a recommendation to boys to read *The Frontiersmen's Pocket Book*, first published by Pocock in 1906.[22]

But even with the encouragement of Mr Haldane and the inspiration of Mr Pocock (whose catalytic roles have only now been recognized), Baden-Powell was still a little distance away from having a blueprint for the world's most successful youth movement.

3. Down to Business (1906–08)

The original short paper which Baden-Powell sent to William Smith under the heading 'Scouting for Boys' has not survived. Smith passed it to the editor of *The Boys' Brigade Gazette*, James M. Hannan, who published an edited version on 1 June 1906. In his introduction Hannan showed no awareness of Scouting's potential but suggested luke-warmly that Baden-Powell's paper might be of interest 'in view of our coming summer camps'. One and a half columns long, the piece was given no particular prominence in the *Gazette*'s June issue and was soon forgotten.

Baden-Powell had still not attempted a proper adaptation of *Aids to*

Scouting for boys, and he remained reluctant to take on so much work until he could be sure of more interest than was currently forthcoming from the Boys' Brigade. 'Chance or fate, or what you will, took me just at this time to stay with Arthur Pearson,' he wrote later, referring to a weekend he spent at Frensham in Surrey in July 1906, as the house guest of the owner of the *Daily Express* and the *Evening Standard*.[1] Chance or fate had really played no part in this visit. He would have stayed with Pearson almost a year earlier if the newspaper proprietor's secretary had not made a mistake over the date.[2] But Baden-Powell pleaded chance rather than calculation because he would later be embarrassed by suggestions that at its inception Scouting had been nothing but a money-making scheme dreamed up by Arthur Pearson and himself. He therefore played down the millionaire's essential role in getting the Scouts started.

Joseph Chamberlain had called Pearson 'the greatest hustler I have ever known', and it was for his undoubted capabilities in this direction that Baden-Powell had first sought him out. Pearson, however, was a man of many parts. While Baden-Powell was staying with him, the magnate impressed him by slipping away to visit a home for crippled children. He also sponsored the Fresh Air Fund – a charity giving East End children days out in Epping Forest.[3] Baden-Powell wrote of Pearson as 'the first public man to whom I spoke of the idea of the Boy Scout Movement'.[4] So he must originally have discussed the Scouts with him in July 1905, a year before he sent his paper to Smith.

Two weeks after staying with Pearson, Baden-Powell was writing about his plans to 'draw up a scheme with a handbook to it for the education of Boys as Scouts'.[5] This is the first mention of the 'handbook', which would become not only one of the world's greatest best sellers but the Boy Scouts' Bible: on one level a 'how to do it' manual, but on another an almost theological statement of purposes and principles. Baden-Powell's weekend in the Surrey countryside brought him appreciably closer to launching the Boy Scouts. But it would still take him a year and a half of hard work and many meetings with his assiduous backer to bring his 'handbook' to press. Meanwhile, he would become entangled with a man whose considerable positive contribution to Scouting would nevertheless cause immense distress.

*

During the very month in which Baden-Powell stayed in the luxuriously appointed house of his future publisher, he received a small package in the post. It contained a quaintly entitled book which he was quick to recognize as a providential windfall. *The Birch-bark Roll of the Woodcraft Indians* had been sent by its author, Ernest Thompson Seton. On the very first page Baden-Powell read: 'This is a time when the whole nation is turning toward the outdoor life, seeking in it the physical regeneration so needful for continued national existence.' Only by living 'the simple life of primitive times', continued Seton, could the ills caused by 'the grind of the over-busy world' be cured.

In his short book Seton set out an adventurous recreation scheme for boys between the ages of 8 and 15, inviting them to identify with his ideal natural man – the Red Indian brave. As he read *The Birch-bark Roll* with mounting admiration, Baden-Powell was unaware that four years after their foundation in America, the Woodcraft Indians had still made very little impression there. He has recently been accused of stealing from Seton the most basic ideas behind the Boy Scout Movement and many details of its programme.[6]

Seton's boys were grouped in 'bands' of 15–50 and were only loosely supervised by an adult 'medicine man'. 'Woodcraft is our principal study,' wrote Seton, 'by which we mean nature-study, certain kinds of hunting, and the art of camping.' Also included were 'triangulation, star-craft, finding one's way, telling direction, sign language, as well as many branches of Indian-craft.' There was an oath of loyalty for new members of 'the tribe' and ten 'laws', the first of which was: 'Don't rebel.' A tuft of black horsehair was called 'a scalp' and was each boy's badge of membership. They played games such as the 'Bear Hunt', 'Spear the Great Sturgeon' and 'Quick Sight'. Tying knots, lighting fires and life-saving drills were among the activities.[7]

What impressed Baden-Powell most was the way in which Seton had fleshed out realistic activities which would keep the boys occupied when camping out. His own Boys' Brigade submission had merely been a list; so he admired details like the scalps, the totems and the tracking-irons (mimicking a particular animal's spoor) which were attached to the human quarry's feet during 'Scouting practices'. But he had already decided that his own Boy Scout would be a self-confident frontiersman rather than a culturally doomed Red Indian. The 'natural man' would have a place, but not centre stage, and he would be represented by the Zulus rather than the American Indians.

On 1 August 1906 Baden-Powell wrote thanking Seton for his book. 'It may interest you to know that I had been drawing up a scheme with a handbook to it, for the education of boys as scouts – which essentially runs much on the lines of yours . . . I should very much like to meet you.'[8] Seton had been put in touch with Baden-Powell by the ubiquitous Lord Roberts, to whom he had written asking for the names of public men who might help him to spread his Woodcraft Indians in Great Britain. (Five tribes were started between 1904 and 1906, but even the most successful had folded by 1908.)[9] Seton also wanted to publicize his new book, *Biography of a Grizzly*, and hoped to persuade some eminent Englishmen to take the chair at several of his lectures. Roberts, whose interest in boys' organizations was well known,[10] had just received Baden-Powell's paper on training boys in scouting and had therefore recommended the hero of Mafeking as the one man Seton had to see.

When they met three months later for luncheon at the Savoy Hotel, Baden-Powell was particularly impressed by what he was told about the Woodcraft Indians' scouting games and their numerous non-competitive badges awarded for personal achievements.[11] One of Seton's future claims of plagiarism would be in connection with these same badges. Scouts in the 5th Dragoon Guards had worn a distinguishing badge, but this hardly compared with Seton's 150 wampum medals made from shells and 'engraved with the symbol or the deed for which it is given'. Later Baden-Powell was in the habit of saying that he adopted his Scout badges of proficiency from the Royal Navy, as well as from Seton's *Birch-bark Roll* and his *Two Little Savages*.[12] But while his earliest Boy Scout badges did look rather like naval insignia – especially those for life-saving, seamanship, pioneering and marksmanship – later badges plainly owed more to Seton's conception. The non-competitive nature of the Scout badge system was directly taken from *The Birch-bark Roll* and is still one of the most attractive features of Scouting.

Another significant 'borrowing' was the identification of each Scout patrol by a totem: usually either an animal or bird whose cry the boys had to be able to mimic; this was exactly Seton's procedure with his 'bands'.[13] Baden-Powell also appropriated five of Seton's excellent outdoor games which, through a genuine oversight, were not acknowledged as his in the first edition of *Scouting for Boys*. He would, however, put this right in the second edition (1909); and in *The Scout* a year later would further acknowledge his 'indebtedness to that great authority on woodcraft for his valuable assistances'.[14]

Unfortunately, by then Seton was arguing that Baden-Powell had agreed at their first meeting to promote the Woodcraft Indians in England, in effect becoming his 'assistant'. Then two years later, ran this argument, he had welshed on his agreement, 'taking my fundamental ideas, and all my work and methods, republishing the substance of my books over your own name, and dropping me out as soon as you thought you could go it alone'.[15] Later Seton wrote for publication: 'General Baden-Powell . . . worked for me for two years and in 1908 gave the movement a great popular boom by changing the name of the Woodcraft Indians to Boy Scouts . . .'[16] Baden-Powell treated Seton's claims with good-natured irony: 'His statement that he and I together organized the Boy Scouts in England in 1908 and in America in 1910 is news to me! However, I am proud to have been associated with it . . .'[17]

From a letter which Baden-Powell wrote to Seton the day after their first meeting, it is very clear that he had always intended to go ahead with his own plans:

I enclose a kind of preliminary notice which I sent out early this year [to William Smith] regarding my scheme of 'Boy Scouts' . . . You will see that our principles seem practically identical – except that mine does not necessarily make its own organization – it is applicable to existing ones: if we can work together in the same direction I should be very glad indeed.[18]

Seton's only 'evidence' that Baden-Powell had agreed to become his 'assistant' was Stephe's spontaneous offer 'to revise the Scouting part of the 7th edition of the *Birch-bark Roll*'.[19]

On 17 June 1907, Baden-Powell told Seton that he was writing a handbook 'much on the lines of my little book *Aids to Scouting*'. He tactfully added that he would 'be proud to be connected as you suggest with your scouting branch'. While the first half of the letter made it obvious that he was pressing on with his own show, Seton later quoted only the latter part, claiming that this proved that Baden-Powell had been eager to work for him in a subordinate capacity. Because Seton was already operating in America – albeit on an extremely limited scale – Baden-Powell intended to make no efforts to export his system to that side of the Atlantic. This had been why he was happy to associate himself with Seton's 'scouting branch'.[20]

Baden-Powell would have behaved more sensitively if he had realized at the outset how insecure Seton was, in spite of his outstanding gifts as an artist and story teller. As a boy Seton had been humiliated by an overbearing father and had remained sane by spending much of his time in the wooded ravines outside Toronto fantasizing about being an Indian brave. English by birth, he felt an outsider in Canada and later in America. He loathed cities and empathized with all threatened beings – animals and humans. Seton signed his letters with a paw print and seldom took a bath or cut his hair.[21]

It agonized this sensitive man that a newcomer to boys' work should, within a couple of years, manage to launch a new movement successful enough to make his own look an irrelevant curiosity. Unable to accept what had happened, he tried to rewrite history. Baden-Powell's love-hate relationship with tribal people long predated his acquaintance with Seton, so the relevance of their survival skills and their rituals of manhood to 'deteriorating' city-dwellers would have occurred to him even if Seton had never sent his book.[22] In his heart Seton must have known that with *Scouting for Boys* Baden-Powell created a world entirely different from that of the Woodcraft Indians; not only because of the famous 'good turn', the Boy Scout name, the uniform and the emphasis placed upon chivalry and patriotism, but because the whole scheme drew in material from every conceivable sphere which could interest a boy from knights in armour to espionage. The world of the Red Indian was a restricted place in comparison with the vast region over which the Boy Scout's imagination was invited to wander.

Seton's most serious accusations should not be taken seriously, nor should Michael Rosenthal's recent argument that Baden-Powell found in the structure of the Woodcraft Indians 'an organizational model that provided solutions for almost every problem he faced'.[23] There were indeed similarities between Seton's Indian 'bands' and Baden-Powell's Boy Scout 'patrols'. Both were placed under a boy leader who was himself under the more distant authority of an adult, but there were many other precedents which Baden-Powell could just as well have chosen to follow. When the *True Blue War Library* was running its Boy Scout stories, the newspaper inaugurated a boys' society called 'The True and Trusty Band'. Members swore to obey various laws, and joined groups of from six to eight under a boy captain. There were secret signs, and badges to be won.[24]

In the 5th Dragoon Guards and in the S.A.C., Baden-Powell had trained men in groups of six under an N.C.O. rather than an officer, and had long been an admirer of the public school system of supervision by senior boys. Seton's bands were considered viable at anything between 15 and 50 boys; Baden-Powell therefore followed his own precedents in determining the number for each Scout patrol. The name itself came from his own book *Cavalry Instruction* (1887), in which he had called all small scouting groups 'patrols'. Nor is Rosenthal correct in thinking that Baden-Powell derived his idea for First- and Second-Class Scouts from Seton's division of his Indians into Braves and Warriors. Scouts in the 5th Dragoon Guards had been divided by ability and knowledge into First and Second Class.[25]

While Baden-Powell was thoughtless and none too scrupulous in his earlier dealings with Seton, he later did his utmost to conciliate. On 23 September 1910 he addressed a large audience of affluent diners assembled in New York by Mr E. M. Robinson and other Y.M.C.A. officials who were then promoting the Boy Scouts in America. (Baden-Powell himself had done absolutely nothing to bring his scheme to the attention either of Robinson or of anyone else in the United States.) As chairman of Robinson's committee, Seton presided at the New York dinner in the Waldorf Astoria. To Baden-Powell's relief the naturalist's introductory remarks about him were surprisingly complimentary. Stephe therefore proceeded to outdo him in generous sentiment: 'You have made a little mistake, Mr Seton, in your remarks to the effect that I am the father of it [Scouting] . . . There are many fathers. I am only one of the uncles, I might say.'[26]

The following day Baden-Powell wrote an equally friendly letter to Seton, approving his incorporation of much of *Scouting for Boys* into the *Handbook of the Boy Scouts of America* for which Seton had written other material. Declining any financial *quid pro quo*, Baden-Powell voluntarily 'renounced his rights in the title in the United States'. He thus sacrificed hundreds of thousands of dollars. Since the Boy Scouts of America needed his official blessing in order to deal with their rivals, he could easily have insisted on their adopting an edited version of his *Scouting for Boys* as their handbook, paying him a handsome royalty for the privilege. Since Seton was chairman of the Boy Scouts of America, Baden-Powell might have been forgiven for supposing that he would also be delighted to be told that 'the Boy Scouts of America is the only association, which I authorize to reproduce for publication my writings in the United States.'[27]

Unfortunately for all concerned Seton would later quarrel with his colleagues in the Boy Scouts of America, accusing them of militarism, over-regulation and the destruction of the outdoor spirit. The B.S.A.'s executive board sacked him as Chief Scout in America after he had held that position for five years. In the public row that followed, Seton lashed out wildly at both the board and Baden-Powell. 'I am quite content to take second place,' he had told Baden-Powell plaintively in 1910, 'but I am not willing to be left out *altogether*.'[28] Having raised no difficulties about Seton becoming Chief Scout in America, and having agreed to the naturalist's name appearing above his own on the title page of the first American *Handbook*, Baden-Powell cannot realistic-ally be accused of having forced Seton out. The truth is that Ernest Thompson Seton was his own worst enemy. By making such sweeping accusations instead of limiting his aims to getting proper recognition for the appropriation of his badge system, Seton guaranteed that he would indeed be 'left out altogether'.

Baden-Powell learned from Seton and the Woodcraft Indians that romantic schemes conceived in a spirit of open opposition to industrial society had no future. Neither the industrialists of Progressive Era America nor Britain's beleaguered ruling class could be expected to see any merit in anything openly subversive. His Boy Scouts scheme would therefore have to promise to make boys not 'noble savages' but the patriotic and morally upright youngsters whom their 'betters' believed the country needed.

Baden-Powell shared Seton's romanticism, but he was also a practical man who knew a lot about the art of persuasion.[29] It would be a mistake to suppose that the promotional material which he soon wrote to 'sell' the Boy Scouts accurately reflected his personal views. At the heart of Scouting lay a whole series of incompatible aims, not the least of which was an undertaking to produce self-assertive independent young men who would nevertheless remain loyal supporters of the *status quo*. Having concealed so much about himself for so many years, Baden-Powell was ideally placed to represent his ideas in the most reassuring rather than the most truthful light.

*

After meeting Seton, Baden-Powell worked fitfully on his handbook during November 1906 but did not manage more than a rough outline. An incident in mid-December came as an encouraging reminder of Scouting's undoubted appeal to children. After inspecting the 4th Cavalry Brigade in Colchester, he stayed with Brigadier-General (later Field-Marshal Viscount) H. H. Allenby, whose son Maurice turned out to have been given instruction in scouting by his governess. Miss Katarina Loveday had been trained as a teacher at Charlotte Mason's House of Education in the Lake District, where *Aids to Scouting* had been on the syllabus since 1905. Allenby told Baden-Powell how Miss Loveday and Maurice enjoyed playing scouting games and often 'ambushed' him by hiding in overhanging branches.[30] (Baden-Powell's need to defeat later charges of militarism against the Scouts would one day lead him to suggest that Miss Mason, a peace-loving educationalist, had been the first person to make him aware of the educational value of Scouting, although his 1902 lecture to the Johannesburg teachers is proof that he had needed no telling.)[31]

Baden-Powell coined the expression 'Peace Scouts' during that November, when he spoke to members of the Birkenhead Y.M.C.A. But a mere two months later in January 1907 he wrote two promotional pamphlets, the first of which pandered to virtually every xenophobic anxiety to have emerged since the Boer War. Yet he was right to suppose that he would get most support from the ruling class if he offered the Scouts as a catch-all cure for 'deterioration', military unpreparedness and party politics (by which he meant the steady growth of support for the Labour Party). The first pamphlet began as follows:

Boy Scouts: A Suggestion

The same causes which brought about the downfall of the great Roman Empire are working today in Great Britain.' These words were spoken the other day by one of our best-known democratic politicians . . . The main cause of the downfall of Rome was the decline of good citizenship among its subjects, due to want of energetic patriotism, to the growth of luxury and idleness, and to the exaggerated importance of local party politics, etc. . . . It becomes incumbent upon every one to turn the rising generation on to the right road for good citizenship. To this end the following scheme is offered as a possible aid towards putting on a positive footing the development, moral and physical, of boys of all creeds and classes, by a means which should appeal to them . . . Under the term 'Scouting', with its attributes of romance and adventure, I suggest instruction in the many invaluable qualities which go to make a good citizen equally with a good scout. These include observation and deduction, chivalry, patriotism, self-sacrifice, personal hygiene, saving life, self-reliance, etc., etc.[32]

The well-known democratic politician was George Wyndham, the Chief Secretary in Ireland from 1900 to 1905. As the author of an introduction to North's *Plutarch*, Wyndham could claim more familiarity with Roman history than most politicians, but in general his true-blue Tory sentiments were out of tune with popular perceptions in the year of the great Liberal landslide. Nevertheless, on this occasion his pessimism struck a common chord not only in the Carlton Club but on the Clapham omnibus. Comparisons of Britain with Rome had become commonplace by 1906, not only as a result of German and American economic progress but because of Japan's victories over Russia in the war in Manchuria. Fears that Japan might one day become a greater power than Britain were dismissed as laughable by most Liberal politicians, but Baden-Powell took them very seriously indeed.

His second pamphlet, *Boy Scouts: Summary of a Scheme*, was more reassuring. He started by holding up the 'Peace Scouts' (pioneers, trappers and prospectors) as heroes for boys to emulate. Through their knowledge of 'woodcraft' such men had learned to 'fend for themselves in the open'. As well as displaying 'courage and endurance', Baden-Powell insisted that they practised 'chivalry' in their dealings with others. (Given the fate of the Red Indians and Baden-Powell's unhappy experiences with hard-drinking colonial 'loafers', this assertion should be considered an example of salesmanship rather than considered belief.) Self-reliance, courage and chivalry, he asserted, 'made the best citizens in a peaceful community'. And since none of these essential qualities was taught in the schools, he described his principal objective as being to supply this deficiency.

Baden-Powell's term as Inspector General of Cavalry ended on 6 May 1907, and shortly afterwards he decided to find out how a combination of scouting games and didactic anecdotes would work in practice. He also needed to know how boys would cope with real camp life. Later that month, on an Irish fishing trip, he happened to meet a stockbroker called Charles van Raalte, who owned Brownsea Island in Poole Harbour.[33] When he was ready to hold his experimental camp this promised to be the perfect place.

From early June Arthur Pearson began to press Baden-Powell to finish the handbook.[34] The newspaper proprietor hoped to bring it out in serial parts during the opening months of the New Year in order to create advance demand for the book when it appeared in volume form in time for the 'camping season'.

Baden-Powell started work in earnest in mid-June at the Izaak Walton Hotel in Dovedale, Derbyshire, and then returned to London, but not to his mother's busy house. Instead he borrowed a cottage picturesquely situated next to the windmill on Wimbledon Common. The Mill House belonged to the Hon. Mrs Timothy (Maria)

Fetherstonhaugh; described as a widow in previous biographies,[35] in reality she was a married woman whose husband was known to his family as the 'East Wind' because of his cold and hurtful behaviour, which had prompted Maria to buy the Wimbledon cottage as a retreat for herself when he was occupying the family's town house in Mayfair rather than his castle in Cumberland. Baden-Powell had first met the Fetherstonhaughs when with his uncle on Malta while the couple had been holidaying in the Mediterranean.

He stayed in the cottage for ten days, and managed during that time – by dint of writing in his own hand and dictating to a succession of shorthand writers – to complete a first draft of *Scouting for Boys*. His benefactress could not resist driving out daily from Mayfair to inspect her famous guest, and was there to his embarrassment when his mother came to tea. But being indebted to her for the services of her cook and servants as well as the use of her cottage, he could hardly prohibit her visits. Incredibly the place boasted a menagerie with resident penguins, owls, marmosets and lemurs.[36]

Baden-Powell breakfasted there with Arthur Pearson on 18 July and lunched with him next day on his return to Prince's Gate. This was less than a week before he was due to set up his camp on Brownsea Island. Pearson never imagined that the camp would be anything but successful, and presented Baden-Powell with special stationery headed: 'Boy Scouts, Scout Camp, Brownsea Island, Poole.' Although members of cadet corps sometimes attended summer camps few Edwardian boys had the chance. To be going camping was exciting enough, but to be invited to go with the country's greatest national hero seemed incredible good fortune to the boys selected by him. His choice of Brownsea Island for this very first Scout Camp was an inspired one since islands had played an important part in adventure stories from *Robinson Crusoe* to *Treasure Island*. Baden-Powell's 9-year-old nephew Donald was typical in being overjoyed by the prospect of living for over a week entirely surrounded by water.[37]

Baden-Powell invited 22 boys, most of them between 13 and 16, to help test his 'scheme'. Lady Rodney provided three; other friends and acquaintances sent their boys. Two were at Eton, two at Harrow, two at Cheltenham and one each at Repton, Wellington and Charterhouse. Since Baden-Powell wanted to see how public school boys mixed with working-class lads, he asked the Boys' Brigade in Poole and Bournemouth for nine boys. The 'invitation' to these locals came as a royal command; one of them recalled: 'We were just told we were going.'[38]

Most would agree that there was little class prejudice, although occasionally each group surprised the other: the public school boys struck the Brigade boys as prissily over-polite, while the Brigade boys sometimes surprised the others by feats such as eating raw cockles. Not yet weaned to oysters, the future Lord Rodney felt sick to watch them.[39] Baden-Powell later liked to describe the boys as coming from 'Eton, Harrow and the East End of London', which was rather hard on those from Poole.[40]

At dawn Baden-Powell would leave his tent, which was distinguished by a cavalry lance stuck in the ground outside. Attached to the shaft was the Union Jack which had flown over his Headquarters in Mafeking. Strikingly attired in below-the-knee-length shorts, golf stockings, a trilby hat and an old S.A.C. shirt, he would wake the boys with several blasts on an African koodoo horn. This had them tumbling out of their bell tents for a quick glass of milk and a biscuit before half an hour of physical training. Then came prayers and the hoisting of the flag, followed by breakfast at eight. After that there were 'scouting practices', 'games' and swimming until lunch, which was followed by more 'scouting practices' until tea. The pace then slackened, but some 'camp games' and a compulsory 'rub down' and change of clothes had to be fitted in before supper at eight.

The 'scouting practices' were carried out with the boys divided into patrols (Wolves, Bulls, Curlews and Ravens, each identified by a distinctive flag). They practised stalking and tracking, putting up tents, constructing simple shelters and stuffing fern mattresses. The boys were also taught how to make 'dampers' of dough – which they mixed in their pockets on Baden-Powell's instructions (a procedure for which several were soundly ticked off on their return home) and then wound round sticks for cooking over a fire. Two patrols raced each other in boats in 'The Whale Hunt' to see which could first spear the wooden 'whale' with a harpoon. The patrols also competed in deer-stalking which pitted them against a human 'deer', able to climb trees and pelt its pursuers with tennis balls. Stalkers hit by a ball were judged to have been 'gored to death' and only 'killed' their quarry if able to hit it three times.[41]

Baden-Powell and Kenneth McLaren, who helped him throughout the camp, were careful never to prolong any activity beyond the boys' attention span. 'We found the best way of imparting theoretical instruction,' Baden-Powell recalled, 'was to give it out in short instalments with ample illustrative examples when sitting round the camp fire or otherwise resting . . . A formal lecture is apt to bore boys.'[42] At the evening camp fire, Baden-Powell would tell 'yarns'. Even at the beginning of the nineteenth century the word 'yarn' had meant, according to the Oxford English Dictionary, 'a marvellous or incredible tale'. Sailors had often told stories while twisting together the yarns or fibres from which ships' ropes were made. So by 1907 the word had a humorously dated quality. This persuaded him that it was quirky enough to be memorable. Words like 'jamboree', 'posse', 'palaver' and 'yarn' would create a characteristic atmosphere for his Movement.

When Baden-Powell stood by the fire each evening his boys crowded around him eagerly. Places like Matabeleland and Ashanti featured in the works of Haggard and Henty, but it was immeasurably more exciting to be told true-life 'yarns' about being hunted by Zulus in the Matopo Hills than to read fictional adventures. With experiences culled from all over the world and three small wars, not to mention a big one, Stephe was in an unrivalled position to entertain his youthful audience. Within a decade professional sportsmen and film actors would usurp the glamour of the military hero, but in 1907 he still reigned supreme, nowhere more so than on a small island off the Dorset coast during that first week of August.

Arthur Pearson sent his senior literary editor to the island for 24 hours; and for Percy Everett a lifelong connection with the Scouts began as he watched Baden-Powell at the camp fire leading the boys in singing a Zulu war chant. This was the Eeengonyama chorus soon to be famous among all Boy Scouts. 'Eeengonyama – gonyama,' sang Baden-Powell loudly, to be answered by the boys singing heartily: 'Invooboo. Yah bo! Invooboo.' This was supposed to mean: 'He is a lion!' 'Yes! he is better than that; he is a hippopotamus!' Everett was mesmerized. 'I can see him still,' he wrote twenty years later, 'as he stands in the flickering light of the fire – an alert figure, full of the joy of life, now grave, now gay, answering all manner of questions, imitating the call of birds, showing how to stalk an animal, fleshing out a little story, dancing and singing round the fire . . .'[43]

Of course the magic of the camp fire could not banish the mosquitoes or the prickly pine-needles in the tents, or the ceaseless burring song of the nightjars. But bearing worse discomforts cheerfully would be very much part of the Scout ethic, as would learning to be considerate to others even when wet, cold and coping with a smoking fire or a leaky tent. In later years Baden-Powell tried to keep in touch with the boys; his favourite, the Harrovian Musgrave Wroughton (Dulce's brother), would come round the world with him on tour in 1912. After going down from Christ Church, Oxford, he would become one of the six Brownsea boys to die in Flanders.[44]

The authors of both histories of the Boy Scouts have implied that there was an inevitable progression from Baden-Powell's conversation with William Smith to the Brownsea Island camp, and then to the foundation of the Movement itself. But at the time Baden-Powell feared that many Edwardians would view as cranky his claim to be able to give boys an education in character by taking them camping and teaching them tracking. Now that he was on half-pay and no longer Inspector General of Cavalry, he had to think seriously about what to do. His mother required regular financial assistance; and fortune still had not smiled upon Baden and Agnes.

In 1906 the Secretary of State for War, Mr Haldane, had murmured about a possible job in the Territorial Army; but if such an offer materialized, ought he to take it or leave himself free for the Boy Scouts? After the camp he was still uncertain whether the Boy Scouts would ever become an organization in its own right. In his pamphlet *Boy Scouts: A Suggestion*, he had described Scouting as 'applicable to any existing organization', but had added, 'Where such organization does not exist a special one can easily be formed.'[45] In his second pamphlet he had seemed to commit himself to 'amalgamation rather than rivalry'. Yet on 30 July 1907, in his first Agreement with Pearson, he undertook 'to lend every assistance to the Boy Scouts' organization'. It is hard to believe that Baden-Powell did not understand the implications of this phrase.[46]

Clearly he did not foresee the huge success of *Scouting for Boys*, since he approached Mr Haldane urgently soon after Brownsea. The Secretary of State for War had just steered his Territorial and Reserve Forces Bill through Parliament, and since recruiting promised to be the single greatest difficulty facing the new force was eager to employ a man still popular enough to draw large crowds wherever he lectured. Haldane therefore invited Baden-Powell to stay with him and his mother at their home in Perthshire and during this stay offered him a Territorial division.[47] The Secretary of State was quite happy for him to delay starting his new job until April the following year, by which time he would have fulfilled his contractual obligation to Arthur Pearson to deliver a nationwide series of lectures on 'Scouting for Boys'.

Baden-Powell tried to make Haldane decide for him whether or not he should accept the Territorial job. He wrote saying that unless the Secretary of State thought him 'especially the man for it', he would rather be pensioned off and spend his retirement 'working up his boys' training scheme'.[48] Since Haldane wanted Baden-Powell, he naturally flattered him into accepting. Admiral Lord Charles Beresford thought Haldane such 'an oily customer' that 'with a wick in his head he would burn for three years'.[49] And there is no doubt that Baden-Powell allowed himself to be smooth-talked into taking a relatively junior job for which any Major-General would have qualified – and this in spite of his recent promotion to the rank of Lieutenant-General.

Stephe would have been in a better position to play for higher stakes with Haldane had he not dreaded finding himself living at home without a job. Command of the Northumbrian Division of the Territorials would however remove him from Prince's Gate, provide him with a regular income and allow him a break from his mother's exhortations to him to try and try again to find a wife.

If Baden-Powell had ever discussed the probable earnings from *Scouting for Boys* with Arthur Pearson he would probably have turned down Haldane's offer; but, incredibly, in their Agreement of 30 July they had left all the financial arrangements undetermined. Like many 'gentlemen' of his day, Baden-Powell looked down upon tradesmen and felt uncomfortable about being paid for doing something which he considered a matter of patriotic duty. This reticence about money suited Arthur Pearson very well; it enabled him to secure the right to publish *Scouting for Boys* and the Boy Scouts' official newspaper without his having to make any mention of royalties either for the pre-publication instalments of *Scouting for Boys*, for the book itself or for the newspaper. The only financial undertaking Pearson made was to pay up to £1,000 of whatever expenses Baden-Powell incurred in publicizing his handbook. If Baden-Powell had talked money, he would have realized why the newspaper proprietor thought the Scouts so commercially exciting. Press interest in the lecture tour would sell the serial parts; publicity arising from the sale of these instalments would in turn sell *Scouting for Boys*, which in due course would create a market for *The Scout* newspaper; the Boy Scouts once up and running as an organization would produce endless purchasers for *The Scout*, for *Scouting for Boys* and for any other Scouting publications which ingenuity might suggest. As the owner of two national newspapers, Pearson knew he could guarantee favourable press coverage for as long as it took to launch the whole package.

Arthur Pearson was not worried that Baden-Powell might stay in the army. The general's absence would simply enable his backer to take fuller control. Baden-Powell had suggested as Manager of the Boy Scouts either his brother Baden or Kenneth McLaren, but Pearson now told him bluntly that they seemed unlikely to be 'good enough really to direct matters'. What was needed, he explained, was 'a thoroughly good organizing head . . . I must see if I can hit upon someone.'[50] He hit upon his senior manager, Peter Keary, who spent his spare time writing self-help manuals such as *The Secrets of Success* in which he advised people 'to weed out friends who were of no value'.[51] Baden-Powell had not yet weeded out 'the Boy' McLaren, and on 12 November he invited him to be the Boy Scouts' first Manager. He hoped that when he himself was in Yorkshire commanding his Territorials, 'the Boy' in London would prevent Keary from assuming autocratic powers. Although his joint management with Keary was never properly defined, McLaren agreed to try. Baden-Powell feared that Keary meant to form his staff into 'a committee of management of the Boy Scouts' and warned Pearson that he 'could never work with a committee'.[52]

Unfortunately for Baden-Powell, Pearson possessed the money and he did not. During the last week of October Pearson had opened an office in Covent Garden with Keary in charge. Baden-Powell ought to have realized that if Pearson paid for this office and its staff, he would expect to control everyone working there, including Major Kenneth

McLaren D.S.O.. Another problem was that the staff would be fully occupied producing a weekly edition of *The Scout* newspaper and would therefore have no time to devote to the Scouts as an organization.

Although Baden-Powell corresponded with the Society of Authors at this time,[53] by mid-November he had agreed in principle to allow C. Arthur Pearson Ltd to retain all the profits of *The Scout* in return for no more than an undertaking to allow him sole use of a couple of pages of the paper for communicating with his Boy Scouts. This was a disastrous arrangement. Almost as foolish was his decision to devote all his share of the profits of *Scouting for Boys* 'to planning out and organizing the Boy Scouts' scheme and . . . its development'. It never seemed to occur to him that, since Pearson's newspaper *The Scout* would be the principal beneficiary of a successful Boy Scouts' organization, Pearson ought to contribute to the costs of this organization rather than leave Baden-Powell to plough *all* his book royalties into it. (The royalties themselves were paid at a perfectly fair rate.) All that Baden-Powell asked of Pearson was that he should pay excess office expenses if his royalties fell short. With *The Scout* soon selling 110,000 copies a week, this hardly worried Pearson. To have started a newspaper based upon another man's ideas without being asked for a licence fee, let alone a royalty, seemed a perfect dream to the magnate. For Baden-Powell it would soon be a nightmare. Fortunately he insisted upon one eminently sensible clause in the Agreement he eventually signed with Pearson on 1 January 1908:[54] the right to terminate or renegotiate the contract after a year, and three months' written notice.

Ironically the qualities which had first drawn Baden-Powell to Pearson were those which guaranteed that he would be worsted in their negotiations, but they ensured that his scheme was properly introduced to the public. Arthur Pearson was never accorded an honoured place in the official Boy Scout history, but he did not brood over it. Even when the Boy Scouts made their debut, his mind was on other things. Like Lord Northcliffe he had decided to buy *The Times*.

IO

SCOUTING FOR BOYS

1. A Book in a Million (1908)

Between November 1907 and February 1908 Baden-Powell gave over fifty public lectures on his Boy Scouts' scheme. By late December he had finished writing the first two 'parts' or instalments of *Scouting for Boys* and went on to write most of the remaining four while he was on the road lecturing. This would have been impossible without the preliminary draft he had written during 1907. When he returned to Wimbledon to complete his writing his mother pronounced the arrangement improper. What must the cantankerous Mr Fether-stonhaugh be thinking? She insisted that her son write at once to the outraged husband. Soon Stephe was able to tell her that Mr Fether-stonhaugh had written 'wishing me a good time. So it's all right.'[1]

Part One of *Scouting for Boys* appeared on bookstalls in the British Isles on 15 January 1908. The cover (see page 586) was by John Hassall, a well-known illustrator who, like Baden-Powell, was a member of the London Sketch Club. He had drawn a boy hiding behind a rock with his Scout staff and Stetson hat intently observing a distant party of smugglers landing from a mysterious ship. The implication was clear: by becoming a Scout a boy would not only read about adventures but would live them too. Because there was virtually no recreation for boys apart from sport, they and their parents bought the little fourpenny pamphlet by the thousand. Arthur Pearson had seen to it that Baden-Powell's lectures received massive publicity, and people had been eagerly awaiting the appearance of the 'Parts'.

Arthur Pearson's influence extended further. While Baden-Powell had been writing, Pearson sent Percy Everett, his senior editor, to lend a hand. Everett had learned his craft on *Pearson's Weekly* (motto: 'To Interest, to Elevate, to Amuse'). Pearson's formula had been copied from *Tit Bits* and involved interspersing uplifting material with curious facts and entertaining anecdotes. To appeal to the semi-literate public created by compulsory education reading matter had to be easy to understand. Everett suggested that the *Pearson's Weekly* pot-pourri approach would also be ideal for a youthful readership, so Baden-Powell divided *Scouting for Boys* into 10 chapters and 28 'Camp Fire Yarns'. This apparent rag-bag of unrelated topics was in reality a cunning blend of entertainment, moral exhortation, practical advice and escapism. A boy could easily skip what did not interest him and pass on to what did.

Baden-Powell began by telling instructors: 'Instruction in Scouting should be given as far as possible in practices, games and competitions. Games should be organized mainly as team matches, when the patrol forms the team, and every boy is playing, none merely looking on.' The boys themselves were addressed directly in 'Camp Fire Yarn No. 1': 'I suppose every British boy wants to help his country in some way or other. There is a way, by which he can do so easily, that is by becoming a Scout.' Then a distinction was made between military 'war scouts' and frontiersmen, who counted as 'peace scouts': 'The trappers of North America, hunters of Central Africa, the British pioneers . . . ready to face any danger, and always keen to help each other . . . The history of the Empire has been made by British adventurers and explorers, the scouts of the nation, for hundreds of years.'[2] Cook, Clive, Baker, Livingstone and Selous all received plaudits.

Baden-Powell switched from patriotism to fiction: the story of Kipling's Kim, condensed as only Baden-Powell knew how. In 1908 no other fictional character was such a dream hero for boys. As a virtual babe-in-arms Kim had been 'hand in hand with men who led lives stranger than anything Haroun al Raschid dreamed of' and had played with 'a mother-of-pearl, nickel-plated, self-extracting .450 revolver'. In Baden-Powell's version the Lama's spiritual search disappeared and the whole story revolved around Kim's work for the Secret Service. Then enter the 'Mafeking Boy Scouts' to indicate every boy's patriotic duty. 'Perhaps you don't see how a mere small boy can be of use to the great British Empire; but by becoming a Scout and carrying out the Scout Laws every boy can be of use. "Country first, self second," should be your motto.'[3]

Next black entertainment: 'The Elsdon Murder', which was solved when an enterprising shepherd-boy 'observed' and memorized the pattern of studs on a vicious-looking gypsy's boots.[4] The many stories in Scouting for Boys involving escape, pursuit and sudden disaster were not unlike the stock adventures in contemporary comics. It therefore seems harsh and humourless of a recent critic to argue that such matters as Burnham's escape from the Matabele, Sherlock Holmes's detective work and the spooring exploits of the American General Dodge 'together establish a context in which warfare, crime prevention, and crime detection implicitly became the normal everyday activities in which human beings engage.'[5] Baden-Powell knew that such stories were of interest precisely because they were so very far from being 'normal everyday activities'.

The same could be said of his yarns about the terrifyingly dedicated Japanese, who 'had been ordered to blow up the gate of a Russian fort'. (In January 1905 the Japanese had captured Port Arthur from the Russians in the war in Manchuria.) This gate could only be destroyed with explosives 'tamped or jammed' tightly against it. 'The Japs "tamped" them by pushing them against the door with their chests; they then lit their matches, fired the charge, and blew up the gates, but blew up themselves in doing so.' Ostensibly an example of inspiring self-sacrifice, this story also fell within the macabre tradition of the 'Bloods' – boys' comics specializing in horror.

The sanguinary fate of the Japanese was followed by the story of two frogs who fell into a bowl of cream and saved themselves by working so hard with their legs that they churned the cream into butter. 'So when things look bad just smile and sing to yourself: "Stick to it, stick to it, stick to it," and you will come through all right.'[6]

At the centre of the whole scheme was the Scout's Oath or Promise, and the Scout Law:[7]

Scout Law

SCOUTS, all the world over, have unwritten laws which bind them just as much as if they had been printed in black and white. They come down to us from old times. The Japanese have their Bushido, or laws of the old Samurai warriors, just as we have chivalry or rules of the knights of the Middle Ages. The Red Indians in America have their laws or honour; the Zulus, the natives of India, the European nations – all have their ancient codes. The following are the rules which apply to Boy Scouts . . . The Scouts' motto is:

BE PREPARED

which means you are always to be in a state of readiness in mind and body to do your DUTY . . .

The Scout Law

1. A SCOUT'S HONOUR IS TO BE TRUSTED.
   If a Scout says 'On my honour it is so,' that means that it *is* so, just as if he had taken a most solemn oath . . .

2. A SCOUT IS LOYAL to the King, and to his officers, and to his parents, his country, and his employers. He must stick to them through thick and thin against anyone who is their enemy or who even talks badly of them.

3. A SCOUT'S DUTY IS TO BE USEFUL AND TO HELP OTHERS.
   And he is to do his duty before anything else, even though he gives up his own pleasure, or comfort, or safety to do it. When in difficulty to know which of two things to do, he must ask himself, 'Which is my duty?' that is, 'Which is for other people?' – and do that one. He must Be Prepared at any time to save life, or to help injured persons. And *he must try his best to do a good turn* to somebody every day.

4. A SCOUT IS A FRIEND TO ALL, AND A BROTHER TO EVERY OTHER SCOUT, NO MATTER TO WHAT SOCIAL CLASS THE OTHER BELONGS.
   Thus if a Scout meets another Scout, even though a stranger to him, he must speak to him, and help him in any way that he can . . . A Scout must never be a SNOB. A snob is one who looks down upon another because he is poorer, or who is poor and resents another because he is rich. A Scout accepts the other man as he finds him, and makes the best of him . . .

5. A SCOUT IS COURTEOUS: That is, he is polite to all – but especially to women and children, and old people and invalids, cripples, etc. And he must not take any reward for being helpful or courteous.

6. A SCOUT IS A FRIEND TO ANIMALS. He should save them as far as possible from pain, and should not kill any animal unnecessarily, even if it is only a fly – for it is one of God's creatures. Killing an animal for food is allowable.

7. A SCOUT OBEYS ORDERS of his parents, patrol leader, or Scoutmaster without question. Even if he gets an order he does not like he must do as soldiers and sailors do, he must carry it out all the same *because it is his duty*; and after he has done it he can come and state any reasons against it: but he must carry out the order at once. That is discipline.

8. A SCOUT SMILES AND WHISTLES under all circumstances. When he gets an order he should obey it cheerily and readily, not in a slow, hang-dog sort of way. Scouts never grouse at hardships, nor whine at each other nor swear when put out . . . You should force yourself to smile at once, and then whistle a tune, and you will be all right. A Scout goes about with a smile on and whistling. It cheers him and cheers other people, especially in time of danger . . . The punishment for swearing or using bad language is for each offence a mug of cold water to be poured down the offender's sleeve by the other Scouts . . .

9. A SCOUT IS THRIFTY, that is, he saves every penny he can, and

puts it into the bank, so that he may have money to keep himself when out of work, and thus not make himself a burden to others; or that he may have money to give away to others when they need it.

A tenth law was added in 1911: 'A Scout is pure in thought, word and deed.'

The Scout Law was to be observed after a boy had taken the Scout's Oath, later known as 'The Promise':

'On my honour I promise that I will do my best
1. To do my duty to God and the King.
2. To help other people at all times.
3. To obey the Scout Law.'

When taking this oath the Scout will stand, holding his right hand raised level with his shoulder, palm to the front, thumb resting on the nail of the little finger, and the other three fingers upright, pointing upwards: this is the Scout's salute and secret sign'[8]

The salute owed something to the army and to the secret signs of the Freemasons.

Baden-Powell's admirers subsequently made much of the fact that his Laws never resembled negative 'thou shalt not' commandments but were always positive. The true significance of this formulation seems to me to be that (rather like a religious convert) a boy who became a Boy Scout was expected to be a changed being, wearing the brotherhood's hat, carrying his pilgrim's staff and knowing the order's secret signs and chants. Thus equipped, he *could be* all the things that the Scout Law states a Scout is.

With 53 Labour M.P.s recently elected, the ruling class must have found the Oath and Laws reassuring. Yet while many boys probably enjoyed the ritual enrolment, human nature does not suddenly change even if fashions and conventions do. From time immemorial boys have lied with facility, have thought adults hypocritical and have resented any attempts to make them appear to be ostentatiously virtuous. Edwardian boys were no different and had they thought, as Michael Rosenthal does, that the Scout Law had been framed to produce 'absolute submission to all officially endorsed forms of authority', they would have shrugged their shoulders. Laws of a kind were insisted upon by all boys' organizations, and if the Scouts had them too that was the way things were; and at least some were unusual. No other body asked its members to smile and whistle 'under all circumstances'. And the prohibition of snobbery was equally novel. Reading the Laws, their parents would have seen that consideration for others bulked as large as military discipline. H. G. Wells recalled that at

11 on his way back to his 'dismal bankrupt home' from school, if
anybody had 'confronted me with a Russian prince or a rajah in all his
glory and suggested he was my equal, I should have laughed him to
scorn'.[9] Only the poorest boys in 1908 felt no pride in being British.
The vast majority of the nation's boys were happy to pledge their
loyalty to the Crown and the Empire.

Far from seeming a strait-jacket of rules, Baden-Powell's scheme
offered freedom beyond anything most of them had ever encountered.
In his Camp Fire Yarn on 'Life in the Open', Baden-Powell recommended that boys go on 'exploring expeditions'. They could walk or
cycle, or in winter, 'they might get along best by skating along the
canals'.

> Scouts in carrying out such a tramp should never, if possible, sleep
> under a roof – that is to say that on fine nights they would sleep in
> the open wherever they may be; or, in bad weather, would get leave
> to occupy a hay loft or barn . . . As a rule you should have some
> object in your expedition . . . Say a mountain in Scotland or Wales,
> or a lake in Cumberland, or possibly some old castle or battle-
> field . . . Keep a log or journal, giving a short account of each day's
> journey, with sketches or photos of any interesting things.[10]

For thousands of boys who had never slept away from home, and
for many more who had never left their home towns even for a day,
this idea of going off with friends on an ambitious expedition was
intoxicating.

Boys found the details of the book wonderfully absorbing: 'If you
are obliged to lie on the ground, do not forget to make a small hole
about the size of a teacup in which your hip joint will rest when you are
lying on your side . . .'[11] Then there were instructions on how to
improvise camping gadgets such as camp candlesticks. Most boys also
relished showing others where they had been and were going by means
of signs chalked on pavements and walls or cut into the bark of trees, all
of which annoyed shopkeepers and farmers. Boys sensed that Baden-
Powell was on their side, trusting them 'on their honour' to behave
well in exchange for unaccustomed freedom. He often quoted the old
scout in Sir Percy Fitzpatrick's *Jock of the Bushveldt*: 'Boys is like pups –
you've got to help 'em some, but not too much and not too soon.
They've got to learn themselves. I reckon if a man's never made a
mistake he's never had a good lesson.'[12]

Baden-Powell was a realist, telling Scoutmasters: 'If you try to
preach to boys what *you* consider elevating matter you will scare away
the more spirited, and those are the ones you want to get hold of . . .
You must be their *friend*; but don't be in too great a hurry at first to gain
this footing . . .'[13] He was convinced that a responsible citizenry
would never be brought into being by threats. 'Discipline is not gained

by punishing a child for a bad habit, but by substituting a better occupation, that will absorb his attention, and gradually lead him to forget and abandon the old one.'[14]

*

Scouting for Boys was published in book form on 1 May 1908 at 2/- in cloth covers and 1/- in paper. Although it is known that it was reprinted four times during the first year, no actual sales figures have survived.[15] But since an edition of 60,000 was printed for the British market less than a year later it is clear that considerably more than that would have been sold in its first year.[16] Sales fluctuated from year to year subsequently but more than 50,000 copies were sold in Britain in 1948, the fortieth anniversary of its first publication, so *Scouting for Boys* was clearly one of the steadiest best-sellers in the history of publishing. Only in 1967 did Pearson's admit that 'the book is possibly on a declining market'.[18] Twelve years later, in 1979, it had finally become an historical curiosity. An edition of 10,000 copies was printed and is still largely unsold.

The publishing history of *Scouting for Boys* in foreign countries is equally impressive. Twenty years after its first publication in Great Britain, the book was in print in 26 countries (not counting all those within the British Empire) in roughly twice that many editions. *Scouting for Boys* has probably sold more copies than any other title during the twentieth century with the exception of the Bible.

*

The plaudits of well-known people and of patriotic societies should be noted *en passant*, but they should not be given serious consideration as prime causes for the Boy Scouts attracting immediate and over-whelming public support. It is difficult today to appreciate that an organization now considered rather staid and conservative was seen quite differently in 1908. In that year, at Lord's Cricket Ground, the amateurs or 'gentlemen' left the field by one gate while the pro-fessionals or 'players' left by another. Baden-Powell's outlawing of snobbery struck many as very nearly revolutionary and the same was true of a uniform consisting of shorts, shirt-sleeves and a cowboy hat. Since boys dressed like men – and 'respectable' men considered stiff collars, waistcoats and hats *de rigueur* – it came as a tonic to be told not 'to shut oneself up from one's neighbours inside one's coat' like a typical Briton, but to be more like the average colonial with his 'free open-air, shirt-sleeve habits'.[18]

To become a Scout,' explained Baden-Powell in *Scouting for Boys*, 'you join a patrol . . . or you can raise a patrol yourself by getting five other boys to join [raised to six or seven in 1909] . . . One boy is then chosen as Patrol Leader to command the patrol . . . several patrols

together can form a Troop under an officer called a Scoutmaster.' And
thousands of boys did just that – formed themselves into patrols after
reading the 'fourpenny Parts' and then went out looking for a
sympathetic Scoutmaster. They pieced together uniforms, 'borrowed'
broomsticks for their staffs, donned an astonishing variety of headgear
and set out for local woodland to teach themselves the arts of tracking,
making shelters and lighting camp fires.

Their Scoutmasters were often kitted-out in an equally bizarre way
with slouch-hats, cavalry boots and bandoliers. They went out armed
with speaking trumpets, bugles or anything they thought might help
them summon their intrepid lads from far and wide. Complaints
poured in from landowners about boys trampling on crops and leaving
gates open. Scouts were chased by bulls and by farmers. In towns they
fared little better.

Like members of an early Christian sect the first Boy Scouts were
subjected to frequent ridicule. One pioneer recalled 'marching out of
the stable yard, and having to push through a mob of spitting and
cheering youths from the nearby slum streets. They had a song about
us which began:

> Here come the Brussel Sprouts,
> The stinking, blinking louts.'[19]

But ridicule seemed a small price to pay for this organized escape from
'repressive schoolmasters, moralizing parsons and coddling
parents'.[20] There was no radio then, no cinema, far too few playing
fields and most schools were tyrannical places. Scouting seemed
heaven-sent to boys and to those who cared about them. F. R. Lucas,
an Edinburgh doctor who ran a club for destitute boys, was typical in
seizing upon Scouting as exactly the kind of constructive recreation he
had been seeking for years. His first attempt at tracking almost ended
with his arrest for allowing his boys to lay thick trails of confetti in the
Royal Park of Holyrood Palace.[21] Minor conflicts with authority,
however, simply increased the Scouts' popularity. But who was
responsible for them? Were they amenable to any authority? And
should just *anybody* be considered a fit person to be a Scoutmaster?

As Baden-Powell freely admitted in 1910, the first two years of the
Boy Scouts' existence had been utterly chaotic. 'It was rather a
mushroom growth . . . and we did not cope with it properly. There
were boys all over seeking for officers [Scoutmasters]; and when there
were many thousands, we thought that it was about time that we did
something for them.'[22] But tied hand and foot to Messrs C. A. Pearson
& Co., what might this something be?

2. 'A Mushroom Growth' (1908–09)

By late February 1908 independent Scout troops already far outnumbered those being started with the Boys' Brigade and the junior
Y.M.C.A.. Kenneth McLaren and his secretary Margaret Macdonald
were rapidly overwhelmed by the volume of requests for Scout hats,
patrol flags, badges, shoulder knots and enrolment cards. They were
soon corresponding with scores of parents of prospective Scouts and
with dozens of would-be Scoutmasters.

Although their situation was hopeless, Peter Keary was not
prepared to take on extra staff until he could be sure that the excellent
sales figures for the 'Parts' of Scouting for Boys would be repeated when
the handbook itself was published. If this meanness had been intended
to bring about McLaren's resignation, it succeeded. In early March 'the
Boy' wrote telling Baden-Powell that he had had enough.[1]

Two weeks after McLaren's departure from the Covent Garden
office, Baden-Powell had to leave London to take command of the
Northumbrian Division of the Territorials. At no cost or trouble to
himself Arthur Pearson had gained control of the Boy Scouts. He had
always thought the idea too valuable to leave in the hands of
uncommercially minded people. In the two official histories of the
Movement it is stated that Kenneth McLaren served a year longer than
he did,[2] which has conveyed the impression that Baden-Powell
retained his authority over his creation throughout 1908. This is
nonsense. He hated Pearson's advertisements for The Scout and
deplored the arbitrary cuts in Scouting for Boys, but learned there was
little he could do.[3] And when The Scout made its first appearance in
mid-April he was appalled to find it just like any 'ordinary boys'
paper'.

Baden-Powell was soon fully occupied in the North. Recruitment
for the Territorials[4] was so slow that even the radical editor of Truth
considered conscription inevitable. The new force was derided both by
Liberals who thought their party's creation of a citizens' army a
betrayal of pacific principles, and by the bellicose National Service
League whose members saw it as a device to trick the public into
supposing compulsory national service unnecessary. The Daily Mail,
the Daily Express and the Morning Post all reviled the Territorials.

Some criticism was richly deserved. Responsibility for the defence of
his area (North and East Yorkshire and Northumberland) was chaotically
divided between the War Office, the regular army's G.O.C. for the
District and himself.[5] There was no local intelligence department and no
liaison between military groups. A raid on the East Coast by German
torpedo boats would have taken all the defence forces by surprise. A year
after his assumption of command there was still no agreed procedure for
raising the alarm if an attack were made out of office hours.[6]

Poor recruitment and the War Office's lack of urgency made Baden-Powell extremely jumpy about rumours of a German invasion. After landing on the Yorkshire coast (so went one popular scenario), they would proceed inland and destroy the industrial towns of the North and the Midlands. Mr Haldane thought the Germans deliberately spread specific rumours so that they could disprove them later. The French too had a vested interest in feeding the British alarmist stories. The more Britain looked to her military preparedness, the better she would be as an ally if and when war finally broke out.[7] Baden-Powell believed that, by scaremongering, he could help the Territorial Army's recruitment drive. On 2 May 1908 he told a gathering of potential recruits that Germany was 'the natural enemy of this country' and could easily land 120,000 troops on the East Coast within thirty hours. His speech was reported in the *Newcastle Daily Journal* and Haldane was questioned in the House of Commons about it. Since serving officers were not permitted to express personal views in public on military matters or politics, Baden-Powell was lucky not to have been publicly rebuked by the Secretary of State.[8]

In August 1908 Pearson decided to involve Baden-Powell in a summer Scout camp, aimed at increasing the circulation of *The Scout*. Thirty readers were to be 'invited' to come camping with Lieutenant-General Baden-Powell on condition that they earned enough 'votes' – these could be obtained by sending in coupons printed in *The Scout*. If they bought a year's subscription they secured 300 votes. Since the greatest number of votes was 29,018, and the fiftieth boy scored 5,350 and yet failed by several thousand votes to be 'invited', it can readily be appreciated how profitable this coupon competition was. Baden-Powell was horrified to learn about the votes and warned Keary that it would 'frighten off poor boys and throw it [the camp competition] into the hands of the richer ones'.[9] The camp itself lasted twelve days and was a success, in spite of its rich boys and the torrential rain lashing the Northumbrian moors.

At Humshaugh Camp Baden-Powell was helped by Captain D. Colbron Pearse, a young officer in the volunteers who had started the 1st Hampstead Scout Troop – one of the earliest in the country[10] (for other early troops see same n. 10, p. 630). He referred to Pearse as his 'Manager' but this was wishful thinking. The man was not employed in the office as acting Manager until November; he would be replaced the following February.[11] All year Baden-Powell had been bombarding Keary with letters of complaint sent to him by members of the public about the lack of organization. Scout committees were springing up all over the country and many were being run by 'unsuitable' people. Most troops took no notice of anyone. Baden-Powell told Keary bluntly that he had to take on somebody at once to travel around vetting local committees and starting new ones where none existed.

Keary recognized that a discredited organization would be damaging to sales. So on 29 September 1908, he authorized Victor Bridges, an under-manager in *The Scout*'s office, to write a letter acknowledging the need for some sort of Scouting organization separate from Pearson's. Bridges offered the job of 'Scout Inspector' to a young man of 22 just down from Queen's College, Oxford, 'on behalf of the Boy Scouts' Organization'. At first he had written 'on behalf of C. A. Pearson Ltd', but had crossed this out after consultation with Keary.[12] The young man received his credentials from Baden-Powell: 'Mr Eric Walker is acting as my representative in the organization of the Boy Scouts' Movement in England. He knows my ideas and intentions with regard to the same, and is willing to give any advice or suggestions that may be desired on the subject . . .' Baden-Powell enclosed a personal note to Walker: 'I look forward to hearing soon of your getting to work in showing local committees how to organize . . . We shall very soon have a proper standard system established. Good luck.'[13] Baden-Powell had never met this man in whom he apparently had such astonishing faith.

Eric Walker first visited the Boy Scouts' office at 33 Bedford Mansions, Henrietta Street, on 21 September 1908, and was shocked by 'the very muddled state of everything'. His first job was to organize a display of Boy Scout camping equipment at Gamages store in High Holborn and it convinced him 'that the whole miserable thing is a commercial venture from beginning to end . . . organized merely to push the weekly rag [*The Scout*].'[14] Days later Walker wrote begging Baden-Powell to break with Pearson's and to do something about the tone of 'the rag'.[15]

The following extract from the Leicester Peace Society's *Journal* is typical of criticism aimed at *The Scout*.

> It opens with 'No. 1 of a thrilling series' which tells of 'Two strong men who make war for a wager'. Blood and thunder prevail, illustrations demonstrate, and revolvers and knives accentuate, the more startling episodes of the sensational tale. 'Curse you!' cried Carr hoarsely (this is a fair specimen of the style adopted by the General's penny dreadful), 'Curse you,' and he made a swift movement to reach the revolver at his belt, but Ali was too quick for him. His razor-edged Kris flashed in the air, and the American with a sharp cry of pain jerked his fingers away streaked with a thin red line.[16]

Small wonder that the suspicion was all but universal that Baden-Powell and Pearson were simply running the Scouts to make money.[17] Since every penny of Baden-Powell's royalties was being swallowed up by office expenses he had every reason to feel aggrieved.

By November Eric Walker was close to resigning. He noted in his diary: 'The General promised to look in during the afternoon, but, after staying ten minutes at Pearson's, rushed away. I was awful sick about it. Things are going from bad to worse. Miss M[acdonald] and myself have practically the whole show to run.' The sudden removal of Victor Bridges – the only man in the office whom Walker respected – made matters still worse.[18]

Walker was a brisk, attractive but rather bulldozing person who hated confusion. His ambition was to persuade Baden-Powell to appoint a 'Boy Scout Executive Committee' as a means of offsetting C. A. Pearson's power. But since Baden-Powell wanted to keep open the possibility of assuming sole command when his army career came to an end, Walker would be disappointed.[19] He was also dismayed when months after Baden-Powell had admitted that the Boy Scouts ought to break with Pearson's he was still dragging his feet about moving into new offices. 'What a muddler old B-P is,' exploded the young man after spending a frustrating day trying to sort out the disputed copyright ownership of the Scout badges with Pearson's lawyer.[20] But although Walker worked incredibly hard, travelling thousands of miles and interviewing scores of potential Scoutmasters and local secretaries, he did not understand Baden-Powell's dilemma.

By the end of the year the royalties from Scouting for Boys were paying the salaries of Walker, Miss Macdonald, Captain D. C. Pearse (the new stop-gap Manager) and W. B. Wakefield (assisting Walker with inspections in the North). If Baden-Powell were to break with Pearson's completely, he would find himself employing typists and messengers and paying office rental, all of which was currently met by his dictatorial backer. With a significant part of his income already earmarked for his mother's upkeep, he could not afford to make himself personally responsible for expenses which might escalate uncontrollably. Unknown to Eric Walker, Baden-Powell was negotiating with Arthur Pearson during December. The magnate said he would pay 10 per cent of The Scout's profits to Baden-Powell's emerging organization as soon as it was incorporated as a private company, but he refused to make any advance payment. Baden-Powell, who had no capital of his own, therefore faced having to find several thousand pounds out of his own pocket for anything up to a year.[21]

Stephe was in a 'Catch 22' situation. In order to end his dependence on Pearson's he would have to appeal for public funds, but in order to appeal for such funds he must be able to show that he was already independent. One way to convince people that the Boy Scouts was an altrustic non-profit-making organization was to acquire the services of a Manager with a reputation for selfless service in the field of boys' work. Mr J. Howard Whitehouse,[22] the former Secretary of Toynbee Hall and present Secretary of the University Mission at Ancoats, Manchester, seemed ideal. Baden-Powell wanted him to run the office and edit *The Scout*, improving its tone as a matter of urgency. But would Arthur Pearson allow *The Scout* to be edited by some worthy boys' club organizer when it was doing so well purveying a diet of sensational stories? Indeed not. Pearson made it impossible for Baden-Powell to engage his new man by again refusing to pay any advance or licence fee in respect of *The Scout*, and by then refusing any assistance with his salary.[23] (Whitehouse later became a Liberal M.P. and Parliamentary Private Secretary to Lloyd George.)

Eric Walker often felt that Baden-Powell 'didn't realize what a big thing he had set afoot',[24] but he *did* realize it and decided to press on and rent separate offices even if he could not guarantee to meet the costs in advance. In April 1909 J. Archibald Kyle, Baden-Powell's recently appointed Manager, supervised the move of the Boy Scouts' organization to offices in Victoria Street, Westminster.

People in adjacent offices would find it 'practically impossible for their businesses to proceed because of ceaseless jumping about and blowing of bugles'[25] but Kyle and his staff were soon on their way to taking control of the Movement nationwide. A carefully planned interview procedure was worked out 'to guarantee that Scoutmasters were fit and proper men'.[26] Baden-Powell toyed with the idea of allowing regional committees to elect the County Commissioners, who would be 'generally responsible for the Movement in their area', but he abandoned the idea and instead 'invited' local worthies to be Commissioners: they included Lords Lieutenant, urban philanthropists, supporters of polytechnics, patrons of boys' clubs and retired or serving officers.[27] Since he was still tied to the North of England, he decided in June 1909 to appoint a Chief Commissioner to act for him. He offered the post to Major-General Edmond Roche Elles, formerly of the Royal Artillery, who before his retirement in 1905 had been a member of the Council of the Governor-General of India.

Elles was chosen with the full approval of Archibald Kyle, the Manager, and was rather like him in character: self-assertive and brusque.[28] County Commissioners had the power to dissolve elected committees in their area, but as Chief Commissioner Elles could dictate to them all – at least in theory. Unfortunately Baden-Powell had not considered what would happen if a County Commissioner who was fully supported by his local committees, councils and district Scoutmasters had a serious difference of opinion with the Chief Commissioner. Would the organization then respect the voices of its grass roots, or would it respond autocratically? The fledgling Movement was being given an administrative structure which was democratic at its peripheries but autocratic at its centre. This inconsistency would bring about a titanic clash that would threaten to wreck the Scouts.

In the month in which Elles became Chief Commissioner, Baden-

Powell met another man whom he decided to appoint to a key position. This was Sir Francis Vane, Bart., who thought it vital to stress the civil as opposed to the military potentialities of Scouting. After recent attacks on the Scouts by Keir Hardie and various nonconformist 'peace' groups, Baden-Powell wanted to make an appointment disarming them. Like J. H. Whitehouse, Vane was a lifelong Liberal who had been connected with Toynbee Hall where during the 1880s he had founded the first working-class cadet corps. Baden-Powell was also delighted to learn that he had been educated at Charterhouse.

Yet Vane, as Baden-Powell would discover, was a disconcerting man. As a serving officer in South Africa he had written a book criticizing his own countrymen for their treatment of Boer civilians. Now he backed the suffragettes and the Peace Society, but paradoxically supported cadet corps as the best means of bringing discipline to the working class. He nevertheless deplored Baden-Powell's encouragement of boys to learn to shoot, and admired his Movement only in so far as it inspired 'unselfish knight errantry'.[29]

Vane's mercurial and imaginative nature appealed to Baden-Powell, but his voluble manner proved anathema to conventional military men like Sir Edmond Elles and his deputy Colonel Ulick G. C. de Burgh. Baden-Powell made Vane his Commissioner for London apparently without considering how he and Elles would get on – nor did he define their precise spheres of influence. To be Commissioner of the capital with its vast population was to be in charge of the equivalent of half a dozen counties, and Vane never felt that he owed any explanation of his actions either to Elles or the Manager, Kyle, who was in Vane's aristocratic eyes a jumped-up office boy. From the beginning Vane wanted to give his local councils the power to run their own affairs and to elect their officials rather than be dictated to by Elles. Because Sir Edmond was a member of the pro-conscription National Service League, Vane mistrusted him from their first meeting.

For Baden-Powell to have tried to employ the radical Whitehouse as his Manager and then only three months later to have made Elles his Chief Commissioner might at first sight seem irrational. But if Scouting could appeal to members of the Y.M.C.A and officers of cadet corps, it was understandable that he should have tried to obtain the services of men whose personal views reflected this wide spectrum. Vane became London Commissioner because of some advice he had given Baden-Powell. 'What you must do,' he had told him, 'is find a common ground for moderate Imperialists and for non-conformists who do not like militarism . . . It will require prophets such as you and I to join the ends.'[30] As a counterpoise to Elles, Baden-Powell can be excused for thinking Vane ideal. But to choose people possessing completely different aims in order to give reassurance to opposing interest groups in society at large is a risky procedure.

3. The Vane Rebellion
(October 1909 to January 1910)

During July and August Sir Francis Vane worked prodigiously hard in London creating representative district associations designed to link the numerous local committees. Many Scoutmasters had wanted to go their own way, and the general mood was one of truculent independence. This situation had been brought about partly by J. A. Kyle's high-handed and tactless methods,[1] and partly by a growing suspicion that Headquarters was too closely involved with military organizations. In May the Battersea Boy Scouts seceded from the Baden-Powell Boy Scouts and formed the British Boy Scouts.[2] Two months later the popular boys' weekly, *Chums*, began to promote the British Boy Scouts as a circulation-boosting device.[3] Vane explained to Baden-Powell that it was vital to move fast to prevent further damage, and urged him to 'understand with how much suspicion and dislike the Headquarters is regarded by a very large proportion of active men in your organization.'[4] This disaffection was not a figment of Vane's imagination and he was right to hold Kyle and Sir Edmond Elles responsible.

Thoroughly sick of Vane's criticisms, Kyle forced a crisis in early November by threatening to resign as Manager unless Baden-Powell dismissed the baronet. When Elles and his deputy de Burgh supported Kyle, Baden-Powell was placed in a very awkward position. Vane was not a paid employee who could be fired with a week's wages, but an aristocratic volunteer who had given a considerable amount of his time to organizing the London Scouts and who might prove very troublesome if asked to resign without any adequate reason being offered. Believing the problem to be as much about personalities as anything else, Baden-Powell warned his Manager that this was a poor reason for dismissal. Kyle simply repeated his threat: 'It must be either Sir Francis Vane or myself.'[5] Baden-Powell ought to have called Kyle's bluff and refused to be blackmailed; but, being fully occupied with his Territorials, he could not face losing his Manager and standing up to Elles who was urging him to 'abolish' the post of London Commissioner on the wholly inadequate grounds that the 'Western Committee' – formed before Vane's appointment – had not recognized him.[6]

Baden-Powell first succumbed to the mounting pressure on 4 November, when he rebuked Vane for having exceeded his authority by seeking to formulate religious policy for the whole Movement. Vane had made no secret of his negotiations with the Bishop of London about the recently formed Church of England (or Diocesan) Scouts; these church troops threatened to become a movement within a movement with their own Scout Law ('A Scout is a Brother to All Diocesan Scouts.'). 'I really understood,' declared Vane, 'that the

making of peace between the warring factions of Scouts *within my area*
was one of the duties of a Commissioner.' He angrily dismissed the
Western Committee as 'the worst administered one' in the capital. He
pointed out that thanks to him the whole of London was now covered
by councils, and advised Baden-Powell to find out what the majority
of men working with him in London actually thought.[7] On 12
November Baden-Powell hinted that he would be grateful for Vane's
resignation. But when it was clear that Vane would go only if sacked,
he dropped this suggestion. 'You go farther than is wanted,' Baden-
Powell wrote lamely, adding, 'A Scoutmaster in Yorkshire told me
this week that he and others wished I was still at the head of the Scouts
and not Sir F. Vane!' He concluded with the mildest of warnings:
'Unless you can assume your proper place as Commissioner, under the
direction of the Chief Commissioner, I must ask you to consider
whether you would not take another post . . .' (The one he suggested
was Commissioner for Colonial branches.)[8]

Vane next suggested the formation of a London Council representing all the local associations. Sir Edmond Elles was acutely embarrassed when the Bishop of London lent his support to this idea; and
although Baden-Powell was impressed by Vane's long and cogently
argued report on the subject, Elles unexpectedly authorized Kyle to
hand Vane a letter of dismissal.[9]

Sir Francis responded by calling a meeting of London Scoutmasters
on 18 November at the Chancery Lane Safe Deposit Office. Baden-
Powell attended and was badly shaken by the Scoutmasters' obvious
devotion to Vane; he left this meeting feeling sure that Vane's 'so-
called crimes were merely over-zeal'. He was very upset that Kyle and
Elles had acted without consulting him, but he could hardly sack his
Manager and Chief Commissioner. 'Kyle's letter of dismissal was very
wanting in tact, and was premature,' he told Elles. 'I have told Vane to
carry on for the present pending our final consideration of the
question.'[10]

But Elles continued to back Kyle and, only two days later, they both
repeated their threat to resign unless Baden-Powell acted against Vane.
So on 20 November Baden-Powell was obliged to write to Sir Francis,
going back on what he had promised just 48 hours earlier. Now he
wrote claiming that 'the meeting on Thursday night proved to me
what I had supposed viz that you have an entirely wrong conception of
your duties as a Commissioner. It is therefore impossible for me any
longer to have confidence in you in that capacity.'[11]

Vane was amazed to find himself dismissed. Why, he asked, had
Baden-Powell failed to state his objection at the meeting? 'Instead of
this you publicly ordered the cancellation and withdrawal of the letter
which the Managing Secretary [Kyle] at Headquarters had written to
me . . . and you requested me to carry on the work . . .'[12] Vane

reminded Baden-Powell that he had offered him another post as recently as 4 November.

Under pressure from Vane to make a specific charge against him, Baden-Powell declared, 'The charge, if you like to call it such, is that you did not suit me . . . I could not trust you.'[13] Totally dissatisfied, Vane pointed out that covert 'insinuations had been made'. 'It is my right to hear what they are,' he told Baden-Powell, 'and it is YOUR DUTY to the cause to see that things are open and above board.' Within days of his dismissal, Vane decided to press on with his own Boy Scouts. 'I have given you every help I could, but the movement is bigger than *the* man, or any man, and God help me I will forward the movement even if the man does wrong.'[14]

Vane now organized a protest meeting of almost 200 Scoutmasters from the London area. Baden-Powell responded with a circular instructing local secretaries and Scoutmasters not to attend on pain of dismissal; he noted in the margin of a draft of this circular: 'Sir F. V. has mistaken his instruction and in his zeal has rather become the administrator of the London District. Instead of organizing the Council, which was to do this, he has started an office of his own to do it.'[15]

Baden-Powell's confusion is painfully apparent. He had made Vane his London Commissioner, not his Inspector for London. He had indeed asked Sir Francis to organize a London Council, which he had been actively engaged in doing. The opposition to centralized councils had originally come from Stephe himself.[16] It was only the row with Vane which finally persuaded Baden-Powell and diehards like Elles that they needed a Council at all. But instead of an elected body, they envisaged one packed with 'invited' public figures; this body would give a spurious appearance of democracy to the organization without actually changing anything.

This was the issue which dominated the meeting called by Vane at the Caxton Hall on 3 December 1909 – should the Movement have an autocratic hierarchy or be run in a democratic fashion? Many speakers acknowledged their indebtedness to their founder, but still believed that the Scoutmasters ought to decide the shape of their own organization. The meeting also resolved that Vane's dismissal be reconsidered pending the formation of a London Council. Fears were expressed that, if Headquarters could arbitrarily dismiss Scout officials, this could endanger their livelihoods. Although tempers ran high, no vote of confidence in Baden-Powell was proposed.

Sir Edmund Elles sent a friend to the meeting as an observer and was distressed enough by his report to write at once urging Baden-Powell to set up a Council. 'This is the only thing that can save the movement from disaster. I only fear that it is too late. With such an organization all this would have been impossible – now it is you against Vane. Kyle's great unpopularity too has much to do with it.'[17] The press was broadly sympathetic to Vane. SCOUTS' REVOLT: LIVELY PROTEST AGAINST 'ONE-MAN RULE' was the *Daily News*'s headline. [18] SPLIT IN THE BOY SCOUT CAMP – VIOLENT ATTACKS ON GENERAL BADEN-POWELL was how the *Daily Express* summarized the situation.[19]

The whole episode was a disaster for Baden-Powell and for the Boy Scouts. He had been lamentably served by Elles, but Stephe alone was responsible for his own indecisive handling of the affair. An eventual inquiry found nothing more damning than the fact that Vane sometimes smelled of whisky.[20] Writing to Evelyn Wood, Baden-Powell mentioned 'various points in his character, which stand against him . . . I could explain this to you, should you desire it, in conversation.' This was exactly the kind of innuendo which Vane feared. He later believed that Baden-Powell had spread rumours that he was a homosexual.[21] By mid-January, under direct threat of proceedings for libel and slander, Baden-Powell felt compelled to put in writing that he had intended 'no reflection on your personal character'. 'As I have explained before, the difference between us was a personal one on a matter of discipline. And, as I have already placed on record, your ability and energy in the discharge of your duty was undeniable.'[22]

Vane's real sin was to have defended himself and thus caused public embarrassment. After years of army life, it was Baden-Powell's instinct to back authority – in this case Headquarters – against a man far more in touch with the feelings of the rank and file. So Baden-Powell vacillated, broke a promise and finally backed nonentities against a highly original man who, while eccentric and egotistical, was a genuine 'knight errant' with an unshakable determination to right wrongs regardless of how many toes he trod on. Six years later, while serving as a reserve officer, he would be strongly advised by officials in Dublin Castle to suppress the truth about the murder of four Irish prisoners in order to save the face of the British military establishment. Instead he went to London to confront the Secretary of State for War, Lord Kitchener, in person; then he returned to Ireland to apologize to the widows on behalf of the army.

A month after his dismissal from the Scouts, Vane accepted an invitation to be President of the British Boy Scouts (the breakaway organization which had started with the Battersea Boy Scouts), bringing with him most of the troops in the London area and the majority of those in Birmingham. Some of the most famous Liberals in the country joined his committee: Sir Francis Belsey, W. T. Stead, Charles Masterman M.P., Barrow Cadbury, Sir Herbert Raphael M.P. and, last but not least, J. Howard Whitehouse, the man Baden-Powell had hoped to employ as his Manager but who was now Liberal

M.P. for mid-Lanarkshire. By early April 1910, with the help of
Chums magazine, the B.B.S. numbered about 50,000 boys and was
supported by the National Peace Council, the Boys' Life Brigade, the
Sunday School Union and Toynbee Hall.[23] Through *Chums* the
B.B.S. was soon spreading to the colonies and this impelled Baden-
Powell to take positive steps for the first time to establish control over
the Movement in the colonies and dominions.[24]

In 1911 Sir Francis Vane's financial affairs – which for some years
had been problematic because of a disputed inheritance – took a turn
for the worse. By subsidizing uniforms and by other acts of generosity
to his Scouts, Vane had over-committed himself and was declared
bankrupt in August 1912.[25] His 'rebel' movement entered a phase of
rapid decline. Baden-Powell was very lucky to have escaped in this
way.

The most enduring consequence of the Vane rebellion was the
alienation of the majority of London's Scoutmasters from Headquarters. When the London Scout Council was eventually formed it
frequently ignored Headquarters' directives, raised its own money and
in the early 1920s ran a magazine, *The Trail*, which published articles
openly critical of Baden-Powell himself. The capital would keep its
own Commissioner until 1965, a quarter of a century after Baden-
Powell's death, and only then was London divided up among seven
individual Commissioners as the founder had wanted.[26]

The Vane revolt convinced Baden-Powell that if the Boy Scouts
were ever to become a democratic organization he would always be in
danger of being voted into a position of powerlessness akin to a
constitutional monarch's – under the thumb of some man of energy
like Sir Francis Vane and his 'cabinet' of elected regional representatives. He was determined that this nightmare should never come to
pass. The Movement's supreme body should therefore be an unelected
council of men of public standing with insufficient time to attend more
than one meeting a year. These 'invited' figures would in turn 'elect' a
small executive committee whose prospective members would already
have been nominated by Baden-Powell. This Executive Committee,
chaired by Baden-Powell or his Chief Commissioner, would appoint
the County Commissioners who would in turn appoint the District
Commissioners. By decreeing that Commissioners should not be
Scoutmasters, Baden-Powell hoped to ensure that their loyalties
would only extend upwards to Headquarters rather than downwards
to the grass roots. Although district committees would consist of
democratically elected members, they could be dissolved by a County
Commissioner. Baden-Powell's later claim that the counties and
districts were 'autonomous units' was false. 'The function of Headquarters,' he stated in a memorandum, 'is merely to define
principles.'[27] In practice the 'principles' of the Movement could be

interpreted as covering a very wide range of practical matters which district committees judged to be of purely local concern.[28]

In March 1911 Baden-Powell met members of Vane's old East London Council and acknowledged that 'they had been frequently snubbed by Headquarters', and matters of direct concern 'done behind their backs' without consultation. He blamed de Burgh and Elles for creating a situation in which it was 'not surprising' that members of the Council had been 'prepared to chuck up the whole thing'.[29]

The loss of London to Vane and the confusion that had preceded this disaster convinced Baden-Powell that he would have to leave the army and devote himself entirely to the leadership of his Movement. He resigned his post with the Territorials on 31 March 1910. At 53 he was embarking upon a second career which would make him more famous than he had ever been in the years immediately after the Boer War.

4. Character Factory or Helping Hand?

In recent years five out of six scholars* who have studied the early Boy Scout Movement have concluded that Baden-Powell's overriding aim was to make efficient future soldiers, and that his interest in good citizenship was secondary and cosmetic. Largely because the British Scout Association has always catergorically denied any military tendency, historians have gone to inordinate lengths to 'prove' what a cursory reading of Baden-Powell's handbook makes obvious: namely that Scouting *did* have military aims among others.

Yet I believe that these 'anti-militarist' historians have overstated their case – just as the most thoughtful and wide-ranging of them, John Springhall, predicted might happen: 'Imbalance,' he wrote wisely, 'is the price to be paid for any attempt at re-adjusting historical boundaries.'[1] I myself am convinced that although *Scouting for Boys* resonates with fear for the future of the British Empire, the kindliness and generosity advocated as the basis for good behaviour was not simply included – as one scholar has claimed – as an expedient façade to conceal the Movement's true purpose from nonconformist and liberal parents.[2] Because none of the scholars employed a biographical approach, they were not in a position to observe how Baden-Powell's interest in good character and in the educational possibilities of Scouting began in South Africa as something quite separate from his later involvement with cadet corps and minature rifle shooting. Through the influence, direct and indirect, of men as different as William Smith, Ernest Thompson Seton, Roger Pocock, Arthur Pearson and R. B. Haldane the two previously distinct strands were finally brought together, as I have shown, in *Scouting for Boys*.

* See note 10 for Chapter Nine, page 627.

The famous passage from *Scouting for Boys* beginning: 'Every boy ought to learn to shoot and obey orders . . .' and the instructions on how to use Scouts' staves as dummy rifles can be contrasted with the passages about 'good turns', 'chivalry', 'saving lives' and 'camping'. This, for example, is how Baden-Powell defines 'character' in *Scouting for Boys*: '. . . a spirit of manly self-reliance and of unselfishness – something of the *practical* Christianity which (although they are Buddhists . . .) distinguishes the Burmese in their daily life.'[3] The balance is fine; but in my view, at its inception Scouting was more a civil than a military institution, both as regards the predominant intention of its founder and in its practice by boys up and down the country. In this last respect there were enormous differences from troop to troop, and in late 1909 – although Baden-Powell had assured the secretaries of Y.M.C.A.s that the Boy Scouts had 'no military tendency whatever'[4] – he was allowing individual Scoutmasters to determine the extent to which their boys took part in military-style activities.[5]

In Sir Francis Vane's opinion Baden-Powell's advisers like Sir Edmund Elles and his deputy Colonel de Burgh were trying to take over the Movement and turn it into 'a recruiting ground for the army'.[6] This would seem to be borne out by a letter written either by Kyle or Elles to the Earl of Meath shortly before he joined the Executive Committee: 'We are a Peace organization, at the present time,' his lordship was told, 'the main reason being that a very large number of people will allow their boys to join the Boy Scouts, who are not in favour of general military service.'[7] Since Baden-Powell could only get to London once a week a for few hours, 'travelling back by night to Yorkshire to save time', it was not surprising that he was losing touch.[8] For example, he had no advance idea of the contents of the programme for the gigantic Crystal Palace rally, and was appalled by the appearance of a Gatling gun and by the shenanigans of the gun-toting Scoutmasters of the Legion of Frontiersmen.[9]

Yet whether or not Baden-Powell's original inspiration had been predominantly civil or military, the Movement itself transcended such considerations from its earliest infancy. In 1913 the editor of the *Manchester Guardian*, after printing a lengthy correspondence in which both possibilities were argued, declared a draw and wrote an eminently sensible leader which has been ignored by all the scholars:

Boy Scouts and Militarism

The dispute might never end, of itself, for both sides are right . . . It is quite true, on the one side that General Baden-Powell has made a few slight attempts in print to influence the Scouts' mind in a militarist or big-armament direction. On the other hand, the general intention and spirit of the movement are unquestionably neither militarist nor anti-militarist, but simply recreative and lightly educational, all the stress being laid on the practice of the good ordinary decencies of boyhood . . . and on the acquisition of 'gumption', or practical sense and alertness of mind. The movement sprang from the mind of a person eminently boyish, and its appeal to the boyish mind, which loves every form of practical ingenuity or 'contraptiousness', has deservedly been enormous . . . It would be the greatest pity if those who do not believe that war is either a school of character or a reputable means of national gain were to stand aloof from a movement so sane and right in all its essentials as Boy Scouting . . .[10]

Great creative achievements – and there can be no question about the Boy Scouts being one – spring from deeper causes than conscious aims. Because of his father's early death Baden-Powell feared that he had missed important advice of a manly kind and had consequently 'mixed a terrible lot of bad with the good I picked up . . .'[11] His subconscious need to control his sexuality by advising others how to deal with 'bad' desires played a most important part in his emergence as adviser-in-chief to the youth of the world. A connection can also be made between Baden-Powell's love of children, his fear of marriage and the comfort he inevitably derived from suddenly becoming honorary father to hundreds of thousands of boys. Avowed aims cannot of course accurately be weighed against unacknowledged subconscious ones. Nevertheless, when a gifted man's deep anxieties about his sexual nature and his personal manliness coincide with a nation's fear of impending decline through lack of virile qualities, the basic ingredients exist for a remarkably potent creative brew.

Baden-Powell was fond of quoting R. B. Haldane's sister, Elizabeth, who had suggested that 'as civilization develops in a people, the men deteriorate under its softening influence and the women come into their own.'[12] With women now entering the professions and the suffragettes destroying that reassuring stereotype of the deferential gentlewoman, men were beginning to glimpse a future in which women would be able to do *their* jobs and there would be no room left for pursuits requiring strength and endurance. In America the new immigrants were out-breeding the old stock; was this the fault of better educated women, or was city 'deterioration' sapping the virility of the nation's well-to-do urban men? Small wonder that when Baden-Powell offered to restore the manliness of nations his words were eagerly seized upon. While American males faced one kind of challenge to their virility, men throughout the thinly held British Empire were engaged in their own Darwinian struggle for survival. His ability to reassure whole nations about their manly prospects must have been a great comfort to Baden-Powell just when a series of

women were refusing to give his own manly credentials their seal of
marital approval.

Another prevalent anxiety, in Britain at least, was the fear that
national unity would be imperilled by the growing political awareness
of the working class. The 53 seats won by the Labour Party in 1906 had
sent a shudder through the British Establishment, so Baden-Powell's
exhortations to working-class boys to be like 'bricks in the wall' of the
Empire and to learn the virtue of public school 'team spirit' would have
been music to the ears of the ruling class. The idea that his Movement
was above all else an agency of social control has recently been argued
at length by Michael Rosenthal in his appropriately entitled book *The
Character Factory*. According to Mr Rosenthal the continuance of the
privileged life of Britain's élite (by contriving 'the complete sub-
missiveness' of the working class) was a natural objective for any man
possessing Baden-Powell's deeply conservative social ideals'.[13] While
he was indeed conservative and often worried lest a shift in political
power might one day leave the nation too divided to defend itself, the
claim that social repression was his principal aim is unwarranted.

Baden-Powell was certainly no Christian Socialist and no radical
philanthropist, but he *did* share some of their motives. Among such
people guilt and fear usually coexisted with more positive desires to
remedy social ills. Like Ruskin, Hughes and Kingsley, Baden-Powell
was a paternalist. He believed that landowners and country gentlemen
had a duty to protect working men from the exploitation of urban
industrialists. 'Gentlemen', in short, *should* lead but should prove
themselves worthy to do so by their chivalry, their kindness and by the
respect which they inspired.[14] While such views were not very
relevant to the political realities of the first decade of the twentieth
century, Baden-Powell was not indifferent to the well-being of the
working-class boys he hoped to attract into the Scouts.*

He hated extremes of affluence and poverty, and his signing away of
the fortune in foreign rights he would otherwise have made out of
Scouting for Boys showed him no hypocrite in this regard. He was
incredulous that 'a rich loafer could pass along the Thames Embank-
ment on his way to a luxurious meal in a sumptuous restaurant and see,
without shame, his fellow, but less fortunate, loafers starving at its
gates.' The worst type of man was the 'rich shirker' who had
'opportunities of usefulness and failed to use them'.[15] Baden-Powell
criticized 'street corner loafers' just as fiercely; but he believed that
these working-class boys were drifting towards 'bad citizenship', yet
only 'for want of hands to guide them the right way towards being
useful'.[16] He thought 'unemployedness largely the outcome of bad
management, about which very little is done in a practical way'.[17]

* The Scouts would however remain predominantly middle- and lower-middle class
(Int. Review of Social History 16 (1971): 125–58).

In *Scouting for Boys* Baden-Powell stated plainly (and was often abused for it) that 'the Socialists are right in wishing to get money more evenly distributed so that there would be no millionaires and no paupers, but everyone pretty well off.' But his fear that in practice Socialism might 'make life a kind of slavery for everybody' persuaded him to drop this passage from the handbook's third edition. However he remained, as he told an acquaintance, 'entirely in sympathy with Socialists in their desire to give any man a fair start in life'.[18] Such remarks are not consistent with the idea that Baden-Powell pioneered the Boy Scouts as a device for brain-washing working-class boys.

The 'Character Factory' was however a metaphor which Baden-Powell himself used on several occasions, most of them during the Great War, to describe his Movement's capacity for 'making' good citizens.[19] As Michael Rosenthal avers, the phrase suggests an intention to produce a standard end product; yet, as with the suggestion that Baden-Powell was 'deeply conservative', the truth about his actual intention is not so simple. 'A boy,' he wrote, 'should take his own line rather than be carried along by herd persuasion . . .'[20] In many of his lists of character ingredients, 'intelligence' and 'individuality' precede 'loyalty' and 'self-discipline'.[21]

Certainly when Baden-Powell decided in 1910 that 'the most important work that the Scout Movement can do lies in getting hold of the vast hordes of slum boys in the great industrial centres of the North Midlands,' his prime motivation was to help them make something of themselves rather than to turn them into 'bricks in the wall'.[22] 'Go into any big works or into any back alley where working lads congregate and hear what they talk and think about,' he told a Scouting colleague, 'and you will come away ashamed at the results of our so-called civilization. But it is not the fault of the boys.'[23] Baden-Powell hoped that the Scout 'tests' and 'badges' would help such boys to develop a pride in their own efforts, which might persuade them to acquire new skills.[24] In this way he managed to combine the Edwardians' pursuit of 'national efficiency' – a Prussian concept which was vague enough to appeal to Fabians and Tory Imperialists – with the libertarian educational ideas which were becoming fashionable shortly before the Great War.

'Dr Montessori,' Baden-Powell wrote in 1914, 'has proved that by encouraging a child in its natural desires, instead of instructing it in what you think it ought to do, you can educate it on a far more solid and far-reaching basis. It is only tradition and custom that ordain that education should be a labour . . . One of the original objects of *Scouting for Boys* was to break through this tradition.'[25] Madame Montessori herself later wrote of Scouting as freeing children 'from the narrow limits to which they had been confined'.[26]

So while the Boy Scouts undoubtedly appealed to Sir Edmond Elles as a semi-military 'Character Factory', the Movement simultaneously

appealed to educationalists and to liberal philanthropists as a disinterested attempt to help boys of all classes widen their overall
perspectives. And whereas scholars have dwelled at great length upon
the role of the militarists within the Movement, the role played by the
philanthropists has been largely ignored.[27]

Arthur Gaddum, the Commissioner for Manchester and South-East
Lancashire, was a millionaire silk merchant who had retired at the early
age of 32 to devote himself to good works. Shortly afterwards, in
1908, he had become secretary to the newly formed Boy Scout
Association in Manchester. Baden-Powell often equated criticism
with disloyalty, yet Gaddum's attacks on the Headquarters Committee as 'dead and completely out of touch' would lead him to try to
get rid of the old members before the Great War ended.[28]

Each year Gaddum used to go and live for a month among the East
Enders who spent their annual holidays hop-picking in Kent. He had
first been persuaded to do this by the Old Wykehamist son of a Liberal
peer, the Hon. Roland Philipps.[29] After going down from New
College, Philipps had worked at Oxford's own 'settlement' in the East
End, teaching illiterate adults to read and organizing boys' clubs. He
was a supporter of the suffragettes and would have contested South
Glamorgan for the Liberals in 1914 had not war intervened.[30] In 1911
Baden-Powell made him his Commissioner for East London, and in
that year Philipps bought a house in Stepney so that he could live in the
slums amongst the boys he hoped to serve. (Philipps was killed in the
war and bequeathed the Stepney house and £15,000 to the Boy
Scouts.)[31]

Anthony Slingsby, another committed Christian and close friend of
Gaddum, became Organizing Secretary for the North of England
from 1911, and joint Manager at Headquarters in 1913. Meanwhile at
Toynbee Hall, where Vane and Whitehouse had once worked, a young
medical student called T. S. Lukis had started a Scout troop and a
Scoutmasters' Council in 1908.[32] To the Movement's great loss,
Slingsby and Lukis would share Philipps's fate in Flanders. Apart from
Arthur Gaddum, the sole survivor of these Christian philanthropists
was H. Geoffrey Elwes, a Colchester solicitor who had worked
voluntarily for the Church of England Men's Society before becoming
editor of the Boy Scouts' *Headquarters' Gazette*. Baden-Powell's
reliance upon such men is clear proof that the movement did not
suddenly lurch towards the National Service League after Vane's
dismissal.

Scholarly emphasis on 'militarism' and the 'Character Factory'
aspects of the Movement has obscured a vital truth about the early Boy
Scouts. Of course Edwardian anxieties about racial deterioration,
working-class disaffection and worsening international rivalry played
their part as motivating factors for Baden-Powell's great invention.

But while fears can be faced and corrective action be taken to allay them, they can just as well be kept at bay by fantasy and escapist dreams. It is therefore very curious that in recent years the Boy Scouts have always been presented as a hard-headed cure for weakening resolution rather than a blessed escape from national and personal self-doubt.

5. Wood-smoke at Twilight: The Great Escape

'Who hath smelt wood-smoke at twilight? who hath heard the
  birch-log burning?
Who is quick to read the noises of the night?
Let him follow with the others, for the Young Men's feet
  are turning
To the camps of proved desire and known delight!'

From 'The Feet of the Young Men',
Rudyard Kipling

During the early 1920s it became customary for these lines to be recited at the opening of camp-fire sing-songs; they sum up the romantic spirit which had been predominant in Scouting from the beginning. John Burns, the first working man to hold Cabinet rank in Great Britain, attacked the Boy Scouts not for their militarism but because they promised the kind of adventure which discouraged boys 'from settling down to ordinary working lives'.[1] Nor was his an isolated voice. The Boy Scouts were also accused of being a refuge from the real world which left ex-Scouts trapped in a perpetual boyhood.[2] For every 'Character Factory' type of criticism, there was one accusing Baden-Powell of irresponsibility for allowing boys too much freedom.

Unlike modern scholars, such critics took no notice at all of what Baden-Powell *alleged* could be achieved by his Movement in the realm of education and character-building. The pseudonymous author of *The Boy Scout Bubble: A Review of a Great Futility* (1912) accused the Scouts of fostering escapism and ridiculed city Scout troops obliged to meet on tracts of waste land:

After a few dead cats and many empty meat-tins have been successfully removed, 'camp fires' are made out of waste paper and an orange box kindly presented by the local grocer. Seated on dust-heaps near these fires, within the sound of tram-cars, railways, and the raucous voice of the itinerant vendor of winkles and pot ferns, little boys play very seriously at being backwoodsmen. Maybe they are far away in thought – far away in the forests of Canada or the Australian Bush . . . We are told that this is character-building, but

I refuse to believe that character will ever be built by unsettling the minds of the young, by turning their thoughts from practical everyday life and the best way to live it, to dreams and visions of a life that not one in a hundred will ever be called upon to live. So strong is the imagination of the youngster that it may be several months before he begins to ask himself what earthly use the knowledge of how to light a damp fire with one match will be to him when he answers an advertisement for a junior clerk . . . It is because romance and make-belief are given such an important place in Scouting that it is so popular with the small boy . . . Semaphore signalling is much more interesting than English history; Latin is not to be compared with marching songs and Zulu incantations . . .[3]

This anti-school, anti-authoritarian streak in Scouting was even noticed by men who later left the Movement to found their own more socialistic and homespun variants. Leslie Paul, the left-wing journalist and a founding father of the Woodcraft Folk, wrote in his autobiography *Angry Young Man*: 'The Scout Movement was the very breath of hope and love and encouragement to many a child . . . I grew up with it as my spiritual home, learning to despise the work of classrooms in favour of the open-air pursuits the movement glorified.'[4] John Hargrave, founder of the breakaway youth movement Kibbo Kift and one of Scouting's most charismatic figures, is usually quoted making accusations of militarism,[5] but nobody ever paid warmer tributes to the Movement's subversive qualities which he attributed to Baden-Powell personally:

He was a mental 'psychic', although he never knew it . . . There was a Huck Finn hidden in Baden-Powell – a kind of backwoods' urchin, or maybe gremlin – that tugged pretty hard and might easily have upset the whole jamboree . . . It broke loose in small exuberances and tricksy quirks . . . It was the Boy-Poltergeist in Baden-Powell – that made rapport with the primitive fraternity gang spirit of boyhood. Like a true poltergeist it rang a bell and rapped on the door . . . And thousands of boys . . . ran after it to camp. They made their escape from a dreary, half-dead commercialized and deadly dull civilization, and during the weekends anyhow pretended to be backwoodsmen . . . Baden-Powell tapped the primitive urge that is cribb'd, cabin'd and confined by civilized herd-conditioning and convention. He tapped it and unlocked it. And for a while . . . it ran free.[6]

Baden-Powell was fond of quoting Robert Louis Stevenson's famous commendation of travel: 'The great affair is to move; to feel the needs and hitches of life a little more nearly, to get down off this featherbed of civilization and to find the globe granite underfoot and strewn with cutting flints.' He also applauded Stevenson's hope that 'there is nobody under thirty so dead but his heart will stir at the sight of a gipsy camp . . .' and that 'youth will now and again find a brave word to say in dispraisal of riches, throw up a situation to go strolling with a knapsack.'[7] The promise of adventurous camping expeditions opened up by *Scouting for Boys* chimed with the mood of many progressive headmasters, who were making 'the simple life' the basis of their educational philosophy. Taking their cue from Rousseau's belief in the innate goodness of 'the natural man', the founders of schools like Bedales and Clayesmore banished decadent luxury and encouraged their pupils to work in the fields as well as in the classroom. Both J. H. Badley and Alexander Devine were deeply influenced by a William Morris style of socialism and encouraged handcraft and civic responsibility above prowess in games. Since neither of these men saw the Boy Scouts as a 'deeply conservative' un-progressive organization but, on the contrary, as a liberating force, both their schools soon boasted Scout troops.[8] Baden-Powell himself never had any use for luxury, having in his bedroom – when he finally had his own home – no furniture except a bed with a hard mattress, a table and an upright chair. He never employed a valet and always preferred to sleep in the open when he could.[9]

The need for a man to renew his links with nature and, in doing so, restore his sense of inner tranquillity, was argued by writers as different as Stevenson, Whitman, Grahame, Edward Carpenter and E.M. Forster. In the year in which the Scouts were founded, Rupert Brooke immersed himself in the New Forest and felt 'for the first time in my life a free man . . . behaving naturally'.[10] Sentiments like these – which militated so heavily in favour of the Scouts – were widespread, and not merely among teachers, faddists and intellectuals. They were largely due to a popular hatred of industrialism and urban society which had been reflected in the writings of Dickens, Mayhew, Ruskin and Morris long before the turn of the century. Of equal and complementary importance had been the school of literature idealizing country life: the novels of George Borrow and the writings of Richard Jefferies and, rather later, the verse of the Georgian poets. Looking back on the period shortly before the Great War, George Orwell would later castigate 'over-civilized' people of that era for 'enjoying reading about rustics because they imagined them to be more primitive and passionate than themselves'.[11]

Baden-Powell used the expression 'over-civilized' to describe boys whose only experience of life was living in a town or city. 'They are accustomed to rely on everyone else for their wants. If they want water, they do not go to a well and draw it: they turn on a tap. If they want light they simply turn the electric switch . . . Through over-civilization our children become weak and unreliant.' Working-class 'townies' would watch other men playing football, and upper-class ones would sink even lower by employing men to run their baths and fold their clothes.[12] Baden-Powell also blamed city life for spawning 'the herd instinct' which had been described in 1908 by the surgeon, Wilfred Trotter, as a force compelling people living *en masse* to seek group approval regardless of common sense.[13] Thus they became, wrote Baden-Powell, easily manipulable by 'the undesirable teachings of the Sunday press, unmoral [sic] cinemas, and easy access to cheap unhealthy pleasures.' 'Nature,' he said, 'was being driven further and further out of the reach of the majority.' With 'the artificial swamping out the natural in life',[14] he was convinced that only his Movement could restore to the children of the industrialized world their birthright of hill, field and forest.

This conception of the countryside was of course the urban romantic view which persists to this day in a country in which many more people live in towns than in rural surroundings. Boys who worked on farms, and therefore knew the drudgery of hoeing turnips and milking at four in the morning, did not often join the Scouts. A trip to the nearest big city was what they craved. The open-air rural bias of Scouting owed much to puritan attitudes to work which had preceded the industrial revolution. The idea that physical labour was morally more elevating than brain work had been taken up by the Christian Socialists and, through Ruskin and his Balliol students labouring on their muddy track outside Oxford, had influenced George Baden-Powell and Cecil Rhodes, who made his own significant contribution to the 'real outdoor work' versus 'unreal office work' debate by combining work of the 'real' variety with the adventure of colonial expansion. Given Baden-Powell's touchstones for character – 'courage, endurance and self-reliance' – it is easy to see why he scorned sedentary work. Only by opening up new territory for agriculture in distant parts of the world could a man find a civil occupation likely to test his manliness.

Imperialists were not alone in feeling sadness at the shift away from physically demanding work in the age of internal combustion and electricity. The psychologist William James detested nationalism, but dreaded 'a world of clerks' and thought that 'human life with no use for hardihood would be contemptible'.[15] Baden-Powell also singled out office clerks for particular derision. 'The nation does not need more clerks in the overcrowded cities of this little island . . . No! The nation wants men and wants them badly, men of British blood who can go out and tackle the golden opportunities, not merely for benefiting themselves, but for building up and developing those great overseas states of our Commonwealth.'[16] Like Froude before him – who had influenced Rhodes and George Baden-Powell – Stephe clutched at the colonies as an escape hatch through which Englishmen unable to afford land at home might escape to become farmers abroad rather than have to endure the humiliating treadmill of an urban office. When he set up a Scout Farm school in 1911, Baden-Powell's hope was to produce future colonists.[17] Emigration was indeed the logical destiny for any boy who took Scouting's message to heart and aspired to live as a frontiersman.

This was very much in the spirit of Charles Kingsley's most famous adventure novel, *Westward Ho!*, which was intended to be 'a symbol of brave young England longing to wing its way out of its island prison, to discover and to traffic, to colonize and to civilize.'[18] The 'island prison' is akin to Kipling's confession to Rhodes that he thought England 'a stuffy little place, mentally, morally and physically'.[19] Baden-Powell agreed. 'It beats me why any Briton continues to live in say, Wigan, when South Africa is open to him.'[19] He considered that 'within our little island there is not sufficient scope for the big-minded men'.[21]

It is essential to recall that some of the world's greatest feats of land exploration took place when Baden-Powell was a boy. He was 14 when Stanley 'found' Livingstone and when the search for the Nile's source was at its height. Inevitably men of his generation were romantically drawn to Africa and other wild places. Yet, as the anonymous author of *The Boy Scout Bubble* had cogently argued, with Imperial expansion effectively ended only a handful of boys would ever grow up to be frontiersmen.

In America a similar problem existed: the 'West' was already a subject for nostalgia rather than somewhere for young men to go. In *Scouting for Boys* Baden-Powell quoted ex-President Roosevelt as saying: 'The out-of-doors man must always prove the better in life's contest.'[22] When influential opinion-makers in industrial nations promoted ideals of manhood which could only be lived out by a handful on the world's shrinking frontiers, boys and men living and working in cities were bound to become unusually susceptible to fantasy. For this reason more than any other, the Boy Scout Movement answered a deep craving: it was the perfect substitute for the dream of manliness and freedom peddled in the boys' comics of the day. Because of its practical hints and 'true life' anecdotes from Baden-Powell's own past, *Scouting for Boys* had been taken by the majority of adults as a practical manual rather than a work of fantasy in the tradition of other masterpieces of adventure from the deceptively down-to-earth *Robinson Crusoe* to the more outlandish *Treasure Island*. In reality Baden-Powell's boy readers imagined themselves only a stone's throw from the frontier freedom of felling trees, killing game and damming rivers. Baden-Powell's success in persuading Roosevelt and Roberts that sickly urban boys could gain the strength and self-reliance of a Daniel Boone from the Boy Scout programme did not make this proposition true. It was pure fantasy too. His determined anti-intellectuality in no way served the material or military interests of an industrial state.

'Too much learning kills common sense,' he wrote confidently, giving as his example the intuitive skill of the native bridge-builders of West Africa who could span a river in a fraction of the time taken by British engineers using their 'complex calculations'.[23] But the future prosperity of industrial nations would depend upon their scientists more than upon an army of self-reliant colonists or heroic explorers, however firm their muscles and sound their characters. This was the unpalatable truth which the Boy Scouts enabled so many men to ignore: brains in a modern society *did* matter more than character, whatever the Rhodes Scholarship examiners might decree.* A civilization dominated by technology would only thrive with the help of men brought up to value science and learning rather than encouraged to despise it.

School and office work were inevitably considered dull and futile in a culture which worshipped adventure. In 1896, Baden-Powell had explained how easily he was diverted from all other matters by thoughts of the veldt:

> . . . somebody in the next room has mentioned the word saddle or rifle, or billy, or some other attribute of camp life, and off goes my mind at a tangent to play with its toys. Old Oliver Wendell Holmes is only too true when he says that most of us are 'boys all our lives'.[24]

Fifty years later in *Death of a Salesman* Biff Loman, who is 'playing around with horses for twenty-eight dollars a week' and confesses himself 'like a boy', urges his successful store manager brother to come West with him. 'Maybe we could buy a ranch . . . men built like we are should be working out in the open.'[25] Prolonging boyish adventure and staving off urban maturity were vitally important unstated aims of the Scout Movement that found an echo in every industrialized country.

In Britain, where there were no ranches to buy, Baden-Powell demonstrated that escape need not be limited to place; a man could also escape in time. Scoutmasters would not require the freedom of the Matopo Hills in order to shake off the shackles of their adult lives. 'All you have to do,' he told then, 'is give rein to your imagination . . . You must see things with your boys' eyes. To you the orchard must, as it is with them, be Sherwood Forest with Robin Hood and his Merry Men

---

* These scholarships to Oxford University created by Cecil Rhodes were awarded for the possession of 'qualities of manhood . . . and moral character' more than for academic aptitude.

in the background; the fishing harbour must be in the Spanish Main with its pirates and privateers; even the town common may be a prairie teeming with buffaloes and Red Indians . . . (Read *The Golden Age* by Kenneth Grahame).'[26]

In *The Golden Age* Grahame summoned up a childhood world freer and more exciting than anything subsequent adult experience could offer. It is significant that Baden-Powell should have recommended to his Scoutmasters a book which so clearly revealed its author's personal longing to escape into childhood.[27] Boys were under no obligation to furnish proofs of manliness as Edwardian men so often felt they were. 'If I were a Boy Again' was the title of one of Baden-Powell's favourite paintings, in which an unhappy father looks at his carefree Boy Scout son and wishes that he could be in his shoes.[28] This picture was used by Baden-Powell as an illustration in pamphlets urging men to join the Movement. As Scoutmasters, he promised that they would be able to 'renew their youth' as 'Boy-Men'.[29]

The sentimental adulation of boyhood which had been a distinctive feature in a wide range of late nineteenth-century novels – the most famous being Mary Louisa Molesworth's *Carrots: Just a Little Boy* (1876) and Frances Hodgson Burnett's *Little Lord Fauntleroy* (1886) – probably owed something to a tendency among adults in uncertain times to seek from their children a security the outside world no longer offered. A prolongation of beautiful boyhood also delayed the onset of interest in the opposite sex. And for all his talk of inculcating manliness, Baden-Powell could sometimes be as whimsical as J.M. Barrie:

> Watch that lad going down the street [he wrote], his eyes looking far out. Is his vision across the prairie or over the grey-backed seas? At any rate it isn't here. Don't I know it? Have you ever seen the buffaloes roaming in Kensington Gardens past that very spot where Gil Blas met the robbers behind the trees? Can't you see the smoke rising from the Sioux lodges under the shadow of the Albert Memorial?

Such sentimentality was not to the liking of character-builders like the Boy Scouts of America's early organizer, Edgar M. Robinson, who detested the cult of the pretty boy who 'is more effeminate than his sister'. For him the tough and lively boys in the 'boy' novels of Twain and Thomas Bailey Aldrich were what was required.

Baden-Powell, however, could easily accommodate such views by leaving the Kensington Gardens of his boyhood for the African veldt of his adult years. His cure for 'weak and unreliant over-civilized boys', he told an American audience in 1910, was 'to put back some of the wild man into the boy'.[30] The Boy Scouts' tests, he explained, were the toned-down equivalent of tribal initiation rites. He never seemed to see any inconsistency in his suggestion that British boys would gain in initiative by learning skills practised in unprogressive societies. This was a strange viewpoint for any supporter of Imperialism to adopt, since it ran directly counter to the popular justification of Empire as a moral mission to improve and educate.

Baden-Powell's enthusiasm for tribal people was counterbalanced by his admiration for medieval knights – not as they had once existed, but as the nineteenth-century antiquarian Kenelm Digby had recreated them. One of Digby's ideas which was to influence Baden-Powell most was a by-product of the eighteenth-century gentry's scorn for money made in 'trade': it was that men of the working class preferred to be commanded by a born gentleman rather than by a mere man of wealth. It would be hard to estimate which was the more inappropriate precept for the youth of a trading nation to follow: the Zulu warrior's inflexible resistance to change or Digby's scorn for money-making. To cram as much romantic material into a single book and then to gain a reputation for having created a sinisterly effective 'Character Factory' is not given to many men. But not many men possess a divided psyche enabling them to argue just as convincingly for self-discipline as for imaginative freedom.

'Give me the man who has been raised among the great things of nature,' he wrote in *Scouting for Boys*. 'I find that those men who came from the farthest frontiers . . . are among the most generous and chivalrous of their race . . . they become "gentle men" by their contact with nature.'[31] This too was pure fantasy, as his experiences among the real settlers of Matabeleland had made abundantly plain. Baden-Powell's frontiersmen, like Digby's gentle knights and Wister's noble cowboys, bore virtually no resemblance to their flesh and blood originals; all were examples of imagination transforming reality.

In October 1909, King Edward invited Baden-Powell to come to Balmoral to be knighted 'for all his past services and especially the present one of raising Boy Scouts for the country'. After the ceremony, the King told the new knight that he intended to review the boys in a few months' time at a mass rally in Windsor Great Park.[32] In fact Edward VII's death in 1910 meant that it was his son, George, who carried out the inspection the following July. And how would Sir Robert Baden-Powell choose to greet his monarch? With his boys drawn up in neat soldierly rows? Hardly – instead he disposed them in two great horseshoes. So on an English summer day, within sight of the battlements of Windsor Castle, 33,000 cowboy-hatted boys (drawn up in Zulu formation and pledged to live by chivalric ideals) awaited the arrival of their King. And when he appeared under the Royal Standard, would they salute in some conventional way?

There was a moment's pause of dead silence and then a sudden roar
filled the air, and the whole mighty horseshoe of boys with one
impulse leapt forward from either side, rushing as only boys can
rush, gathering force as they came, screaming out the rallying cries
of their different patrols, as they came in a whole kaleidoscopic mass
of colour with flags fluttering, hats waving, knees glinting, in the
great charge towards the King. Then, at a sign, the whole mass
stopped its rush, up went a forest of staves and hats, and higher into
the sky went the shrill screaming cheers of the boys in a cry that
gripped the throat of every onlooker . . .[33]

So what were they, in their own minds? Knights-errant vowing to
succour the weak and needy? Zulus greeting their chief with tribal
rallying cries? Future soldiers of the Empire promising allegiance? Or
just boys enjoying the outing of a lifetime? A bit of all these things, just
as Baden-Powell had intended when he had dreamed up his extraordinary scheme only three years earlier.

Reproduced from Punch

THE CAPTURE OF WINDSOR CASTLE
by the Boy Scouts, July 4th, 1911.

II

AN UNEXPECTED MARRIAGE

1. Woes and Widows (1910–12)

Baden-Powell retired from the Army on 7 May 1910 to devote himself entirely to the Scout Movement. A year later he was more rather than less in the public eye. In May he was invited by the recently ennobled Lord Haldane to join a select party of a dozen eminent men chosen to dine with the German Emperor. Four months earlier he had been the guest of the Tsar of all the Russias at Tsarkoe Selo, especially invited by him to explain his Boy Scouts scheme. Several garden parties at Buckingham Palace, the great Rally at Windsor and the unremitting demands of his growing Movement kept him as busy as he had ever been.

Although back in London again and living in his mother's house, he was still travelling a lot and spending frequent days and nights in distant towns. Invariably guards of honour met him at railway stations, along with posses of local newsmen. He hated the 'smart parades and march pasts' usually in prospect. 'I much prefer to see the boys at work in their camps, or engaged in activities like team races, tent pitching or bridge-building.'[1] During 1910 and 1911 he saw precious little of what he preferred; in addition he attended a very large number of meetings (27 in February, March and April of 1910 alone). He once described a typical day on the road as 'a Rat-like Day'. The Rally, which he thought the least offensive part, he compared with the rat's head in a humorous description of a typical visit to a provincial town. 'Then came the body of the thing, the public meeting, not an enlivening show at any time, and when I heard that the Bishop was to preside over it my heart sank.'

The Town Hall was filled with an audience chiefly composed of elderly ladies wearing spectacles that twinkled continuously. The Bishop opened the proceedings with a long prayer followed by a speech from the Mayor. 'Never could he forget,' he said, that 'Sir Powell had founded the Lads' Brigade during the Siege of Lady-smith, and what a night we had when that place was relieved. We had a torch-light procession and Mrs Mullingsworth's mother, she was a girl then, went as Britannia on top of a hansom cab, which

was draped round with white calico to look like a marble pedestal.'
When I was called upon to speak I began on my usual plan of telling
a good story to begin with . . . before going on to the more serious
part of it, at the heart of which a snoring alderman could be relied
upon to cause hilarity.[2]

After enduring dinner with the Bishop – whose home-made sherry
followed by cold beef and pickled cabbage invariably made him feel
sick – Baden-Powell would find himself sheltering from pouring rain
under the porch – nobody having thought to arrange for a car or
carriage. This then was the rat's tail growing thinner and thinner until
he found himself, soaked to the skin, being ushered into 'a cold little
bedroom at the Crossed Keys'.

Baden-Powell attended most rallies and meetings with Eric Walker,
who was by now not only his Scout Inspector but also his personal
private secretary. 'Tall, curly-haired, blue-eyed and very good
looking',[3] Walker emulated his famous master by sleeping in the open
whenever he could; he also walked vast distances and took frequent
cold dips. He considered Baden-Powell the busiest man he had ever
known, and soon found himself writing a large proportion of his
letters.[4] The two men shared a good many prejudices; they both
considered Leicester 'a beastly town, full of socialists, professional
rugger players and knighted boot-manufacturers', and thought
Birmingham little better. Apart from being a stronghold of the rebel
British Boy Scouts, the city's bishop shocked handsome young
Walker with 'his deplorably eastern method of expressing kindly
feelings'.[5] While Baden-Powell usually managed to get to bed early,
Walker was left to cope with elderly aldermen and army officers who
wanted to talk Scouting half the night.

Mercifully there were compensations for a socially ambitious young
man. Baden-Powell and Walker received numerous invitations to stay
with rich landowners, who in increasing numbers were now agreeing
to become County Commissioners. 'Lord Leigh is an excellent host
and a typical English gentleman,' wrote Walker in a characteristic
diary entry. 'Had a ripping night's sleep . . . Stoneleigh is a ripping
old place.' As befitted a Scout Inspector and a Chief Scout, he and
Baden-Powell often amused themselves on train journeys with games
such as 'sketching the history of the little actress next to us – American
boots means been in America; English clothes and lack of accent means
not there long; talk showed she was a chorus girl . . .'[6]

Walker was always impressed by Baden-Powell's good humour and
wondered how he could put up with chairmen of meetings as
disastrous as Sir Jeremiah Coleman, the mustard magnate, or manage
not to lose his temper when, through Walker's own fault, his general's
full-dress uniform was sent on by rail to the wrong town. Walker

implored him to call him a fool when he deserved it, but Baden-Powell simply replied: 'If you don't make mistakes you will never make anything else.'[7] During his six years working for the Boy Scouts (three of them as Baden-Powell's private secretary) Walker would become devoted to his chief and, in spite of an unusually peripatetic life, would never lose touch with him.

With his matrimonial plans virtually in abeyance and life at home no easier than before, it was probably just as well for Baden-Powell that he was so busy during 1911. It was during this period that Eric Walker remarked upon the 'extraordinary attraction he [Baden-Powell] had for the fair sex, although he seems to think very little of them'.[8] In August 1910, Baden-Powell and Walker had taken fifteen boys to Canada on a Scout-promoting trip. If Walker had stayed on for the extra two weeks which his master decided to spend in Canada, hunting moose and canoeing with two muscular lumber-men, he would have felt even more confident that Baden-Powell was destined to be a lifelong bachelor. Soon Baden-Powell was writing enthusiastically about the joys of grilling bass over a camp fire and being with 'men who are men'. Of Ben and Joe, his lumber-men guides, he wrote: 'It is good merely to watch their movements, their handiness and resource.' In his diary, he described 'a splendid full moon night beside a lake as still as looking glass . . . and all three [of us] bedded down on spruce tips in our tent.'[9]

Back in London in September 1911, he found that his room at 32 Prince's Gate had been 'freshly done up' by his mother as an unostentatious tribute to him in his new role of principal provider to the 'family home'.[10] But the situation in Prince's Gate was grim. Frank had developed tuberculosis and now warned that, since he was paying regular doctors' and nurses' fees, he might soon be unable to continue offering financial support for his mother. Meanwhile Warington, urged on by his endlessly patient fiancée, was talking of marrying within the year. George's rich widow was still sending an un-diminished quarterly contribution to her mother-in-law; but since Henrietta Grace had tactlessly criticized her for not bringing up her children properly, this generous subsidy was under threat.[11]

His mother's worsening finances probably explain why in 1911, in spite of his own preference for a young bride, he seriously considered marrying a widow of 50 years. He had met Mrs Juliette Gordon Low in May that year at a luncheon in Lincoln. The daughter of a prosperous American businessman and widow of the son and heir of a Scottish shipping millionaire, she had lost little time in making her interest in Baden-Powell clear to him. Nor had he been slow to introduce her to his mother. Like Baden-Powell, Juliette was a keen sculptor. In late June he invited her to watch, from the Mercers' Hall, the Royal Procession passing through the City on the day of the thanksgiving service for George V's accession. She witnessed the Tercentenary Celebrations at Charterhouse and, in early August, she asked him to stay at her Scottish fishing lodge just before he went on a fishing holiday to Norway.[12] But after his return he did not resume the relationship on the same footing. During June and July he had seen her frequently, as if recognizing the immense advantages that would accrue to his whole family if he chose to make her his bride. Her letters to him plainly intimated that she would have assented if asked. But in the end, as he tried to explain to his mother, he had felt unable to 'take a rich widow . . . A good comrade even without a fortune is what I should like . . .'[13]

A female comrade, like a male one, would of course have to be able to walk long distances and show a predisposition towards the outdoor life. A middle-aged widow would be less likely to fit this particular bill than a younger woman. John Buchan, who also married late in life, invariably made his heroines 'the open-air type, clean-run, boyish and sportsmen'.[14] As early as 1890, Baden-Powell had told his mother that the only girls for him were those keen on walking and shooting.[15] However comradely a woman of Mrs Low's age might have contrived to be in the athletic sense, producing children would still have been beyond her; and no house in Mayfair nor any Scottish shooting lodge could then have been adequate recompense.

Baden-Powell's interest in his nephew Donald was a clear indication of the strength of his paternal longings. Not only had he encouraged Donald – against his mother's wishes – to come on the first three Scout camps, but he had also tried to persuade Frances to let him accompany him to South America in 1909. Although he had failed in this last, he would continue to press her to allow him to take the boy abroad. In 1907 he had told Frances that he would 'gladly take him for the whole of his holidays if you would let him come and live with me'. The thought of bringing up a boy and 'teaching him really to ride, swim, fish, as well as to have manly ideals and thoughts' greatly appealed to him.[16] That had been the attraction of a connection with Lady Rodney: the prospect of helping with the upbringing of her four sons. After the Humshaugh Camp in 1908, Baden-Powell had described his party of boys as 'my family'.[17]

In the dying days of 1912 Baden-Powell went to the theatre with Mrs Mark Kerr, who as Rose Gough had turned down his proposal of marriage.[18] By now her husband's womanizing and ill-temper had become daily facts of life for her. Over the past two years Baden-Powell had quite often gone out alone with her and since he later made a point of telling her that she would be the first to know if ever he became engaged, they probably talked about his marital dilemma. The play they saw was called *Kismet*, but Stephe could have had no presentiment that his own destiny was about to be decided.

2. The Arcadian Girl (January 1912)

In the autumn of 1911 Baden-Powell had been introduced to an American lecture agent, Mr Lee Keedick, who at the tender age of 32 already represented English clients as famous as Sir Arthur Conan Doyle, H. G. Wells and G. K. Chesterton. Ever since his brief visit to America in 1910, Stephe had wanted to return there as part of a world tour. He not only needed to show himself to the thousands of Scouts already enrolled in countries as far apart as Chile, Denmark and Japan, but also to make sure that Sir Francis Vane's movement was not gaining ground overseas. The problem posed by cadet training (already compulsory in Australia and South Africa) was more serious, since it threatened Scouting in all the British colonies. With Keedick's offer of £1,000 for twenty lectures clinched, and free travel promised by several shipping lines, Baden-Powell had hopes of setting his Movement on a sounder footing world-wide *and* returning home with money in hand.

On 3 January 1912 he arrived at Southampton ready to embark on the S.S. *Arcadian*. He was met by his niece and nephew, who had come to wish him *bon voyage* along with 150 Scouts. Baden-Powell was accompanied by three young men whom he variously described as 'my A.D.C.s' and 'my bodyguard'.[1] These were 20-year-old 'Bob' Wroughton (brother of Dulce), who had delayed going up to Oxford in order to come with Baden-Powell; Eric Insole who had been at Harrow with Bob and had just come down from Cambridge; and Noel van Raalte whose father owned Brownsea Island. Their job would be to make all the practical arrangements on the tour, leaving him free to devote his entire attention to his lectures.

Looking down the passenger list, Baden-Powell recognized the names of two prominent surgeons and a couple of distant acquaintances. Then, disconcertingly, he saw 'Mrs A. M. Low', followed by 'Mrs Low and maid. . . .' The second Mrs Low he decided was the result of a printer's inattention. On the first day at sea a strong head wind and steep waves kept most passengers below, but on the following day Baden-Powell was less than delighted to find that the second Mrs Low, far from being a phantom, was none other than his doting widow.[2] She was travelling with friends who occupied much of her attention – which was fortunate since, before spotting her, Baden-Powell had made the acquaintance of an athletic-looking young woman who somehow seemed familiar. It was not her face which he recalled, but the way she walked. He had once made a study of different types of gait in trying to deduce, as native trackers sometimes did from footprints and length of stride, characteristics such as timidity, boldness and so forth. One day in 1909, walking in Hyde Park near Knightsbridge barracks, he had seen a girl striding along with unusually purposeful steps, a spaniel at her heels.

Two years later, on the *Arcadian*, he recognized the same gait in this girl whose name he did not know.

When introduced, I charged her with living in London. Wrong. My sleuthing was at fault; she lived in Dorsetshire!
'But have you a brown and white spaniel?'
'Yes.' (Surprise registered.)
'Were you never in London? Near Knightsbridge barracks?'
'Yes, two years ago.'[3]

Not unnaturally 23-year-old Miss Olave Soames, to whom these remarks were addressed, was astounded by the phenomenal memory which had retained an almost cinematographic record of that earlier glimpse of her. Baden-Powell, who for two decades had hoped to meet genuinely athletic girls, had certainly struck lucky. In the summer months Olave often disposed of ten sets of tennis in a day; she rode to hounds, swam, bicycled, skated, played hockey, squash (usually the preserve of public schoolboys) and went on admirably long walks with her father.

That evening at dinner, Baden-Powell sat next to Olave's father at the Captain's table. His first impression, never subsequently altered, was of an over-serious, bookish man very much older than himself. In reality Soames was only three years his senior. Even though Olave's father shared Baden-Powell's enthusiasm for painting, the two men found conversation difficult.[4] Soames's educational background was impeccable. After Eton he had gone to Cambridge and, while still an undergraduate, had inherited a brewery from his grandfather. He sold it ten years later for almost £300,000, enabling him to live for the rest of his life as a gentleman of leisure.[5] But this brought him little happiness. Being restless and dissatisfied, he moved frequently from place to place, renting historic houses like Renishaw and Cranborne Manor, nursing the illusion that one day he would find somewhere in which he would be content. During Olave's first twenty years, her parents moved house seventeen times. In the winter her father usually went to paint in the South of France or Italy for three or four months and sometimes, as on the present occasion, he took Olave with him for a briefer winter trip.

Whereas Baden-Powell intended to sail on from the West Indies to New York, Soames and his daughter meant to remain in Jamaica until March. As chairman of the ship's Sports and Amusements Committee, Baden-Powell was greatly impressed by Olave's prowess in every kind of deck game – including potato racing.[6] On 12 January, two days after her triumph at a notable Sports Day, Baden-Powell was able to impress her in his turn at a concert given by 'The Atlantic Stars'.[7] But even before he sang 'The Queen of my Heart', Olave had felt strongly drawn to him. 'Had B-P to myself all day till 11.00 p.m.,' she had written in her diary on the 10th. 'Such interesting conversation on religion etc., sitting aft watching phosphorous balls of light whilst other people dance.'

Since 1889, when he had expressed a desire to read some of his father's religious writings, Baden-Powell had rarely attended church and scarcely ever mentioned religion in his letters. Strangely, in talking of such matters at the start of his courtship, he was following a family tradition. His father and Henrietta Grace – who like Olave had been a girl far younger than her future husband – had filled *their* earliest intimate conversations with such talk. But in Baden-Powell's case the choice of subject seems genuinely surprising. With hindsight though, it can be recognized as an example of the remarkable ease he felt in Olave's company right from the beginning. Miss Soames's earnest expression as she listened delighted him, and she herself was no less excited. Just as *she* appeared to be the answer to a prayer for a man with Baden-Powell's preference for the athletic type of girl, *he* was just as clearly exactly what she needed.

Her relationships with young men had all been unsatisfactory. Indeed, one reason for her trip on the *Arcadian* had been, as her mother put it, 'to blow away the dust of unhappy memories'. In the past she had been unable to fall in love with men of her own generation although convinced that she ought to be able to do so. Thus she had often given her suitors signs of strong interest, followed by an alarmed retreat once their ardour had been aroused. Her mother considered that Olave habitually confused pity with love. 'My little girl is *so sorry* for each one who finds her bright nature hard to resist. So, distressing complications arise – and we stumble away from sad appeals.'[8]

For all her father's wealth, Olave had endured an unhappy adolescence and was extremely insecure. Her parents ought to have divorced, but, because their money enabled them to spend long periods apart – Katharine in London and Harold in the country or abroad – they had continued to remain on speaking terms. During Olave's childhood her father had still loved her mother, who had originally married him to escape a life of poverty as a governess or paid companion. Unfortunately their tastes were completely different: he was a reclusive countryman, she a lover of metropolitan life. Harold implored her to interest herself in his landscape painting, but she did not respond. By the time Olave was 12 her parents slept in different bedrooms. Harold would often beg Katharine to come with him on his country walks; but in vain. Eighty years later, their former parlour-maid still remembered how upset he had been at these rebuffs.

Annie Court, the 14-year-old girl in question, had started work with the family in 1904 when they had just moved to Devonshire. She recalled Katharine's unconcealed preference for her son Arthur and her elder daughter Auriol; also her equally obvious rejection of Olave.[9] 'I was always the "runty" one who got pushed out,' Olave remembered. Respectively three and four years older than she, Arthur and Auriol 'were in every way superior to me; I was the dunce of the family.'[10] Not only made to feel intellectually inadequate, she was also led to believe that she was ugly. Until her mid-teens, she was small and thin for her age and wore her hair cut short like a boy's.[11] In reality she was a striking-looking girl with dark lustrous eyes, full lips and an intense, almost mesmeric gaze. Her mother's antipathy to her was due in part to her closeness to her father; while Auriol and Arthur often went to stay in London with their mother for weeks at a time, Olave usually remained in the country with Harold.

Katharine was so much a metropolitan person that, even when walking in the garden, she would wear flowing late Victorian formal clothes with a broad-brimmed Gainsborough hat and gloves. Auriol was always dressed in the height of fashion. By comparison Olave's wardrobe was neglected – not that she minded, since by the time she was 18 she had developed a dislike for conventional female clothing. While Auriol was entering London 'Society', Olave was out shooting with her father or playing squash or tennis with him. In 1908, when he moved to Parkstone just outside Bournemouth, he built a squash court so that he and Olave could play together. In local tennis matches she always partnered him and accompanied him on walks. 'I adored him,' she recalled. 'He and I were great companions . . .'[12] Harold had always hoped that she would be a boy and, in anticipation, had chosen the old Danish name of Olaf. When his 'son' had turned out to be a daughter, he had insisted that she be called Olave (pronounced Olev).[13] In many ways she *was* like a son to him, compensating him for Katharine's theft of the affections of the two older children.

The servants used to call her 'poor little Miss Olave', and for the same reason her father called her his 'little Thumbie'.[14] Just as Olave had been persuaded by Katharine that she was ugly, so lovely little Thumbelina had been told that she was plain by the female cockchafers. Yet Thumbelina revived the swallow who would otherwise have died of cold and he rewarded her by carrying her away from her unhappy surroundings to warm and beautiful lands. Harold too had felt the chill of a loveless marriage and had been warmed by the love of his 'little Thumbie', whom he spirited away to exotic foreign countries in the winter. Yet often he went alone and although Olave needed him, his deep depressions frequently held her at arms' length. In March 1910 Katharine described him as 'almost unhinged by his distressing nerves, in winter and so often besides . . .'[15]

In 1897, in the Lake District, Katharine had met a beautiful young woman called Jean Graham who was gentle, well-read and played the piano exquisitely. After the departure of Olave's former governess,

Katharine somehow persuaded this paragon to come as an informal tutor and companion to the child. Jean, as Olave later affirmed, 'had a big influence on my life as a child . . . I admired her more than I can say . . . She was utterly charming . . . As far as indoor pursuits were concerned, she was everything I wanted to be.'[16] Jean's influence was all the greater on account of Olave's alienation from Katharine. A girl usually learns what it is to be a woman from her mother, but in Olave's case, her mother's indifference to her beloved father and her scorn for the sporting activities they enjoyed together made her reject Katharine as her model for any adult female role that she might ultimately adopt. But Jean Graham, with her accomplishments and femininity, enabled Olave – after her years as a tomboy – to identify with a female. It was therefore a savage blow to her when her idol was suddenly disgraced.

Although Katharine wrote discreetly about the discovery she made in December 1909, her meaning is perfectly clear. 'I will bury deep the ashes of this year. They hold disillusion – a lost friendship. A pitiful wreckage of trust. So – after 12 years – I write farewell to the fair Jean Graham who left me a wiser – and certainly a sadder woman.'[17] Given Katharine's treatment of Harold his affairs were not very surprising, and Olave later told her husband's secretary, Eileen Wade, about this particular liaison. Olave must have felt almost as much betrayed as had her mother: here was the woman whom she had admired more than any other seducing her adored father and making relations between her already unhappy parents even worse. This affair was not Harold's last, and in 1911 and 1912 he became entangled with other women.[18]

One consequence of Jean's disappearance from Olave's life was a corresponding increase in the influence of a very different woman. Sybil Mounsey-Heysham, known to her friends as 'Ba', became a friend of the Soames family in about 1900. Her father owned Branksome Park – a magnificent house in Bournemouth – and a substantial estate in Cumberland where Olave went to stay for the first time in 1903. In that year Katharine Soames wrote of Sybil as 'a clever, original, gentle, manly, astonishing and altogether delightful thing called Ba, who charms equally, sportsman, child, and critical woman – to which sex she officially belongs! This is, however, only a fact she cares to emphasize on rare occasions.'[19] In that psychologically unsophisticated era, even women as prettily feminine as Katharine Soames could accept without embarrassment members of that stalwart breed of English women whose collars and ties, cropped hair and tweeds made them instantly recognizable during the first two decades of the present century. 'Ba' would add to this basic masculine equipment webbing puttees like those later worn in the trenches. When Olave met her, she was widely reputed to be one of the three finest duck shots in the country – the others being the Earl of Leicester and Lord William Percy, who once stayed out all night with her on the

Solway marshes bagging with her a record 64 geese before morning.[20] She used to say that her father's head gamekeeper had taught her all she knew – and she was undoubtedly a knowledgeable ornithologist. She had a gaunt, sharp-featured face and was rather unkempt, with buttons missing from her jackets and shoelaces trailing dangerously. An accomplished amateur violinist, she would swear volubly when she played false notes. Among other eccentricities she used to stuff her pockets with cigarettes, so that she could give them to any soldiers she happened to encounter at railway stations. 'Ba' struck everyone as a vivid and unique character of whom people would say quite matter-of- factly that she ought to have been a man.[21] Indeed, in her house there is to this day an attractive portrait of her dressed in a naval officer's uniform.

Olave found Sybil 'an example and an inspiration'. When she stayed with her, they tramped together on the moors and sailed and shot and rode. At that time Olave had not yet learned to ride side-saddle and was adept at riding bareback. She stayed at Castletown as often as she could, and was there in November 1911 shortly before her cruise on the *Arcadian*.[22] Since she detested her mother's Dresden china view of women and the conventional female elegance of her sister, 'Ba's' absolute indifference to etiquette and fashion was wonderfully liber- ating. Given Olave's later preference for wearing uniform and her disinclination to go to dressmakers, it would appear that Sybil exercised an influence over her greater than any other with the possible exception of her father's.[23] Sybil it was who suggested that Olave take up the violin, and in deference to her mode of dress Olave had taken to wearing puttees in the summer of 1903.[24] Sybil's influence is apparent in a photograph (see third photo-section) which shows a kind of game going on between them. Light-hearted fun perhaps but, with Olave between the shafts of the little carriage and 'Ba' wielding a whip in the driving seat, it cannot but suggest a Svengali-like control by the older woman.

Sadly for Olave, Cumberland was far away and visits were therefore only possible a few times a year. So when her father was in one of his depressions or travelling, she felt terribly lonely. In desperation she used to beg Annie Court, the parlourmaid – the only servant of her own age in her parents' household – to come to her bedroom at night to keep her company. Annie told her she would get into trouble with the other servants for over-familiarity. 'I used to say I can't,' Annie recalled, 'they'll hear me going back, and I'm frightened of the dark.' And in a large Tudor house who could blame her? But Olave told her not to be stupid and gave her her own silver candlestick. 'I used to go because she was so miserable,' recollected Annie.[25]

In the months before her voyage on the *Arcadian*, Olave had found herself increasingly needing to 'hurl herself passionately into every activity to smother dissatisfaction with her life'.[26] Not that she was denied the best that the contemporary theatre or concert halls could offer; she saw Forbes Robertson's Hamlet, watched Nikisch conduct and heard Kreisler play. But always there was the same old problem: how to find somebody she could love. She had begun to suffer from recurrent headaches and other symptoms of 'nerves'; she felt that her existence was meaningless. For a while after her parents moved to Bournemouth, she did what she could to entertain the children at a local convalescent home, but she knew she would never have the patience to be of real assistance to sick children.[27] In 1911 her sister married a rich Scottish tea planter with estates in Ceylon and this placed even greater pressure on Olave to find a man she could love. The pattern of the past repeated itself: another young man proposed and once again she refused. 'I had an awful suicidal fit of the blues,' she wrote in her diary. 'I sat on the sea shore . . . and made my hanky a wet pulp . . . how I wish I could love him enough to be engaged.'[28]

She did become briefly and secretly engaged to her cousin, Noel Soames, during the summer of 1911, shortly before Auriol's wedding; but as usual, within a week she retracted. The same disastrous sequence seemed imminent in December, the victim this time being a young officer in the Shropshire Light Infantry. On this occasion though, Olave escaped with her father on the *Arcadian*, before having to deliver the usual *coup de grâce*. Three days before sailing she had written in her diary, on the first day of the New Year: 'Well, I do hope, Olave, you will have a better year this time than last.' Then on the day her ship sailed: 'There is only one interesting person on board and that is the Boy Scout man.'[29] Her past record might have suggested that he ought to look out. This time, however, Olave was destined to learn something of how her suitors had felt.

3. The Reluctant Bridegroom (January to October 1912)

By 17 January, just two weeks after sailing from Southampton, Olave was confiding to her diary: 'Up before dawn just to see him and kiss him. See Venezuela coast in distance . . . Small talks with various people and the beloved Scout is always there. He gives me a photo album and sketches . . . I adore him.' Six days later matters were going on much the same: 'She pitches like anything, but, oh, I'm so happy all day with him. He sketches away and I talk and we laugh together . . . We feel and think alike about everything. Perfect bliss.'[1]

Nevertheless they had to be circumspect. As Olave herself put it: 'Shipboard romances are notorious and it would not have done for a distinguished General of fifty-five, and the founder of Scouting . . . to be caught flirting with a girl of twenty-three . . . hence the stolen kisses before dawn. Hence the secret little notes that were "posted" in a cleat of one of the lifeboats. Hence the elaborate subterfuge of his going forward on the ship after dinner and my going aft, and meeting secretly at a pre-arranged point on the boat deck.'[2]

Olave described herself at the time of her meeting with Baden-Powell as 'such an ordinary person, not at all clever, with no experience of life whatsoever'.[3] But Baden-Powell, with his long list of friendships with young girls, would have found her lack of sophistication a bonus rather than a drawback. The less mature she was in a conventionally feminine way, the more he was likely to be drawn to her. In spite of her parents' unhappiness, Olave had remained not only naïve and suggestible but open, enthusiastic and eager to commit herself to this man who seemed capable of offering her the kind of paternal guidance and love which her adored but depressive father had only fitfully managed to provide. Baden-Powell had always been successful with adolescents because he genuinely liked them – intuitively understanding, and indeed sharing, many of their anxieties. Because Olave's mother had dispensed with governesses and school-ing for her when she was 12, she had grown used to a life of un-restricted freedom in the country. So the prospect of marrying a man who had pioneered a scheme enabling city boys to enjoy the countryside with as few constraints as possible had strongly appealed to her. In the early days there were a number of troops run by 'Lady Scoutmasters', and Olave soon imagined herself in that role, wearing the Boy Scouts' uniform, rather than that of the recently established girls' Movement.[4] She was a strange compound of child and grown woman, having learned nothing in the formal way but having spent much of her time with unhappy adults. Therefore she could present to Baden-Powell two very different aspects of herself: as a tomboy she could be instructed and led in the same kind of way as he enjoyed directing boys like his nephew; as a sensitive young woman she could treat him with the care and sympathy which she had grown used to lavishing upon her father. Women as unsophisticated girls or caring mothers had never alarmed Baden-Powell, so in this respect Olave and Stephe seemed ideally suited. The girl who had backed away whenever a young man had become too ardent would find an older, more reti-cent man less threatening, just as *his* anxieties would be allayed by a sporting girl whose interest in outdoor comradeship seemed at least as great as her desire for sexual fulfilment.

Comradeship was the theme of the first letter to Olave, written immediately after he sailed on to America, leaving her in Jamaica. He explained that the pain of missing her was 'exactly the feeling I had when my two mates had been killed in Matabeleland'.[5] That he thought of her as a mixture of young woman, male comrade and child friend is apparent in his earliest letters. He had once written to Dulce

Wroughton and the others in much the same way. Shortly before reaching New York, he wrote telling Olave that he was trying to work, 'but you keep putting your oar in and interrupting me . . . but you mustn't do it. Run away and play. I'm fearfully busy and have not time to sit down and write to little girls.'[6]

But regardless of a jocularity reminiscent of his correspondence with children, his seriousness about Olave was not in doubt. The voyage, he told her, had 'brought me the happiest time I ever had'.[7] Being in love, he said, was like having internal stitches which pulled tight when he thought of her.[8]

But judging by everything they wrote, Olave was undoubtedly the more smitten of the two. The only mention *he* made in his diary of their traumatic parting in Kingston, Jamaica was succinct: 'Perfect night on D.T. Pivi!' Olave's version of the same event provides a key to this coded entry. The evening before he sailed, leaving her behind, they had sat together on a little bridge – a 'dangletoes', he had called it (the D.T. in his diary) – and she had cried for several hours at the thought of being parted from him. Hence his abbreviated form of the common Edwardian expression for copious weeping: 'crying capivi'.[9] In the only other contemporary reference to Olave in his diary, Baden-Powell gave no clue that he was emotionally involved.

Not so she. 'He is never out of my mind – unconsciously I feel him always with me and it is heavenly – and yet just too awful to have to wait so long for his return . . .'[10] His letters to her continued to be cheerful and affectionate rather than passionate; the beginning of one written on 5 March from San Francisco is typical: 'Oh! Why aren't you here at this moment! Running through the Sierra Nevada – how silly of you . . . Oh! Fruit trees all in blossom! For goodness sake come and look!'[11] In another letter he asked, after describing his childhood games in Kensington Gardens, whether she was 'perhaps Wendy?' This followed a letter inviting her to go to a performance of *Peter Pan* as soon as he returned.[12] Given his love for Barrie's play this was promising enough, but Olave failed to take account of warning signs.

On 30 January, as the *Arcadian* had steamed towards New York, Baden-Powell had written ominously: 'You agreed with me that it was hopeless to talk or think sensibly while on board this ship – and I have not been able to do so yet . . . But I see the "difficulties" looming very large: especially on my part and that is as regards money – even if my age were forgiven. People can not live on less than 1200 to 1500 and that is pretty low – but I don't see where it is to come from in my case . . .'[13] A few weeks after receiving this missive, Olave opened another so distressing that she tore it up. In it Baden-Powell told her about his brother Frank's illness, and how this prevented him contributing further to Henrietta Grace's household expenses. This meant that her 'beloved Scout' would have to increase his own payments to his mother. 'By the time I have paid my mother's allowance,' she recalled him telling her, 'I shall scarcely be able to keep a dog.' He ended by telling her that she should feel free to marry whomsoever else she might see fit.[14]

This letter was written shortly before one sent to his mother on 16 March.[15] Henrietta Grace was informed that he had just written to Donald, inviting the boy to 'join me when I reach home for a short trip to camp and fish in Norway'.[16] Olave's subsequent version of events was that before meeting her on the *Arcadian*, Baden-Powell had invited Donald to go on this Norwegian jaunt. She wished to give the impression that he would never have contemplated rushing off to Norway or anywhere else immediately after his eight months' tour, unless he had felt bound to do so by a promise made before he had fallen in love with her. It might be supposed that the letter he sent to Donald in mid-March merely confirmed an earlier undertaking; but a letter to Donald's mother dated 30 March rules this out, since in it Baden-Powell was clearly asking her for the first time whether he might take Donald to Norway. He had already decided to spend the briefest possible time in England between returning from his world tour and departing for Scandinavia. 'I hope to get back about 17 August,' he told Frances, 'then I want to go to Norway.' He wanted to teach Donald 'fishing and get the chance of long talks . . . in the place of a father . . .'[17] Baden-Powell would not have formed so definite a plan unless convinced that his mid-March letter to Olave would end their relationship. If he had remained passionately eager to marry her, it is inconceivable that he would have allowed financial considerations to deter him before he had even found out what sort of a dowry she might bring.

In his letter of 30 January, he had mentioned £1,200 as the lowest possible income on which a couple of his and Olave's class could decently get married. As a rich man's daughter Olave could have been expected to bring a dowry producing at least £500 per annum, leaving Stephe a mere £700 to find. Since he had an annual pension of £850 from the army this would have posed no problem. In fact his misrepresentation of his true circumstances was staggering. In 1912 he was no longer giving the British royalties from *Scouting for Boys* to the Scouts' organization, but was receiving them himself to the value of about £750 per annum.[18] (This was in spite of his gift of the copyright to the Scout Association.) His other Scouting copyrights and the Girl Guides' handbook were bringing in at least £700.[19] In March 1910, Arthur Pearson had agreed to pay Baden-Powell half an annual licence fee of £500 a year for *The Scout* and 5 per cent of that paper's annual profits (at least another £250).[20] Then there was his journalism – the *Graphic* paid him £100 in March 1912 – bringing in say £250 in total. Add to that his American lectures, producing £800 after expenses,[21] and a total of

£4,100 from all sources is arrived at. This was almost four times greater than his minimum marriage figure of £1,200.

It was true that he would soon be expected to contribute more to his mother's expenses, but here too he misrepresented the scale. In March 1912, Frank was convalescing in Menton and still paying his mother an allowance. Baden-Powell did not ask her for an accurate estimate of her expenses until he received Olave's outraged reply to his bombshell letter. In September Henrietta Grace would calculate that she would need from him (assuming no further help from Warington and Frank) £500 per annum towards her total annual outgoings of £1,320.[22] So even if Stephe had considered his 1912 income freakishly high, there would have been no genuine financial obstacle to marriage. Furthermore his mother was 88, and on her death her children knew they would inherit the freehold of 32 Prince's Gate. This had been gifted to the family only a month before the *Arcadian* sailed by the wealthy husband of one of Henrietta Grace's oldest friends.[23]

So, although Olave later made out that Baden-Powell had written to her as he had out of an honourable desire to spare her a life of penury, in reality he had been scared off by the intensity of her feelings and had pleaded poverty as a let-out.

After his tours of America and Japan were over, Baden-Powell arrived in Sydney in mid-May to find a letter from Olave in which she poured scorn on his financial worries and told him to find out exactly what was required for running his mother's house, since she was sure she could persuade her father to help.[24] Shaken by her indignation, Baden-Powell returned a contrite reply. 'I know that I ought not to have written to you as I did . . . I was at that time full of those confounded cons and I just rattled them down as they occurred to me . . . Do please forgive. I am trying to find out how things promise at home.' This did not fully commit him, since it was still open to him to suggest later that the expenses reckoned up by his mother were impossibly heavy. Henrietta Grace's possible reaction to Olave clearly worried him. 'I am only afraid that you will be disappointed if I married an ordinary girl . . .', he confided at this time.[25]

Unlike Olave, with her empty days at home, Baden-Powell was so busy on tour that he had little leisure for reflection. In eight months he travelled more than 70,000 miles and gave 41 lectures, 63 speeches and 69 addresses to Scouts. His homecoming on 24 August, and the way in which he spent his time before leaving for Norway three days later, must rule out any idea that he considered himself engaged to Olave. Yet that is what she considered him to be. In William Hillcourt's biography, which was written with Olave's co-operation, it is stated that she knew that Baden-Powell was going to travel straight to Norway with Donald without coming to see her en route.[26] But that seems most unlikely, given how upset she was at his failure to make contact. Looking back, she would never know how to treat this episode. She told Hillcourt that Baden-Powell had informed her father of the engagement *after* his return to England. In her autobiography, published ten years later in 1974, she claimed that he had told her father about their engagement in July *before* his return.[27] But if Baden-Powell had by then given any firm undertaking about marriage, either to her or to her father, it would have been quite impossible for him to have considered spending three days in England, before his departure to Norway with Donald, without making any attempt to see her or even to contact her by telephone. A few days before his return, Olave had been writing joyfully in her diary of her 'heart beating time to these passing seconds – passing quickly at last . . .'[28]

At Southampton, where he landed on the morning of 24 August, he was only a few miles along the coast from Poole. But instead of going to see Olave, he hurried up to London and lunched there with his mother and Frank. Next day he travelled to Guildford to see Sir Edmond Elles, who was still Chief Commissioner and had therefore been in nominal charge of the Movement during his absence. He spent the whole of Monday at Scout Headquarters and the following morning set out for Norway with Donald.[29]

While Baden-Powell was in Norway he received a letter from Harold Soames which, according to Olave, persuaded him to hurry back to England at once. In fact he spent the full two weeks there that he had originally planned.[30] Harold's letter has not survived, but that he sent one can be deduced from the fact that the very moment Baden-Powell arrived back in England on 13 September, he sent a telegram to Soames at Parkstone assuring him that he would be with him that very evening.[31] He made this undertaking in spite of having arrived at Hull at two o'clock that morning, after almost three days of non-stop travel; only a matter of immense urgency could have caused such haste. Whether Soames had made a veiled threat of breach of promise proceedings, or had simply written angrily about the way his daughter had been treated, is beyond knowing. But whatever his communication contained, it was wonderfully effective. As Baden-Powell's ship had approached Hull, he had written to 'Bob' Wroughton (one of his 'young men' on the *Arcadian*) jocularly reproving him 'for not looking after me better' and explaining that he would not be able to attend his birthday celebrations in Northamptonshire because 'I am engaged to Miss Soames.'[32] So he had known even before returning that he would have to marry, whether he liked it or not. Baden-Powell was not an inconsiderate man by nature, so to have treated Olave as he did he must have been in a state of fearful uncertainty. Most of his life he had been 'too young', or too busy, or just disinclined to contemplate marriage. And now, after many years spent trying to find a suitable girl and with success staring him in the face, he had panicked. He had thought she would be discouraged by the problems he had raised, but she had simply tossed them aside. Only panic can explain his flight without a word. Given his lack of enthusiasm for women both anatomically and aesthetically, fear of sexual failure was probably the principal reason for his inability to contact her.

But Stephe was a realist. From the moment he knew that marriage to Olave was inevitable, he put a brave face on it, doubtless comforted by the thought that if any woman could live up to the ideal comradely type he had had in mind for over a decade it was Olave. The Soames's house, Grey Rigg, was a large but undistinguished Edwardian mansion with superb views over Poole harbour. It was just outside the village of Lilliput which Dean Swift, a former resident, had immortalized. Olave's later account of his arrival is characteristic of her way of forcing events to mean what she wanted them to.

She collected Baden-Powell from the station and brought him to Grey Rigg in time for dinner. 'Poor darling in his frantic haste to reach me, he had forgotten his razor! It was amusing, really – the great B–P himself, the man who had given the watchword "Be Prepared" to countless men and boys, being so flustered with love that he forgot his razor! Hardy, our Butler, lent him his own razor, with the result that he cut himself shaving and had to appear at dinner with sticking-plaster on his chin!'[33] That Baden-Powell's 'flustered' condition owed more to a sense of shock than anything else comes over clearly in a letter he sent to Olave from London the following day.

> My life was spread out green and placid like a quiet calm lake when bang comes a dynamite bomb out of an aeroplane . . . and upsets the whole caboodle. And you're the bomb. I can't be the same being who walked the deck of that ship in the North Sea during Thursday night, with a grip clutching his throat with a mighty fear – to find himself on Friday night in a dazed condition in the South of England . . . [34]

Having described his perplexity he went on to parade his new-found happiness, but his 'fear' could have had nothing to do with being refused. Given Olave's determination, he knew Harold Soames could hardly have summoned him to Parkstone with the intention of sending him packing again.

For Soames and for Baden-Powell the occasion must have been an awkward one, and not only on account of the similarity in their ages. Thanks to the hero of Mafeking, Olave's parents had been obliged to endure hysterical scenes during the past month. Her mother would never think him 'a man to be liked'; she attributed his insensitivity to 'a nature hardened by long fighting and much scheming'.[35] Harold Soames quickly consented when his famous guest put the inevitable question; he then said he would settle enough capital on her to produce £1,000 a year. He would have preferred Olave to marry a younger and a richer man, but he did not share his wife's violent prejudice against the Scouts and the Guides.

If the Soames family was not very enthusiastic about Baden-Powell, Henrietta Grace was equally frosty about them. Before his mother first met Olave, Stephe assured her that his bride-to-be would be an 'invaluable adviser . . . and a real playmate', but he warned Henrietta Grace that she 'would probably not see this at first glance'.[36] In July, in writing to his mother, he had expressed himself 'afraid' that she would be 'disappointed' if he married an immature girl instead of a rich and accomplished widow.[37] He was perfectly right. When Olave met Henrietta Grace for the first time on 18 September, she found her 'sophisticated, cold and aloof'. Henrietta Grace was also angry at the flippant way in which her son had announced their engagement, having given no prior indication of any special interest in a particular girl.[38] (Of course he could hardly have explained to his mother how Olave had bounced him into marriage.) 'I had been wondering what to give you as a birthday present,' he had begun his offending letter, 'but I think I've got one now that will please you . . . and that is a daughter-in-law for you!'[39]

Stephe agreed with Katharine Soames that 'a secret marriage' would be preferable to 'a public upheaval in London'.[40] Henrietta Grace, however, was bitterly disappointed that there would be no big ceremony involving the Boy Scouts and her son's two regiments. A quiet ceremony in Bournemouth would be entirely in the hands of Mr and Mrs Soames, who were doubtless very rich but, in Henrietta Grace's eyes, nobodies who had made their fortune in trade. A date six weeks ahead was privately set for the wedding – the press only being told about an engagement. Baden-Powell carried on his usual Scout inspections and regularly visited Olave at Lilliput. He watched her play squash with her father and heard her play the violin; they went on long country walks and attended a few public functions together.[41]

During this period Baden-Powell must have been particularly aware of his lack of real friends. He saw nothing of McLaren and George Noble; he chatted with Eric Walker and A. G. Wade, the new Joint Secretary at Headquarters, but they were both 30 years his junior and hardly friends in any ordinary sense. The only men at the wedding at St Peter's Church, Parkstone, on 30 October, were Baden-Powell's brother Baden, acting as his best man; Major-General R. G. Kekewich, the defender of Kimberley, who was no more than an acquaintance but had become friends with members of the Soames family when they lived in Devonshire; Robert Davidson, Auriol's husband; and Harold Soames. The only women to attend were Katharine Soames; Miss Sie Bower who, with the exception of Sybil

Mounsey-Heysham, was Olave's closest friend; and Agnes Baden-Powell.[42]

Henrietta Grace had excused herself but Agnes, as her representative, was understandably hurt not to be invited to stay overnight with the family before the wedding. She was not even met at the station and had to telephone for a fly. On her arrival a manservant told her that the family was 'not at home', and only changed his tune on hearing her name. Agnes was also distressed when, immediately after the wedding, Katharine Soames left to join her elder daughter at Montacute House, which Bob Davidson was renting for a year. 'No attempt at asking me to the house!' Agnes told her mother incredulously. Nor would Olave and Stephe chat for a moment afterwards, but rushed to catch the next London train.[43] Relations between Olave and Agnes would soon be disastrously bad. 'There was never any love lost between us,' recalled Olave. 'She was a terrible snob and would have liked her brother to have made a much better match.'[44]

On the evening of her wedding day, Olave sat down by the fire in the large Kensington flat which her mother had loaned to them, and wrote in her diary: 'Is it really true, my darling is truly my very own, after three months of waiting and wondering?'[45] Indeed it was, and very much through Olave's toughness and tenacity. At the end of each annual diary, Baden-Powell usually summarized his achievements during the year. Olave would have been amused if she had read, after a long list of the foreign lectures he had delivered, these words: 'Met, marked down, and married Olave.'[46]

4. Settling Down (1912–14)

'I am really very happy, Ma,' Baden-Powell told Henrietta Grace in a letter written on his wedding night.[1] There is often a sense of something forced in his numerous protestations of happiness, and his lavish praise for Olave in every letter to his mother reinforces this impression. His anxiety lest he fail to persuade people of his married happiness at times even entered his dreams, in one of which he was anguished to think that he might not have persuaded Baden 'how happy we were though married . . .'[2]

They spent the first week of November honeymooning at an hotel in Mullion, a small Cornish fishing village on the western side of the Lizard Peninsula. The adjacent coastline is rocky and exposed, but in spite of the season Baden-Powell and his wife stayed indoors as little as possible, going on 'delightful walks . . . taking lunch in our pockets every day, and staying out the whole day in the fresh air'.[3] Yet happy or not – within a month Baden-Powell was too ill to keep social engagements, let alone go for walks. The Cornish climate was not to blame however.

He had last been ill in 1901 when he suffered a nervous collapse brought about by stress and overwork. Since then, apart from an attack of lumbago in 1908 and periodic problems with one of his knees, his health had been excellent.[4] Before the end of November he was suffering from broken sleep and piercing headaches on waking. Although deeply suspicious of the new science of psychoanalysis, he was sufficiently distressed by these headaches to keep a record of the vivid dreams which invariably preceded them.[5] In Chapter Three I quoted passages from several, including one in which he mistook his hotel bedroom and found himself not with Olave but in the company of a young man, who had whistled to him in just the way his wife normally did. Many other dreams involved young men, such as the guardsman who snatched away his whip and asked whether he had ever been 'disciplined'.

Baden-Powell's view of female sexuality as a danger to men emerged in a dream in which he worried as to whether some kitchen maids were 'likely to be dangerous to the morals of my young officers'. Having kept the realities of manhood at bay for so long by seeing manliness in terms of self-restraint, he was at long last confronted with the very situation in which manliness could only be proved by lack of restraint. He had exhorted others to employ will-power to overcome their physical desires; now he would have to use his own will-power to summon up what he had previously been concerned to suppress in others.

Married life did not persuade Baden-Powell to revise his opinion about sexual desire only lasting for a few months during adolescence. But by relegating sex to the position of a transitory function within marriage, linked only to its procreative purpose, he probably increased his chances of finding married life satisfactory. And headaches regardless, his claims to be happy even at the start of his marriage should not be cavalierly dismissed. These headaches would owe most to sexual repugnance and anxiety, but marriage itself must have posed other problems of adaptation for such a long-standing bachelor. Apart from suffering headaches, he was soon running a temperature and appeared to have caught a chill. His doctor blamed 'African fever' brought on by overwork.[6] A relapsing form of malaria, contracted either during the 1895 Ashanti Campaign or in East Africa in 1906, could have laid him low all these years later, but it is curious that he had only been affected by feverish symptoms once before, when he had suffered his nervous collapse in 1901.[7] Since his headaches would persist for years, and long after all signs of fever had disappeared, they must be considered a separate phenomenon. In April the following year, these headaches were as bad as ever.[8] He continued to be plagued by them until he acquired Pax Hill in 1918 and began to sleep on an outside balcony all the year round. He told a friend that 'he used to suffer greatly from headaches until he adopted this way of slumber'.[9] However the additional ration of fresh air was not the only change involved in this arrangement. For the first time since he had married, he was sleeping apart from Olave; and with their family by then completed (their third child having been born in April 1917) his need for procreative performance ceased. Baden-Powell would continue to sleep on his own until his death. Nocturnal separation would not, however, bring about any diminution of their affection for each other – quite the contrary. Their marriage would grow stronger as time passed. Olave's and Stephe's love was founded less upon sexual attraction than upon their complementary needs, a community of interest and mutual respect which together proved more enduring than passion. Permanent companionship and family life with children were what Baden-Powell had wanted and what he got.

When he returned to London from Cornwall, his illness came and went in a perplexing manner. He and Olave stayed in several great houses, which she found an extraordinary and faintly absurd experience. It amused her that her mother was jealous of her social 'success'.[10] Later in his life, Baden-Powell would deny ever having enjoyed the large Edwardian shoots organized on so many aristocratic estates, but his diary suggests otherwise.[11] By mid-December he was too ill to keep any engagements and he only just managed to attend the belated wedding reception which he and Olave laid on at the Mercers' Hall. A Scout choir sang carols and there was a display of presents; 100,000 Scouts had contributed a penny each towards a 20-horse-power Standard landaulette car. Roland Philipps's mother, Lady St Davids, was shocked by Baden-Powell's appearance and offered him the use of Roch Castle in Pembrokeshire for the two weeks over Christmas. A full staff and panoramic views went with this five-storey tower.

Before leaving for Wales Baden-Powell had been able to report to his mother that Olave was proving 'an excellent nurse'. Six weeks later he rather tactlessly told her that 'Olave looks after me like a mother'.[12] Many years later, one of his daughters recalled that her father had often played a game of being a little boy, pretending that Olave was his mother, cross with him over some trifling matter such as not wearing warm enough clothes or getting wet.[13] Olave enjoyed this role, confiding to her diary: 'It is lovely nursing him.'[14] He was her exalted idol, but through his illness she came into her own as his surrogate mother.

Nor was her authority in this role to be taken lightly. By the beginning of the New Year, she was writing to Eric Walker dressing him down smartly for allowing her husband to overwork. 'I don't want to be grandmotherly and possessive,' she told this young man a year or two older than herself, 'but you are "haring round" more than is good for the Chief.'[15] Nor did Olave shrink from sorting out unruly members of the family. After leaving Eton, her husband's nephew Donald struck her as 'thoughtless, careless and lazy'. While staying with his uncle, the boy not only broke Baden-Powell's ejector (an appliance for discharging empty cartridges) and a boomerang presented to him by the Australian Boy Scouts, but missed his train and obliged his uncle to drive him over twenty miles in the dark. Worst of all, Olave caught him kissing her between-maid or 'tweeny'.

> Oh Donald, how COULD you? [she wrote]. You may say what is a kiss – a mere nothing. Yes, perhaps it is to those who know no better and to cads who think it rather fun, and swagger and carry on with low class girls. You aren't one of those though are you. . . ? Try to develop yourself into what you ought to be – a fine manly man and a manly gentleman. Be a *Scout!*[16]

Before going to Wales to recuperate, Baden-Powell had planned to take Olave to North Africa. They sailed in mid-January, bound for Algiers; then leaving the city, they travelled by train to the mountains flanking the Sahara east of Biskra. There they trekked up into the hills on foot accompanied by two armed Arab guides. Baden-Powell was delighted to discover that Olave was 'an excellent Scout in finding her way' Nor was that all. 'She quite astonished the French landlord [at the hotel in Biskra] by her walking powers.' Each day they walked, and in the evening pitched their tents. 'She is a perfect wonder in camp,' he told his mother, 'and is as good as a backwoodsman . . . We always slept out in the open – only one night did we sleep inside our tent – and then only because it was raining.'[17] Best of all, as he also told her, 'Olave conforms her ideas so fully to mine that we have become exactly alike.'[18]

Marguerite de Beaumont, a family friend, recalled that Olave's hero worship had been so intense that she imitated his manner of speech and even his handwriting.[19] Certainly Olave tended to pepper her letters with obsolete slang expressions such as 'my wig' which in 1913 Baden-Powell occasionally used in speech but not in his letters. Grace Browning, another early acquaintance, remembered Olave as gauche enough to expect to be taken seriously when claiming that she and Baden-Powell 'had never had a thought apart'.[20] But such criticism ignores Olave's exceptional vitality and the way in which her lack of formal education and her wandering life had left her open to unconventional ideas. She greatly surprised a journalist from *The Lady* by saying that her children would 'not be educated at all'. And she praised Madame Montessori for 'letting children teach themselves by unfettered choice and experiment'.[21]

When Olave parroted her husband's views, her enthusiasm lent her words conviction. Before her marriage she had felt shy even in the presence of a few strangers, but within a year she felt confident enough to tell Sir William Smith and an audience of several thousands gathered at the Boys' Brigade's annual Albert Hall meeting that his organization's dependence upon drill was turning his boys into machines.[22] How did she do it? asked a friend. 'I felt all the time that *he* was behind me,' was the reply.[23] Baden-Powell's liking for 'cheery' extroverts suited Olave after her years with a depressive father; she loved being 'hearty' and using the slang popular in the services. 'Ripping' would soon be her favourite adjective. 'You refresh me like a fortnight of holiday by the sea,' Roland Philipps told her after one of her breezy letters.[24]

Within weeks of her return from North Africa, her relationship with her mother deteriorated to the point of estrangement – in which unhappy situation the Baden-Powells realized they could no longer remain in Katharine's London flat. Instead they decided to rent a house in the country, which was in any case where they really wanted to live. Near Robertsbridge in East Sussex they found what Olave called 'a modest red brick house'. It had seven principal bedrooms, ample quarters for domestic staff and a fine view of moated Bodiam Castle.

The Baden-Powells started their household with two maids: Annie Court, who had listened to Olave's troubles from the age of 14; and a second maid who stayed only briefly, to be succeeded by Annie's sister Ethel. Their first cook would also be replaced by another of Annie's sisters, Mabel. Soon Annie's brother would come as their chauffeur, and Olave would find herself reassuringly surrounded by Annie's relations.[25] Further consolidation took place when the chauffeur married one of the two nursery-maids and Annie herself married Albert Scofield, the gardener. Annie soon became Olave's lady's maid and virtually her housekeeper.[26] One of Olave's nieces recalled that whereas it was fairly common for a hostess of the day to embrace her female guests on arrival and departure, it was extremely unusual for an employer to embrace a servant – as Lady Baden-Powell would Annie, on going away or returning after a trip.[27] But few servants grew up with their mistresses in the way that Annie had. To have this girlhood friend looking after her home was very consoling to Olave when her links with her family were fraying away.

With so much help Olave never found her ignorance of household matters a handicap. The cook 'used to come in with a slate and say, "We are having mutton today," and that was all I had to do – to agree.'[28] Given Olave's affection for her staff, it was inevitable that they should all become embroiled in Scouting. When the First Ewhurst Scout troop was inaugurated on the Baden-Powells' lawn, Olave became the troop's Lady Scoutmaster with Annie's brother, 'Jack' Court, and Annie's future husband, Albert Scofield, as her Assistant Scoutmasters. Whenever asked about the Girl Guides, Olave would say at this time that her 'chief work and interest centred in the boys' Movement, naturally'.[29]

In the country Baden-Powell remained, as one guest remarked, as busy as ever. 'With the exception of a walk and an occasional excursion with his gun, correspondence, administration and a thousand other urgent things occupy him throughout the day.'[30] He attended numerous meetings at Headquarters, and in 1913 was elected Master of the Mercers' Company.

Sometimes Olave accompanied him to the capital, and they were riding on the top of a London omnibus when she told Stephe that she was pregnant. The baby had been conceived during their camping holiday and would be born on their first wedding anniversary. A boy, he was christened Arthur (after the Duke of Connaught, who had offered to be his godfather), Robert (after his father) and Peter (the name he would actually be called, after Peter Pan). By a sad coincidence he was born on the day of Frances Baden-Powell's funeral, Donald's mother having died at the early age of 47 from kidney failure.[31] Her death was a particular blow to Henrietta Grace, whose income it threatened to reduce – but not for long. The following October she too fell ill. One stroke was followed by another, leaving her conscious but without hope of recovery, and she died a month after her ninetieth birthday.

'Most Scouts know what it is to have a good mother, and the more they like her, the more they dread losing her,' Stephe started his mother's obituary in *The Scout*. Having sought to please her all his life, and remembering everything she had done to advance his career, he felt her loss very deeply. 'There is only one pain greater than that of losing your mother, and that is for your mother to lose you – I do not mean by death but by your own misdeeds . . . Try not to disappoint her . . .' Neither in his private nor in his public life had he ever shamed or disappointed her. He must have felt as if a strong wind, blowing from behind him all his life, had suddenly ceased. 'By acting up to his mother's expectations, many a man has raised himself to the top of the tree . . .'

Successful men and women who have striven to succeed at the behest of an ambitious mother or father often suffer depression after they have achieved the parental ambition or after the parent has died. But it is given to very few men approaching 60 to enjoy the extraordinary range of distractions available to Baden-Powell in the year of his mother's death. Travelling home from London in the autumn of 1913 on any of those busy days during which he attended to the affairs of his world-wide Movement, he would get out at the tiny branch-line station of Bodiam and walk across the fields to be greeted at journey's end by his 'cheery' young wife and red-headed baby son. And then, less than a year later, there was an even greater distraction than parenthood and married life. In the stillness of the Sussex countryside he heard for the first time the muted rumble of the guns in Flanders, pounding out the opening salvoes of the war he had long predicted.

12

'THE BIGGEST EVENT IN OUR NATIONAL HISTORY'

1. Almost a Disaster (August 1914)

Baden-Powell was in Liverpool inspecting Scouts on the day on which the Archduke Ferdinand and his wife died in Sarajevo. But although he had once visited Bosnia on a cycling tour, the news of the assassinations made little impression upon him. He was not alone in failing to discern the coming catastrophe. A month later Lloyd George, then Chancellor of the Exchequer, told the House of Commons that relations with Germany 'were very much better than they had been a few years ago'.[1]

It has recently been argued that from the time of his 'invasion speech' five years earlier, Baden-Powell had been busily preparing for a war which he now 'welcomed . . . as an excellent chance for the Scouts to demonstrate their usefulness'.[2] This is nonsense. Ever since 1909, when Lord Haldane had announced his intention of militarizing the youth movements, Baden-Powell had seen war as a dangerous threat to the Boy Scouts. In that year Percy Everett suggested that to prevent the Scouts being squeezed out (as they might be if cadet training were to become compulsory for all boys), Baden-Powell ought to seek War Office recognition for the Movement. He refused to do so, in case it undermined the Scouts' independence.[3]

By 1910 boys of 14 and over were already obliged to be cadets in Canada, Australia and South Africa. So to save the Movement in the Dominions, Baden-Powell did his best to convince the authorities that Scouting was an ideal prelude to cadet training and would create 'a standard and bond . . . throughout the cadets of the coming Imperial Army'.[4] To lend conviction to this idea, he visited Canada with a mixed party of Boy Scouts and cadets that summer.[5] In 1912 he visited South Africa bearing the same message to General Smuts, the Defence Minister.[6] But in reality, Baden-Powell still considered cadet training to be mechanical and useless; he only said such things to try to salvage something from the wreckage of his hopes in the Dominions. In Australia, his policy of pretending that the Boy Scouts and the cadets were complementary organizations fell apart. In Melbourne the Movement was already split into 'Military' and 'Peace Scout' groupings and by declaring that he would only inspect 'Peace Scouts', Baden-Powell announced the abandonment of his earlier efforts to conciliate the cadets' supporters in Government and in the population at large. By turning away from a rally almost 800 military-style Scouts, he exposed himself to vilification in the Australian press. 'B-P: A SHATTERED IDOL' and 'BREAKS HIS OWN LAWS AND INSULTS AUSTRALIA'S BOYS AND GIRLS' were typical of many unfavourable headlines.[7]

When the Great War started, the British Government looked set to follow the example of the Dominions. Baden-Powell therefore sought to protect the Scouts by arguing that they would make more effective soldiers than cadets because Scouts were taught to show initiative. 'The cadet training imposes collective instructions upon the boys from without; while the Scout Movement encourages self-development . . . from within.'[8] In 1915 he founded a Scouts' Defence Corps for boys over 16, who would be taught marksmanship, but when only 6,000 boys joined, Baden-Powell knew that this corps would be useless as a bargaining counter in future negotiations with the Government.[9] He therefore dreamed up 'Service Scouts', who would start at 15 and would learn signalling and shooting while still involved in ordinary Boy Scout activities.[10] But Gaddum and Philipps reacted so angrily to this idea that he abandoned it,[11] although still trying to impress the Government with any statistics confirming the extent of the Scouts' involvement in the war. (A quarter of a million served and 10,000 died.)[12] By the time the Army Council broke an earlier agreement not to allow boys to be cadets under the age of 15, the war was drawing to a close, so the dire consequences for the Scouts which Baden-Powell had dreaded never came to pass.[13]

War not only threatened the Scouts' present existence, but endangered their long-term future by bringing to a premature end the most ambitious Endowment Appeal ever launched by them. (By August 1914 only one-third of the target had been raised.) Still more damaging would be the loss of the majority of the Movement's Scoutmasters when they joined the armed forces. Far from being excellently prepared for war, as Michael Rosenthal has implied, Baden-Powell's organization had rarely been more chaotic than in August 1914. Two days after war was declared on Germany, he found himself taking the chair at a meeting of Commissioners called to investigate allegations of incompetence and immorality at Head-quarters.[14] One of the joint Secretaries there, Anthony Slingsby, had just resigned because he disapproved of another Secretary, A. G. Wade, 'kissing his typist'. He also deplored Eric Walker's 'swearing and drinking'.[15] A deadlier criticism was made by the Deputy Chief Commissioner, Colonel de Burgh, who thought Wade's paperwork and financial records inadequate. The elderly colonel was standing in for Sir Edmond Elles, who at this moment of crisis was laid up with gout.[16]

Baden-Powell's exoneration of the staff did not end the chaos.

Within a week Wade, Walker and the chief clerk had all joined the army, and most of the younger Commissioners such as Roland Philipps were about to do the same. The Boy Scouts were soon being run by a 60-year old colonel and two 1st Class Scouts from Harrow School. Baden-Powell himself was suffering from the worst headaches he had experienced since the early days of his marriage.[17]

Just before the actual declaration, Baden-Powell had offered the Scouts' services to the Government. Since fears were entertained lest the 80,000 German nationals resident in Britain might suddenly disrupt communications by turning saboteur, the Commissioner for Police and the Postmaster General asked Colonel de Burgh for boys 'to watch telephone trunk lines and telegraphs between London and Dover'. Other boys were soon watching reservoirs, acting as messengers in public offices, hospitals and Red Cross centres and helping the coastguard service. On 6 August, the Admiralty asked for 1,000 Scouts to be deployed on the East Coast; by the end of the war 23,000 would have taken part in 'coast watching'.[18]

Leaving de Burgh to do his best at Headquarters, Baden-Powell toured the South Coast inspecting Scouts working with the coast-guards. But he really wanted to be back in the army and on 10 August he went to see Lord Kitchener, the new Secretary of State for War, and offered to raise a corps of Old Scouts or a battalion of retired S.A.C. men. Kitchener considered private battalions an irrelevance and so advised Baden-Powell to look after the far more important Boy Scouts. Guilt about how he had treated him in the past may explain why this tactless man nevertheless said so many complimentary things about the Scouts that Baden-Powell left the War Office feeling 'very bucked'.[19] After a similar visit General Kekewich – a guest at Baden-Powell's wedding – had gone home and shot himself. But despite Kitchener's advice, Baden-Powell was determined to go to France in no matter what capacity.[20]

2. Being There (1915–18)

Baden-Powell managed to get to the Front in the spring of 1915, ostensibly to inspect his two old regiments but really for the joy of being in uniform again among fighting men. At Rouen, where the British base accommodated 20,000 men, he visited several Y.M.C.A. Recreation Huts. Arriving at one while a concert was in progress, he was spotted at once by the young clergyman introducing the acts who, like several other men, gave him the Scout salute. It swiftly occurred to Baden-Powell that, if he could raise enough money, he could open new huts and staff them not with members of the Y.M.C.A. but with ex-Scouts and Scoutmasters. Then he would be able to come and serve in France (even if that meant serving hot drinks) whenever he felt inclined. In late July he returned to open his first hut near Calais, with funds donated by the Mercers' Company. The first proper Scout Hut was opened at Étaples in December 1915, after which he spent two months working in it.

Olave, however, would usually serve in the Mercers' Hut in Calais while she was in France. She stayed there from early October 1915 until the following January, having left home only four months after the birth of her first daughter, Heather. 'My mother disapproved strongly of the idea of my going,' she recalled. 'It seemed mad and unnecessary to her – another black mark against Scouting.' When Olave returned to England her 2-year-old-son Peter did not recognize her. 'I have never been a doting mother,' she would admit later. 'My darling husband was the person who mattered most in my life. I always put him first and the children a long way second in my affection.'[1] In spite of Olave's mother's fierce opposition to her daughter wearing Scout uniform and working as a barmaid in a recreation hut, Katharine agreed to take in Peter and Heather when Olave went away again. Frail since birth, Peter had been seriously ill with rickets in April 1915. When his mother left for France, he was still sickly and required daily massage for the varicose veins which criss-crossed his stomach. This was done by Annie who, as he himself would say, was more of a mother to him at this age than his real mother.[2]

In France Olave would share digs with other women while her husband stayed in Les Iris, a millionaire's mansion commandeered by the army. During the day he spent a great deal of his time in the Scout Hut, while each evening he would sit with any old Scouts who came in. He sometimes 'read out the day's news, and made explanatory remarks as to the geography and history of incidents'.[3] 'He had a smile and a word of cheer for everyone while he served coffee and buns,' recalled one young soldier. But what was he *really* doing in France? His book, *My Adventures as a Spy*, was published in 1915 and many men believed that his work in the huts was a blind to disarm suspicion. 'We felt certain,' wrote one admiring subaltern, 'that Baden-Powell was at that time one of the great masters of the British Intelligence Service.'[4] This was not an impression that Stephe did much to dispel.[5] It is poignant to think of him exciting such rumours as he poured out cups of coffee, while a few miles away Plumer and Allenby, who had both served under him, were each commanding an Army Corps.

As in his regimental days, Baden-Powell had many private chats with men. He discouraged visits to brothels and warned against masturbation.[6] Soon he became a sort of unofficial father confessor. Given his eagerness to console, it is sad to reflect that his sexual warnings must have made most men feel worse than before.

In France, Baden-Powell used to talk a lot about 'the loyalty to a comrade told in a book called *The Hill*'.[7] This was Horace Vachell's classic novel of romantic friendship at Harrow, in which one boy risks expulsion by selflessly taking the blame for a friend's misdeed. Wilfred Owen also admired *The Hill* and was moved to tears by the account of the death of one of the two close friends in the Boer War. Owen thought of Étaples, where Baden-Powell spent so much time, as the ante-chamber to hell. A place where he saw on men's faces something 'more terrible than terror . . . a blindfold look, without expression like a dead rabbit's'.[8] This same misery persuaded Baden-Powell to disregard his previous mistrust of religious reassurance. In one of his most astonishing performances to date, he took on the role of lay priest and salvationist, administering his own consolatory creed. Salvation, he promised, (sexual misdemeanors notwithstanding) could be obtained through the 'love and service' exemplified by 'the good turn done to a pal in ordinary camp life' and by a man's readiness 'to sacrifice himself to save a comrade under fire'.[9] If they took the 'Promise' as 'Old Scouts', he told men that they need no longer attempt the 'superstitious propitiation of a touchy, bad-tempered deity'. Thus reassured and 'no longer anxious', many scores, he claimed, had 'gone up the line gaily to the Great Adventure'.[10] This closely echoes Peter Pan's words spoken at the end of Act Three, when he is stranded on a rock in the lagoon.

PETER (*with a drum beating in his breast as if he were a real boy at last*): To die will be an awfully big adventure.

Perhaps those 'real boys' at Étaples, most of whom never grew old, derived a measure of comfort from their contact with the founder of Scouting. But there is something very displeasing about this trans-formation of a 'Promise' intended for boys on the threshold of life into a form of Extreme Unction for those about to die, as Owen put it, 'like cattle'.

Baden-Powell heard at first hand about the unimaginable suffering of men who could not be brought in from No-man's Land. For days sometimes, they were left 'crying for water, and screaming with hysteria and pain . . .' He was shown everything: the corpses, the smells, the water-logged trenches and the strangeness of ordinary life going on a mere mile or two away from such horror: 'men ploughing and harrowing in the fields, women working about their cottages, and children playing.'[11] He saw a trainful of cheerfully singing new arrivals leaving Boulogne for the Front. A moment later a hospital train slid into the same station and he reflected that only weeks before its silent passengers had been singing too.[12] At a disinfection centre, where he saw hundreds of naked men 'singing like schoolboys in their tubs', he reflected that most of these 'wonderfully made bodies' would soon be

Still a boy at heart! Canada, 1935.

Establishment figure: magnificent in full dress at St James's Palace levée, 1937.

Left: The strain begins to tell. Baden-Powell with J. S. Wilson of Gilwell at the time of the Indian débâcle, 1937.

Top: A fine send off by local Scouts at Tilbury before he sailed for Australia, 1933.

Left: A Happy Event: Baden-Powell with Betty on her Wedding Day, 1936.

Above: Still sleeping out on his open balcony, 1937.

Treetops when Baden-Powell knew it.

In Kenya, 1940, with his pet hyrax.

On his way to Treetops, Kenya, 1939.

Proud of his boys: Baden-Powell with
three South African Wolf Cubs in
Britain for the Coming of Age Jamboree
1929.

'festering in the fields close around this very bath house . . .'
'Somebody,' he declared, 'ought to be hanged for it.'[13]

But not a word of such revulsion would he ever write for
publication, even after the war. Instead he adopted the typical *Daily
Mail* propaganda line: writing optimistic pieces about British fighting
morale and castigating 'the Hun' for butchering Belgian Boy Scouts.
He would have agreed with Sir Ian Hamilton's instruction to his staff
to 'make it a point of honour [whatever the scale of the disaster they
faced] to maintain a hearty tone of optimism calculated to raise rather
than lower the confidence of the fighting men'.[14] Typical of this mood
was Baden-Powell's 'cheery' wartime greetings card, which depicted
two bare-kneed Sutherland Highlanders leaning into a sleet-laced
wind: 'We are disheartened . . . *I don't think.*'

Selective quotation could make him appear to have been among the
idiotic old men reviled by Siegfried Sassoon for 'glorying in senseless
invective against the enemy'.[15] In reality his feelings towards the
German people had grown warmer between 1909 and 1914. As early as
1907 he had hoped that Donald might go to a German university as
well as to Oxford, so that he should avoid the 'cut-and-dried character
which our English stupid gentlemen suffer from'.[16] In 1909 a group
from the German outdoor youth movement the Wandervogel was
entertained in England by the Boy Scouts, who returned their visit
later in the same year. In 1910 Baden-Powell himself had visited
Germany, and had planned to return in the autumn of 1914. The Girl
Guides visited Germany in 1911 and welcomed to England in April
1914 a party belonging to the Jungdeutschlandbund. Baden-Powell
was on friendly terms with Dr Alexander Lion, the German staff
surgeon, who had translated *Scouting for Boys* into German and thus
laid the foundations for the German Boy Scouts which had enrolled
80,000 boys by 1911.[17]

Yet, while as a human being Baden-Powell deplored the war and
respected the enemy, as a soldier he was fascinated by almost
everything he saw in France. The British goods shed at Le Havre took
his breath away. Extending for sixteen acres under one roof, it
surpassed even the largest wheat store in Chicago and contained
everything from condensed milk to Christmas trees. The scale of the
supply operation defied imagination. Sixty tons of food parcels arrived
every day from the relatives of officers and men, and thousands of
boots, bandoliers and belts were separated from dead owners and
reconditioned for the living.[18]

The Front too never failed to intrigue him – it was as if some endless
version of the Mafeking trenches had spread out across Europe. The
periscopes, the saps and counter-saps and the dug-outs were all familiar
to him. Yet he found it uncanny 'to look over this long tract of country
without seeing a moving thing except an occasional spurt of dirt . . .

and yet knowing that there were thousands of men lying hid'.[19] Three years later, with the war in its final weeks, he drove for miles and was appalled and yet spellbound by the 'miles of jumbled desolation and flattened-out towns'. He could not help finding it 'a wonderful day'.[20]

Although this receives scant recognition, many officers and men found the war exhilarating as well as vile. After being hit several times and shooting four Germans in the space of 90 seconds, Roland Philipps told Baden-Powell: 'I am a pacifist, but by Jingo! That battle was ripping.'[21] Siegfried Sassoon, no supporter of the war, could write: 'I am happy, happy; I've escaped and found peace unbelievable in this extraordinary existence which I thought I should loathe.' He even made common cause with Rupert Brooke, whom he described as 'miraculously right when he said, "death is the best adventure of all – better than living idleness and sinking into the groove again and trying to be happy."'[22]

As a young cavalry officer, Baden-Powell had been heir to a romantic tradition about warfare extending back at least 2,000 years. His faith in the chivalrous ideals of honour, courage and loyalty had survived Game Tree fort but they would not survive the Great War, which he later wrote of as 'this reversion to primitive savagery' and 'a great disgrace'.[23] But while the war lasted he was convinced that it had to be won, so that 'freedom should not be trodden down by military despotism'.[24] In Boston, in February 1912, Baden-Powell had described modern warfare as 'scientific execution' and 'organized murder'.[25] Yet even after Philipps, Lukis, Gamon and Slingsby had all been killed, Eric Walker captured and Olave's brother gravely wounded, he felt no less sure that defeat could never be countenanced. He therefore urged his orphaned nephew Donald to join the army quickly. The war, Baden-Powell told the boy, was 'the greatest event in our national history' and no man had the right to deny himself the chance of serving. Donald joined the Rifle Brigade and, although wounded, survived.[26]

Afterwards, Baden-Powell wrote with absolute conviction about the way in which Britain's young men had 'saved their country'. Michael Rosenthal has accused him of having, through Scouting's ideals, 'encouraged, in World War 1 trenches, the willing acquiescence in their own slaughter of a generation of Britain's future leaders'. Another historian has recently accused the young officers themselves of having been deceived by 'the false ideals' of the public schools and having therefore died 'for all the wrong reasons'.[27] Yet Baden-Powell's awe in the face of so much courage and suffering during those four drawn-out years still seems a more appropriate response. And why confine the search for scapegoats to the Scouts or the public schools? The pressure to conform was created by a whole society. With hindsight the Boys' Brigade, the National Service League, the novels of G. A. Henty, the revival of chivalry, the glamour of imperialism, the leaders in the *Daily Mail*, the belief in the superiority of moral virtue over intellect – all played a part in forming the nation's mood. But without the public schools, without the Scouts (in any numbers) and without Henty's fiction, nationalism did pretty well in France. Forces still scarcely understood were at work in Europe, which had more to do with the mysterious merging of patriotism and religion and the intense commercial rivalry unleashed by the latest phase of the industrial revolution than with easily definable causes.

The spirit of *Scouting for Boys*, for me at least, is not so much summoned up by young officers willingly sacrificing themselves but by a correspondence which Baden-Powell carried on during the war with his former private secretary, Eric Walker. One day in February 1915, Eric had delighted his Chief by landing his Royal Flying Corps aircraft on the Baden-Powells' lawn and breakfasting with them, before flying on to France. A few months later he was shot down behind the German lines and dragged off to prison in Mainz. Soon afterwards he began to send his old friend Professor Stephenson (alias R. Stephenson S. Baden-Powell) a series of coded letters, with the key usually indicated by a deliberate factual mistake. By giving Peter Baden-Powell's age as 7 instead of 2, Walker meant Baden-Powell to decipher the letter by selecting each seventh word, counting on from the verb 'begin' near the start of the letter. On the surface the letters would be bland but not nonsensical. Baden-Powell was asked, in these hidden messages, to send a pair of wire-cutters concealed inside a ham,[28] cigarettes containing a powerful narcotic (to paralyse his guards) and an air cushion with a blue and red cover. The cushion was intended to hold several days' supply of water and the coloured cloth was to be worked by a fellow prisoner – who had been a tailor in peacetime – to mimic the facings of a German officer's overcoat. This bogus garment actually enabled him to escape and the air cushion served not only as a water bottle but as extra flotation when he swam the Elbe. Sadly, Eric was soon recaptured. The wire-cutters arrived after the Armistice, too late to help him. Walker had won an M.C. before his capture and no sooner was he released than he volunteered to fight for the White Russians. This was the authentic spirit of *Scouting for Boys* in action: ingenious, adventurous and all the more endearing for being a little dotty.[29]

This same spirit is also epitomized by the affectionate pride which Baden-Powell took in his boys.

The outstanding memories of my experience with the night patrol [he recalled, after visiting some Sea Scouts on coastguard duty] were darkness and 'Excuse me Sir'. It was 'Excuse me Sir' when my small guide warned me of the step as we started out into the night.

'Excuse me Sir,' he warned me of a deep hole in the track . . . Then with a more compelling, 'Excuse me Sir,' this lad suddenly turned aside and ascended a rise on which there stood a farm-house, one of whose windows was lit . . . I followed close to see the fun. A peremptory knock on the door was followed by a civil but very firm request that the light should at once be screened. That seemed all right and I turned away to pursue our journey but found that my guide had stopped behind. When he rejoined me I asked him the reason for the delay. It was, 'Excuse me Sir, but I do not trust those people one yard. . .'.[30]

The Times History of the War would devote a whole chapter to the Scouts' war work and the Prime Minister David Lloyd George would pay fulsome tribute to the boys' 'honour, straightness and loyalty'; but Baden-Powell's vignette speaks volumes more.

13

THE FAMILY MAN

1. No Place Like Home (1916–19)

In April 1916 the owner of Ewhurst Place, the Baden-Powells' rented house, was killed in action, obliging them to move. The fifteenth-century black and white half-timbered farmhouse which they soon found in Surrey was picturesque but too small and too low-ceilinged. So they set out on fresh forays. The day after the Armistice was signed, they bicycled into the Hampshire village of Bentley and were soon being shown over a large red brick house at the end of a wooded drive.

It is typical of Baden-Powell's love of myth-making that he should have encouraged stories about his having stumbled upon his future home by chance.[1] Visiting Farnham, he and Olave had called upon some distant cousins who told them that a suitable house was for sale in nearby Bentley.[2] Two weeks later, on 3 December 1918, the owner was delighted to accept their over-generous offer of £4,500, which they raised with the help of £1,000 given them by Olave's father and a bank loan secured against Baden-Powell's quarter-share in his mother's house. Baden-Powell had a genius for names; and since he had first seen the house the day after the re-establishment of peace, he changed the lugubrious-sounding Blackacre Farm into the brightly apposite Pax Hill.

It was important that the leader of a worldwide youth movement dedicated to the virtues of a healthy outdoor existence should live in an unspoiled place. And, although Bentley is an undistinguished village straggling along the old London to Winchester Road, the house itself is protected by its half-mile drive and the surrounding countryside makes up for other shortcomings. Close at hand the river Wey meandered through lush water-meadows, while a short walk from the house were woods and open downland. Pax Hill had been built at the turn of the century in rural 'stockbroker Tudor' style for the owner of a famous Holborn toy-shop. After twenty years its timbers and brickwork had mellowed, while its rambling length and irregular roofline gave it a pleasantly idiosyncratic air. The Baden-Powells added two new wings: one for servants and one for guests, as well as a large music room known as 'The Barn'. This last was designed by Baden-Powell himself to house a grand piano and to be a display room for his heads of African game, his spears, shields, caskets, presentation swords and Scouting memorabilia. In the guests' bathroom, he

modelled in plaster of Paris along the wall above the bath a bas-relief
frieze of a river with fish in it. All the children were later encouraged to
add their own sub-aquatic contributions of rocks, worms, crabs,
tadpoles and so forth.[3]

Pax Hill would be Baden-Powell's home during the years of his
greatest fame. Paramount, Gaumont and British Movietone would all
film him there in his shorts, doing his exercises on his balcony and
relaxing in shirtsleeves in the garden. Journalists invariably commented on the beauty and peacefulness of the place, and Baden-Powell
himself often followed their example. 'Pax' seemed wonderfully
appropriate during the 1920s and 1930s, when world peace was the
Movement's primary objective, and it was adopted by Scouts and
Guides in many parts of the world as the name for their huts and camp-
sites. Most leaders of the Movement throughout the Empire and in
other countries visited the house and usually echoed the sentiments of a
South African Scoutmaster 'whose memory of my few days there was
all of roses and sunshine and the sort of joyous peace which God sends
to a home where only selfless loving-kindness, sincerity, and good will
abound'.[4] Visitors would comment upon their host's simple but busy
life, and many mentioned his friendly and gentle manner. Some would
go further, praising his saintliness and modesty – this last a tribute to
the increasingly spiritual tone of his public pronouncements.

His changing physical appearance also played a part in this transition
from soldier to sage. Until the early twenties his expression had often
seemed guarded and secretive, as if he were playing a game of poker.
John Hargrave noticed this in 1916: 'The soldierly Bluff King Hal
manner took a lot of people in, but the slightly slit-eyes . . . were quick
and cunning . . . something round, and smooth and smilingly
imperturbable looked out at you through those quick-glancing
eyes . . .'[5] Hargrave, however, liked 'the way he wore his cowboy hat
raked a-jaunty . . . and the way his trim moustache seemed to be fixed
forever in a smile of friendly interest and enquiry'. Grace Browning
remembered feeling that there was something 'foxy' and not quite
trustworthy about Baden-Powell when she first met him before the
Great War. His subsequent metamorphosis into one of the world's
best-loved men struck her as uncanny, as if he had somehow succeeded
in becoming someone else.[6]

But whatever the relative degree of artifice and authenticity in his
new persona, he made a lasting impression upon countless people, so
much so that when the mask occasionally slipped the effect would be
doubly disconcerting. One Australian Scout official – who had just
discovered that Baden-Powell's kindliness extended to putting out for
the birds (to use in their nests) the hair he had just trimmed from his
head – was appalled when the Chief Scout unexpectedly lost his temper
over some trifling matter. 'His anger was devastating.'[7] At times

Baden-Powell's 'cheeriness' was only assumed with an effort, but his famous 'boyishness' was often genuine. One regular visitor remembered him sometimes embarrassing his children by bringing out his numerous decorations and 'poring over them, not as a man, but as a boy'.[8]

Some guests found Pax Hill scruffy and uncomfortable, and complained that Olave knew next to nothing about entertaining. Many were shocked to discover that the sheets were only changed if slept on by the previous guests for more than a night or two.[9] But while some thought the house poorly furnished, those who came to Pax Hill as to a shrine considered walls covered with Zulu spears and walking sticks carved by the Chief Scout's hand of much greater interest than had they been hung with Impressionist paintings. When foreign visitors were due to arrive, gifts from the Scouts of that particular country were hastily retrieved from cupboards and prominently displayed. The majority of Scouting folk found their time at Pax Hill vividly memorable. They were astonished to discover that the Chief rose at five in the morning, having slept out on his balcony. If rain or snow blew in, he pulled down a green canvas awning and hooked it to the balustrade. His morning ritual involved five minutes of deep breathing, trunk twisting and knee bending. Then he would slip into his 'cold gravy'-coloured Jaeger body suit which combined a jacket and trousers in a single garment, like a cross between a boiler suit and a modern track suit. He would peel himself an apple and settle down to two hours work on his weekly articles for *The Scout* and *The Headquarters' Gazette*.[10] At half-past seven he would take a cold bath, always rubbing himself dry afterwards with a stiff partially starched towel which he believed improved the circulation.[11] Then he dressed and, either accompanied by Olave or alone, took the dogs for a brisk two-mile walk.

After a light breakfast – usually a baked apple or stewed fruit, followed by porridge – he read *The Times* carefully and then with his secretary, Eileen Nugent, went through his post which often amounted to 50 letters. Miss Nugent, who in 1920 married Major A. G. Wade, one of the joint Secretaries at Headquarters before the war, became much more to the family than the Chief's personal secretary. In 1922, she and the major moved to Ash Cottage in Bentley, which was a mile from Pax Hill and only minutes away after her employer gave her the little Standard car which he had bought in the war to save petrol. After working in the Scouts' Appeal Fund office, she had become the Chief Scout's secretary when Eric Walker joined the Royal Flying Corps.[12] Eileen was 'the right sort', having been at Cheltenham Ladies' College, and ingenious too in the best Scouting tradition. She soon mastered Baden-Powell's epistolary style so completely that he allowed her to compose, sign and send many letters on his behalf, without reference to him, when he was away or ill. 'How you manage to catch hold of his way of writing, I don't know,' wrote Olave admiringly.[13] Eileen's version of his signature became so skilful that it remains exceptionally difficult to detect.[14] She also mastered his journalistic style and became adept at converting old articles and parts of books into new material for re-publication in newspapers and journals.

Apart from his work for Scouting publications Baden-Powell regularly contributed to the *Daily Mail*, and Eileen wrote at least a third of these articles. By 1932 he was paying her a third of his fee, and the whole fee 'for articles you make up in my absence'.[15] She put together the entire text of his last two books, as he willingly acknowledged. 'I think you made an excellent book of it. Well done! and THANK YOU!' he wrote on receiving a copy of *More Sketches of Kenya*.[16] During Baden-Powell's and Olave's numerous trips abroad, Mrs Wade was in charge of Pax Hill and the servants, paying bills and dealing with any crisis that might arise. On one occasion, when the house's electrical wiring was discovered to be dangerous, she supervised the rewiring of the whole place. As Olave said: 'These sort of things are not what people would ordinarily give a "private secretary" to do I imagine!! But then you aren't that – you are just our mainstay!!!'[17] Not unnaturally the Baden-Powells were horrified when, after the Armistice, Eileen threatened to give up her position so that Eric Walker could return to his old job.[18] For all his good looks and athletic prowess Eric had never been able to write in his master's style, nor deal with his office work with such effortless efficiency.

During the mid-twenties the Headquarters' Committee pressed Baden-Powell to allow his biography to be written. 'I can't help thinking it would be better left till I'm dead,' he told Percy Everett, his publications adviser.[19] He realized that a biography might help the Movement by generating public interest, but still thought the disadvantages more compelling.[20] 'The whole idea of journalistic battening on one's intimate relationships is repugnant to me.'[21] But once Everett had hit upon Mrs Wade as the Chief Scout's official biographer, all problems seemed to melt away. Eileen, like Everett, was a trustee for the Baden-Powells' children's trust fund and was named as an executor in the wills that Baden-Powell and Olave made at this time. Her loyalty and discretion guaranteed that the biography would be uncontroversial.[22] As well as being her Chief's biographer and his major domo in his absence, Mrs Wade produced fishing wristwarmers for him, modelling clay and the famous ham for Eric Walker's wire-cutters. She made appointments with doctors, chiropodists and newspaper editors; bought steamer and rail tickets, booked hotels and found out how he should wear each new decoration as it was awarded to him.[23] As with Annie, upon whom the family were equally dependent (in her case for looking after their physical needs), they could be very generous. At Christmas Eileen often received £25.[24] And for Annie, Olave spent many hours making a magnificent family scrapbook, the equal of any she produced for her children. Olave also offered Eileen and Annie garments that had ceased to fit her, or which she rarely wore.[25] But such offers soon ceased. After the birth of her own children Eileen became extremely fat; and in any case, as time passed Olave bought fewer and fewer new clothes, preferring to patch up those she already had.[26]

For all Eileen's help, Baden-Powell worked exceptionally hard at his numerous projects, going up to London at least three times a week. In 1921 he wrote his book *Rovering to Success* (entirely without Mrs Wade's involvement). In it he offered young men advice about how to avoid various pitfalls: drink, gambling, loose women and political extremists. Olave typed the manuscript during November,[27] including the chapter in which her husband asserted that sexual attraction between men and women only lasted 'several months'. His young readers were warned never to confuse 'animal lust' with 'human love'. If Olave took all this seriously – and there is nothing to indicate that she did not – she would not have felt hurt when Baden-Powell moved from her bedroom out on to his open-air balcony. It seems unlikely that they indulged in physical relations after the birth of their third child Betty in 1917. Before going to his solitary bed for the night, Baden-Powell would visit his wife's room for what she described as "armchairs" – just lying in each other's arms, revelling in being together.'[28] It would be hard to think of a better synonym for an entirely passionless embrace.

While he normally called her 'Mum', she called him 'Bin', which was short for Robin. (In his earliest letters to her he had represented himself pictorially as a little robin.) She also called him 'Dindo', her personal version of 'darling' which he often applied to her. On his return from London, she always rushed out to him with a stream of affectionate greetings.[29]

Several friends felt that Olave would have been nothing without her husband, and that he was therefore quite literally everything to her.[30] His awareness of this led him to write her a number of letters in case he died suddenly. He wrote the first on 31 January 1916 in France, when he had been badly shaken by the inconsolable grief of the wife of a Canadian officer who had just died of his wounds in the hospital at Étaples. Having failed to console the widow after the funeral, Baden-Powell found himself imagining how devastated Olave would be if anything happened to him. With considerable psychological insight, he wrote about how he would deal with the situation if *she* were to die before *him* – a most unlikely event.

When I have found myself more and more in love with you . . . I have realized, only in part perhaps, how awful will be the break when it comes . . . I have asked myself would it be better to live, as some couples do, on easy terms of friendship so that when the parting comes it is not so knock-down a blow to the survivor? My answer has been No – this glorious love between us is worth any shock that can come later . . . If the blow has to fall on me, I feel that by Being Prepared for it in this way I shall be able to bear it in looking on it as the price I have naturally got to pay for having had the best and happiest life that any man ever had. Will you see it in the same light?[31]

Both Olave and Stephe had a liking for strenuous country activities such as cutting reeds in the river bed, clearing mud off the drive, hedge clipping and applying gigantic drums of weed killer to various parts of the garden. They also shot together and walked long distances, blackberrying or simply enjoying the countryside.[32] Rather surprisingly Olave did not often ride, as she had in childhood, even when her children acquired ponies and horses. But she did play tennis regularly and organized games of hockey in which a Pax Hill team made up of servants and family would take on local village opposition.[33] Baden-Powell himself took no part in these proceedings, but he did take up folk dancing with the rest of his family. His own favourite pursuit during these years was fishing. With other local landowners he founded the Bentley B-P Fly Fishing Association, which was responsible for stocking and caring for five miles of the river Wey. He also enjoyed salmon fishing, and paid an annual visit to Scotland or the West Country for this.

Nobody meeting the outward-going Baden-Powells during their early years at Pax Hill would ever have suspected that they had just lived through a double tragedy which, for Olave at least, might have been expected to cause total prostration. On 16 December 1918, she received a phone call from her mother in Lilliput. Olave's father 'had disappeared'. Harold had gone out early in the morning on one of those long walks which Olave had once shared with him, and had not come back. On New Year's Day, Baden-Powell told Donald that 'it now appears he had been suffering a great deal from insomnia and it is feared that in his panic he went off and drowned himself in the sea'.[34] Katharine, he said, was 'bearing up well'. That Olave's mother should have taken her husband's death in this manner is not surprising, given his love affairs and depressions. But Olave had been far closer than any other member of the family; she knew that he had been lonely after her marriage and that he had missed her. Yet in reply to condolences from Eric Walker, she wrote a letter which must have struck him as unsentimental to say the least. 'If one looks at it dispassionately, one realizes that in many ways it is a merciful release . . . One has to be

horribly sane these days.'[35] Later, as part of her policy of being
'horribly sane', she described her father's action as 'splendid . . . as he
was becoming a BURDEN to Monna [Katharine] and to him-
self . . .'[36]

Unlike Olave, her sister Auriol seemed traumatized by her father's
death. Already grief-struck, she caught Spanish influenza in March
1919. At 10.30 p.m. on 5 April, Annie answered the phone at Pax Hill
to be told that Auriol had slipped away unnoticed from the private
nursing home where she was being treated for depression and the
physical after-effects of influenza.[37] She had made her way to the
nearest railway track, where she had flung herself under the wheels of
the first train to pass. When Harold had 'disappeared', the family had
represented it as a bathing accident. Now Auriol was said to have died
of influenza and even 55 years later, this was the impression which
Olave gave in her autobiography. The truth was kept from Auriol's
three daughters, even as adults until at last in 1974 Clare, Auriol's
middle daughter (by then nearing the end of her own life), wrote to
Olave asking her to put in writing how her mother had died.
Reluctantly Olave did so, explaining that her sister had taken Harold's
death to heart. She also told her about a more general depression which
might have been caused by the war.[38] In writing to Auriol's eldest
daughter, Christian, whom Olave loved as much as any of her own
children, she said: 'DON'T let it worry you, Darling. It is SO long
ago . . . Funny that Clare should want to know about it in writing!! I
HAD to answer her question, as she asked it point blank – But I haven't
thought about it for YEARS!!'[39] Olave attended her sister's funeral,
but a dozen years later she would refuse to see her mother buried –
neither would she attend her beloved husband's funeral, nor her son's.
Death remained terrifying to her, although apparently so effectively
blotted out.

In 1918 Baden-Powell had come across the writings of the French
psychotherapist, Emile Coué, and thought his theory of 'auto-
suggestion' proof that 'one can cure oneself not only of weakness of
character or fear, but even of illness. Suggestion is what can be done by
one person to another – as one does to a child who has fallen down and
hurt himself . . . You get the child to suggest for himself that though
he fell he is not after all hurt and so he cures himself . . .'[40] Olave's
suggestion to herself that she was not hurt by these two personal
disasters owed something to Baden-Powell's admiration for Coué.
When his favourite daughter Heather began to weep over comparatively trifling annoyances, he made her repeat over and over again
Coué's famous incantation: 'Every day, in every way, I am getting
better and better.'[41] Coué's philosophy buttressed Baden-Powell's
mistrust of self-analysis; the cure, he remained sure, did not lie in
giving scope to the emotions but in distracting the mind with activity

and in not 'giving in' to grief or anger. The Baden-Powells' devotion to Boy Scout 'cheeriness' made them both practise it to the point of parody. To have tried to imagine why Heather wept, or why Peter often suffered from fits of anger, would not have seemed profitable to them. After all, with his mother's 'help' Baden-Powell had mastered his anger as a child; and Olave, with *his* help, had not only conquered her feelings of inferiority but had remained 'sane' when two of her closest relations had killed themselves.

2. Parental Pains and Pleasures (1915–22)

Katharine Soames could not behave with Olave's objectivity. Her favourite daughter's death seemed the worst fate that could have befallen her, and she thought Olave heartless to go ahead with a previously planned tour of North America. Moreover she also considered Olave unnatural to have left her children for months at a time during the war – particularly in view of Peter's ill-health. As well as suffering from varicose veins, he had a weak back and a limp; he was also subject to regular attacks of vomiting and feverishness, with consequent weight loss.[1]

Although Katharine disapproved of her daughter's protracted absences, these would have caused little consternation at a time when upper-middle-class children were invariably brought up by nannies. Peter did not walk until he was three but his childhood rickets did not cause lasting damage. Nevertheless, the vomiting and fever continued. At first the two doctors consulted diagnosed his illness as gastric influenza, but Peter's continuing weakness obliged them to change their minds. A year and a half after these attacks had first caused concern, Peter was x-rayed. No organic abnormality was revealed and Baden-Powell was reassured to hear that all the boy needed was 'solid food and exercise';[2] but in spite of this regimen Peter's vomiting continued. By the last day of 1916 Heather, at eighteen months, weighed more than Peter who was over twice her age.[3]

During the late summer of 1916 the Baden-Powells decided to rent a house in Bexhill on the south coast for Peter and Heather to live in under the care of a trained nurse and an assistant.[4] They evidently thought that 'bracing sea air' would cure Peter, where 'solid food and exercise' at home had failed. For Heather, who needed no fresh air cure, the separation from her parents was thought necessary so that Peter should not feel lonely. At 3 and 1½ respectively, both children felt their exile acutely, even though their parents visited them at weekends, Scouting commitments permitting. If Annie or Hilda had been allowed to go with the children, they would have been less upset. Annie was horrified to learn that Miss Anderson, the nurse in Bexhill, punished them severely if they wet their beds.[5]

When 'sea air' also failed to bring about an improvement in Peter's health, Baden-Powell decided to seek fresh medical opinions. In January 1917, after the children had been away for five months, he was told by a Dr Kent that Peter's vomiting and other stomach pains were 'probably due to neurosis'.[6] Sadly Dr Kent did not recommend the boy's immediate return to Pax Hill but instead, plainly holding the over-strict Miss Anderson responsible for his neurosis, he urged Baden-Powell to send the boy to a well-run private nursing home. So, on 20 January, Peter was sent to Miss Keogh's establishment in the same town. Since it would have been nonsensical to admit a healthy child, Heather returned home. At this time Olave was pregnant with her third child, which she and Baden-Powell hoped would turn out to be a second son; in anticipation they called the unborn baby 'David'.[7] With his sister back home again and the new baby 'son' about to join her there, it is not surprising that, isolated in Bexhill, Peter felt rejected by his family and furious with this interloping 'brother' who was about to replace him. Shortly before Olave gave birth, he warned his father that he had 'got a gun to shoot the new baby'.[8] Baden-Powell noted this remark in his diary without comment, but he seems to have got the message since two weeks later Peter came home. Stephe described returning to Pax Hill after a rally: 'Got home to find Olave with Peter and Heather all sitting in bed together drawing pictures, and making at the same time the best picture I have ever seen in my life.'[9]

It was perhaps fortunate for Peter that 'David' turned out to be Betty. The whole family was together again from May until September, when Peter returned briefly to Bexhill before coming home for good. Not that periods of separation from his parents ceased. From April to June 1919, Olave and Stephe toured North America, and they would return there for a similar period in 1923. From January to April 1921, they were in India and the Far East. The memory of the Bexhill separation obviously haunted Peter, because many years later he recalled being at Little Mynthurst Farm (his parents' briefly rented Surrey farmhouse) when his father was away:

> I thought I saw him walking down the road so dashed out, arms waving wildly and with loud cries of 'Daddy! Daddy!' But it was not father at all, and I could have sunk through the earth with shame and disappointment. However he did come home later, and so anxious was I to see him that I shoved my head well and truly out through the bars of our nursery window and became stuck fast. I yelled, and screamed so much, that my father's first act on entering the house was calmly to fetch a screwdriver and unfasten one of the bars to release me . . . Before and during my early school days, I often suffered much agony of mind when my parents went off on long tours abroad.[10]

On Christmas Day 1918, Baden-Powell gave Peter his first lesson in tracking and thought he made 'a promising start'.[11] But in other directions Peter's first steps were less promising. He was very slow in learning to read and, worse still in his parents' eyes – given their love of extroverts – remained very silent and shy. Heather soon drew better than her brother; and when they learned to ride, she immediately displayed superior aptitude. Baden-Powell's love of both drawing and riding deepened the bond between him and Heather. Because Peter was weaker than Heather, he could not even get his own back in a scrap. One of his school friends later recalled thinking that Heather was treated as if *she* were the son of the family.[12] While Baden-Powell was closest to Heather, Olave made Betty her favourite and rejected Peter. Heather confirmed that her mother used to be 'scandalously anti-Peter'.[13] Annie thought Olave resented him for being sickly, since she secretly felt guilty about giving her adored husband an imperfect son. Katharine Soames muttered about the boy's father having been too old, and certainly that was what most of the servants thought.[14] For Baden-Powell himself, with his fetish about boys and young men needing to 'look after the germ' which would be their future son, *his* son's ill-health was very distressing. In a vain effort to strengthen the boy, he gave instructions to Annie that he should drink a broth largely consisting of the blood pressed out of beefsteaks.[15]

Early in 1919 Olave wrote of her hope that 'Peter would be a credit to us'.[16] This echoed the letters received shortly after Peter's birth, when several friends 'hoped the son will prove worthy of his Father'.[17] In jocular mood, Baden-Powell would ignore the boy's frailty and describe him as 'a fine young recruit for the 13th [Hussars]'.[18] Very early in Peter's life Baden-Powell began to see his son in dynastic terms, as potentially the ideal Scout, and decided to involve him in the Movement even before he was old enough to be enrolled. In 1918 he requested Eileen Wade to 'get Wolf Cub totem poles prepared on the pattern already made (with earrings and a few keyring tabs), a lock of Peter's hair to be wired on to the tuft between the ears of each. To be sent to the Chief Scout in each Overseas Dominion for competition by Wolf Cub packs.'[19] These bizarre totems were not a success and were soon forgotten. Baden-Powell also arranged for Scout Shops to stock photographs of Peter at his christening and, later, as a 'typical' Wolf Cub.[20] Any child burdened with such expectations would have had difficulty in living up to them, even given the advantages of good health and above-average intelligence. But for a boy who was physically frail and intellectually backward, these high parental hopes rapidly became a nightmare. Even outings on ponies could end in humiliation. Baden-Powell would walk with the children as they rode and send them on ahead 'to spy out the land'. This was a test in 'powers of observation' in which Peter often came last, behind his younger sisters.[21]

When Peter was 7, his father – with night tracking in mind – began to teach him about the position of the stars. By mid February 1920, he was able to note in his diary: 'Peter now knows Orion, Sirius, and the Great Bear.'[22] This had been achieved only after many hours out on the balcony together after dark. Peter and his sisters realized very early that their father was a famous man, as the numerous honours which were continually showered upon him made clear. They attended a number of presentation ceremonies and 'stood solemnly to attention throughout the ordeals'.[23] To be alone with this revered person and instructed by him in fishing, astronomy or tracking was inevitably stressful. Peter tried hard but his efforts – if witnessed by Olave or either of his sisters – were often greeted with derisive cries of 'Oh, Peter!'[24] But although saying little, he was not crushed. His nurse insisted upon his wearing a pair of buttoned boots which took a long time to put on and fasten, but one day when he was 7 he hurled them through the largest window in the music room. In great trepidation the nurse went to Baden-Powell to tell him what had happened, but he grinned at her and said: 'Thank God he had the guts to do it.'[25]

While daunting in some ways, Baden-Powell was marvellous with his children in others. He played at being animals with them, telling them to adopt the persona of a bear, lion, pig or whatever came to mind. Then they had to enact the character of the beast named, while he joined in as another animal. On other occasions he encouraged them to try to get around the sitting room without setting foot on the floor.[26] Often at breakfast-time he would recite ditties and yarns, such as the story of the little Irish boy who merely asked for more pudding when gently told by his mother that his dog, Paddy, was dead. Later she heard terrible tantrums. 'Paddy's dead,' the little chap sobbed. 'I tried to tell you at lunch,' his mother murmured. 'Och,' said the boy, 'I thought you said Daddy.'[27] Stephe drew inventive and amusing little scenes for all his children and encouraged their drawing. Peter's efforts were usually the least acomplished, although he always did his best. No image of the boy's desire to please is more poignant than his farewell to his parents when he was 6 and they were leaving for America. As their car swung up the drive, Baden-Powell glanced back at the house and saw Peter standing rigidly to attention in the doorway, saluting him.[28]

In 1921 the three daughters of Olave's dead sister Auriol came to spend roughly half their holidays at Pax Hill; the rest of the time they lived with their grandmother. Christian, the eldest at 9, was a year older than Peter and tall for her age. At 8, Clare was the same age as Peter but stood a full head taller. Yvonne, a pretty curly-haired 3-year-old, was the youngest. While it might be supposed that this sudden influx of two large and capable girls and one adorable little one would have made Peter feel even less confident, the effect was beneficial. As the only boy among all these girls he enjoyed a special status and, with so many children about, he suffered less parental pressure. As home to six children, Pax Hill – with its varying number of horses (rarely less than four) and its assorted dogs, cats, rabbits, doves, ducks and chickens – was a wonderful place to grow up. From 1919 whenever Olave and Stephe were away, the children felt secure in the hands of 'Nursie' (Hilda Court, Annie's sister-in-law), Kathleen (Hilda's sister) and of course Annie herself. One of Heather's earliest memories was of Ernest Court ('Nursie's' husband), who had been the Baden-Powells' chauffeur since they had first owned a car, suddenly reappearing at Pax after the Armistice wearing his fur-lined flying-suit. Heather thought he was either a bear or 'the enemy from the war'. 'The Bear', as Ernest was known from that day forth, would soon live in 'The Den' – the small house which Baden-Powell designed for him and 'Nursie' in the grounds. Although Court had become an officer in the Royal Flying Corps, he had never thought of anything except returning to the Baden-Powells' service. The other servants thought just as highly of their employers.

When the Baden-Powell children followed their Davidson cousins to boarding school in 1922, they left behind a happy childhood world only partly dependent on the presence of their parents. Peter was the first to go, in January. As if realizing that his son's departure marked the end of an era, Baden-Powell wrote with uncharacteristic gloom after depositing him: 'The drive home was like coming back from his funeral.'[29]

14

WHAT TO DO WITH THE GIRLS

1. Can Girls be Scouts? (1909–10)

During the Great War the Girl Guides' organization was convulsed by a power struggle, from which Olave Baden-Powell emerged as a figure almost as commanding within *her* Movement as her husband was within *his*. To understand how they became respectively the king and queen of Scouting and Guiding, it is necessary to go back a little.

The official history of the Girl Guides firmly states that Baden-Powell 'hardened his heart against all imitations by girls of the game he had invented for boys of the country'. Supposedly he turned a Neloonian blind eye to the thousands of girls who took up Scouting during 1908 and 1909, until actually confronted by a party of 'Girl Scouts' at the Crystal Palace Rally on 4 September 1909. Only then, according to the official historian, did he recognize the need for a movement for the girls of the world. He is also credited with an early revulsion against the very idea of girls using the sacred word 'Scout' in their collective name.[1]

In fact as early as 1907, in his first Boy Scouts' Scheme pamphlet, he had described Scouting as the basis 'for an attractive organization and valuable training for girls'.[2] In *The Scout* in May 1908, he asked rhetorically under his own name: 'CAN GIRLS BE SCOUTS?' and replied firmly, 'I think girls can get just as much healthy fun out of Scouting as boys can . . . and prove themselves good Scouts in a very short time.'[3] By September 1908 his enthusiasm for Girl Scouts had not diminished. 'I have had several quite pathetic letters from little girls asking me if they may share the delights of a Scouting life with the boys. But of course they may! I am always glad to hear of girls' patrols being formed . . .'[4] This contrasts strangely with the official historian's contention that, from the beginning, Baden-Powell thought it 'obvious that the girls' movement . . . must be run separately from that of the boys . . . and find a name of its own.'[5]

Until now, he has never been credited with having initially envisaged a programme virtually identical for boys *and* girls. Since Baden-Powell's regimental days, he had urged men to learn the traditionally feminine skills of cooking and sewing. For the daughters of leisured families to learn to do the same, so that they would not have to depend upon servants for their very survival, seemed sound common sense to him. And if Scouting could confer character upon men, why should it not do the same for women who, in his opinion, were unnecessarily mollycoddled and therefore ruined as companions for men?[6] They needed fewer social graces and more of Olave's sporting and outdoor capabilities.

But while Baden-Powell remained adamantly opposed to girls being treated as 'dolls',[7] his attitude towards Girl Scouts began to cool as Establishment fears that he would coarsen young ladies became apparent. In a statement headed 'Girl Scouts' which appeared in *The Scout* on 16 January 1909, he claimed he felt 'very guilty at not yet having found time to devise a Scheme of Scouting better adapted for them [girls]', but that he hoped 'to get an early opportunity of starting upon it'.

Up until early August 1909 Baden-Powell continued to write about Girl Scouts, and in the second edition of *Scouting for Boys* he suggested a uniform of blue flannel shirt, blue skirt and matching knickers.[8] But by late August he had decided to change the name to Girl Guides and it seems likely that his mother played a part in this. On 18 June he had sent her 'an idea for Scouting for Girls for your criticism'.[9] Henrietta Grace had already complained about Scout Camps being too tough for Donald, and now advised her son strongly not to make toughness a central feature of a movement for girls.[10]

By late August Baden-Powell had not only decided that it would be inappropriate to call girls 'Scouts', but had also made up his mind to create a different programme and a separate organization.[11] In the November issue of *The Headquarters' Gazette*, he published a short piece entitled: 'The Scheme for Girl Guides', whose object would be to make girls 'better mothers and guides to the next generation'. To propitiate his critics, he conceded that the Scouting programme set out in *Scouting for Boys*, although suitable for all boys 'does not apply equally well to all girls, even when altered in detail to suit the sex. With girls it has to be administered with greater discrimination; you do not want to make tomboys of refined girls, yet you want to attract and thus to raise the slum girl from the gutter.'

Nevertheless, in the *Headquarters' Gazette* he stated: 'Girls must be partners and comrades rather than dolls,' including among the proficiency tests for girls: *Stalking, Cyclist, Electrician, Clerk, Telegraphist, Swimmer, Pioneer, Sailor* and *Signaller*, which were all listed as the same tests 'as for Boy Scouts'. Boys and girls also shared badges for *Musicians, Artists, Tailors, Cooks* and *Florists*. Apart from *Nursing Sister* and *Nurse*, fewer concessions were made to defenders of the refined girl than he made out.

But the new emphasis on nursing was significant. In the *Headquarters' Gazette* he suggested that 'this scheme might be started either independently, or possibly as a cadet branch or feeder to the Territorial Organization of Voluntary Aid'. The Voluntary Aid Detachment scheme was inaugurated by the War Office in August 1909 to provide nursing care for wounded Territorials in the event of an invasion. VADs were administered by their local branch of the Red Cross and trained by the St John Ambulance Association. The fact that Baden-Powell was prepared to consider letting another organization provide the administrative machinery for the Girl Guides shows that he was not at this time interested in trying to run the Guides himself as a sister movement to the Boy Scouts.

In 1909 he had not yet retired from the army, and his trouble with Vane had evidently left him wondering whether he could successfully run the Boy Scouts let alone a second movement for girls. Nevertheless, before the year ended he had decided to leave the army and to devote himself to the Scouts. With more time on his hands and perhaps recalling the failure of the Boys' Brigade to promote and administer the Scouts, he began to take steps to organize the Girl Guides himself. He was encouraged at the outset to find that the majority of the 6,000 Girl Scouts who had already enrolled were prepared to adopt the new name, albeit reluctantly.

When Baden-Powell asked his sister Agnes to form a Girl Guides' Committee, he was content to see her adopt a much more ladylike approach than he had thought desirable before being criticized in the press for failing to understand that 'girls are not boys'.[12] Unfortunately for Agnes, her brother's views would prove changeable after his marriage.

2. The Rise and Fall of Agnes Baden-Powell (1910–24)

One of Agnes's early publications was entitled 'A Mother's Reply' which took the form of a mother's letter to an impetuous Girl Guide daughter. Short skirts, the erring girl was told, might be suitable for vaulting gates, but 'violent jerks and jars' could fatally damage 'a woman's interior economy'. A girl going in for 'rough games and exposure' would soon have 'rough and worn hands', which were fine for workmen but not for nurses or pianists. 'Do you know that there are more girls nowadays with hairy lips than formerly, and I believe it is due to the violent exercise they take?' The daughter was particularly urged not to use 'silly vulgar slang, such as "topping" and "ripping", and "what ho!" etc. (all picked up from boys)'. Olave, who used all these expressions, would not have been amused. Agnes recorded her own agreement with 'the mother's' sentiments and promised that, just as the Scouts developed manliness, so the Girl Guides would 'make for womanliness'.[1]

Yet however cautious the official line Baden-Powell and his sister adopted in order to commend the Girl Guides to the public and to the

Establishment, the girls managed to enjoy themselves. Hemmed in at home by numerous petty restrictions, they were thrilled to get away – even if only to a church hall with some girls of their own age – for a few hours. Short skirts were banned and, for the sake of future wounded Territorials, Guides were obliged to bandage and re-bandage each other repeatedly. They also had to spend hours practising bathing babies (large dolls doing duty for the genuine article), but they *did* sometimes manage to observe wild life and to try some tracking. Many early Guides dressed in flamboyant unofficial uniforms; a former Devonshire Guide recalled 'the open-mouthed astonishment of an old lady as I walked past her in the full glory of my – in those days – *short* blue skirt, white blouse, belt of gold braid, navy blue hat, with a chin-strap, turned up at one side with a bit of my mother's feather boa, long gloves, a haversack on my back and grasping a stout pole about five feet long'.[2]

Agnes Baden-Powell was 52 years old when she became President of the Girl Guides and started to assemble a committee of charitably inclined ladies. She and a secretary, Miss Margaret Macdonald – who had worked for 'the Boy' McLaren when he was the Scouts' Manager – operated from a small office in Scout Headquarters. Agnes's long years as unpaid secretary to her mother and her brothers had given her some organizational experience, but hardly enough for the immense task of running the rapidly expanding Girl Guides. Nevertheless from April 1910 for six years, she held committee meetings and travelled up and down the country choosing Commissioners and Secretaries.[3] To be received like royalty wherever she went to inspect Guides was bliss to her after having lived for so long in the shadow of her brothers. In the late summer of 1910 Agnes was pressed to write a handbook for the Guides and, in her foreword, she acknowledged that she had written *The Handbook for the Girl Guides* 'with Lieutenant-General Sir Robert Baden-Powell'.

Agnes took many passages verbatim from *Scouting for Boys* and supplemented them with chapters on nursing, child care and house-keeping. The handbook set out all the Guide proficiency tests and prescribed a standard uniform. Girls were advised against mastur-bation as strongly as boys. Under the heading 'When in Doubt Don't', they were warned that 'bad habits' quickly lead to 'blindness, paralysis and loss of memory'.[4] Given the Establishment's attitude to the suffragettes, it is not surprising that girls were also warned against 'dishonourable actions' such as 'deceiving superiors', most of whom would have been men. Trade Unions were treated even less sym-pathetically than they had been in *Scouting for Boys*. Activities recommended for 'really well-educated women' included 'taking up translating, dispensing to a doctor or in a hospital', or becoming 'stockbrokers, house decorators, agents, managers of laundries, accountants or architects'.[5] Among more adventurous heroines such as a French woman aviator and Joan of Arc, Elizabeth Garrett Anderson and Marie Curie were also held up for emulation. Although Girl Scout patrols with names like 'Wildcats' and 'Nighthawks' were gone for ever, and 'Elves' and 'Pixies' now took their place, the toned-down girls' Movement was still appealing enough to draw an astonishing half-million girls by the late 1920s. (By then there would be 200,000 more Guides and Brownies in Britain than Boy Scouts and Cubs.)

The success of the Guides convinced both Baden-Powell and Olave that Agnes could not be left in control. As a first step on the road to replacing her sister-in-law, Olave offered her services to the Girl Guides' Committee on 14 September 1914. Mrs Wade remembered the occasion well, since her office adjoined the committee room. 'Mrs Lumley Holland [the committee's chairman] was wearing a fur cape and a black bonnet with bugles, after the fashion of Victorian days . . . Lady Baden-Powell, slim and charming in turquoise blue, looked altogether too young for this set-up, and possibly that was why she was told that the Guides were getting on very nicely and needed no extra help.'[6] Charming she may have looked, but Olave did not harbour charming thoughts as she said goodbye.

Mrs Lumley Holland was a well-known figure in the world of fashionable charity work – a general's widow, 'Lady of the Manor' of a Kentish village and the owner of a house in Wilton Crescent. Agnes had known and respected her for many years. In her autobiography Olave claimed that her husband had been incensed enough to demand Mrs Lumley Holland's resignation, which he had secured at their first meeting. He had been helped, she said, by 'observing' how nervous the lady was from the trembling of her egret feathers.[7] In reality, matters had not been so easily resolved. Baden-Powell did indeed call on Mrs Lumley Holland, but the chairman stood her ground and refused to resign.

After having put up with two more disagreeable meetings, on 17 December Mrs Lumley Holland faced an astonished Baden-Powell across the teacups with an open threat of blackmail. If he 'ejected the present Girl Guide Committee', he was told that, 'some of them might turn nasty, and expose dishonesty on Agnes's part, in keeping £100 sent on to her by Miss du Pré for the Girl Guides and only forwarding £10 to the fund.' Baden-Powell was also taken aback to learn that Mrs Lumley Holland 'had something far worse about Agnes in black and white'. She would not, however, divulge what this was. When Stephe angrily quizzed his sister, she excused her appropriation of most of the donation by saying that the donor had said it was 'for her to use as she thought best'. Agnes had decided that it would be 'best' to 'pay herself', which was bad enough, but he was more alarmed by his inability to find out anything from his sister about the graver secret matter.[8] No evidence exists to suggest what this could have been; but if worse than embezzlement it must have been genuinely reprehensible.

Only when Baden-Powell obtained a Charter of Incorporation for the Girl Guides, making it an equal and equivalent organization to the Boy Scouts, was he able to reorganize Mrs Lumley Holland's Committee. But even then the changes he was able to make were not as sweeping as he would have liked. Although he became chairman, Agnes remained President and the truculent Mrs Lumley Holland was elected on to the new ten-strong Executive Committee as Head of the Overseas and Foreign Department: a far from insignificant post given the growing number of Guides abroad. In the end this redoubtable woman retired of her own free will in November 1916, a full two years after the hero of Mafeking's first onslaught.[9]

Although older than Agnes, Stephe nevertheless thought that the Guides needed a younger leader, and that Olave would do a better job. He had been badly shaken by Mrs Lumley Holland's accusations against his sister. For her part, Olave had disliked her sister-in-law since her own earliest visits to Henrietta Grace's house. 'Agnes,' she recalled, 'resented me from the start but had to tolerate me . . . She was always fluffing round her mother when I was there, listening, snooping,' and trying, Olave was sure, to poison Henrietta Grace against her.[10] Olave now saw Agnes as the single obstacle standing between her and her ambition to be to the Guides what her beloved husband was to the Scouts. Neither she nor Stephe would ever forgive Agnes for allowing Mrs Lumley Holland to deliver so comprehensive a snub – offering the founder's wife absolutely nothing to do in her husband's new Movement.

Baden-Powell was alarmed by the possibility that if he should suddenly die, Agnes might manage to foist herself on the Movement as Chief Guide. He therefore left written instructions saying that he thought her 'unfitted' for that role.[11] By late 1919, Agnes had hinted that she might abandon the Presidency if her brother either paid her off or offered alternative employment. But Baden-Powell found these terms unacceptable. He suspected that his sister was clinging on simply in order to deny Olave her due. To justify her own campaign against her sister-in-law, Olave would describe her as an incompetent, who had done 'no definite organizing at all, and always went behind the back of the Committee . . .'[12]

To blacken Agnes's reputation further, Olave unblushingly wrote about the 1912 *Handbook* as if her husband had never had anything to do with it. 'Robin and I called it "The Little Blue Muddly",' she wrote in her autobiography.[13] Muddles there undoubtedly were, but largely because a Movement based upon adventure had through no fault of

Agnes's been watered down to suit the cautious inclinations of influential Edwardians. Agnes had demonstrated considerable skill in sitting on a far from stable fence, buffeted on one side by the suffragettes and on the other by reactionaries. She herself, with her hobbies of ballooning and bicycle polo and her undoubted artistic talents (she designed many of the early Guide badges), was no typical Edwardian spinster; she struggled so vigorously to retain her position in the Guides because it had given her an authority unlike anything she had ever enjoyed when running hither and thither at her mother's behest. In her eyes, her famous brother and his young wife already enjoyed much that she would never have – a home of their own, children and financial independence. By trying to take away the one occupation which gave her a sense of purpose, they seemed to be bent upon destroying her.

As the battle reached its crisis in December 1919, Mrs Mark Kerr (the former Rose Gough, now a member of the Committee) came to see the Baden-Powells 'to plead for Agnes'.[14] But Baden-Powell and Olave were determined to be rid of her, and, at long last on 15 January 1920 after a vote against her in Committee, Agnes's will crumbled and she accepted the honorary title of Vice-President. She continued to cling to her seat on the Committee, but in January 1924 her brother managed to dislodge her.[15] She told him that her originating role in the Movement was mocked by her honorary rank and asked instead to be granted the title of 'Commandant General'. Baden-Powell and the Committee threw this proposal out.[16]

Later that year, when the first World Camp for Foreign and Imperial Girl Guide Leaders was held in Hampshire, Baden-Powell and Olave wrote to Agnes telling her that she would not be welcome. While Baden-Powell addressed the assembled women on 'friendship', his sister hid in a shrubbery to avoid being seen by him. Suspecting that she might come, Olave had ordered Grace Browning – a member of the Committee – to use her tracking skills to follow her sister-in-law around and stop her grousing to any of the leaders of foreign contingents. At the end of the day Olave was enraged to learn that Agnes had nevertheless managed to 'tell some foreign heads that she [Olave] had pushed her out'. Baden-Powell told the camp commandant to inform all senior Guide leaders that Agnes 'was not to be relied on' and was 'not responsible', but the damage had been done.[17] When he next met his sister, he warned her that a repetition of such remarks would cost her her Vice-Presidency.

But by then Agnes was past caring. She went uninvited to a Girl Guide garden party at Buckingham Palace, and when a lady-in-waiting tried to turn her away on her brother's instructions, she shouted and screamed and refused to go. A fortnight later at the Guiders' Training Centre in the New Forest, she publicly accused

Olave of brutality. Banned from all Guide premises, she invited foreign Guiders to tea at her flat and told them about her persecution.[18] With their help she subsequently launched herself on a tour of Canada and the United States, describing herself as 'the founder of the Girl Guides' in spite of a flurry of telegrams from her brother contradicting this.[19]

Although Olave was the driving force behind the long vendetta against Agnes, Baden-Powell backed his wife at every turn. Perhaps Agnes had genuinely been 'unfitted' for the principal executive position in the Guides, but that had been no reason for refusing her an honorable titular role which would have salved her pride. When all that Agnes had left was her Commissionership for Dunmow in Essex, Olave persuaded the Committee to send her 'a memo asking her to resign' which, as she admitted, 'though not the right or usual way of removing a C.C., it does save *us* from having to do it!!!'[20] Olave's vindictiveness did not even stop there. On discovering that Agnes was still inviting young Guiders to her flat, she told them that they could not hope to remain on friendly terms with *her* if they accepted Agnes's hospitality.[21]

In June 1916 Baden-Powell had insisted that the Committee appoint Olave County Commissioner for Sussex. She had set to work with a zeal that astonished Agnes and her colleagues and within months had established an effective county administration, with District Commissioners and local Secretaries all in place. Her youthful good looks and almost evangelical fervour had won her a devoted following among Sussex Guiders. The impact which she made later that year at a County Commissioners' conference was such that she was elected Chief Commissioner – a very important position since it would entitle her to choose County Commissioners.

In February 1918, Agnes was powerless to prevent her young sister-in-law from being elected Chief Guide. Nor was she able to stop her sacking her office secretary, Miss Macdonald, who had been with her since the earliest days of the Guides. In 1917 Olave had dedicated her book on *Training Girls as Guides* 'to Margaret Macdonald . . . who has done so much for the Girl Guide movement from the beginning'. But after dismissing her a year later, she described this paragon as 'jealous, troublesome and careless'.[22]

While Olave was responsible for the witch-hunt against those who had served on Agnes's Committee or under her in any other capacity, Baden-Powell was perfectly aware of what was going on. 'We don't quite like her tone, you know,' Olave confided to Percy Everett. 'The Chief and I really don't think that it would do to let Miss Macdonald come back . . .'[23] Eileen Wade felt that, while Olave was always subservient to Baden-Powell when policies were discussed, *she* often led *him* where personalities were concerned.[24]

In August 1916 Baden-Powell inspected the Guiders' Summer Camp run by Mrs Agatha Blyth, the founder of the Girl Guides' Officers' Training School. Afterwards he congratulated her on 'the right spirit being abundantly present'.[25] The following year, with Mrs Blyth's help, Olave wrote a book on Guide training and subsequently decided that she ought to take charge of the Training Department herself. So, regardless of what he had said so recently, at Olave's instigation Baden-Powell wrote to Mrs Blyth informing her that her training school's 'spirit' was 'out of harmony with the movement'. Olave then condemned her in her absence at the next Commissioners' Conference – whereupon Mrs Blyth's entire Committee resigned in sympathy, to be promptly replaced by four of Olave's close friends.[26] Agatha Blyth (like her three older sisters who had founded Roedean) was a dedicated woman who had worked hard to make the Guiders' school a success and had spent considerable sums of her own money on the venture. Unfortunately she had been a member of Agnes's Committee and a personal friend of Mrs Lumley Holland. Mrs Blyth's secretary at the school confessed that she had lost her belief in 'the Guide spirit' and in the reality of the Baden-Powells' desire to help others. 'It's a pity they talk so much, it would be preferable if they lived up to it.'[27]

Baden-Powell had thought it vital to take over the Girl Guide Training Department as part of his drive to establish total control over the girls' organization. But that does not excuse the inept way in which the sackings were done. Since he now chaired most meetings of the Committee, he was also involved in the sacking of Miss Macdonald's successor, Miss B. G. Anson who, in Olave's words, 'got above herself . . . and had to be gently slipped out'.[28] It would be a recurring pattern with Olave to 'adore' the women she appointed and then to fall out with them as soon as they expressed a personal point of view conflicting with her own. The same thing would happen with Miss Muriel Montgomery, the red-haired Canadian who succeeded Miss Anson. In the end even Olave's personal secretary, Lettice Hill, who worked for her for nineteen years and was a great favourite – accompanying her on long walks in the country around Pax, and even being forgiven for wearing make-up in her presence – fell from grace.[29] This rejection was so painful that Miss Hill never once mentioned to Lord Renton, her friend and employer for over a decade after the war, that she had known the Baden-Powells.[30]

So Agnes Baden-Powell was not the last to suffer on account of Olave's insecurity. Unless she was flattered and her authority accepted without question, she could be more ruthless than her husband had ever been. Yet once she had established her authority so effectively, a new ambition would nearly undo what she and Baden-Powell had achieved with so much effort.

3. At the Court of Queen Olave (1919–30)

In the early years of her marriage, Olave had still depended heavily upon the companionship of girlhood friends such as 'Ba' Heysham and Sie Bower. Both had often stayed at Ewhurst and Little Mynthurst, but when Guiding became important to Olave her new circle of intimates was made up entirely of leading figures in the Guide world. To start with there had been Muriel Messel, her county secretary in Sussex who, although being the spoiled and self-willed daughter of a rich financier, had exactly the bubbly extrovert personality which Olave liked most. With their shared scorn for conventional female attire and Muriel's immense capacity for hard work, they made a formidable team. Olave had just appointed her to sit on her new Training Committee when Muriel unexpectedly died of pneumonia.[1]

Olave had then been on the point of moving to Pax Hill, where she would be within a few miles of Lady Helen Whitaker, her County Commissioner for Hampshire. She had first met Lady Helen in 1917 and had immediately taken to her. Both Olave and Baden-Powell were keen for senior figures in the Movement to be 'the right sort' and as an earl's daughter, Lady Helen undoubtedly fitted the bill. She was the same age as Olave, attractive, amusing and diplomatic. Her unhappy marriage was already all but over, and she needed diversion.[2] Olave recommended her for the highest positions in the Movement and she was soon made Deputy Chief Commissioner for the South of England and Head of Publications and Kindred Societies (the department responsible for liaison with bodies like the Y.W.C.A.). In addition she became Commissioner for British Guides in Belgium, Germany and France.

Lady Helen developed a loving friendship with Miss Ann Kindersley, who was District Commissioner for Newbury and, as Lady Helen's deputy in Europe, often travelled with her. Romantic friendships between senior Guide officials and ordinary Guiders were sufficiently common to excite little comment and Mrs R. B. Eggar – who ran the Guides in the Baden-Powells' village of Bentley – referred without any embarrassment to Miss Kindersley as Lady Helen's 'constant companion'. The two women acted together in a number of medieval pageants, one of which took place in Bentley and was attended by the Baden-Powells. On that occasion Lady Helen appeared as the 'Liege Lady' and Ann as her 'Wench'. Afterwards Helen always wrote to Ann as 'My darlingest Wench' and ended her letters 'so very much love my Wench darling, Your very loving Liege'.[3] They wrote to one another about the pain of separation and the joys of being together. Since Olave saw so much of Lady Helen and the two friends often visited Pax together, she could hardly have been in ignorance of their love for one another.[4]

In the early 1920s it was still possible for educated women to be ignorant of the sexuality underlying romantic friendships. By 1930 *The Well of Loneliness* prosecution and increasing public awareness of the works of Havelock Ellis and Freud had made unselfconscious love between women impossible. But during the Great War and immediately after it, popular girls' fiction such as Angela Brazil's school novels was still full of crushes between girls and between members of staff. Many early Guide leaders were alumni of schools like Roedean and St James's, Malvern, where they had learned to imitate the life in boys' public schools. They often left such institutions 'as gauche as men in personal relationships, their hair cut short (the Eton crop), their breasts squashed flat, their clothes severe, with boys' nicknames, boyish attributes and using boys' slang'.[5] Olave herself was not immune to such influences. Apart from flattening her breasts and concealing any hint of cleavage with handkerchiefs, she promised herself that she would cut off most of her hair as a reward for organizing all the counties of England.[6]

Two other 'constant companions' were prominent members of her Committee: the Hon. Mrs Walter (Fflorens) Roch, the wife of a back-bench Liberal M.P., and a Scottish spinster, Miss Clementina Anstruther Thomson. Mrs Roch lived very little with her husband and had nothing in common with him; she and Clementina were rarely apart. During the war they organized the Girl Guides in London and gave joint classes in drill and public speaking at the first Girl Guide training school. Mrs Roch ignored all adverse comments about her companion's masculine appearance and style of dress.[7] Nor was Olave with her devotion to 'Ba' Heysham inclined to worry about masculine attire or manly ways of speaking. As she explained to Mrs Wade, she rather liked a Guider to have 'a nice deep voice'.[8] For many women, either unhappily married or unmarried, or simply valuing friendships with other women, the Guide Movement was a blessing. Olave herself was never interested in children and enjoyed Guiding far more for the adult companionship it offered. Baden-Powell had a far greater interest in boys than Olave ever had in girls.

In February 1918, Olave went to France as a member of a small team of 'representative women' deputed to report on the Women's Auxiliary Army Corps, after some sections of the press had impugned the girls' sexual morals. She had taken a great liking to Dame Helen Gwynne-Vaughan, who was then Chief Controller of the W.A.A.C. It had then occurred to Olave that the Guides would gain greatly in national kudos if they could boast a few well-known women as members of their Committee. After the war she invited Dame Helen to join the Guides' Committee; she accepted and soon became Vice-Chairman. Like many of the women who held key positions in the Guides (Olave included), Helen had been much closer to her father than to her mother. Just as had happened to Rose Kerr, Helen's father (also an army officer) had died when she was a child – and, as with Rose, this remembered relationship became increasingly important as she grew older.[9] During a distinguished academic career, Helen had felt impelled to turn her back on her scientific work in order to join the women's army in emulation of her long-dead father. Exceptional devotion to a father either dead, absent or emotionally distant also characterized the childhood of Dame Katharine Furse, the post-war Assistant Chief Commissioner who, like all the others, had married a considerably older man. As a student Dame Helen had married her departmental professor and had then insisted on living apart from him except during vacations.[10] (He died after only four years of marriage as did Dame Katharine's husband, the painter Charles W. Furse.) None of these women was maternal, and both Olave and Katharine admitted their difficulties in this direction; they all shared a preference for uniform over ordinary female clothing.

Dame Katharine, who had founded the Women's Royal Naval Service and the V.A.D., was much more famous than Dame Helen and therefore seemed a more alluring catch. But unlike Helen, she was not sure if she wanted to have anything to do with the Guides. Olave wooed her most humbly during 1919, and at last in November Katharine intimated that she would consider being the director of a residential training school for Guiders if that were on offer. 'Oh, I DO like your idea,' replied Olave. 'It would be absolutely ideal . . . and would make a real Mecca of Guiding.'[11] But then Katharine abruptly changed her mind. Unabashed, Olave continued her wooing: 'Oh! I shall go on wanting you badly till the end of the chapter . . . How much I want to hear just a wee line . . . to say that there is still a chance.'[12] It was not until the spring of 1922 that Katharine finally decided to work with Olave as her Assistant Chief Commissioner. 'Your coming in now is to me the greatest joy and comfort, and I have never been more happy,' Olave told her in late May.[13]

Katharine was a large, splendid, open-minded woman, with two grown sons whom she had brought up – as she herself put it – more as a father than as a mother.[14] She was the youngest daughter of the famous art critic and essayist, John Addington Symonds, now better known as the author of a private diary giving an unvarnished account of homosexual life in Victorian England. Only when Katharine went to a psychoanalyst in her late forties did she at last understand 'not only why my father was not interested in me, but also why, during my early childhood, I was so sure that I was a boy'. She recalled finding contentment only when 'accepted as the boy of the family'.[15] As an adolescent she had found some of her father's albums of pornographic photographs and had pasted her own picture in amongst the nude sailors and soldiers. She took to wearing a sailor's uniform and imagined growing up to be one of these men whom her father had desired.[16] With no view of herself as a woman and no sexual feelings towards men, she married in a state of confusion – surprised to be asked, and flattered but far from enraptured.[17] As a young woman she had formed a series of 'intense attachments' and 'most passionate hero-worships' with members of her own sex, but in spite of her strong attraction to women she never thought of herself as exclusively homosexual. 'There are intermediate grades as varied as are the shades of colour.'[18] She shared this ambivalence with women like Helen Whitaker and Ann Kindersley, who both married at the end of their lengthy attachment (Lady Helen – for the second time – to a general, inevitably older than herself; and Ann to a bishop). But open-minded though she was, Dame Katharine was disconcerted by the 'sentimental intimacies' which she observed between Guiders and even Commissioners. She censured public kissing and embracing as 'unsuitable in a uniformed body of women', since 'the girls might follow their Guiders' example'.[19]

The plan was to make Dame Katharine Chief Commissioner as soon as she knew enough about the Movement to take over the administration, thus giving Olave greater freedom as Chief Guide to travel. To start with, everything went well. 'All the Commissioners love her already, and have simply taken her right into their hearts and work,' Olave told Percy Everett in October.[20] Katharine embarked upon a programme of public appearances and rallies in various parts of the country and when she was in Cumberland, Olave suggested that she stay with 'Ba' Heysham. This was so successful that Katharine vowed to return within weeks. 'Do give my love to your dear delicious hostess,' wrote Olave. 'I KNEW you would like her! I have known and loved her so long and felt sure you would find her delightful.'[21] Katharine wrote regularly to Olave during her tour, addressing her as 'Dear Ma'am' – this royal and yet familiar greeting delighting the Chief Guide. In late December Katharine went back to Switzerland where she had been brought up and where she worked for three months of the year for Sir Henry Lunn's travel company. Her departure marked the high-spot of her relations with Olave; they exchanged photographs and Olave admitted that she missed Katharine 'really a big lot'. Just before Christmas 1922, Olave told Katharine that 'never in my wildest dreams and my fondest hopes could I have imagined you would be and do what you have done . . . I knew you were the one person in the world worth having.'[22] Not knowing that Olave's close friendships often began at this white-hot pitch and then cooled with equal rapidity, Katharine felt euphoric. There was, however, one anxiety that weighed upon her even in Switzerland: Olave had another favourite, who would have to be dealt with if Katharine's ambitions for monopolizing her affections and for making the Guides a more socially responsible body were to be fulfilled.

Olave had introduced Katharine to Helen Whitaker and Alice Behrens in August 1919 as the two most important women in the Movement after herself.[23] Alice by then was Deputy Chief Commissioner for the North and County Commissioner for North-East Lancashire. But by the time Katharine had made up her mind to become actively involved, Alice had considerably increased her powers by becoming Head of Training and Guider-in-Charge at Foxlease (the Hampshire country house where Guiders went for their training, and where the women who would train the Guiders were themselves trained). The removal of Agatha Blyth had shown that the Baden-Powells appreciated the importance of controlling the Training Department, therefore Alice's appointment was proof of the highest favour. Since Katharine believed that the way in which an organization trained its leaders determined what kind of organization it became, she decided to stay at Foxlease as soon as she returned to England.

Alice was no intellectual, unlike Katharine. She had none of Katharine's administrative skills, and she never attempted to make impressive speeches about the Guide Movement's role in society as Katharine did. But she was warm, impetuous, totally unselfconscious and able to inspire passionate loyalty and enthusiasm in the majority of women who came to train at Foxlease. The daughter of a philanthropic textiles millionaire, Alice herself (when her father was Lord Mayor of Manchester) had often used his official car without his consent to take dirty clothes and linen from the slums to the free laundry she had started.[24]

In 1919 Katharine had told Olave that, if she joined the Guides, she would like to run a residential training centre. So some of the dislike she soon felt for Alice was inevitably due to jealousy. She was, however, genuinely dismayed by the atmosphere of fanatical keenness which Alice generated. The Guiders worked at the various tests they were set – whether on tracking, knots or camp hygiene – with astonishing enthusiasm. Watching Alice striding out in the New Forest with these young women, imitating for their benefit the calls of birds and larger animals (including the laughing jackass), made Katharine think of children at play rather than adults in training as future leaders of the nation's girls. 'Look up not down/ Look out not in,' sang the Guiders joyfully as they returned from the woods. Alice always joined in the singing and put herself through all the Guiders' tests. Katharine found herself feeling increasingly isolated.

Olave liked Foxlease because of its 'Guidy' atmosphere, by which she meant she thought it an intimate, homely, cheerful and lively place. 'Guiding is a Game; Guiding is Fun; Guiding is an Adventure,' both Olave and Alice would say in their speeches. To be Alice's guest at Foxlease was one of Olave's great pleasures. So when Katharine, after her week there, condemned the keenness which Olave found so

exhilarating as 'a disease and a madness', the Chief Guide was very
upset.[25] Katharine claimed that Alice's regime encouraged women,
even married ones, to sacrifice everything for Guiding, 'even to desert
their homes in the rush after the distractions offered by Guide
activities'.[26] 'The first aim of Guiding,' she told Olave, 'should be to
make them happier in their homes because they have new ideas for
making home a jollier and more interesting place.' Instead the Guiders
returned 'to ordinary life like lost souls', their minds stuffed with
'Guide Dope'. Katharine also castigated Alice for wasting money and
for trying to force Protestant Christianity down the throats of Jews and
Catholics. And as for the Guiders themselves – even the 'Diplomaed
Guiders' or 'Dips', who had been trained to teach new Guiders – they
were shockingly arrogant. On the platform at Brockenhurst station
they had terrified fellow passengers by 'their selfish, inconsiderate,
rude behaviour   singing Guide songs at the top of their voices . . .
and [on the train] taking seats from old people.'[27]

Olave first of all wrote back making light of these criticisms. The
'Dips' were very young; they had been uncontrollable even before
Alice started on them; and time and maturity would improve them in
the end.[28] But Katharine kept up her onslaught and a month later was
delighted to learn from Olave that she was 'trying to persuade Alice
Behrens to go right away for three months abroad and NOT TO
TOUCH Guides during that time.'[29] This was a wonderfully
welcome development, but as the months passed Alice stayed on at
Foxlease and the 'Dips' remained as indifferent as ever to their civic
responsibilities.

In November Katharine stayed at Foxlease again to see what changes
had taken place. She found the selection procedures as bad as ever, and
'a horrid system of "unofficial reports" and tittle tattle' being
employed by Alice to determine who was eligible to try for the highest
diploma qualification, 'The Red Cord'.[30] Katharine was convinced
that Alice was deliberately inventing excuses for refusing to allow
lower-middle-class girls to go on Red Cord Courses. One girl in
particular, whom Alice had rejected, Katharine had thought so
outstandingly well qualified that she wrote to Olave on her behalf,
asking the Chief Guide to set aside Alice's decision. With her letter
Katharine enclosed detailed recommendations for the reform of all
selection procedures.[31]

Olave had sought her husband's advice when she received
Katharine's earlier unfavourable verdicts on Foxlease, and she sought
it again after receiving Katharine's request to reverse Alice's judgement. 'About the Training and Diploma Judging etc.,' Olave replied,
'I am waiting really for the Chief to be able to cogitate upon it too . . .
He and I fully agree with you about the need for some change in the
system of judging.' Sensing that the Baden-Powells were almost on the

point of sacrificing Alice and surrendering the Training Department to her, Katharine waited anxiously for their decision on the wronged Guider, Miss Vachell. But their verdict proved a severe disappointment. 'We can't possibly go back on Alice Behrens's decision about Vachell NOW,' Olave informed her. "cos it would be unthinkable to give a person the job to do and then let her down by saying she is wrong.'[32]

Katharine's instincts told her that if she accepted this rebuff meekly, she would never convert any of her opinions into concrete reforms. She therefore fired off a letter threatening resignation on the grounds that she could not honestly go on publicly promoting a Movement without a committee having the power to act as a court of appeal in individual cases of injustice. Olave responded characteristically in this emergency: 'Oh, oh, NO, please. You DON'T mean it! Please think it over more . . . Let us meet to talk about it.' She was coming up to town the following week and asked if she might 'come and sleep in your house that night?' Katharine agreed. Baden-Powell now wrote to Katharine too, begging her to stay on and suggesting that she ought not to resign 'unless you feel that we are not working on right lines . . .'[33] This gave Katharine an inkling of the man's shrewdness. Would she be wise to resign over what could easily be represented as a clash of personalities rather than a basic point of principle? Had he guessed that her envy of Alice was partly to blame?

Her meeting with Olave confirmed Katharine's opinion that the Movement could not be reformed while Baden-Powell and Olave ruled as 'King and Queen'. Well-connected court favourites like Alice would always be invulnerable while the committee rubber-stamped all the Baden-Powells' decisions. The Movement was clearly 'an Autocracy with the Shadow of a Democracy to meet public opinion'. As a 'proprietory concern' belonging to the ruling couple, 'helpers were only used to push it along, without in any way controlling its policy'. After Olave had gone, Katharine wrote: 'If I consent to continue as Assistant Chief Commissioner I must put aside my own views and follow blindly, standing for something over which I have no control and on which my views are not really wanted. At the same time I love the Chief Guide . . .'[34]

Katharine allowed Olave to persuade her to delay a final decision until she returned from Switzerland in the spring of 1924. By then Olave had come to a decision of her own. Katharine had not turned out to be the warmly supportive and uncritical assistant she had wanted, but fortunately that was exactly what loyal and unassuming Alice Behrens had been all the time and still was. As soon as Katharine heard the first rumour that Olave intended to make Alice her Chief Commissioner, she was thankful that she had not resigned. Since she would never agree to serve under Alice, who in national terms was a nonentity, Olave would have to sack her before being able to appoint her favourite. When Olave at last wrote telling Katharine that she meant to reorganize her Commissioners and to abolish the Assistant Chief Commissionership, Katharine replied: 'You often remind me of the White Queen in Alice in Wonderland, "Off with their heads." So now I am added to the derelicts of whom I think there are already too many in the Guides . . . You must do what you think best for the Movement and explain it as best you can – But if people ask me why I have been disrated I shall have to tell them what I know of it and that won't be easy.'[35] Katharine then wrote to Dame Helen, the Chairman of the Executive Committee, reminding her that under the Guides' Royal Charter the appointment of the Chief Commissioner did not rest with the Baden-Powells but with the Committee.[36]

Faced with choosing between a vitriolic public fracas or back-tracking over Alice's appointment, Olave took Baden-Powell's advice and backtracked. With Olave powerless to harm her, Katharine allowed herself the luxury of writing a long letter of advice to Alice about how to run her training courses. Then, with an eye to the future, she started to cultivate the Head of the Overseas Department and to use her work for Lunn to make more contacts with leaders of the Guides in Europe.[37] By the autumn she had joined the International Committee at Guide Headquarters and was pointing to 'the need for some independent international entity'.[38] Although her attempt to reform the British Guides had come to nothing, Dame Katharine finally defeated the Baden-Powells' determined opposition to her new aim of setting up and leading a separate Girl Guide World Bureau. Baden-Powell and Olave were also forced to give way to her over Alice Behrens who, instead of being made Chief Commissioner, was sent to Australia to reorganize the Movement there. An uninspiring compromise candidate was chosen for the top job.

After Katharine became Chairman of the World Council of Guides and Director of the World Bureau – defeating Rose Kerr, Baden-Powell's preferred candidate – the Chief Scout prevented the Dominions from being represented on the World Council except through the Overseas Department at Girl Guide Headquarters. He also made it clear in the late 1920s that he would never permit the World Council to become an international representative government for the Guides.[39] Katharine tried to force Olave to take a greater interest in European Guiding by persuading the Council to elect her 'World Chief Guide'. 'To my mind you are Chief Guide of each country,' Katharine told her, 'and you have therefore an obligation to the Guide Movement of each country as such. Sometimes you appear to me to be completely Empire in mind . . . All our work will be wasted if the feeling continues that the Anglo-Saxons are trying to dominate the World Association.' During the early 1930s Olave actively canvassed against the election of individual women to the World Council if she thought them too independent-minded; this led to worse relations with Dame Katharine.[40]

Olave always acted on Baden-Powell's instructions in connection with Katharine's organization. His great fear was that the World Committee would become a policy-forming body. As founder of the Movement, he believed that all policy had to flow from him. When the Council formed a research sub-committee in 1932 to study and advise on the future direction of the Movement, he was appalled. 'It means practically the taking over of the direction of the Movement by the World Committee.'[41] Baden-Powell also worried about what he described as 'over organization', which was, he suggested, 'very satisfactory to some reformers but not to the girls. Too much organization kills the spirit.'[42] Dame Katharine perhaps did not make fair allowance for the genuineness of his fears. When the Council was formed, Britain – with almost half a million Guides – had significantly the largest number in the world. Out of 40 countries with some kind of Girl Guide organization, 22 had fewer than 1,000 members each. After Britain, America and the Dominions accounted for the greater part of the remaining quarter of a million Girl Guides and Girl Scouts in the world. Katharine countered by blaming Anglo-American exclusiveness for Guiding's comparative failure in Europe and by suggesting that it had to be promoted internationally and shown to be international, rather than Imperial, before it could grow there.

Katharine Furse did more than anyone else to set in motion the Movement's gradual emancipation from its founder's autocratic control. Without this development, she had been sure that the Scouts and the Guides would not develop identities truly their own. She nevertheless underrated what Baden-Powell and Olave had achieved before she became actively involved with Guiding herself. A wise friend of Olave had advised her to remember that 'in such a personal thing as Guiding, back history counts such a lot . . . inevitably when you think the only organization started with the Baden-Powells and their friends . . . In the old days no one knew anything and so to a great extent it was the personality of the person that counted – that's where Alice Behrens came in.'[43]

Olave had been right to consider Alice a remarkable person, and it was Guiding's misfortune that she never became Chief Commissioner. But Katharine was remarkable too with her very different aptitudes. With greater wisdom and less favouritism, Olave might have managed to retain both their considerable talents for the benefit of the British Guides. In 1928 Alice married the now elderly Arthur Gaddum of the Scouts' Headquarters' Committee – like herself a member of Manchester's manufacturing aristocracy. She never returned to Guiding. After her departure and Dame Katharine's

European defection, Olave abandoned her search for the perfect friend and assistant. This was a relief to her husband, who thenceforward felt able to rely upon her not to endanger the family's dominance by too close an involvement with any individual within the Movement.

15

WIDER STILL AND WIDER

1. American Dreams and Nightmares (1910–31)

Between 1908 and 1914 Scouts and Guides spread throughout the British Empire, including all the Dominions. They could also be found in Scandinavia, France, Germany, Austria, Holland, Poland, Portugal, Russia, Switzerland, Italy and Greece. Both Movements were popular in South America, the Balkans and even in Japan. But their most striking success outside Great Britain was in America, where by 1918 there were already 300,000 Scouts, and almost a million a decade later.[1]

Scouting first spread to the United States without any encouragement from Baden-Powell. In 1910 he visited Canada and was invited to New York by Edgar M. Robinson of the Y.M.C.A., who had recently persuaded the Chicago publisher, William D. Boyce, to let the 'Y' take over the Boy Scouts of America, which he had first incorporated. Robinson and his colleagues were determined to stop the Scouts being abused as a circulation gimmick by the Hearst newspapers. When they asked Baden-Powell to support them, he most generously signed over his rights in *Scouting for Boys* and agreed to let them use his Movement's uniform and variants of his badges without any form of payment.[2]

In 1912 he returned to America for a lecture tour which he had arranged through a New York agent. When James E. West, the new Executive Secretary of the Boy Scouts of America, heard that the founder of Scouting had contracted to deliver twenty lectures in America but none of them to Scouts and their supporters, he was appalled. He at once entered into negotiations with Mr Keedick, the lecture agent, to see if he could buy him out and turn Baden-Powell's visit into a fund-raising exercise for the Scouts. For $20,000 West and his Executive Board managed to purchase thirteen of the lectures; and for so large an investment they expected Baden-Powell to give his lectures and speak at numerous luncheons and dinners. Unlike the British Scouts, the Boy Scouts of America was employing paid organizers, and so depended upon a constant stream of donations for the salaries. Although Baden-Powell was exhausted by giving so many lectures, he allowed West to bully him into these unwelcome extra commitments.[3]

Only rarely did he refuse to play the game, as in Nashville where he 'escaped via the luggage lift' and left the town rather than face the Governor of the State, the local Scout committee and a band when they came to serenade him late in the evening at his hotel.[4] He found it unbelievable that what had started in such a haphazard way in England should have spread so far. 'Every town, wherever we go,' he told his mother, 'seems to be full of its Scouts and Scoutmasters, and they all seem to look upon me as their head.'[5]

The America of his dreams was still a wild untamed place, and the people were resourceful, honest and energetic. Just as in the Colonies he had commended the freedom from English class distinction, in America he applauded relaxed social attitudes. He was welcomed by successive Presidents of the United States and some of the country's richest men. In 1912 he met President Howard Taft at the White House, had a long conversation with Andrew Carnegie and then visited Theodore Roosevelt at his house in Oyster Bay. Here surely was the archetypal frontiersman turned statesman. Sitting with the ex-President by a great log fire, surrounded by his big game trophies, Baden-Powell studied 'the strong and burly figure of my restless host' as Roosevelt 'rocked violently in his rocking chair' and affirmed that 'what counted in a nation as in a man was character'.[6] Roosevelt would soon be given the honorary title of 'Chief Scout Citizen'.

Yet in 1912, America was no longer Cody's land. And the direction in which James E. West (soon to be Chief Scout Executive) began to take the Boy Scouts of America was one Baden-Powell deplored. West was not an outdoor man, which was not his fault since he had been born with a deformed foot, but his obsession with bureaucratic control was a different matter. In Baden-Powell's opinion the organization of Scouting ought to be free of 'red tape', and as little like the management of a business as possible. Yet business seemed to be the model on which West based his entire operation. By paying all his Scout officials as members of 'an organized profession', West – according to Baden-Powell   had lost the altruistic spirit of a 'voluntary movement' in which individuals give their time to serve the community.[7] Almost as bad was West's encouragement of vast 'community gatherings', which left no scope for a sense of adventure. American boys were hampered too by numerous regulations governing the amount of equipment which had to be taken on expeditions and the exact ratio of adult supervision. Baden-Powell described such highly organized camps as 'Parlour Scouting'.[8]

Stephe cared more for the United States than for any other country outside the British Empire, but still felt unable to attack West in public to ensure that changes occurred. The man was a cripple, and had been brought up in an orphanage. Furthermore, West had been vilified in the press by Thompson Seton just when the naturalist had accused Baden-Powell of plagiarism. Baden-Powell had thus been forced to be

James West's ally. [9] Seton summarized his 'true' history of Scouting in America with the phrase: 'Seton started it, Baden-Powell boomed it, and West killed it.'[10]

In 1915, 1927, 1937 and 1940, Seton attacked Baden-Powell in the press and on each occasion West (a lawyer by training) was ready to parry the blows. When Seton finally wrote an autobiography in which all his old claims were repeated, West subjected Mr Scribner to such intense pressure that the publisher surrendered unconditionally and 'agreed to eliminate all reference to the origin of Scouting'.[11]

But while Baden-Powell remained silent on such matters his disapproval of the Boy Scouts of America meant that, when he returned briefly in 1919, 1923, 1926 and 1930, he spent more time with the Girl Scouts than with the boys. In truth West was only partly to blame for Baden-Powell's increasing disillusion. In 1912 the spirit of small-town America had seemed unimpaired; but when he returned during the 'roaring twenties' to be fêted in Chicago he saw another side of America. The mayor honoured him with a police motorcycle escort and drove him at 70 m.p.h down the centre of Michigan Avenue, 'the biggest thoroughfare in the world and the most densely crowded with traffic'. As pedestrians leapt for their lives and the sirens screamed, the mayor confided to Baden-Powell that his police shot gangsters whenever they could 'since if merely arrested juries would not convict for fear of gang reprisals'. Baden-Powell would be equally depressed by the popularity of gangster movies and crime novels.[12]

In 1930, he was caught up in a violent street demonstration in New York. A civic reception in his honour ought to have taken place at the City Hall, but had to be cancelled. The trouble – caused by a mob of unemployed men – was not principally aimed at him, although he did see several placards bearing legends such as 'SMASH THE BOY SCOUTS'. To his amazement, the police turned out 'armed with clubs, machine guns, and tear gas bombs, supported by the fire brigade with their hoses playing on the mob'. Since extracts from his speech were to have been broadcast, he was driven to a recording studio where a vital technician proved to be absent. He returned next day, and was told to reduce his speech to three minutes; while struggling to oblige, he was pestered by a couple of female reporters whose persistence made him feel ill. He left New York for the last time upset, exhausted and only slightly mollified by Franklin D. Roosevelt's courteous farewell.[13]

Increasingly, Baden-Powell feared the cultural impact of the world's greatest economic power. In the 1920s hysterical British women routinely welcomed Hollywood stars on their arrival at London's Waterloo Station. 'Yet into this same railway station have come soldiers and sailors, back from hell, who fought for us and saved their country, but who are allowed to slide in unnoticed and unpraised.'[14]

Then there were the American-inspired publicity stunts, the solo flights, the speed records – all angled at the film news cameras. In Britain too, instant celebrities came and went in the American fashion.

Other exports from the United States which he deplored were jazz, cocktails, high heels, nail varnish and, particularly, lipstick which in his youth had been associated with prostitutes. 'What is the difference between a cow chewing the cud and a man chewing gum?' he would ask rhetorically. 'The cow looks intelligent.'[15] He knew intuitively that these fads meant the end of the deferential society in which a code of ethics could be handed downwards with a reasonable chance of finding acceptance. His advocacy of the simple life would be drowned out by the commercial values of America. 'A rich man,' he would often say during the 1920s and 1930s, 'is not the man with the most money but with the fewest wants.' He reproached people for wanting 'to possess, rather than to enjoy the world around them'.[16]

Stephe's own favourite film, however, remained an American production: *The Covered Wagon*.[17] The image of whole families on the move, braving hardship and danger as they lumbered westward in their wagons, was one that both touched and saddened him, since it recalled America before 'over-civilization' had destroyed the virtuous pioneering spirit.

2. The Empire: White and Black (1912–36)

In America, as in other foreign countries, Baden-Powell saw his role as a concerned adviser. In 1920 the Boy Scouts' International Bureau was founded under a British Director and all Boy Scout organizations were expected to register – only one body being officially accepted in each country. But from that point onwards these organizations were their own masters.

In the British Empire, however, matters were quite different, as became apparent in 1918 when 'Imperial Headquarters' was the name chosen for the new Boy Scout offices in Buckingham Palace Road. 'Imperial Headquarters,' Baden-Powell wrote three years later, 'is responsible to the Privy Council that each branch to which we give authority to act is working on right principles.'[1] Colonies and States were expected to run their own organizations without supervision unless these 'right principles' were threatened, in which case Baden-Powell's personal intervention would be required. This happened much more often than is generally supposed, and many of his tours were concerned with laying down the law as well as with ceremonial duties.

In Sydney in 1912 he asked Mr. T. R. Roydhouse, the chairman of the New South Wales Scout Council, to resign because – as the proprietor of the *Sydney Sunday Times* – he was giving the impression that Scouting in the state was being run as a circulation-boosting device. Roydhouse obliged the Chief Scout.[2] Baden-Powell aimed to keep control in the Dominions by personally appointing State Chief Commissioners and making them answerable to Imperial Headquarters. In 1931, he was requested by the State Scout Council in Victoria to dismiss their self-willed Chief Commissioner, Captain F. A. White, who had ignored the unelected Council set up by Imperial Headquarters and had formed his own committee of 'Elected Scoutmasters', which he considered sovereign in the state. Since Baden-Powell's system of rule from afar (which depended upon London authorizing all key state appointments) would not survive if men like White opted for local democracy, he was determined to sack him; and since he was neither young nor in good health, Baden-Powell (himself 74) told him to resign.[3]

When White merely promised to consider his position, Baden-Powell let it be known that a 24-year-old tutor at Adelaide University would take over as Chief Commissioner. But White rallied support so effectively that Baden-Powell was obliged to abandon his young favourite, leaving the state's Scouting affairs in a worse state than when he had arrived.[4] White's warrant was summarily withdrawn by Imperial Headquarters a few months later, although he had increased the number of Scouts in South Australia from 250 to 6,000 in less than eight years.

Like Sir Francis Vane, White had failed to understand Baden-Powell's determination to maintain his hold over the Scouts' organization in every part of the Empire. Not that he only thought of this as a personal matter. Loyalty to the Mother Country was equally involved. Men like Captain White had to go because they threatened Scouting's capacity to remind boys throughout the white colonial Empire of their common British heritage.

In Australia, New Zealand and Canada (in spite of the French Canadians), Baden-Powell felt confident of his authority. But in South Africa and India, where race was an issue, matters were different. By 1912, without his sanction, decisions had been made by white Commissioners in Barbados and Demarara to prevent black boys being Scouts. In Trinidad there were separate troops for blacks and whites, and in South Africa all the troops were white. By 1926, all the white Provincial Commissioners in South Africa had rejected requests from groups of Africans, Cape Coloureds and Indians wishing to be recognized as Boy Scouts. Since the South African Government supported this line, Baden-Powell accepted that for the time being the Scouts must remain a monopoly of the white population.[5]

In 1926 the Archbishop of Cape Town told him in person that the Boy Scouts would be destroyed in South Africa if he allowed blacks to join. His Grace reminded him of the fate of the Boys' Brigade and the Church Lads' Brigade, which when they had attempted to become multi-racial had seen all their white boys removed by their parents.[6] Baden-Powell was also warned by Government officials that the Boers would opt out of the Scouts and form their own youth movement. In spite of Baden-Powell's attempts to prevent this, in 1931 the Boer-dominated South African Government introduced their own scheme for boys of Dutch descent: the Voortrekkers.

The four Provinces of South Africa formed a Union Scout Council in 1923, but did not trust one another enough to vote this body any powers. In Natal, Scout officials considered local blacks and Indians better educated than in other parts of South Africa. The Chief Commissioner E. II. Clemmans and his deputy H. V. Marsh pro-posed – as a first step towards a fairer system – allowing Indians to become Boy Scouts but in segregated troops. If this did not provoke a white boycott black and coloured troops could then be sanctioned.[7] Such views proved anathema in the Transvaal where Scout officials had already formed a separate movement for blacks called the Pathfinders. In 1927, Baden-Powell refused to allow the Transvaalers either to 'control' or 'administer' this new grouping; they could give them 'assistance' but no more than that. He knew that, if there were ever to be blacks and whites in a single movement, he would have to refuse the Pathfinders official status.[8]

The Natal Scout Council refused to start Pathfinder troops and in 1927 began to register Indians as Boy Scouts. In response a Transvaal Scoutmaster, Mr G. W. Dickinson, caused Baden-Powell further difficulties by asking him to take charge of the Paladins, a movement he had started for Cape Coloureds (most of whom had refused to join the Pathfinders).[9] Baden-Powell was not going to be tricked into approving this separate movement, even when the rapid spread of the Paladins in the Cape Colony caused a crisis. The line taken by Mr C.L. Mansergh, the Provincial Commissioner for the Cape Colony (where there were more coloureds than in any other part of South Africa) was that unless the South African Government decided 'to lay down a definite policy', he would ignore the Paladins. He certainly did not feel justified in 'assisting' them.[10] This infuriated the Transvaal leaders who were only interested in 'taking charge' in the Cape to stop coloured boys there from wearing the standard Boy Scout uniform, which they would do unless supplied with Paladin and Pathfinder gear from Johannesburg. Indian troops in Natal were already wearing ordinary Boy Scout uniforms. While Baden-Powell dreaded the existence of large numbers of native troops responsible to no Scouting authority, he was reluctant to allow the reactionary Transvaal Scout Council to exercise any authority in the Cape.

In September 1926 Baden-Powell came out to South Africa for six

months, determined to sort out these grave problems. He concentrated on the white leaders, rarely making contact with the blacks and
coloureds about whom the fuss was supposed to be. On one occasion,
however, he met a deputation of nine Cape Coloureds from Kimberley who wanted to start some troops of Boy Scouts. These men asked
him why, since there were black Boy Scouts in Uganda and Indian
Boy Scouts in India, there should be no African Boy Scouts in South
Africa. 'They spoke remarkably well and one could not help
sympathizing with them,' noted Baden-Powell. One man reminded
him of the services performed by the Cape Boys during the Matabele
Campaign; another had served in the Machine-Gun Corps in Flanders.
Shaken by this encounter, Baden-Powell injudiciously told them that
they 'could rest assured that their application has my full sympathy'.
He noticed that 'they seemed very pleased'.[11] But this pleasure would
be short-lived.

Two weeks later the Commissioner in Salisbury, Southern
Rhodesia, warned Baden-Powell of the dangers of taking what such
men said at face value. 'Coloured people,' he insisted, 'are keen to join
the Scout movement *because* it is white . . . Politics are behind this.'
Time and again Baden-Powell was urged not to be tricked by black or
coloured politicians, who would use his concessions to embarrass the
South African Government.[12] All Baden-Powell's life he had been
inclined to respect authority, but 'the native question' still left him
feeling guilty and dissatisfied. Just before sailing, he wrote: 'The
question stands with the politicians just where it did 20 years ago. They
do not look forward to what is due to the native.'[13] At sea, homeward
bound, he met a fellow passenger who disabused him of any idea that
the South African Government was neutral. President G. S. Botha,
this stranger told him, on the authority of Miss Botha whom he knew,
'hated us [the Scouts]'.[14]

Within a month of his return home Baden-Powell began to press the
Transvaalers to follow the Natal Council's plan of one Boy Scout
Movement with parallel but separate branches for whites, blacks,
Indians and coloureds – all to be called Boy Scouts and to wear the one
uniform.[15] He made no progress at all and ought to have risked sacking
their leaders, but since he still hoped to avoid the formation of a
separate Boer youth movement he stayed his hand.

After the South African Government's creation of the Voortrekkers,
there was less need to conciliate the Boers. Clemmans and the Natal
Scout Council decided to admit blacks as well as Indians to the
Movement, as full Boy Scouts entitled to wear the uniform and
badges. 'To suggest that the ideals and name can only apply to
Europeans . . . is absolutely opposed to the spirit of Scouting,' Natal's
leaders told the South African Scout Council.[16] They were at once
ostracized by the rest of the white Movement.

The Pathfinders' leaders reacted to this new situation by applying to the Boy Scouts' International Bureau for 'official recognition as an equivalent and autonomous organization in Southern Africa'.[17] Still believing that he could somehow persuade the South African Scout Council to come to an agreement with the liberals of Natal, Baden-Powell blocked a decision and promised to come out to South Africa in 1936 to help all the parties to find a way out of the current impasse. He was in poor health even before he contracted malaria while sailing down the East African coast; and at 79 he no longer had the energy to out-manoeuvre or crush opponents like Sir Reginald Blankenberg (the former secretary to the South African High Commissioner in London), who now chaired the Transvaal Scout Council.

He *ought* to have let the Pathfinders and Paladins (outside Natal) register with the International Bureau and to have declared the Natal Council the official centre of approved Scouting in South Africa. But he recoiled from breaking up the white Movement and instead offered Blankenberg a compromise on 'control' over the 'equal and parallel' black and coloured branches. The South African Scout Council was to be granted 'general supervision' over all the branches.[18] The Pathfinders naturally refused to accept this unless they were to be properly represented on the Council.[19]

The solution which Baden-Powell finally worked out with the white South African Scout Council was that there would be two Councils, one for the white and one for the non-white Boy Scouts. In the event of a dispute, they would come together as a joint Council, but with the whites possessing a small in-built majority. Since no other terms were acceptable to Blankenberg, Baden-Powell and the Pathfinders' leaders accepted this arrangement. On the uniform and badges Baden-Powell was more successful; the Scout hat and other items would be identical for all branches, except that each would wear a different hat-band. All boys in South Africa would be within one Movement and would be called Boy Scouts.

Baden-Powell would always be affected by the views on race current in his youth; but over the years he progressed a long way. In this connection, he liked to quote J. R. Lowell's famous dictum: 'There are two kinds of people who never change their opinions – the foolish and the dead.'[20] Indeed his opinions on race changed considerably during the last decade of his life. He knew he had failed in South Africa, although he did not say so in public. Shortly after his return to England he wrote to Lord Clarendon, the British Governor-General at the Cape, admitting that he feared 'lest questions which affect the Movement as a whole in South Africa are liable to become directed by a triumvirate in Johannesburg'.[21] Baden-Powell made this admission after Sir Reginald Blankenberg and his cronies had dissuaded his first two choices for the Chief Commissionership of South Africa from taking up the post. He had earlier told Blankenberg that the Chief Commissioner would be over all the non-European Scouts as well as over the whites. Blankenberg wanted Chief Commissioners for 'each of the parallel organizations . . . the whole idea being to keep them entirely separate . . .'[22] Eventually, to Blankenberg's disgust, Baden-Powell appointed the liberal Clemmans. He and his deputy were decent people who believed that 'public opinion in Natal had changed very much for the better in regard to colour within recent years', and were determined not to be 'inconsistent in carrying out our Scout principles'.[23] Sadly, the future of South Africa would not lie in the hands of such men.

In the Southern States of America during this period there were no integrated Scout troops. In 1918 the Boy Scouts of America's expert on race relations stated that it was futile to expect Southern whites to allow blacks to become Boy Scouts even in segregated troops. The Executive Board allowed the Southern whites to veto the formation of black troops, even when they offered to call themselves names such as the 'Young American Patriots'. In the north segregated troops were also the norm, although by the 1930s some integrated troops existed.[24]

★

After South Africa the Dominion closest to Baden-Powell's heart was India, and here too there was a 'colour question'. As early as 1916, he expressed himself in favour of Indians becoming Boy Scouts,[25] but when the Viceroy Lord Chelmsford vetoed the idea,[26] Stephe accepted the ban.

The situation was transformed by the emergence of a most unexpected champion of would-be Indian Boy Scouts. During her extraordinary career Mrs Annie Besant had been an atheist, a freethinker, a birth control pioneer, a Fabian socialist and the spiritual leader of the Theosophists. Throughout the 1920s, as President of the Indian National Congress, she was a dauntless campaigner for Indian Home Rule. During the course of 1916 Mrs Besant, whose Theosophists ran a number of schools, started some troops of Indian Boy Scouts in Madras and Benares. The Governor of Madras, Lord Pentland, considered her a dangerous political agitator and interned her.

After her release, Mrs Besant castigated Baden-Powell for toeing the official line.[27] When her Scouts began to multiply in thousands, Lord Pentland arbitrarily declared himself President of the Boy Scouts of India and began to promote his own Scouts in a bid to stop the spread of Mrs Besant's. The Y.M.C.A. did the same and by 1918 had 200 Scoutmasters in training. But by then Mrs Besant's boys numbered over 20,000. Baden-Powell knew it would be absurd not to attempt 'to get all the various Indian organizations together', and in spite of the

Viceroy's hostility he decided 'to take the Indian boys into the Movement . . .'[28] He arrived in India on 7 January 1921, determined to unite with Mrs Besant – a courageous and well-timed decision since it coincided with her brief period of support for the Government's constitutional reforms. However, there were plenty of influential people eager to stop him doing a deal with 'that horrible woman'.[29]

The highlight of his visit was a great rally to which Mrs Besant had promised to bring several thousand of her Scouts. These and Pentland's Scouts had by now amalgamated but there were other groups of Indian boys also at the rally, such as the pro-Independence Seva Samiti. The ceremony did not quite go to plan. 'It was arranged that Mrs Besant would come out into the centre and take from me the Scout Promise. With all the dramatic force at my command I called upon her . . . to repeat after me the words of the Promise. At that moment my mind wandered . . . and for the life of me I could not remember the words . . . There was an awkward pause.' Luckily Mrs Besant, 'picturesque in native costume', whispered the words, 'which I then roared out in ringing tones'.[30] A few months later he had the imagination to write to Mrs Besant to ask her for stories about native Indian heroes which he wished to include in a new Indian edition of *Scouting for Boys*.[31]

★

During the 1920s and 1930s, Baden-Powell travelled to Canada three times and to New Zealand twice. Nor were the countries of Europe forgotten – most being visited more than once during this period. That he attempted so much during his late sixties and seventies was due entirely to his unrelenting sense of duty. Long after other men had retired, he was coping with the honours and the absurdities of official visits. 'At Tenerife, directly we arrived, Scout Commissioners appeared with bouquets, but nobody knowing English . . . one simply could not do anything but grin.' On ordinary occasions, he and Olave found 'there was always so much talk about so little'.[32] The constant rallies and functions and the added strain of staying with Governors or national figures were very wearying for him during tours of two or three months' duration.[33] Expenses apart, Baden-Powell was never paid anything for his years of toil as World Chief Scout.

16

THE SPIRIT VERSUS THE FORM

1. Committee Men and Boy Men (1917–25)

In the summer of 1918, a Winchester Scoutmaster wrote to Baden-Powell deploring the 'schoolmasterly' type of mind that was 'de-souling' Scouting by 'throttling' it with routine. '"Spirit" is what matters – "form" must be elastic enough to allow the spirit to express itself adequately in whatever conditions it is trying to work.'[1] Baden-Powell was so struck by this letter that he subsequently gave numerous Scouting speeches on the theme of 'The Spirit versus the Form'.

At the end of the Great War, with so many of his promising young Commissioners and Scoutmasters dead, Baden-Powell had been left with an elderly Headquarters' Committee which Arthur Gaddum accurately described as moribund and out of touch.[2] As Baden-Powell looked at these soberly suited and wing-collared gentlemen sitting round the Committee table, they appeared more like the directors of a bank than the leaders of a vigorous youth movement. Their actions as well as their appearance convinced him that they cared less for the spirit than for the form.

In India in 1921, Baden-Powell had met and taken a liking to a fat and cheerful businessman who had been helping Mrs Besant with her boys. Sir Alfred Pickford, whose self-confident public manner belied his sensitive nature, had made a fortune in jute before returning to England in 1922. After buying a substantial Surrey estate where he settled down with his spinster sister, he offered his sevices to Baden-Powell and was soon the Chief Scout's most valued member of the Headquarters' Committee. Throughout the 1920s Baden-Powell considered 'Pickie' his heir apparent, and consequently Sir Alfred was frequently subjected to petty attacks in Committee by envious members.[3] He chaired a Publicity and Appeals Sub-Committee which the main Headquarters' Committee arbitrarily dismantled without speaking to him first, effectively throwing away two years' work. Baden-Powell was infuriated, but although he was now even more determined to get rid of the 'dead wood', he would find it impossible to do so while a majority of the Committee fell into that category.[4]

'Pickie' was constantly urging Baden-Powell to bring in 'new blood'. He had been particularly upset by the sniping of a septuagenarian Committee member who had helped raise much of the money for the new Headquarters' offices and was therefore considered beyond reproach. In 1917 Baden-Powell had unsuccessfully attempted to persuade Percy Armitage to resign, but the old man was still on the Committee in 1930.[5]

Baden-Powell deplored the Committee's slowness in launching the Rovers or Senior Scouts. Olave came home one day to find him 'raging at the rotten way in which the Committee try to put on the brake and the disgracefully ungrateful manner in which they behave'. 'It is too horrid, and boring and sickening,' she complained to Percy Everett.[6] Stephe and Olave were also sickened by the Committee's lack of sympathy towards the Girl Guides, best illustrated by their refusal in 1919 to accommodate the Guides' small office in the Boy Scouts' magnificent new building – except at an exorbitant rent.[7] Another incident which upset Baden-Powell was Major A. G. Wade's resignation in 1924; Wade had become joint Managing Secretary in 1912, and had resumed his old post after having had 'a good war' (he won the M.C.). He had always shared Baden-Powell's scorn for red tape and paper-work. If he knew he was going to incur expenses, he applied for them in advance and never thought it necessary to give an itemized breakdown afterwards. Colonel A. D. Acland (a former director of W. H. Smith), who became the Boy Scouts' Treasurer in 1921, had other ideas and did not consider a gentleman's word sufficient discharge. Wade resigned over this issue; and although Baden-Powell was eager to undo the damage, he failed.[8]

In 1922 Baden-Powell decided that the term 'Scoutmaster' was too formal for the 'elder brother' relationship which ought to exist between boys and their adult leaders. He much preferred the term 'Scouter', which had already been informally adopted by progressive Commissioners. In inviting men of national standing to sit on the Council, Baden-Powell later paid a price by having so many of them on the Executive Committee. The Earl of Meath, who had dreamed up Empire Day and founded the Duty and Discipline Movement, was 81 in 1922 and an extremely active Committee member. He loathed the term 'Scouter' and was determined to stop its implementation. Several members wrote to Baden-Powell telling him that if Lord Meath moved his resolution ('Respectfully requesting the Chief Scout to cease to use the term "Scouter" in official documents or speeches'), they would support it. The resolution was indeed moved by Meath and carried by a substantial majority, whereupon Baden-Powell wrote icily to the Committee:

> With regard to Lord Meath's wish to re-open the question of 'Scouter' . . . It seems to me still rather open to question whether the matter was not one for me rather than the Committee, since it has to do with the spirit and *intention of Scouting*, rather than with the rules and organization of the Movement . . . I am afraid that I must

still maintain that 'Scouter' is the only one I can employ to state my
meaning, and since it is not approved for official use, I will use it
merely as an expressive nickname.[9]

A year later Baden-Powell won approval for his favoured word, but
his annoyance with the Committee lingered on and was not improved
by their half-hearted endorsement of his new oath of loyalty for
Scouters. This was called the Ipise Test ('*ipise*' in Zulu means whither)
and its purpose was to guard against communists or perverts entering
the Movement – though why such people should not have been
prepared to swear that they were neither of these things was never very
clear.

The Committee was not alone in condemning the incantation of the
Ipise Test as absurd mumbo-jumbo. Nevertheless Baden-Powell
persevered with it for a couple of years before giving way.[10] Although
on this occasion the Committee had been right, it was Baden-Powell's
particular genius to be able to mix the prosaic with the strange. His
decision to base his training for younger boys (in the 8–11 age range)
upon the anthropomorphic goings-on of the animals in a work of
children's fiction is a perfect example. The stories in the *Jungle Books*
had at once suggested the rituals which guaranteed the success of the
Wolf Cubs.

> The call of the pack all over the world is 'We'll do our best'; so when
> your cubmaster comes into the circle you chuck up your chin and,
> all together, you howl out – making each word a long yowl; 'A-ka-
> la – We-e-e-e-ll do-o-o-o our-u-ur BEST.' Yell the word 'best'
> sharp and loud and short and all together.

The coded abbreviations of 'Do your best' and 'Done our Best',
chanted as 'Dyb, dyb, dyb' and 'Dob, dob, dob', gave the Cubs a
secret ritual of their own. Instead of being a pale imitation of the
Scouts, the Cubs had a strong identity from the beginning. That all this
was Baden-Powell's doing is certain. *The Wolf Cubs' Handbook* was
already in proof by the time he approached Kipling for permission to
use the *Jungle Books*. Kipling was normally exceptionally chary of
allowing his work to be quoted or exploited, so his decision to let
Baden-Powell make such extensive use of the *Jungle Books* is proof of
his admiration for the man. Baden-Powell mailed the proofs of the
handbook to Kipling on 28 July 1916, and Kipling accepted his
workmanlike adaptations without a single editorial suggestion.[11]

The invention of the Wolf Cubs was of a piece with his determination to make the Movement less formal and more responsive to the
needs of the boys themselves. 'If God made the boy a creature of
extreme and restless energy, with an inquisitive and eager mind, a
sensitive little heart, and a romantic imagination, it is up to you to

make full use of these instead of crushing them,' he told prospective Cubmasters.[12] Although 'the Cub gives in to the Old Wolf', the overall emphasis was on self-discovery rather than discipline – with acting, drawing and modelling receiving plenty of attention. 'Model the head of a monkey, only take care you don't make it too much like yourself!' Such jokes could be made by 'boy men' and 'elder brothers', but hardly by the authoritarian 'officer Scoutmaster' of the Movement's earlier days.

In 1920 Baden-Powell wrote to Lord Hampton, the Assistant Chief Commissioner: 'I want to urge all County Commissioners to expand their camping arrangements and get woodcraft well to the fore as our prime activity everywhere.'[13] During the war he had appointed John Hargrave, a young Quaker, as the Commissioner for Camping and Woodcraft. Hargrave advised him that the only way 'for getting ahead with nature-craft' was to 'buy up chunks of nature and form open-air training schools . . .'[14] He suggested Epping Forest and it was there, six months later, that an Essex District Commissioner learned that Gilwell Park, a decaying eighteenth-century house with over 50 acres of woodland, was for sale. A Scottish rubber magnate, Mr W. F. de Bois MacLaren, offered to buy the estate as a camping ground for East End boys and as a training school for Scouters.

From the time of his first visit to Gilwell, Baden-Powell wanted to make the place more important than Headquarters. If Buckingham Palace Road was where the 'form' of the Movement was determined by the Committee men, Gilwell Park would be where the Movement's 'boy men' would guard 'the fountain head of the Scouting spirit'.[15] At Gilwell Scouters were to 'learn boyhood as boy men'. In his diary he noted, 'the right spirit causes the Movement to run itself – no dependence on Imperial Headquarters needed'.[16] It was a bit like the nonconformist belief in an individual's direct access to God: a Scouter possessing the true spirit would need no priestly guidance from anyone, least of all an old codger on the Committee.

Once the Scouts had acquired Gilwell – in no small measure due to John Hargrave's urgings – the question arose as to who should run it. When Baden-Powell made Hargrave Commissioner for Woodcraft in 1917, he was not put off by his youth (he was 23 at the time) nor by the fact that he had not been to a public school. Not even the young man's pacifism had discouraged him. Hargrave had served as a stretcher-bearer at Gallipoli; and, given Baden-Powell's usual insistence on it being the patriotic duty of every citizen to *fight* for his country, by his own standards he was being exceptionally broadminded in promoting Hargrave to such an important position. But in 1918, the Chief Scout hesitated to hand over Gilwell to his handsome young Commissioner.

Hargrave was an utopian who craved a way of life combining Seton's tribal dreams with a revival of medieval arts and crafts. He would tolerate industrial processes only provided they were used to free whole populations for his ideal outdoor life. Impressed initially by Hargrave's charismatic personality and his artistic talent, Baden-Powell's unease about his new Commissioner's 'ultra views, and the possibility of his going off at a wrong tangent' had grown steadily.[17] In Hargrave's *Wigwam Papers* (a series of articles which appeared in *The Scout* during 1916), he introduced a new category of 'Woodcraft Scouts' who would wear a loose sweater with buckskin fringes and moccasins. In spite of his problems with Seton (which flared up again in 1917), Baden-Powell noted tolerantly in his diary: 'Saw Hargrave – no objection to his getting names of troops doing Seton Woodcraft in Scouting, but don't make it a branch of the Movement.'[18]

It is stated by those scholars who have studied the matter that Hargrave's rebellion was caused by the continuing militarism of the Scouts.[19] Hargrave himself certainly said so during 1920 and 1921; but his rift with Baden-Powell really dates from late February 1919 when, according to his own history of his breakaway movement, he held his first meeting of 'like minded men'.[20] That same February Baden-Powell had told Hargrave that he did not mean to appoint him Camp Chief of Gilwell Park.

In 1920, under the pseudonym of 'White Fox', Hargrave began a series of articles for the London Scout Council's official organ *The Trail*. Quoting the socialist newspaper *Our Circle*, he attacked the Scout Movement for its militarism and its church connections.[21] He declared it absurd, in view of Baden-Powell's public pronouncements on the evils of war, that the 1919 revised edition of *Scouting for Boys* should retain references to shooting. In private, Baden-Powell conceded that such passages ought to have been omitted.[22] But with the evidence mounting that Hargrave was planning his own movement, Baden-Powell could not afford to be conciliatory. In August 1920 Hargrave became Head Man of the Kindred of the Kibbo Kift (an archaic Kentish dialect phrase meaning 'proof of great strength'), so his expulsion from the Boy Scouts the following January was hardly abrupt. Nor is it factually correct to suggest, as one scholar has done, that Hargrave began to organize his movement only after being expelled from the Scouts.[23]

Hargrave would have been a disastrous Camp Chief for Gilwell and might have done the Scouts serious damage if appointed. He was autocratic, vain and many of his views – such as on the 'natural' inequality of the sexes and the role of leaders in society – were of greater interest in Germany than in his own country.[24] Although his defection made Baden-Powell look over-trusting and gullible in the eyes of the Committee, the Chief Scout accepted what had happened philosophically and wrote: 'It is such a pity that so promising a young fellow, with his undoubted talents should go off the rails. I have done a lot to try to win him onto the sensible line.'[25] This was nothing but the truth.

But Baden-Powell did not allow his failure with Hargrave to persuade him to play safe over Gilwell. He was still determined to find a man epitomizing the Scout spirit, with none of the 'rules and regulations' savour of Headquarters about him.

In 1908 a 16-year-old pupil at Lichfield Grammar School had started a Scout troop. His name was Francis Gidney. He went on to Cambridge, graduating in 1914 in which year he volunteered. In France he was promoted to the rank of Captain, was seriously wounded and invalided out of the service before the Armistice. Frank Gidney at once struck Baden-Powell as the perfect 'boy man'. Although his angular bespectacled face was sad in repose, he had a boyish sense of humour and was a natural enthusiast. Appointed Camp Chief of Gilwell in May 1919, he immediately displayed a showman's love of circus tricks and entertainments, as well as a fascination with tree climbing and log cabins. Gidney's 'camp fires' at Gilwell would be enlivened by exhibitions of axe- and knife-throwing, as well as by 'shooting' displays in which concealed pins rather than bullets popped strings of balloons. He encouraged amateur dramatics and kept a resident quartet of singing Rovers. 'Gidney brought a touch of controlled lunacy to the place,' recalled an early helper.[26] The boys who visited Gilwell adored him, as did the many trainee Scouters.

He was so amusing and cheerful that, when offering him the job, Baden-Powell had never guessed that the war had broken his health, leaving him a slowly dying man. Nor had he been aware of the precariousness of his marriage. Mrs Gidney was a twice-married former actress who had never been accepted by Gidney's family;[27] she cared little for Scouting and could not settle at Gilwell. But ill-health and domestic unhappiness did not stop Gidney devising excellent training courses for Scouters on subjects as diverse as camp gadgets, bridge building, axemanship and camp hygiene. While Gidney played the part of the Scouter, the Scouters-in-training became the boys of his patrol. The Scouters camped in their patrol and spent the whole of their eight days together.[28] They had to learn how to train their boys through games. The spectacle of bank managers, shop-keepers and clergymen solemnly building bridges with sticks and twine, and then sitting sedately on logs in semi-circles listening to the jovial Frank Gidney explaining how to imitate animal calls, was certainly memorable.

Scouters who passed Parts I (theory) and II (practice) of the three-part course (Part III being administration) were entitled to their Wood Badge, which consisted of two wooden beads on a leather thong. (See p. 134 for the origin of these beads.) In addition Gidney invented a Gilwell scarf, which was grey with a patch of Maclaren tartan in

honour of the Scottish benefactor who had purchased the place. This
was awarded to all men who had passed Part II, and it could be worn
instead of the usual Scout neckerchief.[29]

Baden-Powell came to Gilwell frequently, sleeping out in a
hammock at first and later in a caravan. 'As far as the eye can see
beneath the trees – are tents and more tents,' he observed enthusiastically. 'Among them half-naked men and boys are busy about the little
nothings that go to make camp life so fully occupied. And everywhere
the air is humming with the songs and whistling of happy lads.'[30] A
koodoo horn which Baden-Powell had acquired in Matabeleland was
used to sound reveille; and whenever he was there, Stephe himself
would blow it.[31] If he wanted to impress a potential benefactor, he
would bring him to Gilwell 'to see Scouting in action'.[32] Each
weekend anything between 50 and 500 boys would be encamped.
Scouts still there on Sunday evenings would try to avoid being 'landed
with "Lemonade Duty"', a boyish euphemism for the job of
syphoning urine from the camp-site lavatories into a 200-gallon
container, then wheeling it to the main gate and tipping its contents
down the drain there.

When more and more letters from Gidney's grateful graduates
began arriving at Headquarters, members of the Committee felt
alarmed and resentful. If Gidney and his assistants were really defining
what Scouting ought to be in practice, what were they supposed to be
doing at Headquarters?

2. Paradise Lost: The Battle for Gilwell (1920–23)

The Committee's battle to wrest back the powers that its members
feared they had lost to Gilwell began with some minor skirmishing. As
early as October 1919, the Committee had been notified that Gidney
thought himself inadequately paid; although Baden-Powell agreed
with him, two years later nothing had been done.[1] While successfully
blocking any increase in his salary, the Committee also meant to cut to
a bare minimum his expenditure on Gilwell, where he was erecting log
cabins, decorated gates and totem poles. The Committee muttered
about extravagance, but was soon presented with a much better excuse
for intervening at Gilwell.

Gidney's marital difficulties and the death of one of his children
obliged him to take time off in December 1921, and this gave the
Committee the perfect opportunity to take charge at Gilwell. The
Chief Training Officer, Major J. A. Dane, who was a Committee
member but not, as it happened, an enemy of Gidney, was deputed to
act as Camp Chief at Gilwell while Gidney was away. This was
resented by Gidney's deputy Alan Chapman who, because he was

running the training courses in Gidney's absence, felt that *he* ought to have been made acting Camp Chief.[2] On Gidney's return Chapman resumed his old status, but an ominous precedent had been established. Training could no longer be said to flow solely from the 'fountain head of Gilwell' when the Chief Training Officer at Headquarters could replace the Camp Chief and discharge all his administrative duties. It seems likely that Baden-Powell had given Gidney verbal guarantees of protection from interference by Headquarters because, when serious conflict broke out in the autumn of 1922, he did his best to prevent the Committee bludgeoning Gidney into submission.

Colonel Alfred D. Acland, the Treasurer, who had already so much offended Major Wade, was determined to enforce strict business methods upon the staff at Gilwell. Baden-Powell, who enjoyed fishing on Acland's estate,[3] tried to keep the peace in an even-handed way. 'It is no good to put off good men by too close an insistence on business methods if we can ensure economy and efficiency in another way,' he told Acland in November 1922. 'I believe we can do it through the spirit of "playing the game" on the part of Gidney and Lucas [office manager at Gilwell] . . . I am confident that they will work in close touch with you – largely because they are not forced to.'[4] This merely infuriated both men.

Gidney's real antipathy to Acland and the Committee was due not to their advocacy of financial efficiency but to their plan to implement a policy of 'dual control' at Gilwell which would leave him in charge of training there but not in charge of management; this would be under another resident official, who would be his equal rather than his subordinate, as in the case of the present office manager. If this change were to take place, Gidney knew that he would be Camp Chief only in name. Gilwell would really be controlled by the Chief Training Officer, the Treasurer and the Headquarters' Committee.[5]

Baden-Powell tried to fudge the issue. Gidney, he argued, should remain in sole charge as Camp Chief, but Dr F. R. Lucas – who ran the office – 'should be given a free hand to be fully responsible for his department'.[6] Gidney had no doubt that the 'free hand' promised to Lucas was a euphemism for placing him directly under Headquarters. Sensing that Dane's sympathy for Gidney would cause problems if the conflict worsened, Baden-Powell persuaded him to resign as Chief Training Officer in December and appointed himself in his place. In a letter to Gidney, originally drafted for Dane to send, he assured the Camp Chief that he would not give Acland 'overall control'. Baden-Powell also promised to 'represent' Gilwell on the Committee. 'I am willing to be responsible that there will be no lack of either efficiency or economy as a result of trusting to the spirit of "playing the game".' Exactly what this 'trust' would be worth in practice Gidney reckoned he knew when he received a letter from Dane, written at Acland's insistence, and sent days before Dane's resignation. This letter was nothing but a list of questions concerned with expenditure of a footling kind. 'Who gave the order for the entrance gates to be put up? Who gave the order for the office cupboard?'[7]

The chaos of his private life made everything infinitely worse for Gidney. His wife was ill; and in September 1922 he went with her, as she wished, to America for three months, returning to England for a similar period before spending a further six months in the United States.[8] Baden-Powell discussed Gidney's future with him on three separate occasions during December 1922 and managed to dissuade him from resigning, which he said he wanted to do.[9] In Gidney's absence Baden-Powell arranged for Gilwell to be run by Rodney Wood, a handsome Old Harrovian in his late twenties who owned property in the Seychelles and had been a game warden in Nyasaland.[10] He would be assisted at Gilwell by Gidney's deputy, Alan Chapman.

From March to May 1923 Baden-Powell was in Canada, and in his absence he asked Percy Everett to help Wood and Lucas with administration at Gilwell. Everett had been on the Headquarters' Committee for many years and was an ultra-efficient Treasurer of the Girl Guides. Somehow he combined all this with being Managing Director of Pearson's. On Baden-Powell's return to England, Everett told him Gilwell was in chaos and that 'dual control' was absolutely essential there.[11] He urged him to start the new system before Gidney returned from America, since he would be sure to do his utmost to stop it.[12]

Although the full changes were going to leave Gidney's deputy, Chapman, without a job, Baden-Powell (who had not told him this) wrote appealing to him to help him push through a few vaguely defined measures before Gidney returned.[13] Suspecting what lay behind this, Chapman refused. Gidney too was left in the dark about the real nature of the impending changes, and Baden-Powell failed to mention them either when they lunched together on the day of his return or, a few days later, when he and 1,000 Scouters went to Gilwell as Gidney's guests for the annual Scouters' Reunion. Baden-Powell enjoyed his two days there, applauding 'the splendidly cheery spirit' he found everywhere.[14] He decided to break the bad news to Gidney on 3 October at Pax Hill, and for moral support he invited his efficiency expert, Percy Everett, to stay overnight too. The encounter was tense. Gidney soon sensed that Everett was using the financial issue as a cloak to take over training as well as administration.

Until now Part I of the Wood Badge (the theoretical part of the Scouters' training) had been administered by Gilwell, with Chapman and Gidney appointing all the examiners. Everett argued that, by permitting this, Headquarters had in effect handed over control of the

Movement's future to the two men. Gilwell under Gidney, claimed Everett, had become an autonomous 'clique within the Movement'.[15] After his troubles with Vane and Hargrave, Baden-Powell was hypersensitive to the possibility of charismatic individuals acquiring too much power – and Gidney had certainly allowed some very 'weird forms of dress' that were alarmingly reminiscent of Hargraves's buckskin-fringed sweaters and moccasins.[16] Such matters weighed more with Baden-Powell than badly-kept accounts.

On the morning after this confrontation Gidney felt too ill to go into London with Everett and Baden-Powell, who both had appointments there. Instead he left Pax Hill later in the day. At first he indicated that he would accept being placed under the Head of Training, especially since Baden-Powell himself now held that position. But when he heard that his deputy Chapman was to be sacked as part of the new arrangements, he sent in his resignation. Baden-Powell expressed himself shocked and distressed; but when Gidney reaffirmed that he accepted all the changes except the removal of his deputy and promised to withdraw his resignation if Chapman were re-employed, Baden-Powell refused to allow him this one concession[17] – even though Gidney had orginally urged Chapman to give up a steady job in order to come to Gilwell. Baden-Powell had been thoroughly convinced by Percy Everett that in the past Chapman had actively encouraged Gidney to reject all changes out of hand.

In the aftermath of the affair, James E. West (who had been entranced by Gidney when he had been in the United States) asked Baden-Powell if he would mind his offering Gidney a job with the Boy Scouts of America.[18] Baden-Powell dissuaded him by representing Gidney as being on the verge of a nervous breakdown, though in the same letter he conceded that he was 'an outstanding personality' and 'a genius at training', and had resigned 'mainly from a misunderstanding with myself'.[19] Gidney's departure brought a spate of resignations from men who had trained under him; Gidney himself sent out a circular alleging 'the very gravest provocation' by Headquarters, and suggesting 'a public Scout enquiry into the causes which led to our resignations'.[20]

Unfortunately for his cause, he was too ill to attend when the propriety of his treatment was discussed at a Commissioners' Conference. Major Dane, the former Head of Training, moved that an enquiry be held, but he was out-voted. His plea that Chapman be allowed to attend in Gidney's place was also rejected by the meeting after Gidney's enemy, Colonel Acland, moved that this would be out of order. In the end the meeting voted for a motion proposed by Sir Edmond Elles and seconded by Colonel Acland, expressing absolute confidence in Baden-Powell's handling of the affair and condemning Gidney for 'gross insubordination'.[21] To have ended up depending upon support from old men like Elles against 'the new blood' for which he had so fervently appealed two years earlier was painfully ironic.

The Hargrave and Gidney troubles effectively ended Baden-Powell's hopes for a self-regulating Movement animated by its own unfettered 'spirit' and run by 'cheery boy men'. Scoutmasters had become Scouters, but the Committee had made sure that in matters of finance and policy it was the master. It probably amused Baden-Powell when the 81-year-old Lord Meath decided to take his Wood Badge at Gilwell; but after sacrificing Gidney to the Committee, he must have sensed that his own exhortations to Meath and the rest of them 'to keep the Movement abreast of the times' now had a distinctly hollow ring. The situation improved during the 1930s with a number of capable men in key positions, but very few of them were under 50 years of age.[22] Baden-Powell would never again criticize the Committee in public, nor try to set up a less rule-bound counterpoise as he had endeavoured to do at Gilwell.

Gidney died from the effects of his war wounds at the age of 36, only five years after leaving Gilwell. Before that his marriage had foundered. He worked briefly as a master at a preparatory school in Bournemouth before returning to his parents' house to die. On his deathbed he wrote forgivingly to Baden-Powell – the perfect Scout to the end. 'I have tried to "smile and whistle" through it all,' he declared, echoing Baden-Powell's famous exhortation. He asked to be remembered to Baden-Powell's children, particularly Heather.[23] The Frank Gidney Memorial Log Cabin was opened by Baden-Powell at Gilwell on Easter Day 1930.

In his heart, Baden-Powell knew that much had been lost with Gidney. In 1935 he laid the blame for a drop in the number of Scouters attending Wood Badge courses on J. S. Wilson, the new Camp Chief. A former senior police officer in Calcutta, Wilson was tough, efficient and commendably tight with money. Unfortunately, as Baden-Powell himself admitted, 'Wilson's personality and manner seemed to have a quelling effect, especially upon the more diffident Scouters. His strong character, which will stand no nonsense, is coupled with a certain shyness or aloofness.'[24] Numbers in the Movement as a whole were dropping in the mid-1930s, and Baden-Powell believed that this was partly due to Scouting having become too formal. 'It is ceasing to attract,' he told Percy Everett, 'owing to want of the genial spirit of making Scouting a well directed *game*.'[25] During the Second World War Wilson became Director of the Boy Scouts' International Bureau. Unknown to anyone outside the Secret Service, he was also organizing British Intelligence in Norway. For a spymaster an aloof personality was ideal, but not for a Camp Chief.

Gidney and Wilson were dedicated men, as were most of those who worked under them; but the place which Baden-Powell described as 'our Mecca of Scouting' did have two spectacular staffing failures which illustrate the immense difficulty with which the Movement always had to contend in weeding out unsuitable men. Robert Patterson, who became an Assistant Camp Chief at Gilwell in 1920, had run a Scout troop in Northern Ireland for nine years and was married, with a daughter. By 1915 he was Deputy Provincial Commissioner for Eastern Ulster and a respected leader of the Movement in Northern Ireland.[26] He came to live at Gilwell without his family and was soon placed in charge of the boys' camping field. During the summer he slept in the small first-aid hut near the gate of the main field, so as to be close to the boys in his charge. They always called him 'Doctor' Patterson, as did most of the staff, under the mistaken impression that the initials F.L.S. (Fellow of the Linnean Society) which he invariably added to his name meant that he was a medical doctor.[27] (Members of the public interested in botany could become 'fellows' on payment of a fee.) In February 1921 the Headquarters' Gazette recorded him as giving 'a very fine talk on: "Sex teaching and the realization of God through Nature", illustrated by some really remarkable slides.'[28] In March 1921 he was appointed Assistant District Commissioner for Epping Forest, and in June he delighted everyone by giving Gilwell 'a magnificent hospital tent'.[29]

When war widows such as the mother of a 15-year-old Westminster boy wrote to Baden-Powell asking his advice about their sons' masturbation, Stephe always knew to whom they should be sent. 'I am leaving for France tomorrow,' he told Mrs Nash, the Westminster boy's mother, 'or I would offer to see your son myself and have a chat. But if he would care to try camping at our school of Woodcraft in Epping Forest, he would find lots of healthy comradeship . . . We have also, in addition to our staff of Woodcraft instructors, one – a doctor – who as "Uncle" to the boys is able to accept their confidences and to give advice that is very helpful since it is human as well as medical . . . If you care to communicate with Dr Patterson he will endeavour to meet your wishes.' This reply was also in response to the woman's additional plea to be 'put in touch with a man who understands boys as you do', and would be 'safe to take him hiking, or boating'.[30]

In August 1922 some boys complained to Gidney about the irksome thoroughness of the nocturnal 'physical examinations' carried out by Dr Patterson in the medical hut. A few days later Baden-Powell noted in his diary: 'Breakfast with Gidney. Heard why he parted with Patterson.'[31] The Scouting community at large, however, heard nothing at all. Mr Patterson went quietly.

Patterson's successor, a young Irishman called H. D. Byrne, was appointed by J.S. Wilson and seemed entirely satisfactory as custodian

of the camping field. After a decade of apparently blameless service, he
went abroad to the Jamboree at Gödöllö in Hungary. While he was
away, the Gilwell office boy found a fat diary in Byrne's room and
discovered it to be filled with detailed descriptions of sexual encounters
with boys. When Byrne returned on the boat train, Wilson was
waiting at Waterloo Station to dismiss him as quickly as possible.[32]
Although Baden-Powell stated publicly that flogging might be a
deterrent to Scouters tempted to abuse the trust placed in them,[33] he
allowed Patterson and Byrne to escape unscathed. Headquarters
evidently preferred not to let it be known that for almost fifteen years
the one job in the Movement requiring men of unimpeachable in-
tegrity had been occupied by a succession of active paederasts.

Baden-Powell went on visiting Gilwell regularly and would later
choose the style of Baron Baden-Powell of Gilwell when he was
elevated to the peerage. But there was always a cloud of disappointment which cast a shadow over that formerly sunlit landscape after
Gidney and Patterson had shown, in their different ways, how
dangerous it was to locate 'the spirit' of the Movement in a single
shrine.

3. The Sage of Scouting (1917–35)

For a brief period immediately after the Great War, Baden-Powell
made speeches about the need to prepare for 'The Trade War after the
War' since 'commercial dominance is Germany's aim'. Because British
education ignored commerce, he proposed new badges 'of a directly
useful kind', for salesmanship, engineering, accountancy and surveying. The Government, he said, ought to promote 'organized education
in technical skill'.[1]

However, Baden-Powell soon abandoned this return to 'national
efficiency', sensing its unpopularity in a country reacting against
further calls for effort and self-sacrifice. Nor was his heart really in it.
In 1919 he had drawn public attention to 'the disgrace to our so-called
humane civilization of poverty, disease and squalor . . . sanctioned as
inevitable in our midst'. He knew that the Labour Party was 'bound to
have an important say in the Government of the country in the near
future', and set out to win over the Party's leaders. George Lansbury
rebuffed him in 1923 but spoke out publicly in favour of the Scouts in
1929, the year in which Ramsay MacDonald – by then Prime Minister
– submitted Baden-Powell's name to the King for ennoblement.[2] In
August 1920 Baden-Powell ended his parting message at the First
International Jamboree:

Brother Scouts, I ask you to make a solemn choice . . . The War has taught us that if one nation tries to impose its particular will upon others, cruel reaction is bound to follow. The Jamboree has taught us that if we exercise mutual forbearance and give and take, then there is sympathy and harmony. If it be your will, let us go forth from here fully determined that we will develop among ourselves and our boys that comradeship, through the world wide spirit of the Scout Brotherhood, so that we may help to develop peace and happiness in the world . . . Brother Scouts, answer me. Will you join in the endeavour?

The ringing cry of 'Yes' which he received on that summer afternoon would be the first of many, after the promotion of international peace became his first priority.

His chosen weapon was the International Jamboree – a word which, until he adopted it in 1920 to describe a gigantic Scout gathering, had been American slang for 'a noisy revel, carousal or spree'.[3] In 1916, Baden-Powell had written of the need for 'an International Rally to mark the tenth anniversary of the Movement, to be held in June 1918, provided the war is over. Objects – to make our ideals and methods more widely known abroad; to promote the spirit of brotherhood among the rising generation throughout the world, thereby giving the spirit that is necessary to make the League of Nations a living force . . .'[4]

Because the war continued until the autumn of 1918, the Jamboree was held in 1920. Its location was the ugly concrete exhibition hall at Olympia in west London, where the floor was covered with a foot of earth so that tents could be pitched and displays mounted. At considerable expense stage carpenters and painters were employed to create a pirate's ship, a forest setting suitable for the enactment of scenes from *The Jungle Book* and a mountain pass zig-zagging down from the rafters. Baden-Powell wanted to encourage enthusiasm for Shakespeare, so he offered prizes for the best performance of an act from any of his plays. Similar prizes were offered for folk dancing and historical pageants. Foreign contingents gave demonstrations of their own arts and culture. Bugle bands played, stamp collections and scrapbooks were displayed, trek-carts raced and Gilwell-style bridges were built. The sight of 5,000 boys of over a dozen nationalities all in the same arena, repeating the words of the Scout Promise after Baden-Powell, made a profound impression on all those who witnessed it. Lord Northcliffe visited Olympia twice and 'wept openly at the sight of the boys'.[5] Naturally the *Daily Mail* and *The Times* rhapsodized over the Jamboree and the unprecedented publicity lured tens of thousands of would-be spectators, hundreds of whom had to be turned away daily. On the eighth and final day, before he gave his closing speech on the subject of peace and tolerance, Baden-Powell

walked across the arena through a lane of national flags, flanked by two
women impersonating Columbia and Britannia. A Scout stepped
forward and piped: 'We, the Scouts of the World, salute you, Sir
Robert Baden-Powell – Chief Scout of the World!' Although this was
described as a spontaneous event, it had been well-rehearsed; Baden-
Powell had dreamed up the title for himself long before the war. But
the pandemonium after his speech, when he was chaired across the
arena by wildly cheering boys, *was* unplanned.

After the Jamboree, Baden-Powell loomed far larger in the public
imagination than he had previously. Ironically the Jamboree cost the
Scouts £14,000 and left them almost bankrupt; an appeal cleared this
debt, but it would be almost a decade before the Movement became
fully solvent again.[6] It is easy to understand why many people thought
it hypocritical to stigmatize Gidney for small-scale financial mismanagement while at the same time condoning the way in which the
Committee had allowed a potential gold-mine to lose money.
Nevertheless Baden-Powell and the Committee remained determined
to press on with similar spectaculars. Official approval of the Jamboree
may well have influenced them. On 23 December Baden-Powell
received a letter from the Premier, David Lloyd George, announcing
the award of a baronetcy.[7] Adults seemed to have been more
impressed than boys by the Jamboree; in the following year the
number of Scouts in Great Britain fell by 3,000, but an extra 1,000
Scouters offered their services.[8]

In 1922, 60,000 Cubs and Scouts assembled at Alexandra Palace to
greet the Prince of Wales on his return from his world tour, with a
ceremony called 'The Posse of Welcome'. The press responded
favourably again – as did George V, who promoted Baden-Powell to
the highest rank in his personal order of chivalry. Already K.C.V.O.,
Baden-Powell was now gazetted G.C.V.O.

The year 1924 brought the Imperial Jamboree at Wembley, the
World Camp at Foxlease and the Second International Jamboree in
Denmark. At these events Baden-Powell coupled pleas for peace and
world brotherhood with denunciations of the Great War.

> The present unsatisfactory conditions in the world are the after-
> effects of war – that war that was to have ended wars . . . But we
> have more nations in rivalry with one another than there were
> before, and more armed men in the world ready for war than ever
> existed in history. We civilized peoples, with our education and our
> churches, have little to be proud of in having committed this
> reversion to primitive methods of savagery for settling our
> disputes . . . Schools merely continue their teaching of academic
> history, largely restricted to the more creditable doings of their own
> particular country, and with little regard to that of other

nations . . . The war and its upset of old ideas has given the opportunity for implanting entirely new ones. Buddha has said: 'There is only one way of driving out Hate in the world and that is by bringing in Love.' The opportunity lies before us where in place of selfishness and hostility we can enthuse good will and peace as the spirit in the coming generation . . . We in the Movement can prove by example that such a step is possible . . .'[9]

There were four million Scouts and Guides in the world in 1929, when Imperial Headquarters organized a coming-of-age Jamboree to celebrate 21 years of Scouting. Held in Arrowe Park, Birkenhead, it was attended by 30,000 Scouts forming 71 separate contingents. This international event was celebrated as an affair of state, with a service of thanksgiving in Westminster Abbey during which Baden-Powell read the lesson to a congregation of 3,000 Scouts. The Prince of Wales spent 2½ hours at the Jamboree. The Prime Minister came and declared that: 'No social development of our time is more attractive in its aim or more far reaching in its effect than the growth of the Boy Scout Movement.'[10] George Lansbury ate his previous words of criticism in public; the Archbishop of Canterbury came to bless the proceedings and began his sermon with the words: 'Twenty-one years ago a soldier dreamed a dream . . .,' and ended it, 'Behold this dreamer cometh not alone, but with a comradeship of two million boys . . .' The Scouts gave Baden-Powell a Rolls Royce bought with pennies contributed by boys from all over the world, a portrait of himself painted by David Jagger and a cheque for £2,800. The Government gave him a peerage.

There has been some debate about whether or not Baden-Powell wanted this honour. John Hargrave was certain that he had always longed to be ennobled;[11] and he certainly lost little time in ordering Pax Hill writing paper augmented with a coronet. But Olave was adamant that he had fully intended to decline the honour until persuaded by the Duke of Connaught that he owed it to the Movement to accept, since it was conferred on Scouting as well as upon himself.[12] On the evening of 31 July, the day after receiving the Prime Minister's letter, Baden-Powell allowed J. S. Wilson to send a telegram of acceptance. In a letter he had written earlier in the day but had not mailed, he had described himself as 'undeserving of further honours' and had suggested that Everett and Pickford should receive some recognition in his place. There was, however, no word of firm refusal in this letter.[13] The following day, in a letter which *was* sent, he wrote: 'If it were considered necessary that I, *as a figurehead of the movement*, should receive some outward mark of the King's approval, a far lesser award would be appreciated . . .'[14] But by then the Prince of Wales had already announced the grant of the peerage in a speech at the Jamboree, so the issue had already been decided. Claude Fisher,

Baden-Powell's press secretary, was present the evening before when he made up his mind to accept. Fisher, J. S. Wilson and Mrs Wade had all urged him 'to accept for the sake of the Movement'. Fisher recalled him saying: 'Well, if I must, I am *not* paying any fee for it – if they want to honour Scouting they should not expect payment.'[15] Much of Baden-Powell's correspondence with the Prime Minister's private secretaries was concerned with the thousand or so pounds in fees which new peers were generally obliged to pay. At last, on 26 August, he was informed that the usual fees would be waived in his case.[16] Given his many attempts to secure honours for his leading helpers in the Movement, it would be wrong to suppose that Baden-Powell was insincere when he subsequently suggested that he would have preferred to see them rewarded. His efforts on behalf of Everett began in October 1923, and he wrote six times about him between then and 1930 when Everett was eventually knighted.[17]

Stephe was torn in opposite directions. He adored awards and honours, yet knew that they were alien to the simple life he advocated. He also knew that his fame was already such that a peerage was beside the point. He simultaneously enhanced his reputation as a man who cared little for material things, when in reply to an enquiry about the kind of gift he would like from the Scouts of the Irish Free State he begged a pair of braces. These were presented soon after the Rolls Royce. Often thereafter he would refer to the braces to illustrate the maxim that the happiest man is the one with fewest wants.[18]

Although Baden-Powell played his part consummately at every Jamboree, he was well aware of the absurdity of many of the ceremonies. At Arrowe Park, the Jamboree ended with a vast parade in which 'the boys of the different nations were all mixed together and formed in a great circle with files of Scouts in lines radiating from the centre to the rim like so many spokes'. At the hub of this human wheel Baden-Powell's task was 'to bury an axe – the axe of war and ill-will – and then to hand out to the leading boy of each spoke a golden arrow – the sign of peace and goodwill – to be passed from one to the other until it reached the head of a national contingent.' Then he gave an emotional speech enjoining the boys to: 'Go forth from here as ambassadors of goodwill and friendship.' As in his acting days, when he had tried to affect the most stony-faced members of the audience, he delivered his appeal to an inscrutable boy opposite him who disappointingly looked 'preternaturally unmoved'. He supposed it had been his misfortune to choose a foreigner but in fact – as he liked to recall – he had delivered 'the main force of his remarks' to the only deaf-mute present amongst at least 40,000 boys.[19] Claude Fisher remembered an incident which had convulsed the hundreds who witnessed it. A photographer had been 'pestering the Chief, who was standing in the Royal Box watching a rehearsal. After a while Baden-

Powell told him to go. The man continued pestering and to the delight of those who saw it, Baden-Powell, then over 70, chased the man out of the arena.'[20]

Baden-Powell made hundreds of speeches in which international goodwill was the keynote. In 1936 he urged schoolmasters to take care lest they inculcate a patriotism 'that stopped at their own country, and thus inspired jealousy and enmity in dealing with others. Our patriotism should be of the wider, nobler kind which recognizes justice and reasonableness in the claims of others . . .'[21] At the Fifth World Jamboree in Holland, he said in his closing address: 'We have been called a Boys' Crusade, the Crusade of Peace . . .'[22]

Most of his major speeches were filmed and the sight of an old man in shorts with a benign expression urging tolerance and fraternal goodwill upon his vast international audiences still has the power to move. The way in which these huge crowds of boys warmed to him, cheering his words and waving hats and staves aloft, is very poignant when one remembers that such scenes took place on the eve of a war in which so many of them would die. In 1938 Baden-Powell's name was submitted to the Nobel Peace Prize Committee for consideration for the following year's award. But the 1939 Prize would turn out to be one of Hitler's many unnoticed casualties.

Katharine Furse described him with more than a hint of tongue-in-cheek as 'the inspired mystic of Scouting', but this was actually how he was seen by millions.[23] This image owed much to his growing tendency to represent Scouting as a form of religion. 'Scouting is nothing less than applied Christianity,' he had written in the intro-duction to a pamphlet entitled *Scouting and Christianity* in 1917. In 1921, he wrote an article entitled 'The Religion of the Woods', in which he argued that observing the beauties of nature was the best way in which to apprehend God and that no one religion held a monopoly of truth. This made him very unpopular with churchmen. A cleric who overheard Alan Chapman at Gilwell describing the Scout Movement as 'a bigger thing than Christianity' told Baden-Powell that, if he himself thought so, he would destroy the Movement as a national institution.[24] Bishop Joseph Butt, auxiliary bishop to the Roman Catholic Archbishop of Westminster, accused Baden-Powell of 'sweeping with one magnificent gesture the Christian Revelation, Mohammedanism, and all the rest, into a heap of private opinions which do not matter much.'[25] In the next edition of the *Headquarters' Gazette*, Baden-Powell obliged his horrified Committee by assuring readers that it was 'not his intention to attack Revealed Religion or to suggest a substitute for it'. But he never regretted what he had said, nor that he had invited Muslims and Buddhists to recite prayers at Gilwell. He quoted Carlyle as saying: 'The religion of a man is not the creed he professes but his life – what he acts upon, and knows of life, and his duty in it. A bad man who believes in a creed is no more religious than the good man who does not.'[26] Baden-Powell's public refusal to countenance the exclusive claims of any one religion was accompanied by increasingly fervent references to 'God' in his speeches.[27] For all his anti-clericalism, there was a lot of the spoiled priest in him. He was more his father's son than a superficial view of his opinions might lead one to suppose.

At the first International Moot (or gathering of Rovers) in the Albert Hall in 1926, Baden-Powell – like some medieval Grand Master of a militant religious order – took the boys through 'the whole ceremonial of an esquire being made into a knight . . . and then carried out the ceremonial of promoting a Scout to be a Rover.' He asked the boys to imagine themselves going through a vigil in a chapel alone for the night.

> The lights were turned down until that great hall was dark and you could have heard a pin drop . . . and I gave out just a few thoughts for them to think to themselves in the dark . . . 'You are crossing the threshhold in life, which you will never cross again, going from boyhood into manhood; think what are you going to do in life. You are thinking of making money, or a career or something: that is the wrong end to think from. Think from the other end. In your last hours, when you have to look back on your life, ask, 'What have I made of my life? Have I wasted it? Have I done my best with it, that life that God has loaned me for these few years?' Work backwards and then you will see what is worthwhile taking up in life.[28]

He told boys: 'There is only one success in life, and that is Happiness; and true happiness comes out of service.'[29] 'Service' became the principal ingredient in many of his speeches during the 1920s.

'Most of our social troubles,' he wrote in 1920, 'are the result of selfishness; our narrow patriotism . . . our class differences.'[30] He was sure that unless boys were shown an example of unselfishness by unpaid Scouters, they would not grow up with any feelings for community service. In 1938 he put 'moral courage' as the first prerequisite for "character", followed by 'judgement to see the right and pluck to stand up for it'.[31] The philanthropic sentiments expressed in his 'Laws for Me when I am Old', written at the age of 8 under his mother's influence, were more evident in the writings of his old age than in those dating from the early years of the Movement.

Baden-Powell's antipathy towards competition in schools dovetailed with his determination that badges should be awarded for effort rather than for any fixed level of attainment. This sounds exclusively radical, but his discouragement of competition also had the effect of maintaining the status quo. 'So many people take things too seriously,' he complained. 'They are always looking like a greedy boy at dinner –

to see what other people have got, and thinking themselves wronged because they are not so well off. They forget that life is only a temporary affair after all. It will soon be over and what does it matter if one has had a little more than another, as long as you have all enjoyed it?'[32]

As he left behind the age at which it seemed worthwhile 'to order a new evening coat', he reflected upon the futility of possessions.[33] His own simple tastes were not affectations; nor was the morality he commended. Like all his family he had been wildly ambitious when young, but old age brought a genuine change – albeit with an element of play-acting about it. He still travelled in his Rolls Royce and loved dressing up in all his finery of orders and medals. Years after his death, Mrs Wade would recall him most vividly when she was gardening in the autumn.

I thought of how frequently I had seen the Chief, in his garden at Pax Hill, burning hedge-clippings, and how he had once remarked, as he applied bellows to a flickering flame: 'That's what I'm always trying to tell them – there's a spark of good in the toughest of these chaps and the Scouter's job is to find it and fan it into a flame.' He stood back, his shabby garden hat on the back of his head, his eyes full of smoke and watched for a moment . . . For me time stood still while he spoke, to be recalled every time I see a sulky fire or smell the smoke rising from a garden heap.[34]

17

STORMS AND SUNSHINE

1. Father and Son (1922–40)

Things that have made me Gulp:
Gorse bush against blue sky,
Kamchyugu 4 a.m.,
News that I have got a son,
Sunset in the Orange Free State.[1]

Untitled note by Baden-Powell c. 1913

Baden-Powell's many trips with Donald and his determined efforts to be a father to the boy can be seen in retrospect as a kind of trial run for the real thing: bringing up a son of his own. And the whole process of fatherhood was all the more significant to him because of his own father's early death.[2] When Peter was 8, Baden-Powell announced in public that it was every father's duty 'to make your boy a better man than you yourself by teaching him all that you know, and what to aim for and what to avoid.'[3]

Character building[4] was based upon the assumption that the mind's major faculties such as intellect, emotion, will and conscience could be improved by appropriately uplifting activities, rather as muscles could be strengthened by exercise. Conscience could be galvanized by the daily good turn, and intellect be sharpened by observation and deduction. Baden-Powell set out such ideas in numerous charts, of which the draft on p. 587 is a typical example. He subscribed to the Victorian belief that people could improve their character by consciously choosing a virtuous course and rejecting baser urges.

In 1918 Herbert Jenkins the publisher had written to Baden-Powell suggesting he produce for publication a series of 'Letters to Peter'. The letters need not, he had added reassuringly, be 'actual' ones.[5] The commercial attraction of letters which would be seen by the public as model advice for any young boy was obvious, and emphasized the extremely sensitive position which Baden-Powell and Peter were in. On this occasion Baden-Powell wrote back saying that he was too busy,[6] but the same suggestion was made by Percy Everett seven years later on behalf of Pearson's. By then a great many 'actual' letters existed. 'There is something intimate about them that I don't care to expose to publication,' he explained in his letter of refusal.[7] Peter was then only 12, so Baden-Powell's reticence was not due to his having given the boy explicit sexual warnings. The truth was sadder. By then Baden-Powell already knew that the ideal father-and-son relationship of his dreams would never be realized. Nor would it ever be possible to demonstrate the wonderful character-building qualities of the Cub and Scout training through the exemplary development of his own boy.

When Peter came home for the spring holidays after his first term at his preparatory school, his father thought he detected 'a wonderful change in him from child to boy in ten weeks'. But after two weeks' fishing in Scotland, Baden-Powell returned to Pax Hill to be told by Olave that the change had been less wonderful than they had at first supposed. On consecutive days Baden-Powell took his son for long walks and 'began correction of the slackness and selfishness apparent in him'. A separate talk on 'truth speaking' was combined with a visit to a nearby kingfisher's nest.[8] The boy was 9 and his father 65 when these conversations took place.

Peter was enrolled as a Wolf Cub by his father in October 1921. Exactly a year later Baden-Powell arranged that his son should lead the Prince of Wales into the arena at the Alexandra Palace for the 'Posse of Welcome' ceremony, which was attended by 50,000 Scouts and Cubs. Peter, whose shyness had already started to distress Baden-Powell, found it a terrifying experience.[9] After this highly publicized event, he was often called the 'Chief Cub' by his sisters.[10]

The lack of rapport between Peter and his father comes across in Baden-Powell's diary account of taking the boy out for the first time shortly after he went away to his prep school. (He would visit him at school roughly once every three weeks.) 'Olave and I motored over to Dane Court. Our first sight of him since he went to school. He was quite shy and reserved at first – told us a bit about school as we drove over to Charterhouse – but never asked a question about home. Saw football: Charterhouse *v* Westminster. Tea in Guildford restaurant and back to school 5.30, where he left us without a word of goodbye. Quaint little chap.'[11] Other engagements permitting, Baden-Powell always tried to attend the twin pinnacles of the Charterhouse sporting calendar: the Winchester cricket match and the Westminster football. He had played in goal against Westminster and, by taking his 9-year-old boy to see the game, must have impressed upon him the hope that one day he would play in this very match. In many ways Baden-Powell was sensitive to what interested boys and what their priorities were. It is therefore sad that he should have chosen to take Peter from one school to another on his very first day out – and not just to any school, but to the one where Peter knew that he was expected to go and where his father – as one of the most famous living Old Boys – was always welcomed by the headmaster like royalty.

Most boarding preparatory schools during the 1920s imposed a spartan regime upon their inmates: beatings, cold baths and plenty of sport. Dane Court, however, which Baden-Powell had chosen for Peter after looking at many other schools, was not at all like this. Its most famous Old Boy might be Henry Rider Haggard, but under the enlightened rule of Mr H. F. Pooley and his Danish wife, Michaela, there was nothing rugged about the place. Augustus John, no conformist, had sent his five sons there, and the atmosphere was friendly and relaxed. Sports were not fervently pursued; and tree climbing, Cubbing and end-of-term plays were all encouraged.[12] So too was bicycling.

Baden-Powell decided to deny Peter a bicycle, 'partly so as not to spoil him by giving him everything he wants, and partly so that it would not take him away from games'. Mrs Pooley told Baden-Powell firmly that there was 'no danger of either' and advised him to send the bicycle at once. She then broke it to him that although he had seen Peter in gym displays, he was not strong enough 'to play ordinary games; but was keen in his own way'.[13] Baden-Powell sent the bicycle.

At the end of the same term he and Olave attended Prize Giving and saw Peter collect a prize for French. This was Mr Pooley's subject and the prize was given, in the best Scouting tradition, for effort rather than attainment. Pooley told the Baden-Powells that Peter was also 'doing well at Latin, improving in quickness, and really trying'.[14] Both he and Michaela felt that, if the boy could only be encouraged and his self-confidence boosted, he would catch up much of the ground lost during his series of childhood illnesses. Whenever Baden-Powell called at the school, the Pooleys did their best to persuade him 'not to expect too much of him particularly at games'.[15]

If Peter had been merely average athletically and average in class, Baden-Powell would probably have been well content. But unfortunately his belief that with effort and auto-suggestion anyone could cure himself of weakness of character, and even illness, did not help him to accept the reality of his son's difficulties.[16] Another problem was posed by Stephe's elevation of physical fitness to the status of a major component in 'character'. Remembering his own boyhood boating adventures and his later exploits in India and Africa, he could not help feeling that a boy who remained physically unadventurous was a poor thing.[17]

Baden-Powell's first thought on being created a baronet had been to scribble down in his diary: 'Sir Peter!'[18] The boy was his heir and nothing could alter that. His urgent desire to 'improve' him persisted throughout Peter's childhood; he bought a tent for him, took him fishing and tried to 'strengthen' his powers of deduction by discussing 'the Bournemouth murder'. This case had been solved as a result of forensic attention paid to some motor-car tyre tracks.[19] Then there were visits to the Tower of London, to the National Gallery ('but nothing attractive for him beyond Frith's "Derby Day'"), and to the Royal United Services Institute where the Ashanti Blood Bowl and the Wolf howitzer from Mafeking were on show. When Peter was 10, he was taken to his first pantomime and his father described watching his happy face as an experience he 'would not have missed for £1,000'.[20]

Every year or two, Baden-Powell would take Olave and the children on a spontaneous camping expedition. In September 1923 he selected a wooded area on the map near Havant and drove there, finding on arrival that these woods were part of a private estate. 'We boldly drove up to the house and called on the owner . . .' Permission on this and on other occasions was invariably given once Baden-Powell's identity had been established. Olave slept alone in the 'Palace' tent (so called because it had originally sheltered the Prince of Wales for a night at the Wembley Jamboree). Baden-Powell bedded down in a caravan while Peter and the two girls had a tent each, as later did their dog Shawgm. When their chauffeur 'Bear' Court was driving them, he would sleep in yet another tent pitched on the far side of the Rolls Royce.[21] They camped at Havant for three days, while making excursions to see the *Victory* and the *Queen Elizabeth* in Portsmouth harbour and then crossing to the Isle of Wight, where they caught a bus to Seaview and then 'lazed and paddled on the beach'.[22]

In spite of such excursions Peter remained very shy. His embarrassment when his father visited him at school was due partly to the curiosity of the other boys, but his diffidence owed more to Baden-Powell's lectures which in January 1925 shifted for the first time towards sex. 'I had a paternal talk with Peter on the Scout Laws No. 1 and 10,' he noted in his diary on 19 January. These were in his opinion the most important Laws, being respectively: 'A Scout's Honour is to be trusted' and: 'A Scout is clean in thought and word and deed.' Between making arrangements to start a trout hatchery at nearby Isington, Baden-Powell continued lecturing his son on these matters, although a bout of unexpected vomiting which prostrated Peter on the 20th prevented him from making it three days in a row. Next day he subjected Peter to another 'long talk on the Scout Laws and told him that he was not yet ripe for a Scout – must improve in cleanliness and courtesy. He seemed to grasp it.'[23] The Boy Scouts, Baden-Powell had always maintained, were uncompetitive and prided themselves on welcoming boys of all abilities and giving them a chance to gain a sense of achievement. It was ironic indeed that he should have stopped his own son from transferring at the normal age.

When Peter was 3, Baden-Powell had sketched him sitting on a toy rocking-horse with a rucksack on his back. He had written under the sketch: 'Peter off on service, in heavy marching order, mounted.' The rucksack was a full-sized one, very nearly as large as the boy.[24] Ten years later the burden Peter was carrying was fear that he would fail his father in everything he tried to do; perhaps he would never make a good Scout, nor even pass the examination for Charterhouse. He sat the exam in June 1927 and a few days later Baden-Powell noted: 'Peter passed a poor exam for Charterhouse – and is to be seen by Lower Master for approval or otherwise.'[25] The approval followed in due course, so Peter had scraped in. The fact that the final decision was touch and go in spite of the school's natural desire to assist such a famous Old Carthusian ought to have given Baden-Powell pause to wonder whether the place would suit Peter. But no such doubt seemed to have occurred to him.

His son's arrival at Charterhouse gave Baden-Powell an excuse to increase the number of his already regular visits. By the middle of Peter's first term he had already visited him four times, on several occasions driving his house guests over from Pax Hill for the Sunday service in Charterhouse chapel. He brought a party to see the Westminster match, when the visitors provokingly won by five goals. Peter was looking well but admitted that he had been thrashed too, not on the sports field but 'for being insufficiently up in Charterhouse "notions"'. In layman's terms he had failed his fagging test, which would have incorporated every kind of information about the school, both trivial and significant. As a pointer to the powers of memory which he would bring to bear upon his academic work, this was not a propitious start.

Peter was soon struggling in class and by 1928 was thought to be over a year behind his age group. In the summer of 1929 Baden-Powell began searching for a suitable tutorial establishment where his son could spend most of the holidays trying to reduce the leeway.[26] The following March he finally decided to throw in the towel and wrote telling Peter's housemaster, Mr M. J. Chignell, that he could no longer hope that Peter would pass into the Civil Service or, as Olave later put it, 'into anything in which energy and brains are essential'. His father hoped he might get to Sandhurst, but even the modest examination required for that establishment seemed likely to be beyond him, unless he were sent full-time to a competent crammer. 'So long as he is in a crowd, he will just drift happily along without making any personal effort,' opined his mother, who thought him 'slack and helpless'.[27]

From about 1930, Baden-Powell came to accept that 'physiological changes in various glands' governed adolescent behaviour more than he had previously supposed. But he still failed to make any concessions to Peter on account of this.[28] Nevertheless he was more sympathetic towards Peter than was Olave. Ursula Kearsley, one of Baden-Powell's godchildren, used to stay at Pax Hill from time to time and was shocked by how 'savage, awful and terrible his mother could be to him'.[29] In fairness to Olave, Peter could be exasperatingly careless – as when he let the horses get out on the road, leaving his mother to bicycle after them and effect a daring capture; or when he jumped some hurdles in a field where several dozen ewes were about to lamb. This escapade cost Baden-Powell a considerable sum of money, since many still-births ensued. Then there was the day on which he broke his pony's knees through careless jumping.[30]

In April 1931 Peter was sent to Chillon College, near Montreux in Switzerland, to be coached for the Sandhurst entrance exam. In the meantime he would have to pass his School Certificate in English and mathematics, which he ought to have managed at Charterhouse. Chillon had been recommended to Baden-Powell by the Bishop of Fulham (a keen supporter of the Scouts) because of its 'high moral tone'.[31] Baden-Powell was therefore shocked to learn that, only a month after his arrival, Peter had been seen kissing a maid. Then, two nights after being reprimanded for this, he was caught flirting with *two* maids in their quarters. The headmaster of Chillon told Peter to write to his father about the incident, but he had been unable to bring himself to do so. Baden-Powell spent several days at Chillon with his son in July, on his way to a rally of 2,000 Austrian Boy Scouts. Before he left, he noted: 'Peter promised, and shook hands on it, to take himself in hand.'[32] But on reflection, Baden-Powell decided that this assurance was far from watertight and decided to remove him from Chillon.

Baden-Powell's feelings about 'calf-love' and his horror of boys surrendering to 'animal instincts' had not changed since 1922 when he had written *Rovering to Success* – in part as an advice manual for Peter. The risk of Peter's becoming seriously involved with a servant, and even impregnating her, was not one Baden-Powell felt inclined to take. Never having been attracted to women himself and still considering sexual attraction a brief adolescent phase, he found his son's behaviour puzzling and unsavoury. He had very much hoped that the boy would not develop 'girlitis' until he was ready to marry; but here he was chasing after girls while still a schoolboy.

Stephe felt that, with the help of a resident tutor, his son might be kept safely celibate at home and still be coaxed into passing his School Certificate, thus qualifying for Sandhurst. One of these tutors was the eldest son of Peter's former headmaster at Dane Court. Peter Pooley was 21 when he came to Pax Hill to help Peter Baden-Powell, and found him 'a very sweet boy' and not difficult to teach.[33] William Mather (now Sir William) had been a friend at Dane Court and continued to see Peter in later years; he remembered his fits of rage caused by frustration over his physical limitations. But although Peter was bullied, he was no coward and would stand up to stronger boys.[34] In one sport Peter did excel: this was shooting, in which he represented Charterhouse just as his father had done.

For Peter, Baden-Powell devised a 'self-measurement' chart on which the boy was meant to enter his achievements under headings

such as 'Truth', 'Swimming', 'Running' and 'Jumping'. Quite how he
was supposed to measure his improvements in truthfulness was not
apparent.[35] A little later, Baden-Powell was telling him to treat getting
on in life as if he were climbing a ladder: 'Make each month a step in
your ladder – put down on the last day of the month what you have
gained during that month in the way of knowledge, or prizes, or
badges . . . Then at the end of the year you will be able to look back
and see how far you have gone towards your aim.'[36] This was more of
a tribute to Henrietta Grace's success-oriented methods than to his
own public pronouncements on the need for boys to think more about
the welfare of the community than about their own careers.

Shortly before Pooley began to tutor Peter, news came through that
he had failed his School Certificate again. His time at Chillon had been
a disaster in every way. In desperation, Baden-Powell wrote to the
Duke of Connaught asking him whether he could persuade the War
Office to let Peter sit the Sandhurst exam without having passed his
School Certificate. The Duke obliged by commending Peter to the
Army Council, but Baden-Powell never heard from them.[37] Consequently Peter was sent to a crammer near Farnham, but failed again in
April 1932, leaving Baden-Powell no choice but to give up or to find
out what 'influence' might achieve. The same day he wrote to Lieu-
tenant-General Sir Ivo Vesey, the Director of Staff Duties at the War
Office, asking whether Peter might be excused School Certificate as a
basic qualification for Sandhurst.[38] This was a far cry from the Baden-
Powell who had so adamantly told his sister-in-law Frances that if the
parents of candidates for the S.A.C. 'tried to bring interest to bear and
quoted high connections: it damns the candidate's chances at once'.[39]
Within a few days of writing he was invited to the War Office for a chat
with Colonel W. G. Lindsell, the Assistant Director of Personnel.
Lindsell said that Peter would have to take his School Certificate again
in July, but that if he were to fail the War Office might be able to help.
This, however, would have to be kept secret. To cement his relations
with Lindsell, Baden-Powell asked him to a Mercers' Banquet a few
days later.[40] In late June Peter 'passed' his medical examination for the
army, although he was below the requisite height and his chest
measurement was too small. It was assumed that by the time he passed
out of Sandhurst he would have grown sufficiently.

Peter sat the Sandhurst examination and his School Certificate (yet
again) in July 1932. On 10 August, while both he and his father were at
the Hague after Scouting festivities in Austria and Switzerland, a
telegram arrived announcing that the boy had passed for Sandhurst.
That Lindsell had pulled strings seems likely, given Baden-Powell's
immediate desire to write to him on receipt of the good news.[41] A few
days later, Baden-Powell wrote to the Military Secretary at the War
Office proposing Peter for his own beloved 13th Hussars.

In June 1932, at a Guide Rally in Regent's Park, Olave invited a young London Guider to lunch with her at Guide Headquarters the following week. Josephine Reddie was 25, had given Guiding lectures in America and had corresponded with Olave about the Movement in the United States.[42] On the day in question, Olave found that she had Peter on her hands and, being tied up with appointments all afternoon, felt reluctant to leave him wandering about in London by himself until he was due to join her at St Paul's Cathedral for a Guide thanksgiving service. Could Josephine perhaps look after him in the meantime? Like any good guider, she was delighted to help the Chief Guide; and because she was an attractive young woman, Peter was equally enthusiastic. They spent most of the afternoon on the top of a bus travelling around London and laughing a lot.[43] Peter would not have seen Josephine again had she and her widowed mother not gone out to Adelboden in Switzerland soon afterwards for the opening of a chalet donated to the International Guide Movement by the widow of a Bostonian banker. There Josephine found herself staying at the Nevada Palace Hotel with all the Baden-Powells, also in Switzerland for the chalet's opening. The young people all thought the hotel magnificent with its golf course, swimming pool, tennis courts and resident jazz band. On his first day there Baden-Powell recorded 'having tea with Mrs Ready [sic] and her daughter'. Preoccupied with preparing his speech for the chalet's opening, he did not notice how much time Peter was spending with Mrs 'Ready's' girl.[44]

The family stayed for almost a week at Adelboden and during that time Josephine also got to know Peter's sisters. Both Heather and Betty were still schoolgirls and felt rather flattered by Josephine's interest in them. From Holland, on their way home, they wrote her chatty letters about their lack of suitable clothes for the glittering functions which they were expected to attend. Heather wrote of her longing to have a full-length mirror, and described how she and Betty had been obliged to smile their way through a three-hour-long Dutch banquet without being able to speak a word of the language.[45]

On 2 September, Baden-Powell drove Cadet the Hon. A. R. P. Baden-Powell to enrol at Sandhurst. They both lunched with the Commandant, Lieutenant-General Sir Reginald May, whom Baden-Powell was soon inviting to visit Pax Hill. He was delighted to discover that the Director of Studies at the college was Major Claude Nicholson, a nephew of his former Chief Staff Officer in the S.A.C.. Given the struggle it had been to get Peter to Sandhurst, Baden-Powell was under no illusions about the importance of being on friendly terms with his instructors.

Like his sisters, the 19-year-old Peter had also been corresponding with Josephine, and on his first Saturday at Sandhurst he caught a bus to London to meet her at Hyde Park Corner. On every available free afternoon, he would return to London and they would lunch or dine at

Lyons' Corner House. Josephine lived with her mother in a flat in Fitzjohn's Avenue, in Hampstead, which was inconveniently far away; and in any case both of them would have found her mother's presence inhibiting. So instead they used to go to her doctor uncle's house in Harley Street; he and her aunt were understanding people who allowed them time alone together. This was a great blessing, since Josephine had by now fallen in love with Peter. He had been smitten with her from the beginning.

Baden-Powell meanwhile fondly supposed that Peter was working hard during his spare time. Early in December he went with Percy Everett, General Godfrey-Faussett, the Commissioner for Rovers, and Miss Majendie who ran a scheme for the unemployed, to see Church Parade at Sandhurst. 'I saw <u>Peter for the first time in H.M. uniform!</u>', he wrote proudly in his diary. By then Peter had already told Josephine that he could not cope with the technical aspects of his training – finding the mapwork and theory of gunnery totally beyond him. He knew he ought to prepare his father for the worst, but could not face it.

By mid-November Olave had discovered that Peter was seriously involved with Josephine, and therefore invited her and her mother to Pax Hill so that she could scrutinize them more closely.[46] Although Olave made no early move to end the relationship because Peter was so much younger, Josephine sensed a certain coldness. She mentioned this in a letter to Heather, who replied that as far as she and Betty were concerned 'we like you sharing Peter with us . . . Why on earth shouldn't you?' Heather was at the Sandhurst Ball at which Peter danced almost constantly with Josephine.[47] In early December Olave wrote pleasantly to Josephine, addressing her by her nickname 'Baba' which Peter always used and asking her to stay on 20 December, the day Peter came home from Sandhurst. 'I have a sort of shrewd suspicion that that would make his home-coming happier!' This was a thoughtful invitation for which Peter was grateful; he was given the letter to post and added a marginal note: 'Yes, my darling!!! *I AM [HAPPY]*!!'[48]

Sadly Josephine's stay was a miserable one. Annie caught Peter on his way to Josephine's room during the night and reported him to Olave; and at breakfast time the following day a letter arrived from Sandhurst with the news that he had failed his first examination there. His father groaned aloud and banged his fist on the table. Then he rounded on Josephine and blamed her for distracting Peter. Being six years older than the boy, Baden-Powell said she should not have led him on. After everything he had done to get Peter to Sandhurst, Baden-Powell was beside himself. Josephine and Peter could have told him that he might have spared himself a lot of disappointment if he had only selected a career for Peter which did not involve examinations.

But Stephe had got it into his head that Peter's only chance of earning a living lay in gaining a commission and then making a lucrative marriage. Unfortunately Josephine's mother had recently let slip in conversation with Baden-Powell that she was not, as he had previously supposed, a rich widow but a poor one – her husband having been a Professor of Music at the Royal Academy and not a businessman.[49] Josephine's comparative poverty had been niggling at the Baden-Powells throughout December, and his failure in his examinations finally persuaded them that they would have to end this unsuitable romance.

On 4 January 1933, after posting a letter to Josephine asking her 'to let Peter alone',[50] Olave took him and the girls to the *Yeomen of the Guard*, before depositing him at the King Edward VII Hospital for Officers. He had been suffering from a torn cartilage for several weeks, and his parents saw his five-week immobilization as a heaven-sent opportunity. If they could dissuade Josephine from visiting him, they might be able to end the affair. The hospital was run by its formidable founder, Sister Agnes Keyser, with whom Baden-Powell and Olave had a private word on the day of Peter's operation. Sister Agnes struck Baden-Powell as 'most motherly' and the perfect person 'to deal gently with Peter's love affair', possibly because she had once had an affair with Edward VII.[51] However, Josephine had no intention of abandoning Peter while he was in hospital and turned up two days after his operation at the same time as Baden-Powell. An unpleasant situation was smoothed over by Sister Agnes, whom Baden-Powell thought 'most helpful and understanding'.[52] Josephine did not feel so well-disposed towards the woman, but kept in touch with Peter by letter and their affair continued after his discharge. Olave and Baden-Powell discussed matters with May Mackie, the mother of one of Peter's Charterhouse friends. Olave liked Mrs Mackie for her sensible and forthright manner,[53] and thought she might succeed in 'dissuading Josephine' where she herself had failed. In the event, Mrs Mackie fared no better.

On 8 April Baden-Powell wrote in his diary: 'I had a talk with Peter. Pointed out danger of his love-making with Josephine. He agreed to stop it and to my writing to tell her.' Baden-Powell then concentrated on money, telling Peter that he would not be able to support a wife for at least ten years – nor would he have any chance of getting into the army if he spent his time dreaming of Josephine. Surely he could see that this was a crucial period demanding exceptional sacrifices on his part? Baden-Powell was horrified to learn during this interview that Peter had actually proposed to Josephine. Did he not realize that she might sue for breach of promise? Did he want to blight himself with the authorities at Sandhurst and with the War Office? Josephine knew that Peter was frightened of his father and had always half-suspected that, at the first real pressure from him, Peter would give her up. His failure to object to his father writing to her certainly looked like the end.[54]

Baden-Powell misjudged Josephine, who would never have dreamed of suing Peter. She was shocked by his father's letter, which was clearly written with this fear in mind. He told her of 'most distasteful rumours' about her relationship with Peter having 'come to us from very unexpected quarters', and went on: 'This is not good for your reputation, and, though there is of course no engagement, yet if the rumour got say to the War Office, or the regiment, that he was engaged it would bar him from getting a commission.' Undoubtedly an early marriage would have harmed his prospects, but the idea that an engagement would have denied him a commission was simply untrue. Stephe disingenuously suggested that Olave, in attempting to persuade her 'to let Peter alone', had only been trying to reduce the time they spent together rather than demanding a complete ban; by going on as before, Josephine had let Olave down. Baden-Powell said that he too had had faith in Josephine, 'but I'm afraid my expectations were not well founded, and this boy-and-girl comradeship was becoming a sloppy sentimentality (which is no more love than my boot).'[55]

Earlier Baden-Powell had written to Major Nicholson at Sandhurst about Josephine, saying that it would help if he could write back requesting that the affair should be given up in the interests of the boy's future. Nicholson obligingly wrote along these lines, enabling Baden-Powell to give Peter a salutary shock.[56] He mentioned this communication in his letter to Josephine as proof that his anxiety was justified, and ended by asking for her 'frank assurance that you will cease communicating with him or seeing him . . .'[57] Knowing that Peter had agreed to let his father send this letter 'on his behalf', Josephine saw no point in fighting. She wrote back agreeing to cooperate, and a few days later heard from Baden-Powell that Peter had been shown her letter and 'quite understands from it that it is best for you both to cease all communication right away. So you will not feel hurt at his not writing.'[58]

By August that year Peter seemed to be getting over his blighted affair. Olave had organized a summer cruise for 650 Guiders and Scouters on a liner, which would call at ports in Holland, Poland and all the Scandinavian countries for quayside rallies. In amongst all the speech-making about peace and international goodwill, Olave and Stephe managed to find time for separate chats with their son 're his character and future'. A few days later they were rebuking him for failing to go to bed when told to, but instead choosing to 'hang around with girls'.[59] Peter, 20, and Baden-Powell, now 76, were inhabiting different worlds. Heather and Betty, who also found most of the

Guiders and Scouters excruciatingly dull, had formed a B.Y.T. Club (for Bright Young Things) and invited anyone who looked young and lively to join.[60] Back home, Peter was given another formidable lecture before returning to Sandhurst for what was certain to be his last term if he failed his exams again.

On 23 November, Baden-Powell was inundated with irate letters from peace-loving Scouters who had taken exception to a speech he had made earlier in the week advising young men to join the Territorials. In his swollen post-bag, he also found a letter from Major Nicholson warning him that Peter had very little chance of passing out as a commissioned officer. To complete his misery, he had an agonizing ulcer in his mouth and was beginning to suffer pain every time he urinated. Nevertheless he set off for London at once in the hope of seeing the Hon. John W. Downie, the High Commissioner in London for Southern Rhodesia, he had now pinned all his hopes on getting Peter into the British South Africa Police. On arrival at Downie's office he learned that the High Commissioner had been called away unexpectedly. 'A bad day altogether,' he commented in his diary.[61]

However, he managed to see Downie a few days later and was relieved to find him accommodating. If Peter passed a medical, he was assured that there would be no problem. A week later Baden-Powell told Peter about his imminent departure for Rhodesia and found him 'fully agreeable'. His father would have been most surprised if he had not been. In his opinion, members of frontier police forces led 'a fine outdoor life with lots of interesting adventure about it'.[62] With its routines of 'reveille' and 'stables', a body like the B.S.A.P. was the next best thing to a cavalry regiment.

Baden-Powell's trouble with his bladder was by now causing him constant pain and he was obliged to use a catheter and bag whenever he went out. His brother Frank was dying, and his brother Baden had just survived a heart attack and was still in a precarious state. At this depressing time, Stephe had another delicate interview in prospect. Two years earlier, his old friend Colonel John K. Spilling and his wife had told him that being childless they wished to leave their fortune to the young Baden-Powells.[63] Spilling had commanded the 13th Hussars during the late 1880s and had been delighted to hear about Peter's 'choice' of the army as a career; he had hoped almost as fervently as Baden-Powell himself that Peter would one day be a subaltern in their old regiment. Baden-Powell's only comment in his diary after disabusing Spilling was: 'They were very disappointed.'[64] He allowed his personal chagrin to overcome his judgement and let slip certain details about events leading up to Peter's failure which persuaded the Colonel and his lady to think again about their wills. When Peter came to see the Spillings in person, he made matters worse by not appearing sufficiently mortified over failing to become a Hussar.[65] To him, the 83-year-old Colonel was an unendurable old fogey whose disdain for colonial police forces was sickeningly patronizing. Two weeks later, sensing that he had said too much, Baden-Powell wrote to Spilling telling him that Peter 'is only backward' and 'roughing it in South Africa will make a man of him'.[66] Unfortunately the damage had been done. Both the Spillings died within the next four years, leaving Heather and Betty £20,000 between them and Peter nothing.

On 12 December at the Charterhouse Founder's Day Dinner, Baden-Powell thought 'the headmaster's speech smacked of mutual admiration in excelsis'.[67] But his bladder pains had been excruciating that evening. When his brother Frank lay dying that Christmas, Stephe was too ill to visit him. By then he was frantic about Peter again, since the Rhodesian medical officer had refused to pass him because of his varicose veins. Baden-Powell sent for the certificate he had obtained from Sir Crisp English, the consulting surgeon at St George's Hospital; this had secured entry to Sandhurst and, to his joy, was again successful.

On New Year's Day 1934 Betty was rushed into a Farnham nursing home with appendicitis, and the next day her father was admitted to the King Edward VII Hospital for Officers to have his bladder investigated. After an exploratory operation, his surgeon diagnosed an enlarged prostate and advised removal. The operation took place on 20 January and seemed to go smoothly, but five days later Baden-Powell haemorrhaged and had to have a transfusion. His temperature rose to 105 degrees, and he suffered severe rigor which lasted over an hour. On 9 February a similar relapse occurred and once again he nearly died. Olave was naturally distraught. It was not until 3 March, five days before he returned home, that she managed to get through a whole day without weeping with anxiety and exhaustion.[68]

When Peter left for Rhodesia on 23 February for his new life in the British South Africa Police, his mother did not come to see him off at the London docks, although by then Baden-Powell's condition was no longer causing concern. He made a complete recovery, but was very weak until the autumn. Peter did not see his father again for almost two years and when he did, Baden-Powell and Olave were sailing down the eastern seaboard of Africa bound for Durban in a steamship which called en route at the port of Beira in Mozambique. Peter managed to get 48 hours' leave and travelled overnight from Salisbury to be there to greet his parents at the quayside. Olave was suffering from malaria and Baden-Powell was about to succumb to it, so their reunion was not ideally timed. His mother, who felt 'like a chewed rag', thought him 'grown in body, but, dear boy the same age as when he was at Charterhouse'.[69] Peter must have found it hard to appear light-hearted since he had something on his mind which he could not bring himself to tell them. He was planning to get married within the next two weeks to Carine Crause Boardman, a South African girl from Johannesburg whom he had met soon after leaving England in 1934.

When his parents travelled up from South Africa to Rhodesia in April 1936, he joined them for a week's leave and accompanied them to Bulawayo, Mafeking and the Kruger National Park Game Reserve. Before returning to Salisbury, he had the bizarre experience of being solemnly warned by both of them against marrying on the rebound. He had married Carine four months earlier and by now knew that she was pregnant. He may have considered telling the truth but, faced with this familiar bombardment of advice, thought better of it.[70]

Peter finally decided to inform his parents of his marriage in January 1937. The reason he chose to do so just then, when his mother and father were leaving England for a lengthy tour of India, seems likely to have been his recent discovery that his sister Betty was pregnant too. She had married in September of the previous year and, while Peter got on well with Heather, his relations with Betty were more distant – largely because she identified so closely with her mother who remained, as Peter knew, his most unforgiving critic. To announce to his parents the birth of the first Baden-Powell grandson – a boy, and therefore a future Lord Baden-Powell – a few months before Betty gave birth would, he thought, knock the wind from her sails.[71]

Olave and Baden-Powell were shocked and wounded by their son's secret marriage. Knowing that he still kept in touch with Josephine (who had just married a young curate), Olave felt no qualms about corresponding with her, seeming unaware of the irony of complaining to Josephine about 'the rotten way' Peter had behaved. 'But now we are putting his dreadful deficiencies behind us, as far as we can.'[72] The Baden-Powells' immediate problem was whether to tell people that they had connived in his deception (troopers in the B.S.A.P. were not allowed to marry for three years), or admit that they had not known that Peter had married and had a son. Not unnaturally, they chose to put it about that they had 'kept Peter's secret'. Baden-Powell hated this pretence because he would never have lied for Peter. On the very day he learned about the marriage, he wrote to his son's commanding officer telling him the truth; he also wrote to Peter advising him to confess to his colonel. These letters were posted from Marseilles on 13 January.[73]

Peter was probably not surprised when his parents chose to announce the birth of his son to their friends as a postscript to their announcement of the birth of Betty's daughter. 'And now here is this other most important bit of news about Peter . . .' Olave, who had written this, ended by saying that congratulations would be out of order since it was such old news.[74] An acrimonious correspondence ensued, in which Peter blamed his mother for the breakdown of trust and Baden-Powell rebuked him for trying to hold his mother responsible for what had been his own fault.[75] Nevertheless, hoping to help Peter get into the Rhodesian Civil Service, he wrote to Sir Herbert Stanley, the Governor of Southern Rhodesia, on his behalf. That Peter swiftly acquired a job in the Native Affairs Department was probably due to this letter.[76]

Baden-Powell and Olave spent the winter of 1937/38 in Kenya, and in March Olave flew down to Rhodesia to see Peter's family. She reported back enthusiastically and, while distressed by Carine's South African accent, found her 'an excellent housewife'.[77] Stephe was too ill to travel on this occasion, but a month later met his daughter-in-law and his grandson Robert for the first time at Beira on his way to South Africa. He thought Carine 'exactly the wife for Peter' and admitted that 'he had shown better sense than I gave him credit for in finding her'.[78] He declared that Peter had filled out into a well-built man, and that Robert was 'the best baby of his age in the world . . .' Baden-Powell was with Peter and his family for three days, and during that time made his peace with his son. He would see him only once again, in Kenya the following February, when Peter's and Betty's families joined him at Nyeri for two weeks. During this final reunion, Baden-Powell was relaxed and affectionate towards Peter and Carine and delighted in playing with the 3½-year-old Robert.

Soon afterwards Baden-Powell sent Peter a cheque for just over £3,000 – this gift being equal to half his total assets.[79] Several months earlier he had given him £500. When Peter's uncle, Baden, had been dying in the summer of 1937, Baden-Powell had made sure that he left the bulk of his estate to Peter.[80] In this way, he tried to make up for his inadvertent part in losing Peter his share in Colonel Spilling's estate. Of Baden-Powell's last half-dozen letters one would be to Carine, enclosing a birthday present of £15 for Robert and another to Peter in time for his birthday.[81] Unlike her husband, Olave would never truly make her peace with her son.

Given his relations with Peter, it is ironic that Baden-Powell should simultaneously have been urging Scoutmasters to give their boys responsibility and trust them. Trust was what Peter never enjoyed. His failures were deemed to be due to his lack of effort rather than to his lack of aptitude; and because his parents never would believe that he was doing his best, he was subjected to repeated humiliations. The price Baden-Powell and Olave paid was to be deceived and rejected. At Dane Court and earlier Peter had missed his parents terribly when they went away, and on their later tours he did not bother to write. 'That rascal Peter had not written to us once,' Baden-Powell told Mrs Wade sadly in 1931.[82]

In 1939 Baden-Powell wrote congratulating Percy Everett on his grandson, another Peter, gaining a Winchester scholarship. 'The boy is bound to be a success.'[83] His dreams for *his* Peter had been too powerful for his own good. In an ideal world, Peter would have restored his youth to him by re-enacting and even improving upon his achievements: Captain of Football at Charterhouse; passing into the cavalry not second, as he had done, but first; marching crisply across the parade ground to receive the Sword of Honour at Sandhurst; playing polo not just for the 13th Hussars but for the army. What pleasure even part of this would have given Baden-Powell. If only his old military cronies had had occasional cause to congratulate him upon his son's progress rather than commiserate with him for his failings. Even in the dire national emergency of 1940, Peter would be rejected by the army as unfit.

But the Peter with whom Baden-Powell finally came to terms was not a projection of his own wishes but the man himself. Against the odds, Peter had grown up to possess many of the virtues of the perfect Scout. He was modest, unselfish, kind, the reverse of snobbish and so little concerned with protocol that he would often cause consternation by arriving at the House of Lords wearing shorts and with a rucksack on his back.[84]

2. We Fancy We be Wise (1933–38)

Baden-Powell ended his brief autobiography with an envoy entitled 'Vesperascit' (it becomes evening), which was meant to convey the warm and peaceful afterglow of a well-spent life.

> I write this sitting in my garden at the close of a perfect day in late September . . . with the sunset giving a new tone to the lights and shadows across the woodlands . . . There is a scent of roses in the air – and sweetbriar . . . A bee hums drowsily by, hiveward bound. All is peace in the house at dusk, as night closes down . . . it is good to laze, honestly half-tired, and to look back and feel that though one has had one's day it has, in spite of one's limitations, not been an idle one . . . Through an upper window comes the laughing chatter of the young folk going to bed. Tomorrow *their* day will come. May it be as happy a one as mine has been. God bless them! As for me – it will be my bedtime soon. And so – GOOD NIGHT!
> Sleep after toyle, port after stormie seas,
> Ease after warre, death after life, doth greatly please.[1]

This was published in 1933, when Baden-Powell's troubles with Peter were at their height. The quotation more truthfully reflecting his thoughts and feelings at this time was one he culled from the *Fishing Gazette* and with which he prefaced his book:

What fools we be when young. We fancy we be wise, forgetting that the old boys have graduated in the varsity of the world, the greatest varsity of all, and each day we should learn from them.[2]

And alas Peter was very far from being the only 'fool when young'. The number of Scouts in Great Britain had started to decline in 1934, and went on doing so throughout 1935 and 1936. The average had only been 3 per cent for each of these years, but in his bones Baden-Powell sensed that something significant had happened. The loss of 'the genial Gilwell spirit', once generated by Gidney, could only be a partial explanation.[3] An article by 'a Holborn Rover', published in *The Scouter* in June 1935, came much closer to explaining what he feared.

Have you ever taken a couple of your blokes (sorry, I forgot I was writing for *The Scouter*) your boys to a prize fight? Horrified? Ha, ha! Something is attracting our boys, and it is something on what we class as the 'outside' of Scouting. Right, then let's start right away and bring it on the 'inside' . . . Lots of Scoutmasters like to feel that their boys are blue-eyed little angels, who long for tenderfoot revision and an evening with their s.m. . . . but do they? [Not according to the author, who urged Scouters to take boys to] . . . skating rinks, prize fights, dirt track races, talkies, since as soon as they regard you as part of all these things on the 'outside', you will have much less trouble holding them from the 'inside' . . . Ever had a chap cry off playing football for your troop because Chelsea are at home? Why not? Chelsea won't be playing at home next week, and it does us all good to watch experts . . . It's all very well in theory to say, 'My lads never put anything before their duty,' but don't be too broken hearted if they do.[4]

But Baden-Powell *was* broken-hearted – not because boys liked to please themselves (they always had done) but because within a few decades their expectations and interests had changed. When the Brownsea boys had set out on their adventure there had been very few swimming pools and playing fields, only a handful of ice rinks and cinemas and no radio. Very few boys had ever travelled out of their home town or county, and hardly any owned anything as expensive as a bicycle. But during the 1930s the Scouts and Guides (whose numbers had dropped as steeply as the boys') were having to compete with numerous other pursuits. And there was another problem – adolescents were not only better informed and more sophisticated than a quarter of a century earlier, but inclined to be suspicious of public men and women who urged them to think first of the community. The Depression and high unemployment made such calls sound hypocritical. The Scoutmaster and the old military man were becoming figures of fun – as witness, in the *Evening Standard*, David Low's

Colonel Blimp with his diehard remarks and walrus moustache. 'Mad dogs and Englishmen go out in the midday sun,' sang Noel Coward, epitomizing the educated young's ironic attitude towards the Empire.

Baden-Powell was thoroughly bewildered. One day he felt sure that the Movement needed 'young men' as Scouters, rather than 'old gentlemen merely interested in improving the morals of the younger generation',[5] and the next he was angrily accusing youth movements of casting aside older men.[6]

While age had worsened his problems with Peter, it seemed (at least to start with) to have had no effect upon his relations with his daughters. His rejection of genteel Edwardianism had freed Heather and Betty to ride and spend as much time out of doors as they liked. He encouraged them to be tough, and took Heather to the Army Physical Training School at Aldershot as often as he took Peter. When she was 6, she fell heavily on her elbow from her pony on to the brick border of a rose-bed. Her father was summoned and between her sobs Heather managed to ask: 'Do Brownies ever cry?' When he told her that they did not, she 'looked up at him, chin quivering, and tried to be brave', as he carried her and her broken arm into the house.[7]

Appropriately Heather was sent to St James's, Malvern, where the headmistress – a 6-foot giant who had also founded the school – decreed that Girl Guiding and games should be accorded as much attention as academic work. Betty was sent to another school, Westonbirt, where the headmistress had been the Guides' Chief Commissioner for Scotland. When she left, Betty was at once transferred to St James's. Both girls were well able to cope with the spartan regime.[8] Because Olave had never been sent away to school herself, she had no idea how embarrassing it was to arrive with a trunk containing old-fashioned flannel vests and combinations instead of ordinary light modern underwear. Heather was also nauseated by the brand of 'carbolic' toothpaste which her mother thought suitable for all her children. Nor did Olave have any feel for the kind of everyday clothes which the girls wanted to wear in the holidays.[9]

But while Heather did well at school and loved both her parents, she suffered from bouts of weeping which struck them as alarming enough to require the help of a psychologist. During her last year at St James's she was sent to a Dr Patrick Leahy, who was unable to be of much assistance.[10] Her problems probably dated back to her period of separation from her parents at Bexhill during the war; nor could it have helped her that her mother so plainly preferred Betty and her niece, Christian Davidson, who had spent much of her time at Pax Hill since her mother's suicide. While Heather could ride to her heart's content, Olave was always petrified in case Christian harmed herself.[11] Olave made no secret of such preferences, even calling Betty 'my Betty' in letters to friends and giving Heather no such distinction. Betty was very like Olave physically, with the same dark eyes and hair and the same self-confident way of speaking. By contrast Heather, in spite of her success at school, was shyer and would later dislike speaking in public and talking to journalists. Because Baden-Powell did not expect anything specific from his daughters in the way that he expected achievements from his son, his relations with them were better.

But when Heather ceased to be a child her father still thought of her as one, although by then she was longing to emulate her eldest cousin. While Christian was speeding away to hunt balls with young men in sports cars, Baden-Powell was taking his 'beloved Heatherums', aged 18, to *Toad of Toad Hall*.[12] A year later, however, she was presented at Court and was at last able to begin to get her own back on Christian. She found herself longing to escape from the overwhelmingly wholesome atmosphere of home. Where else except at Pax Hill would visiting friends have to remove their lipstick and chip off their nail varnish before arriving? And her mother could make life so difficult at dances and parties. William Mather recalled taking a girl into the garage to kiss her in the back of the Rolls Royce. Suddenly Olave appeared, shining a torch through the glass and shouting at him to leave the house.[13]

When Heather met a handsome and raffish army officer with a Sunbeam sports car and a reputation for philandering, she was entranced. She went to several balls as his partner during the autumn of 1933 and then, with her father conveniently out of the way in hospital (and her mother constantly by his side), she managed to see a great deal more of him. On 20 March 1934, only ten days after Baden-Powell's return home following his prostate operation, Heather's engagement to Lieutenant G. E. ('Geordie') Lennox-Boyd of the Highland Light Infantry was announced in the newspapers.

Although Heather kept her feelings to herself, her father soon sensed that she was unhappy. He had little faith in women's abilities to choose men discriminatingly and at once suspected that his daughter had made a mistake.[14] He therefore contacted the Scout District Commissioner for Lymington (which was not far from Geordie's home village) and learned that it was rumoured locally that the young man had another girl. Being too ill to go himself, Baden-Powell at once sent Olave to see the colonel of the Highland Light Infantry to try to find out as much as possible about Lieutenant Lennox-Boyd. To her horror, she learned that Geordie had recently fallen on his head at a point-to-point and had undergone a character change so severe that his future in the army would remain uncertain until he went before a medical board in June.[15] With trouble looking inevitable, Olave went to see the Spillings to prepare them gently. She also wrote to Geordie, on Baden-Powell's instructions, telling him that the wedding could not take place until the results of the medical were known.[16] In the meantime Heather had been sent away to stay with friends.

The Baden-Powells hoped to have won themselves enough time to plan and launch a proper offensive. Baden-Powell got in touch with the Lymington Scouts again and learned that Lennox-Boyd had a reputation for 'flirting, unpopularity with his men, indebtedness and irresponsibility'. All this was confirmed by a previous girl friend whom Olave managed to run to earth in Petersfield.[17]

Geordie got wind of these enquiries and wrote demanding that Olave make 'specific charges' against him and send the names of those who had slandered him. Alarmed by this threat of litigation, Olave replied that she had no 'specific charges' to make, but was simply worried about his prospects of returning to the regiment.[18] At this point five national newspapers telephoned to find out whether the wedding was on or off. Olave told them that it was still on, but would have to be postponed because of their impending world tour.[19] At this inauspicious moment, Geordie did what Baden-Powell had dreaded most – passed his medical and rejoined his regiment.

Sensing that it was already too dangerous to put pen to paper in any material way, Baden-Powell invited Geordie to come to Pax to discuss the situation. Geordie came on 21 June with his brother, Alan, who at once demanded the names of Geordie's slanderers. A formidable character, Alan had been President of the Oxford Union and at the age of 27 had been elected Conservative M.P. for mid-Bedford.[20] (In the 1950s he would be a Tory minister, and subsequently a life peer.) When Alan pointed out that his brother's career and reputation were being endangered by unfounded rumours, Baden-Powell told him reassuringly that nothing he had heard amounted to more than youthful irresponsibility. In that case, countered Alan, he would not mind letting him have the names of his informants. Baden-Powell refused, but still managed to persuade the brothers that it would be in all their interests to leave matters as they were until after the end of his world tour. Alan agreed to consider this, provided that the rumours ceased and that the family's clear intention was for the marriage to take place as soon as possible after they returned to England.[21]

From Baden-Powell's point of view any time gained was precious. Heather was still in love, but the longer the delay the greater would be his chances of convincing her that marrying Geordie would be folly. Given his reputation for chasing women, there was even a chance that he might become seriously entangled with someone else while they were all away on tour. In mid-June Baden-Powell felt well enough to take Heather to Scotland for a month's fishing. Years later, Heather would applaud his cleverness in patiently fishing and sketching with her rather than attempting a direct trial of wills.[22] By the time she returned to Pax, she was almost ready to give up Geordie. And by mid-September, her father finally had her agreement to his writing to Lennox-Boyd to suggest that the engagement be broken off. These three months had also given Geordie time for reflection; he now decided that marrying Heather would be likely to bring him more pain than pleasure. Provided the blame for the broken engagement were to be equally shared, he would raise no objection to calling it off. On 13 October, what Baden-Powell called 'Heather's disengagement' appeared in *The Times*.[23] Geordie would never marry anyone; he died during the Second World War, taking part in a cloak-and-dagger sabotage mission in occupied France.

The 'Geordie débâcle' combined with the decline in the number of Scouts and Guides to have a disillusioning effect on Baden-Powell. When Betty wrote to him in August 1935 complaining about his attitude towards the young, he told her that just 'because others of your generation are fools, there is no reason why *you* should be a fool too'. When *he* had recognized that his mother's 'philosophy was right', he had 'guided himself by her almost entirely'. He ended by telling Betty that he meant to put flowers on his mother's grave the very next day, which he did.[24] His disappointment with Heather led him to recommence work on a manuscript which he laid aside early in 1930, after a few months of sporadic writing. This was *Rovering and Rangering*, which he intended to publish as a new and expanded edition of *Rovering to Success* adapted for both sexes.[25] When completed, the manuscript exhibited most of the faults of *Rovering to Success* and few of its virtues. His warnings to girls about the dangers of 'siliasity' (a new disease afflicting the female sex) were puerile and condescending, and the prejudices voiced against young women were more pronounced than anything he had written since the turn of the century. The new 'mania' for 'make-up' and 'face painting' he attributed to an all but universal female weakness for 'self-advertisement'. He accused 'young people of the silias breed' of affecting 'eccentricity or loudness of dress, or behaviour, simply to attract attention. They call it daring; others call it silly.' This was sorry stuff from the man whose own efforts 'to attract attention' had included dressing up as a woman and placing his head on a postage stamp. Baden-Powell would owe a considerable debt to Headquarters for vetoing publication.[26] Just when his writing had degenerated to this banal level he was awarded the nation's highest honour, the Order of Merit. But the 'boy man' was still able to assert himself. Returning from the Palace with his order, Baden-Powell was spotted by some Scouts. Telling the chauffeur to stop, he jumped out to show the admiring boys his newest decoration.

Baden-Powell's weariness with the young had not a little to do with his health. During the mid-thirties, he experienced a worrying loss of energy which would later be attributed to a heart condition.[28] Yet while he was ill more often than the female members of the family, he focused anxiety upon *them*. His particular phobia was breathing through the mouth. This 'condition', in his opinion, made sufferers look stupid and damaged their health by admitting germs which would otherwise be caught in the 'nasal slime'.[29] So in the early years of his marriage, when he was suffering from terrible headaches, he persuaded his perfectly healthy wife to have an operation on her nose.[30] Later Baden-Powell corresponded with a Wimpole Street specialist on 'the dangers of young people neglecting the care of their noses', and subsequently insisted upon Betty having the same operation.[31]

During 1936 in South Africa, when Baden-Powell was ill with malaria and Olave and Betty were away together on Guide inspections, Heather stayed behind and nursed her father. This was the tour during which Baden-Powell settled the South African Scouts' constitution and visited Mafeking for the last time; an event of real interest to the girls, who had grown up hearing numerous anecdotes about the place and having met many of their father's officers at the regular Mafeking reunions. It was, as Heather put it, 'a funny little place, with bumpy roads and sad little shops'. Baden-Powell tried to find Game Tree fort, but the bush had sprung up so thickly around it that his efforts were in vain. The suburbs now sprawled further, the trees had grown taller and many of the old 'Siegeites' had died. There was still no statue to him in the town. Baden-Powell visited the cemetery, pausing longest in front of the headstone of Private Webb, a Headquarters' orderly whose death had upset him at the time. Only here, among the graves, was there any indication that the Siege had ever taken place.[32]

Not many hours out from Cape Town on the return voyage to Britain, Betty made the acquaintance of a 28-year-old District Officer who was stationed in a remote region of Barotseland and was returning for six months' home leave in England. Gervas Clay and Betty managed to snatch enough time together to fall in love.[33] Shortly after the family's return to Pax Hill, Olave took Betty off again on a Guiding tour of Scandinavia, and before long had learned that Gervas had proposed. To Olave's credit, given her love for Betty – and the fact that Gervas would be taking her to one of the least accessible parts of South Central Africa – she made no attempt to discourage Betty once convinced that her daughter was in earnest. She was swayed by several strange coincidences: she herself and Baden-Powell had also met on board ship and, just like Stephe and her, Gervas and Betty also shared a common birthday. Baden-Powell's immediate response was to write to Clay 'urging him to defer publishing the engagement for the present'. The thought of being subjected to another shambles like the Lennox-Boyd saga appalled him.

He first heard about the engagement when he received a letter from Olave while he was inspecting Scouts in the North of England. By the

time he returned to Pax, Olave was back there too; and he found Betty
at the gate waiting to tell him that she was determined to marry Gervas
before he sailed for Africa in six weeks' time. The following day
Baden-Powell interviewed Gervas in his study. Because Olave had
already thrown her support behind the match and because Clay was
serving the Empire in a far-flung outpost (exactly the sort of job which
he had spent so much time commending), he felt he could not sensibly
oppose a marriage.[34]

Gervas found his future father-in-law a daunting proposition
because of his age and fame. When offered a glass of flat beer at
luncheon, dare he ask for another? And was Baden-Powell serious
about wanting him to bring a gun on his next visit so that he could
shoot a rabbit which had been destroying the lawn? He brought the
gun, but was tormented by fears of missing the animal or earning the
great man's displeasure by shooting it while sitting. But when the
Chief Scout roared: 'There he is!' Gervas shot the sitting rabbit and
earned nothing but praise. Given Baden-Powell's saintly public
reputation, Gervas was surprised to learn that Olave disliked being
driven by her husband since he swore so much. He was also
disconcerted to discover that Baden-Powell did not shake hands with a
firm grip; and worse than that, that the hero of Mafeking's hands were
soft and rather puffy in spite of his vigorous morning exercises.[35]

Betty's magnificent wedding took place on 24 September 1936 in
Bentley Church with 400 guests. Outside Major Wade and the
Farnham Fire Brigade 'kept the photographers and their lady-touts
under control'.[36] Afterwards, with Betty and Peter gone and Heather
often away, it was clear that Pax Hill's days as a family home were
over. Yet when the as-yet-uncrowned Edward VIII offered a free life
tenancy of the sumptuously furnished King's House at Walton-
on-Thames, Olave and Baden-Powell turned it down. Pax Hill still
meant too much to them.[37] They would have been much better off if
they had accepted the royal offer, but both of them retained a
happy-go-lucky attitude towards money. Even when Katharine
Soames died, leaving her money to her nieces and her 'wearing
apparel' to Olave (this being her revenge on her for wearing Guide
uniform), Olave recovered quickly.[38] She would often complain
about lack of money but continued to maintain her staff, quite rightly
so since 'something always turned up'. In 1933 it was a legacy of £5,000
from an admirer of the Movement, then two years later one of Olave's
uncles left her twice that amount.[39] In 1937 a Belgian peace prize and a
Silver Wedding cheque from the Scouts and Guides together brought
in another £5,000. In late 1936 the Baden-Powells intended to continue
with their old routines and certainly had the financial wherewithal to
do so.

It was Baden-Powell's last tour of India which finally persuaded him that the time had come to abandon his active role in the Movement. His arrival in India in January 1937 coincided with the approach of the provincial government elections agreed to by the British Parliament in the Government of India Act (1935). In eight provinces these seemed certain to be won by Gandhi's Indian National Congress. Indians would have no say in foreign policy, but Baden-Powell could see that in domestic matters they would soon share power with the Viceroy. It was a most delicate moment and he was warned by Lord Linlithgow, the Viceroy, to be extremely careful in his public speeches and not to recognize any nationalist 'Scouts' without consulting him first.[40] Two days later Linlithgow showed Baden-Powell over the House of Assembly; he listened in on the proceedings and was depressed to hear an Indian with an Oxford accent describing England and South Africa as foreign countries.[41] That afternoon he opened the All-India Jamboree attended by 5,000 Scouts from all over the subcontinent. The unofficial Scouts still far outnumbered the official ones, and both of their largest representative bodies supported the Indian National Congress. Although Baden-Powell knew they favoured independence, he still felt these organizations were beneficial to Indian boys and so gave serious consideration to their request to him 'to show approval of them – as Chief Scout'. Since this was not exactly 'recognizing them', Baden-Powell put it to Linlithgow, who advised him very strongly against making any such statement.[42]

It was a relief to him to get away from Indian politics to revisit some of the haunts of his youth. The 13th Hussars (now the 13th/18th) were at Risalpur and here, on his eightieth birthday, Baden-Powell – in a borrowed uniform and mounted on a placid charger – rode out for his last full dress parade.[43] With the regiment due to mechanize later in the year, there would be few more of these parades for anyone. He found it almost eerie to visit Meerut and Muttra again and to see once more the bare rocky hillsides of the Khyber Pass. When he watched a large field compete for the Kadir Cup, it was exactly 54 years since 'Ding' MacDougall had won the trophy for him. He followed the heats high up on a howdah strapped to an elephant's back.

> Looking down at those little groups of keen young fellows, alert and on their toes for a run, with the silent line of beaters behind them, behind the phalanx of elephants, pressing inexorably forward through the swishing grass, I thought is this real? Am I awake or dreaming of the past? I felt that I might come to and find myself returning to consciousness on an operating table.[44]

He visited the bungalow at Meerut where he and 'the Boy' McLaren had lived so happily and found it occupied by 'a charming boy' who turned out to be none other than Nigel Dugdale, a son of Miss Turner (later Mrs James Dugdale), whom he had met in India in 1898 and had hoped he might one day marry. Writing to Colonel Sidney Kennedy of the 13th/18th Hussars after returning to Delhi, he described his time with the regiment 'as a sort of reincarnation . . . hearing reveille sounding, the bungalow, horse parade, the hunt meeting, the frontier mountains – it was all of life to me . . .'[45]

In Queen Victoria's heyday the British Raj had appeared as fixed and immutable as the planets, but now it scarcely seemed likely to outlive its former servant R. S. S. Baden-Powell. Of all that company of martial youth, he alone was left. They were all dead now – McLaren, MacDougall, Dimond, Smithson, Spilling, Christie and Noble.

In part, it was this sense of already belonging to history which persuaded him that enough was enough; but the incident that really brought it home to him took place on his return. At a press conference in the Rubens Hotel, while answering some general questions about his Indian tour, he remarked that the coming generation of Indian boys would need the Scout Movement's unique training in 'character, health and national unity'. Various Indian nationalist reporters took this to mean by implication that Baden-Powell thought Indian boys peculiarly lacking in 'character'. That they were able to do so was due to an astonishing gaffe. Baden-Powell said that the principal obstacle to the Scouts prospering in India was the absence of any word in Hindustani 'that actually stood for honour in its best sense'. Within ten days a tidal wave of criticism swept through the Indian press, and in England too Baden-Powell was caught up in the backwash. He found himself receiving reproachful letters from the Viceroy and the Secretary of State for India, as well as from Scout Commissioners in the subcontinent who suddenly saw years of work in ruins.

Only J. S. Wilson, who had been blamed for destroying the 'cheery' spirit at Gilwell, enjoyed Baden-Powell's discomfiture. He described the Chief Scout 'as rather like the naughty boy who has stolen the farmer's apples and refuses to admit that he has done anything wrong'.[46] The Commissioner for Bombay, Sir Byranjee Jeejeebhoy, was soon writing to a fellow Commissioner telling him that given Baden-Powell's extreme unpopularity in the city, the only way to save the Scout Association there would be to announce its severance from Imperial Headquarters.[47] This was soon done in Bombay and in almost every other province. It hurt Baden-Powell terribly to have gone to India intending to strengthen the recognized Scout Association, only to find that he had actually accelerated its destruction.

On 9 August 1937 Baden-Powell concluded his address to 27,000 Scouts, assembled for the Fifth World Jamboree in the Netherlands, with a personal farewell: 'Brother Scouts, the time has come for me to say good-bye . . . We are meeting for the last time – some of us. I am in my eighty-first year and am nearing the end of my life . . . You are at the beginning of yours' – he paused, suddenly emotional – 'but in this there is no cause for melancholy, but rather the opposite . . . it is an occasion of thanksgiving for a very happy existence.'[48] Unlike Captain Hook in *Peter Pan*, Baden-Powell would not repeat his farewell speech. The time had really come.

3. *Baden-Powell and the Dictators (1933–40)*

Earlier in his farewell speech Baden-Powell had referred to the Dutch Jamboree as a 'Crusade of Peace'; but as he knew all too well, the prospects for world peace were steadily worsening. At the 1929 Jamboree Italian and German boys had camped along with the rest. In 1933, at Gödöllö in Hungary, there had been no Italians and although a large German contingent had been expected, they too had failed to arrive.[1] The continuing absence of the Germans and Italians in Holland was a personal disappointment to Baden-Powell, since he had for several years been advocating a policy of keeping in touch with the Hitler Jugend.

Since this policy has recently been used to support the allegation that Baden-Powell wished 'to include' the Hitler Jugend within the international Scouting community because he felt that the Nazi organization 'shared so many of Scouting's ideals', it is most important to examine the development of Baden-Powell's thoughts on this subject.[2] As a prelude to this allegation, Michael Rosenthal argued that Baden-Powell entertained 'conceptions of Jewish character that are unacceptable for anybody to hold'.[3] In combination these charges are very much deadlier than either would have been alone, especially since it is never stated that all Baden-Powell's supposedly 'unacceptable' utterances and writings *preceded* the rise of Hitler and the persecution of the Jews. Before arguing either of these claims, Rosenthal implied that Baden-Powell had a general admiration for dictators by pointing to his earlier praise for Mussolini. Yet he neglects to mention that before the rise of Hitler, Mussolini had had many eminent admirers all over the world.

At a time when the British popular press was still inclined to describe the Bolsheviks as godless murderers and thieves, Baden-Powell was not alone in thinking that Mussolini had saved Italy from a bloody communist revolution. On meeting the Duce, Winston Churchill had said: 'If I were Italian, I am sure I would have been with you from the beginning to the end in your struggle against the bestial appetites of Leninism.' Austen Chamberlain took Mussolini yachting; the Archbishop of Canterbury and Mahatma Gandhi called him respectively 'the one giant figure in Europe' and a 'superman'. Across the Atlantic Thomas Edison pronounced him 'the greatest genius of the modern age'.[4]

In 1927 Mussolini decided to absorb the Italian Boy Scouts into his state youth organization, the Balilla. Baden-Powell had particular reasons, however, for not wishing to object too loudly. The Italian Scouts had never been recognized by the International Bureau – being the last remaining vestige of Sir Francis Vane's once proud worldwide organization. So Hubert Martin, the Bureau's director, advised him not 'to associate himself officially with Sir Francis Vane's protest'.[5] In addition, 1927 was the year in which Britain severed diplomatic relations with the Russians after the scale of Soviet support for the striking miners had been made public. To attack Mussolini's anti-communist youth movement at such a time therefore seemed impolitic. Baden-Powell himself had just received a coffin sent by the Young Communist League of Great Britain.[6]

Eric Blair's (George Orwell's) contemporaries at Eton may have smiled at the communist tracts reaching most schools in the country, but Baden-Powell did not.

Question: Can a Boy Communist be a Boy Scout, comrade?
Answer: No, comrade.
Question: Why, comrade?
Answer: Because, comrade, a Boy Scout must salute the Union Jack, which is the symbol of tyranny and oppression.[7]

Nor was the Chief Scout flattered when told by the secretary of the Young Communists' League that there were two million Russian boys in training as 'Red Pioneers . . . on the lines of the Boy Scouts but with better ideals'. Their oath was directly modelled on the Scouts' Promise and commanded them to 'uphold the cause of the workers and peasants of the whole world'. Their motto was a more specific version of 'Be Prepared': 'Be ready for the struggle of the working class.'[8]

Baden-Powell's admiration for Mussolini was therefore grounded in his hatred of communism. His meeting with the Italian dictator came about as the result of an audience arranged for him with Pope Pius XI in March 1933, at which he had over-optimistically hoped to enlist the Pontiff's help to stop the formation of separate Catholic Canadian Scouts. Since Baden-Powell was going to be in Rome, the director of the International Bureau had urged the Foreign Office to secure an appointment with the Duce during the same visit.[9] Stephe found Mussolini 'not a bit the bombastic or commanding figure' he had expected; instead he was 'small, rather stout . . . but genial and human'. Although he doubted whether the Balilla were truly volunt-ary, he was nevertheless impressed by the sheer scale of the operation. Nor could he help being flattered when the dictator told him that he had based his youth movement on the Scouts.[10]

After visiting the principal centre where the adult leaders were trained, Baden-Powell decided that the movement's prime objective was to bring character-training into the scope of national education. In an enthusiastic article published in the *Daily Telegraph*, he wrote of the Balilla as not only demonstrating that Scouting too 'could be made a definite part of national education', but also as showing that this 'experiment' was actually taking place. This was nonsense, as he later admitted when in reply to a letter from Sir Francis Vane he described the Balilla as 'cadets pure and simple'.[11] There was no woodcraft, no emphasis on good citizenship and, as he soon conceded, the Balilla was not voluntary.[12] When Baden-Powell saw the massive resources available to a state-financed youth movement, he could not help fantasizing about a similarly subsidized Scout Movement. Would it really destroy the virtues arising from the voluntary principle if the Government were to finance the Movement as part of the nation's educational system? The idea both tantalized and disturbed him.[13]

His initial reaction to the Balilla coincided with Hitler's coming to power in Germany, but before the brutality of his regime was recognized in other parts of Europe. Two years later, Baden-Powell was still blind to what was going on in Germany and, remembering the hyper-inflation and near civil war in that country, he felt justified in praising 'the dictators in Germany and Italy' for having 'done wonders in resuscitating their people to stand as nations'.[14] He was not in a position to condemn Hitler for dissolving the independent youth organizations in Germany, since there had been no officially recognized Boy Scouts there when he came to power. The Freishar and the Neudpfadfinders (the organizations which most closely resembled the Scouts) appeared perfectly willing to merge with the Hitler Jugend.[15]

By 1935, Baden-Powell was feeling confused about how he ought to react to the two dictators' youth movements. In that year he criticized them for aiming 'to harness the spirit and suppress individuality' – while he, by contrast, 'believed in promoting the desire from within the boy rather than imposing upon him from without'.[16] In 1937, he condemned 'the unity being promoted [in Germany and Italy] by enforcement and the repression of individual ideas', pronouncing it to be no more than a 'surface unity, not coming from the heart of the people'.[17]

Mr Rosenthal would have us think that Baden-Powell decided to maintain a policy of keeping in touch with the Hitler Jugend until 1937 because he approved of that organization's ideals. Undeniably, during 1934 and 1935 Baden-Powell did publish some laudatory remarks about the Jugend – even though more of his writings were critical. In 1937 his suspicions of 'mass suggestion' deepened, and he was certainly not being complimentary when he described Hitler as using 'huge pageants for hypnotising his people'.[18] A few months earlier he had agreed with Stanley Baldwin that: 'Freedom for the common man, handed down by our forefathers, is in jeopardy in our own land because it has been taken away from the common man in other lands.'[19]

Baden-Powell was persuaded by Mrs Mark Kerr and Dame Katharine Furse that the only way to influence the Germans was to keep in touch with them. Hubert Martin and the International Committee argued that on the contrary isolation and rebuffs would be 'more likely to bring about a genuine Scout Movement in Germany . . .'[20] But Baden-Powell blamed this attitude for having prevented the emergence of a genuine Scout Movement in Germany in the past. In September 1935, Mrs Kerr (now chairman of the World Committee) visited Germany with a party of Guides and Rangers. She was entertained by the Bund of Deutscher Mädel (the feminine equivalent of the Hitler Jugend) and, although shocked by clear evidence of anti-semitism, was touched by the warmth of the welcome given them by ordinary Germans. She felt strongly that the best corrective would be 'for groups of them to come outside their own country to see a more normal state of things'.[21] This was also Dame Katharine's view.[22] Lord Somers (the Deputy Chief Scout) invited members of the Hitler Jugend to come and camp on his estate in Herefordshire, while J. S. Wilson of Gilwell was another leader who favoured continuing contact.[23] So when Baden-Powell joined in and advocated closer links with the Jugend he was not alone – although that is the impression given by Michael Rosenthal, who confines his attention to the opposition of Hubert Martin and the International Committee.

Somers, Furse and Wilson were ardently anti-Nazi but, like the majority of their compatriots, misguidedly believed that war could be avoided if Chamberlain's policy of appeasement were followed. Like Baden-Powell, they felt that children should not be punished for the sins of their parents; and that although ostracizing adult organizations might make sense, it would be morally wrong to treat children in the same way. Baden-Powell also believed that 'it makes us at Head-quarters look a little ridiculous if we decree against fraternising while our boys are keeping up and extending friendships with the German boys through Scouts, school journeys, gliding clubs, Y.M.C.A., camping clubs etc..'[24]

Neville Chamberlain's flight to Munich and the apparent success of his mission convinced Baden-Powell that the policy of contact and friendship had been vindicated.[25] Appeasement is the true explanation for Baden-Powell's desire to maintain links with the German youth movement, rather than any fondness for the Jugend's ideals. If it seems implausible tht he should ever have been won over to Chamberlain's docile foreign policy, the article he wrote in *The Scouter* immediately after the Prime Minister's return from Munich puts the matter beyond doubt.[26] Baden-Powell hardly ever advised young men to join the

Territorials,[27] and although he had become keener on mass physical training by 1936, he did not recommend military training for the young.[28] The country's danger was greater than it had been before the First World War, but he remained silent on the need to 'be prepared'. But as he told Betty, 'the one great blessing of being old is one doesn't worry but is in the position of a looker on.'[29]

On the night of 9 November 1938 (*Kristallnacht*), widespread and well-organized attacks were made on Jewish homes, shops and synagogues in Germany and Austria. Members of the Hitler Jugend were prominent in these brutal acts. Neither Baden-Powell nor any of the Scout and Guide leaders who had supported him ever again wrote or spoke a word in favour of maintaining contact with the Hitler Jugend. It is one of history's paradoxes that a man who urged greater preparedness before one world war, and was blamed for it, was blamed again when he urged conciliation before another. It seems to me that Michael Rosenthal's scathing condemnation of Baden-Powell's policy trivializes a real dilemma. 'Giving up the possibility of extending Scouting's connections to another youth movement, particularly one that shared so many of Scouting's ideals, was not something Baden-Powell took lightly.'[30] No indeed – he sat down and wrote an article for *The Scout* entitled 'Why I should fight.'

And did Baden-Powell, as Mr Rosenthal claims, entertain 'conceptions of Jewish character that are unacceptable for anybody to hold'? One of the problems in considering the justice of such an emotively phrased statement is the way in which popular opinions on the subject changed so much during Baden-Powell's long life. There was strong anti-semitism in France, Russia, Romania, Poland, Austria and Germany from the 1880s until the Great War. Although anti-semitism was not as pronounced in the British as in the French Army – there having been no catalyst such as the Dreyfus case – Jews were not welcomed in exclusive regiments. Rosenthal is quite right in arguing that in the early years of the century Baden-Powell shared a belief widespread among his brother officers that Jews were entering the service 'to gain a position in society'. Stephe undoubtedly described this prejudice in a way that showed he shared it, but he was also prejudiced against rich tradespeople's sons taking commissions for exactly the same reason. He and many other officers were frightened by the power of new money and the way in which it was undermining the position of the old gentry in the army. A great many tradesmen's sons were forced out of smart regiments and most were gentiles. Although Rosenthal does not go into details, the passage he quoted was specifically concerned with the case of a Lieutenant Mocatta who had been told that he was not wanted by the subalterns of the 14th Hussars. As Inspector General of Cavalry, Baden-Powell was asked to sort out the trouble. By today's standards his energetic search for a more enlightened regiment would seem quite inadequate; but at the time, his behaviour would have been thought over-tolerant by many of his contemporaries. If he had made an example of the anti-semitic subalterns, it is very likely that there would have been resignations in the 14th Hussars and in other cavalry regiments and he would have been censured by senior officers for unnecessarily jeopardizing discipline in the army. It would effectively have ended his career.[31]

While ignoring the real dilemma which Baden-Powell faced, Mr Rosenthal also neglects to say that he was on excellent terms at this very time with Miss Lydia Sassoon whose father, as befitted one of the capital's richest Jews, owned a magnificent house in Grosvenor Place. Baden-Powell took her out on a number of occasions and gave her a specially made brooch that he himself had designed around a Mafeking bullet. If Miss Sassoon's family had realized that Baden-Powell was actively searching for a wife, they would probably have been less welcoming to him. In 1908, with her parents' blessing, she married into an Austrian Jewish family. Another family with whom Baden-Powell was on friendly terms was that of a German-Jewish diamond merchant, Karl Ernst Rube; he often stayed with the Rubes at their shooting lodge in Scotland and went to concerts with them in London.[32]

Mr Rosenthal seems to read too much into the examples he advances as proof of anti-semitism. In 1920 Eric Walker sent Baden-Powell a 'Report' from Russia, exhibiting virulent anti-semitic feelings. (This was the period when Bolshevism was often represented in the press as a German-Jewish plot.) Rosenthal commented: 'While Baden-Powell is guilty of none of Walker's excesses, it is clear from a variety of comments that Walker's vision was not essentially different from his own.'[33] But what were these comments? I have read through Walker's papers, and there is no evidence that Baden-Powell ever reacted to the report. Nor has any comment survived in Baden-Powell's papers. Another example which Mr Rosenthal advances to prove Baden-Powell's anti-semitism is a remark made in a letter about a Mr Weinthal, a South African Jewish supporter of the Boy Scouts: 'He is a Jew by descent, but not in practice and I think he is wholeheartedly out for the good of the show and not for himself.'[34] This is undoubtedly anti-semitic. But at a time when Jews were routinely stereotyped either as shopkeepers or businessmen too busy with money-making to have any interest in anything else, or as intellectuals with little respect for British history or culture, it hardly seems evidence of an attitude 'unacceptable for anybody to hold'.

Baden-Powell was undoubtedly guilty of swallowing, for a time, the ridiculous German-Jewish conspiracy theory which was given wide currency by the press in America and Britain in the years after the Great War. In 1924 he wrote an article in which he described Moscow as being 'under German-Jew direction'. Since he thought he was stating a fact he was astonished to be rebuked by a Mr A. Yellin, the Chairman of the Boy Scouts' Association in Jerusalem.[35] His failure to concede Mr Yellin's point about the offensiveness of the phrase –which linked the Jewish people both to Europe's most unpopular nation and to the western world's most unpopular ideology – was due to his habitual disinclination to admit a fault rather than to exceptionally powerful anti-Jewish feelings. Because a number of Lenin's colleagues were German Jews, Baden-Powell stuck by his statement, but at the same time expressed sorrow that his remark had been taken 'even indirectly as an attack on Jews generally, for I have on the contrary the greatest admiration for the race'.[36]

Michael Rosenthal compares a drawing of a *nouveau-riche* Jewish-looking woman – which Baden-Powell included in his short book *Life's Snags and How To Meet Them* – with 'caricatured figures in the German anti-semitic publications of the 1930s'. Since the book was published in 1927, six years before Hitler became German Chancellor, this is misleading. When criticized for this drawing at the time, Baden-Powell vehemently denied that he would ever 'sit down and deliberately draw caricatures of Jews or any other race'.[37] But in spite of this assertion, the drawing seems by far the best shot in Mr Rosenthal's locker. When Baden-Powell thought of people who flaunted their wealth in a vulgar and ostentatious way, the example which came most readily to mind was of a *nouveau-riche* Jew. This was anti-semitic. Yet in the world of real people rather than stereotypes, his perceptions were different. Just after the outbreak of war he wrote in *The Scouter* of his great good fortune in having found 'a perfectly excellent Jewish doctor . . . driven out of Germany . . . who has treated me with marked ability'.[38] Given the intimacy of a doctor's relations with his patients, it would have been strange indeed for a convinced anti-semite to have chosen a Jewish physician. Baden-Powell could be prejudiced and was guilty of occasional anti-semitic remarks, but in my judgement this does not merit grave condemnation, given his background and the date.

Mr Rosenthal's most interesting but least investigated claim is that Scouting shared 'many ideals' with the fascist youth movements. There would have to be truth in this since Mussolini had told Baden-Powell that he had based his movement on the Scouts. In the form in which Baden-Powell sold it to the Edwardian establishment, with the emphasis upon duty, discipline and self-sacrifice, Scouting held an obvious appeal to authoritarian governments of the right or left. The Promise, together with the use of carefully chosen vignettes of national history and culture incorporated into a programme which stressed the need for physical fitness and self-reliance, was sure to interest any regime eager to guarantee that boys would one day fight for their country.

The romantic appeal of the frontiersman in Scouting had also struck an immediate chord with Hitler, who recommended the works of Karl May to his general staff. (Karl May, 1842–1912, wrote forty volumes of Western adventures.) A dictator bent upon territorial expansion would naturally applaud the virtues of colonists of the kind Baden-Powell had represented as the backbone of the Empire in *Scouting for Boys*. The British imperialist view of the Empire's subjects in the non-white protectorates and colonies as 'lesser breeds' must have been of compelling interest to anyone with Hitler's racial preoccupations. Although it was not Baden-Powell's fault that twenty years after he wrote *Scouting for Boys* Hitler and Mussolini should have found aspects of the book germane to their purposes, he was naïve not to recognize earlier than he did their perversion of his aims.

It is fortunate for Baden-Powell's reputation that Michael Rosenthal appears not to have read his diary entry for 6 October 1939. The Second World War was in its earliest phase, and Baden-Powell had recently borrowed a copy of *Mein Kampf*; had he been an admirer of Hitler he would have acquired one many years earlier, but now he wanted to get to know the enemy. He wrote: 'Lay up all day. Read "Mein Kampf". A wonderful book, with good ideas on education, health, propaganda, organization etc. – and ideals which Hitler does not practise himself.'

As the story of an adventurer with a capacity for action unrivalled since the age of Napoleon, *Mein Kampf* – if not 'wonderful' – is certainly a remarkable document. Writing in his private diary at the age of 82, Baden-Powell would not have seen the need to choose his words carefully. It would be ridiculous to suppose that his use of that exceptionally ill-chosen adjective implied approval of Hitler's territorial ambitions, which had plunged Europe into war and which were so clearly signposted in the book. When Hitler had occupied what was left of the Czech state in March 1939, Baden-Powell had concluded that the dictator had 'developed megalomania'.[39] So Baden-Powell's failure in the diary entry to comment upon the evidence of megalomania in *Mein Kampf* does not mean that he thought of Hitler in any other light. Similarly his failure to remark upon the book's obsessive anti-semitism should not be taken to imply tacit approval. When in the mid-thirties Baden-Powell had been treated by a titled lady to a lecture on 'the Jews' secret plans for ruling the world', he had dismissed her as 'an eccentric'.[40] 'What we want,' he had written a decade earlier, 'is broad-minded leadership rather than restrictive dictatorship – a democracy founded upon good-will . . .'[41]

The 'good ideas' which Baden-Powell discovered in *Mein Kampf* and listed under 'education, health, propaganda and organization', for the most part bore a surprising resemblance to his own ideas on these subjects. At times it is hard to avoid the conclusion that Hitler had been heavily influenced by him. The following, on education, is from *Mein Kampf* but could equally well have been taken from any of Baden-Powell's early Scouting speeches: 'It [German education] was fashioned as a one-sided system with a view to mere knowledge and very little with a view to producing practical ability. Still less score was set on formation of character, very little on encouraging the joy of responsibility, and none at all on cultivation of will power and decision.'[42] The borrowings, however, went both ways. In November 1933 Baden-Powell had quoted approvingly from *Mein Kampf* in *The Scouter*, but without being aware of the fact. Instead, he described his source as 'a manifesto recently published in Germany'. Since the book was already well-known in 1933, it is most unlikely that he would have published an unacknowledged extract if he had known its origin. In the 1930s, Baden-Powell became increasingly worried about the prevalence of sex in films and in advertising. He was sure that this was having 'a deteriorating effect . . . on our lads'.[43] The passage he quoted from *Mein Kampf* was on this theme:

> Today all our life in public is like a forcing bed for sexual ideas and attractions . . . Anyone who has not lost the capacity for entering into the souls of the young will realise that it must lead to their very great injury.[44]

As regards 'propaganda', Baden-Powell would have found *Mein Kampf* interesting because Hitler claimed to have learned all he knew of this art from British exponents during the Great War. In praising Britain's will to fight in spite of her lack of 'any national army', Hitler seemed to recognize, as Baden-Powell had always done, the limits of coercion.[45]

Like Baden-Powell, Hitler detested 'industrialization' and phrased his dislike in very similar terms. Baden-Powell had cited as 'a national disgrace' the fact 'that there is permanent squalor, misery and poverty on a vast scale in our so-called well ordered community, in which there also exists wealth, happiness and luxury.'[46] Hitler declared that 'a nation, half of which is in misery, worn with care, or indeed corrupt, makes a picture so bad that no one can feel pride in it.'[47]

Because of this similarity of viewpoint in various areas, it was perfectly possible for Baden-Powell to praise *Mein Kampf* without agreeing with any of the basic tenets of National Socialism – such as, most obviously, the mission of the German nation to be the world's master race. The claim that the Hitler Jugend shared 'many of Scouting's ideals' might seem to be supported by Baden-Powell's remarks about *Mein Kampf*: but while a shared preoccupation with character training and physical hardihood does amount to one kind of similarity, the fundamental moral ideals of the two organizations could hardly have been more distinct. Whereas a Scout promised 'to help others at all times' and 'to be a friend to all, and a brother to every other Scout, no matter to what country, class, or creed, the other may belong', National Socialism was opposed to international cooperation. Following Nietzsche, it rejected the basic tenets of Christianity and Judaism, denying the social and spiritual necessity for human societies to uphold absolute standards of ethical behaviour. To move from this to Baden-Powell's 'good turns' and his exhortation to boys to aim for 'something of the *practical* Christianity which (although they are Buddhists . . .) distinguishes the Burmese in their daily life' is to step into a different moral world.[48] Hitler offered an escape into nationalism and the merging of individual identity within that of the all-conquering Third Reich; Baden-Powell offered an escape into the backwoods of a romanticized and kindlier pre-industrial world.

In 1927, Baden-Powell had published an appeal for Scouters: 'Whoever you are . . . it is in your power to do something for the boy . . . You can probably draw a sketch, or mend a clock, or collect butterflies . . .'[49] These were scarcely the qualifications which Hitler and Mussolini would have looked for in their youth leaders.

Not to be able to recognize evil in a national ruler is a grievous fault in a prime minister or a foreign secretary, but in the leader of a worldwide youth movement dedicated to international friendship it is not a fatal flaw. The most striking single illustration of Baden-Powell's naïvety in this regard concerns his continued use of the swastika as his emblem of thanks to individuals who had helped the Movement. As early as 1912, after his engagement to Olave, he had given her a Scout 'Thanks Badge' in the form of a swastika with the Scout fleur-de-lys superimposed. In June 1933, only months after Hitler had become German Chancellor, Baden-Powell wrote about his own use of the swastika and how the word meant 'good luck' in Sanskrit. He suggested that, if the hooked cross was used with the rectangular projections pointing clockwise, it was a sign portending good. But if the projections pointed anti-clockwise, it was an ill-omened sign. He did not mention Hitler's use of this ancient sun symbol, but implied that the German swastika was the anti-clockwise version.[50] This was confirmed by Olave, who later described the Scouts' swastika as 'right-handed' and the Nazi sign as 'left-handed'. In fact the Nazi cross was exactly the same as the Scouts', both being right-handed. (A failure of Baden-Powell's legendary 'powers of observation' seems responsible for this misconception.) Although Baden-Powell had been at pains to differentiate his swastika from Hitler's very early on – an attitude incompatible with uncritical admiration – he was nevertheless determined not to abandon *his* sign, just because the Germans had adopted it. In February 1935, Baden-Powell obstinately decided to have more swastika 'Thanks Cards' printed. Nobody was going to stop him using the symbol he had adopted almost 30 year earlier.

But as might have been predicted, he was soon obliged to change his mind. Reports reached him that several wearers of the 'Thanks Badge' had been assaulted while travelling in central Europe. He never used the device again after the autumn of 1935.[51]

18

UNDER MOUNT KENYA

1. The Last of England (1935–38)

In the spring of 1936, over a year before Baden-Powell had made his decision to retire from the limelight, Olave had confided to Eileen Wade that Africa had 'caught' them 'badly again', and that they both longed to return.[1] On their way to South Africa during 1935 they had spent two weeks at Nyeri in Kenya, where Eric Walker (Baden-Powell's personal secretary before the Great War) had started an hotel. After his adventures in the war and fighting for the White Russians, Eric had briefly been a 'rum-runner' during Prohibition and had travelled widely, not settling down until his marriage in 1926. He had then come out to Kenya with his wife Lady Bettie (one of the Earl of Denbigh's seven daughters), intending to become a coffee planter. But when they found that there were hardly any tolerable hotels in the White Highlands, they had instead decided to become hoteliers.

The Outspan was planned as a series of bungalows around a central building housing a bar, dining room and sitting rooms. A common enough system today, but in 1935 the idea was novel. Sitting out on the veranda of their bungalow, the Baden-Powells gazed across a garden ablaze with red and yellow cannas and showers of blue jacarandas towards the slopes of Mount Kenya.[2] On their third day, Eric drove them ten miles to the 'Tree Top', a two-roomed house he had built in a big tree overlooking some drinking pools in a clearing. Baden-Powell somehow climbed the 30-foot ladder to reach the balcony and was thrilled to look down on a network of 'well-beaten paths converging on this point. We wore rubber shoes and talked in whispers and watched. . . Animals appeared generally at intervals of half an hour from ten o'clock till two. . .'[3]*

Baden-Powell found Nyeri a magical place, and before he left talked to Eric about the possibility of coming out to Kenya every winter. 'We have collected nearly a mile of stone ready for building your cottage,' Eric told him the following year.[4] Two years later, in November 1937, the Baden-Powells sailed once more for Africa to spend the winter there. The day after his arrival at the Outspan, Stephe took to his bed with a sore throat, a headache, a chesty cough and lumbago. On Christmas Eve, and for three nights thereafter, he found it almost

---

* Treetops, much expanded by then, became famous at the time of the accession of Queen Elizabeth II, who was staying there on the night her father died.

impossible to sleep. One of these nights was 'made bearable by Olave reading me to sleep with gruesome details of Spilsbury's post-mortem deductions in the Crippen case'.[5] On New Year's Day Olave called in Dr Alec Doig, who owned a small local nursing home. He diagnosed a 'tired heart', but ruled out heart disease; the other ailments he put down to general exhaustion and a chill caught at sea. Apart from prescribing a course of injections, he did his best to explain to Baden-Powell that 'absolute rest was essential, permanently'.[6] This diagnosis was repeated by a doctor working with the Scottish Medical Mission, and also by a specialist who flew out from Nairobi. This doctor explained to Olave that Baden-Powell's heart had 'a slight leak and was slightly enlarged', which was confirmation of a faint murmur Doig had detected.[7] Nevertheless, by the second week in February Baden-Powell seemed so much better that Olave felt safe to book their passage back to England in mid-April.

At this time Eric wrote confidentially to Percy Everett, warning him that in his opinion Baden-Powell could die at any time and would certainly never again be able to give the Movement even nominal leadership.[8] A letter from Olave to Everett made it look all but certain that Baden-Powell would choose to end his days in Kenya. 'He is so happy! Percy, it is just HEAVEN being alone here like this together, un-get-at-able and quiet, and in this divine climate we just adore this place, and shan't want to leave it.'[9] Baden-Powell lazed in the sun and read Bulldog Drummond, a life of Foch and a history of the first Boer migrations from the Cape.[10]

He and Olave finally sailed from Mombasa in early May, reaching Southampton on the 21st. They were met by Heather, Mrs Wade and about 50 journalists and photographers. A. W. Hurll (soon to be General Secretary of the Scout Association) was also there to welcome the Chief Scout; he went on board and found him lying on his bunk with his shirt collar open and his tie undone. The Chief struck Hurll as being a very sick old man, so much so that he was scared that he might collapse while walking down the gangway or passing through customs. He nervously asked him how he was feeling, but Baden-Powell brushed the question aside. Then, with collar fastened and tie knotted, he swung himself off the bunk and by force of will impersonated a man many years his junior. Hurll was both moved and appalled to see him bound down the gangway with sprightly steps. As soon as he was in the car after this feat, Baden-Powell crumpled.[11]

At Pax Hill there was a characteristic letter from Eric awaiting him. 'Remember to take an aeroplane to Africa when things begin to hot up in Europe; there could be no point in your staying to have gas and bombs dropped on you . . .' Before leaving the Outspan, Baden-Powell had agreed to invest £600 in the hotel, in return for which Eric would build him a bungalow. It was never openly admitted that he was preparing to leave England for the last time – and to start with he did little to show that this was his intention. Then in late August one of his few remaining close friends died suddenly of heart failure. Colonel George E. N. Booker was never a 'best friend' in the sense that McLaren had been, but they had both been in the 5th Dragoon Guards and Baden-Powell often shot over his land in Somerset. Because Booker was ten years younger, the shock of his death was all the greater, and two days after learning that he was dead Baden-Powell began to put his own papers in order. In the end the sheer size of the task seemed to overwhelm him and he allowed the Wades to remove 'wheelbarrow loads of stuff'.[12] Most of this material was eventually sold to the Boy Scouts of America by Major and Mrs Wade, and now forms an important part of that organization's stupendous collection of Baden-Powell manuscripts. They sold other papers to Mr Paul Richards, an American collector, and donated some to the British Museum.

The gold casket presented to Baden-Powell when he received the freedom of the City of London was among the many items which he now sent to Imperial Headquarters to start a museum of Scouting memorabilia.[13] His abandonment of his old way of life was underlined when he failed to attend the unveiling of the 5th Dragoon Guards' memorial in Aldershot, but lay instead in his rose garden reading *Gone with the Wind*. He went fishing occasionally but tired very quickly. Since he disliked keeping the chauffeur on duty in the evening, Mrs Wade often used to 'take the little car and lurk somewhere near the bottom of the drive' so that she could claim to be passing by chance. Then she could give him a lift up to the house without arousing his suspicions.[14]

The thought that gave him most pleasure was that Eric Walker was building his bungalow for him. 'We are longing to get back,' he told Eric, 'and the bad weather here is doing its best to encourage us to go.'[15] Baden-Powell cited the Czechoslovakian crisis as another reason for hurrying back 'to the peace of Nyeri'.[16] When Dame Katherine Furse talked to Olave about her impending departure, she thought the Chief Guide seemed 'distraught and disgruntled'. Olave told her about 'their delightful house in Kenya', but then said that it was 'very boring for her that the Chief has to live so sheltered a life because she wants people to stay'.[17] For anyone as addicted to activity as was Olave, the prospect of retirement at 48 was frightening. For a time she hoped that Christian, her favourite niece, would come back with them. But Christian had just had an operation on her back and did not in the end feel well enough to leave in October.[18] A sad day was the one on which Olave handed over their favourite labrador to the vet to be destroyed. 'The poor old dog had lately gone deaf as well as totally blind, and was evidently bewildered and wretched,' Baden-Powell recorded.[19]

When Heather arrived at Pax Hill to drive her parents to the West India Docks, she found her father 'like a schoolboy eager to start on the journey home for the holidays. . .' She dined with them on board and felt miserable, but her parents seemed not to notice. Olave talked about visiting England in the spring of 1940, but Heather had a strong premonition that her father would never return.

2. Paxtu: Only Peace (1938–41)

The Kenyan White Highlands in which Baden-Powell would spend his final years are best known today as a backdrop for the doings of adventurers like Denys Finch Hatton, who organized safaris for the romantically inclined rich between the wars, and for the exploits of big game enthusiasts like Ernest Hemingway. The first British settlers, who hacked their farms out of the bush early in the century, had little in common with the socialite arrivals of the 1920s – the 'veranda farmers' – who cared more for pleasure than for the manly virtues which Baden-Powell had always associated with the lives of colonial settlers. He would not live long enough to read about Lord Erroll's murder, nor witness the subsequent exposure of upper-class adultery, drug-taking and alcoholism which shamed the whole colony during the trial of Sir Jock Broughton. Baden-Powell's only dealings with the 'Happy Valley set' would be when he wrote a letter of condolence to Erroll on the death of his second wife, Molly.[1]

Nyeri was to the east of the Aberdare Mountains and therefore not in Happy Valley itself, but the countryside was no less alluring. After the dust and thorn and red rocks of the plains came miles of lush grassland, like an endless English park; yet parkland with a difference, for here grew wild fig and olive, and although settlers sometimes remarked a similarity with the landscape of the west of Scotland, brightly coloured birds and the perpetual scent of mimosa emphasized the difference. The air was diamond clear and marvellously bracing, and the sun invariably shone.

On a typical day, after breakfasting on paw-paw and poached eggs, the Baden-Powells would wander out into their garden to 'sit happily gazing at the heavenly view, the mountain for ever changing colour, clouds rolling up and hiding the peak, and then getting swished away again'.[2] This was Mount Kenya, which being over 17,000 feet high was often capped with snow. Baden-Powell sent home for a telescope so that he could look more closely at its distant slopes. Olave would often drive him round Nyeri or out on to the Sangana Plain, with frequent halts to look at particular views. 'This life here,' Baden-Powell told Mrs Wade, 'is as near perfection as one could get in this world. We are so tired of saying to each other how wonderfully lovely it is that we have now adopted the expression "och!", which means a whole mouthful.'[3]

Baden-Powell had at first decided to call his bungalow Paxtoo – in the sense of it being both Pax too and Pax two. He made it a triple pun when he finally settled on Paxtu. *Tu* in Swahili means only and his new home, he implied, would bring *only* peace and not the constant activity which had previously given his life its meaning. He often described his bungalow as 'a shack', but typically added 'we find it in every way excellent'. Not for him then the home comforts of those settlers belonging to what Evelyn Waugh described as 'a community of English squires established on the Equator', with their chintz-covered sofas, ancestral portraits, family silver and hunting prints. His shack was simply furnished and consisted of a central sitting room, with glass folding doors giving on to a veranda; two bedrooms, each with its own bathroom, and at the back a servants' pantry.[4]

The social life at the Outspan Hotel was not exciting – the other residents being the snobbish younger son of an obscure peer and his lady, an amiable old colonel, a retired bank manager and and an elderly widow.[5] One person Baden-Powell chose to see fairly often was Colonel Charles Stockley, who had won the D.S.O. and the M.C. in the Great War and now took daring close-up photographs of elephants and lions. Although he admired Stockley for having built his house with his own hands and for surviving on £300 per annum, the intrepid colonel was thought rather a ruffian locally.[6] Another retired officer to whom Baden-Powell took a fancy was Major Steele, again no 'veranda farmer', having 'carved a charming home and farm out of the jungle'. Baden-Powell visited him in spite of warnings that Steele had committed the unforgivable sin of 'going native'; the major lived with an African mistress.[7] Even in old age Baden-Powell retained his lurking admiration for people who had had the guts to flout convention and go their own way.

Because Baden-Powell thought Kenya incomparable, he was distressed to find Eric Walker 'restless and rather depressed'. 'Goodness knows why,' he confided to Mrs Wade, after listing Eric's reasons for happiness: his 'lovely charming wife', his 'two lovely girls', and the many attractions of the Outspan which, tree house apart, boasted a golf course, billiard room, squash courts and marvellous vegetable gardens.[8] But depressed or not, Eric was still a fine showman. When he drove guests out to the Tree Top in his old Chevrolet truck he often made an adventure out of the trip, leaving the vehicle some distance from the clearing (engine still running for a quick getaway if need be) and then leading his visitors from bush to bush with an admonitory finger to his lips. Scared by the thought of being charged by an unseen rhinoceros, they obeyed blindly.[9]

Eric regularly played chess with Baden-Powell and often sat up with him at night when he was ill. He thought it a privilege to help the old man in and out of his fishing boots whenever he felt well enough to visit the Thega River. Eric's wife, Lady Bettie Walker, used to say that her husband's priorities were Baden-Powell first, his own family some distance behind and his business trailing badly in third place.[10] When Italy entered the war and there was a real danger of an invasion of Kenya from Ethiopia, Eric 'used to keep just behind Baden-Powell's house a car loaded up with petrol, oil, blankets and food, ready to set off at a moment's notice'.[11] Meanwhile Eric's two daughters Honor and Susan, who were 11 and 8 respectively, became Baden-Powell's last child friends. He used to invite them to tea with respectful formality, treating them to a display of ambidextrous drawing and, when he was confined to bed, waggling his toes for their amusement. To the very end he kept up his habit of sleeping with his feet outside the bedclothes.[12]

His relations with his own family were less relaxing. While his attitude towards Peter was no longer disapproving and he was relieved that Betty's marriage seemed so happy, he remained anxious about Heather. The previous autumn she had brought to Pax Hill a new boy friend; but because they had been busy packing up the house, John King had made little impression upon her parents, who had nevertheless noticed that he drove a sports car but had no job. In fact he had recently failed to qualify as a chartered accountant. Heather came out to Kenya in the spring of 1939, bringing with her a letter from John to her father asking if he might announce their engagement. On arriving she left this envelope on her father's table, but found it the following morning still unopened. She had told him that it was from John, so he had known what it contained. Even after learning that John had played in goal for Charterhouse, Baden-Powell refused to give any answer until his daughter was due to leave.

Heather had another slightly less delicate mission: she had been asked by Mrs Wade to find out whether her father wanted to be buried in Westminster Abbey since the Dean had earmarked a space and needed to know whether he should reserve it. Thank you but no, Heather was told. Before she left, Baden-Powell told her not to consider marrying until John had qualified as an accountant. When she went to kiss her father goodbye, he was sitting on the veranda 'busily painting a picture of the garden, framed by tall gum trees and Mount Kenya'. This would be Heather's last sight of him.[13]

When the war started, Heather joined the W.A.T.S. as a staff car driver and would sit in her general's Humber, when she was not busy, writing to her parents with a pad of airmail paper propped up on the steering wheel.[14] Her father did not change his mind about John until after the fall of France. When the airmail service between Britain and Kenya was suspended, he cabled Heather telling her that she could announce her engagement or marry 'if and when John is in H.M. Service'. To his amazement, nine days later he received a cable from her telling him that she had married.[15] John had apparently been accepted by the R.A.F. a few days after the arrival of Baden-Powell's new terms. It was a token of Heather's fondness for her father (and perhaps also a feeling of contrition about her previous broken engagement) which had led her to fall in with his wishes. Being above the age of consent, she could have married John at any time she pleased.

By August Olave was writing of the war having 'come a good deal closer to us. We have our dug-outs ready to hop into and black-out always at night.'[16] For anyone of Baden-Powell's age, born only a few years after the British and French victory over Russia in the Crimea, the catastrophic rout of June 1940 was an unbelievable humiliation. It was as if all the worst nightmares of the Allied commanders of the Great War had suddenly been realized. In May and June he went to church for the first time in many months. With Britain's survival in the balance and him so old and far away, what else could he do but pray?

Eric Walker lied about his age and thus secured for himself 'a minor job in the R.A.F.' which he told Baden-Powell was 'far too cushy'.[17] When Major Wade cabled, begging to be commended to the War Office, Baden-Powell replied rather insensitively, since Wade was over 20 years his junior: 'Both of us backnumbers. I cannot commend to W.O.'[18] Eric he treated more gently: 'If you try to push yourself on, they may elect to push you out! Go slow.'[19] But Eric ignored his idol's advice and somehow landed the plum job of Intelligence Officer to the 1st South African Division in East Africa. He served in this capacity throughout the Ethiopian Campaign and in the Western Desert in 1941.[20]

The Italians, who outnumbered the British in southern Ethiopia and on the Kenyan border by at least 40,000 men, managed to bomb Isiolo, only 150 miles north of Nyeri, which thenceforth had to be considered a target with its large military hospital.[21] In September Baden-Powell wrote with pride to Major Burnham, his old associate in Matabeleland, describing the 'fine force we have up here of the sons of the men we knew in Rhodesia and South Africa, who have taken up arms for the further security and welfare of the country we know so well.'[22] 'The Italians,' he predicted, 'will have a tough job in dealing with them.'[23] Sadly for him, operations in which he would have taken such pride did not begin until after his death. He was, however, able to follow the progress of the Battle of Britain. Knowing exactly what was at stake, he noted down in his diary throughout the critical month of

August the number of planes shot down on both sides and the numbers engaged.[24] In early September, past and present met when a young South African airman appeared on the veranda at Paxtu and introduced himself as the son of Miss Hill (later Mrs Wimble) who had been the matron at Mafeking.[25]

On 15 September, Baden-Powell made what would prove to be his penultimate effort on behalf of the Scouts. He had heard from Percy Everett that there were plans afoot in Britain to start a National Youth Training Movement, and that the King had given his blessing to the project.[26] This sounded uncommonly like a British version of the Balilla; if created, this monster would swallow up the Boy Scouts just as the cadets had threatened to do in the Great War. Baden-Powell thought the best ammunition he could give Everett for fighting it would be a revised version of his interview with Mussolini. Thus he could combine anti-Italian propaganda with a defence of the virtues of British voluntary organizations. On 16 September, a few days after Dr Doig had warned Olave that her husband might die at any moment,[27] Baden-Powell wrote a long memorandum headed 'Youth Training Movement'. In it he attacked all compulsory state movements as repressive, lacking spiritual heart and designed solely to achieve mass cohesion at the expense of individual character. Whether his arguments influenced the British Government is not clear; but no British Youth Training Movement ever materialized.

In early October Baden-Powell drew his last Christmas card. This would be his final service to the Scout Movement. In it he depicted Hitler being swept away by a large broom, and wrote as his seasonal message: 'Out of evil good will come. We owe a statue to Hitler, he has done more than any man ever to consolidate our nation at home and overseas and has given us friends in America and in all the countries he has ravaged; such wide friendship will help to bring world peace so soon as he and his war clouds are swept away . . . Stick it out! Play up to the Scouts' slogan *Sleeves up!* and with *Tails up go to it to win the war*, and after that to bring about peace with goodwill and happiness for all.'[28] During the First World War, he had concentrated upon vilifying the enemy. It was symptomatic of his new outlook that during the darkest year of the Second World War his final printed words should have been about peace and happiness.

The gentler Baden-Powell of the Kenyan years also had a reformed attitude towards wildlife. He was frequently upset by the slaughter of game; and even when a man was killed by elephants several miles outside Nyeri, he was appalled when a game warden shot five of them. 'Beastly I call it.'[29] He was convinced that, when elephants attacked humans, the animals had invariably been annoyed or threatened first.

The animal which Olave bought for five pence in Nyeri and which became the best loved of all Baden-Powell's many pets may also have been partly responsible for his increasingly sympathetic attitude towards all living things. This creature was a hyrax – a nocturnal mammal about the size of a rabbit, but tail-less and with smaller ears, sharp fangs, and possessing what Olave described as 'the loveliest feet, with their sort of little kid gloves for climbing up trees'. Hyrie, as Olave called him, started very much as her pet. 'He sleeps IN my bed – against the pillow or festooned round the top of my head.' But later, when Baden-Powell spent occasional days in bed, he would lie 'looking out at the mountain and hugging Hyrie (who has adopted him more!) in his arms'.[30] Olave wrote about their 'Hyrie worship' and sometimes devoted whole letters to his doings. He was house-trained like a cat and lived on a curious diet of roses, apple rind, plum or mulberry leaves and chocolate. Being nocturnal, he would often go out 'roofing', spending whole nights on roofs or under eaves. Baden-Powell used to fret about his absences and was afraid some predator might catch him; so each afternoon Olave would endeavour to tempt him home. He never seemed to annoy either of them although he always shrieked and squawked when they listened to the wireless. Baden-Powell would forgive him worse acts of delinquency. 'After feeding out of my hand, Hyrie suddenly attacked me and bit me in both legs and I bled like a pig.' He excused his pet because 'the tea trolley had annoyed him'.[31] The next day, the back of one of Baden-Powell's knees was badly swollen and he recorded a sudden rise in his temperature. For Hyrie's sake, he was capable of almost superhuman feats. 'Taking Hyrie home from a walk on the lead, he slipped away. I *ran* after him for 20 yards and secured him – but at night my heart ached steadily.'[32] Dr Doig attributed Baden-Powell's feverishness and nausea, which had started in mid-June, to an infection. He did not, however, single out Hyrie's bites as a possible cause.[33] Nor was the radium treatment which Baden-Powell was now having for his facial skin cancer considered; although today radium is routinely expected to cause nausea. That he needed this treatment was never in doubt though, since there were times when his eyelids suppurated so profusely that he could not see to read or write, but had to sit in darkness with his eyes covered. Fortunately when treated he would remain trouble-free for six months or so. A more troublesome affliction was the eczema which began in 1938. After eight months of itching torment, Baden-Powell discovered a Jewish refugee living only a few miles outside Nyeri. Within a week Dr Piorskowski's ointment had cured his hands and arms – leaving only his legs affected.[34]

To be able to use his hands freely again was a great blessing, since he dreaded inactivity. Apart from executing numerous small sketches and watercolours, he began a series of large oils of wild animals. In November 1939, he exhibited five of these in Nairobi and he was still working on similar paintings in the summer of 1940. Olave called them his 'masterpieces' and he became irritable if anyone had the temerity to criticize them. Eric's brother-in law, Miles Fletcher, certainly regretted suggesting that the head of the buffalo in one of the 'masterpieces' was not anatomically correct.[35] When Baden-Powell was not painting, he was writing semi-humorous accounts of life in Kenya with accompanying illustrations. These were published either in *The Scout*, or on the *Daily Mail*'s children's page. Mrs Wade made three collections in book form, adding her own crucial contributions to the text. They were: *Birds and Beasts of Africa* (1938), *Paddle Your Own Canoe* (1939) and *More Sketches of Kenya* (1940). Baden-Powell looked forward to the publication of each with keen anticipation.[36] In late September, he started to assemble 'a collection of snaps and scraps of memory', which he hoped would be published after the war.[37] He was dictating one of these to Olave's niece, Christian Davidson (who had at last come out to stay with them in Nyeri) only three days before he entered the half-life of his final illness.[37]

Olave found life 'unreal' away from the war and England. She heard of Pax Hill being requisitioned by the army. 'It does seem odd somehow that all this should be going on, and our home being broken up . . . and us here . . .'[38] She was very upset when her husband became 'peevish and irritable'. Although she knew how ill he was, she still found the change in him incredible, 'since always he had been so patient and loving'.[39]

With Christian her 'niece-cum-daughter' now at Paxtu,[40] Olave felt safe to leave Baden-Powell for a few days while she took Betty (who had arrived with Christian) on a few days' tour of local Girl Guide groups. On 5 November Baden-Powell developed a wheezy cough which, had Dr Doig heard it, he would have associated with congestive heart failure. (As the heart grows weaker fluid collects in the lungs.) At three in the morning, Christian heard a crash and ran to her uncle's bedroom. He had been coughing badly and had fallen out of bed and banged his head. He spent the following day in bed, and was still there when Olave returned. On 7 November, Baden-Powell felt slightly better, and wrote in his diary: 'Had almost an appetite for dinner. Walked in garden with Christian 50 yards – quite enough!' This was the last entry he ever made. Next day he felt very weak and breathless and Dr Piorskowski – who happened to be staying at the hotel – injected him with coramine, a respiratory stimulant.

Stephe walked out on to his veranda for what would turn out to be the last time on 8 November and lay there all day. He grew steadily weaker over the next few days and could only be persuaded to drink soup or other liquids with difficulty. The Governor of the Colony, Sir Henry Moore, had been told by Dr Doig a few days earlier that the Chief Scout's death was imminent. He therefore sent a cable to the

Archbishop of Canterbury, who wrote to Sir Percy Everett about
dates for a memorial service. His Grace confided that it would suit him
if Baden-Powell were to die before 27 November, since after that he
would have no space in his diary until mid-December. [41] Somehow the
news reached Fleet Street and Olave was suddenly inundated with
thousands of messages of sympathy. Percy Everett also upset her by
reviving the question of burial in Westminster Abbey, which in his
opinion the founder's greatness demanded. 'But Percy,' she replied,
'don't you think it would be DREADFUL to bury that dear man in
that dark dank mausoleum, in the midst of the noise and filth and
crowds and buildings of a city, when instead he might be in the quiet of
Gilwell with birdsong and wind in the trees . . .' Her plan was for him
to be buried in the cemetery at Nyeri, 'and there he will lie near me, till
after the war, when perhaps you will all like to have him back in
England.'[42]

Unexpectedly the crisis passed. Dr Piorskowski agreed to stay on at
the Outspan, and secured the services of two South African nurses
from Nyeri's military hospital. 'It is heartbreaking to see him like this,'
Olave wrote on 24 November. He was too weak to hold a pen or lift a
cup. But against all predictions he was still alive on the last day of the
year, and had even sat in a chair on Christmas Day and listened to the
King's broadcast to the Empire.[43] Then came another relapse. When
he was in pain, he seemed to fight for life; Olave therefore feared most
the times when the pain subsided and lassitude overwhelmed him. Life
to him had always been about making *something* even out of the most
unpromising circumstances. Now, too weak to feed himself and
feeling perpetually sick, he wanted to die.

In the village, Olave watched the preparations for his military
funeral. With round-the-clock nursing cover and her dying husband
almost always asleep, she existed in limbo. She sat beside him, went
for walks, wrote letters, gardened and even played tennis. All this time
she was consoled by her favourite niece. 'Christian is MARVEL-
LOUS, and goodness itself, and manages me QUITE wonderfully.
She is an absolute ROCK to lean upon.'[44]

Hanging over Olave was another problem. Percy Everett and the
Headquarters' Committee wanted to bring out 'an authorized life' as
soon as possible after her husband's death. Everett and Sir Alfred
Pickford had invited her to write this book, and had pressed her hard
during the spring and summer. 'I have neither the time, *nor* the ability,'
she told them in May; and then in August more bluntly still: 'I get
absolutely sick of my typewriter as it is, and haven't had time to read a
book for the last YEAR – (and before that for about 25 years!!) – and so
I simply could not face such a task.' She had hoped that they would
commission Mrs Wade. But now it seemed that the Committee had
asked a stranger, Mr E. E. Reynolds, the acting editor of *The Scouter*,

to write the life. It was chilling for Olave to realize that even before her husband was in his grave she had lost all influence over the Scouts' Committee.[45]

On 6 January, Baden-Powell understood when Olave told him that British and Australian troops in North Africa had followed up their success at Sidi Barrani with another decisive victory over the Italians. Although she did not think him significantly worse, the 7th turned out to be his last full day. She played tennis up at the hotel during the afternoon, so it was a shock to be told on her return by the nurse, Sister Ray, that she doubted whether he would live through the night. Olave sat up for several hours and then went to bed. At 2.30 in the morning on the 8th, Sister Ray woke her and said, "He is going."

'I went to his room and just sat by his bed and watched the dear darling's life ebbing away. He was quite unconscious and still, breathing slowly and in gusts, white and thin. Sister Ray sat on the other side of the bed holding his pulse – just flickering.' At 5 a.m Olave returned to bed feeling very cold. 'I lay wide awake and shivering in my bed, listening.' At 5.45, Sister Ray said quietly, 'He's gone.' Olave asked if he had spoken or opened his eyes. The sister shook her head. His breathing had simply stopped. 'That was all.'[46]

*

During the Great War Baden-Powell had been distressed enough by the thought of the misery his death would cause Olave to sit down and write a letter of consolation in case he were to die suddenly. Ten years later he wrote again. 'I know the parting will have to be bitter . . . we have to pay something for the good time we have had, and it is the one who stays that has to pay. But if it were me to stay I should pay it gladly . . .'[47] Shortly after Dr Doig's pessimistic prognostication in September 1940, he had written a final shaky but perfectly legible note:

> Dindo darling, I don't know whether my increasing and unaccountable weakness of the last few weeks may mean the beginning of the end . . . I have had a most extraordinarily happy life, most especially in those last twenty-seven years of it which you have made so heavenly and successful for me . . . The fact of having to leave you is the one pang that haunts me . . . especially because it will mean a terrible break in your own life. One thing that comforts me is that you are so sensible that you will see it in its right proportion as a natural thing that had to come, and you will face the ordeal with courage . . . I am glad to think that you have the best form of consolation before you in the shape of plenty of work with the Guides . . . If I know that you will not let it grieve you unduly I shall die all the happier, my D.[48]

Olave found these letters in his desk in a large envelope marked 'In the

event of my death'.[49] Thirty-six years later to the day, and a few
months before her own death, she wrote to Christian who had been
with her at Paxtu on the day Baden-Powell died. 'You too will be
thinking of that OTHER Jan 8th, at Paxtu . . . I still can hardly BEAR
what I felt like that day, and for weeks and months afterwards . . .'[50]

Baden-Powell had had good cause to feel anxious about Olave, and
not only because her father and sister had killed themselves. Her horror
of death was such that she had refused to witness her mother's burial.
In 1941, she was still three decades away from speaking to Christian
about her mother's suicide. Christian attended Baden-Powell's funeral
as her aunt's representative; Olave herself remained 25 miles away,
dazed with grief.

As soon as Eric Walker had heard that Baden-Powell was dying, he
obtained leave and hurried back from Eritrea, arriving only 'to find
him in his coffin in the cottage I had built for him . . . I paid him the last
service that anyone could. I went to the pantry, collected a duster, and
tin of metal polish, and shone up the tarnished plate on his coffin, and
am not ashamed to say that with the polish were mixed salt tears.'[51] It
was the kind of service which Baden-Powell would have appreciated.

In the first week of January, Eileen Wade was producing a morale-
boosting pantomime in Bentley with the local Scouts and Guides as her
actors. 'Everything was ready; then on January 8th I walked into my
office and found the cable. We postponed the performance, but only
until after the funeral . . . I went through my part with a numb feeling
inside, and it was not until later that I suddenly awoke to the realization
that my job had ended and there would be no more letters.'[52]

Olave and Christian stayed on in Nyeri for several months, and then
in May set out on a three-months' tour in a £60 Dodge 'which was
virtually tied together with string'. They visited Tanganyika, Uganda,
Rhodesia and the Congo before returning to Kenya. With Christian's
help, Olave survived the black despair which had overwhelmed her
after Baden-Powell's death. She sailed for England in 1942; and saw
the ships immediately on either side of hers torpedoed. Alone in
London the day after landing, she walked away from Victoria station
shocked by the extent of the bombing. With Pax Hill in the hands of
the army, she had no home. She wanted to pray somewhere, so walked
down Victoria Street to Westminster Abbey but found it locked, so
went on past the Houses of Parliament and on to Westminster Bridge:
'I stopped in the middle and leaned over the parapet, staring at the
water. I was tempted to jump in; it would be one way out of my
loneliness. But I didn't . . . I remembered Robin's charge to me in his
letters. I must carry on the work he had started.'[53]

19

EPILOGUE

1. Curbing the Beast and Reclaiming the Child

In 1958 Cecil B. De Mille announced his intention of making Baden-Powell's life the subject of a motion picture, with David Niven in the title role.[1] Shortly afterwards the mogul's death put paid to the project, but it is not hard to imagine how the Founder's life would have been presented: the devoted son, the philanthropic young officer, the self-sacrificing general inventing the Scouts as the natural response of a boyish and benevolent nature to the deprivation of Edwardian city youth. Of course, by way of compensation for so much piety there would have been his humour and his showmanship and a colourful cast of thousands in four continents; but on the brink of the 1960s the film could only have been a resounding failure. By 1979 roughly 500,000,000 people had been Scouts or Guides, but such is the destructive power of hagiography and changing beliefs that in that year neither Baden-Powell nor his Movement rated an entry in reference books such as the *Penguin Dictionary of Twentieth-Century History*.

Today renewed sympathy, in some circles, for 'character building' and 'Victorian values' might seem to favour some kind of recanoniz-ation for a man whose long reign as a secular saint ended with a mixture of mockery and execration. Yet eagerness to praise or condemn historical figures invariably tells would-be apologists or critics more about themselves and their own society than about the man or woman under scrutiny. When faced with a life which reveals as much about the nature of Victorian and Edwardian fears and longings as Baden-Powell's, what matters is to understand its messages.

When Henrietta Grace trained her children to be good and obedient, she was following the practice of her day.[2] Wordsworth's and Blake's vision of childhood as a time of higher spiritual perception had done nothing to temper the evangelicals' view of the individual child as innately sinful. When Stephe, after long separation from his mother, had given vent to fits of rage, she had seen it as her duty to curb his anger.[3] Fearful of losing her love, he repressed his true feelings and curried favour as the family wit and buffoon. To ensure that they were loved, her sons competed with each other to be good, and then as men to win the 'race for honours'.[4] Since George, Baden and even Frank had been more highly favoured, Stephe had tried hardest of all to please. Yet jealousy and anger do not simply go away when forbidden by a parent whose love cannot be risked. They reappear as self-hatred or aggression. Because the ability to express anger is essential for the development of an independent personality, its systematic prohibition places a child in a situation in which secret fantasies of violence offer the only possible escape.

When John Hargrave (whose own showmanship made him suspicious of other men's public masks) studied Baden-Powell's bluff and amusing exterior, he was aware of 'another self . . . which stood apart and watched the neat, genial Baden-Powell personality from a distance and told it what to do. This other self was cold and calculating, and, when necessary, entirely ruthless.'[5] Others had also sensed a frightening hidden presence: in reality a concentration of those emotions which Henrietta Grace had outlawed. On the surface Stephe was cheery and straightforward, and yet at school he had no close friends. He had loved his brother who died, yet never mentioned him afterwards. It was his mother's boast that after babyhood Stephe 'never cried, but took everything with a most unchildlike calm and self-control'. Forbidden to express his need for her, he learned to insulate himself from feeling; and yet anger and longings for revenge remained. How else explain his apparent enjoyment of botched executions in India and his short stories which, with few exceptions, culminate in violent death either by accident or execution.[6] Writing was one way of discharging long-pent-up childhood hatred. Another was by delegating it to others such as executioners (often sub-consciously), or even by acting out, as in the case of Chief Uwini.

Of course most young officers enjoyed blood sports and longed to fight, but the passionate, patently sexual delight experienced by Stephe was of a different order – with the moment of killing best of all. Grasping his pigsticking spear, what joy to 'give him *one* and feel it go in beautifully in exactly the correct spot'.[7] How thrilling at last to be brave enough to shock his mother with descriptions of violence in nursery language. 'Now shut your ears and hold your eyes, and scream. One spear I gave him . . . came out through his "tummy" and stuck into the ground – that was a pretty vicious one!'[8]

In Victorian school novels the ultimate test of comradely devotion was to take the blame for a friend's crime.[9] In Stephe's 'Test of Friendship' the proof of devotion was to kill a wounded comrade at his urging before the Matabele closed in. ' "Now old friend, just get your revolver, I'm longing for it. Oh! for God's sake." '[10] Murder as an act of love, performed by a narrator bearing Baden-Powell's military code-name.

It would be tedious to recount in how many places he sought out the local executioner during his travels. Typically in Canton, in 1912, he ran the man to earth and negotiated the purchase of his beheading sword. In Ashanti the executioners told him grisly anecdotes.[11] Baden-Powell would recount such horrors jocularly or in a neutral tone. His accounts of corporal punishment would be equally merry or matter-of-fact, and again there would be drawings.[12] Sometimes these would be based on what he had seen; at others they would be imaginative, as with the execution of the Zouave which he had been so anguished to miss.[13]

Battlefields would always be a magnet to him – Indian, South African, North American, Franco-Prussian and, above all, those of the Great War. In 1929, he took Peter (then 16) on a two-day tour of Verdun followed by a day at the Marne. The boy felt sick and depressed.[14] In 1932 Baden-Powell returned home from Switzerland via Verdun, taking the whole family.[15] And so it went on throughout his life: the macabre visits and his habit of recording unusual forms of execution or death, ranging from a novel form of strangulation in Tunisia to the fate of a workman who fell down one of the steep metal water-collecting slopes on Gibraltar and burst into flames with the friction.[16] Even in extreme old age when gravely ill, he recorded in his diary that Olave helped him to sleep by reading gruesome details of Spilsbury's post-mortems.[17]

Since most young upper middle-class men of that era had been taught that love was conditional upon obedience, and had been handed over to servants for their nurture before being sent away to school, it was not surprising that many shared the same anger (if not the same fantasies). Yet to suppose that Baden-Powell – or anyone else whose feelings of helplessness and anger were eased by witnessing the suffering of others – lost his humanity would be much mistaken. He and his male contemporaries were drawn to the cult of 'manliness' not because their hardness and self-reliance made them natural votaries, but because its taboo on tenderness offered them a defence against dependence. The battle Baden-Powell later fought against 'milksops' was a repetition of the war he had waged against the defenceless child he had once been. Only by rooting out all tender emotion had he been able to defend himself against the terror of his mother's heart 'growing cold'. And although he withstood the many hardships of life in India, the death of 'the Boy's' mother revealed the fragility of his manly armour.

Baden-Powell and his brother officers fought their emotions so fiercely because their survival seemed to depend on it. In his eyes self-mastery ('that deeper form of subordination of one's own desires')[18] not only protected a man from grief and tenderness but enabled him to master the anger always threatening to erupt. If an officer struck a private soldier a single half-hearted blow, he could be ruined by a word. The army knew the crucial value of self-discipline and so did Baden-Powell.

A 'self-mastering' man could even defeat his sexual desires. Mentally self-castrated, he would neither masturbate nor succumb to girlitis, nor the love that dare not speak its name. But even 'bad thoughts' had to be banished. 'For this a man must use his self-control to switch off all that is impure from his mind.' And if he failed, declared Baden-Powell, he would have to struggle with 'his conscience and his shame'.[19] Having so much anger within him, and such unacceptable sexual feelings, his personal struggle had required advice-giving, rigorous self-denial and compensating fame on an epic scale. And even then, the emphasis which his mother had placed upon being good had required additional appeasement of his conscience for entertaining those bad thoughts.[20] Founding the Boy Scouts had furnished much-needed counterbalancing goodness.

Baden-Powell's influence was so great because his experience, and consequently his anxieties, exaggerated similar fears acutely present below the surface of his contemporaries' awareness. Well-disciplined Victorian children only had to look at the drunken, dirty and promiscuous poor to know what instincts had to be caged. Their parents – whose beliefs had been savaged by Darwinian biology – clung all the harder to the stability of family life and evangelical moral values. With motherhood fast becoming a sacred institution and connubial love a substitute for threatened faith, the sexual double standard (obvious to anyone who used his eyes in central London) reinforced the idea of woman as angel or outcast and sex as the great contagion. Mothers, sisters and other young girls were consequently idealized because untainted. Love of a 'pure' woman was the supposed ideal of every 'clean' young man; and yet in practice male comradeship was far more important. This caused anxiety not only to men who suffered temptation, but also to an Establishment entirely wedded to the value of all-male schools, all-male professions and an economic system requiring prolonged celibacy. Small wonder that Oscar Wilde's trial unleashed such savage emotions. Only deep insecurity can explain the panic caused by public disclosure of facts which so many men hid from themselves.

Wilde and other 'decadent' *fin de siècle* poets and artists had seemed to threaten an entire culture with their self-indulgence and effeminacy. Their antithesis was the ideal soldier living simply, ignorant of art and intellectual matters, disciplining his mind and body and placing his love of country above all else. Such a man was proof against degeneration inseparable from soft urban living. He personified the self-control which society would need if anarchism, socialism and sexual licence were not – as Max Nordau put it – to lead 'to its certain ruin because too worn out and flaccid to perform great tasks'. And when such fears in Britain were at their height during the disastrous Boer War, no soldier epitomized that saving manly spirit more perfectly than R. S. S. Baden-Powell.

The reason for Imperial Britons dreading eclipse by other nations so intensely was their belief that national 'greatness' depended upon 'character' rather than upon technology, natural resources or size of population. The Japanese seemed to prove the point when they defeated mighty Russia – a small nation of small men bringing down a colossus simply by dint of discipline and dedication. Empires decayed from within, morally, as Rome had decayed. Character was everything and yet it was threatened on every side – and nobody knew that better than Stephe, who had fought so long and hard to keep out the moral enemies which threatened him. 'Be Prepared' was not just the perfect motto for an Edwardian youth movement but for an entire era in which so many different fears were linked.

When calling to mind those cohorts of manly men filling the stalls night after night at performances of *Peter Pan*, and the eager 'boy men' who became the first Scoutmasters, it is clear that aggression was very often not the only survivor of a highly disciplined upbringing. The child they had striven so hard to cast out, when bent on making men of themselves, was still lurking in the wings. He had been kept alive in Stephe's case by practical jokes and make-believe and those reviving escapes into the wilds.

The pressure on boys to abandon the comforts of feminine care and love before ready to outgrow their childishness stemmed from widespread anxiety about their future manliness. When great stress was also laid upon them to succeed, as happened to all Henrietta Grace's sons, the message was plain: mother prefers success to enjoyment. For many men, Baden-Powell among them, the Boy Scouts provided a blessed illusion of reclaiming their stolen childhoods.

2. *Values and Illusions*

Until his last illness Baden-Powell continued to have absolute faith in a man's ability to control his thoughts and emotions through will-power. In his own nature the desire to conform coexisted with the need to escape. I have argued in an earlier chapter that his genius lay in fashioning from this conflict a Movement which brilliantly reconciled these two needs. The backwoods represented an escape from maturity into a safe boys' world, away from women and competitiveness. The character-building represented social constraint and was addressed to realizing the organization's ostensible aim of furnishing society with kindly and responsible citizens.

After the Second World War 'character-building' came to be thought of among many educated people as sinister, comical or simply archaic. This may explain why a man who had such an immense impact on the social history of so many nations has been denied serious attention for so long. Freud is in no small way to blame, since one of his greatest achievements was to cut through the web of self-deception and rationalization which the Victorians' belief in will-power had encouraged. 'The deeply rooted belief in psychic freedom and choice,' he wrote, '. . . is quite unscientific and must give ground before a determinism which governs mental life.'[1] In the name of will-power and self-control countless lives were undoubtedly ruined and great stores of resentment, self-hatred and emotional inhibition piled up. The sheltered Victorian middle-class home was as often filled with guilt and morbid terror as with peace and harmony.

Yet moulded though we are by conditioning and impelled by unconscious processes, Baden-Powell's belief that we can change ourselves and our society for the better is of great value in the post-Freudian world. In fact if *will* is an illusion, this is something which individuals will have to ignore if they are to save the planet. Used creatively rather than manipulatively (and the idea of helping others is surely creative), the effects of will can be benign. Modern man's sense of individual helplessness is far more dangerous.

Baden-Powell saw society in Victorian terms and held it to be the duty of the élite to set standards and help their inferiors. He therefore deplored the failure of the Edwardian plutocracy to acknowledge their moral responsibilities. He always thought industrialism unnatural. His ideas about good citizenship were framed when social inequality was far greater than it is today, so it is not profitable to speculate about his reactions to contemporary admiration for market forces. As an utopian he was never concerned with the practicalities of economic life and thus maintained many of the prejudices against trade and new money which had been commonplace in his youth. Nevertheless it seems safe to conclude that his ideal of the self-sacrificing gentleman – caring more for the fate of the disadvantaged than for his own profit or advancement – would not have made him a whole-hearted supporter of 'the enterprise culture'.

Baden-Powell believed in the power of example. If men thought their leaders honourable and honest, they would be more likely to respect what they said. He thought it his duty to hand down moral advice (indeed felt compelled to do so), and was in no way inhibited by the fact that his own life was invariably more comfortable than those of the recipients of his pep-talks. 'Happiness doesn't come from being rich,' he told the Girl Guides in his last message, 'nor merely from being successful in your career: nor by self-indulgence . . . The real way to get happiness is by giving out happiness to other people. Try and leave this world a little better than you found it.'[2]

He urged Edwardian boys to consider the civilians' Albert Medal for saving life a greater honour than the military Victoria Cross. It was possible, he said, to display heroism in ordinary life by never passing by on the other side when a fellow citizen was in danger. He believed that children needed to identify with heroic figures in order to wish to behave rightly. Like other influential men of his era, he conceived of honour almost as a physical possession – like, say, an incalculably precious coin – which could only be lost at enormous cost to its possessor. This would occur if at some moment of crisis an individual failed to live up to his personal code. (This sentiment is very strong in the works of Kipling and Conrad.) The men who remained behind on the decks of the *Titanic* rather than risk swamping any of the lifeboats bearing away the women and children were actuated by it – as Baden-Powell had been when resolutely radiating confidence to the towns-people of Mafeking, although his heart was in his boots.

Today the heroes of the tabloid press reflect the values of a society more concerned with 'making it' and 'flaunting it' than with loyalty, self-sacrifice and honour – values which would have been thought as applicable to a Roberts as to a Livingstone. The ideal of the fair and incorruptible Imperial administrator inevitably involved self-deception given the nature of imperialism itself, but there were enough quixotic protectors of the weak – among the bigots and self-servers, working behind the scenes of British rule – to lend conviction to the moral pronouncements of public men. Of course the promotion of selflessness as a social ideal was helpful to a ruling class eager to retain its privileges, but the caveat that their own behaviour had to prove them worthy was not without value. In relative terms Edwardian society was both immensely poorer and more law-abiding than our own.

Whether a society gains more than it loses when the balance shifts from paternalism to permissiveness depends upon the social maturity of its citizens and the values they respect. Speaking in July 1988 at the Oxford Union, the Home Secretary Mr Douglas Hurd argued that the inculcation of 'personal responsibility, self-discipline and civic duty' ought to be given priority in the schools and not 'thrust into some tiny timetable ghetto of its own'. It should instead 'pervade the curriculum and become an integral part of school life'.[3] Eighty years earlier and in similar terms, Baden-Powell had blamed the schools for not touching on such matters and had offered the Scout Law as a remedy. It is as true now as it was then that, when a society appears to reward and admire people whose buccaneering values are not at all the same as those virtues which are officially endorsed, the 'pervasive' powers of the latter are unlikely to prove very strong. In this important respect the hero of Mafeking had the advantage of Mr Hurd.

*

If Baden-Powell had survived the Second World War he would have been moved to learn that the Boy Scouts in Occupied Europe had played an important part in the various resistance movements, carrying food and messages and distributing underground newspapers. Sixty-five such boys were shot in Czechoslovakia and an unknown number during the Warsaw uprising. Ten were sentenced to death in Bergen, Norway, while eight out of the twelve Norwegians involved in the famous raid on the 'heavy water' installations at Vermork in 1943 were ex-Scouts. Groups of former Scouts had come together to form troops in places as infamous as Buchenwald, Lublin and Changi.[4] In Britain during the Blitz, Scouts worked with the emergency services and, by the time Baden-Powell died, had been awarded two George Crosses and five George Medals. In their founder's argot, they 'Played the Game'.[5]

In the post-war era the Scouts in Britain would rediscover neither the magic and vitality of the early years, nor the prestige and sense of purpose generated by Baden-Powell's great Jamborees in the 1920s and 1930s. The Cubs and Beavers (Junior Cubs) today outnumber their seniors, the Scouts, by over 200,000; and this long-standing trend extends to the Guides who are now outnumbered by the Brownies. At almost 620,000, the girls in Britain number nearly 100,000 more than the boys. But in the wider world the boys' Movement has expanded beyond its founder's dreams – proving sufficiently adaptable and attractive to draw 16 million members in more than 150 countries. In 1945 there were 4½ million Scouts in the world. Today there are very nearly 4 million in America alone, and 6 million in the Far East. This last figure (nearly 40 per cent of the world Movement) would have staggered Baden-Powell most of all, in spite of his enduring admiration for the Japanese.[6]

3. Brave New World

Lady Baden-Powell devoted the rest of her life to her husband's Movement, travelling hundreds of thousands of miles before ill-health finally ended her self-imposed duties in the early 1970s. She never accepted her husband's death and consoled herself with the spirit messages conveyed to her by two mediums. Cynthia, Lady Sandys (a member of the Guides' International Committee during the Great War) wrote down messages from 1942 onwards, as if taking direct dictation from the dead man. The living Baden-Powell, who had always had a keen sense of the ridiculous, would have been appalled had he ever known that it would one day be asserted that he predicted the arrival of 'much higher grades of beings' in flying saucers. Nor would he have relished reports of his conversations with George VI and Christ. Olave was convinced that unless Lady Sandys and Mrs Bedford (who made contact in trances via a spirit messenger) had helped her, she 'could not have gone on . . .'[1] She slept with Baden-Powell's horse-blanket on her bed, kept all his combs and brushes,[2] and wrote happily about 'my grave' in Nyeri and her longing to be 'inside the ground there too'.[3]

One of Olave's first acts after her husband's death had been to send a cable to Peter telling him that he ought not to take his father's title 'since there was only one Lord Baden-Powell'.[4] Peter ignored this. In 1942 when he returned to England from Rhodesia, intent on finding a permanent home, he did not tell his mother he was back but instead went to stay with the now married Josephine Reddie, whose husband was a curate in Esher.[5] He came intending to stay a few weeks, but remained under Josephine's roof for a year and a half. His son Robert, then 11, was with him and stayed on with Josephine for a further year after his father returned to southern Africa, where his wife and other son and daughter had been living in the meantime.[6]

Olave felt guilty about leaving Robert with Josephine instead of having him at her grace and favour apartment in Hampton Court Palace where she had plenty of room. Yet although she then enjoyed Annie's services, she repeatedly failed to do anything significant for her grandson when his father was back in southern Africa, preparing to bring the rest of his family to England. In October 1948, she wrote typically to Josephine: 'I can do nothing about him this year!'[7]

Eventually Peter bought a house near Farnham (within a few miles of Pax Hill), and moved there with his whole family in 1950. That August Olave, who had been chided by Josephine, was able to tell her that she was 'seeing Peter very occasionally'.[8] The frost had thawed a little more by the mid-1950s but relations never became cordial. 'He will always naturally have a "complex", and know unconsciously what I felt about him,' Olave told Christian.[9]

In 1961 Peter became gravely ill with leukaemia. He seemed to be responding to treatment a year later but, ironically, his continuing interest in Scouting hastened his demise. In September 1962 he attended the Gilwell Reunion and caught a chill after spending the night in his father's old caravan. A heavy cold became bronchial pneumonia which, in his enfeebled state, brought on a heart attack.[10] Olave saw her son for the last time in November but, although she doubted whether he would be alive when she returned, she still departed on a tour of the Far East. She received a cable on 9 December saying that he was dead, but did not return for his funeral which was conducted by Josephine's husband, Norman Pollock. Later Olave wrote to Eileen Wade telling her how thankful she was to have had very few letters of sympathy. 'I hope that there won't be any more.'[11] Olave had never been a hypocrite. She had repaired her relations with Heather, and was always on excellent terms with Betty and Christian.

A few months before Peter's death, she herself suffered a heart attack but recovered sufficiently to continue her punishing schedule of unpaid work. Seven years later, at the age of 80, she visited over a dozen countries as part of the Guide Movement's Diamond Jubilee celebrations. Baden-Powell had worked on into his eightieth year and she could do no less. By the late 1960s she had become profoundly pessimistic about the state of the country, and not only because the traditional Boy Scout uniform had been scrapped and the Scout Law abbreviated. 'It is horrid here now,' she wrote to Christian in Kenya, 'with prices soaring, people cross and angry, strikes every few days (it is CHAOS in London) and morals and morale pretty poor . . . It is sad to see this country going DOWN so, and of course with Rhodesia, and all the mismanagement of Anguilla etc. this country with its present government is distrusted, despised and disliked.'[12] When Labour was returned to power again after the destruction of Edward Heath's government by the miners, her despondency deepened. She and her friends on fixed incomes had suffered badly in the recent inflation but would soon be much worse off after the dramatic rise in the oil price and the failure of the 1974 Labour Government to persuade the trade unions to honour their agreements over wages.

Old friends like Eric Walker who returned to England on visits could not afford to go to restaurants or stay in any of the hotels they remembered.[13] 'Everybody talks about MONEY these days, and that they are going to be SHORT,' she told Christian, adding that she was astonished by the apparent wealth of the people she saw on the television at Ascot and Wimbledon.[14] The kind of elderly people she knew, who had been County Commissioners in the Scouts and Guides several decades earlier, were nowhere to be seen. But most of them had been in public service rather than business. At least her grandson Robert was doing well in the City, after a period selling alcohol and motor cars. Olave had been rather sniffy and grand when Robert married, but as her health began to fail from 1970 onwards she became almost pathetically grateful to her grandson and his wife, Patience, for their kindness.[15]

In 1974 she moved from Hampton Court to an old people's home outside Guildford 'where 40 of us old crocks are all waiting for the end'.[16] She suffered from diabetes and increasing weakness, particularly in her legs, but remained stoical. Only the national malaise depressed her. 'Such gloom and squabblings . . . and striking and parading with banners. Isn't it strange to think back even TWENTY years and to see what changes have taken place.'[17] The bloodshed in the newly independent African states grieved her almost as much as events at home. A few months before her death, she was horrified when M.P.s (and not just on the Labour Government side) voted themselves a large salary increase at a time when other people were suffering so much from the effects of inflation.[18] Britain seemed to her to be ungovernable, and the spirit of cooperation and the national pride which she remembered so well gone for ever. It consoled her to turn to her Guide magazines with their praise of kindliness and good deeds.[19]

Olave died on 25 June 1977, aged 88, and her ashes were flown to Kenya and buried in her husband's grave. The presence of a vast crowd of Africans including leading members of the Kenyan Government at her funeral service in All Saints Cathedral, Nairobi, was perfectly natural – but extraordinary too, in view of her husband's activities in Ashanti and Matabeleland. By 1977 Baden-Powell already seemed an historical figure from an era of Britain's history too far distant in time and thought to be linked to the present by anything as tangible as flesh and blood – and yet there sat his two daughters in the congregation.

In his own lifetime Baden-Powell witnessed almost unbelievable changes in every field of human experience; indeed it is hard to think of many men whose careers and thinking shed as much light on so wide a range of social and historical phenomena: the male role and the relationship between the sexes, Imperialism, the scramble for Africa, anti-urban romanticism, militarism, race, fascism, warfare, character-building and the priorities of education. Nor has any other social institution encapsulated so much of what is thought of (rightly or wrongly) as quintessentially British as Baden-Powell's Boy Scouts – social idealism coupled with fear of social change, romanticization of the past, suspicion of business, love of adventure, fear of sex, admiration for amateurism, mistrust of intellect, the association of happiness with virtue and the certainty that if adult life is about no more than growing old and making money, then so much the worse for adult life.

For all his obsessions and compulsions, Baden-Powell remains a dazzling, complicated and life-enhancing figure who did, as John Hargrave affirmed, 'a vast amount of good in the world'.[20]

APPENDIX I

Admiral Smyth's Legitimacy

Joseph Smyth's claim was finally rejected by the Treasury Commissioners, on the evidence of the Lieutenant-Governor of Crown Point and Ticonderoga, who deposed that the deeds and other papers produced by him were forgeries. But when Mr Maskelyne resumed his researches in earnest in 1905 (employing two American researchers), he was not interested in whether Joseph had ever owned the property he claimed. Instead he scrutinized Joseph's evidence to the Commissioners on the number of his children and their dates of birth.

In 1783 Joseph had sworn to having a wife and two children, and to having once had a total of six children, four of whom 'he had lost through want'. When Joseph's wife, Caroline, swore an affidavit five years later in July 1788, she stated that she 'married her husband in England in 1780 . . . and has two children'. This was very odd, since, if the two children mentioned by Joseph Smyth in 1783 ever existed (and were not invented to excite the compassion of the Commissioners), they could not have been the same as either of the two children mentioned by Caroline Smyth in 1788. The Admiral stated on a number of occasions that he had been born on 21 January 1788, and Maskelyne deduced that the Admiral's sister Elizabeth had been born in 1789. This is what he told George Baden-Powell on the basis of the inscription on Elizabeth (née Smyth) Murray's tombstone, which gave her age as 49 in 1838, the year of her death.

Maskelyne believed that Joseph had lied about his two children in 1783, and that Caroline had lied in 1788, since by his reckoning Elizabeth was not born till 1789. The four 'lost' children of Joseph's 1783 testimony, if they had ever existed, could only have been the issue of an earlier marriage. So what of this first Mrs Smyth? Was she dead? And if she was, could it be proved? Neither of the American researchers was able to come up with any answers.

Maskelyne had good reason to be perplexed, but he had been wrong about Elizabeth's date of birth; the tombstone had been inaccurate. Writing to his wife from Canada in August 1788, Joseph Smyth had asked her to wish his 'dear little Betsy well' and likewise 'the little stranger'. Betsy was plainly Elizabeth, born in 1787 (not 1789), and the 'little stranger' was the Admiral, who had been born after Joseph's departure for North America in 1787. He had gone, it was said, to try to find conclusive proofs for his claims. But Elizabeth's real date of birth showed that Caroline's testimony in 1788 had been reliable. The two children could perfectly well have been legitimate too, if the first Mrs Smyth was dead and if the second Mrs Smyth had been formally married (which Maskelyne had failed to prove).

Henrietta Grace and the rest of the family were not, however, aware that Maskelyne had got Elizabeth's birthday wrong, and were therefore given a very bleak report. Joseph and Caroline were both represented as perjurers and, because Joseph Smyth had left England in 1787 and Elizabeth (as he thought) was born in 1789, Joseph could not have been her father. Nor did Maskelyne find it hard to suggest a candidate for this role.

In 1787 Smyth's friend and fellow refugee, James Earl, an indigent artist, had been living with Caroline and Joseph at 42 Great Peter Street, Westminster. He was still there when the Admiral was born in 1788, and in August of that year, in his last known letter to his wife, Joseph Smyth sent greetings to Earl. Since Caroline married James Earl, according to the Admiral, in 'about 1789', and Maskelyne could find no hard evidence to prove that Joseph Smyth had died by then, this inevitably made him suspect that Caroline had always known that her marriage to Smyth was invalid. In December 1789, the supposed year of the marriage to Earl, Caroline had written to the Commissioners pleading for more time in which to produce the necessary evidence – a strange letter to write if she had thought Smyth dead.

With a 'husband' either dead or unable to return to England (because he would have been prosecuted for fraud if he had), Caroline's plight was desperate enough to make marriage to Earl – who was making a living of sorts out of his pictures – seem like salvation. By 1793, when the Admiral was 5, he and his sister had been joined by two half-sisters and a half-brother. Then, a year later, James Earl packed his bags and sailed for America, leaving his wife and children in England. He may have intended to send for his family if his fortunes improved; but they never did. He died in Charleston in 1796.

In 1802, shortly after Caroline married for the fourth time, the Admiral, aged 14 now, ran away to sea as cabin boy on a West Indiaman. This then was the astonishing chronicle unfolded to the family by the diligent Mr Maskelyne: a thrice married mother (if all, or any, of her marriages had been valid); two husbands leaving for America and never returning, and one of these probably guilty of forgery and fraud; and all this set against a background of unremitting poverty and frequent moves from boarding house to boarding house. At last they knew why Admiral Smyth had been so vague about his parentage.

An ironic consequence of Henrietta Grace's insecurity about her father's origins was the way in which it denied her the opportunity to make public capital out of her kinship with her father's half-sisters and half-brother. The last of these, Augustus Earle (he added a final 'e' to his surname), became a noted painter of Antipodean scenes and sailed with Darwin on the *Beagle* as the captain's personal draughtsman. Earle's sister, Phoebe, married the artist Denis Dighton, and herself painted flower pieces for the Queen. Since one of Henrietta Grace's sons became an artist she might have been expected to invoke Phoebe's name to gain him royal patronage. That she did not do so, was entirely due to her determination to keep the family skeletons securely locked away.

(The Sources for this Appendix are on p. 647.)

APPENDIX II

Baden-Powell's Affidavit on the Origins and Sources
of Scouting for Boys

On 24 May 1918, Baden-Powell swore an affidavit ('Deposition as to Origins of Scout Movement')[1] at the American Consulate General in Cavendish Square, London, to be used by the Boy Scouts of America in their case against the United States Boy Scouts in the Supreme Court of New York County. The former body expected to win their case if they could establish that Baden-Powell was the Movement's undoubted founder and had conferred upon them the exclusive right to use the name, uniform, badges and other paraphernalia of *his* Movement in America. I did not refer directly in the text to Baden-Powell's affidavit account of his founding of the Boy Scouts and his alleged sources for the book *Scouting for Boys*, because it is so full of inaccuracies; but since it has been relied upon unquestioningly by the authors of both official histories of the Scouts (and was supported by Baden-Powell himself until his death), it demands attention.

It has not been understood that the context of the affidavit was Thompson Seton's disastrous quarrel with the Executive Board of the Boy Scouts of America in 1915. Because Seton knew that the BSA's legitimacy depended upon their connection with Baden-Powell, and upon his unassailable status as founder, he (Seton) decided to tell the American press that his ideas had been stolen by Baden-Powell in order to torpedo the BSA's attempt to secure an American Scouting monopoly.[2] Baden-Powell therefore decided to leave nothing to chance in his testimony. Too much was at stake for the truth to be told. If the BSA lost their case, then there would be repercussions everywhere and he might ultimately lose control over the name and uniform even in Britain. Fortunately for Baden-Powell, Seton did not know that the magic words 'Boy Scout' had first made their appearance in a boys' comic.

In his affidavit Baden-Powell accurately described how, while with the 13th Hussars and the 5th Dragoon Guards, he had come to see Scouting as a means of 'developing character as well as field efficiency'. Then he continued:

> During the South African War, 1899–1900, Major Lord Edward
> Cecil, my Chief Staff Officer, organized the boys of Mafeking as a

corps for general utility on scout lines rather than those of cadets and the experiment was an entire success. The experience taught one that if their training was made to appeal to them, boys would learn rapidly and also that boys were capable of taking responsibilities to a far greater degree than was ordinarily believed . . .

After describing his patrol system in the South African Constabulary, and implying that there had been many more S.A.C. badges than there actually had, he went on:

On my return to England in 1903, I found that, among others, Miss Mason, head of a training school for teachers, had adopted *Aids to Scouting* as a textbook for their instruction and education as a step to character training. In 1904, I schemed some ideas for scouting as a training for boys. In 1905, I had a conversation with Sir William Smith, the founder of the Boys' Brigade, as to adapting the idea for boys, and I offered to write a book for them . . .

Now the inaccuracies: Lord Edward Cecil had never trained the existing Mafeking Cadet Corps on 'scout lines'. In 1927, BP stated in a private letter dictated to his secretary Mrs Wade and signed by her on his behalf: 'The boy messengers were not Boy Scouts . . . but more in the nature of cadets . . .'[3] In his eagerness to claim that scout training had been applied to boys before Seton had invented his Woodcraft Indians in 1902, Baden-Powell had given Cecil a niche in Scouting history which his lordship had never earned (and, since he had recently died, was not now going to disclaim). Similarly Baden-Powell, in order to deny his debt to Seton over the Scout badges, swore in the affidavit that his proficiency badges had been inspired by those devised for the S.A.C. A decade later he would admit that Seton's badges had furnished most of his originals.[4]

Although Baden-Powell did not discover until 1906[5] that Miss Charlotte Mason had made the activities described in *Aids to Scouting* part of the curriculum at her teacher training college, he claimed in his affidavit to have learned this in 1903. (Miss Mason had not come across the book until 1905.)[6] This not only placed his discovery of Scouting's educational significance long before his first meeting with Seton, but also stole some of Sir William Smith's thunder for having suggested that he adapt *Aids to Scouting* for use by boys. He further reduced William Smith's importance by placing his suggestion in 1905 rather than 1904. Baden-Powell would repeat the 1905 date in his autobiography.[7]

Before writing *Scouting for Boys*, Baden-Powell claimed in the affidavit to have studied '. . . the principles adopted by the Zulus and other African tribes, which reflected the ideas of Epictetus, and the methods of the Spartans, ancient British and Irish for training their boys. I also looked into the Bushido of the Japanese as well as the more modern methods of John Pound for dealing with boys, and Jahn for their physical culture, as well as those of today put into practice by Sir William Smith, Seton Thompson [sic], Dan Beard and Jahn more especially . . .' Two years earlier in 1916, Baden-Powell had compiled a similar list including Cu Chulainn (the mythological ancient Irish boy hero) and the Maoris and Red Indians. In a list in 1915, he had included the Pacific Islanders and Kenelm Digby's *Broadstone of Honour* as major influences, as well as the usual cast of Seton, Smith and Beard. In 1920 he added Professor Baden Powell, Dr Arnold of Rugby and W. T. Stead. Pestalozzi made an appearance in a list of 1918.[8]

In citing numerous influences Baden-Powell seems to have had three main aims: 1) to reduce the importance of living individuals like Seton and Smith; 2) to give Scouting a respectable educational pedigree at a time when educational methods were under intense debate; 3) to give the impression that *Scouting for Boys* had been the result of lengthy study and deliberation rather than a burst of rapid and spontaneous writing.

Of the influences cited, Seton stands clear of the field, with Digby, Arnold, Smith, Professor Powell and the Zulus all having an undoubted but lesser right to be there. John Pound (1766–1838) the Portsmouth cobbler who had taught children practical subjects along with the three 'Rs', seems to have had no direct influence; and the same can be said of W. T. Stead and Pestalozzi, whom Baden-Powell only learned about four years after he had written his book.[9] Friedrich Ludwig Jahn's pioneering of gymnastics in German schools may well have persuaded Baden-Powell to include a full section on physical exercises. At Charterhouse, it is possible that Stephe learned to admire the Stoic philosophy of Epictetus with his emphasis on endurance and abstinence. Daniel Carter Beard's 'Sons of Daniel Boone' had no real impact outside the field of gadgets and games; but the boys of another American, Byron Forbush (neglected in Baden-Powell's lists), probably impressed him. Called 'The Knights of King Arthur', their chivalrous programme prefigures much of the Scout Law. Roger Pocock of the Legion of Frontiersmen and Frederick Burnham, the scout, were similarly neglected.

None of Baden-Powell's detailed accounts of the origin of the Boy Scouts was written until eight years after the Brownsea Camp, so in the text I concentrated on the period itself rather than on discrepancies in retrospective material.

(The Notes to this Appendix are on p. 647.)

APPENDIX III

Lord Baden-Powell's Medals, Decorations and Orders

Ashanti Star Medal	1895
Matabele Campaign Medal	1896–97
South African War Queen's Medal	1899
Companion, Order of the Bath	1900
South African War King's Medal	1901
Knight Commander of the Order of the Bath	1909
Knight Commander of the Victorian Order	1909
Chilean Order of Merit	1910
Coronation Medal (King George V)	1911
Knight of Grace of St John of Jerusalem	1912
Knight Grand Cross of Alfonso XII (Spain)	1919
Grand Commander of the Order of Christ (Portugal)	1920
Grand Commander of the Order of the Redeemer (Greece)	1920
Storkos of the Order of Dannebrog (Denmark)	1921
Order of the Commander of the Crown (Belgium)	1921
Baronetcy	1922
Commander of the Legion of Honour (France)	1922
Grand Cross of the Victorian Order	1923
Order of Polonia Restituta (Poland)	1927
Knight Grand Cross of Order of St Michael and St George	1927
Order of Amanullah (Afghanistan)	1928
Order of Merit, First Class (Hungary)	1929
Order of the White Lion (Czechoslovakia)	1929
Order of the Phoenix (Greece)	1929
Peerage: Barony	1929
Grand Cross of the Order of Merit (Austria)	1931
Grand Cross of Gediminus (Lithuania)	1932
Grand Cross of Orange of Nassau (Holland)	1932
Commander of the Order of the Oak of Luxembourg	1932
Red Cross of Estonia	1933
Grand Cross of the Order of the Sword (Sweden)	1933
Grand Cross of the Order of the Three Stars (Latvia)	1933
Jubilee Medal (George V)	1935
Grand Cordon of Legion of Honour (France)	1936
Order of Merit	1937
Coronation Medal (George VI)	1937
Awarded Wateler Peace Prize	1937

FREEDOMS of the following Cities:

Newcastle on Tyne, Bangor, Cardiff, Harwich, Kingston on Thames
   (1903), Guildford (1928), Poole (1929), Blandford (1929), London
   (1929), Canterbury (1930), Pontefract (1933).

HONORARY DEGREES:

Doctor of Law Edinburgh University (1910)
Doctor Toronto University (1923)
Doctor McGill University, Montreal (1923)
Doctor of Civil Law (DCL) Oxford University (1923)
LL.D. Liverpool University (1929)
LL.D. Cambridge University (1931)

Part I.

Price 4d. net

SCOUTING FOR BOYS BY B-P

LIEUT. GEN. BADEN POWELL C.B.

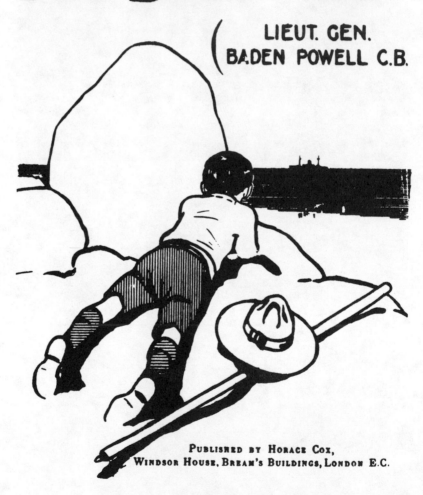

PUBLISHED BY HORACE COX,
WINDSOR HOUSE, BREAM'S BUILDINGS, LONDON E.C.

Front cover, Part I, "Scouting for Boys"
Published Jan. 15, 1908. Design by John Hassall.

A typical character-building chart devised by Baden-Powell

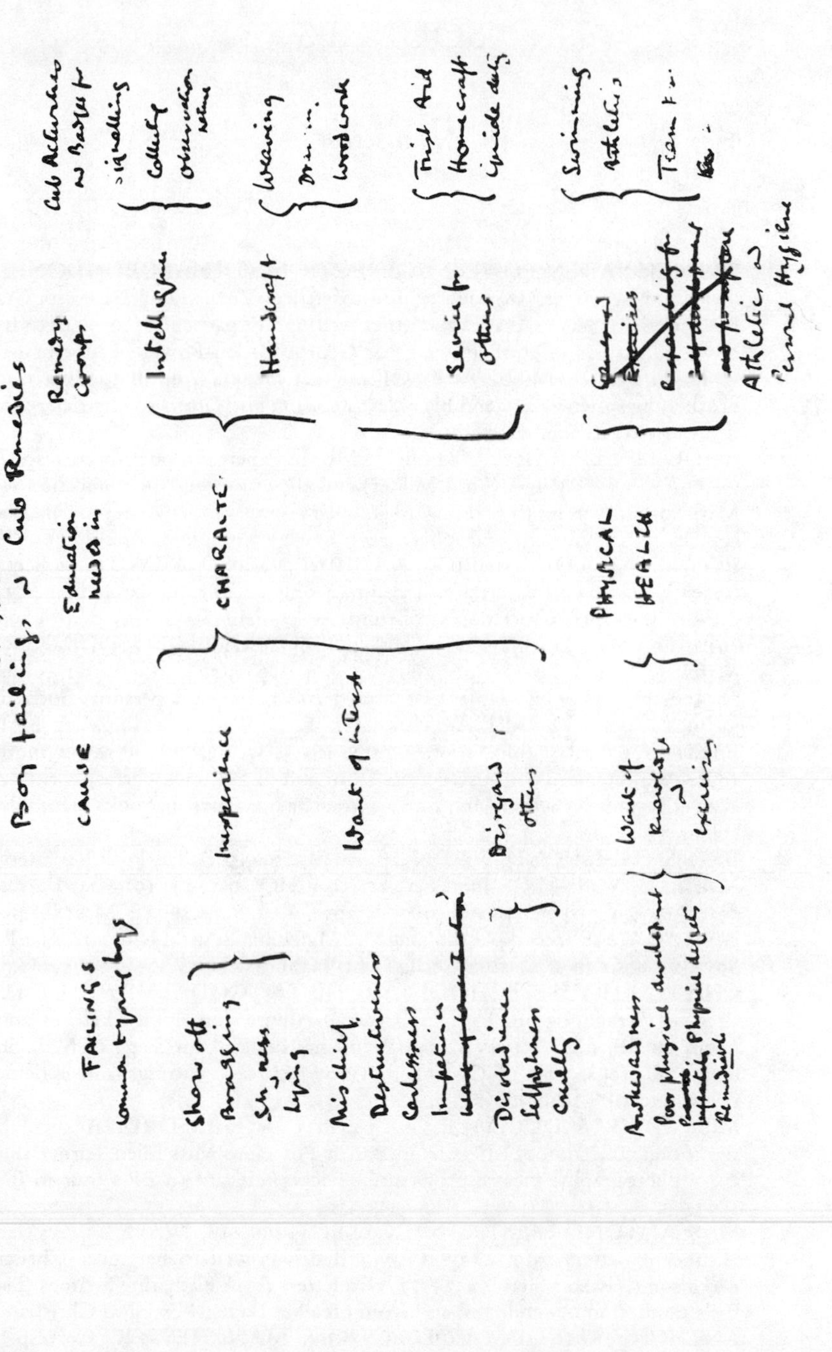

DIAGRAM

Boy failings & Cub Remedies

FAILINGS & common types	CAUSE	CHARACTER	Education Needs in	Remedy Groups	Cub Activities & Badges

Show off
Bragging
Shyness
Lying

Inexperience

Intelligence

Signalling
Collecting
Observation
Nature

Mischief
Destructiveness
Carelessness
Impatience

Want of interest

Handcraft

Weaving
Drawing
Woodwork

Disobedience
Selfishness
Cruelty

Disregard of others

Service to others

First Aid
Home craft
Upside down

Awkwardness
Poor physical development
Lethargy Physical defect
Remedied

Want of knowledge & exercise

PHYSICAL HEALTH

Corrective Exercises
Cultivation of natural powers
Athletics & Personal Hygiene

Swimming
Athletics
Team for all

SOURCES

Manuscript

1. FRANCIS BADEN-POWELL COLLECTION, FULHAM, LONDON. The finest and largest private collection in existence. Virtually all Henrietta Grace BP's surviving letters, diaries and other writings: of particular relevance to BP's boyhood; papers of Prof. Powell, Sir George Baden-Powell, Lady (Frances) Baden-Powell, Donald Baden-Powell and many letters from BP to his favourite brother, his sister-in-law and his oldest nephew; also letters to Henrietta Grace from Jowett, Ruskin, Dodgson etc.

2. BODLEIAN LIBRARY, OXFORD. Milner Papers. Important corresp. between Sir Alfred Milner (Lord Milner) and BP 1899–1903, in connection with Mafeking and the South African Constabulary; letters from Milner to Chamberlain, Hely-Hutchinson, Gell, Nicholson, Lawley, containing opinions on BP.

3. BOY SCOUTS OF AMERICA, MURRAY, KENTUCKY. This collection (recently placed on 15 reels of microfilm) is only equalled in size and quality by the British Scout Association's collection. It contains BP's daily diaries 1902–1940; most of his illustrated travel and campaign diaries 1887–1937; top copy of Mafeking Staff Diary 25 July 1899–13 Aug. 1900; sketches, water colours, photographs; huge assortment of first draft articles and personal notes and jottings preserved by Maj. A. G. and Mrs E. K. Wade in 1938, when BP left England for the last time; approx 2,000 letters written by BP to his mother 1877–1914; hundreds of misc. letters from and to BP, incl. corresp. with Mrs Wade, Thompson Seton, Mrs. E. K. Wade, Arthur Pearson; books, pamphlets, ephemera.

4. BRITISH LIBRARY, LONDON. BL Ad Mss 50255, Baden-Powell's letters to Maj. A. G. Wade M.C., Joint Sec. at Scout HQ 1912–14, 1919–24; BP diary notes 1904–12; sketches and m/s scraps. Weil Papers, Ad Mss 46848–9, Benjamin Weil's records of the Siege of Mafeking, several letters from BP to Snyman; notes to Weil from Cecil, Stent, Hanbury-Tracy.

5. CHARTERHOUSE SCHOOL ARCHIVES, GODALMING. Dr Haig Brown's Scrapbook, Edward F. Brown's Album containing sketches and a poem by BP, misc. letters from BP, an m/s descript. of Siege of Mafeking, theatrical progs, vols of *Carthusian, Greyfriar,* press cuttings and ephemera relevant to BP's schooldays.

6. MISS PAMELA DUGDALE COLLECTION, FAIRFORD. A small but significant collection of letters from Baden-Powell to Miss Ellen Turner 1897–1940; photographs, theatre progs and reviews relevant to BP's tour in India 1897–99.

7. MRS ANTONIA EASTMAN COLLECTION, N. WALES. Very large number of letters from Lady (Olave) Baden-Powell to her niece Christian Davidson (Rawson-Shaw) 1925–77; also letters from Katharine Soames (Lady BP's mother) to her children, and from Heather Baden-Powell to Christian.

8. ANTHONY GADDUM COLLECTION, MANCHESTER. Corresp. of

Arthur Gaddum (a very influential early Scout Commissioner); letters from BP, and most leaders of the Boy Scout Movement 1910-1928.

9. CENTRAL LIBRARY, HOVE. Wolseley Papers, which include BP's letters to Field-Marshal Viscount Wolseley 1896-1903.

10. MRS HONOR HURLY COLLECTION, AUCKLAND, NEW ZEALAND. The papers of Eric G. S. Walker (BP's private secretary 1909-1914), including his diaries from 1908–1911, corresp. with BP and Lady Baden-Powell, 1908–1974, code letters sent to BP in Great War.

11. 13/18th ROYAL HUSSARS REGIMENT, YORK. Regimental Scrapbooks, letters, sketches, press cuttings.

12. KENT COUNTY ARCHIVES, MAIDSTONE. Powell Mss. Deeds and legal documents of the Powell family, relevant to the finances of Prof. Powell, Mrs Baden-Powell and her family (deposited by Mr S. K. M. Powell 1963).

13. MRS ANTOINETTE LUNN, RINGWOOD. Letters from BP to Dulce and Musgrave Wroughton.

14. MAFIKENG MUSEUM, BOPHUTHATSWANA. Material connected with Siege, photographs, letters, sketches, and excellent unpub. diaries of J. R. Algie (Town Clerk), Mrs Ina Cowan, Serg. R. V. Hoskings (Protectorate Regt.), Mr H. Martin, Mother Mary Stanislaus (Mother Superior of Convent), Mr R. Urry (bank clerk); minutes of Town Council, press cuttings, ephemera.

15. MISS J. MOORE COLLECTION, HARPENDEN. All the surviving papers of Agnes, Frank and Augustus Baden-Powell; a number of BP's boyhood letters, and some of his mother's papers.

16. NATIONAL ARMY MUSEUM, LONDON. BP's diaries and official corresp. as Inspector General of the South African Constabulary, 1900–03, and I.G. of Cavalry for Gt Britain, S. Africa and Egypt 1903–07; 13th Hussars Scrapbook 1878–91, South African Scrapbook late 1880s, Malta Scrapbook, Ashanti Scrapbook (cuttings, drawings), microfilm of illustr. Ashanti Diary in Kumasi, Ghana. Roberts Papers, incl. many letters and telegrams from Lord Roberts to Baden-Powell, 1900–07.

17. NATIONAL ARCHIVES OF ZIMBABWE, HARARE. BP's Matabeleland Album, containing letters, orders, official documents, sketches, and cuttings from the 1896 Matabele Campaign.

18. NATIONAL LIBRARY OF SCOTLAND, EDINBURGH. Letters from BP to Viscount Haldane and his family 1907–29.

19. RICHARD H. NICHOLSON COLLECTION, WHITCHURCH, HANTS. Papers of Maj. the Hon A. Hanbury-Tracy (BP's Intelligence Officer at Mafeking and in Western Transvaal), incl. the Mafeking Day Book (an outstanding historical document in which is recorded every message sent or received during the Siege); an unbiased t/s account of the Siege by H-T; letters from BP, Roberts, Hanbury-Williams, Plumer, Bell, and a complete sequence of intelligence reports smuggled into the town by African spies.

20. PAUL C. RICHARDS COLLECTION, TEMPLETON, MASS. Very large collection of letters from BP and Lady BP to Mrs E. K. Wade; other letters to Mrs Eggar, Lord Edward Cecil, Arthur Poyser etc.; Scouting memorabilia.

21. PUBLIC RECORD OFFICE, KEW. Colonial Office and War Office communications concerning the campaigns in Zululand 1888, Ashanti 1895-6, and Matabeleland 1896. Also BP's dealings with the CO and WO in 1899, and from 1900–03 as I.G. of the S.A.C. and 1903–7 as I.G. of Cavalry (see notes for refs).

22. RHODES UNIVERSITY LIBRARY, GRAHAMSTOWN. Charles G. H. Bell's Mafeking Diary; letters to C. G. H. Bell in Siege, incl. many from BP, Vyvyan, Goold-Adams etc.

23. SCOUT ASSOCIATION ARCHIVES, SOUTH KENSINGTON. Virtually all BP's Scouting papers, including diaries kept on tour, thousands of carbon

duplicates of letters on every imaginable subject; fragments of a diary kept in Malta 1891; his Territorial Diaries 1808–09; corresp. with colonial and foreign movements; corresp. with Sir F. Vane; Lord Somers, Sir Percy Everett (the Everett Papers include an unbroken sequence of BP's letters from 1908–1940). Numerous scrapbooks, both Scouting and personal, incl. BP's finest Mafeking Album; Committee Minutes etc.

24. SCOUT ASSOCIATION OF SCOTLAND, EDINBURGH. BP's corresp. with Maj. K. McLaren during Siege of Mafeking.

25. SOUTH AFRICAN LIBRARY, CAPE TOWN. BP's Album relating to Swaziland Mission 1888, includes letters, sketches, cuttings; BP's Zululand Campaign Album, 1888, letters, sketches, official communications, photographs.

26. SMALLER COLLECTIONS. Africana Museum, Johannesburg, Mr Ian Bassett, the Hon. Mrs G. Clay, Mr W. Beckwith, Mrs Y. Binning, Mrs D. Cairns, Mrs Carp-Moore, Mr R. Chignell, Mr S. Copeland, Lord Downe, Mr C. Dymoke Green, Mr P. E. Gipps, Mrs D. Hargrave, Major T. Morley, Mr J. H. Morrison, Mrs J. Pollock, Scout Association of New Zealand, Mrs C. Shoolbred, Commodore D. Smyth R.A.N., Major J. Wade, Col. John Walton, Mr J. S. Winthrop Young.

27. UNIVERSITY OF BRISTOL LIBRARY, SPECIAL COLLECTIONS. Dame Katharine Furse's Papers. A large collection of letters from BP and Lady BP to Dame Katharine Furse 1919–38, and copies of her replies.

28. UNIVERSITY OF DURHAM. BP's letters to the 4th Earl Grey.

29. SIR JOHN VYVYAN BT COLLECTION, TRELOWARREN, CORNWALL. Col. Sir C. B. Vyvyan Bt's Papers. Matabeleland, 1896, incl. several letters from BP; Mafeking papers: Vyvyan was BP's Base Commandant, and as Chief Engineer was in charge of laying out the town's defences. Many notes and letters from BP in connection with defences; plans of the town's trenches and gun emplacements. Before the Siege, Vyvyan was BP's Intelligence Officer and kept a detailed diary.

30. RODNEY WARINGTON-SMYTH COLLECTION, FLUSHING, CORNWALL. Papers relating to Admiral Smyth's ancestry and the Baden-Powell family's efforts to prove his legitimacy.

31. YALE UNIVERSITY LIBRARY, NEW HAVEN. BP's letters to Frederick Russell Burnham, deposited by the Burnham family.

PUBLISHED WORKS

1. Books by Baden-Powell

1883 *On Vedette.*
1885 *Reconnaissance and Scouting.*
1885 *Cavalry Instruction.*
1889 *Pigsticking or Hoghunting* (1923 re-issue: *Pig-Sticking or Hog-Hunting*).
1896 *The Downfall of Prempeh.*
1897 *The Matabele Campaign.*
1899 *Aids to Scouting for N.C.O.s and Men.*
1900 *Sport in War.*
1901 *Notes and Instructions for the South African Constabulary.*
1907 *Sketches in Mafeking and East Africa.*
1908 *Scouting for Boys.*
1909 *Yarns for Boy Scouts.*
1910 *Scouting Games.*
1912 *Handbook for Girl Guides* (with Agnes Baden-Powell).
1913 *Boy Scouts Beyond the Seas.*
1914 *Quick Training for War.*
1915 *Indian Memories.*
      My Adventures as a Spy (1924 re-issue: *The Adventures of a Spy*).
1916 *Young Knights of the Empire.*
      The Wolf Cub's Handbook.
1918 *Girl Guiding.*
1919 *Aids to Scoutmastership.*
1921 *What Scouts Can Do.*
      An Old Wolf's Favourites.
1922 *Rovering to Success.*
1927 *Life's Snags and How to Meet Them.*
1929 *Scouting and Youth Movements.*
1933 *Lessons from the Varsity of Life.*
1934 *Adventures and Accidents.*
1935 *Scouting Round the World.*
1936 *Adventuring to Manhood.*
1937 *African Adventures.*
1938 *Birds and Beasts of Africa.*
1939 *Paddle Your Own Canoe.*
1940 *More Sketches of Kenya.*

2. Biographies and Other Works

ADAMS, W. S., *Edwardian Portraits*, London 1957.

AITKEN, W. FRANCIS, *Baden-Powell, The Hero of Mafeking*, London 1900.

ALDERSON, E. A. H., *With Mounted Infantry and the Mashonaland Field Force*, London 1898.

AMERY, L. S. (ed.), *The Times History of the War in South Africa*. 7 vols., London 1900–1909.

ANGLESEY, MARQUESS OF, *A History of the Cavalry* (1816–1919), London 1986.

ANNAN, NOEL, *Roxburgh of Stowe*, London 1965.

ARENDT, HANNAH, *The Origins of Totalitarianism*, New York 1951.

ARROWSMITH, R. L. (ed.), *A Charterhouse Miscellany*, London 1982.

ARTHUR, G., *Life of Lord Kitchener*, 3 vols., London 1920.

———, (ed.), *The Letters of Lord and Lady Wolseley 1870–1911*, London 1922.

BADEN-POWELL, HEATHER, *A Family Album*, Gloucester 1986.

BAILLIE, Maj. F. D., *Mafeking. A Diary of the Siege*, London 1900.

BALFOUR, A. J., *Decadence*, Cambridge 1908.

BARR, P., *The Memsahibs*, London 1976.

BATCHELDER, W. J., and BALFOUR, DAVID, *The Life of Baden-Powell*, London 1929.

BEGBIE, HAROLD, *The Story of Baden-Powell*, London 1900.

BIRCH, AUSTIN, *The Story of the Boys' Brigade*, London 1959.

BRENDON, PIERS, *Eminent Edwardians*, London 1980.

'British Officer', *Social Life in the British Army*, London 1900.

BROOKFIELD, ARTHUR M., *Annals of a Chequered Life*, London 1930.

BROWN, H. E. HAIG, *William Haig Brown of Charterhouse*, London 1908.

BULPIN, T. V., *The White Whirlwind*, London 1961.

BURNHAM, Maj. F., *Scouting on Two Continents*, London 1926.

BUTLER, SIR WILLIAM F., *Autobiography*, London 1911.

BUSHELL, W. F., *School Memories*, London 1962.

CALLWELL, Maj-Gen. Sir C. E., *Stray Recollections*, London 1923.

CARPENTER, HUMPHREY, *Secret Gardens*, London 1985.

CHESNEY, GEORGE, 'Battle of Dorking', *Blackwood's Magazine*, March 1881.

———, *The Dilemma*, 2 vols., London 1876.

CHILDERS, ERSKINE, *War and the Arme Blanche*, London 1910.

CHOLMONDELEY, ESSEX, (ed.), *In Memoriam Charlotte M. Mason*, London 1966.

CHURCHILL, WINSTON S., *Great Contemporaries*, London 1939.

COLLIS, HENRY, with FRED HURLL and REX HAZLEWOOD, *B-P's Scouts: An Official History of the Boy Scouts Association*, London 1961.

COMAROFF, JOHN L., (ed.), *The Boer War Diary of Sol T. Plaatje*, London 1976.

COMFORT, ALEX, *The Anxiety Makers*, London 1967.

COOKE, E. T. and WEDDERBURN, A., *The Works of John Ruskin*, London 1903–12.

CORSI, PIETRO, 'The Methodology of Science and the Question of Species in the Works of the Rev. Baden Powell', unpub. Ph.D. thesis, Oxford 1980.

CRAUFURD, A. M., *A Nurse's Diary in Besieged Mafeking*, Crampton's Magazine, London 1900.

DARK, SIDNEY, *The Life of Sir Arthur Pearson*, London 1922.

DAVEY, ARTHUR, (ed.), *The Defence of Mafeking and Ladysmith*, (incorporating the Siege Diary of Samuel Cawood), Johannesburg 1986.

DELANY, PAUL, *The Neo-pagans*, London 1987.

DE MONTMORENCY, H., *Sword and Stirrup: Memories*, London 1936.

DIGBY, KENELM HENRY, *Broadstone of Honour*, London 1822.

DOYLE, A. CONAN, *The Great Boer War*, London 1900–1902.

DREWERY, MARY and BADEN-POWELL, OLAVE, *Window on My Heart*, London 1973.

DRYBROUGH, T. B., *Polo*, London 1898.

DUNAE, PATRICK A., 'Boys' Literature and the Idea of Empire', *Victorian Studies*, 1980.

DUNBAR, J., *J. M. Barrie*, London 1970.

EAGAR, W. McG., *Making Men: The History of the Boys' Clubs and Related Movements in Great Britain*, London 1953.

ESHER, VISCOUNT, *Journals & Letters*, London 1914.

EVERETT, PERCY W., *The First Ten Years*, Ipswich 1948.

FABER, G., *Jowett* London 1957.

FARWELL, BYRON, *For Queen and Country*, London 1982.

FLETCHER, J. S., *Baden-Powell of Mafeking*, London 1900.

FLINT, J. E., *Cecil Rhodes*, London 1976.

FLOWER, LILLAR, 'Born in a Zoo', unpub t/s, *c.* 1960.

FOSTER, REV. MICHAEL J., *The British Boy Scouts* (booklet), Aylesbury 1987.

———, *The Use of the Name Boy Scouts in Boys' Literature (1899–1906)* (pamphlet), Aylesbury 1987.

FREUD, SIGMUND, *Civilization and its Discontents*, revised ed. J. Strachey, London 1979.

The Frontiersman's Pocket Book, London 1914.

FURSE, DAME KATHARINE, *Hearts and Pomegranates*, London 1940.

FUSSELL, PAUL, *The Boy Scout Handbook and Other Observations*, London 1982.

GANN, L. H. and DUIGNAN, P., *Burden of Empire*, London 1968.

GARDNER, BRIAN, *Mafeking: A Victorian Legend*, London 1967.

GATHORNE-HARDY, JONATHAN, *The Public School Phenomenon*, 597–1977, London 1977.

'Gentleman Private', *Six Months in the Ranks*, London 1883.

GIROUARD, MARK, *The Return to Camelot: Chivalry and the English Gentleman*, London 1981.

GODLEY, GEN. SIR ALICK, *Life of an Irish Soldier*, London 1939.

GODLEY, R. S., *Khaki and Blue*, London 1935.

GRAVES, ROBERT, *Goodbye to All That*, London 1929.

GREEN, MARTIN, *Dreams of Adventure: Deeds of Empire*, London 1980.

GREENE, GRAHAM (ed.), *The Spy's Bedside Book*, London 1957.

GRIFFIN, F. W. W., *The Quest of a Boy: A Study of the Psychology of Character Training*, London 1927.

———, *Rover Scouting*, London 1930.

GRINNELL-MILNE, D. W., *Baden-Powell at Mafeking*, London 1957.

HALL, G. STANLEY, *Adolescence*, New York 1904.

HAMILTON, ANGUS, *The Siege of Mafeking*, London 1900.

HAMILTON, GEN. SIR IAN, *Listening for the Drums*, London 1944.

HANLEY, H. A., *Dr John Lee of Hartwell*, Buckingham n.d.

HARGRAVE, JOHN, *The Confessions of the Kibbo Kift*, London 1927.

———, *The Great War Brings It Home*, London 1919.

HARINGTON, GEN. SIR C., *Plumer of Messines*, London 1935.

HAVELOCK ELLIS, H., *Little Essays of Love and Virtues*, London 1922.

HEADLAM, CECIL (ed.), *The Milner Papers Vol. I: South Africa–1899; Vol. II: South Africa 1899–1905*, London 1931, 1935.

HILLCOURT, W. and BADEN-POWELL, O., *Baden-Powell: The Two Lives of a Hero*, London 1964.

HOLMS, JOHN, *The Army in 1875*, London 1876.

HONEY, J. R. de S., *Tom Brown's Universe: The Development of the English Public School in the Nineteenth Century*, London 1977.

HOWARTH, PATRICK, *Play Up and Play the Game*, London 1973.
HUXLEY, ELSPETH, *The Flame Trees of Thika*, London 1959.
HYNES, SAMUEL, *The Edwardian Turn of Mind*, Princeton 1968.
IZZARD, MOLLY, *Helen Gwynne-Vaughan*, London 1969.
[JAMES, LIONEL], *Intelligence Officer. On the Heels of De Wet*, Blackwood 1902.
JEAL, TIM, *Livingstone*, London 1973.
JENKYNS, R., *The Victorians and Ancient Greece*, Oxford 1981.
JONES, E. A., *The Loyalists of New Jersey; Their Memorials, Petitions, Claims, Etc. From English Records*, New Jersey 1927.
KEARY, PETER, *The Secrets of Success*, London 1906.
KIERNAN, R. H., *Baden-Powell*, London 1939.
KERR, ROSE, *The Story of the Girl Guides*, London 1932.
KINCAID, D., *Social Life in India (1608–1937)*, London 1938.
KINSEY, A. C., POMEROY, W. B. and MARTIN, C., *Sexual Behaviour in the Human Male*, London 1948.
KINGSLEY, CHARLES, *Westward Ho!*, London 1855.
KISCH, H. M., *A Young Victorian in India*, London 1957.
KRUGER, RAYNE, *Goodbye Dolly Gray: the Story of the Boer War*, London 1959.
LAQUEUR, WALTER Z., *Young Germany: A History of the German Youth Movement*, London 1967.
LE MAY, G. H. L., *British Supremacy in South Africa 1899-1907*, Oxford 1965.
LEONARD, A. G., *How We Won Rhodesia*, London 1896.
LODGE, H. CABOT, *Correspondence of Theodore Roosevelt and Henry Cabot Lodge*, New York 1923.
MACKENZIE, NORMAN, 'Sweating It Out with B-P', *New Statesman* (15 October 1965).
MACLEOD, DAVID I., *Building Character in the American Boy*, Madison, Wisconsin 1983.
MANGAN, J. A. and WALVIN, J. (eds)., *Manliness and Morality*, Manchester 1987.
MAUDE, CYRIL, *Behind the Scenes with Cyril Maude*, London 1927.
MAURICE, MAJ-GEN. SIR FREDERICK and GRANT, M. H., [Government], *History of the War in South Africa, 1899–1902*, 4 vols, London 1906–1910.
MEINTJES, JOHANNES, *President Steyn*, Johannesburg 1966.
MILLS, ELLIOT, *The Decline and Fall of the British Empire: Appointed for Use in the National Schools of Japan, Tokyo, 2005*, London 1905.
MIDGLEY, J. F. (ed.), *Petticoat in Mafeking: the Letters of Ada Cock*, Johannesburg 1974.
MILNER, VISCOUNTESS (formerly Lady Edward (Violet) Cecil), *My Picture Gallery 1886–1901*, London 1951.
MORRIS, A. J. A., *The Scaremongers*, London 1984.
MORRIS, BRIAN, 'Ernest Thompson Seton and the Origins of the Woodcraft Movement', *Journal of Contemporary History* 5 (1970) 183–94.
NEILLY, J. EMERSON, *Besieged with B-P: Siege of Mafeking*, London 1900.
NEVILL, P. B., *Scouting in London, 1908–1965*, London 1966.
NEWSOME, DAVID, *Godliness and Good Learning*, London 1961.
NEWTON, A. P., and WALKER E. A., *The Cambridge History of the British Empire*, vol. viii, Cambridge 1936.
'NOEMO, CAPTAIN', *The Boy Scout Bubble: A Review of a Great Futility*, London 1912.
O'MEARA, LT-COL. W. A. J., *Kekewich in Kimberley*, London 1926.
PAKENHAM, THOMAS, *The Boer War*, London 1979.
PARKER, P., *The Old Lie: the Great War and the Public School Ethos*, London 1987.
PAUL, LESLIE, *Angry Young Man*, London 1951.
PEACOCK, ROGER S., *Pioneer of Boyhood: The Story of Sir William A. Smith, Founder of the Boys' Brigade*, Glasgow 1954.
PHILIPPS, R. E., *Letters to a Patrol Leader: The Scout Law*, London 1916.

PIENAAR, PHILIP, *With Steyn and De Wet*, London 1902.
PIMLOTT, J. A. R., *Toynbee Hall: 50 Years of Social Progress*, London 1934.
POCOCK, ROGER, *Chorus to Adventurers*, London 1931.
POLLOCK, MAJ. A. W. A., *With Seven Generals in the Boer War*, London 1900.
POWELL, EDGAR, *The Pedigree of the Powell Family*, London 1891.
RANGER, TERENCE, *Revolt in Southern Rhodesia, 1896–7*, London 1967.
REYNOLDS, E. E., *Baden-Powell: A biography of Lord Baden-Powell of Gilwell*, London 1942.
——, *The Scout Movement*, London 1950.
RICHARDS, PAUL C. (ed.), *The Founding of the Boy Scouts as Seen Through the Letters of Lord Baden-Powell*, East Bridgewater, Mass. 1973.
RICHARDSON, F. M., *Mars without Venus*, London 1981.
ROBERTS, B., *Churchills in Africa*, London 1900.
ROBERTS, FREDERICK, LORD, *Defence of the Empire*, London 1905.
——, *A Nation in Arms*, London 1907.
ROSE, KENNETH, *The Later Cecils*, London 1975.
RUSKIN, JOHN, *The Winnington Letters*, London 1969.
ST GEORGE, HILARY, *The Left Handshake*, London 1949.
SANBORN, F. B. (ed.), *Memoirs of Pliny Earle M.D.*, Boston 1898.
SANSOM, J. G., *The Worlds of Ernest Thompson Seton*, New York 1976.
SCHREINER, OLIVE, *Trooper Peter Halket of Mashonaland*, London 1897.
SETON, ERNEST THOMPSON, *The Birch-bark Roll of Woodcraft*, New York 1906.
——, *Two Little Savages*, New York 1903.
SMITH, T. d'ARCH, *Love in Earnest*, London 1970.
SPIERS, EDWARD M., *The Army and Society (1815–1914)*, London 1980.
SPRINGHALL, JOHN O., 'The Boy Scouts, Class and Militarism in Relation to British Youth Movements, 1908–1930', *International Review of Social History* 16 (1971): 125–58.
——, *Youth, Empire and Society: British Youth Movements, 1883–1940*, London 1977.
——, FRASER, BRIAN, and HOARE, MICHAEL, *Sure and Steadfast: A History of the Boys' Brigade, 1883–1983*, London 1983.
STORR, ANTHONY., *Sexual Deviation*, London 1964.
SYKES, F. W., *With Plumer in Matabeleland*, London 1897.
THUILLIER, SIR H. F., *The Principles of Land Defence*, London 1902.
TORDOFF, W., *Ashanti under the Prempehs*, London 1965.
TROTTER, WILFRED, *The Herd Instinct, Sociological Review*, 1908.
TRUDGILL, E., *Madonnas and Magdalens*, London 1976.
TRUSTRAM, M., *The Victorian Army: Women of the Regiment*, London 1984.
TUCKWELL, W., *Pre Tractarian Oxford*, Oxford 1909.
TURNER, E. S., *Boys Will be Boys*, London 1948.
TWAIN, MARK, *Roughing It*, London 1872.
——, *Life on the Mississippi*, London 1876.
USBORNE, RICHARD, *Clubland Heroes*, London 1953.
VACHELL, HORACE A., *The Hill*, London 1905.
VANE, FRANCIS FLETCHER, *Agin the Governments*, London 1929.
——, *The Boy Knight*, London 1910.
VANCE, NORMAN, *Sinews of the Spirit*, London 1985.
WADE, E. K., *The Piper of Pax*, London 1924.
——, *The Story of Scouting*, London 1935.
——, *27 Years with Baden-Powell*, London 1957.
WALKER, ERIC G. S., *Treetops Hotel*, London 1962.
WALKOWITZ, J. R., *Prostitution in Victorian Society*, London 1980.
WARD, W. E. F., *Britain and Ashanti 1874–1896, Transactions of the Historical Society of Ghana*, vol. xv (ii).

WARWICK, PETER (ed.), *Black People and the South African War*, London 1980.

———, (ed.), *The South African War*, London 1980.

WAUGH, ALEC, *The Loom of Youth*, London 1917.

WEIR, C. J., *The Boer War: A Diary of the Siege of Mafeking*, Edinburgh 1901.

WESTLAKE, AUBREY T., *Woodcraft Chivalry*, Weston-Super-Mare 1917.

WHALLEY, G. F., *With Plumer to Mafeking*, London 1900.

WHITEHOUSE, J. H., (ed.) *Problems of Boy Life*, London 1912.

WIENER, M. J., *English Culture and the Decline of the Industrial Spirit 1850–1980*, London 1982.

WILKS, I., *Asante in the Nineteenth Century*, London 1975.

WILLAN, BRIAN, *Edward Ross: Diary of the Siege of Mafeking*, Cape Town 1981.

———, *Sol Plaatje: South African Nationalist 1876-1932*, London 1984.

WILLIAMS, W. W., *The Life of General Sir Charles Warren*, Oxford 1941.

WILSON, LADY SARAH, *South African Memories*, London 1909.

WULFSOHN, L., *Rustenburg at War*, Johannesburg 1987.

YOUNG, FILSON, *The Relief of Mafeking*, London 1900.

YOUNG, WINTHROP, *The Grace of Forgetting*, London n.d.

NOTES

Abbreviations used in Notes

A	Agnes Baden-Powell (BP's only sister, 1858–1945).
Aitken	*Baden-Powell, The Hero of Mafeking*, W. F. Aitken (London 1900).
Augustus	Augustus S. Baden-Powell (BP's brother who died aged thirteen, 1849–1863).
Baden	Major Baden F. S. Baden-Powell (BP's youngest brother, 1860–1937).
Beghie	*The Story of Baden-Powell*, H. Beghie (London 1900).
BL	British Library.
BP	Robert Stephenson Smyth Baden-Powell, O.M., 1st Baron Baden-Powell of Gilwell (1857–1941).
BPD	Baden-Powell's basic daily diary kept from 1902 to 7 Nov. 1940. In annual vols, owned by the Boy Scouts of America. Microfilm Reels 1–4.
BP's Scouts	*BP's Scouts: An Official History of the Boy Scouts Association*, H. Collis, F. Hurll, R. Hazlewood (London 1961).
BSA	Boy Scouts of America, specifically their vast collection of Baden-Powell papers.
CO	Colonial Office files and papers in the Public Record Office at Kew, London.
DB	Mafeking Day Book, being the daily register of all incoming and outgoing communications during the Siege, owned by Mr R. H. Nicholson.
Eastman	Collection of letters (1925–77) written by Lady Baden-Powell to her niece, Christian Davidson (later Mrs Rawson-Shaw), owned by Mrs Antonia Eastman.
EP	A dozen volumes of letters from Lord and Lady Baden-Powell to Sir Percy W. Everett (1908–1941 and beyond).
EWD	The Diaries of Eric G. S. Walker 1908–1912. Walker was a Scout Inspector from 1908, and in 1909–14 was private sec. to BP.
F	Francis (Frank) Smyth Baden-Powell (youngest of BP's three older brothers, 1850–1933).
FBPA	Mr Francis Baden-Powell's archive of family papers.
Frances	Lady (Frances) Baden-Powell (née Wilson, married to Sir George).
G	Sir George S. Baden-Powell, K.C.M.G., M.P. (the second oldest of BP's brothers, 1847–1898).
Gardner	*Mafeking: A Victorian Legend*, Brian Gardner (London 1966).
GH	Government History of the War, i.e. *History of the War in South Africa 1899–1902*, Sir F. Maurice and M. H. Grant (eds.), 4 Vols (London 1906–10) 'Written by direction of His Majesty's Government'.
GL	Authentic 300-page typescript copy of letters exchanged during the Siege of Mafeking by Major A. J. Godley and Mrs Godley, courtesy of Dr Brian Willan.

HC   Mrs Honor Hurly's Collection, comprising the diaries and papers
                of her father Eric G. S. Walker.
HFA   *Baden-Powell: A Family Album*, Heather Baden-Powell (King),
                (Gloucester 1986).
HG   Henrietta Grace Baden-Powell (1824–1914). BP's mother.
Hillcourt   *Baden-Powell: the Two Lives of a Hero*, W. Hillcourt and O. Baden-
                Powell (London 1964).
I.M.   *Indian Memories*, R. Baden-Powell (London 1915).
JM   Miss Joan Moore's Collection of Baden-Powell papers.
JPC   Mrs Josephine Pollock's Collection.
KF   Dame Katharine Furse.
Kerr   *The Story of the Girl Guides*, Rose Kerr (London 1932).
KFP   Dame Katharine Furse's Papers.
MP   Milner Papers.
NAM   National Army Museum.
NAZ   National Archives of Zimbabwe.
OBP   Lady (Olave) Baden-Powell (1889–1977).
Pakenham   *The Boer War*, Thomas Pakenham (London 1979).
PCR   Paul C. Richards Collection.
Piper   *The Piper of Pax*, E. K. Wade (London 1924).
PRO   Public Record Office, Kew.
R 1–15   Microfilm reel numbers of the Boy Scouts of America's collection.
RCWSA   *Royal Commission on the War in South Africa* (4 Vols) 1903.
RHN   Richard H. Nicholson's Collection.
Reynolds   *Baden-Powell: A Biography*, E. E. Reynolds (London 1942).
Reynolds SM   *The Scout Movement*, E. E. Reynolds (London 1950).
Richards ed.   *The Founding of the Boy Scouts as Seen Through the Letters of the Lord
                Baden-Powell*, Paul C. Richards (ed.) (East Bridgewater, Mass.
                1973).
Rosenthal   *The Character Factory: Baden-Powell and the Origins of the Boy Scout
                Movement*, Michael Rosenthal (London 1986).
RP   Lord Roberts's Papers, NAM.
TH   *The Times History of the War in South Africa (1899–1902)* see L. S.
                Amery (ed.) in Bibliography.
27 Years   *27 Years with Baden-Powell*, E. K. Wade (London 1957).
SAA   British Scout Association's Archives.
SD   Baden-Powell Military Staff Diary 1899–1900.
V of L   *Lessons from the Varsity of Life*, R. Baden-Powell (London 1933).
V of L t/s   The original uncut typescript of the above autobiography.
W   Warington Baden-Powell (BP's oldest brother, 1847–1921).
Window   *Window on My Heart*, Mary Drewery and Olave Baden-Powell
                (London 1973).
WO   War Office files and papers in the Public Record Office at Kew,
                London.

Chapter One
THAT WONDERFUL WOMAN
1. Miracles and Nightmares

1. *Rovering and Rangering* t/s 1937, R8 BSA.
2. *Lessons from the Varsity of Life*, BP (London 1933), 17.
3. Harold Begbie, *The Story of Baden-Powell* (London 1900).
4. Sarah Tooley in *The Lady's Realm*, May 1900.
5. HG to G 9 May 1869, FBPA.
6. BP's obit for HG in *The Scout*, Oct. 1914.
7. HG Journal 1844-5, 146, FBPA.
8. Later Sir James Fitzjames Stephen.
9. HG Journal 1844-5, 104-13.
10. HG Journal 1844-5, 117.
11. *Dr John Lee of Hartwell*, H.A. Hanley (Buckinghamshire Record Office, n.d.), 12-14, 25.
12. A to Frances, 27 May 1908, FBPA.
13. *Dr John Lee of Hartwell*, 27.
14. *Born in a Zoo*, Lillar Flower/Mrs Charles Bethune (unpub t/s c.1960); and information from Miss S.J. Flower.
15. G.A. Maskelyne to G, 22 Nov. 1892, JM.
16. *The Loyalists of New Jersey; Their Memorials, Petitions, Claims, etc. From English Records*, E.A. Jones (New Jersey 1927) 204-205; PRO AO 13/41, AO 13/111.
17. *Memoirs of Pliny Earle M.D.*, ed. F.B. Sanborn (Boston 1898), 378-79.
18. This claim appeared as recently as 1980 in the Baden-Powell entry in *Burke's Peerage*.
19. Athelystan Glodrydd, Prince of Fferlys; G to HG, 20 Oct. 1888, FBPA; G would christen his son Donald Ferlys.
20. For HG's courtship and marriage see her diary ending Feb. 1845, and her résumé dated May 1847, FBPA.
21. HG Diary 11 May 1846, FBPA; *Pre-Tractarian Oxford*, W. Tuckwell (Oxford 1909) 168; HG's Notes for Journal 1849-56: 16 Jan. 1851.
22. HG Diary 23-29 June 1847, FBPA.
23. 'The Methodology of Science and the Question of Species in the works of the Reverend Baden Powell', Pietro Corsi (unpublished Ph.D. thesis 1980), 204.
24. HG Diary 21 Sep. 1853, FBPA.
25. HG Notes for Journal 1849-56: misc. refs. May to Sept. 1850 and 1851, FBPA.
26. HG Diary 4 May 1853, FBPA.
27. HG Diary 21 Dec. [error for 31] 1852, FBPA.
28. HG Diary 16 June 1852, FBPA.
29. HG Diary 11 Mar. 1854, FBPA.
30. BP to HG 19 Sept. 1884, BSA; HG's Diary 25 July 1861; A to Frances 23 Jan. 1901, FBPA.
31. *Lady's Realm*, May 1900; Begbie, 20.
32. Supp. to *The King* 26 May 1900; Album [43], SAA.
33. H.F. Brown's Album, Charterhouse Archives.
34. Tuckwell, 170-1.
35. HG to G 12 Apr. 1860, FBPA.
36. Note by HG June 1860, FBPA.
37. *Jowett*, G. Faber (London 1957), 231.
38. *The Piper of Pax*, E.K. Wade (London 1924), 14; *Aberdeen Herald* 21 July 1860.
39. W.H. Flower to ed. *The Times* 7 Dec. 1869.
40. HG Diary 16-25 June 1853, FBPA.
41. B. Jowett to HG 20 June 1860, FBPA.

2. Poor Little Stephe (1857-68)

1. *Baden-Powell*, W.F. Aitken (London 1900), 15.
2. Evidence for this in FBPA and JM, which together contain all HG's surviving papers, including diaries, journals and many letters from her to George, Frank, Agnes and Augustus.
3. HG to Annarella Smyth 23 Feb. 1861, FBPA.
4. HG to Annarella Smyth 1 Aug. 1861, FBPA.
5. HG to G 17 Jan. 1861, FBPA.
6. Augustus to HG 8 June 1861, JM.
7. Supp. to *The Sphere* 26 May 1900.
8. Augustus to HG 11 Mar. 1862, JM.
9. Augustus to HG 17 Mar. 1862, JM.
10. HG to Augustus 10 Apr. 1862, JM.
11. Augustus to F 19 Apr. 1862, JM.
12. HG to Augustus 2 Aug. 1862, JM.

13. HG to Augustus 1 Apr. 1862, JM.
14. HG to G 24 Feb. 1863, FBPA.
15. HG to Annarella Smyth 9 Mar. 1863, FBPA.
16. Augustus's will, JM.
17. Note by HG June 1869; HG to G 1 Nov. 1863, FBPA.
18. HG to G 20 Apr. 1869, FBPA.
19. HG to G 1 Nov. 1863, FBPA.
20. Ibid.
21. HG to 'My darling boys' 8 Sept. 1864, FBPA.
22. HG to G 19 Sept. 1859, FBPA.
23. Note by HG Oct. 1853, FBPA.
24. HG Diary 8 Nov. 1853, FBPA.
25. Original in SAA.
26. HG to G 11 Nov. 1863, FBPA.
27. HG to G 9 May 1869, FBPA.
28. HG to 'My dear sons' 26 Nov. 1869, FBPA.
29. HG Diary 14 July 1853, FBPA.
30. Supp. to *The King* 26 May 1900.
31. *The Scout* Oct. 1914.

3. Clinging Together

1. HG Diary Sept. 1869, FBPA.
2. Property deeds and other legal papers of Powell family, Kent Archives Office, Maidstone, U934. Presented by S.K.M. Powell of Speldhurst.
3. *Baden-Powell: The Two Lives of a Hero*, William Hillcourt and Olave Baden-Powell (London 1964), 4; numerous notes by HG 1861, viz 23 Feb. 1861, and long financial history compiled for W in 1914 when HG made her last will: all in FBPA.
4. Note by HG 4 Apr. 1873, FBPA.
5. HG to sons 23 Oct. 1869, FBPA.
6. HG to G 4 Sept. 1869, FBPA.
7. HG to G 11 Aug. 1869, FBPA.
8. HG to sons 5 & 6 Nov. 1869, FBPA.
9. Hilda BP to Peter BP 21 Apr. 1945, FBPA.
10. Note by HG n.d. but 1863, FBPA.
11. HG Diary 12 Apr. 1874, FBPA.
12. HG Diary 23 Nov. 1875, FBPA.
13. HG to W Feb. 1869; HG to G 4 Sept. 1869, FBPA.
14. HG to G 28 May 1869, FBPA.
15. HG to G 1 Nov. 1863, FBPA.
16. HG to G 11 Aug. 1869, FBPA.

17. Hilda BP to Peter BP 21 Apr. 1945, FBPA.
18. BPD 1927–30, e.g. 21 Apr. and 2 May 1930.
19. F to HG 5 Dec. 1882, JM.
20. *The Pedigree of the Family of Powell*, Edgar Powell (London 1891).
21. HG to Frances 8 Sept. 1906, FBPA.
22. HG to Frances 20 Apr. 1902, FBPA.
23. BP to HG 20 Oct. 1881, BSA.
24. BP to G 3 Feb. 1886, BSA
25. *Pedigree* (as n. 20 above).
26. HG to G 28 Oct. 1869, FBPA.
27. HG to G 15 July 1869, FBPA.
28. HG to G 28 Oct. 1869, FBPA.
29. HG to G 15 July 1869, FBPA.
30. HG to G 11 Aug. 1869, FBPA.
31. HG to sons 26 Apr. 1869, FBPA.
32. HG Diary 2 Nov. 1853, FBPA.
33. HG Diary 13 Aug., 17 Oct. 1875, FBPA.
34. HG Diary 3 Aug. and 15 Dec. 1874, FBPA.
35. HG to G 7 Oct. 1869, FBPA.
36. HG to G 16 May 1869, FBPA.
37. HG Diary Feb. & Mar. 1874, FBPA.
38. BP to Vere Stent 23 Mar. 1900, BSA.
39. BP's comment on remarks of Dean Inge in *Evening Standard* 19 Dec. 1923, TC 21 SAA.
40. *T.L.S.* 24 Sept. 1964.
41. 'Elder Brother' draft article 1919, R7 BSA.
42. Viz BP to Vere Stent (n. 38 above).

4. Stephe at School (1868–76)

1. Notes by HG 21 Dec. 1852 and Oct. 1853, FBPA; *Piper*, 18.
2. Rose Hill Reports, File: Founder's Education, SAA.
3. E. Abbott (F's tutor) to HG 13 Dec. 1870, FBPA.
4. Note by HG Mar. 1870, FBPA.
5. Duke of Marlborough to HG 22 June 1870; Fettes offer: Album [43], SAA.
6. State of the Public Schools and Charterhouse: *Tom Brown's Universe*, J. de S. Honey (London 1972); *The Public School Phenomenon*, J. Gathorne-Hardy (London 1977); *A Charterhouse Miscellany*, R.L.

Arrowsmith (ed.) (London 1982); *William Haig Brown of Charterhouse,* H.E. Haig Brown (London 1908).

7. *Indian Memories,* BP (London 1915), 1–2.

8. *A Charterhouse Miscellany,* 93.

9. Original t/s *V of L* 92–101, R9 BSA.

10. Unpub. m/s account of BP's Charterhouse days by E.H. Parry (1921), R13 BSA.

11. *Rovering to Success,* BP (London 1922), 238–9.

12. Minute Book of Druids, Charterhouse Archives; *Greyfriar* Apr.1914, article on Druids by Robert Graves.

13. E.H. Parry (see n. 10 above).

14. G.H. Rendall's remark see *Goodbye to All That,* Robert Graves (London 1929; my refs Penguin reprint 1957), 39; footballing friend (see n. 11 above).

15. *Agin the Governments,* Sir Frances Vane Bt. (London 1929), 18–19.

16. Ibid 19.

17. E.H. Parry.

18. *Rovering to Success,* 24.

19. *Roxburgh of Stowe,* Noel Annan (London 1965), 10.

20. *William Haig Brown of Charterhouse,* 64.

21. *With an Eye to the Future,* Osbert Lancaster (London 1967), 43–44.

22. *School Memories,* W.F. Bushell (London 1962), 51–54; *Charterhouse Miscellany,* 111.

23. *William Haig Brown of Charterhouse,* 77.

24. *V of L,* 24.

25. *Roughing it,* Mark Twain (1872), quoted in *Dreams of Adventure: Deeds of Empire,* Martin Green (London 1980), 83; *Reconnaissance and Scouting,* BP (London 1884).

26. Hillcourt, 26; File: Founder's Education, SAA; shooting team see HG Diary 16 July 1874, FBPA; Album [43], SAA.

27. 'When I was at School . . .' m/s n.d., R7 BSA.

28. *V of L* t/s, R9 BSA.

29 E.H. Parry.

30. *V of L* t/s, R9 BSA.

31. Cutting in W. Haig Brown's Scrapbook, Charterhouse.

32. Begbie, 48.

33. *V of L* t/s, R9 BSA.

34. Ibid.

35. Ibid.

36. BP to Rosetta Flower n.d., copy in SAA.

37. Recollections of A.H. Gipps, 'Gownboys 1868–72', P.E. Gipps Coll.

38. Begbie, 38f.

39. *Carthusian* Feb. 1876.

40. Press cutting interview with Haig Brown 'Baden-Powell as a Schoolboy', n.d. but 1900; Old Carthusian to ed. *Daily Telegraph* 19 May 1900.

41. Begbie, 46.

42. E.H. Parry; Recollections of A.H. Gipps.

43. *Roxburgh of Stowe,* 16; *Memoirs,* Lord Chandos (London 1962); *An Edwardian Youth,* L.E. Jones (London 1955).

44. E.H. Parry.

5. Choosing a Career (1876)

1. *V of L,* 13, 23.

2. Hillcourt, 33.

3. *Piper,* 31.

4. HG Diary 13 June 1874, 21 Jan., 22 Feb., 27 Mar. 1875, FBPA.

5. Information given by HG to *The King,* 26 May 1900.

6. *Portrait of an Age,* G.M. Young (London 1936), 98.

7. B. Jowett to HG 20 June 1860, FBPA.

8. HG to G 4 Sept. 1869, FBPA.

9. Ibid.

10. HG to G 2 Oct. 1869, FBPA.

11. HG to G 29 May 1869, FBPA.

12. HG Diary 20 Dec. 1875, FBPA.

13. *V of L* t/s, R8 BSA.

14. Begbie, 55; *Baden-Powell,* W.F. Aitken (London 1900), 25; supplement to *The Sphere,* 26 May 1900; etc.

15. *Westminster Gazette* 20 Sept. 1912.

16. Dean Liddell to HG 15 Oct. 1876, FBPA.

17. *Indian Memories,* 3.

18. A receipt for fees and caution money paid to the Univ. of Oxford on 12 May (see Hillcourt n. 32 p. 425) may

have been an exam fee – the caution money being required because he was resident in Oxford for the duration of the exam. But it may mean that he would have been admitted as an unattached student in October had he presented himself for matriculation.

19. BP to G 28 Apr. 1884, BSA; *V of L* t/s, R8 BSA.
20. Undated press cutting A.H. Gipps collection, but early Dec. 1906.
21. File: Founder's Army Career, SAA; Album [43], SAA.
22. Unpub. t/s on Education, p. 12, TC 23 SAA.
23. *V of L* t/s R8 BSA.
24. HG to G. 16 May 1869, FBPA; in 1902 A sold 5 letters from Ruskin to her (1866–83) at Sotheby's: see *The Works of John Ruskin*, ed. E.T.Cooke and A. Wedderburn, 1903–1912 vol. XXXVII, 734; Ruskin to HG 19 Oct. 1869, FBPA.
25. Ruskin to M. Bell 1 Jan. 1863, *The Winnington Letters*, J. Ruskin (London 1969).
26. *English Culture and the Decline of the Industrial Spirit 1850–1980*, M.J. Wiener (London 1982), 37–9.
27. *The Return to Camelot: Chivalry and the English Gentleman*, M. Girouard (London 1981), 136.
28. BP to Peter Keary 17 March 1908, Letter No. 30 in *The Founding of the Boy Scouts through the Letters of Lord Baden-Powell*, ed. P.C. Richards (Massachusetts 1973).
29. HG Diary 27 Mar. 1853, FBPA.
30. Girouard, 222.
31. BP to HG 23 Nov. 1898 and BP's many letters to G, BSA.
32. G's letters to HG, 1866–72, FBPA.
33. *Burden of Empire*, L.H. Gann and P. Duignan (London 1968), 28–9; Girouard, 223; Note by BP on Rhodes and Ruskin, quoting Oxford speech, R8 BSA.
34. HG Diary 20 May 1858, FBPA.
35. 'A Yachting Adventure' in *Adventures and Accidents*, BP (London 1934); Begbie 27; Hillcourt 30.
36. *V of L* t/s, 453, R8 BSA.

Chapter Two
SERVANT OF THE RAJ
1. Heat and Dust (1876–79)

1. G. Noble unpub. t/s Army Reminiscences, 1–7, Dowager Lady Gainford Coll.
2. Hillcourt, 37.
3. *I.M.*, 9.
4. *Piper* 36; *I.M.*, 13.
5. *I.M.*, 17.
6. BP to HG 4 May 1877, BSA.
7. *I.M.*, 174; Indian m/s 00993, R9 BSA.
8. *I.M.*, 229.
9. BP to G 13 Apr. 1877; BP to HG 4 May 1881, BSA.
10. Hillcourt, 38.
11. *V of L* t/s, 456, R8 BSA.
12. Album [43]: draft article for 13th/18th Hussars Journal, SAA.
13. *The Memsahibs*, P. Barr (London 1976); *Social Life in India (1608–1937)*, D. Kincaid (London 1938); *A Young Victorian in India*, H.M. Kisch (London 1957).
14. *The Dilemma*, T.G. Chesney, vol. i, (London 1876), 243–4.
15. BP to HG 17 July 1877, BSA.
16. BP to G 17 Apr. 1877, BSA.
17. Christie and family are often mentioned in BP's letters to HG 1877–1879, BSA.
18. 'The Founder and His Family', unpub. t/s, E.K. Wade, R15 BSA.
19. Quoted in *Baden-Powell*, E.E. Reynolds (London 1942), 24, 29.
20. Begbie, 57; Aitken, 31.
21. BP to family 18 May 1877; BP to HG 7 Apr. 1877; BP to G 27 Apr. 1877, BSA.
22. BP to HG 5 June 1877 and 19 May 1881, BSA.
23. BP to HG 14 Aug. 1877, BSA.
24. BP to family 18 May 1877; BP to G 17 Apr. 1877; BP to HG 19 June, 21 Aug. 1877, BSA; riding masters see *Boot and Saddle*, H. de Montmorency (London 1936).
25. *For Queen and Country*, Byron Farwell (London 1982), 132ff, 151.
26. BP to G 19 Apr., to family 25 June 1877; BP to HG 17 May 1878.
27. *I.M.*, 32.

28. G. Noble autobiography m/s, 26, Lady Gainford Coll.
29. Note to trader in 13th Hussars Scrapbook, NAM 6411–1–15.
30. BP to HG 25 May 1877; BP to family 12 Sept. 1877, BSA.
31. G. Noble t/s, 29.
32. *I.M.*, 93–7.
33. Acting in India m/s, R7 BSA.
34. BP to HG 30 Nov. 1877, BSA; M.A.P. 13 Jan. 1900.
35. *Annals of a Chequered Life*, A.M. Brookfield (London 1930).
36. BP to family 16 June 1878, BSA.
37. Ibid.
38. BP to HG 15 July 1878, BSA.
39. BP to family 22 July 1878, BSA.
40. BP to family 8 Nov. 1880, BSA.
41. *I.M.*, 162.
42. BP to HG 7, 12 Apr., 17 July 1877; 4 Oct. 1878, BSA.
43. BP to HG 24 June 1878, BSA.
44. BP to HG 3 Sept. 1878, BSA.
45. BP to HG 5, 14, 19, 29 Nov. 1878, BSA.

2. Home to Mother (1879–80)

1. BP to HG 29 July 1878, BSA.
2. BP to A 13 Aug. 1878, BSA.
3. Social Scrapbook: dinner guest list 22 July 1879, FBPA.
4. G to HG 10 Oct. 1878, FBPA.
5. G to HG 22 Jan. 1878, FBPA.
6. G's biog. details, FBPA.
7. G. Noble m/s 61–62.
8. *V of L* t/s, 51, BSA.
9. *I.M.*, 167–8.
10. *V of L* t/s, 51ff, BSA.
11. *Court Journal*, Feb. 1880.
12. *V of L*, 36–38.
13. See Ch. Four, Section 7: Spies and Butterflies.
14. BP to G 11 May 1877, BSA.
15. BP to family 18 Dec.; BP to A 4 Sept. 1882, BSA.
16. Letter pasted in 13th Hussars Scrapbook, NAM.
17. Cast list: Lord Chamberlain's Plays B.M. Ad MS 53233. Mrs King played Mathilde (nicknamed Marguerite) de Meridor in *Faustine* at Bristol and at the Olympic in London. Her address was at the head of her letter.

18. BP to HG 20 Mar. 1884, BSA.
19. Quoted Hillcourt, 46–7.
20. BP to G 3 Oct. 1880, BSA.
21. BP to HG 10 Oct. 1880, BSA.
22. Army List Apr. 1883. No record of court martial in PRO or in Royal Artillery Archives (Lacy had been in R.A.).
23. For voyage, see BP to HG 10, 17 Oct., 4, 8 Nov. 1880, BSA.

3. Blood and Friendship (1880–82)

1. BP to HG 2 Dec. 1880, BSA.
2. *I.M.*, 129.
3. G. Noble t/s 34–5.
4. G. Noble t/s 43.
5. BP to family 24 Dec. 1880, BSA.
6. G. Noble t/s Section iii, 15.
7. *I.M.*, 132–3.
8. BP to family 8 Apr. 1881, BSA; *I.M.*, 132.
9. BP to family 8 Jan. 1881, BSA.
10. *I.M.*, 134.
11. BP to family 8 Jan. 1881, BSA; *V of L* t/s, 615, R8 BSA.
12. *I.M.*, 135–8; BP to family 2, 8 Jan., 27 May, 2 June 1881, 21 June 1882; G. Noble t/s Section iii, 3.
13. 'A Test of Friendship', *The Windsor Magazine*, Oct. 1896.
14. G. Noble m/s, 41.
15. BP to family 2 June 1881, BSA.
16. G. Noble m/s 42–3.
17. BP to family 21 June 1881, BSA.
18. A.H.R. Ogilvy to his father 29 Aug. 1881, Sir David Ogilvy Bt Coll.
19. BP to family 14 Aug. 1881, BSA; *I.M.*, 126.
20. BP to family 8 Sept. 1881, BSA.
21. BP to HG 8, 20 Sept. 1881, BSA.
22. BP to HG 20 Sept. 1881, BSA.
23. BP to A 9 Sept. 1881, BSA.
24. BP to family 12 Oct. 1881, BSA.
25. *V of L* t/s R8 BSA.
26. BP to HG 10, 18, 26 Dec. 1881, 12 Feb., 1 Apr. 1882, BSA.
27. BP to HG 4 Dec. 1882, BSA.
28. BP to A 15 Jan. 1882, BSA.
29. BP to family 28 Jan. 1882, BSA.
30. *Sport in War*, BP (London 1900), 134–40.
31. BP to family 29 Apr. 1882, BSA.
32. *Sport in War*, 'The Ordeal of the Spear', 83–118.

33. BP to A 9 July 1884, BSA.
34. BP to family 30 May 1884, BSA.
35. BP to A 21 Aug. 1883, BSA.
36. BP to F 22 May 1882, BSA.
37. BP to family 22 May 1882, BSA.
38. BP to family 1 June 1882, BSA.
39. *I.M.*, 33-4.
40. *Polo*, T.B. Drybrough (London 1898), 193.
41. *I.M.*, 169.
42. *V of L* t/s, 64, R8 BSA; BP notes for E.K. Wade for *Piper of Pax*, Maj. James Wade Coll.
43. BP to HG 7 Apr. 1877, BP to family 25 June 1877, BP to G 2 Oct. 1880, BSA.
44. BP to HG 22 Sept. 1883, BSA.

4. A Scout Must Be. . . (1882–86)

1. BP to G 12 Feb. 1882; BP to HG 16 Sept. 1882, BSA.
2. *Reconnaissance and Scouting*, BP (London 1884), 1.
3. Ibid, 63–38.
4. Ibid; *Cavalry Instruction*, BP (London 1885), 176.
5. *Reconnaissance and Scouting*, 36.

Chapter Three
MEN'S MAN
1. 'My Best Friend in the World'

1. *Eminent Edwardians,* Piers Brendon (London 1979), 217–18; *The Character Factory: Baden-Powell and the Origins of the Boy Scout Movement,* Michael Rosenthal (London 1986), 48.
2. BP to Frances 5 May 1901, FBPA.
3. M/s by BP headed 'Eggs and Germs' on the subject of marriage, reproduction and friendship between men and women and men and men, TC 41 SAA.
4. BP to HG 11 Oct. 1886, BSA.
5. BP Diary of trip from Colchester to Metz 10–30 Jan. 1887, R4 BSA.
6. Notice of Reward . . . Return to Chief Constable of Colchester, 13th Hussars Scrapbook 1878–91, NAM 6411-1-15.
7. Incomplete press cuttings 25 and 26 Feb. 1895, 13th Hussars Scrapbook, 13/18 Hussars Regimental Coll.

8. BP Indian Diary 12–20 Apr. 1898, R5 BSA.
9. Elizabeth Miller's (née McLaren) Visitors' Book for Sauchrie, Maybole, Ayrshire, Mrs Jennifer May Coll.
10. Guest list in scrapbook compiled by Mary Louise Landon (sister of McLaren's wife) still kept at Creaton House, Northants, Dr L. Davies Coll.
11. BP to J.S. Nicholson 27 April 1900, R9 BSA; 5 letters to Commandant Snyman, April 1–10, Weil Papers, vol. iii, Ad Ms 46850 BL.
12. BP to HG 3 Apr. 1900, BSA.
13. BP to McLaren 1 Apr. 1900, Boy Scouts' Assn of Scotland, 18 letters from BP to McLaren 1–14 April by courtesy of Mr David Jefferies.
14. As n.11 above.
15. BP to HG 26 Dec. 1901, BSA.
16. BP to HG 7 June 1902, BSA.
17. BPD Mar. 8–11 1903; Creaton Scrapbook.
18. BP Inspector General of SAC's Papers; Corresp. with London Office 1902–03, NAM 6411-1-2.
19. BP to Dulce Wroughton 4 Nov. 1904, Mrs A. Lunn Coll.
20. BP to HG 2 Nov. 1904, BSA.
21. Hurlingham Club Polo Committee Minutes 23 Mar. 1909; *Polo at Home and Abroad,* T.F. Dale (London March–Aug. 1909).
22. McLaren to BP 12 Mar. 1908, BSA.
23. *The Buteman*, obit., 26 Sept. 1924; death cert. 20 Sept. 1924; BPD 20 Sept. 1924.
24. BPD 1 Dec. 1926.
25. Ibid, 8–9 Dec. 1926.
26. Mafeking Scrapbook, SAA.
27. BP to McLaren 20 Oct. 1902, NAM 6411-1-2.
28. BPD 17 Oct. 1926, 5 Feb. 1936.
29. *Greyfriar*, vol ii, no. 6, fifth in BP's 'My Hats' series.
30. BP to Miss Collier 22 Mar. 1933, SAA.
31. BPD 1–3 Sept. 1938.
32. Maj. A.G. Wade to Mr Place, Scout Assn's Publicity Dept., n.d. but 1950s, SAA.
33. Explanatory note signed 'OBP 1944

when sorting', attached to note about Sergt Mills, TC 95 BP Finances: Army Pension; letters written to BP by close friends, Colonel H.G. Kennard, formerly 5 DG, were returned to him by OBP in 1944, information Mr Noel Brack, Kennard's son-in-law.

34. Information Miss Pamela Dugdale, owner of BP's letters to her mother when she was Miss Ellen Turner.

35. Present Lord Baden-Powell to author 9 Jan. 1983.

36. BPD 11 July 1926.

37. Death certs of Ethel Mary McLaren (1957) and Enid Blackith (1978); Mr Alfred Longmate letter to author, 15 Oct. 1983.

38. Dr Nora O'Leary (physician to Eilean Woodford before her death), interview with author 14 Aug. 1983.

39. Eilean McLaren/Woodford's marriage cert. 1942.

40. Information Christopher Woodford.

41. Creaton Scrapbook, see n. 10 above.

42. Diary of Major H. de Montmorency, who shelled the hospital in error, PRO/WO 108/185.

43. See n. 13 above.

44. See n. 18 above.

45. Miss Faith Ratcliff.

46. W. Anstruther-Thomson, L.R.J.S. Battye, E.L. Braithwaite, C.W. Cotterell-Dormer, T.G. Cuthell, F.S. Dimond, W.A. Grant, G.J.W. Noble, A.H.R. Ogilvy, T.B. Phillips, J.K. Spilling, H.J.J. Stern, J.T. Wigan.

47. V of L, 269.

48. Misc. letters of Redmond Wawand (1st cousin of J.R.P. Gordon) to his father Col. A.R.B. Wawand, Mrs Ann Crothers Coll.

49. BP to McLaren 11 Apr. 1900, Mafeking Scrapbook, SAA.

50. Roundell Palmer Selborne, 1st Earl, 1812–95.

51. The Victorians and Ancient Greece, R. Jenkyns (Oxford 1981), 88.

52. An analysis of this subject has appeared recently in a collection called Manliness and Morality (eds.) J. A. Mangan and J. Walvin (Manchester 1987) (Chapter Six by Jeffrey Richards '"Passing the love of women": manly love and Victorian society').

2. 'The Finest Creature'

1. Rovering to Success, 120.

2. Esp. Rudyard Kipling, M. Seymour-Smith (London 1989); That Singular Person Called Lear, Susan Chitty (London 1988).

3. Sexual Behaviour in the Human Male, A.C. Kinsey, W.B. Pomeroy and C. Martin (Philadelphia and London 1948).

4. BP to HG 20 Mar. 1884, BSA.

5. Lt-Col. Rawlins to Sec. of Scout Assn 2 May 1941; Lady's Realm, May 1900.

6. Miss Caroline Heap (later Mrs A. Slade-Baker) was close to BP in Malta: 'plain but pleasing' quote in letter BP to HG 20 Oct. 1890, BSA; the 'big and handsome' girl was a Miss Carpenter, whom BP met on 22 Nov. 1908 and went out with for several months thereafter (BPD, BSA).

7. BP to HG n.d. except Apr. 1889, BSA.

8. BP Diary, trip to Algeria/Tunis, vol.ii, 21 April–12 May 1893, R4 BSA.

9. BP Diary, trip to Tunisia Apr. 1891, R4 BSA.

10. V of L, 270; BP to HG 28 Oct. 1912, BSA.

11. Clubland Heroes, R. Usborne (London 1953), 101.

12. Information Mrs K. Lessiter (nursemaid Pax Hill 1919–22); Mrs E.K. Wade (BP's secretary 1914–41).

13. Draft t/s, Rovering and Rangering, n.d but 1938, R8 BSA.

14. The Hon. Norah and the Hon. Faith Dawnay mentioned in BP to HG 13 Feb. 1886; 9 letters to Winifred and Lesley Winter, sold at Sotheby's 13 Mar. 1979; Miss Dulce Wroughton born 1887; her father was a neighbour of Maj. and Mrs Landon, Kenneth McLaren's parents-in-law.

15. BP to Dulce Wroughton 12 May 1903, 31 Mar. 1907, 7 Apr. 1908, Mrs A. Lunn Coll.

16. See Chapter Eight, Section 1.
17. BP to HG 6 Apr. 1884, BSA.
18. See *Sexual Deviation*, A. Storr (London 1964); *Madonnas and Magdalens*, E. Trudgill (London 1976).
19. BP to G 21 Feb. 1893, FBPA.
20. 'A Chosen Twelve', unpublished t/s, John Hargrave, being 12 studies of eminent men of whom was BP, Mrs Diana Hargrave Coll.
21. 'Eggs and Germs', BP, m/s, TC 41 SAA.
22. *Rovering to Success*, 122–3.
23. As n. 21 above.
24. *Rovering to Success*, 103.
25. 'A Scout is Clean . . .' m/s n.d, BP, R12 BSA.
26. *Rovering to Success*, 122–3.
27. Draft t/s 'Nature and Naturalness of Movement' 1920, TC 21 SAA.
28. 'A Dirty Age', unpub. m/s approx. 1928, R7 BSA.
29. *Rovering to Success*, 120.
30. BP Diary Blida to London, May 1893, R4 BSA.
31. Draft letter to press n.d., file Pats and Pinpricks 2, SAA.
32. M/s account of dream 16 Jan. 1915, file: Founder's Dreams, SAA.
33. Quoted in *Mars Without Venus*, F.M. Richardson (London 1981).
34. 'The Order of the Bath,' 23 Feb. 1929 unpub. m/s, R11 BSA.
35. As n. 25 above; *Rovering to Success*, 111.
36. *Prostitution in Victorian Society*, J.R. Walkowitz (London 1980) 4; *The Army in 1875*, John Holms (London 1876), 122; *Women of the Regiment*, M. Trustram (London 1984), 26–7, 122f; *For Queen and Country*, B. Farwell (London 1982), 226.
37. 'School of Leadership' unpub. m/s n.d. but *c.* 1920, R15 BSA.
38. *V of L* t/s, 599, R8 BSA.
39. Eric G.S. Walker Diaries (hereafter EWD) 25 Apr. 1910, HC.
40. *Birkenhead and Cheshire Advertiser*, 24 Nov. 1906.
41. 'Life in the Backwoods' t/s, R7 BSA.
42. *V of L* t/s, 106, R9 BSA.
43. Untitled m/s advocating migration to Australia or South Africa, n.d. but *c.* 1925, R7 BSA.
44. 'Short Run in the Himalaya Hills' June–July 1898, R5 BSA.
45. Great War Diary 31 Mar. 1915, Reel 6 BSA.
46. R.G. Goodes to 'Dear Sir' 29 Sept. 1978, TC 111 SAA.
47. *The Scouter* 1934, 262.
48. BPD 15 Nov. 1919.
49. BP to A.H. Tod 18 Nov. 1919, TC 35 SAA.
50. E.E. Harrison (Master of the Charterhouse) to author 18 Sept. 1985; Mrs Freake (former librarian Charterhouse) to author 31 July 1985; phone conversation with Dr Ian Blake (Curator of the Charterhouse Museum) 7 Sept. 1984. On 29 Oct. 1923, Tod recorded handing over to the then librarian, J.L. Stokes, a specific number of named albums as a permanent gift. Since the album listed by Tod as 'figure studies' was missing when I visited the library, I began asking questions, and only then learned what had happened.
51. E.E. Harrison to author 18 Sept. 1985.
52. *Love in Earnest*, T. d'Arch Smith (London 1970), Chap xix.
53. Henry Scott Tuke's registers are in the Victoria & Albert Museum.
54. T. d'Arch Smith's *Love in Earnest* (London 1970) is the best introduction to this neglected branch of art.
55. Jenkyns, 284.
56. *Rovering to Success*, 122.
57. File 'Grey Lists': Mar. 1938 Confidential Memo on homosexuality by BP, SAA.
58. BP to Col. J.M. Maugham (Chief Commr. New South Wales) 2 Feb. 1935, TC 49 SAA.
59. Interviews with author, Chilland, Hampshire, 28 Apr, 15 Dec. 1984.
60. Viz BPD 11 Nov. 1921, 2 Sept. 1922.
61. BPD 9 Jul. 1932; 'Gilwell Park' t/s draft, 1932, TC 26 SAA.
62. R. Patterson sacked in 1922 and H.D. Byrne in 1933.
63. *The Scouter*, Jan. 1923.
64. Draft memo from BP on Public Schools and Scouting, dated 1916 by former archivist but written in 1917, TC 27 SAA.

65. Quoted Gathorne-Hardy, 333.
66. Ibid, 335.
67. *Loom of Youth*, A. Waugh (London 1918 ed.), 59.
68. Ibid, 60–1.
69. Oscar Wilde to Sir M.W. Ridley (Home Sec.) 2 July 1896, *Selected Letters of Oscar Wilde*, ed. Rupert Hart-Davis (Oxford 1979).
70. BPD 28 Mar. 1928.
71. Wheatley Cobb Diaries; *Tuke Reminiscences*, ed. B.D. Price (Royal Cornwall Polytechnic Society 1983); d'Arch Smith, 16, 68, 129, 158 n. 54.
72. BP to Col. J. Hanbury-Williams 14 Sept. 1899, R15 BSA.
73. *V of L*, t/s, 637, R8 BSA.
74. BP to family 17 June, 3 Sept. 1881; playbill 29 Sept. 1882, BSA; South Africa and Malta Album, containing photo of BP in gym display on Malta 1890–3, NAM 6411-66.
75. BP to family 5 Sept. 1877.
76. *I.M.*, 8; BP to family 9 June 1881, BSA.
77. Farwell, 132–3.
78. BP to HG 25 Mar. 1881, BSA.
79. *Six Months in the Ranks*, A Gentleman Private (London 1883), 85.
80. BPD 19 June 1925, 18 Nov. 1931.
81. BP to family 12 Sept. 1877, BSA.
82. *V of L* t/s, 30, R9 BSA.
83. *Social Life in the British Army*, A British Officer (London 1900), 152–3.
84. *The Army in 1875*, J. Holms (London 1876), 108; *The Victorian Army; Women of the Regiment*, M. Trustram (London 1984), 27.
85. *The Other Love*, H. Montgomery Hyde (London 1970), 158–61.
86. See *Scandal*, H. Montgomery Hyde (London 1976); *The Cleveland Street Affair*, C. Simpson, L. Chester, D. Leitch (London 1977); *Father and Son*, J.R. Ackerley (London, Penguin ed. 1984), 176.
87. *Churchill: 1874–1915*, T. Morgan (London 1983), 70–1.
88. Draft for address to public school boys. *c.* 1927–8, R7 BSA.
89. BP to HG 5 Sept. 1883, BSA.
90. 'In Barracks' in *The Greyfriar*, 186, *c.* 1885, file: Founder's Journalism, SAA.
91. Diary of Austrian Manoeuvres 2 Sept. 1891, R4 BSA.
92. 'The Religious Aim' t/s *c.* 1927, R15 BSA.
93. Untitled draft for speech in Sweden, n.d. but 1937, R7 BSA.
94. BP to Rev. T. H. Hennessy 7 May 1910, TC 22 SAA.
95. Edward Bolger to BP 4 Aug. 1922, TC 2 SAA.
96. F.E. Bennet to BP 12 June 1921, TC 1 SAA.
97. Address at Waldorf Astoria 23 Sept. 1910, R15 BSA. Address 'The Educative Possibilities of Scouting', 1911, R12 BSA.
98. *Civilization and Its Discontents*, S. Freud (London 1979, ed., revised J. Strachey), 69.
99. BPD 6 Aug. 1914.
100. File: Founder's Dreams, SAA.
101. *The Scotsman*, 'Baden-Powell: Personal Recollections' by Arthur Poyser 13 Jan. 1941; undated note, PCR.
102. Dream 15 Aug. 1916, SAA.
103. Dream n.d. but listed 18, so *c.* Jan. 1915, SAA.
104. Dream 3 Mar. 1917, SAA.
105. Dream 17 Jan. 1915, SAA.
106. *Goodbye to All That*, 23.
107. Gathorne-Hardy, 194.
108. *Robert Graves: His Life and Work*, M. Seymour-Smith (London 1982), 22.
109. Information re R.H. Musk: Major J.A.F. Barthorp (of Bentley) to Archivist NAM 1 Jan. 1979; telephone calls and correspondence with Mr Archie Knight (Bentley); Mr E. Palmer and Mrs J. Cotterell, relations; Musk not employed by BP attested by Mrs E.K. Wade and Mrs Annie Scofield; date of death of Musk and various press cuttings from solicitor Stevens & Bolton.
110. *Rovering to Success*, 120.
111. Viz BP Diary Italy, Albania, Greece and Sardinia 30 Dec. 1893, R4 BSA; BPD 14 Oct. 1921, 17 Oct., 16 and 27 Nov. 1926, 16 May 1931.
112. Diary Bosnia and Herzegovina, 29 July 1892, R4 BSA.
113. Diary Italy, Albania, Greece and Sardinia 30 Dec. 1893, 5 and 7 Jan. 1894, R4 BSA.

114. *V of L*, t/s, 436, R8 BSA.
115. BP to 'Dear Sir' 10 July 1902, TC 95 SAA.
116. BP to G 20 Jan. 1886, FBPA; *Quetta Gazette* 12 Aug. 1881; cast list *Timothy to the Rescue*, 29 Sept. 1882; BP to G 5 Feb. 1886, BSA.
117. Diary trip to Tunisia 27 Dec. 1890, R4 BSA.
118. Diary trips to Tunisia Dec. 1890, Nov. 1891, Apr. to May 1893, R4 BSA; *V of L*, 70–72.
119. *Sport in War*, BP (London 1900), Chapter on Hadj Ano was originally pub. in the *Badminton Mag.*
120. Diary of a visit to the Franco-Prussian battlefields, 16 January 1887, R4 BSA. BPD 5 Feb. 1929; *Times* House Journal, July 1962; letter to Author from Dep. Archivist, *The Times*.
121. BP to P. Keary 6 and 17 Mar. 1908, Richards ed.; Keary to BP n.d. except Sat, R11 BSA.
122. Original t/s of *Scouting for Boys*, 26 Dec. 1907–24 Feb. 1908, SAA.
123. Ibid.
124. Lecture on 'Continence' by Dr Schofield, Manchester Scoutmasters' Conference 1911, R12 BSA.
125. *Rover Scouting*, F.W.W. Griffin (London 1930), 127; *The Quest of a Boy; A Study of the Psychology of Character Training*, Griffin (London 1927); *Little Essays of Love and Virtue*, H. Havelock Ellis (London 1922), 52, 58.
126. *Rovering to Success*, 106.
127. BP to family 5 May 1881, BSA.
128. BP to Keary 17 Mar. 1908, Richards ed.

Chapter Four
IN THE BALANCE
1. The Ambitious Adjutant (1882–84)

1. *I.M.*, 24–6; obit. *Daily Telegraph* 27 Nov. 1911.
2. BP to HG (insert for F) 13 July 1883; BP to HG 22 Sept. 1883, BSA.
3. BP to HG 22 Sept. 1883, BSA.
4. BP to HG 15 Aug. 1883, BSA.
5. BP to G 25 Dec. 1883, BSA.
6. *Morning Post*, 16 Jan. 1884.
7. BP to HG early Feb. 1884, 01011 BSA.
8. Lady Downe to Lady Sefton 5 Feb. 1884, Downe Coll.
9. BP to HG 16 and 20 Mar. 1884, BSA.
10. BP to G 13 May 1884, BSA.
11. BP to HG 30 Aug., BSA.
12. 'The Ordeal of the Spear' and 'The Polo Cap' appear to be the only survivors from this period.
13. M/s 'Chota Hazri', R7 BSA.
14. BP to G 25 Dec. 1883, BSA.
15. BP to HG 21 June 1882; BP to A 30 Aug. 1883, BSA.
16. BP to G 28 Apr. 1884, BSA.
17. BP to HG 18 Oct. 1883, BSA.
18. BP to family 4 Feb 1883, BSA.
19. *V of L* t/s, R8 BSA.
20. As n. 7 above.
21. BP to HG 8 Mar. 1884, BSA.
22. BP to HG 2 Mar. 1881, BSA.
23. BP to family 4 May 1881, BP to HG 15 Aug. 1883, BP to Baden 13 May 1885, BP to HG 6 July 1885, BSA.
24. BP to HG 19 Aug. 1882, 11 May 1884, BSA.
25. BP to HG 19 May and 2 June 1881, BSA.
26. Quoted in *Boys Will Be Boys*, E.S. Turner (London 1948), 95.
27. BP to HG 13 July 1883, BSA.

2. Marking Time (1885)

1. 3 Aug. 1881, Convention of Pretoria.
2. BP to HG 1 Apr. 1882, 8 Mar. 1884, 28 Apr. 1885, BSA.
3. G. Noble m/s, 57–60.
4. BP to Baden 13 May 1885, BSA.
5. G's letters to HG 1885; G to HG 12 Mar. 1885, FBPA.
6. G to HG 28 Apr. 1885, FBPA.
7. Joseph Chamberlain to Sir Edward Russell 5 Nov. 1885, Lady Rennell of Rodd Coll.
8. G to HG 2 July 1885, FBPA.
9. Ibid.
10. BP to HG 8 Mar. and 28 Apr. 1885, BSA.
11. BP to HG 11 May and 6 July 1885, BSA.
12. 'South Africa Re-Visited' m/s, R8 BSA.

13. BP to G 6 Apr. 1885; BP to A 14 Apr. 1885, BSA.
14. Undated notes prepared for Mrs Wade by BP while she was writing his biography *The Piper of Pax*, Major James Wade Coll.
15. *Rovering to Success*, 56; *V of L*, 96.
16. *V of L*, 96.
17. Shooting trip near Inhambane 9 Aug. 1885, R4 BSA.
18. Ibid 10 July–7 Sept. 1885; BP to HG 22 Nov. 1885, BSA.
19. *Fifty Years of Scouting in Pinetown*, M. Macartan (Durban 1963), 2.

3 'A Fresh Start' (1885–87)

1. HG to F 2 Feb. 1887, JM.
2. BP to G 5 Nov. 1885; BP to A 7 Nov. 1885, BSA.
3. BP to HG 6 Nov. 1885, BSA.
4. G to HG 8 Nov. 1885, FBPA.
5. G to HG n.d except Oct. 1885, FBPA; HG to F 3 Feb. 1887, JM.
6. G to HG 15–22 Nov. 1885; G to HG 27 June 1886, FBPA.
7. G to HG 3 Dec. 1885, FBPA.
8. HG to F 3 Feb. 1887, JM.
9. Note dated 20 April 1895, HG purchases 'Venice at Sunset', JM.
10. BP to HG 2 Jan. 1886, BSA.
11. BP to G 12 Jan. 1886, BSA.
12. *V of L* t/s, 467, R8 BSA.
13. BP to HG 13 Feb. 1887, BSA.
14. BP to HG 5 Sept. 1883, BSA.
15. BP to HG 30 Dec. 1885, BSA.
16. BP to G 3 Feb. 1886, BSA.
17. e.g. *The Case of the Dixon Torpedo* from *Martin Hewitt Investigator*, Arthur Morrison (London 1894).
18. Hillcourt, 73.
19. BP to G 17 Aug. 1886, BSA.
20. BP to G 12 Aug. 1886, BSA.
21. *My Adventures as a Spy*, BP (London 1915), 92; *V of L* t/s, 214, R8 BSA.
22. BP to G 28 Aug. 1886, BSA.
23. *V of L*, 123–4.
24. BP to G 3 Nov. 1886, BSA.
25. BP to HG 6 Nov. 1886, BSA.
26. BP to G 4 Sept. 1886, BSA.
27. BP to G 3 Nov. 1886, BSA.
28. HG to Frank n.d. but late Jan. 1887; HG to F 2 Feb. 1887, JM.
29. BP to HG 13 and 17 Feb. 1886, BSA.

30. *V of L* t/s, 461, R8 BSA; Hillcourt, 77.
31. BP to G 31 Oct. 1887, BSA.
32. Hillcourt 77–8.
33. *V of L* t/s, 463–4, R8 BSA.
34. BP to G 1 Sept. 1887, BSA.
35. HG Diary 1874, various refs.
36. BP to HG 10 July 1889, BSA; *V of L* t/s, 466, R8 BSA.
37. G to HG 18 Jan. 1888, FBPA.
38. Lord Wolseley to G 15 Feb. 1888, FBPA.

4. With Uncle Henry and the Zulus (1888)

1. Message to G in BP to HG 15 Feb. 1888, BSA.
2. BP to HG 3 Dec. 1888, BSA.
3. BP to HG 25 Mar. 1888, BSA.
4. *Born in a Zoo*, t/s, 40–50.
5. BP to HG n.d. but late Apr. 1889, BSA.
6. *Cape Punch*, cuttings in South African Scrapbook NAM.
7. BP to G 19 Oct. 1888, BSA; *V of L*, 145.
8. G to HG 4 Feb. 1885, FBPA.
9. G to HG 25 Apr. 1885, FBPA.
10. BP to HG 5 Feb. 1888, BSA.
11. See entries for Dinuzulu and Cetewayo in *Dictionary of South African Biography*; *The Cambridge History of the British Empire*, vol. viii (Cambridge 1936); BP Zululand Scrapbook, South African Library; BP Zululand Diary, June 1888, 00042 R4 BSA.
12. *V of L* t/s, 477, R8 BSA; BP Zululand Diary 2 Sept. 1888, John Dunn: *Dictionary of South African Biography*.
13. *V of L* t/s, 478, R8 BSA.
14. *V of L* t/s, 'South African Travel', no p.n., R9 BSA.
15. BP Zululand Diary 7–12 July 1888, R4 BSA.
16. *Piper*, 68.
17. R.F. Thurman (Camp Chief, Gilwell) to 'My Dear Bob' 19 Oct 1959, Gilwell box file, SAA.
18. BP to G 22 July 1888, BSA.
19. BP to G 17 June and 22 July 1888, BSA; Sir Arthur Havelock to Lord Knutsford 27 Oct. 1888, PRO CO 417/194.

20. BP to G 23 June 1888, BSA.
21. *Army and Navy Gazette*, 15 Sept. 1888.
22. Lord Wolseley to Smyth n.d. except July 1888, Album [43], m/s fragments, SAA; BP Zululand Diary 29 Aug. 1888, R4 BSA.
23. BP to G 28 July 1888, BSA.
24. Lord Wolseley to P.U.S. at W.O. 9 Oct. 1888, WO 32/7838, CO 417/194.
25. *V of L* t/s, 489–92, R8 BSA.
26. Ibid 492.
27. BP Zululand Diary 11 Aug. 1888, R4 BSA.
28. Havelock to Smyth 15 Aug. 1888, PRO CO 427/2 343.
29. Notes written by BP for Mrs Wade for *Piper of Pax*..
30. Havelock to Rosmead (HC Cape) 22 Aug. 1888 CO 427/2.
31. BP to G 6 Sept. 1888, BSA.
32. G to Harriette Colenso 20 Aug. 1885, Colenso Papers, Natal Archives.
33. Frances Colenso to Harriette 13 Sept. 1888, Natal Archives.
34. *Times of Natal*, 28 Nov. 1888.
35. As n. 29 above.
36. BP to G 3 Aug. 1888, BSA.
37. BP Zululand Diary 10 Sept. 1888, BSA.
38. BP to HG 3 Oct. 1889, BSA.

5. The Lure of the Dark Interior (1888–90)

1. BP to HG 26 Dec. 1888 and 27 Feb. 1889, BSA.
2. M/s in Major J. Wade Coll.
3. BP to HG late Apr. 1889, BSA.
4. *Scouting for Boys* (London 1909 2nd ed.), 179.
5. BP letters to HG and G Apr. to July 1889, BSA.
6. BP to G 12 Feb. 1889, BSA.
7. BP to HG 7 May 1889, BSA.
8. BP to W 17 Feb. 1889, BP to HG 30 Apr. 1889, BSA.
9. Smyth to HG 21 Apr. 1889, BSA.
10. BP to G 23 May 1890, BSA.
11. BP to HG 3 Oct. 1889, BSA; Hillcourt, 86.
12. *Cambridge History of the British Empire*, vol. viii, 526f; BP Swaziland Album; *Pall Mall Budget*, 'A Chat

with General Joubert', 28 Aug. 1890.
13. Details of report for de Winton in BP to G 19 Oct. 1889, BSA.
14. *V of L* t/s, no p.n., R8 BSA.
15. Ibid.
16. Ibid.
17. Ibid.
18. *Sport in War*, 46.
19. Smyth to BP 17 Dec. 1889, BSA.
20. BP to G 5 Jan. 1890, BSA.
21. Sir F. de Winton to G 12 May 1890, BSA.
22. Lord Wolseley to BP 18 Sept. 1889; BP to HG 7 Dec. 1889, BSA.

6. The Prisoner of Malta (1890–93)

1. F.W. Foley to BP (re *V of L*) 20 Apr. 1933, TC 3 SAA.
2. A. Constance Gifford to BP 26 Mar. 1934, TC 42 SAA.
3. *St Paul Pioneer* interview with BP, Mar. 1912, R6 BSA.
4. Begbie, 185.
5. Aitken, 49.
6. *Piper*, 80; *St Paul Pioneer*.
7. Reynolds, 43.
8. As n. 1 above.
9. 'Pirates in Malta' m/s, TC 21 SAA.
10. BP to HG 7 June 1891, BSA.
11. BP to HG 24 Mar. 1890, BSA.
12. BP to HG 21 Aug. 1890, BSA.
13. Supp. to *The King*, 26 May 1900.
14. Information from Mrs Pauline Bridger-Turner, granddaughter.
15. BP to HG 20 Oct. 1890, BSA.
16. Malta Diary t/s, SAA.
17. *Malta Times*, 13 Feb. 1891, report of Lady Dingli's Country Dance.
18. Diary: Austrian manoeuvres and return to Malta 11 Sept. 1891, 00050 R4 BSA.
19. BP to G 21 Feb. 1893, FBPA.
20. BP to HG 3 Mar. 1893, BSA.
21. Aitken, 51.
22. BP to Ellen Turner 27 Dec. 1902, Miss Pamela Dugdale Coll.
23. BP to HG 9 June 1890, BSA.
24. Malta Diary 12 Jan. 1891, SAA.
25. BP to G 25 May 1892, BSA.
26. BP to HG 12 Oct. 1890, BSA.
27. BP to G 15 June 1891, BSA.
28. BP to HG 30 Nov. 1892; BP to family 28 Jan. 1893, BSA.

7. Spies and Butterflies (1890–93)

1. *My Adventures as a Spy*, 95-6.
2. Ibid.
3. BP to HG 24 Mar. 1893, BSA; see notes 4 and 5 below.
4. Diary: Algeria and Tunisia, vol.ii, 24 Apr. 1893, R4 BSA.
5. Ibid 28 Apr.
6. Ibid 7–11 May.
7. *My Adventures as a Spy*, 52–3.
8. *The Spy's Bedside Book*, ed. Graham Greene (London 1957), 12.
9. Ibid, 220.
10. *My Adventures as a Spy*, 57.
11. Diary: trip through Bosnia and Herzegovina, vol. i, 6–11 Aug. 1892, R4 BSA.
12. Diary: Algeria and Tunisia, 12–13, 25 Apr. 1893, R4 BSA.
13. *My Adventures as a Spy*, 72; *The Spy's Bedside Book*, 33.
14. Diary: Austria, Switzerland and Italy, vol. ii, 30 Aug. 1892, R4 BSA.
15. BP Staff Diary, Territorial Army, 1 May 1909, TC 209 SAA.
16. Malta Diary, 2 Feb. 1891.
17. *The Scaremongers*, A.J.A. Morris (London 1984), 156–7.
18. Album 'Army 2', May 1908, SAA.
19. BP to Lord Grey n.d. 1916, University of Durham.
20. BP to P.W. Everett, 15 Jan. 1924, Everett Papers, SAA.
21. Viz short stories like 'The Ordeal of the Spear' and 'A Test of Friendship'.

8. Lord Wolseley's Man at Last (1893–95)

1. BP to G 19 Mar. 1891, 20 June 1892, 13 Mar. 1894; BP to HG 20 Oct. 1892, BSA.
2. BP to HG 11 Mar. 1893; BP to G 20 June 1893, BSA.
3. G to HG 3 Sept. 1892; G to HG 18 Nov. 1891, FBPA.
4. BP to HG 16 Mar. 1895, BSA; G to HG 23 Nov. 1893; Frances to HG 17 Jan. 1894, FBPA.
5. BP to HG 2 and 3 Oct. 1893; BP to A 22 Oct, 1893, BSA.
6. BP to G 20 Jun. 1893, BSA.
7. BP to G 13 Mar. 1894, BSA.
8. G to HG 9, 12, 13 Apr. 1893, FBPA.
9. BP to HG 18 Sept. 1895, BSA.

10. Letters to author from Mr Christie-Miller 15, 22 July 1985.
11. Reynolds, 46.
12. Diary: Italy and Albania, vol. i, 27 Dec. 1893 to 9 Feb. 1894, R4 BSA.
13. G. Noble m/s, 73.
14. Reynolds, 47.
15. *The Downfall of Prempeh*, BP (London 1896), 36.
16. BP to HG 14 Nov. 1895, BSA.
17. BP to HG 20 Nov. and 11 Dec. 1895, BSA.
18. *V of L*, 161.
19. BP to G 15 Aug. 1893, BSA.

Chapter Five
THE COMING MAN
1. 'A Grand Thing for Me': The Ashanti Campaign (1895–96)

1. *Britain and Ashanti 1874–1896*, W.E.F. Ward, in *Transactions of the Historical Society of Ghana*, vol. xv (ii), 133.
2. Ibid, 135.
3. Ibid, 155.
4. *Ashanti under the Prempehs*, W. Tordoff (London 1965), 59–60.
5. Ward, 157.
6. *Downfall of Prempeh*, 18.
7. Farwell, 116.
8. Ibid, 117.
9. Ashanti Diary/Scrapbook 22 Nov. 1895, facsimile in NAM.
10. *V of L* t/s, 514, R8 BSA.
11. *Piper*, 94.
12. *V of L*, 162.
13. *V of L* t/s, 517, R8 BSA.
14. *Downfall of Prempeh*, 56–7.
15. *Livingstone*, Tim Jeal (London 1973), 123, 149 etc.
16. Farwell, 109.
17. BP to Lord Wolseley 18 Jan. 1896, Wolseley Papers, Central Library, Hove.
18. 'High Strategy: A Moral of the West Coast', t/s, R7 BSA.
19. *Downfall of Prempeh*, 78.
20. General Orders in Ashanti Diary/Scrapbook, NAM.
21. Ashanti Scrapbook (drawings and press cuttings), 6501–18–2 NAM.
22. Viz Stanley on the Emin Pasha Relief Expedition.

23. As n. 18.
24. Ibid.
25. *V of L*, 163.
26. *On the South African Frontier*, W.H. Brown (London 1899); *The Flame Trees of Thika*, Elspeth Huxley (London 1959).
27. *Downfall of Prempeh*, 71.
28. Ibid. 13.
29. Hillcourt, 110.
30. BP to Wolseley 18 Jan. 1896, Hove.
31. *Downfall of Prempeh*, 94–6.
32. *Edwardian Portraits*, W.S. Adams (London 1957), 111.
33. J.P.R. Gordon to BP 11 Jan. 1896, Ashanti Diary/Scrapbook, NAM facsimile.
34. *Downfall of Prempeh*, 108.
35. Ibid., illustration, based on an original by BP, facing p. 120.
36. Tordoff, 69.
37. Ibid, 70.
38. *Asante in the Nineteenth Century*, I. Wilks (London 1975), 661.
39. *Downfall of Prempeh*, 25–28; I. Wilks 592–8.
40. BP to F 18 Jan. 1896, BSA.
41. Ibid.
42. R.S. Curtis Album, and original drawing by BP, W. Beckwith Coll.
43. BP to Wolseley 18 Jan. 1896, Hove.
44. BP to HG 21 Dec. 1895, BSA.
45. BP to Constance Smyth 3 Apr. 1896, BSA.
46. Social Scrapbook, guest list, FBPA.
47. *V of L*, 166.

2. Mistake in Matabeleland (1896–97)

1. G to HG 16 Nov. 1895, FBPA.
2. *V of L* t/s, 548–9, R8 BSA; *Piper*, 96.
3. *Revolt in Southern Rhodesia 1896–7*, T. Ranger (London 1967), 171; Sec. of British South Africa Co. to Chamberlain 20 Apr. 1896, CO 417/197.
4. Ibid, CO 417/197.
5. Sir George Baden-Powell's 'Hall Book': Lord Wolseley's name appears on 14 Apr. 1896.
6. *Downfall of Prempeh*, 190 (G's afterword 'Policy and Wealth in Ashanti' 181–99).
7. *How We Won Rhodesia*, A.G. Leonard (London 1896).
8. Ranger, 103.
9. *The Matabele Campaign*, BP (London 1897), 15.
10. *With Plumer in Matabeland*, F.W. Sykes (London 1897), 42f.
11. Ranger, 129.
12. Sykes, 27–8.
13. *Trooper Peter Halket of Mashonaland*, O. Schreiner (London 1897), 77.
14. BP Matabele Album, National Archives of Zimbabwe [NAZ].
15. *Matabele Campaign*, 8.
16. BP Report to Sir Frederick Carrington, NAZ.
17. *The Campaign in Rhodesia*, BP (Dublin 1897), 8–9.
18. BP Diary 27 May and 3 June 1896, R4 BSA.
19. *Matabele Campaign*, 22–3.
20. BP Report to Carrington, NAZ.
21. *Matabele Campaign*, 23.
22. Ibid, 24.
23. A.W. Jarvis to his sister 12 July 1896, Durham University.
24. *Matabele Campaign*, 69; Sykes, 268.
25. Ranger, 237.
26. *Matabele Campaign*, 67.
27. BP Diary 5 Aug. 1896, R4 BSA.
28. Ranger, 239.
29. BP to HG 23 Aug. 1896, BSA; *Matabele Campaign*, 73; *The White Whirlwind*, T.V. Bulpin (London 1961), 323f.
30. BP to HG 23 Aug. 1896, BSA.
31. BP Diary 22 Aug. 1896, R4 BSA.
32. *Cecil Rhodes*, J.E. Flint (London 1976), 206.
33. *Dreams of Adventure, Deeds of Empire*, Martin Green (London 1980), 389.
34. BP Diary 5 Jan. 1897, R4 BSA.
35. Ranger, 260–1.
36. *The Campaign in Rhodesia*, 10; *Matabele Campaign*, 15; Ranger 260.
37. *Matabele Campaign*, 30.
38. Ibid, 84.
39. Ibid, 85.
40. Evidence to Court of Inquiry: affidavit sworn by Major H.M. Ridley, NAZ.
41. BP to Carrington 13 Sept. 1896, NAZ.
42. BP Matabele Album, 87, NAZ.
43. BP Diary 12 Sept. 1896, R4 BSA.
44. Ibid 13 Sept.

45. *V of L* t/s, 58 R8 BSA.
46. Rosmead to Carrington 19 Sept 1896, teleg. 871, BP Matabele Album, NAZ.
47. Rosmead to Chamberlain 19 Sept. 1896, PRO CO 879/47; BP's evidence to Gwelo Inquiry, NAZ.
48. Rosmead to Chamberlain 22 Dec. 1896, PRO CO 879/47.
49. *7th Hussars Regimental History*, 134–5.
50. Carrington to BP 28 Sept. 1896; NAZ.
51. BP to HG 1 Nov. 1896, FBPA.
52. BP to G, 14 June 1896; BP to C.B. Vyvyan 29 June 1896; BP Matabele Album, NAZ.
53. BP Diary 13 Nov. 1896, R4 BSA.
54. *Truth*, 22 Oct. 1896.
55. BP Diary: Tunisia and Algeria 7 Apr. 1891, vol. i, R4 BSA.
56. Ibid, vol. iii, 17–19 May 1893.
57. *Greyfriar*, no. vii, 'My Hats Series: The Algerian Hat', written 1893, 152–3.
58. See PRO CO 879/47 and CO 417/172.
59. BP Diary 24 July 1896, R4 BSA.
60. *Matabele Campaign*, 32, 102, 107.
61. *The Campaign in Rhodesia*, 18.
62. Ibid, 19.
63. BP to HG n.d., but after 14 June 1896, BSA.
64. G. Noble t/s, final unpaginated section.
65. *Matabele Campaign*, 79.
66. BP Diary 11 Sept. 1896, R4 BSA.
67. *Matabele Campaign*, 83.
68. Green, 254.
69. *V of L*, t/s, 30, R9 BSA.
70. *Matabele Campaign*, 41.
71. Ibid, 26.
72. *Matabele Campaign*, 83.
73. Ibid, 55–6.
74. *V of L* t/s, Travel Section, unpaginated, R9 BSA.
75. *Aids to Scouting for N.C.O.s and Men*, BP (London 1899), 124.
76. *Matabele Campaign*, 133–5.
77. *With Mounted Infantry and the Mashonaland Field Force*, E.A.H. Alderson (London 1898).
78. Interview in M.A.P. (Mainly about People), 13 Jan. 1900.
79. Ibid.
80. Reynolds, 62.
81. Aitken, 75.

3. Indian Interlude (1897–99)

1. BP to HG 7 Feb. 1897, BSA.
2. *V of L* t/s, unpaginated, R7 BSA.
3. Wolseley to G n.d. except Sat, but mid-1897, BP Matabele Album, 116, NAZ.
4. Album: Observations in Novaya Zemlya; Social Album, FBPA.
5. Lord Montagu to G 9 May 1897, FBPA.
6. *V of L*, 182.
7. BP to HG 7 Mar. 1897, BSA; M. Dillon to DP 16 Dec. 1896 and 24 Mar. 1897, Matabele Album, NAZ.
8. Begbie, 173.
9. Will of Edward Sargeaunt, 1929, Somerset House; draft for obit. of Sargeaunt by BP, BSA.
10. *V of L*, t/s, 593, R8 BSA.
11. *The Scouter*, Dec. 1951, Lt-Col. G.A. Swinton-Home.
12. BP Diary 9 Nov. 1896, R4 BSA.
13. Reynolds, 72.
14. *V of L* t/s, 599, R8 BSA.
15. *V of L*, 82.
16. BP to HG 4 Apr. 1899, BSA.
17. BP to HG 28 Feb. 1897, BSA.
18. BP to HG 5 Apr. 1898, BSA.
19. BP to HG 8 Apr. 1897, BSA.
20. BP Kashmir Diary, vol. iii, 16 June 1898, R5 BSA.
21. *Simla Times*, 1 Sept. 1897.
22. Hillcourt, 151.
23. BP's letters to Ellen Turner are owned by her daughter Miss Pamela Dugdale.
24. Wun Hi & Co. to Ellen Turner 15 Dec. 1897, Dugdale Coll.
25. BP to HG 7 Sept. 1897; photograph in Dugdale Coll: Geisha Picnic at Bendochy, Mashobra, 11 Sept. 1897.
26. BP to Ellen Turner, 6 Sept. 1903, Dugdale Coll.
27. HG to BP 28 Dec. 1897, BSA; G to HG 16 Nov. 1895, FBPA.
28. *V of L*, 41–2.
29. *I.M.*, 75.
30. Reminiscences, Dugdale Coll.

31. BP to HG 27 Nov. 1897, BSA.
32. BP to HG 11 Dec. 1897, BSA.
33. Hillcourt, 147.
34. *V of L,* 194–5.
35. *I.M.,* 211.
36. BP to HG 2 Aug. 1897, BSA.
37. Ibid.
38. *V of L* t/s, 259–60, R8 BSA.
39. Undated R8 BSA; Hillcourt dates it 16 Jan. 1899.
40. As n. 11 above.
41. *Christian Science Monitor,* 3 May 1941, 'B-P as I Knew Him' by H.G. Kennard; Ellen Turner's reminiscences, Dugdale Coll.
42. BP to G 8 Mar. 1885, BSA.
43. BP to HG 19 Sept. 1884; BP to G 6 Jan. 1885, BSA.
44. Secret Memo from Col. W. Everett AAG prepared for DMI and Lord Lansdowne, 1 July 1899, PRO WO 32/7852.
45. BP Kashmir Diary: A Short Run in the Himalayan Hills, 19 to 21 June 1898, R5 BSA.
46. *I.M.,* 288.
47. Ibid, 289.
48. As n. 45, 21 June 1898; *I.M.,* 175.
49. *Rovering to Success,* 177–8.
50. *Matabele Campaign,* 84.
51. BP to Ellen Turner 30 May 1897, Dugdale Coll.
52. BP Kashmir Diary, vol. iii, 25 Aug. to 6 Sept. 1897, R5 BSA.
53. Hillcourt, 153.
54. Published as *Aids to Scouting for N.C.O.s and Men* (London 1899).
55. BP to HG 23 Nov. 1898, BSA.
56. HG to BP 25 Nov. 1898; Frances to HG 7 May 1904; H. Wilson to Frances 9 May and 21 July 1904, FBPA.
57. BP to HG 20 Apr. 1899, BSA.
58. BP to A 22 Jan. 1899, BSA.

Chapter Six
THE HERO
1. A Visit to the War Office (May to July 1899)

1. HG to Frances 3 Apr. 1899, FBPA.
2. A to HG 6 and 24 Mar. 1899, JM; HG to Frances 3 Feb. 1900, FBPA.
3. A to W 2 Sept. 1898, FBPA.
4. HG to A 3 Sept. 1898, JM.
5. A to HG 24 Aug. 1898, JM.
6. BP Diary: India and England, May and June 1899, R5 BSA.
7. *V of L,* 198–9.
8. Ibid, 199.
9. *Southern Echo,* 18 Sept. 1912.
10. Information Miss Mary Mackenzie, Fawley Green, Henley.

2. Mission Impossible (July to Sept. 1899)

1. *The Milner Papers; Vol 1; South Africa 1897–1899,* C. Headlam ed. (London 1931), 508.
2. Secret Memo prepared by Col. W. Everett for DMI and the Sec. of State for War, 1 July 1899, PRO WO 32/7852.
3. Ibid.
4. Ibid.
5. *The Boer War,* T. Pakenham (London 1979), 398–99.
6. Rosenthal, 30.
7. *Eminent Edwardians,* Piers Brendon (London 1980), 226.
8. *History of the War in South Africa,* vol. i, Sir F. Maurice ed. (London 1906) 'Written by direction of His Majesty's Government', 455–6 (hereafter Government History/GH).
9. Col. J. Hanbury-Williams to Col. E.A. Altham 31 May 1895, CO 417/275.
10. BP's 'General Orders: Mafeking' Album, Cable 84, 20 July 1899, WO 079/8697, NAM; RCWSA, 19 Mar. 1903, 452, No. 19822.
11. Gen. Sir E. Wood's Orders to BP 7 July 1899, WO 32/7852.
12. *V of L* t/s, 624, R8 BSA.
13. *The Later Cecils,* K. Rose (London 1975), 189; Hanbury-Tracy: *Burke's Peerage* 1899.
14. *V of L* t/s, 628, R8 BSA. The best and most detailed information about BP's officers is in Major A.J. Godley's letters to his wife and hers to him before and during the Siege, t/s version of original lent by Dr B. Willan.
15. Hillcourt, 157.
16. BP to Arnold (solicitors) 21 Dec. 1900, Private Coll.
17. 'Standing Orders' in Mafeking Scrapbook, vol. i, SAA.

18. *V of L* t/s, section called 'Initial Difficulties', 525–6, R8 BSA; War Office Memo signed A. Graham to Colonial Office, 7 July 1899, CO 417/295.

19. Milner to Hon A. Lawley 10 July 1899, dep. 219 f49, Milner Papers, Bodleian Library, Oxford.

20. W. Hely-Hutchinson to Milner 8 July 1899, dep. 211, MP.

21. BP Indian and Mafeking Diary 26 July 1899, R5 BSA.

22. For Milner's views, see his correspondence with Hely-Hutchinson, Lord Selbourne and Philip Gell, June–Oct. 1899, MP.

23. Mrs Godley to A.J. Godley 10 Aug. 1899, GI

24. BP to Lord Wolseley 8 June 1901, Wolseley Papers, Hove.

25. RCWSA, 19 Mar. 1903, 423.

26. Ben Weil in conversation with Vere Stent, Apr. 1900, Weil Papers, Ad Ms 46850 BL.

27. *Life of an Irish Soldier*, A. Godley (London 1939), 71–2.

28. *Mafeking; A Victorian Legend*, B. Gardner (London 1966), 40; *My Picture Gallery 1886–1901*, V. Milner (formerly Lady Edward Cecil) (London 1951), 125–6.

29. Mrs Godley to Godley 11 Apr. 1900, GL.

30. A.W. Jarvis to Lord Grey 29 July 1899, Univ. of Durham.

31. BP Staff Diary (SD) 1 Aug. 1899, R5 BSA.

32. Ibid 2 Aug. 1899.

33. Diary of Vet. Captain J. Moore (1899–1900), 11 Aug. 1899, Mrs Carp-Moore Coll.

34. RCWSA, p. 426, ref. 19843.

35. Hanbury Williams to BP 25 Aug. 1899, R.H. Nicholson Coll.

36. Ibid.

37. Godley to Mrs Godley 5 Sept. 1899, GL.

38. Godley to Mrs Godley 8 Mar. 1900, GL.

39. *I.M.*, 191.

40. Moore Diary, 24 Oct. 1899.

41. Gardner, 122.

42. As n. 11.

43. SD 17 and 29 Aug. 1899; Indian and Mafeking Diary 9 and 20 Aug., 11 Sept.; *Edward Ross, Diary of the Siege of Mafeking* [hereafter Ross], B. Willan ed. (Cape Town 1981), 241.

44. SD 19 Aug. 1899.

45. SD 20 Aug., 10 Sept., 3 and 10 Oct. 1899.

46. RCWSA, 427–8, ref. 19880–2; R.N.R. Reade to Col. F.J. Davies 22 and 23 Aug. 1899, RHN; Col. C.B. Vyvyan's Intelligence Diary 8, 12, 15 and 16 Sept. 1899, Vyvyan Papers, Trelowarren, Mawgan, Cornwall.

47. SD 24 Sept. 1899.

48. SD 15, 18 and 21 Aug. 1899.

49. SD 27 Aug.

50. SD 29 Aug.

51. 'The Siege of Mafeking' t/s by Captain the Hon. Algernon Hanbury-Tracy, RHN.

52. SD 2 Sept. 1899.

53. SD 9 Sept. 1899.

54. SD 10 Sept. 1899.

55. Gardner, 42; Rosenthal, 34–5, quoting Gardner.

56. Viz Hillcourt, 161; Rosenthal, 34.

57. *V of L*, 202.

58. Quoted in SD 12 Sept. 1899.

59. BP to Hanbury-Williams 15 Sept. 1899, R5 BSA.

60. SD 20 Sept. 1899.

61. SD 23 Sept. 1899.

62. SD 26 Sept. 1899; Reade to Hanbury-Tracy 16 Sept. 1899, RHN.

63. SD 12 and 19 Sept. 1899.

64. B-P quoted in *Cape Argus* 13 Sept. 1900.

65. SD 1 Oct. 1899.

66. Maj. H. de Montmorency Diary, PRO WO 108/185.

67. Rosenthal, 34–5.

68. As n. 11; Col. Everett to Lansdowne, 1 July 1899, PRO WO 32/7852.

69. RCWSA, 423.

70. Rosenthal, 35.

71. BP to Hanbury-Williams 15 Sept. 1899, R5 BSA.

72. BP to Wolseley 14 Aug. 1900, Hove.

73. Ibid.

74. Gardner, 54.

3. *Preparing for the Worst (Sept to Oct 1899)*

1. BP Report for Lord Roberts 6 June 1900, NAM.
2. Vyvyan to DMI 30 Sept. 1899; Vyvyan to sister Mollie 21 May 1900, Vyvyan Papers.
3. Lawley to Milner 11 Nov. 1899, MP.
4. Godley, 67, 73.
5. Vyvyan to BP 21 Sept. 1899; Vyvyan Diary 9 Oct. 1899.
6. Brig. Sir J.E. Edwards (Intelligence Div.) interviewed by Sir B. Liddell Hart, Liddell Hart Archives, King's Coll., London Univ; Paul Rycart to Ivy and George 7 Sept. 1900, Acc 762 (2) 1–5, Middlesex Records.
7. Vyvyan Diary 19 Sept.; Ross, 238–9.
8. Godley to Mrs Godley 6 Oct. 1899, GL.
9. SD and Vyvyan Diary, late Sept. and early Oct, numerous refs to numbers.
10. Vyvyan Diary, 1 Oct. 1899.
11. GH, vol. iii, 145.
12. BP Report for Roberts 6 June 1900, NAM.
13. SD 13 Mar. 1900. For details of armed blacks see n. 15 in Ch. Six: *6. Black Warriors in a White Man's War.*
14. SD 18 Aug., 2 Oct. 1899.
15. Bentinck to Hore 28 Oct. 1899, Mafeking Scrapbook, SAA.
16. Godley to Mrs Godley 6 Oct. 1899, GL.
17. BP to HG 8 Oct. 1899, BSA.
18. SD 7 and 8 Oct. 1899.
19. SD 3 Oct. 1899.
20. Godley to Mrs Godley 6–8 Oct. 1899, GL.
21. *The Siege of Mafeking*, J.A. Hamilton (London 1900), 50.
22. Ross, 17; *The Boer War Diary of Sol T. Plaatje*, ed. J. Comaroff (London/Cardinal ed. 1976), 93, 115.
23. Diary of J.R. Algie, 29 Jan. 1900, unpub. t/s, Mafikeng Museum, Bophuthatswana.
24. 'General Orders' 7 Oct. 1899.
25. SD 6 Oct. 1899; *The Listener*, 13 Oct. 1937.
26. Ross, 17.
27. *Times History of the War in South Africa*, [hereafter TH], vol. iv, ed. L.S. Amery (London 1906), 578.
28. BP to Cronje 30 Oct. 1899, Mafeking Scrapbook, SAA; Ross, 34, 27 Oct. 1899, indicates some mines were genuine.
29. *South African Memories*, Lady Sarah Wilson (London 1909), 79.
30. Godley, 73.
31. Milner to Lord Selborne 18 Oct. 1899, dep c 686 f189, MP.
32. Gardner, 48.
33. Godley to Mrs Godley 12 Oct. 1899, GL.
34. Ross, 15.
35. *Besieged with B-P. Siege of Mafeking*, J.E. Neilly (London 1900), 27.
36. Telegram from Hanbury-Williams quoted SD 12 Oct. 1899.
37. SD 12 Oct. 1899; *Goodbye Dolly Gray: The Story of the Boer War*, R. Kruger (London 1959), 69; Notes for author compiled by Mrs Audrey Renew, curator Mafikeng Museum.
38. Algie 13 Oct. 1899; SD 13 Oct. 1899.
39. Godley, 73.
40. *Mafeking: A Diary of a Siege*, F.D. Baillie (London 1900), 18.
41. A. Renew's notes; Baillie, 16.
42. Diary of Lt. Hubert Swinburne, p. 3, Mrs. J. Browne-Swinburne Coll.
43. Hamilton, 59.
44. Ibid.
45. Swinburne, 2; SD 14 Oct. 1899.
46. SD 15 Oct. 1899.
47. Hamilton, 59.
48. Godley, 73.
49. H. de Montmorency Diary, p. 39, PRO WO 108/185; Gardner, 70.
50. Dr J.H. Breytenbach to author 5 Apr. 1984.

4. *The Siege of Mafeking: First Phase (Oct to Dec 1899)*

1. Neilly, 26.
2. *Petticoat in Mafeking; the letters of Ada Cock*, J.F. Midgeley ed. (Johannesburg 1974), 17 Oct. 1899, p.28.
3. *A Nurse's Diary in Besieged Mafeking*, A.M. Craufurd (London 1900), 16 Oct. 1899.
4. J.R. Algie, 16–18 Oct. 1899.

5. Godley to Mrs Godley 20 Oct. 1899, GL.
6. Godley, 64.
7. Hamilton, 73; Godley to Mrs Godley 20 Oct. 1899, GL.
8. Craufurd, 18 Oct. 1899.
9. SD 18 Oct. 1899.
10. Swinburne, 2.
11. SD 19–20 Oct. 1899.
12. Neilly, 45–6.
13. Baillie, 34.
14. Godley, 75.
15. Diary of Sergeant R.V. Hoskings, 31 Oct. 1899, unpub. t/s, Mafikeng Museum.
16. SD 31 Oct. 1899; *Standard and Diggers' News*, n.d. in vol. i Mafeking Scrapbook, SAA; figures for Doer casualties in Hamilton, Baillie, Ross and Swinburne are wildly inaccurate.
17. Hoskings 31 Oct. 1899.
18. Diary of Ina Cowan, 28 Oct. 1899, unpub. t/s, Mafikeng Museum.
19. TH has 45; Hanbury-Tracy 45; Baillie 57; Hamilton 44; Plaatje 70; Hanbury-Tracy's figures are usually accurate.
20. Hanbury-Tracy t/s.
21. J.R. Algie, 8 Dec. 1899.
22. See too Ina Cowan 31 Oct. 1899.
23. 'Mafeking Notes' n.d. (includes detailed account by BP of attack on Cannon Kopje), R5 BSA.
24. GH, vol. iii, 153; Defence Plan in Vyvyan Papers.
25. Hoskings, 31 Oct. 1899.
26. Remark by BP in *Sketches in Mafeking and East Africa*, quoted Gardner, 229.
27. In *V of L* and *Adventures and Accidents* respectively.
28. BP to Kekewich 11 Oct. 1899, RHN.
29. BP to Rhodes 16 Nov. 1899 in Mafeking Album, SAA.
30. Vyvyan Diary 26 Sept. to 16 Oct. 1899.
31. Hanbury-Tracy t/s, 10.
32. Godley, 84.
33. Brian Willan agrees in 'The Siege of Mafeking' in *The South African War*, ed. P. Warwick (London 1980), 141; Dr Breytenbach to author 5 Apr. 1984 suggests 5,400.
34. *V of L*, 204.
35. RCWSA, 424.
36. Hanbury-Tracy t/s; Godley, 84.
37. Mafeking Day Book, RHN [hereafter DB] 2 May 1899 states 2,600.
38. DB 16 Mar. 1900.
39. SD 16 Feb. 1900; Godley to Mrs Godley 23 Nov. 1899; Swinburne 4 Apr. 1900.
40. DB BP to CSO (Lord Kitchener) 20 Mar. 1900.
41. DB (1218) BP to Plumer 3 Feb. 1900.
42. C. Moberley Bell to Hamilton 27 Apr. 1900, Letter Bk 23, *Times* Archives; DB (1042) 12 Oct, (1046) 12 Oct. 1900; SD 6 Oct. 1900.
43. SD 19 Apr. 1900.
44. Weil to Stent 24 Apr. 1900, Weil Papers.
45. SD 17 Sept. 1899.
46. SD 15 Feb. 1900.
47. Ross, 96–7.
48. Neilly to Sir D. Straight 16 Nov. 1899, RHN.
49. 'We had one blessing. . .': Neilly, 95; Baillie, 259.
50. Vere Stent, t/s n.d. but Dec. 1899, Charterhouse Archives.
51. Hamilton, 192–5.
52. Viz Ross, 78.
53. Draft lecture to officers (probably at Army School of P.T.) c. 1920, R15 BSA.
54. Hoskings 31 Oct. 1899.
55. SD 23, 26 Nov. 1899; SD 7, 30, 31 Jan. 1900.
56. Godley, 79.
57. Godley to Mrs Godley 20 Apr. 1900, GL.
58. Diary of H. de Montmorency, p. 64, WO 108/185.
59. A.M. Craufurd 6 Apr. 1900.
60. BP to Lady Downe 25 June 1900, Downe Coll.
61. SD 13 Oct. 1899.
62. Letter from Mrs Lynn Immelman (d. of Mr Fodisch, mechanic and shell-maker in Siege) to author 4 Feb. 1985.
63. SD 15 Nov. 1899.
64. Swinburne 16 May 1900.
65. TH, vol. iv, 586.
66. Hamilton, 120–1.

67. Rosenthal, 37.
68. Hamilton, 141–3.
69. Ibid, 134–5.
70. Hanbury-Tracy t/s; Appendix in vol. iii GH.
71. Diary of Dr W. Hayes unpub. t/s, 8 Dec. 1899, Cape Archives.
72. Baillie, 141.
73. Plaatje, 24 Jan. 1900, 105.
74. Ibid, 7 Dec. 1899, 64.
75. Diary of C.G.H. Bell, unpub. t/s, 86, Rhodes University Library.
76. Diary of Mr R. Urry, unpub. t/s, 18, Mafikeng Museum.
77. Lady S. Wilson, 88.
78. Ross, 115.
79. Diary of Albert J. Shimwell, 31 Dec. 1899, 6 Feb. 1900, Rhodes University Library.
80. Hoskings, 25.
81. Baillie, 175, 224.
82. BP List of Accidents and Injuries, 00081 R5 BSA.
83. *The Relief of Mafeking*, F. Young (London 1900), 268.
84. *With Seven Generals*, A.W.A. Pollock (London 1900).
85. Ross, 75.
86. Ross, 161.
87. Plaatje 29 Oct. 1899, 34.
88. Godley to Mrs Godley 28 Nov. 1899, GL.
89. SD 23 and 28 Nov. 1899.
90. SD 2 Mar. 1899; Ross 169.
91. Mr H. Martin 29 Nov. 1899, p. 7, unpub. t/s, Mafikeng Museum.
92. Craufurd, 16 Dec. 1899.
93. SD 19 Nov. 1899.
94. SD 23 Nov. 1899.
95. SD 22 Dec. 1893.
96. SD 23 Dec. 1899.
97. SD 24 Dec. 1899.
98. Godley to Mrs Godley 24 Dec. 1899, GL.
99. Viz Godley to Mrs Godley 20 Apr. 1899; BP to Vyvyan 11 May 1900, Vyvyan Papers.
100. Swinburne 20–1.
101. SD 2 Dec. 1899; Hanbury-Tracy t/s, 26.
102. SD 24 Dec. 1899.
103. DB (1167a) BP to J.S. Nicholson 24 Dec. 1899.
104. Hanbury-Tracy t/s, 26ff.

105. Swinburne, 30 Dec. 1899, 20.
106. Hamilton, 177ff; Hoskings, 26 Dec. 1899, 15; Hanbury-Tracy t/s 26–8; SD 26 Dec. 1899.
107. Swinburne, 27 Oct. 1899, 11–12.
108. Hoskings 27 Dec. 1899; Ross, 78.
109. SD 26 Dec. 1899; Ross, 79.
110. Algie, 80; Craufurd 25 Dec. 1899; Cowan, 25 Dec. 1899.
111. Ross, 79.
112. Ross, 78; BP in 'Mafeking Notes' n.d., R5 BSA.
113. Ross, 80; Baillie, 97; BP to Godley 11 Mar. 1901, Private Coll.
114. DB (1228) BP to Plumer 10 Feb. 1899.
115. BP Report to Lord Roberts, NAM.
116. 'Mafeking Notes' n.d., R5 BSA.

5. *Starving the Blacks to feed the Whites?*
   (Nov. 1899 to April 1900)

1. Pakenham 406–10.
2. *Observer*, Sunday Plus, 26 Aug. 1979.
3. See SD 1 and 30 Jan. 1900, by which last date the oat-grinding experiment had been made (see 23 Jan.) but still not put into practice.
4. SD 22 Nov. 1899.
5. SD 22 and 23 Nov. 1899.
6. *Mafeking Mail*, 2 Jan. 1900.
7. SD 7 Jan. 1900.
8. Plaatje, 2 Jan. 1900, p. 97.
9. SD 10 Jan. 1899.
10. Plaatje, 2 Jan. 1900.
11. Hoskings, 27 Feb. 1900.
12. BP only put pressure on Bell to agree to his commandeering African livestock in Apr. 1900. See BP to Bell 23 and 26 Apr., Bell Papers, Rhodes University Library.
13. SD 3 Dec.; 1, 15. Jan.; 5 Feb.; 14 Apr.; Algie 11–12 Mar. 1900; Hanbury-Tracy 10 Dec. 1899; 29 Jan.; 9 Mar. 1900; *Mafeking Mail*, 16 Feb. 1900; Plaatje 13 Jan. 1900, 100–101.
14. BP to Bell 13 Jan. 1900, Bell Papers; Plaatje 13 Jan. 1900.
15. Algie, 11 Mar. 1900.
16. SD 16 Apr. 1900.
17. SD 4 Mar. 1900. (On 22 Nov. 1899 [SD] BP had written: 'Meat and

groceries [excluding breadstuffs] are
so plentiful that for the moment they
do not matter . . .') On 26 Feb.
there were 1,211 sheep and goats,
which had only declined to 830 by 1
Apr., see Animal Census SD 16 Apr.
18. SD 30 Jan. 1900 records 135,000 lbs
tinned meat and 26,600 lbs tinned
fancy meats and fish.
19. SD 15 Feb. 1900.
20. Ross, 96–7.
21. SD 20 Mar., 4 Apr. 1900.
22. SD 21 Apr. 1900.
23. SD 4 Mar. 1900.
24. DB (1255) BP to CSO (Lord Kitchener) 1 Mar. 1900.
25. *Mafeking Mail*, 21 Jan. 1900.
26. SD 1 Feb. 1900.
27. Pakenham, 407; SD 15 Nov. 1900.
28. Hamilton, 249–50.
29. Plaatje, 10 Feb. 1900, 115.
30. Pakenham, 407.
31. DB (1222) CSO Cape Town to BP
21 Jan. 1900, recd.Mafeking 8 Feb.
32. Bell Diary 9 Feb. 1900, Rhodes
University Library.
33. Plaatje 10 Feb. 1900, p. 115.
34. DB (1226) BP to CSO 10 Feb. 1900;
DB (1228) BP to Plumer 10 Feb.
1900.
35. DB (1224) BP to Plumer 11 Feb.
1900.
36. SD 21 and 23 Feb. 1900.
37. Bell to BP 15 Feb. 1900, Bell Papers.
38. BP to Bell 15 Feb. 1900, Bell Papers.
39. Bell Diary 20 Feb. 1900.
40. Algie 23 and 27 Feb. 1900.
41. Ryan to Vyvyan 1 Mar. 1900,
Vyvyan Papers.
42. Bell Diary 1 Mar. 1900.
43. Pakenham, 407; Algie, 23 Mar.
1900.
44. SD 25 Feb. 1900.
45. Plaatje 27 Feb. 1900, 124–125.
46. DB (1236) BP to Plumer 6 Mar.
1900.
47. SD 12,13 Mar. 1900; Bell Diary 14
Mar. 1900; Plaatje 17 Mar. 1900,
140.
48. DB (1315) BP to CSO 7 Apr. 1900.
49. Bell Diary 8 Apr. 1900; DB (1339)
Plumer to BP 13 Apr. 1900.
50. *The Boer War: A Diary of the Siege of
Mafeking*, C.J. Weir (Edinburgh
1901), 13 Apr. 1900.

51. Baillie, 237.
52. DB (1361) BP to Plumer 24 Apr.
1900; DB (1370) Plumer to BP 2
May 1900.
53. Bell Diary 21 Apr. 1900.
54. DB (1336) Plumer to BP 19 Apr.
1900; Bell Diary 26 Apr. 1900; SD 8
Apr. 1900.
55. Neilly, 228.
56. BP to Bell 17 Mar. 1900.
57. Pakenham, 408.
58. Neilly, 227–9 as quoted by Pakenham, 408, with major omissions
distorting the sense.
59. Neilly 228–9, second and crucial
passage omitted by Pakenham.
60. Rosenthal, 40–1; *Black People and the
South African War*, P Warwick
(London 1983), p. 13; n. 14 on p.
190; *Eminent Edwardians*, P. Brendon
(London 1979), 231–2: ('Of course,
no one now denies that the Africans
were reduced to starvation . . .'; *Sol
Plaatje* (biog), B Willan (London
1984)· Dr Willan accurately writes
about free soup kitchens, but still
cites Pakenham as reliable on black
feeding – e.g. p. 84 and n. 26 on p.
400.
61. Rosenthal, 40–1.
62. Neilly, 231–2.
63. SD 13 Mar. 1900.
64. Bell Diary 21 Apr. 1900.
65. Ross, 194.
66. Bell Diary 20 Mar. 1900.
67. Ada Cock, 27 Mar. 1900; Bell Diary
30 Mar., 9 May 1900.
68. Baillie, 209–10.
69. Viz Algie 16 Mar. 1900.
70. Quoted in Ross, 241.
71. *Black People and the South African
War*, 37.
72. Hanbury-Tracy t/s.
73. Craufurd, various dates in Mar. and
Apr.
74. C.J. Weir, 27 Feb. 1900.
75. Bell Diary 21 Feb. 1900.
76. Report to Lord Roberts 18 May
1900.
77. Rosenthal, 43.
78. Ada Cock, 8 and 17 Apr. 1900.
79. Ross, 112; Swinburne 19 and 28 Feb.
1900.
80. Hoskings, 6 Mar. 1900.

81. Plaatje, 22 Feb. 1900, 121–2.
82. Martin, 28 Apr. 1900.
83. Hoskings, 27 Feb. 1900.
84. C.J. Weir, 18 Feb. 1900.
85. DB (1342) Nicholson to BP 15 Apr. 1900: message repeats verbatim telegram, dated 9 Apr., from Roberts to BP.
86. DB (1345) BP to Roberts 20 Apr. 1900.
87. SD 20 Apr. 1900; DB BP to Plumer 21 Apr. 1900 and BP to Roberts 2 May 1900, also see above p. 291. Algie, 18 Apr. 1900.
88. Craufurd, 1 Apr. 1900.
89. Ada Cock, 13 Apr. 1900.
90. Ross, 219.
91. Rosenthal, 41.
92. Ada Cock 8 and 17 Apr. 1900.
93. Hamilton, 287–8.
94. B. Willan in *The South African War* ed. P. Warwick, p. 154.
95. Hamilton, 215–17.
96. Bell to Cecil 27 Oct. 1899, Bell Papers.
97. Bell to Cecil 22 Jan. 1899, Bell Papers.
98. Ross, 74.
99. Ibid, 223.
100. SD 2 Apr. 1900.
101. SD 17 Mar. 1900.
102. Plaatje, 29 Mar. 1900, 249–50.
103. Ross, 220.
104. Rosenthal, 43; Pakenham, 403.
105. Information: J.R. Dovell (Dep. Gov., Parkhurst Prison) to author 23 Apr. 1986; J.R. Hamilton (Medical Director, Broadmoor Hospital) to author 10 Jul. 1986.

6. Black Warriors in a White Man's War (Oct. 1899 to Apr. 1900)

1. Neilly 96–8: full text signed on behalf of Cronje by his American surgeon John E. Dyer.
2. Hanbury-Tracy t/s.
3. SD 2 Nov. 1899.
4. Bell Diary 4 Nov. 1899.
5. Ross, 41.
6. Vyvyan to Inspector Marsh 7 Nov. 1899, Small letters books 58–62, Vyvyan Papers.
7. Vyvyan to O.C. Right Troop 10 Nov. 1899; Vyvyan to Cecil 11 Nov. 1899, Vyvyan Papers.
8. Ross, 53.
9. Hamilton, 242–3.
10. A. Renew's notes for author.
11. See the numerous notes from BP to Vyvyan in Vyvyan Papers.
12. Ross, 173.
13. Bell Diary 8 Apr. 1900; SD 9 Apr. 1899.
14. Plaatje, 12 Nov. 1899, 41–2.
15. Numbers of Armed Africans and Coloureds: notes compiled for author by Mrs A. Renew, Curator Mafikeng Museum; Ross, n. 17, p. 17; BP Report to Lord Roberts; SD 14 Nov. 1899, gives total black pop. as 7,500. The number of armed Barolongs in the stadt can be deduced from no. of free soup tickets issued; SD 11 Jan. 1900 states 404; Ross, p. 187, states 400. Number in Black Watch given in SD 7 Nov. as 37. Since BP's figure of 30 for the Cape Boys was under half the true figure, his estimate for Black Watch was almost certainly much too low. P. Warwick in *Black People and the S.A. War*, p. 32, sets the figure at 60 and rising throughout Siege. Mrs Renew estimates 200–300. In his Report to Roberts, BP divides his '300 cattle guards, watchmen etc.' into three groups: 1) Capt. Mackenzie's Zulus, i.e. the Black Watch; 2) Mr Webster's Fingoes; 3) Cpl Abrams' Barolongs. Since we know (see Ross 187) Abrams' force of 400 was supposed to number 100, and from an extant photo in Mafikeng Museum that Webster's men were 70 strong, this would put the Black Watch at 130. Given BP's habitual underestimation of all black groups, 200 seems likely. The Cape Boys numbered 68, GH, vol. iii, 202; from 7 Nov. 1899, BP called them the Colonial Contingent. The total of armed blacks in Mafeking was thus about 750.
16. Ross, 187.
17. See SD 7 Nov. 1899.
18. RCWSA, 19875.
19. *Sol Plaatje*, B. Willan (London 1984), 89.

20. Hanbury-Tracy t/s, 21–22; TH, vol. iv, 591–7.
21. Neilly, 98.
22. Neilly 102 (BP to Cronje 30 Oct. 1899).
23. DB (1098) BP to Cronje 14 Nov. and to Snyam 8 Dec. 1899.
24. Minutes by Sir H. Just, Sir F. Graham and Joseph Chamberlain 28 Sep. 1899, CO 179/206/26305.
25. *Black People in the S.A. War*, 20.
26. SD 22 Jan. 1900.
27. *Black People in the S.A. War*, 39–41.
28. Lawley to Milner 14 Dec. 1899, MP.
29. DB (1484) BP to Nicholson 4 Dec. 1899; DB (1182) BP to Plumer 6 Dec. 1899.
30. DB (1484) BP to Roberts 19 June 1900; DB (1485) Roberts to BP 19 June 1900.
31. *Sol Plaatje*, B. Willan, 88–9.
32. General Orders, 24 May 1900, NAM.

7. *The Siege of Mafeking: Final Phase (Jan. to May 1900)*

1. Lady Sarah Wilson, 200; *Mafeking Mail*, 11, 25 Feb. 1900.
2. Godley to Mrs Godley 16 Feb. 1900, GL.
3. Godley to Mrs Godley 7 Jan. 1900, GL.
4. Ross, Crauford, Cock etc.
5. Rosenthal, 31; Gardner, 112.
6. Rosenthal, 31.
7. Mafeking Album, SAA.
8. Baillie in *Pall Mall Gazette* 19 Apr. 1900.
9. Baillie, 203.
10. Husband to 'My dearest wife' 15 Apr. 1900, Ba 40, Univ. of the Witwatersrand.
11. Algie 10 Dec. 1900; Ross, 69.
12. Ross, 64.
13. Ross, 133.
14. BP to HG 24 Nov. 1899, BSA.
15. BP to Godley 11 Mar. 1901, Private Coll.
16. SD 10 and 29 Mar. 1900; Ross, 223.
17. BP to HG 24 Nov. 1899, BSA.
18. Ross, 112.
19. SD 30 Apr. 1900.
20. Hillcourt 197 and n. 132.
21. Ibid.
22. African spies, see Bell to BP 24 and 26 Apr. 1900, Bell Papers; Baillie, 243, 246.
23. J. Moore Diary 31 Mar. 1900; TH, vol. iv, 207.
24. DB (1306) Plumer to BP 1 Apr. 1900.
25. Hanbury-Tracy to Capt. H. Llewellyn 4 Apr. 1900, Major T. Morley Coll.
26. Aitken, 150.
27. DB (1366) Plumer to BP 1 May 1900 recd. Mafeking 4 May.
28. SD 30 Apr. 1900; Hamilton (30 Apr.), 286–7.
29. RCWSA 19895.
30. DB (1370) Plumer to BP 2 May 1900.
31. DB (1346) BP to Plumer 21 Apr. 1900.
32. DB (1369) BP to Roberts 2 May 1900.
33. Mafeking Album, SAA.
34. Ross, 223–4.
35. Lady Sarah Wilson, 204–7.
36. Craufurd, 12 May 1900.
37. *V of L* t/s, 682, R8 BSA; SD 12 May 1900.
38. Hamilton, 293.
39. Godley, 81.
40. SD 12 May 1900.
41. Ibid.
42. Baillie, 259.
43. *Mafeking Mail*, 14 May 1900; Baillie (260) said Eloff had 700; TH, vol. iv, 594, estimated 225.
44. DB (1378) BP to Plumer 12 May 1900.
45. Quoted in *Sketches in Mafeking*, and referred to in BP to HG 21 May 1900, BSA.
46. Bell to BP 26 Apr. 1900, Bell Papers.
47. TH, vol. iv, 594–5.
48. *Mafeking Mail*, 14 May 1900.
49. Godley to Mrs Godley 13 May 1900, GL.
50. SD 12 May 1900.
51. Gardner 187; Pakenham, 413.
52. Hamilton, 299.
53. *Mafeking Mail*, 14 and 16 May 1900; SD 12 May 1900.
54. Craufurd, 13 May 1900.
55. Hamilton, 306.
56. Godley to Mrs Godley 13 May 1900, GL.

57. Hamilton, 306f; *Mafeking Mail* 14 May 1900.
58. Ross, 227.
59. Godley to Mrs Godley 18 May 1900. (In this letter Godley reported that a telegram from Kruger had been found after the Relief in the Boer Laager saying as much.)
60. R. Urry Diary, 15 May 1900, Mafikeng Museum.
61. Baillie, 269–70.
62. Gardner, 189.
63. Ross, 229–30.
64. GH, vol. iii, 181.
65. Speech to Eton O.T.C. *c.* 1914–16, R7 BSA.
66. Lady Sarah Wilson, 209–10.
67. R. Urry Diary, 12 May 1900.
68. TH, vol. iv, 219; Brig. Mahon's Report to Roberts 23 Aug. 1900, NAM.
69. TH, vol. iv, 221; *Goodbye Dolly Gray,* 296.
70. Lady Sarah Wilson, 214.
71. Baillie, 278–9; Gardner, 12–13.
72. Hamilton, 315.
73. Filson Young, 264–5.
74. Gardner, 194.
75. SD 15 May 1900.
76. SD 20, 22 Apr. 1900.
77. Lady Sarah Wilson, 217; Filson Young, 212.
78. Filson Young, 274–5.
79. *With Plumer to Mafeking,* G.F. Whalley (London 1900).
80. H. de Montmorency Diary WO 108/185.

8. *Hero in a Chilly Fog (1900)*

1. From *Great Contemporaries,* Winston Churchill (London 1939).
2. Hillcourt, 203.
3. HG to A 30 Nov. 1899, JM.
4. F to Frances 2 Mar. 1900, FBPA.
5. A to Frances 3 Mar. 1900, FBPA.
6. HG to A 4 Nov. 1899, JM.
7. HG to A 4, 20, 21 Nov. 1900, JM.
8. HG to Frances 2 Dec. 1899, FBPA.
9. Mrs Singleton to Lt H.T.C. Singleton n.d. Mar. 1900, Mrs Y. Binning Coll.
10. Lord Wolseley to George Wolseley 17 May 1900, William R. Perkins Library, Duke University.
11. Algie 18 Oct. 1899.
12. Quoted by Gardner, 67; Rosenthal, 31.
13. Mafeking Album, SAA; Hillcourt, 175.
14. Godley to Mrs Godley 22 Mar. 1900, GL.
15. BP to HG 10 Apr. 1900, BSA.
16. SD 12 Apr. 1900.
17. Godley to Mrs Godley 10 Apr. 1900, GL.
18. BP to HG 27 June1900, BSA.
19. BP to HG 10 Oct. 1900, BSA.
20. BP to HG 11 Jan. 1901, BSA.
21. BP to HG 21 July1902, BSA.
22. Ross, 188 and n. 29.
23. BP to HG 3 Apr. 1900, BSA.
24. Mrs G to Godley 11 Apr. 1899, GL.
25. Godley, 79–80.
26. *V of L,* 210.
27. Ross, 192; *Mafeking Siege Views* (1900).
28. Ross, 90, 132, 136, 194.
29. Ross, 64–5.
30. Ross, 47–8.
31. Godley's Siege Letter Books 14 Sept. 1899–17 May 1900: entries in Dec. and Jan. Sold Sotheby's 1986.
32. SD 15 Mar. 1900.
33. SD 20 Mar. 1900.
34. BP to Vyvyan 29 Apr. 1901, Vyvyan Papers.
35. Mrs N. Winter to Vyvyan 15 Sept. and 2 Dec. 1912, Vyvyan Papers.
36. *Mafeking Mail,* 29 Mar. 1900.
37. *The South African War,* ed. P. Warwick, 144ff.
38. Roberts to Kitchener 4 May 1901, PRO 30/57 20.
39. Brig. Sir J.E. Edwards interviewed by Sir B. Liddell Hart, 11 Apr. 1930, King's Coll., London.
40. *The South African War. . . ,* ed. P. Warwick, 158; Gardner 89f, 92f, 141.
41. GH, vol. iii, 192–3.
42. Gardner, 153.
43. DB (1274) BP to Plumer 17 Mar. 1900.
44. DB (1283) BP to CSO 22 Mar. 1900.
45. DB (1289 & 1295) BP to Plumer 26 Mar. 1900.

46. DB (1299) BP to Plumer 30 Mar. 1900.
47. DB (1226) BP to CSO 10 Feb 1900; DB (1228) BP to Plumer 10 Feb. 1900.
48. *Pall Mall Gazette*, 19 May 1900.
49. BP to Mr Methuen, 20 Jan. 1901, SAA.
50. BP to HG 21 July 1902, BSA.
51. *Pall Mall Gazette*, 19 May 1900.
52. Hamilton, 289.
53. GH, vol. iii, 184–5.
54. BP to Hanbury-Tracy 23 Nov. 1900, RHN; Hanbury-Tracy t/s, 40–1.
55. *The Principles of Land Defence*, Sir H.F. Thuillier, (London 1902), 98.
56. BP to Godley 23 May 1918, sold Sotheby's 1986.

Chapter Seven
THE GENERAL
1. *Commander in the Field*
(June to Aug. 1900)

1. *Goodbye Dolly Gray*, 452.
2. Hillcourt, 209.
3. BP to Gen. Sir A. Hunter 25 May 1900, R9 BSA.
4. Ibid; GH, vol. iii, 551.
5. BP to Roberts 9 June 1900, R9 BSA.
6. BP Report: Operation of the Frontier Force 18 May–28 Aug. 1900, t/s, NAM.
7. DB (1501) Milner to BP 26 June 1900; SD 19 June 1900.
8. Notice to Burghers 14 June 1900, RHN.
9. DB (1465) Roberts to BP 1 June 1900.
10. TH, vol. iv, 224; GH, vol. iii, 230; Plumer to BP 18 June 1900, RHN.
11. BP to Roberts 9 June 1900, R5 BSA; BP to CSO 14 June 1900, R5 BSA.
12. BP to HG 19 June 1900, BSA.
13. DB (1498) BP to Roberts 24 June 1900; DB (1486) Roberts to Carrington 19 June 1900.
14. TH, vol. iv, 345.
15. BP to Roberts 29 June 1900, WO 105/15; DB (1505) Baden-Powell to Roberts 27 June 1900.
16. SD 2 July 1900.
17. SD 3 July 1900.
18. Ibid.
19. SD 4 July 1900.
20. Roberts to Hanbury-Tracy 5 July 1900, RHN.
21. Hanbury-Tracy to Mil. Sec. 6 July 1900, RHN.
22. Roberts to Hanbury-Tracy 6 July 1900, RHN.
23. DB (1518) Hanbury-Tracy to Mil. Sec.[Pretoria] 7 July 1900.
24. Proclamation 6 July 1900; Hanbury-Tracy to Mil. Sec. 6 July 1900, RHN.
25. Roberts to Sec. of State for War 10 July 1900, RHN.
26. BP to Roberts 6 July 1900, WO 105/15.
27. *My Picture Gallery*, V. Milner (London 1951), 201.
28. TH, vol. iii, 349; SD 10–16 July 1900; DB (1551) BP to Roberts 16 July 1900.
29. DB (1534) Roberts to BP 12 July 1900.
30. TH, vol. iv, 352.
31. Ibid, 354.
32. Ibid, 355.
33. *Goodbye Dolly Gray*, 342.
34. General Orders, 12 July 1900, R5 BSA.
35. Gardner, 222.
36. General Orders, 14 July, R5 BSA.
37. DB (1551 & 1557) Roberts to BP 16 and 17 July 1900.
38. DB (1537 & 1546) Roberts to BP 13 and 15 July 1900.
39. DB (1553) Roberts to BP 16 July 1900.
40. BP to Roberts 25 July 1900, WO 105/15; *Rustenburg at War*, L. Wulfsohn (Johannesburg 1987), 41–2.
41. DB (1568) Methuen to Roberts 22 July 1900.
42. DB (1570a) Methuen to BP 22 July 1900; (1571) BP to Methuen 23 July 1900; SD 24 July 1900; TH, vol. iv, 357.
43. *Goodbye Dolly Gray*, 486–94.
44. Rosenthal, 44.
45. DB (1574) BP to Roberts 24 July 1900.
46. DB (1578) Roberts to BP 24 July 1900.
47. DB (1579) BP to Hore 25 July 1900.
48. DB (1583) BP to Roberts 26 July 1900.

49. DB (1593) Roberts to BP 26 July 1900.
50. DB (1594) BP to Roberts 29 July 1900.
51. Roberts to BP 29 July 1900, Roberts Papers 1252, NAM.
52. DB (1613) I. Hamilton to BP 3 Aug. 1900.
53. Pakenham, 458, quoting Rawlinson Diary Nov.–Dec. 1900.
54. Milner to Brodrick 5 Nov. 1900, Brodrick Papers, PRO 30/67/6.
55. DB (1579) BP to Hore 25 July 1900.
56. *Goodbye Dolly Gray*, 452.
57. SD 7 Aug. 1900; BP Report: Operation of the Frontier Force, 18 May to 28 Aug. 1900, t/s, NAM.
58. TH, vol. iv, 361; Wulfsohn, 43.
59. DB (1620) BP to Hamilton 6 Aug. 1900.
60. DB (1619) Roberts to Hamilton 6 Aug. 1900.
61. Roberts to Carrington No. C. 032, 6 Aug. 1900, 11. 30 p.m., 1424 RP, NAM; Roberts to Hamilton, 1425 RP, NAM.
62. TH, vol. iv, 361.
63. Roberts to Sec. of State for War 17 Aug. 1900, 776 RP NAM.
64. *The Great Boer War*, A.C. Doyle (London 1900–2), 494.
65. Gardner, 223; *Goodbye Dolly Gray*, 452.
66. SD 5 Aug. 1900.
67. Roberts to Hamilton 8 Aug. 1900, 1467 RP, NAM.
68. Roberts to BP 1 Aug. 1900, 1285 RP, NAM.
69. GH, vol. iii, 335.
70. Notes by Baden Baden-Powell, R13 BSA.
71. Roberts to BP 14 Aug. 1900, 1611 RP NAM.
72. Godley 90; GH, vol iii, 360; Mafeking Box 3: 4 pp of m/s written at Commando Nek 18 Aug. 1900, SAA.
73. TH, vol. iv, 430.
74. Roberts to BP 17 and 18 Aug. 1900, 1665, 1691–2 RP, NAM; Roberts to Kitchener and Hamilton 17 Aug.
75. Roberts to BP 18 Aug., 1696, RP, NAM.
76. BP Report: Operation of Frontier Force, 18 May to 28 Aug. 1900, t/s, NAM.
77. Roberts to Paget 22 Aug. 1900, 1785, RP, NAM.
78. BP to Roberts 23 Aug. 1900, copy in Godley Papers sold Sotheby's 1986.
79. As n. 76.
80. Hanbury-Tracy t/s, re Warmbad 24 Aug. 1900; GH, iii, 368–9.
81. *V of L*, 215.
82. Rosenthal, 45.
83. Roberts to BP 14 June 1900, RHN.
84. BP to Roberts 9 June 1900, R5 BSA.
85. Roberts to Milner 4 July 1900, MP.
86. Roberts to Queen Victoria, 21 Aug. 1900, copy in RP, NAM.

2. Constabulary Duty to be Done (Sept 1900 to March 1903)

1. *Annals of a Chequered Life*, A.M. Brookfield (London 1930).
2. *V of L* t/s, Ch. vi, R7 BSA; BP to HG 7 Sept. 1900, BSA.
3. BP to HG 10 Sept. 1900, BSA.
4. Milner to Chamberlain 13 Sept. 1900, CO 879/65 f636.
5. Ibid 24 Sept. 1900.
6. Milner to Roberts 13 Sept., copy in MP.
7. WO Memo 27 Oct. 1900, CO 879/65.
8. BP to Milner 3 Oct. 1900; Milner to BP 4 and 7 Oct. 1900, CO 879/65.
9. Chamberlain to Milner 4 Oct. 1900; Proclamation of Org. of SAC, 22 Oct. 1900, CO 879/65.
10. Hillcourt, 220.
11. *V of L*, 218.
12. SD 11 Nov. 1900, NAM.
13. *A History of the Cavalry* (1816–1919), Marquess of Anglesey (London 1986), 360.
14. Milner to Roberts 26 Nov. 1900, CO 879/65.
15. BP to McLaren 2 Nov. and 14 Dec. 1902, IG SAC Letter Book, NAM.
16. BP to McLaren 26 Aug. and 6 Sept. 1902, NAM.
17. Milner to Chamberlain 4 Nov. 1900, CO 879/65.
18. *V of L*, 219.
19. Milner to BP 19 Nov. 1900, CO 879/65.

20. R.S. Curtis Scrapbook, W. Beckwith Coll.
21. *Goodbye Dolly Gray*, 426.
22. TH, vol. v, 247.
23. Ibid.
24. Rosenthal 45–6, esp. Kitchener to Roberts 5 Apr. 1901.
25. TH, vol. v, 271.
26. Pakenham, 498, quoting Smith-Dorrien and Allenby.
27. Kitchener to Brodrick 22 Mar. 1901, PRO Kitchener Papers, 30/57/22/Y.
28. TH, vol. v, 258ff; Pakenham, 487, 494, 511
29. Roberts to Kitchener 2 July 1901, RP, NAM.
30. TH, vol. v, 260–1.
31. Ibid, 324t; Pakenham 356t.
32. Baden Baden-Powell biog. notes on BP, R13 BSA; Lt-Col. W. Beevor to HG 12 July 1901; BP to HG 27 June 1901, BSA.
33. Kitchener to Roberts 24 May 1901, RP, NAM.
34. Milner to Chamberlain 3 Dec. 1901, dep. 171 f43, MP.
35. Roberts to Kitchener 20 July 1901, PRO 30/57.
36. Kitchener to Roberts 17 Aug. 1901, RP, NAM.
37. Milner to Chamberlain 3 Dec. 1901, MP.
38. Brodrick to Kitchener 3 Jan. 1902, PRO 30/57.
39. M.M. Hartigan: Recollections for E.E. Reynolds, not included in Reynolds's 1942 biog. of BP, TC 95 SAA.
40. Ibid.
41. *V of L* t/s, R7 BSA.
42. *V of L*, 226; BP to Mr Methuen 20 Jan. 1901, TC 95 SAA.
43. Hartigan Recollections, SAA.
44. BP to HG 19 Sept. 1884; BP to G 6 Jan. and 6 Mar. 1885, BSA.
45. BP to Twynam 22 May 1902, SAC Organization, NAM.
46. *Pall Mall Gazette*, 12 Feb. 1902.
47. BP to Lord Lambton 11 May 1902, SAC Org., NAM.
48. BP to Frances 24 Jan. 1901, FBPA.
49. Hartigan Recollections, SAA.
50. BP Notes to SAC Troop Officers: 27 June 1901, SAC Org., NAM.
51. SD 13 Feb. 1902, Transvaal Archives, Pretoria.
52. *V of L* t/s, 618–19, R8 BSA.
53. BP to Mr Methuen 20 Jan. 1901, TC 95 SAA.
54. *Youth, Empire and Society*, J. Springhall (London 1977), 56–7.
55. *V of L* t/s, R7 BSA.
56. *V of L*, 245.
57. Hartigan Recollections, SAA.
58. BP to HG 15 Oct. 1900, BSA.
59. BP Diary 21 Sept. 1902, BSA.
60. Hartigan Recollections, SAA.
61. Roberts to Brodrick n.d. Dec. 1902, Midleton Papers, PRO 30/67 f10.

Chapter Eight
HOME COMES THE HERO
1. To Wed or Not to Wed

1. G to HG 17 June 1898, FBPA.
2. HG to Frances 27 July 1902, FBPA.
3. BP to Baden 15 Feb. 1902, FBPA.
4. Baden to HG 12 Feb., 12 Dec. 1903; Baden to Frances 29 Apr. 1905, JM.
5. Sir W. Berry to HG 12 June 1901; HG to Berry 12 May 1902; A to HG 6 Oct. 1900, JM.
6. A to HG 29 Aug. 1900, JM.
7. HG to Frances 15 Sept. 1913, FBPA.
8. F to Frances 19, 23 Dec. 1907, FBPA.
9. BP to HG 14 Apr. 1902, BSA.
10. BP to HG 25 Apr. 1901, BSA.
11. BP to HG 11 Feb. 1901, BSA.
12. *V of L*, 268.
13. Maud B-P (Mrs Moore) BBC Radio Talk Feb. 1957, t/s FBPA.
14. See BP to Harold Wilson 14 Apr. 1900, FBPA; James Elliot conversation with author 10 Apr. 1986; recollections of Mrs Barbara Halsey (Orr-Ewing), letter to author 13 Apr. 1986; Veronica Lady Gainford (Noble) letter to author 8 Sept. 1983.
15. 'Eggs and Germs' m/s note, TC 41 SAA.
16. *Rovering and Rangering* draft t/s, R8 BSA.
17. BP to HG 20 Mar. 1884, BSA.
18. BP to Dulce Wroughton 7 Apr. 1908, Mrs A. Lunn Coll.
19. As n. 15.
20. Quoted by Rose Kerr in *The Guide*, vol. xiv, 23 Feb. 1935.

21. BP Diary 26 Dec. 1910, BSA.
22. BP to HG 2 Aug. 1904, BSA.
23. BP Diary 12–17 Mar. 1905, BSA.
24. Miss Rosemary Kerr (daughter) interviewed by author 22 Sept. 1983; Mrs Sonia Heathcoat-Amory (née Denison) to author 14 July 1985.
25. Information Mrs Annie Scofield (Lady BP's maid/housekeeper during 1904–52).
26. Miss Grace Browning, interview with author 13 May 1985.
27. Rose Kerr to Olave BP n.d. and 19 Mar. 1925 (returned to Rose by Olave).
28. Information Miss Rosemary Kerr.
29. BP to HG 18 Sept. 1895, BSA.
30. Mr John Christie-Miller to author 15, 22 July 1985.
31. Mr C. G. Sowerby to author 23 Nov. 1985.
32. BP Diary 2 Nov. 1906, BSA.
33. Commander Claude Sclater R.N. Retd. to author 17 July 1985.
34. Winthrop Young: Recollections, t/s dated 1941, SAA.
35. BP to Lady Young 12 July 1905, J. S. Winthrop Young Coll.
36. As n. 34.
37. *The Grace of Forgetting*, Winthrop Young (London n.d.).
38. As n. 34.
39. BPD 1 Apr. 1905; BP to HG 14 Aug. 1904, BSA.
40. BPD 11, 20 Aug. 1906.
41. BPD 22, 23 and 25 Jan. 1906.
42. BPD 19–22, 27 Apr., 3 May, 4 July 1907; the present Lord Rodney and his sister have no papers relating to their grandmother.
43. Hillcourt, 309–12.
44. BPD 10 Feb. 1905; *Stratford-upon-Avon Herald*, obit. for Mrs Leggett 9 Oct. 1931.
45. BPD 10, 11 Feb. 1905; BP to HG 4 Mar. 1905, BSA.
46. *The Carthusian*, Aug. 1899 (report of performance on 26 June).
47. *Who was Who in the Theatre*, Sybil Carlisle.
48. Barrie Notebook, quoted in *J.M. Barrie*, J. Dunbar (London 1970), 278.
49. Notes in the *Peter Pan* Paris Acting ed. (1908).
50. *Window on My Heart*, O. Baden-Powell and Mary Drewery (London 1973), 78; BPD 10 Jan. 1913.

2. Cavalry Chaos (1903–07)

1. *V of L* t/s, 313, R9 BSA.
2. Ibid, 865.
3. *V of L*, 248.
4. *Cavalry Journal*, vol. i, 1906, 49–51.
5. Red covered album [Army], SAA.
6. BPD 19 Jan. 1905, BSA.
7. Quoted in *V of L* t/s, 871, R9 BSA.
8. Hillcourt, 232.
9. BP I.G. Diary 29 July 1905, NAM.
10. Anglesey, vol. iv, 388.
11. Roberts to Kitchener 28 Jan. 1904, RP, NAM.
12. Anglesey, vol. iv, 389–90.
13. Ibid., 54–60.
14. BP I.G. Diary 17 Aug. 1903, NAM.
15. Ibid., 8 Nov. 1903.
16. Report on German Cavalry Manoeuvres, 20 Oct. 1903, preface by Roberts, BP I.G. Papers, NAM.
17. BP's Report was intended to replace Haig's Part iv. of *Cavalry Training*; BP I.G. Diary 8 Oct. 1903; *Pall Mall Gazette*, A.C. Doyle to ed. 6 Apr. 1910.
18. Anglesey, vol. iv, 407.
19. Ibid., 408.
20. RCWSA, 19 Mar. 1903.
21. BP to WO 10 Mar. 1904, WO 32/6782.
22. BP Territorial Diary, vol ii, 10 July 1908, TC 209 SAA.
23. *The First World War*, A.J.P. Taylor (London 1963 Penguin ed.), 86.
24. BP I.G. Diary 31 Aug. 1906, NAM.

3. The Nation in Peril (1903–04)

1. *Southport Visitor* 28 Mar. 1903; *Kelly's Guide to the Titled and Official Classes* (1906).
2. BP I.G. Diary: April 1904 résumé of events describes BP's inspection of Boys' Brigade in Liverpool (14 April) as 'made under Lord Roberts's instructions', IG Papers, NAM.
3. *The Salford Reporter*, 6 Feb. 1904.
4. *Correspondence of Theodore Roosevelt and Henry Cabot Lodge*, ed. H. Cabot

Lodge (New York 1923), 1103–4.

5. *Scouting for Boys*, 1909 ed., 194.
6. Ibid., 16f.
7. BP 'Deposition as to the Origins of Scout Movement', affidavit of 24 May 1918, sworn at American Consulate, London.
8. Ross, 209; information from Mrs A. Renew, Mafikeng Museum.
9. Details on Mafeking Cadet Corps, BP SD 7 Oct. 1899; General Orders Nos. 165 and 178; Mafikeng Box, information from Mr L. B. Webster, SAA.
10. *Southport Visitor*, 28 Mar. 1903.
11. *Pioneer of Boyhood*, Roger S. Peacock (London Sec. of BB from 1902) (London 1954); *The Boys' Brigade and Scouting*, pamphlet 1983.
12. As n. 2 above.
13. BP I.G. Diary 29 Apr. 1904, NAM.
14. Ibid., 12 Apr.
15. Hillcourt, 248.
16. *Making Men*, W. McG. Eager (London 1953), 325.
17. BP Notes in diary form 30 Apr. 1904, given to Major and Mrs Wade, Ad Ms 50255 BL.
18. Hillcourt 165, 222; *Aids to Scouting* sales figures, TC 3 SAA; Memo re sales from Gale & Polden 4 Sept. 1941, SAA.
19. *Boys' Brigade Gazette*, 1 June 1904.

Chapter Nine
THE BOY MAN TAKES HIS BOW
1. In the Beginning there was a Name: The Boy Scouts (1900–03)

1. BP to HG 13 Apr. 1877, BSA.
2. *Scouting for Boys* (1909 ed.) 25, 193, 195.
3. *Making Men*, 112–13,.
4. BP to 'My dear boys' 23 July 1900, *Jamboree* March 1949.
5. BP to HG 7 June 1902, BSA.
6. Album (43); *Jamboree* March 1948.
7. Scrapbook, Lord Baden-Powell Coll.
8. Damaged untitled newspaper cutting, n.d. but early Sept. 1900, R13 BSA.
9. *Johannesburg Star*, 10 July 1902.
10. The historians are Michael Rosenthal (see bibliog.); J.R. Gillis (see *Youth and History*, New York 1974); Samuel Hynes (see bibliog.); John Springhall (see bibliog.); Anne Summers (see 'Militarism in Britain before the Great War', *History Workshop*, Autumn 1976). A sixth historian, Allen Warren, has recently countered these ideas (see bibliog.). I applaud Dr Warren's effort to redress the balance, and think him right to try to rescue the civil aims of the Movement in the pre-Great War period, but I agree with Dr Springhall that Warren has weakened his argument by ignoring most of the contradictory facts advanced by his opponents. A synthesis of the views of both sides comes closer to the truth. Much of Dr Warren's most telling material is from 1911–1920 (the second part of his twenty-year span) by which time BP was stressing the educational and civil aims of the Movement in order to fight off the threat of compulsory cadet training (see Ch. 12. 1). The years from 1902 to 1909 give a more reliable indication of BP's original purposes – and there the balance between civil and military aims is far more finely balanced than Dr Warren would seem to concede.
11. Ibid., 7 July; Memo to SAC 15 Feb. 1902, original t/s, NAM.
12. BP in *Headquarters' Gazette*, Nov. 1914, 319.
13. BP Scouting Diary 26 July 1912, TC 53 SAA; Scouting Diary 1 Dec. 1926, TC 9 SAA; Document: 'Should it ever be necessary to refute this . . .', and cutting from *John Bull*, n.d., but 1913, TC 42 SAA; papers re E.P. Carter in Transvaal Archives 1903–07.
14. *Boys of the Empire*, 27 Oct. 1900–06 Jan. 1901, PP, BL; *The Use of the Name Boy Scouts in Boys' Literature* (1899–1906) Rev. M.J. Foster (London 1986).
15. Letters re *Boys' Empire League* (1901–03), Dep. 181, 198–203, MP.
16. I am indebted to the Rev. M.J. Foster for drawing the *True Blue War Library* to my attention.
17. Pearson to BP 10 Sept. 1907, R11 BSA.

18. BP to G.H. Mair, Dep. of Information, 5 June 1917, TC 42 SAA.
19. BP to Sec. of *Scout Press* 4 July 1916, replying to letter of 20 June 1916, R15 BSA.

2. Liberals and Frontiersmen (1904–06)

1. BPD 26 Nov. 1906.
2. Information on Warre from Mr P.H.S. Lawrence, Curator, Eton College Museum.
3. *Eton College Chronicle,* 8 Dec. 1904.
4. 'Knights and Retainers: The Earliest Version of Baden-Powell's Boy Scout Scheme', M. Rosenthal, *Journal of Contemporary History,* Vol. 15, (1980), 603–17; also *Character Factory,* 54f.
5. *Eton College Chronicle,* 8 Dec. 1904.
6. *The Scaremongers,* A.J.A. Morris (London 1984), 109.
7. I.G. Scrapbook 28 July, 4 Aug., 27 Oct., 14 Dec. 1905, SAA.
8. *Cardiff Times,* 17 June 1905.
9. BP I.G. Diary 19 May 1906, NAM.
10. *The Countess of Warwick,* M. Blunden (London 1967).
11. BP to P.W. Everett 22 May 1932, EP.
12. BP Affidavit: Origin of the Scouts, 24 May 1918, SAA.
13. *The Army and Society (1815–1914),* Edward M. Spiers (London 1980), 279.
14. Viscount Haldane introducing speech before Baden-Powell's address to R.U.S.I. members 29 Mar. 1911, *Journal of the R.U.S.I.* May 1911.
15. *Chorus to Adventurers,* Roger Pocock (London 1931), 37ff.
16. *Morning Post,* 26 Dec. 1904.
17. Legion uniform regulations pub. 1927; *The Frontiersman's Pocket Book* (1909 ed.).
18. See also *The Frontier Post,* Dec. 1984.
19. *Scouting for Boys* (1909 ed.), 11.
20. Photograph in *Headquarters' Gazette* of Scoutmasters and Boy Scout officials at Crystal Palace Rally Sept. 1908 includes many members of the Legion; photograph in SAA of 1909 'Legion of Frontier Boy Scouts, Ealing, West London'; J.A. Kyle in *The Trail* (May 1922 122ff) lists Scoutmasters who were members of the Legion.
21. *The Scout,* 18 Apr. 1908.
22. *Scouting for Boys* (1909 ed.), 97.

3. Down to Business (1906–08)

1. 'Origins of the Boy Scouts and Girl Guides', t/s c. 1920, R8 BSA.
2. BPD 15 July 1906.
3. *Sir Arthur Pearson,* S. Dark (London 1922), 104f.
4. Ibid., 84, quoting BP's obit. of Pearson.
5. BP to E.T. Seton 1 Aug. 1906, BSA; Hillcourt, 256.
6. W.H. Storer to BP 10 Feb. 1908, TC 42 SAA; *The Scout* 5 Feb. 1910. Allegations of plagiarism in: 'Ernest Thompson Seton and the Origins of the Woodcraft Movement', Brian Morris, *Journal of Contemporary History* Vol. 5, (1970), 183–94; Rosenthal, 64–81.
7. *The Birch-bark Roll of the Woodcraft Indians* (New York 1906), 11–17.
8. BP to Seton 1 Aug. 1906, BSA.
9. W. H. Storer to BP 10 Feb. 1908, TC 42 SAA.
10. W.J.B. Conway to BP n.d. but July 1929, TC 46 SAA.
11. BPD 30 Oct. 1906.
12. Viz *Boys' Life,* 'How the Scouts' Badges Originated', July 1928.
13. *Scouting for Boys* (1909 ed.), 33.
14. *The Scout,* 5 Feb. 1910.
15. Seton to BP 24 June 1910, BSA.
16. 'The Boy Scouts in America', E.T. Seton, n.d. draft article, R13 BSA.
17. BP to J.E. West 5 Feb. 1916, R15 BSA.
18. BP to Seton 31 Oct. 1906, BSA.
19. *The Scout,* 5 Feb. 1910.
20. BP to Seton 17 June 1907, R11 BSA; BP in Waldorf Astoria speech 23 Sep. 1910: 'I purposely have not tried to advocate the idea in this country because I thought you already had your Seton Indians.' R15 BSA.
21. *The Worlds of Ernest Thompson Seton,* J.G. Sansom (New York 1976).

22. *Matabele Campaign*, 55–6.
23. Rosenthal, 72ff.
24. Details in *True Blue War Library* from Apr. 1900 (e.g. 1 Oct. 1900, 24 Dec. 1900 etc.).
25. *V of L* t/s, 850, R9 BSA.
26. BP's Waldorf Astoria speech 23 Sept. 1910, R15 BSA.
27. BP to Seton 24 Sept. 1910, TC 118 SAA.
28. Seton to BP 24 June 1910, BSA.
29. BP R.U.S.I. lecture, 29 Mar. 1911, Haldane's introductory remarks about BP.
30. BP's remarks about 'A Field Marshal's Governess' are in *In Memoriam Charlotte M. Mason*, ed. Essex Cholmondely (London 1966).
31. BP Affidavit on origins of Scouts 24 May 1918, SAA; *V of L*, 271.
32. *The Scout Movement*, E.E. Reynolds (London 1950) [hereafter Reynolds SM], 9–10.
33. BPD 19 May 1907.
34. BPD 5 June 1907.
35. Viz Hillcourt, 262.
36. Information on Mrs Fetherstonhaugh from her gt-grandson Mr T.R. Fetherstonhaugh; also BP letters to HG 15, 16, 17, 20 July 1907; BP to Miss Lucy Lyttelton 21 July 1907, The Karpeles Manuscript Library, Santa Barbara, California.
37. Donald B-P interviewed in *The Eagle and Boys' World*, 22 July 1967.
38. Interview with Arthur Primmer, TC 80 SAA.
39. T.A. Bonfield to T.B.A. Evans-Lombe 3 Jan. 1970, Evans-Lombe Coll.
40. Viz 'I saw the start of the Boy Scout Movement' t/s, circa 1936, R9 BSA.
41. *Jamboree*, New Series 8, vol. ii, Aug. 1947, 270–1: E. E. Reynolds quoting BP; also Hillcourt, 271.
42. Reynolds, 271.
43. Quoted Reynolds SM, 19.
44. Other public school boys who died: R. Grant, W. Rodney, Marc Noble (1st World War). J.M. Evans-Lombe (2nd World War). Brigade Boys: A. Blandford (1st World War); A. Collingbourne of wounds after Armistice.
45. Reynolds SM, 9–10, pamphlet 'Boy Scouts: A Suggestion' 1907.
46. 'Boy Scouts Scheme' pamphlet; agreement with Pearson 30 July 1907, R11 BSA.
47. BP to HG 1 & 2 Sept., 1 Oct. 1907; BPD 15 Nov. 1907.
48. BP to HG 1 Oct. 1907 BSA.
49. *Scaremongers*, 228.
50. Pearson to BP 10 Sept. 1907, BSA.
51. *The Secrets of Success*, P. Keary (London 1906), 7.
52. BP to Pearson 19 Nov. 1907, R11 BSA.
53. Viz Society of Authors to BP 21 Oct. 1907, R11 BSA.
54. Agreement with Pearson's 1 Jan. 1908, R6 BSA.

Chapter Ten
SCOUTING FOR BOYS
1. A Book in a Million (1908)

1. BP to HG 30 Dec. 1907, BSA.
2. *Scouting for Boys*, (2nd ed. 1909), 12; [I use this ed. because it incorporates the contents of the 1st ed. with several important additions].
3. Ibid., 25.
4. Ibid., 27–9.
5. Rosenthal, 168.
6. *Scouting for Boys*, 221–2.
7. Ibid., 48–9.
8. Ibid., 39.
9. From *An Experiment in Autobiography*, H.G. Wells (London 1934), 99.
10. *Scouting for Boys*, 58.
11. Ibid., 105.
12. Ibid., 293.
13. Ibid., 294–5.
14. Ibid., 295.
15. BP in 1909 Diary, on preliminary pages, lists his 1908 achievements as including 4 eds of *Scouting for Boys*. R. Brandon of Pearson's writing to R. Hazelwood 31 Dec. 1954 admits no sales figures have survived. When Pearson's (14 Feb. 1957) created a news event by presenting BP's grandson with the 'millionth copy', their figure was probably an immense underestimate (source: photo of Hon. Robert Baden-Powell re-

ceiving the 'millionth copy', Topical Press AD. 911 Hulton Pic. Lib.).

16. 30,000 cloth, ditto paper cover printed 1909, see contract dated 16 Feb. 1909, TC 1 Folder 1 SAA.

17. R. Brandon to K. Stevens, Scout Assn, 20 March 1967, TC 79 SAA.

18. *Scouting for Boys*, 213.

19. *Angry Young Man*, Leslie Paul (London 1951), 51.

20. Ibid., 53.

21. *BP's Scouts: An Official History of the Boy Scouts Association*, H. Collis, R. Hazlewood and F. Hurll (London 1961), 44.

22. BP's Waldorf Astoria speech 23 Sept. 1910, R15 BSA.

2. 'A Mushroom Growth' (1908–09)

1. McLaren to BP 12 Mar. 1908, R12 BSA.

2. Hillcourt, 289, 292; Reynolds SM, 64.

3. BP to Keary 12 and 13 Mar. 1908, in *The Founding of the Boy Scouts as Seen Through the Letters of Lord Baden-Powell*, ed. P.C. Richards (East Bridgewater, Mass. 1973) [hereafter Richards ed.].

4. BP Territorial Diary (TD) Apr-May 1908, TC 209 SAA.

5. TD 5 Feb. 1909, SAA.

6. TD 5 Feb. and 5 June 1909, SAA.

7. *Scaremongers*, 156–7, 159.

8. Album (Army 2), containing cuttings and letters, SAA.

9. BP to Keary 29 Mar. 1908, Richards ed.

10. Article by Pearse in bound vol. of 1st *Hampstead's magazine*, 1910–12, p. 9, (Burgh Ho., Hampstead) indicates troop was founded between 15 and 30 Jan. 1908. Ist Glasgow Troop has cert. of regist. 26 Jan. (File: First Troop, SAA). On 25 Jan. *Birkenhead News* reported formation of 2 Birkenhead troops the day before. (These were not registered until Feb.) These 4 troops all have a claim to have been Britain's first.

11. Eric G.S. Walker's Diary [EWD] 14 Nov. 1908, Mrs H. Hurly Coll; BP to HG 24 Aug. 1908, BSA.

12. Victor Bridges to Walker 29 Sept. 1908, HC.

13. BP Note of Introduction for Walker 5 Oct. 1908; BP to Walker 4 Oct. 1908, HC.

14. EWD 7 Oct. 1908.

15. BP to Keary 17 Sept. 1908, Richards ed.

16. *Leicester Peace Society Journal* in EWD n.d. but Sept. 1908.

17. BP to Everett 6 Sept. 1908, Everett Papers SAA; EWD Oct. and Nov. 1908.

18. EWD 18 Oct. and 6 Nov. 1908.

19. EWD 15 Dec. 1908; BP to Pearson 19 Nov. 1908, R11 BSA.

20. EWD 18 Nov. 1908.

21. Draft for future Agreement with C.A. Pearson 1 Dec. 1908, EP; BP to Pearson 21 Jan. 1909 and Memo 22 Jan. 1909; BP to Keary 7 Feb. 1909; BP to Lord Blyth 8 Nov. 1909, R11 BSA.

22. Information on Whitehouse *Making Men, Who was Who*; J.S. Dearden (Curator Ruskin Galleries, Bembridge School) letter to author 14 Sept. 1988.

23. BP to Keary 12 Feb. 1909, R11 BSA; BPD 2 Feb. 1909.

24. EWD 2 Oct. 1908.

25. Bott & Stennet Ltd to BP 20 Dec. 1909, (File: Headquarters SAA).

26. Original pamphlet in PCR.

27. Everett to BP 17 May 1909 (BP's comments in margin), EP, SAA.

28. EWD 21 and 23 Dec. 1908, 12 Jan., 5 Feb., 18 June 1909.

29. *Agin the Governments: Memories and Adventures of Sir Francis Vane Bt*, Sir Francis Vane (London 1929), 193; *The Frontiersman* Feb. 1910, p. 21.

30. Vane to BP 21 Dec. 1908, TC 66 SAA.

3. The Vane Rebellion (Oct. 1909 to Jan. 1910)

1. Kyle to H. Moore May–June 1909 various letters, TC 66 SAA.

2. *The British Boy Scouts*, Rev. M. Foster (Pamphlet 1987), 3.

3. Kyle to BP 10 Nov. 1909 TC 66 SAA.

4. Vane to BP 19 July 1909, TC 66 SAA.
5. Kyle to BP 10 Nov. 1909, TC 66 SAA.
6. Elles to BP 12 Nov. 1909, TC 66 SAA.
7. Vane to BP 6 Nov. 1909, TC 66 SAA.
8. BP to Vane 14 Nov. 1909, TC 66 SAA.
9. BP to Vane (unsent draft letter) 17 Nov. 1909, TC 66 SAA.
10. BP to Elles n.d. but 19 Nov. 1909, TC 66 SAA.
11. BP to Vane 20 Nov. 1909, TC 66 SAA.
12. Vane to BP 22 Nov. 1909, TC 66 SAA.
13. BP to Vane 24 or 25 Dec. 1909, TC 66 SAA.
14. Vane to BP 24 and 25 Nov. 1909, TC 66 SAA.
15. T/s n.d. but late Nov. 1909, TC 66 SAA.
16. EWD 12 and 15 Dec. 1908.
17. Elles to BP 4 Dec. 1909, TC 66 SAA.
18. *Daily News*, 4 Dec. 1909.
19. *Daily Express*, 4 Dec. 1909.
20. BP to Elles n.d. but 19 Nov. 1909, TC 66 SAA.
21. Vane to BP 4 June 1910, TC 66 SAA.
22. BP to Vane 15 Jan. 1910, TC 66 SAA.
23. British Boy Scouts headed stationery TC 66 SAA; *Chums* 6 April 1910; Foster, 8–9.
24. BP to C.C. Branch 11 Aug. 1911, TC 32 SAA.
25. *The Times*, 8, 31 Aug., 10, 18 Oct. 1912.
26. *Scouting in London* (1908–1963), P.B. Nevill (London 1966); Papers of the Committee of the London Scout Council esp. BP's letters to A.G. Barralet Nov. 1922.
27. Memo on Function of Headquarters (1924) TC 32 SAA.
28. BP's fullest views on organization and democracy: paper on organization 1932, 01000 R9 BSA; On Reconstruction of Headquarters Organization, Jan. 1918 TC 32 SAA; BP Scouting Diary Australian visit 15 June 1912, TC 49 SAA.
29. BP Inspection Order Book 11 Mar. 1911, Ad Ms 50255a BL.

4. Character Factory or Helping Hand?

1. *The Boy Scouts, Class and Militarism in Relation to British Youth Movements, 1908–1930*, J.O. Springhall, *International Review of Social History* 16 (1971), p. 158.
2. Rosenthal, 192.
3. *Scouting for Boys*, 292.
4. BP to Town Clerks & YMCA Secs 28 Oct. 1907, Richards ed.
5. BP to Capt MacIlwain 9 Dec. 1909 R11 BSA.
6. *The Boy Knight*, Sir Francis Vane (London 1910), p. 1.
7. Kyle or Elles to Earl of Meath 3 Aug. 1910, TC 42 SAA.
8. HG to Frances 5 July 1909, FBPA.
9. EWD 4 Sep. 1909.
10. *Manchester Guardian*, 24 Oct. 1913.
11. 'Scouting: The Parents' Point of View', draft t/s, *c*. 1930, R7 BSA.
12. M/s quotation attributed by BP to Emma [a mistake for Elizabeth] Haldane (sister of R.B. Haldane), R8 BSA.
13. Rosenthal, 8, 104.
14. 'The Boy Scout Movement' draft article, *c*. 1920, TC 21 SAA.
15. *Workers and Shirkers*, pamphlet, reprinted from *Pearson's Magazine*, 1910 and 1911.
16. 'Boy Scouts Scheme' pamphlet (1907): 'Play the Game: Don't Look On'.
17. 'The Educational Possibilities of Scouting', lecture by BP to the Scoutmasters' Training Course, 1911, R12 BSA.
18. BP to J. Metelerhamp 14 Nov. 1911, R11 BSA.
19. Rosenthal, 6, 284 n. 2.
20. *Rovering and Rangering*, t/s, R8 BSA.
21. Viz 'Scouting in its Tenth Year' (1917), in which lecture 'intelligence' heads the list of character ingredients, R7 BSA.
22. BP to A.G. Wade 25 Nov. 1910, Ad Ms 50255 BL.
23. BP to Col Leslie n.d. but 1910–14, R15 BSA.
24. As n. 17 above.
25. M/s on Education by BP n.d. but context indicates 1913–14, TC 21 SAA.

26. Tribute from Madame Montessori 2 Sept. 1939, Lord Somers Papers SAA (enclosed in letter BP to Somers 12 Nov. 1939).

27. Allen Warren in *Sir Robert Baden-Powell, the Scout Movement and citizen training in Great Britain, 1900–1920 (English Historical Review* April 1986) is the only scholar to touch on them (footnote 2 p. 377).

28. Gaddum to BP 23 Sept. 1917, Gaddum Papers, Anthony Gaddum Coll.

29. R. Philipps to Gaddum 19 Nov. 1913, Gaddum Papers.

30. *Haverford West Telegraph* 17 Apr. 1913.

31. See Philipps Papers, SAA.

32. *Toynbee Hall: 50 Years of Social Progress*, J.A.R. Pimlott (London 1934), ch xi.

5. *Wood-smoke at Twilight:
The Great Escape*

1. J. Burns in *The Sunday Times*, 22 Aug. 1920.

2. E.A. Brett-James (quoting Gerald Heard) to BP 9 May 1937, TC 41 SAA.

3. *The Boy Scout Bubble: A Review of a Great Futility*, Captain Noemo (London 1912), 25–7, 46.

4. Leslie Paul quoted Reynolds SM, 69.

5. Viz Rosenthal, 245; Springhall, *Youth Empire and Society*, 62.

6. 'A Chosen Twelve', unpub. t/s by J. Hargrave, incl. essay on BP, Mrs Diana Hargrave Coll.

7. Quoted in articles 'The Call of the Open' and 'The Brotherhood of Nature', 1931; *Rovering to Success* 212.

8. *The Neo-pagans*, Paul Delany (London 1987), 13f, 67; Gathorne-Hardy 316–17; Devine to BP 24 July 1925 TC 27 SAA.

9. 'The Founder and His Family', E.K. Wade, unpub.t/s, n.d. but *c.* 1945–50, R15 BSA.

10. Delany, 57.

11. See 'Inside the Whale', George Orwell (1940).

12. BP Waldorf Astoria speech 23 Sept. 1910, R15 BSA; 'The Call of the Wild', *Greyfriar*, July 1911.

13. 'The Herd Instinct', Wilfred Trotter, *Sociological Review* (1908).

14. 'A Possible Aid to Education' n.d. R7 BSA.

15. Quoted in *Building Character in the American Boy: The Boy Scouts, YMCA and their Forerunners 1870–1920*, David I. MacLeod (Wisconsin 1983), 45.

16. BP address to Army P.T. Instructors *c.* July/Aug. 1923, R7 BSA.

17. *Boy Scouts's Farm: A National Need and Remedy* pamphlet, 1911, R12 BSA; BP advocacy of emigration to S. Australia 22 June 1912, TC 49 SAA.

18. *Westward Ho!*, Charles Kingsley (London 1855), 10.

19. Quoted in *Dreams of Adventure, Deeds of Empire*, Martin Green (London 1980), 286.

20. *V of L* t/s, 311, R8 BSA.

21. 'Look Wide', t/s, R7 BSA.

22. *Scouting for Boys*, 56–7.

23. 'Common Sense' m/s n.d., R7 BSA.

24. *The Matabele Campaign*, 83.

25. From Act One of *Death of a Salesman*.

26. *Scouting for Boys*, 297–8.

27. Humphrey Carpenter in *Secret Gardens* (London 1985) develops this idea in detail, esp. 177f.

28. 'If I were a Boy Again' painted by Ernest S. Carlos 1911.

29. 'Old Scouts' t/s 1919, TC 27 SAA; Pamphlet 'About those Boy Scouts' (1927).

30. BP Waldorf Astoria speech 23 Sept. 1910, R15 BSA.

31. *Scouting for Boys*, 56.

32. BP to HG 3 Oct. 1909, BL BSA; BPD 3 Oct. 1909.

33. *Adventures and Accidents*: 'A Scouting Thrill', 166f.

Chapter Eleven
AN UNEXPECTED MARRIAGE
1. *Woes and Widows (1910–12)*

1. BP to Sir William Hoy 27 Jan. 1926, TC 53 SAA.

2. 'A Rat-like Day' m/s, n.d.. R7 BSA.

3. *27 Years with Baden-Powell*, E.K. Wade (Gloucester 1957), 15.

4. EWD 21 Feb. and 14 Mar. 1910.
5. EWD 6 Oct. 1909.
6. EWD 27 Feb. 1910.
7. EWD 13 June 1910.
8. EWD 25 Apr. 1910.
9. *Greyfriar*, July 1911 'Scouting'; BPD 15, 21 Sept. 1911.
10. BPD 13 Sept. 1911.
11. HG's letters to F 1905–13, FBPA.
12. Hillcourt, 309–12.
13. BP to HG 5 July 1912, BSA.
14. *Clubland Heroes*, Richard Usborne (London 1953), 101–2.
15. BP to HG 20 Oct. 1890, BSA.
16. BP to Frances 11 Aug. 1907, FBPA.
17. BP to Frances 29 Aug. 1908, JM.
18. BPD 29 Dec. 1911.

2 The Arcadian Girl (Jan. 1912)

1. BP to HG 3 and 6 Jan. 1912, BSA.
2. Scrapbook 1912, Girl Guides' Assn; Hillcourt, 320; 6 letters to HG Jan. 1912, BSA.
3. *V of L*, 269–70.
4. BPD 4 Jan. 1912; BP to HG 3 Jan. 1912, BSA.
5. Record of Harold Soames's Estate at Somerset House.
6. Anonymous friend of BP to E.E. Reynolds, Olave BP File SAA.
7. Scrapbook 1912, Girl Guides' Assn.
8. 'Arthur's Book': a handwritten account of her youth, marriage and family life presented to her only son by Katharine Soames, Mrs Diana Cairns (née Soames) Coll.
9. Mrs Annie Scofield (née Court) interviews with author 14, 22 Jan. 1984.
10. *Window on my Heart*, Olave Baden-Powell and Mary Drewery London 1973), 24 [hereafter *Window*].
11. *Window*, 21.
12. *Window*, 31–2.
13. OBP to Josephine Pollock (née Reddie) 22 Jan. 1943, Mrs Pollock Coll.
14. Mrs Scofield interviews.
15. 'Arthur's Book' March 1910.
16. *Window*, 19, 27, 33.
17. 'Arthur's Book' Dec. 1909.
18. *Window*, 56; OPB to Christian Rawson-Shaw (née Davidson)

1 Mar. 1961, Mrs Antonia Eastman Coll.
19. 'Arthur's Book' Aug. 1903.
20. Undated press cutting sent to author by 'Ba's' nephew's widow Mrs Marjorie M. Gubbins.
21. Three letters to the author from Mrs Hope M. Chance, sister-in-law of Norah Chance, 'Ba's' companion; Mrs M. Gubbins to author 7 Dec. 1983.
22. Castletown guest book: Castletown, Rockcliffe, Cumberland.
23. Four interviews with Mrs E.K. Wade, 1983 and 1984.
24. 'Arthur's Book' 12 Aug. 1903, photograph of picnic.
25. Interviews with Mrs Scofield.
26. *Window*, 48.
27. *Window*, 51–3.
28. *Window*, 54.
29. *Window*, 65.

3 The Reluctant Bridegroom
(Jan. to Oct. 1912)

1. OBP Diary 17 and 23 Jan. 1912, quoted Hillcourt, 323, *Window*, 68–9.
2. *Window*, 69.
3. Ibid., 68.
4. *The Story of the Girl Guides*, Rose Kerr (London 1932), 163: this reference was cut from subsequent editions.
5. BP to OBP 26 Jan. 1912, quoted *Window*, 71-2.
6. *Window*, 73.
7. Ibid., 74.
8. BP to OBP 26 Jan. 1912, quoted *Window*, 71.
9. BP Diary 25 Jan. 1912, BSA; *Window*, 71.
10. OBP Diary 9 Feb. 1912, quoted *Window*, 75.
11. BP to OBP 5 March 1912, quoted Hillcourt 327; *Window*, 76.
12. *Window*, 78–9.
13. BP to OBP 30 Jan. 1912, quoted *Window*, 74.
14. *Window*, 76–7.
15. In *Window* Olave dated the arrival of this undated letter as 9 days after the arrival of one written on 5 Mar. So it

was probably written on 14 or 15 Mar.

16. BP to HG 16 Mar. 1912, BSA.
17. BP to Frances 3 Mar. 1912, JM.
18. Between 1909 and 1911, The Boy Scouts Assn. raised almost £10,000 by public appeal. On 24 May 1910 BP signed contract with Pearson's for 3rd ed. of *Scouting for Boys*. (The previous ed. of 60,000 copies printed in 1909 had already sold out.) The new 1910 ed. was 40,000 in paper at 1/- per copy and ditto in cloth at 2/- per copy. BP's royalty was a straight 25%; so on a sold-out ed. he would make £1,500. Agreement for new ed. signed in 1913, so the old one had sold out within two years giving BP £750 per annum from this one title. Details of contracts TC 1, Folder 1, and EP.
19. In Everett Papers, vol. xiii, 41–3, under 'Baden-Powell Problems', (n.d. but 1941), Percy Everett explained that, after the separation of the Scouts from Pearson, BP had received *Scouting for Boys* and *Girl Guiding* royalties. In 1912, he also had in print *Yarns for Boy Scouts* and *Scouting Games*. He was also the nominal editor, on a royalty, for a popular series of boys' books (*B-P's Books for Boys*). Contract with Hannaford Bennett & Co., EP. Precise earnings not listed until end of 1915 (back of diary) and end of 1917.
20. Kyle to Pearson's 12 Mar. 1910, BSA; BP to Everett 15 Dec. 1912, EP.
21. The actual sum earned was £845.
22. HG's listing of 'Family Income, Expenditure and Taxes for 1912', JM; received by BP 23 Sept. 1912 (BPD).
23. Edward Heywood to HG 21 Dec. 1911, JM.
24. *Window*, 77; Hillcourt, 329.
25. BP to HG 5 July 1912, BSA.
26. Hillcourt, 333.
27. *Window*, 77.
28. OBP Diary 17 Aug. 1912, quoted *Window*, 82.
29. BPD 25–28 Aug. 1912.

30. *Window*, 83; BP to HG 4 Sept. 1912, BSA; BP to Frances 30 Mar. 1912, FBPA.
31. *Window*, 83; BPD 13 Sept. 1912.
32. BP to M. Wroughton 12 Sept. 1912, Mrs A. Lunn Coll.
33. *Window*, 83–4.
34. Ibid., 84.
35. 'Arthur's Book', Sept. 1912.
36. BP to Olave 17 Sept. 1913, quoted *Window*, 85–6.
37. BP to HG 5 July 1912, BSA.
38. *Window*, 86.
39. BP to HG 14 Sept. 1912 BSA.
40. 'Arthur's Book', Sept. 1912.
41. BP Diary 21, 25, 29 Sept. etc; *Window*, 85–6.
42. *Window*, 90–1.
43. A to HG 31 Oct. 1912, JM.
44. *Window*, 86.
45. OBP Diary 31 Oct. 1912, quoted *Window*, 91.
46. BPD after 30 Dec. 1912 'Summary of Year.'

4. Settling Down (1912–14)

1. BP to HG 30 Oct. 1912, BSA.
2. File: Founder's Dreams, SAA: 3 Mar. n.y.
3. BP to HG 5 Nov. 1912, BSA.
4. BP to HG 30 May 1908, BSA.
5. File: Founder's Dreams: BP's final comments after accounts of dreams often refer to these headaches; also *Window*, 93–4, 114; Hillcourt 337; misc. letters to HG Dec. 1912; BPD 1912.
6. BP to Mercers' 28 Dec. 1912, Mercers' Company Archives; BP to Frances 10 Jan. 1913, FBPA.
7. Lt-Col. Beevor to HG 12 July 1901; Hillcourt, 224.
8. Viz BP Diary 13 Apr. 1913.
9. *The Scotsman*, 'Baden-Powell: Personal Recollections', Arthur Poyser, 13 Jan. 1941; also note in BP's hand n.d. connecting new sleeping arrangements with cure of headaches.
10. *Window*, 93.
11. Viz BPD numerous dates Nov. 1909.
12. BP to HG 13 Dec. 1912; BP to HG 8 Feb. 1913, BSA.

13. The Hon. Betty St Clair Clay (née BP) in film *Scouts!*, produced Mike Murphy 1984, BBC2 transmitted 1985.
14. *Window*, 94.
15. OBP to Walker n.d. but early 1913, HC.
16. OBP to Donald 18 Oct. 1916, FBPA.
17. BP to HG 31 Jan. 1913, BSA.
18. BP to HG 8 Feb. 1913, BSA.
19. Interview with author, 21 June 1984.
20. Interview with author, 15 Aug. 1984.
21. *The Lady*, 19 Feb. 1914: profile by Marion Holmes.
22. *Window*, 99.
23. *The Guide*, Rose Kerr profile of OBP, vol. xiv, 45.
24. Roland Philipps to OBP 16 Mar. 1916, Philipps Papers, SAA.
25. *Window*, 97.
26. Interviews with Annie Scofield 14, 22 Jan. 1984.
27. Interview with Mrs Yvonne Broome (née Davidson) 9 Aug. 1984.
28. *Window*, 97.
29. As n. 21 above.
30. Herbert Jenkins, quoted Hillcourt, 337–8.
31. Notes on causes of death of G and Frances, FBPA.

Chapter Twelve
'THE BIGGEST EVENT IN OUR NATIONAL HISTORY'
1. Almost a Disaster (Aug. 1914)

1. *Morning Post*, 24 July 1914.
2. Rosenthal, 227, 229.
3. BPD 26 July 1910.
4. BP to Lord Lanesborough 9 Jan. 1910, TC 9 SAA.
5. S.F. Irwin Diary, (8 Lord Roberts's Boys and 7 Boy Scouts went with BP to Canada in Aug. 1910: see BP's Canadian Scrapbook) TC 9 SAA; BPD 27 July 1910.
6. BP Scouting Diary 26 July 1912; t/s draft dated Aug. 1912, notes on the Boy Scout Movement in South Africa, TC 53 SAA.
7. *Trafalgar News*, 27 June 1912; mani-festo issued by the BP Boy Scouts Organization in Victoria, 13 Mar. 1912: information from A.R. Milne M.B.E., Victoria Branch Archivist.
8. Everett to BP 21 June 1915, TC 3 SAA; *Times Ed. Supp*, 4 July 1918, 'Cadets, Scouts and Guides'.
9. Census 1913 137, 776 Boy Scouts in UK; Springhall in *Boy Scouts, Class and Militarism*, 153 n. 1, states that only 40% of 137, 776: i.e. 55,110 were eligible. So 6,000 was 10. 9% of 55,110.
10. See BP to A.G. Wade 20 July 1915, on 'Service Scouts' as a compromise between 'compulsory military training and extension of school training views', Ad Ms 50255a BL. In committee C.C. Branch and the Rev. W. Twining also opposed 'Service Scouts'.
11. BP to Arthur Gaddum 10 Jan., Philipps to Gaddum 8 Aug. 1915, Gaddum Papers, and letters (1915–16) in Philipps Coll; BP Diary Summary 1915, also Diary 8, 13, 29 Dec. 1915. BSA.
12. 'Boy Scouts and the Country', t/s, PCR; 'Scouts in War', t/s, R7 BSA.
13. Memo on Cadets 10 Sept. 1918, t/s dictated by BP R13 BSA; BPD 20 June, 5 Sept. 1918; notes of meeting with Lord Scarborough, R11 BSA.
14. BPD 6 Aug. 1914.
15. A. Slingsby to A. Gaddum n.d Aug. 1914, Gaddum Papers.
16. De Burgh War Diary 23 Aug. 1914, R11 BSA.
17. BPD 6 Aug. 1914, visits Dr Jackson about headaches.
18. De Burgh War Diary 6–8 Aug. 1914, R11 BSA; Reynolds SM 78–9.
19. BPD 8 Aug. 1914, BSA; 'The War', t/s, R8 BSA.
20. *Window*, 101.

2. Being There (1915–18)

1. *Window*, 103–4.
2. BPD Apr. 1916; *Window*, 105; Annie Scofield interviews.
3. 'Mercers' Arms' carbon t/s, 1918, TC 118 SAA.
4. *The Scout*, Spencer Leeming, 19 Feb. 1948.

5. BP to Burnham 17 Aug. 1914, Burnham Papers.

6. BP speech at YMCA in London 1917, R7 BSA.

7. 'A Poser', draft by BP, 14 Apr. 1917, R11 BSA.

8. *Collected Letters of Wilfred Owen* (London 1967), 506, 521, 536, 570-1.

9. 'The Religious Aim' t/s approx 1927, R15 BSA.

10. YMCA Hon Sec. to BP 31 Jan. 1916, quoting BP's pamphlet for 'Old Scouts', which the 'Y' thought blasphemous, TC 95 SAA.

11. 29 Mar. 1915 BP War Diary, R6 BSA.

12. 21 July Ibid.

13. 31 Mar. Ibid.

14. Quoted in *The Old Lie: The Great War and the Public School Ethos*, P. Parker (London 1987).

15. *Siegfried Sassoon's Diaries: 1915-1918*, ed. R. Hart-Davis (London 1968), June 1917, p. 176.

16. BP to Frances 11 Oct. 1907, FBPA.

17. BPD 2 Oct. 1908; BP to Keary 12 Sept. 1908, Richards ed.; *Young Germany*, W.Z. Laqueur (London 1962), 73.

18. 5 April 1915 BP War Diary, R6 BSA.

19. Ibid, July–Aug.

20. BPD 27 Oct. 1918.

21. Philipps to BP 5 Mar. 1916, Philipps Papers.

22. *Siegfried Sassoon's Diaries: 1915-1918*, 2, 4 Apr. 1916.

23. Chief Scout's speech at opening of World Camp at Foxlease 1924 (official programme p. 7).

24. 5 April 1915 BP War Diary, R6 BSA.

25. *Boston Post*, 2 Feb. 1912.

26. BP to Donald 7 Jan. 1916, 17 Apr. 1917, FBPA.

27. Rosenthal, 281; *The Old Lie*, 283-4.

28. BP to Miss Nugent (later Mrs Wade) 15 Feb. 1918, R11 BSA.

29. Code Letters in HC 6 Sept. 1915, 9 May, 16 Sept., 27 Dec. 1916, 22 Dec. 1917, 8 Sept. 1918.

30. 'A Night Patrol', Aug. 1917, t/s, R7 BSA.

Chapter Thirteen
THE FAMILY MAN
1. *No Place Like Home (1916–18)*

1. *Baden-Powell: A Family Album*, Heather King (Gloucester 1986) [hereafter HFA], 2-3; *Window*, 117.

2. BPD 12 Nov. 1918.

3. *Window*, 121; HFA 7; *27 Years with Baden-Powell*, E.K. Wade (Blandford 1957) [hereafter *27 Years*], 46-7.

4. *27 Years*, 51-2.

5. 'A Chosen Twelve, unpub. t/s, J. Hargrave.

6. Grace Browning, interview with author 15 Aug. 1984.

7. *The Victorian Scout*, W.D. Kennedy, 'A Camp Fire Yarn on BP', Feb. 1941.

8. 'Recollections', Ann Kindersley, m/s, C.J. O'Ferrall Coll.

9. Miss Jean Harrap conversation with the author 10 Aug. 1983; Katharine Furse to Sybil Rocksavage 4 Dec. 1925; interview with the Hon. Mrs Heather King 29 Nov. 1984.

10. HFA, 8; *Window*, 125.

11. Mrs K. Lessiter interview with author 18 June 1984.

12. *27 Years*, 15.

13. OBP to Mrs Wade Good Friday 1915, PCR.

14. Discussion between author and Paul. C. Richards, who had talked about this with Mrs Wade when he bought many of Mrs Wade's Baden-Powell letters.

15. BP to Mrs Wade n.d. (but 1932), PCR.

16. BP to Mrs Wade 12 May 1939, Maj. James Wade Coll.

17. OBP to Mrs Wade 18 May 1935, PCR.

18. OBP to Mrs Wade 19 Nov. 1918, PCR.

19. BP to Everett (draft) 25 Jan. 1924, PCR.

20. BP to Everett 15 Jan. 1924, EP.

21. BP to Miss Collier 22 Mar. 1933, SAA.

22. *The Piper of Pax* published in 1924 was just that.

23. Misc. notes to Mrs Wade, R11 BSA, PCR and James Wade Coll.

24. Maj. A.G. Wade Occasional Diary viz Jan. 1931, James Wade Coll.
25. Viz OBP to Mrs Wade n.d. but Jan. 1920, PCR.
26. Mrs Lessiter interview with author 18 June 1984.
27. BPD 5 Nov. 1921.
28. *Window*, 126.
29. Interviews with Mrs Annie Scofield, Mrs Lessiter, the Hon. Mrs King and Mrs Wade.
30. Interviews with Miss Grace Browning and the Hon. Mrs Elizabeth Coke, 22 Sept. 1984.
31. BP to OBP 31 Jan. 1916, quoted *Window*, 191.
32. BPD 22 June 1920, 20 Sept. 1921, 1 Dec. 1924.
33. 'Reminiscences' of Mr D.P. Eggar sent to author 30 Feb. 1985.
34. BP to Donald 1 Jan. 1919, FBPA.
35. OBP to Walker mid Jan. 1919, HC.
36. OBP to Christian (Rawson-Shaw, née Davidson) 23 Aug. 1974, Mrs Antonia Eastman Coll.
37. Mrs Annie Scofield interviews with author Jan. 1984.
38. OBP to Christian 23 Aug. 1974, Eastman.
39. OBP to Christian 5 Sept. 1974, Eastman.
40. Various notes and cuttings under heading of 'Auto-Suggestion and Mr Coué', Pats and Pinpricks, File 1, SAA.
41. Hon. Mrs Heather King interview with author 29 Nov. 1984.

2. Parental Pains and Pleasures (1915–22)

1. BPD Apr.–May 1916, *Window*, 105.
2. BPD 10 Dec. 1916.
3. BPD 31 Dec. 1916.
4. Details of Bexhill house and staff BP Diary 18 Oct. 1916; first reference to children there 30 Sept. 1916, but OBP had been in Bexhill in June making arrangements.
5. Interviews with Mrs Annie Scofield.
6. BPD 4 Jan. 1917.
7. Various letters to Miss Nugent, Jan.–April 1916, PCR; *Window*, 105.
8. BPD 16 April 1917.
9. BPD 28 April 1917.

10. 'The Father I Knew', Peter BP in *Boys' Life* 1961.
11. BPD 25 Dec. 1918.
12. Brig. W. Collingwood to author 28 Dec. 1983.
13. The Hon. Mrs Heather King interview with author 29 Nov. 1984.
14. Mrs Annie Scofield interviews with author Jan. 1984.
15. Ibid.
16. OBP to Donald 1 Jan. 1919, FBPA.
17. H. Wilson to BP 28 Nov. 1913, FBPA.
18. BP to Mrs Cuthell, 31 Oct. 1913, Mrs F. Turnbull Coll.
19. BP to Miss Nugent n.d. but 1918, R11 DSA, DP to Walker 24 Feb. 1918, HC.
20. BP to Miss Nugent n.d. but 1914, James Wade Coll; BP to Mrs Wade n.d. but *c.* 1922, R11 BSA.
21. HFA, 21.
22. BPD 17 Feb. 1920.
23. HFA, 33.
24. Hon. Mrs Betty Clay interviews with author 28 Nov. 1983, 13 Dec. 1984.
25. Mrs K. Lessiter interviews with author 18 June 1984.
26. Ibid.
27. HFA, 14–15.
28. BPD 22 Apr. 1919.
29. BPD 20 Jan. 1922.

Chapter Fourteen
WHAT TO DO WITH THE GIRLS
1. Can Girls be Scouts? (1909–10)

1. *The Story of the Girl Guides 1908–1932*, Rose Kerr (London 1932, repub. 1976), 14, 29 [hereafter Kerr].
2. 'Boy Scouts Scheme' 1907 Pamphlet, R12 BSA.
3. *The Scout*, 16 May 1908, 'Can Girls be Scouts?'
4. *The Scout*, 12 Sept. 1908.
5. Kerr, 30.
6. 'Rangers', 'Haven't women got as much character as men?' R8 BSA .
7. BP to ed. *Morning Post*, 9 Aug. 1913.
8. *Scouting for Boys* (1909 ed), 41; BPD 9 May 1909 BSA.
9. BP to HG 28 June 1909, BSA.

10. Annie Scofield recalled HG in 1913 warning BP about this, so her views in 1909 would have been more pronounced.
11. Everett to BP 27 Aug. 1909. BP's comments were written on the margin and then sent back to Everett.
12. *Spectator*, 4 Dec. 1909.

2. The Rise and Fall of Agnes Baden-Powell (1910–24)

1. Attached to Pamphlet 'B' (1910 Girl Guides' Assn), 'Mother's letter' dated 11 June 1909.
2. Kerr, 39.
3. A's letters to HG 29 May 1910–12 Feb. 1913 in JM contain numerous refs to Girl Guides' business.
4. *The Handbook for Girl Guides*, BP and A (London 1912), 340.
5. Ibid., 394.
6. *27 Years*, 26.
7. *Window*, 109.
8. BPD 2 Oct., 16 Nov., 3 Dec., 17 Dec. 1914, BSA.
9. BPD 23 Dec. 1916; Kerr, 89–90.
10. *Window*, 86.
11. BPD 24 Apr. 1919.
12. OBP's 'Private History of the Movement', written for Dame Katharine Furse, 1924, Furse Papers [hereafter FP], Bristol University Library, Special Colls.
13. *Window*, 108.
14. BPD 23 Dec. 1919.
15. BPD 17 Jan. 1924.
16. BPD 20–21 Mar. 1924.
17. BPD 6, 20, 21 July, 11 Aug. 1924; Miss Grace Browning interview with author .
18. BPD 9, 15–19 July 1928.
19. BPD 22, 28 Sept. 1931.
20. OBP to Everett, 11 Oct. 1924, EP; OBP to Katharine Furse [KF] 19 June 1923, FP.
21. Mrs Josephine Pollock interview with author 1 Feb. 1984.
22. As n. 12 above.
23. OBP to Everett 6 May 1918, EP.
24. Mrs E.K. Wade interviews with author 12 Aug., 14 Oct. 1983, 14 Jan. 1984.
25. BP to Mrs A. Blyth 16 Aug. 1916, Mrs Camilla Shoolbred Coll.
26. Mrs Blyth to OBP 1 Sept. 1918; Miss Baird to Miss Gumpert 22 Oct. 1918; the 4 new members were Alice Behrens, Lady Helen Whitaker, Muriel Messel, Mrs Kerr.
27. Olive Crosby to Mrs Blyth 30 Aug. 1918, Shoolbred Coll.
28. As n. 12 above.
29. OBP to Everett, 27 Nov. 1938, EP; the Hon. Mrs Heather King interview with author 29 Nov. 1984.
30. Lord Renton to author 5 July 1984.

3. At the Court of Queen Olave (1919–30)

1. Information, Ann, Countess of Rosse, niece of Muriel Messel; photographs of Muriel in OBP's 1918 Scrapbook, GG Assn; BPD numerous refs to Muriel 1916–18.
2. Information Miss Grace Browning.
3. Early history of Hampshire Girl Guides and leading figures by Mrs Eggar, m/s, J.H. Morrison Coll; viz Helen Whitaker to Ann Kindersley 14 Aug. 1924, C.J. O'Ferrall Coll.
4. BPD 9 Aug. 1924; A. Kindersley's Guiding Diary/Scrapbook, and letters, C.J. O'Ferrall Coll.
5. Gathorne-Hardy, 291–2.
6. Kerr, 93; Mrs K. Lessiter interview with author.
7. Grace Browning interview with author; Kerr, 93, 162; C. Anstruther Thomson to Agatha Blyth n.d. but Sept. 1918, Shoolbred Coll.
8. OBP to Mrs Wade 26 Aug. 1940, PCR.
9. *Helen Gwynne-Vaughan*, Molly Izzard (London 1969).
10. Ibid., 105.
11. OBP to KF 18 Nov. 1919, FP.
12. OBP to KF 17 Feb. 1922, FP.
13. OBP to KF 22 May 1922, FP.
14. *Hearts and Pomegranates*, Katharine Furse (London 1940), 262.
15. T/s draft of *Hearts and Pomegranates*, 1–3, DM 190, FP.
16. Ibid., 116.
17. *Hearts and Pomegranates*, 183.
18. T/s draft DM 190–1, 159, FP.

19. *The Commissioners' Book* (1926), Dame KF writing in, p. 24.

20. OBP to Everett, n.d. but *c*. 3 Oct. 1922, EP.

21. OBP to KF 28 Nov. 1922, FP.

22. OBP to KF 17 Dec. 1922, FP.

23. OBP to KF 15 Aug. 1919, FP.

24. Miss Mary Gaddum's letters to author 1983–7; privately printed family history of the Behrens family, Anthony Gaddum Coll; information from Violet, Lady Merthyr.

25. KF to OBP 26 May 1923 (copy), FP.

26. Ibid.

27. KF to OBP 18 June 1923 (copy), FP.

28. OBP to KF 24 June 1923, FP.

29. OBP to KF 19 July 1923, FP.

30. KF to Lady Delia Peel 1 Oct. 1925 (copy), FP .

31. KF to OBP 12 Nov. 1923 (copy), FP.

32. OBP to KF 30 Nov. 1923, FP.

33. OBP to KF 30 Nov. 1923; BP to KF 3 Dec. 1923, FP.

34. Memo by KF 9 Dec. 1923, FP.

35. KF to OBP 22 Feb. 1925 (copy), FP.

36. KF to Helen Gwynne-Vaughan 11 Mar. 1925 (copy), FP.

37. KF to OBP 17 July, 17 Aug. 1925 (copies), FP.

38. KF to Mrs Essex Reade 31 Aug. 1925 (copy), FP.

39. 'Suggested Constitution of a World Committee' by BP, t/s, 1927, FP .

40. KF to OBP 13 July 1930 (copy); OBP to KF 13 Mar. 1932, FP.

41. Memo to KF from BP 1 Aug. 1932, FP.

42. Memo to KF from BP 5 Sept. 1932, FP.

43. Mrs G. Strode to KF n.d. Jan. 1925, FP.

Chapter Fifteen

WIDER STILL AND WIDER

1. American Dreams and Nightmares (1910–31)

1. Statistics British Scout Assn. and Boys Scouts of America.

2. E.W. Robinson to BP 24 May 1910, and other corresp. with Robinson and with J.E. West 1910–11, R11 BSA.

3. BP to West 24 Nov. 1911; West to BP 9 Dec. 1911, 2 Feb. 1912, R11 BSA

4. BPD 23 Feb. 1912.

5. BP to HG 23 Feb. 1912, BSA.

6. Black Album 'A', containing m/s fragments, SAA.

7. BP to M. Maure 12 Mar. 1930, R11 BSA.

8. Memo to West, Howse, and Head, June 1927, R7 BSA.

9. BP's corresp. with West, viz West to BP 11 Dec. 1915, R15 BSA.

10. *New York Times*, 6 Dec. 1915, TC 42 SAA.

11. BP to West 18 June 1940; BP to West 1 Sept. 1940; R11 BSA.

12. *V of L* t/s, 152–7, R9 BSA; BP to Mrs Wade 27 Apr. 1926, R11 BSA.

13. Diary of US visit 6–8 Mar. 1930; BP's report to Committee of the Council 11 Apr. 1930, TC 54 SAA.

14. *Rovering to Success*, 40.

15. Pats amd Pinpricks, File 1, SAA.

16. 'Success is Open to the Poorest' (1928) article, TC 21 SAA.

17. BPD, visits to *Covered Wagon*, 18 Sept., 4 Oct. 1923; OBP 1923 Scrapbook, GG Assn., Col. McCoy's visit to Gilwell Oct. 1923.

2. The Empire: White and Black (1912–36)

1. BP to Col. D. Cosgrove 6 June 1921, S. Assn of N.Z.

2. Roydhouse Papers, Bungaroo District, S. Assn of Austr; BP Scouting Diary of Australian Visit 1912, TC 49 SAA.

3. BP Scouting Diary of Australian Visit 1931, 22, 26 April, 13 May, TC 49 SAA.

4. Ibid, 15 May.

5. BP to Col. H.S. Brownrigg 2 Dec. 1916, TC 53 SAA; BP to H.W. Soutter 13 Jan. 1916, TC 53 SAA.

6. BPD 20, 27 Sept. 1926, BSA.

7. Founder Tours: 'Colour Question', BP South African Diary 20 Sept. 1926, TC 9 SAA.

8   Sir A. Pickford to F.H. Hodgkinson 13 June 1927, TC 6 SAA.
9   BP South African Diary 26 Nov. 1926, TC 9 SAA.
10. Ibid, 29 Sept. 1926; F.H. Hodgkinson to BP 30 Mar., 6 July 1927, TC 53 SAA.
11. BP South African Diary 3 Oct. 1926, TC 9 SAA.
12. Ibid, 13 Oct.
13. Ibid, Note: 'Native Question', 1 Apr. 1927.
14. Ibid, 2–3 Apr. 1927.
15. BP to J.C. Ferguson 3 May 1927, TC 53 SAA.
16. H.V. Marsh to S.A. Scout Council 16 May 1935, TC South Africa [hereafter SA] SAA.
17. J.D. Rheinault Jones to International Bureau 15 Aug. 1935, TC SA, SAA.
18. BP to Sir R Blankenberg 18 Feb. 1936, TC SA, SAA.
19. Granville Walton to BP 6 Mar. 1936; Rheinault Jones to BP 28 Jan. 1936, TC SA, SAA.
20. Pats and Pinpricks, File 2, SAA.
21. BP to Lord Clarendon 31 July 1936, TC SA, SAA.
22. Blankenberg to BP 21 Apr. 1936, TC SA SAA.
23. Memorandum by H.V. Marsh on Non-European Scouts 6 Aug. 1935, TC SA SAA.
24. MacLeod, 214–215.
25. BP to Gen. E.S. May 8 May 1916, TC 51 SAA.
26. W.P. Pakenham-Walsh to BP 14 Dec. 1916, TC 51, SAA.
27. Mrs Besant in *New Indian* (local daily ed.) 19 Dec. 1917.
28. BP to R.B. Chapman 16 Feb. 1920, TC 51 SAA.
29. Sir R. Scallon to Sir E Elles n.d. but March–May 1918, TC 51 SAA.
30. BPD 30 Jan. 1921, BSA; *V of L*, 295–6.
31. BP to Mrs Besant 2 Dec. 1921 (copy), TC 51 SAA.
32. OBP to Mrs Wade 24 Feb. 1929, PCR.
33. Ibid, 2 June 1935, PCR.

Chapter Sixteen
THE SPIRIT VERSUS THE FORM
1. Committee Men and Boy Men (1917–25)

1. J. Benson to BP 19 July 1918, R11 BSA.
2. A. Gaddum to BP 23 Sept. 1917, Gaddum Papers.
3. BPD 16 May 1924, 9 April 1925, 17 Aug. 1926; BP to Dymoke Green 17 Aug. 1926, Dymoke Green Coll; information Mr C.H. Pickford.
4. BP to Elles 20 Nov. 1917, Dymoke Green Coll.
5. BP to Everett 15 Dec. 1930, EP.
6. OBP to Everett 13 Sept. 1918, EP.
7. BP to Everett 8 Dec. 1918, EP.
8. BP to Everett 20 Apr. 1924, EP.
9. BP to C.C. Branch 8 June 1922, R7 BSA.
10. Mr Rex Hazlewood interview with author 16 Feb. 1985.
11. Kipling to BP 29 July 1916, J.H. Morrison Coll.
12. 'The Secret of True Education: The Principle', Wolf Cub pamphlet, n.d. SAA.
13. BP to Lord Hampton 20 Oct. 1920, TC 415 SAA.
14. Hargrave to BP 18 Apr. 1918, TC 37 SAA.
15. BP Report to Headquarters Exec. 30 Jan. 1920, TC 26 SAA.
16. BPD 21 July, 2 Sept. 1922, BSA.
17. BP to Everett 25 July 1917, EP.
18. BPD 28 June 1918, BSA.
19. Viz J. Springhall *Boy Scouts, Class and Militarism* (1971) p. 154; Rosenthal 244ff.
20. Kinlog (Hargrave's History of the Movement), Museum of London.
21. *The Trail* Sept. 1920, 'The Words of White Fox', 272.
22. BP to Everett n.d. but Nov. 1920, EP.
23. *Boy Scouts, Class and Militarism*, 154.
24. For Hargrave's influence in Germany see *Young Germany*, W.Z. Laqueur (London 1962), 136–7.
25. BP to Gaddum 7 Nov. 1920, Gaddum Papers.
26. E.E. Reynolds' note on History of Gilwell, t/s, TC 112; Don Potter interview with author 6 Aug. 1984.

27. BPD 24 Apr. 1938; information Don Potter.
28. Reynolds SM, 109.
29. *BP's Scouts: An Official History of the Boy Scouts Association*, H. Collis, F. Hurll and Rex Hazlewood (London 1961), 90.
30. Draft for article on Gilwell, pub. in *Daily Tel.* 1932, TC 26 SAA.
31. Viz BPD 2 Sept. 1922, BSA.
32. Mr Hazlewood interview with author 16 Feb. 1985.

2. *Paradise Lost: The Battle for Gilwell (1920–23)*

1. BP to Gidney Oct. 6–10 1919, TC 26 SAA.
2. Memo by Maj. J.A. Dane 1 Dec. 1921, TC 26 SAA.
3. OBP to Everett 11 Oct. 1924, EP.
4. BP to Acland 10 Nov. 1922, TC 26 SAA.
5. Gidney to Acland 13 Nov. 1922, TC 111 SAA.
6. BP to J.S. Wilson 29 Oct. 1923, TC 26 SAA.
7. Dane to Gidney 13 Dec. 1922, TC 26 SAA.
8. BPD 6 Sept., 9 Nov., 6 Dec. 1922.
9. Ibid, 6, 12, 15 Dec. 1922.
10. Don Potter interview; Register of Old Harrovians; other information TC 26 SAA.
11. Everett to BP 10 July, 8 Aug. 1923, TC 26 SAA.
12. Ibid.
13. BP to A. Chapman 11 July 1923 TC 26 SAA.
14. BPD 22, 23 Sept. 1923.
15. BPD 3 Oct. 1923; Everett to BP 10 July, 29 Aug. 1923, EP; Memo by BP 28 Sept 1923; BP Report to Headquarters on Gilwell 9 Nov. 1923, TC 26 SAA.
16. Memo for Rodney Wood and Chapman 9 Mar. 1923, TC 26 SAA.
17. Gidney to BP 25 Oct. 1923, TC 26 SAA.
18. West to BP 28 Nov. 1923, TC 26 SAA.
19. BP to West 14 Nov. 1923, TC 54 SAA.
20. Gidney to Commrs. 2 Nov. 1923, TC 26 SAA.

21. Report of Commrs.' Conference 2 Nov. 1923, TC 112 SAA.
22. Hubert S. Martin, Dir. Internat. Bureau from 1920; Col. Granville Walton, Commr. for Rovers from 1930; Charles Dymoke Green, Gen. Sec. from 1917; J.F. Colquhoun, Wolf Cubs Commr. from 1927; Lord Hampton, Ch. Commr.
23. Gidney to BP 26 Jan. 1928, TC 26 SAA.
24. BP to Lord Somers 15 Nov. 1935, Somers Papers SAA.
25. BP to Everett n.d. but 20 Oct. 1935, EP.
26. *A History of Scouting in Northern Ireland*, compiled by Margaret Bell. File Criticisms: Robert Patterson to BP n.d. but late 1919 or early 1920, SAA.
27. E. Allan to J. Thurman 22 Apr. 1967, TC 111 SAA.
28. *Headquarters' Gazette*, Feb. 1921.
29. Ibid, June 1921.
30. Mrs Nash to BP n.d. but July 1920, BP to Mrs Nash 20 July 1920 (appreciations of *Rovering to Success*), TC 2 SAA.
31. BPD 2 Sept. 1922.
32. Information Don Potter; J.S. Wilson, Gilwell t/s, lent by his daughter Miss Margaret Wilson.
33. *The Scouter*, Jan. 1923, 2.

3. *The Sage of Scouting (1917–35)*

1. 'Senior Scouts: Proposal for new badges, t/s, R9 BSA; 'Lesson of Three Years' War', t/s, 1917, R8 BSA.
2. Rt. Hon. George Lansbury M.P. to BP 4 July 1923, TC 26 SAA; Reynolds SM, 142.
3. Reynolds SM, 116; OED Jamboree.
4. *BP's Scouts*, 97.
5. BPD 18 Aug. 1920.
6. *BP's Scouts*, 99–100.
7. BPD 23 Dec. 1920.
8. *BP's Scouts*, 265–6.
9. *The World Camp* (1924) official prog., 7–8.
10. D. Lloyd George t/s (1929), PCR.
11. 'A Chosen Twelve', J. Hargrave.
12. OBP interviewed by W. Hillcourt,

file: Founder's Honours and Awards, SAA.

13. Unsent letter, BP to H.G. Vincent (P.M.'s Private Sec.) 31 July 1929, file: Founder's Hons etc, SAA.

14. BP to Vincent 1 Aug. 1929, file: Founder's Hons etc, SAA.

15. 'Looking Back', Claude Fisher, article 1983, SAA.

16. H.G. Vincent to BP 26 Aug. 1929 (File: Founder's Honours and Awards, SAA).

17. BPD 1 Oct. 1923, 28 June 1927, 13 May, 14 July, 13 Dec. 1929.

18. 27 Years, 121.

19. 'Jamboree', m/s 1929, R8 BSA.

20. 'Looking Back', Claude Fisher, article 1983, SAA.

21. Untitled speech on Boy Scouts, 1936, R8 BSA.

22. Transcript of closing speech 22 Sept. 1937, R9 BSA.

23. KF to Dr Gilbert 1 Feb. 1948 (draft not sent), FP.

24. H.G. Elwes to BP 21 Nov. 1921, TC 25 SAA.

25. Bishop J. Butt to H.G. Elwes 30 Nov. 1921, TC 25 SAA.

26. 'The Aim of the Scout and Guide Movement', t/s, c. 1921, R7 BSA.

27. Viz address to Rover Moot at Kandersteg 2 Aug. 1931 R7 BSA.

28. Address to Boy Scouts of America, 1926, R9 BSA.

29. T/s on 'Service' c. 1922, TC 21 SAA.

30. 'Look Wide', t/s, address for 1920 Jamboree, R7 BSA .

31. Untitled t/s on 'Education' c. 1937–8, R7 BSA.

32. 'See the Funny Side', m/s, n.d. but 1920s, TC 21 SAA.

33. Pats and Pinpricks, File 2 SAA.

34. 27 Years, 84–5.

Chapter Seventeen
STORMS AND SUNSHINE
1. Father and Son (1922–40)

1. Pats and Pinpricks, m/s note, n.d., file 2 SAA.

2. 'Scouting: The Parents' Point of View', m/s, n.d. but 1920–30, R7 BSA.

3. Rovering to Success, 129.

4. First ref to 'character building' in OED dates from 1886: R.W. Burchfield's supp. to 1972 ed 1.482.

5. H. Jenkins to BP 11 March 1918, TC 5 SAA.

6. BP to Jenkins 15 Mar. 1918 (copy), TC 5 SAA.

7. BP to Everett 2 July 1925, EP.

8. BPD 30 Apr., 1 May 1922.

9. Window, 139.

10. The Hon. Mrs Betty Clay interviews with author 1983–4.

11. BPD 18 Feb. 1922.

12. Sunrise, Dane Court School's mag. centenary ed. 1967.

13. BPD 17 May 1924.

14. BPD 26 July 1924.

15. BPD 20 June 1925.

16. BP's notes appended to article about Coué, 'Heal Thyself': by auto suggestion, Pats and Pinpricks, File 1 SAA.

17. Evident in Waldorf Astoria speech, R15 BSA; 'Chota Hazri', m/s Aug. 1932, R7 BSA.

18. BPD 23 Dec. 1920.

19. BPD 30 Aug. 1922.

20. BPD 9 Jan. 1923.

21. HFA, 27, 31.

22. BPD 10–14 Sept. 1923.

23. BPD 21 Jan. 1925.

24. Hillcourt, 372.

25. BPD 1 July 1929.

26. BPD 2 July 1929.

27. BP to M.J. Chignell 30, 29 Mar. 1930; OBP to Chignell 28 Apr., 5 May, 21 Aug. 1930, R. Chignell Coll.

28. Dr Molito's paper on the chemistry of adolescence given at Swedish Rover Moot Aug. 1937, BSA.

29. Information Mrs Ursula FitzGerald (née Kearsley, godchild to BP's ADC Capt. Harvey Kearsley).

30. BPD 24 May 1930, 26 Dec. 1928, 31 Mar. 1929.

31. H.S. Martin to BP 22 July 1930, TC 53 SAA.

32. BPD 23–24 July 1931.

33. Peter Pooley conversation with author 31 July 1984.

34. Sir William Mather interview with author 25 Sept. 1984.

35. 'Peter: Self Measurement', 01010, R9 BSA.

36. 'Success in 1933', R12 BSA.

37. BPD 26, 29 Aug. 1931.
38. BPD 19 Apr. 1932.
39. BP to Frances 24 Jan. 1901, FBPA.
40. BPD 22 Apr., 10 May 1932.
41. BP to Mrs Wade 13 Aug. 1932, R11 BSA.
42. OBP to Miss J. Reddie 18 Feb. 1932, Mrs J. Pollock Coll.
43. Mrs Josephine Pollock interview with author 1 Feb. 1984.
44. BPD 30 July 1932.
45. Heather to Josephine 13 Aug. 1932, JPC.
46. Peter to Josephine 13 Nov. 1932, JPC.
47. Josephine's dance card; Heather to Josephine n.d., JPC.
48. OBP to Josephine 6 Dec. 1932, JPC.
49. Mrs J. Pollock interview with author.
50. BPD 4 Jan. 1933.
51. Ibid, 6 Jan.
52. Ibid, 8 Jan.
53. Ibid, 30 Mar.; conversation with Brig. W. Collingwood and Sir A. Mackie Dec. 1983.
54. Mrs J. Pollock interview with author.
55. BP to Josephine 8 Apr 1933, JPC.
56. BPD 12 Apr. 1933, BSA.
57. BP to Josephine 8 Apr. 1933, JPC.
58. BP to Josephine 14 Apr. 1933, JPC.
59. BPD 15, 24 Aug. 1933.
60. Hon. Mrs Heather King interview with author.
61. BPD 23–24 Nov. 1933.
62. 'They've a Good Life in the BSAP', m/s 27 June 1936, R12 BSA.
63. BPD 16 July 1931.
64. BPD 3 Dec. 1933.
65. Hon. Mrs Heather King interview with author.
66. BPD 30 Dec. 1933.
67. Ibid 12 Dec.
68. OBP to Mrs Wade 3 Mar. 1934, PCR.
69. OBP to Mrs Wade 25 Dec. 1935, PCR.
70. BPD 19–27 Apr. 1936.
71. Peter to Josephine 24 Feb. 1938, JPC.
72. OBP to Josephine 9 July 1937, JPC.
73. BPD 9, 13 Jan. 1937.
74. Announcement, 24 June 1937, typed by OBP on Pax Hill headed paper, file Baden-Powell Family, SAA
75. BPD 14 July 1937.
76. Ibid, 2 Apr.
77. OBP to Mrs Wade 28 Feb. 1938, PCR.
78. BP to Dymoke Green 25 April 1938, Dymoke Green Coll.
79. BPD 30 Mar. 1940 BSA.
80. Maj. B.F.S. Baden-Powell's will (1937) Somerset House; OBP to A.G. Wade n.d. but 1938, 01065 BSA.
81. BPD 18, 24 Oct. 1940.
82. BP to Mrs Wade 11 June 1931, R11 BSA.
83. BP to Everett 23 June 1939, EP.
84. The Rev. and Mrs Norman Pollock interview with author 1 Feb. 1984.

2. 'We Fancy We be Wise' (1933–38)

1. V of L, 316.
2. Ibid, 11.
3. BP to Everett n.d. but late Oct. 1935, EP.
4. The Scouter, June 1935.
5. HFA, 59.
6. 'Youth in these days', m/s, n.d. but 1933–4, R7 BSA.
7. HFA, 9.
8. For life at St James's, Malvern (late 1920s) see Mercury Presides, Daphne Vivian (London 1954), 64–6; a rosier view exists in I Was There, ed. Alice Baird (Worcester 1956).
9. The Hon. Mrs Heather King interview with author.
10. Ibid; BPD 20 Apr. 1932.
11. OBP to Christian Davidson 4 Jan., n.y., Eastman.
12. BPD 2 Dec. 1932.
13. Sir William Mather interview with author 25 Sep. 1984.
14. 'Rovering and Rangering' t/s, R8 BSA.
15. BPD 18 Apr. 1934 BSA; Hon. Mrs Heather King interview.
16. OBP to Everett 20, 29 Apr. 1934, EP.
17. BPD 6 May 1934.
18. Ibid, 1 June.
19. Ibid, 14 June.

20. Kelly's *Handbook of the Titled and Official Classes*, 1934.
21. BPD 21 June 1934.
22. HFA, 47.
23. BPD 19 Sep., 13 Oct. 1934.
24. BP to Betty 2 Sept. 1935, Hon. Mrs Betty Clay Coll.
25. BPD 26 Sept. 1929; 29 Nov. 1937; 10 Mar. 1938.
26. Mrs Wade to Col. Granville Walton 24 Mar. 1938, TC 2 1938.
27. BPD 16 Oct. 1937.
28. BPD 16 Oct. 1937.
29. Kashmir Diary, vol i, 1 Aug. 1898, R5 BSA; *Scouting for Boys*, 181.
30. BP to A. Godley 28 June 1916, Private Coll; BPD 25–26 June 1916.
31. BP to Dr O. Lewin 18 Sept. 1923, TC 37 SAA; BPD 6 May, 28 Nov. 1929, 6 Dec. 1932.
32. HFA, 79.
33. HFA, 82.
34. BPD 16, 18–19 Aug. 1936.
35. Gervas Clay interview with author 13 Dec. 1984.
36. BPD 24 Sept. 1936.
37. *Window*, 173.
38. Ibid, 158.
39. E. Whitehead and Arthur Soames.
40. L. Impey's Report 1 Feb. 1937, TC 51 SAA.
41. BPD 3 Feb. 1937.
42. BPD 2, 15 Feb. 1937; Memo 'Seva Semiti' n.d., R11 BSA.
43. HFA, 86.
44. 'Kadir Cup' t/s 1937, R7 BSA.
45. BP to Col. S. Kennedy 7 Mar. 1937, 13th Hussars Coll.
46. J.S. Wilson to KF 28 May 1937, FP.
47. Sir B. Jeejeebhoy to C.H. Tyrrell 16 Aug. 1937, TC 51 SAA.
48. HFA, 99; Reynolds SM, 179–80.

3. Baden-Powell and the Dictators (1933–40)

1. *Window*, 163.
2. Rosenthal, 278.
3. Ibid, 268.
4. Quoted in Richard Collier's *The Rise and Fall of Benito Mussolini*, 92.
5. H.S. Martin to BP 27 Apr. 1927, TC 51 SAA.
6. Memo 19 Oct. 1927, TC 109 SAA.
7. 'Boys' Weeklies', George Orwell, 1939.
8. BP's notes of his meeting with William Rust, 28 Oct. 1927; BP to Maj.-Gen. Tudor 12 Oct. 1920, TC 48 SAA.
9. BPD 20 Jan. 1933, BSA.
10. HFA, 40; BPD 2 Mar. 1933 BSA; 'The Balilla', draft article, Mar. 1933, TC 21 SAA.
11. BP to Sir F. Vane 24 Apr. 1933, TC 51 SAA.
12. 'The Balilla' draft article, Mar. 1933, TC 21 SAA.
13. BP to K.A. Curtis 27 Dec. 1933, file: Criticisms, SAA.
14. Fragment of article, n.d. but mid-1930s, R9 BSA, quoted Rosenthal, 277.
15. Laqueur, 133–4, 153, 201; BP to Herr F. Fink 19 Feb. 1923, TC 50 SAA.
16. Untitled draft, n.d. but mid-1930s, R9 BSA.
17. 'National Unity', draft n.d. but Aug.-Sept. 1937, R9 BSA.
18. *The Scouter*, Oct. 1937.
19. Ibid, Feb. 1937.
20. H.S. Martin to BP 22 Aug. 1935, TC 50 SAA.
21. Report of tour of Germany by Mrs Mark Kerr, Sept. 1935, FP.
22. Report of visit to Germany, Dame KF, 1937, FP.
23. Lord Somers to KF 25 Aug. 1938, FP.
24. BP to H.S. Martin 8 Oct. 1937, Somers Papers, SAA.
25. KF to Dame Helen Gwynne-Vaughan 19 Sept. 1938, FP.
26. *The Scouter*, Oct. 1938.
27. His speech at Bentley Ex-Service-men's Annual Dinner in Nov. 1933 was exceptional.
28. BP to Everett 11 Nov. 1934, EP; *The Scouter*, Oct., Nov. 1934.
29. BP to Betty n.d. but Sept. 1938, Hon. Mrs Betty Clay Coll.
30. Rosenthal, 278.
31. BP Inspector General of Cavalry's Diary, May 1906, NAM.
32. BP to HG 6 Mar. 1904; BPD 28 Feb. 1904; information R. Weisweiller

(grandson): Miss Sassoon married 4 Aug. 1908 Gustave Weisweiller; Rube family, BPD esp. Nov.-Dec. 1905.

33. Rosenthal, 269.
34. Quoted Rosenthal, 269.
35. A. Yellin to ed. *The Scouter* 7 May 1924, TC 22 SAA.
36. *The Scouter*, July 1934.
37. BP to J. Newmark 23 June 1927, TC 46 SAA.
38. *The Scouter*, Oct. 1939.
39. 'Why I Should Fight' pub. Mar. 1939, but written several months earlier.
40. BPD 22 Sept. 1937 re Lady (Gertrude) Scott.
41. BP to ed. *T.L.S.* 13 Aug. 1921.
42. *Mein Kampf*, 108–9 (Paternoster Library ed. 1935).
43. Pats and Pinpricks, n.d. but probably 1929, File 2 SAA.
44. Extracts from *Mein Kampf*, 112–13, pub. in *The Scouter*, Nov. 1933.
45. *Mein Kampf*, 66, 70.
46. 'Camp Craft' t/s, Dec. 1919, TC 43 SAA.
47. *Mein Kampf*, 127, 168.
48. *Scouting for Boys*, 292.
49. 'About Those Boy Scouts', pamphlet 1927, SAA.
50. 'The Swastika for Good Luck', draft article, 1 July 1933, R12 BSA.
51. BP to Mrs Wade 26 Feb. 1935, PCR; *BP's Scouts*, 275.

Chapter Eighteen
UNDER MOUNT KENYA
1. The Last of England (1935–38)

1. OBP to Mrs Wade 3 May 1936, PCR.
2. HFA, 67.
3. BPD 4–5 Dec. 1935.
4. Walker to BP 10 Feb. 1936, HC.
5. BPD 22–27 Dec. 1937.
6. BPD 1 Jan. 1938.
7. BPD 23 Jan., 1 Feb. 1938; OBP to Everett 2 Feb. 1938 EP.
8. Everett to Walker 4 Feb. 1938 (copy), EP.
9. OBP to Everett 4 Feb. 1938 EP.
10. BPD 17 March 1938.

11. Mr A W 'Fred' Hurll interview with author 14 Mar. 1985.
12. BPD 1–4 Sept. 1938; Maj. A.G. Wade to Mr Place, Scout Assn. Publications Dept. n.d., TC 83 SAA.
13. BPD 5 Oct. 1938; *BP's Scouts*, 278.
14. 'The Founder and His Family', Mrs Wade t/s. R15 BSA.
15. BP to Walker 8 July 1938, HC.
16. BP to Walker 29 July and 9 Oct. 1938, HC.
17. Note headed 'Secret': an account by KF of a conversation with OBP on 7 June 1938, FP.
18. OBP to Walker and Lady Bettie Walker 10 Oct. 1938, HC.
19. BPD 8 Sept 1938.

2. Paxtu: Only Peace (1938–41)

1. BPD 13 Oct. 1939.
2. OBP to Mrs Wade 1 Jan. 1938, PCR.
3. BP to Mrs Wade 16 Dec. 1938, R11 BSA.
4. Described in letter to Cyril Maude quoted in 'Paxtu', a pamphlet published by the Kenyan Boy Scout Assn. n.d. but *c.* 1965; 'Paxtu' in BPD 14 Feb. 1938, earlier he had called it Paxtoo in letters to Eric Walker.
5. Information on residents from Mrs Joan Martin, who worked at the Outspan in the late 1930s and early 1940s.
6. BPD 1939–40, many refs viz Dec. 1939; HFA, 109.
7. BPD 12, 21 Aug. 1939.
8. BP to Mrs Wade 6 Dec. 1935, R11 BSA.
9. Sir W. Mather interview with author; BPD 5 Mar. 1939.
10. Mrs H. Hurly (née Walker) to author 21 March 1988.
11. *Treetops Hotel*, E.G.S. Walker (London 1962), 90.
12. Mrs H. Hurly to author 21 Dec. 1983.
13. HFA, 108–9.
14. HFA, 113.
15. BPD 15, 24 June 1940.
16. OBP to Everett 8 Aug. 1940, EP.
17. Ibid, 3 Oct.

18. BPD 25 May 1940.
19. BP to Walker 17 Sept. 1940, HC.
20. Mrs Hurly to author 27 Jan. 1987.
21. BPD 26 Sept. 1940.
22. BP to Major Burnham 22 Sept. 1940, Burnham Papers.
23. BP to Dacre Smyth 21 Oct. 1940, Dacre Smyth Coll.
24. BPD 8, 11 Aug. 1940.
25. BPD 3 Sept. 1940.
26. Everett to BP 24 Apr. 1940, EP.
27. *Window*, 188; in BPD 10 Sept. 1940 BP records examination by Doig; OBP to Mrs Wade 14 Jan. 1941 gives day as 9 Sept., PCR.
28. BP finished this card on 3 Oct. 1940.
29. BPD 3 June 1939.
30. OBP to Mrs W. 21 May 1940, PCR.
31. BPD 17 June 1940.
32. BPD 28 June 1940.
33. BPD 16 Sept. 1940.
34. BPD 27 July, 12 Aug. 1939; OBP to Mrs Wade 5 Aug. 1939, R11 BSA.
35. Lady Victoria Fletcher to author 29 Feb. 1984.
36. Viz BP to Mrs Wade 5 Aug. 1939, James Wade Coll.
37. BPD 4 Nov. 1940.
38. OBP to Mrs Wade 16 Dec 1939.
39. *Window*, 188.
40. OBP to Everett 16 Nov. 1940, PCR.
41. Cosmo Lang Cantuar to Everett 15, 18 Nov. 1940, EP.
42. OBP to Everett 20 Nov. 1940, EP.
43. *Window*, 189.
44. OBP to Mrs Wade 14 Jan. 1941, PCR.
45. OBP to Everett 31 May, 8 Aug. 1940, PCR; OBP to Mrs Wade 4 Jan. 1940.
46. OBP to Mrs Wade 14 Jan. 1941, PCR; *Window*, 189; Hillcourt, 417.
47. *Window*, 193.
48. Hillcourt, 415–16; *Window*, 193–4.
49. OBP to Mrs Wade 14 Jan. 1941, PCR.
50. OBP to Christian Rawson-Shaw (née Davidson) 8 Jan. 1977, Eastman.
51. Walker to OBP 14 Apr. 1968 (copy), HC.
52. *27 Years*, 150.
53. *Window*, 200–1.

Chapter Nineteen
EPILOGUE
1. Curbing the Beast and Reclaiming the Child

1. Olave to Christian Rawson-Shaw 29 Nov. 1958, Eastman.
2. HG to G 19 May 1869, FBPA.
3. HG to G 17 Jan. 1861, FBPA.
4. BP to HG 8 Mar. 1884, BSA.
5. 'A Chosen Twelve', J. Hargrave, unpub. t/s, Mrs Diana Hargrave Coll.
6. 'A Test of Friendship', 'The First Spear', 'The Algerian Hat', 'The Afghanistan Helmet'.
7. BP to G 28 June 1883, BSA.
8. BP to HG 21 June 1882, BSA.
9. Viz *Tom Brown's Schooldays* and *The Hill*.
10. 'A Test of Friendship', first pub. *Windsor Magazine*, Oct. 1896.
11. Canton: *V of L* t/s, 14, short separate section 'Canton 1912', R9 BSA; Ashanti: *V of L* t/s, 531, R8 BSA.
12. BP Scrapbook (Ashanti press cuttings and drawings), NAM 6501–18–2.
13. BP Algerian Diary, vol iii, 17–19 May 1893, R4 BSA.
14. Peter at Verdun, BPD 15–16 April 1929.
15. BP to Mrs Wade 13 Aug. 1932, Betty delighted BP by finding some finger bones, R11 BSA.
16. Tunisian Diary 5 Nov. 1891, 00051 R4 BSA; BPD 28 Feb. 1929.
17. BPD 27 Dec. 1937.
18. 'Educative Possibilities of Scouting', draft address 1911, R12 BSA.
19. *Rovering to Success*, 110.
20. Pats and Pinpricks, File 2, SAA.

2. Values and Illusions

1. *General Introduction to Psychoanalysis*, Sigmund Freud, trans. Joan Riviera (New York 1938), 95.
2. BP's Last Message to Girl Guides, 1940.
3. Report of Home Sec's visit to Oxford, *The Independent*, 12 July 1988.
4. For an account of the Scouts in the 2nd World War, see *The Left*

Handshake, Hilary St George (London 1949); *Changi*, see *The Victorian Scout* (Australian Scout Assn., 1941).

5. 'They Were Prepared: Boy Scouts' National Service' (1941 SAA).
6. Statistics from SAA.

3. Brave New World

1. Flying Saucers Message written by Lady Sandys, 8 July 1969; George VI and Christ: OBP to Christian 3 Sept. 1953, Eastman.
2. Mrs K. Lessiter interview with author.
3. OBP to Christian n.d. (1946), 16 Apr. 1949, 7 Jan. 1965, Eastman.
4. Mrs Kim Doig to author 3 Feb. 1984.
5. Mrs Josephine Pollock interview with author; OBP to Christian 5 June 1949, Eastman.
6. Mrs Josephine Pollock interview with author.
7. OBP to Josephine 15 Oct. 1948, JPC.
8. OBP to Josephine 18 Aug. 1950, JPC.
9. OBP to Christian 15 Mar. 1953, Eastman.
10. *Window*, 232; Carine, Lady Baden-Powell to Grace and William Hill-court 15 Nov. 1962, R11 BSA.
11. OBP to Mrs Wade 20 Dec. 1962, PCR.
12. OBP to Christian 3 July 1969, Eastman.
13. Walker to OBP 12 May 1974 (copy), HC.
14. OBP to Christian 10 July 1974, HC.
15. Contrast OBP to Christian 26 July 1964 with 21 July 1974, Eastman.
16. OBP to Mrs Hurly 15 Mar. 1977, HC.
17. OBP to Christian 14 Feb. 1977, Eastman.
18. Ibid.
19. OBP to Christian 2 June 1974, Eastman.
20. 'A Chosen Twelve'. J. Hargrave t/s., Diana Hargrave Coll.

Sources for Appendix I

The American Loyalist Files in the P.R.O., AO 13/111, contain Caroline's letters to the Commissioners and a number of Joseph's to her. Rodney Warington Smyth of Flushing, Cornwall, possesses all Mr Maskelyne's notes and researches into the Admiral's antecedents. Information about the Earl (Earle) family in *Memoirs of Pliny Earle, M.D.*, F.B. Sanborn (ed.), Boston 1898, and in the introduction to *Narrative of a Residence in New Zealand* by Augustus Earle (E.H. McCormick, ed., re-issued Oxford 1966).

Notes to Appendix II

1. Copy of Affidavit, SAA.
2. 'The Boy Scouts in America' by E.T. Seton, Reel 13 BSA.
3. E.K. Wade for Sir R. Baden-Powell to L.A.C. Davis 8 July 1927, TC 42 SAA.
4. 'How the Scouts' Badges Originated' by R. Baden-Powell, TC 21 SAA.
5. BP's Diary 14 Dec. 1906, BSA.
6. *The Story of Charlotte Mason 1842–1923*, E. Cholmondeley (London 1960), 99–100.
7. *Lessons from the Varsity of Life*, R. Baden-Powell (London 1933), 274.
8. BP to Sec. of *Scout Press* 4 July 1916, Reel 15 BSA; 'History of the Boy Scouts' (1915), BSA; Annual Report (1918); t/s dictated by BP 'The Origin of Scouting', file: Origins of Scouting, SAA.
9. BP to Col. Elliot 18 Oct. 1911, TC 42 SAA.

INDEX

Compiled by Douglas Matthews

NOTE: Ranks and titles are generally the highest mentioned in the text.

All the drawings on these end-papers, except the *Cape Punch* cartoon, are by Baden-Powell (© *Scout Association*).

DATE DUE

Badge
front of h

Staff w
patrol flag

Lanyar
and whist

Shirt o
sweater.